KEOS

RESULTS OF EXCAVATIONS CONDUCTED BY
THE UNIVERSITY OF CINCINNATI
UNDER THE AUSPICES OF
THE AMERICAN SCHOOL OF CLASSICAL STUDIES AT ATHENS

VOLUME XII

AYIA IRINI: AREA B

BY

NATALIE ABELL

LOCKWOOD PRESS
ATLANTA, GEORGIA
2021

Library of Congress Cataloging-in-Publication information

Names: Abell, Natalie, author.
Title: Ayia Irini : Area B / by Natalie Abell.
Description: Atlanta : Lockwood Press, 2021. | Series: Keos ; volume XII | "Results of excavations conducted by the University of Cincinnati under the auspices of the American School of Classical Studies at Athens." | Includes bibliographical references and index.
Identifiers: LCCN 2021003140 (print) | LCCN 2021003141 (ebook) | ISBN 9781948488570 (hardback) | ISBN 9781948488679 (pdf)
Subjects: LCSH: Ayia Irini Site (Kea Island, Greece) | Excavations (Archaeology)--Greece--Kea Island. | Kea Island (Greece)--Antiquities. | Pottery, Aegean--Greece--Kea Island. | Bronze age--Greece--Kea Island. | Civilization, Aegean.
Classification: LCC DF221.K36 A24 2021 (print) | LCC DF221.K36 (ebook) | DDC 939/.15--dc23
LC record available at https://lccn.loc.gov/2021003140
LC ebook record available at https://lccn.loc.gov/2021003141

© 2021 by Department of Classics, University of Cincinnati
ISBN 9781948488570 (hardback)
ISBN 9781948488679 (PDF)
All rights reserved.

This paper meets the requirements of ANSI/NISO Z39.48-1992 (Permanence of Paper).

KEOS

VOLUME XII

AYIA IRINI: AREA B

Dedicated to the memory of Aliki Bikaki

TABLE OF CONTENTS

List of Figures ix
List of Plates x
List of Color Plates xii
List of Tables xiii
Acknowledgments xv
Abbreviations xvii

I. INTRODUCTION 1
    A Brief History of Ayia Irini 1
    Excavation of Area B 3
    Terminology 4
    Formation Processes 6
    Recovery and Selection 7
    Goals and Methodology 8
    Presentation of Finds 9

II. STRATIGRAPHY, ARCHITECTURE, AND POTTERY 27
    Overview of Remains in Area B 27
    Room B.1 28
    Room B.1 Catalogue 34
    Room B.2 (+ B.3 and B.4) 59
    Room B.3 64
    Rooms B.2, B.3, and B.2/B.3 Catalogue 65
    Room B.4 104
    Room B.4 Catalogue 107
    Room B.8 112
    Room B.8 Catalogue 112
    Alley AB 113
    Alley AB Catalogue 122
    Summary of Occupation in Area B 141

III. CERAMIC FABRICS AND FORMING METHODS 147
    Local Geology 147
    Macroscopic Fabrics 148
    Petrographic Analysis 152
    Forming Methods 156

IV. EARLY BRONZE AGE CERAMIC ANALYSIS 165
    Overview of Period III Pottery 165
    Synchronisms 166
    Fabrics 167
    Manufacture 169
    Ceramic Importation Patterns 170
    Summary 171

V.	MIDDLE BRONZE AGE CERAMIC ANALYSIS	173
	Timing of the MBA Foundation	173
	Overview of Period IV Pottery	175
	Synchronisms	178
	Fabrics	181
	Manufacture	184
	Importation and Consumption Patterns	186
	Summary	189
VI.	PERIOD VI CERAMIC ANALYSIS	191
	Overview of Period VI Pottery	191
	Synchronisms	197
	Fabrics	199
	Manufacture	203
	Importation and Consumption Patterns	204
	Summary	205
VII.	PERIOD VII CERAMIC ANALYSIS	207
	Overview of Period VII Pottery	207
	Synchronisms	216
	Fabrics	218
	Manufacture	223
	Importation and Consumption Patterns	224
	Summary	226
VIII.	AREA B, AYIA IRINI, AND THE WIDER AEGEAN	227
	Production and Consumption Patterns at Ayia Irini	227
	Conclusions	238

Appendices

I.	Concordance of Room Numbers	239
II.	Concordance of Inventory Numbers to Catalogue Numbers	239
III.	Ware Designations	247
IV.	Descriptions of Macroscopic Fabric Groups	250
V.	Petrographic Descriptions	265
VI.	Fabric Group Munsell Colors	316
VII.	Results of Wave-Dispersive X-ray Fluorescence	318
VIII.	Excavation Unit Information	324

References ... 329
Index ... 345

LIST OF FIGURES

Fig. 1.	Map of the central Aegean; inset map of Kea (Keos)	2
Fig. 2.	Map of the northwestern coast of Kea	3
Fig. 3.	Comparison of chronological phases at Ayia Irini with other Aegean sites	4
Fig. 4.	Plan of LBA Ayia Irini, showing location of Area B	5
Fig. 5.	Trench plan of Ayia Irini	6
Fig. 6.	a. Plan with location of test pits in Alley AB and Period IV Wall X; b. Plan of Alley AB	7
Fig. 7.	Section 1, House B (Rooms B.2–B.4), facing NW toward Wall H	11
Fig. 8.	Section 2, House B (Room B.1), facing NW toward Wall H	11
Fig. 9.	Section 3, Room B.1, facing NW toward Wall H	12
Fig. 10.	Section 4, Room B.1, facing NE toward Wall I	12
Fig. 11.	a. Section 5, test pit in Room B.1 below Wall I, facing SE toward Wall J; b. Plan and section of test pit below the Wall H foundation in Room B.1, facing NE toward Wall I; c. Section 6, Room B.2/B.3 facing SW toward Wall O	13
Fig. 12.	Section 7, Room B.2, facing SW toward Wall O	14
Fig. 13.	Section 8, Rooms B.2–B.4, facing NW toward Wall H	14
Fig. 14.	a. Section 9, 1961 test pit in Alley AB, facing SW toward South Alley, facing SW toward South Alley; b. Section 10, Wall AF in the Room B.2 test pit, facing NE toward Wall I; c. Section 11, Room B.4, facing SW toward Wall O	15
Fig. 15.	Section 12, Room B.1 and 1975 test pit in Alley AB, facing SW toward Wall O and South Alley	16
Fig. 16.	Harris matrix of excavation units in Room B.1	17
Fig. 17.	Harris matrix of excavation units in Rooms B.2, B.3, and B.2/B.3	18
Fig. 18.	Harris matrix of excavation units in (a) Alley AB and (b) Room B.4	19
Fig. 19.	Plan of Period III architecture in Area B	20
Fig. 20.	Period IV architecture below Alley AB and Room B.1	21
Fig. 21.	House B: Phase 1 (Period VI)	22
Fig. 22.	House B: Phase 2 (Period VI)	23
Fig. 23.	House B: Phase 3 (Period VII)	24
Fig. 24.	House B: Phase 4 (Period VII)	25
Fig. 25.	Walls that continued to be visible and new construction that postdate the Period VII destruction of House B	26
Fig. 26.	Pottery from B03-829, B03-828, B03-825, B602CL, B03-826, and B601CL	36
Fig. 27.	Pottery from B601CL	40
Fig. 28.	Pottery from B601CL and B610CL	44
Fig. 29.	Pottery from B610CL and B609CL	46
Fig. 30.	Pottery from B609CL	50
Fig. 31.	Pottery from B609CL	52
Fig. 32.	Pottery from B609CL and B608CL	54
Fig. 33.	Pottery from B608CL	56
Fig. 34.	Pottery from B03-824, B03-823, and B03-822	68
Fig. 35.	Pottery from B03-821 and B03-821 etc.	70
Fig. 36.	Pottery from B03-820	72
Fig. 37.	Pottery from B03-819 and B03-818	73
Fig. 38.	Pottery from B03-818, B03-817, B03-815 etc., B03-814, B03-813, B03-812, B03-810, and B603CL	74
Fig. 39.	Pottery from B603CL	80
Fig. 40.	Pottery from B603CL and B607CL	82

Fig. 41.	Pottery from B607CL and B606CL	86
Fig. 42.	Pottery from B606CL	90
Fig. 43.	Pottery from B606CL and B604CL	92
Fig. 44.	Pottery from B604CL	96
Fig. 45.	Pottery from B604CL, B605CL, and B03-72	102
Fig. 46.	Pottery from B03-70	108
Fig. 47.	Pottery from B03-71a, B03-148, B03-806, and B03-805	110
Fig. 48.	Pottery from B03-805, B03-804, B03-803, B03-802, B800/801CL, B03-799, and B797/798CL	124
Fig. 49.	Pottery from B795/a/796CL and B791/793CL	128
Fig. 50.	Pottery from B03-790, B03-789, B03-788, B03-786, B03-785, and B648CL	130
Fig. 51.	Pottery from B648CL, B03-97, B03-96, and B03-94	134
Fig. 52.	Pottery from B647CL, B646CL, B03-87, and B03-88	138
Fig. 53.	Number and relative proportions by ware of common shapes in published Period IV deposits	174
Fig. 54.	Number and relative proportions by ware and general shape of imported vessels in published Period IV deposits	175
Fig. 55.	Number and relative proportions by ware of common shapes in published Period V deposits	187
Fig. 56.	Number and relative proportions by ware and general shape of imported vessels in published Period V deposits	188
Fig. 57.	Number and relative proportions by ware of shapes other than handleless cups in published early Period VI deposits	192
Fig. 58.	Number and relative proportions by ware of common shapes other than handleless cups in published later Period VI deposits	194
Fig. 59.	Number and relative proportions by ware and general shape of imported vessels in published Period VI deposits of both phases	196
Fig. 60.	Number and relative proportions by ware of common shapes, other than handleless cups in published Period VIIa deposits	208
Fig. 61.	Number and relative proportions by ware of common shapes, other than handleless cups and tripod jars in published Period VIIb deposits	209
Fig. 62.	Number and relative proportions by ware of common shapes other than handleless cups and tripod jars in published Period VII deposits of all phases	210
Fig. 63.	Number and relative proportions by ware and general shape of imported vessels in published Period VII deposits of all phases	212

LIST OF PLATES

Pl. 1. a. Areas A and B at the beginning of excavation from the east-northeast.
b. Room B.2/B.3 during excavation in 1961 from the northeast.
c. Rooms B.1 and B.2/B.3 from the east, showing the Period VII destruction deposit.

Pl. 2. a. Room B.2/B.3 from the east, showing the Period VII destruction debris.
b. Rooms B.1 and B.2/B.3 from the northeast, showing the Period VII destruction deposit.
c. Room B.1 from the west, showing the Period VII destruction debris.

Pl. 3. a. Room B.1 from the southwest, showing the lower part of the Period VII destruction debris.
b. Room B.1 from the northeast, showing architecture from House B: Phases 1 and 2.
c. Room B.2/B.3 from the east, showing EBA Wall AB and Walls O, T, AA, and J from Phases 3 and 4 of the LBA house.

Pl. 4. a. Rooms B.2 and B.1 from the southwest, showing EBA Wall AB and Walls I, J, K, and AA from Phases 3 and 4 of the LBA house.
b. Eastern edge of Rooms B.3 and B.4 from the southwest, showing EBA Wall AD extending under Period VII Walls T and J.
c. Room B.2 from the north, showing EBA Wall AB and Walls AA and J from Phase 3 of the LBA house.

Pl. 5. a. House B from the east, with LBA cross walls labeled.
b. House B from the southeast, with LBA walls (except long walls H and J) labeled.
c. House B from the south, showing Rooms B.1, B.2, and B.8.

LIST OF PLATES

Pl. 6
a. Room B.1 from the southeast, showing LBA Wall H built on top of the Wall H foundation, a possible Period IV wall.
b. Rooms B.2/B.3 and B.4 from the east.
c. Room B.2/B.3 from the southeast, showing Walls P, T, R, AA, and the Wall AA buttress.

Pl. 7.
a. Room B.2/B.3 from the southeast, showing Walls P, T, R, AA, and the Wall AA buttress.
b. Room B.2 from the southeast, showing the large stones of the Wall H foundation under Wall H.
c. Room B.1 from the southwest, showing the corner of Walls I and J.

Pl. 8.
a. Room B.1 from the south, showing the large stones of the Wall H foundation under Wall H.
b. Room B.1 from the northeast, after excavation.
c. Room B.8 from the south-southeast, showing the intersection of Walls I and J.

Pl. 9.
a. Northeast part of Alley AB in 1975 from the northeast, before the test pit was opened.
b. Area of the 1975 test pit in Alley AB, below the four stones in the center of the photograph, from the northwest.
c. Northeast part of Alley AB in 1975 from the southwest, before the test pit was opened.

Pl. 10.
a. Northeast part of Alley AB in 1975 from the northeast, before the test pit was opened.
b. Flat stones embedded in red mud under the slabs of Drain 1 in Alley AB, from the northwest.
c. At a level slightly lower than in the previous photo from the northwest, showing more tightly packed stones.

Pl. 11.
a. After excavation unit B03-767 from the southeast, showing the relationship of Street 1 to House A Wall E.
b. End of excavation unit B03-767 from the southeast, showing the relationship of Street 1 to House A Wall E.
c. Upper part of the loose soil and stones in the Wall H foundation trench, from the northeast.

Pl. 12.
a. Upper part of photo shows fallen stones found in B03-781, beneath layer of red soil, from the southeast.
b. Pebble layer (Street 2) found in B03-785 from the southeast.
c. Second paving level of Street 2 from the southeast.

Pl. 13.
a. A shallow layer of packed stones that abutted Wall E1 beneath Street 2, from the southeast.
b. Wall X beneath Wall H from the northwest.
c. Test pit in Alley AB from the northeast.

Pl. 14.
a. Test pit in Alley AB from the southwest, showing Wall H above Wall X and the northeast scarp.
b. Test pit in Alley AB from the south.
c. Period IV Wall E1 beneath Period VI Wall E of House A, from the east.

Pl. 15.
a. Test pit in Alley AB from the northeast, showing Wall H above Wall X, a possible Period III wall in the southwest scarp, and Wall E1 beneath Wall E of House A.
b. Test pit in Alley AB from the southwest.
c. Test pit in Alley AB from the east, showing Period IV walls and Drain 2, as well as a possible Period III wall in the southwest corner of the test pit.
d. End of the test pit in Alley AB, from the northeast.

Pl. 16.
a. Test pit in Room B.2 from the southwest, showing Wall AF below Wall K and Period III destruction debris.
b. Test pit in Room B.2 from the southeast, showing Period III destruction debris between Walls AB and AF.
c. Test pit in Room B.2 from the northwest, showing Period III destruction debris between Walls AB and AF.

Pl. 17.
a. Test pit in Room B.2 from the southwest, showing pithos (**232**) underwater.
b. Test pit in Room B.2 from the southwest, showing pithos (**232**) half submerged in seawater.
c. Test pit in Room B.2 from the northeast, showing Wall AB.

Pl. 18.
a. Bikaki and a workman pumping water from the flooded test pit in Room B.2.
b. Test pit in Room B.2 during excavation from the northwest.
c. Test pit in Room B.2 from the southwest, showing large, flat slab.

Pl. 19.
a. Sketch of Room B.2/B.3 and B.4, showing the relationships between walls and "Floors" a and b.
b. Section and plan of Wall AB and the spur of Wall AF, from the west.
c. Sketch of Walls AB and AF below Room B.2.

Pl. 20.
a. Section of test pit in Alley AB from excavation notebook, showing the relationship of strata and architectural features to Walls H and X.
b. Section of test pit in Alley AB, showing the relationship of strata and architectural features to Walls E and E1.

Pl. 21. Objects from B03-829, B03-828, B03-825a, B03-825, B602CL, and B03-826.

Pl. 22. Objects from B601CL.
Pl. 23. Objects from B601CL and B610CL.
Pl. 24. Objects from B610CL and B609CL.
Pl. 25. Objects from B609CL.
Pl. 26. Objects from B609CL and B608CL.
Pl. 27. Objects from B608CL, B03-830, and B03-824.
Pl. 28. Objects from B03-823.
Pl. 29. Object from B03-822.
Pl. 30. Objects from B03-822 and B03-821.
Pl. 31. Objects from B03-821 etc.
Pl. 32. Objects from B03-820 and B03-819.
Pl. 33. Objects from B03-818, B03-817, B03-816, B03-815 etc., and B03-814.
Pl. 34. Objects from B03-814 etc., B03-813, and B03-812 etc.
Pl. 35. Objects from B03-812, B03-810, and B603CL.
Pl. 36. Objects from B603CL and B607CL.
Pl. 37. Objects from B03-108, B03-809, and B606CL.
Pl. 38. Objects from B606CL.
Pl. 39. Objects from B606CL.
Pl. 40. Objects from B606CL and B604CL.
Pl. 41. Objects from B604CL.
Pl. 42. Objects from B604CL, B605CL, B03-72, and B03-70.
Pl. 43. Objects from B03-70 and B03-71a.
Pl. 44. Objects from B03-148, B03-506, B03-806, B03-805, B03-804, B03-803, B03-802, B800/801CL, and B03-799.
Pl. 45. Objects from B797/798CL, B795/a/796CL, and B791/793CL.
Pl. 46. Objects from B03-790, B03-789, B03-788, B03-786, B03-785, B649CL, and B648CL.
Pl. 47. Objects from B03-97, B03-96, B03-94, B647CL, B646CL, B03-87, and B03-88.

LIST OF COLOR PLATES

Color Pl. 1. Photomicrographs of probable and possible local fabrics, PFG 1 and 2A–C.
Color Pl. 2. Photomicrographs of imported fabrics, PFG 2D, 3, 4, 5A–G.
Color Pl. 3. Photomicrographs of imported fabrics, PFG 5H, 6, 7, 8A–D.
Color Pl. 4. Photomicrographs of imported fabrics, PFG 8E, 9–14.
Color Pl. 5. Plan of the southeastern part of Ayia Irini, showing walls and major features of all Bronze Age phases in Area B.

LIST OF TABLES

Table 1.1. Schematic chronology of Ayia Irini 3
Table 1.2. System of notation used in this volume 10
Table 2.1. Room B.1 combined lots (CL) 28
Table 2.2. Room B.1 deposit summary 29
Table 2.3. Rooms B.2, B.2/B.3, B.3, and B.4 combined lots (CL) 60
Table 2.4. Rooms B.2, B.3, and B.2/B.3 deposit summary 61
Table 2.5. Room B.4 deposit summary 105
Table 2.6. Alley AB combined lots (CL) 114
Table 2.7. Alley AB deposit summary 115
Table 3.1. Macroscopic fabrics with their distinguishing characteristics 149
Table 3.2. Summary of petrographic fabric groups and proposed regions of origin 158
Table 4.1. Overview of vessels in Period III lots in Area B according to macroscopic fabric group 168
Table 4.2. Relative proportions of imported vessels according to probable regions of production
in Period III deposits in Area B 170
Table 5.1. Period IVa synchronisms 179
Table 5.2. Period IVb synchronisms 179
Table 5.3. Period IVc synchronisms 179
Table 5.4. Period V synchronisms 180
Table 5.5. Overview of vessels in Period IV lots in Area B according to macroscopic fabric group 182
Table 5.6. Relative proportions of imported vessels according to probable regions of production
in Period IV deposits in Area B 183
Table 5.7. Rough estimate of the proportion of Period IV imports in Area B lots 184
Table 5.8. Relative proportions of wares in Period IV 185
Table 5.9. Common tablewares in published Period V deposits 188
Table 6.1. Early Period VI synchronisms 198
Table 6.2. Later Period VI synchronisms 198
Table 6.3. Overview of vessels in Period VI lots in Area B according to macroscopic fabric group 200
Table 6.4. Relative proportions of imported vessels according to probable regions of production
in Period VI deposits in Area B 202
Table 6.5. Rough estimate of the proportion of imported Period VI pottery in Area B lots 202
Table 6.6. Common tablewares in published Period VI deposits 204
Table 7.1. Period VIIa synchronisms 217
Table 7.2. Period VIIb synchronisms 217
Table 7.3. Period VIIc synchronisms 217
Table 7.4. Overview of vessels in Period VII lots in Area B according to macroscopic fabric group ...219
Table 7.5. Relative proportions of imported vessels according to probable regions of production
in Period VII deposits in Area B 223
Table 7.6. Rough estimate of the proportion of imported Period VII pottery in Area B lots 224
Table 7.7. Common tablewares and rhyta in published deposits of Period VII 225

ACKNOWLEDGMENTS

Excavations at Ayia Irini on the Cycladic island of Kea began in 1960 under the direction of John L. Caskey of the University of Cincinnati, under the auspices of the American School of Classical Studies at Athens (ASCSA). Aliki Halepa Bikaki oversaw excavation in a large part of the southeastern sector of the site, initially all designated as Area B. There, she discovered an LBA house (House B) and the Temple. Although the Temple was separated out from Area B in its records and publication schedule, Aliki was entrusted with the publication of the rest of Area B, namely the LBA House B and Alley AB, which separated House B from House A, as well as the EBA and MBA deposits below them. Aliki worked toward the publication of Area B until 2008, when she passed the assignment to me. I am grateful to Aliki for entrusting me with this project, and I am thankful to Jack Davis both for recommending me to Aliki and for his unflagging support of my work.

Aliki was an excellent archaeologist, and any success in this study is owed in large part to her diligence in excavating, observing, recording, and interpreting the story of Area B as it was uncovered. Over the course of decades spent analyzing the Area B remains, Aliki built up a collection of notes and drawings that she provided to me. I obtained additional excavation records from the Kea Excavation archives at the ASCSA and the University of Cincinnati. Carol Hershenson, Natalia Vogeikoff-Brogan, and Jeffrey Kramer provided access to and assistance with the archives. John Wallrodt helped me to create a database and manage my digital data.

Aliki's notes included stratigraphic sections, architectural plans and sketches, a working catalogue of ceramics and small finds, and prose summaries about some aspects of the area that seem to have been intended for her eventual publication. She had compiled summary descriptions of all the excavation units for the major deposits, including lists of elevations and finds and basic dating. A group of notes and sketches described the excavation and stratigraphy of the 1975 and 1976 test pits in detail. She had also located some ceramic comparanda, especially for Period III and Period VII deposits. Stratigraphic sections drawn by Aliki have been digitized. She also sketched the architecture and emerging stratigraphy in the excavation notebooks; some of those sketches are included here when they provide additional evidence for the interpretation of the stratigraphy or architecture (Pls. 19, 20).

The plans that Aliki drew were based on the architects' field sheets. Site architects were Lloyd Cotsen, Charles K. Williams, Roger Holzen, and W. Willson Cummer; the architectural drawings adapted for this volume were not signed or initialed unless otherwise noted. Aliki used modified versions of the field sheets to show walls, features, and the placement of test pits, as well as to compile elevations. Information from her plans has been incorporated into phase plans (Figs. 19–25), drawn from the architects' field sheets, with the exception of the Period IV plan (Fig. 20), which existed (unsigned) in the Kea archives at the ASCSA.

Aliki created a preliminary catalogue of ceramics and small finds for all of the combined lots in Area B and for the test pit in Alley AB. All ceramics that she numbered for her catalogue have been included here. Descriptions are mine, unless otherwise noted. Many additional sherds have also been included in my catalogue. Thanks are owed to Stella Bouzaki, Nelly Lazaridou, Tasoula Voutsina, Kostas Chionatos, Sotiris Maras, Yannis Lavdas, and Petros Petrakis who mended objects for the excavations during the 1960s and 1970s. Aliki's drawings of ceramics and small finds have been inked and are presented in the figures. Many additional drawings were prepared by Lily Bonga and Mary-Jane Schumacher, through the assistance of Tom Brogan and the INSTAP Study Center for East Crete. A few drawings are the work of John Bouda, Alice (Fäthke) Berbner, and Alison Rittershaus. All photos are courtesy of the Kea Excavation archives. Photographs that are not attributed to a particular photographer in the captions were taken during excavation or study seasons between 1960 and 1989. Most were taken by either John L. Caskey or E. Tucker Blackburn, although some photographs were taken by other excavators and researchers; in any case, the photographers' names were not recorded. Photos taken by me are noted in the captions.

I have been influenced significantly by Aliki's interpretations, both those in her notes and those that were shared with me in person. She had completed extensive work toward reconstructing the stratigraphy, and, in most instances, I have come to the same or similar conclusions. In the few cases where I did not follow her reasoning, or where I disagreed with her interpretations, I have included her ideas alongside my own.

Many colleagues allowed me to access comparative ceramics in collections and museums in Greece, including Natalia Vogeikoff-Brogan, Sylvie Dumont, Robert Pitt, Catherine Morgan, Vance Watrous, Jeffrey Soles, Eleni Nodarou, Doniert Evely, Eleni Hatzaki, Caroline Jeffra, Barry Molloy, Jo Day, Florens Felten, Walter Gauss, Rudolphine Smetana, Kostas Kalogeropoulos, Kim Shelton, Salvatore Vitale, Žarko Tankosić, Nikos Papadimitriou, Anna Philippa-Touchais, Gilles Touchais, Alexandra Christopoulou, Katia Manteli, Marisa Marthari, and the staff of the National Archaeological Museum, as well as the archaeological museums of Paros, Naxos, and Melos. My ideas have been influenced by fruitful conversations about ceramics, the Bronze Age, and the Cyclades with those colleagues and others, including my former professors, especially Jack Davis, Eleni Hatzaki, Gisela Walberg, and Kathleen

ACKNOWLEDGMENTS

Lynch, as well as Emily Egan, Emilia Oddo, Lynne Kvapil, Joanne Cutler, Jill Hilditch, John C. Overbeck, Donna May Crego, Miriam Caskey, Irene Nikolakopoulou, Carl Knappett, Kim Shelton, Ioanna Galanaki, Peter Pavúk, Salvatore Vitale, Štěpán Rückl, Tobias Krapf, Anthi Balitsari, Deb Trusty, Jennifer Moody, Margarita Nazou, Maria Anastasiadou, Myrto Georgakopoulou, and Maria Koutsoumbou. I warmly thank Evi Gorogianni for welcoming me to Kea and sharing her extensive knowledge of Cycladic ceramics over the course of several seasons together in the apotheke. I am grateful to Evi, as well as to David Wilson, Rodney Fitzsimons, Joanne Cutler, Jill Hilditch, Carl Knappett, Peter Pavúk, Michael Lindblom, Jeremy B. Rutter, John C. Overbeck, Donna May Crego, and Miriam Caskey for sharing unpublished work.

Macroscopic fabric groups were developed initially in consultation with Jill Hilditch in relation to the system she established for Period V–VII pottery from the Northern Sector (Hilditch, forthcoming). Jill's help and willingness to consult with me on macroscopic and petrographic fabrics were pivotal in enabling me to complete this work. Michalis Sakalis of the Fitch Laboratory of the British School at Athens prepared the petrographic slides. The petrographic study began at the University of California, Berkeley, where I was sponsored by Kim Shelton. Ted Peña kindly gave me access to his microscope. The bulk of the petrographic analysis took place at the University of Michigan. Dawn Johnson, Christopher Ratté, and T. G. Wilfong provided lab space in the Kelsey Museum of Archaeology. The petrographic study was completed at Lawrence Livermore National Laboratory, where my work was facilitated by Scott Tumey and Susan Zimmerman. Vangelio Kiriatzi, Zoe Zgouleta, and Carlotta Gardner of the Fitch Laboratory and Dimitris Michailidis and Panagiotis Karkanas of the Wiener Laboratory enabled me to access their microscopes, cameras, and comparative slide collections. The petrographic work was much improved through consultation with Vangelio Kiriatzi, Eleni Nodarou, Michael Galaty, Bartek Lis, Anthi Balitsari, and Noémi Müller, in addition to Jill. The WD-XRF analysis was undertaken by Noémi Müller at the Fitch Laboratory. Evi Margaritis and Nikos Kounadis analyzed a soil sample from inside a pithos (**232**), work that was enabled by Dimitris Michailidis at the Wiener Laboratory.

Specialists examined several categories of non-ceramic finds from Area B; their names are noted in parentheses in the catalogue when they have provided information about an object. George Rapp, Ian Whitbread, and Robin Torrence provided information on some stone objects. Myrto Georgakopoulou examined metal and metallurgical objects; one was also sent to the University of Cincinnati Department of Geology, where it was probably analyzed by Reuben Bullard. Jenny Coy and John L. Caskey identified the type of bone used for some objects; other bone objects were given types or dates based on a preliminary study by Olga Krzyszkowska. Some fragments of painted wall plaster were discussed by Katherine Abramovitz Coleman in her dissertation; others were examined by Lyvia Morgan, who shared her notes with me. Aliki, on the basis of her own records and Coleman's analysis, also drew sections that note the locations of fragments of painted wall plaster (Figs. 9, 11:c, 13, 14:c).

Much of the initial work for this project took place during a year that I spent in Greece as a Fulbright Fellow at the ASCSA. I am grateful to the members of the Fulbright office, especially Nicholas Tourides and Artemis Zenetou, as well as the staff of the ASCSA, including Karen Bohrer, Maria Tourna, Natalia Vogeikoff-Brogan, and Leda Costaki. Maria Pilali and Ioanna Damanaki helped me with my many permit applications. Permissions were granted by William Johnson, Peter van Minnen, and Jack Davis of the University of Cincinnati and by Marisa Marthari, Panagiotis Hatzidakis, Dimitris Athanasoulis, and Maria Koutsoumbou of the KA´ Ephoreia. My research was enabled through the assistance of the staff of the Kea Archaeological Museum, especially Eleftheria Morfoniou, Eleni Tsiogka, and Lefteris Lepouras. I am grateful to the faculty and staff of the University of Cincinnati Department of Classics and the Burnam Classics Library, especially Jacquie Riley, Mike Braunlin, David Ball, and Cade Stevens, as well as the University of Michigan Department of Classical Studies and the library staff, especially Zachary Quint and Beau Case.

Figures and plates were compiled by Lorene Sterner of the Kelsey Museum of Archaeology, who also optimized the drawings and photos for publication. Bruce Worden prepared several figures and plates, as well. Anna Belza, Jami Baxley Craig, Michael Koletsos, and Lauren Oberlin helped with data checking and editing. Elena Gwynne helped with the index. I thank Jack Davis, Eleni Hatzaki, Tom Brogan, Gerald Cadogan, Michael Galaty, Carol Hershenson, and the two anonymous reviewers for their comments on the manuscript. Susan Ferrence and Phil Betancourt also offered feedback and clarified several parts of the publication process. Jennifer Sacher provided crucial support during the final stages of revising and editing. Lisa Nevett, Michèle Hannoosh, and Artemis Leontis gave me much helpful advice and support during the last stages of manuscript preparation, as well.

Philip and Noelle Auerbach allowed me to use their house on Kea during one season, the spectacular view from which helped to inspire many of the following pages. Funding was provided by the University of Cincinnati, Institute of International Education, ASCSA, Archaeological Institute of America, and University of Michigan; the final stages of analysis and writing were undertaken while I was supported by fellowships from the Loeb Classical Library Foundation and the American Council of Learned Societies.

I am grateful to the many people who have worked and collaborated with me on Kea, including those mentioned above, as well as Shannon LaFayette Hogue and Joanne Murphy, whose patience and support were fundamental to the completion of this project. Lastly, I thank Scott Tumey for his encouragement at every stage of researching and writing this volume.

ABBREVIATIONS

Abbreviations for publications follow the list of the *American Journal of Archaeology*
(http://ajaonline.org/submissions/abbreviations).

EXCAVATION RECORDS

AB Stratigraphy	Bikaki, n.d. "General Alley AB Stratigraphy Notes"
H-E Results	Bikaki, n.d. "Brief Diagram of Results in Test H-E"
Notecards	Bikaki, n.d. Notecards
Test H-E Pottery Notes	Bikaki, 1976. "Test H-E Pottery Notes"
B604CL Pottery Notes	Bikaki, n.d., "B604CL Pottery Notes"
B606CL Pottery Notes	Bikaki, n.d., "B606CL Pottery Notes"
B608CL Pottery Notes	Bikaki, n.d., "B608CL Pottery Notes"
Summary (Miscellaneous)	Bikaki, n.d., "Summary"
Coleman, 1970 Notes	Coleman, "Frescoes/Plaster. Kassie's Notes as of June 1970"

CHRONOLOGICAL TERMS

EBA	Early Bronze Age	EM	Early Minoan	EH	Early Helladic	EC	Early Cycladic
MBA	Middle Bronze Age	MM	Middle Minoan	MH	Middle Helladic	MC	Middle Cycladic
LBA	Late Bronze Age	LM	Late Minoan	LH	Late Helladic	LC	Late Cycladic

OTHER TERMS

ASCSA	American School of Classical Studies at Athens	max.	maximum
ca.	circa	min.	minimum
CL	combined lot	mm	millimeter/s
cm	centimeter/s	μm	micrometer/s
D.	diameter	perf.	perforation
DOL	dark-on-light	pres.	preserved
est.	estimated	rest.	restored
FM	Furumark Motif Number (Furumark 1941)	RKE	rotative kinetic energy
		SDL	Seismic Destruction Level at Akrotiri (Marthari 1984, 1990)
FS	Furumark Shape Number		
g	gram/s	Th.	thickness
H.	height	WD-XRF	Wave-dispersive X-ray fluorescence
ICP-AES	inductively coupled plasma atomic emission spectroscopy	VDL	Volcanic Destruction Level at Akrotiri (Marthari 1984, 1990)
L.	length	vs.	versus
LOD	light-on-dark	W.	Width
m	meter/s	Wt.	weight

ABBREVIATIONS

FABRIC TERMS

Macroscopic and petrographic fabric groups are described in detail in Chapter 3 and Appendices IV and V.

a	angular	opt act	optical activity
CF	coarse fraction	PBS	Pink-Brown Soapy
CSW	Coarse, with Shiny, White Inclusions	PFG	petrographic fabric group
DV	Dusty, Volcanic	ppl	plane polarized light
el	elongate	r	rounded
eq	equant	RBM	Red-Brown Metamorphic
FF	fine fraction	sa	subangular
FST	Fine, Non-Micaceous, Sand-Tempered	sr	subrounded
FV	Fine, Varied	tcfs	textural concentration features
MFV	Micaceous, Fine, Varied	wr	well-rounded
MxM	Mixed Micaceous	xpl	cross-polarized light

ABBREVIATIONS IN FIGURES 53–63 (SHAPE AND WARE)

Amph	amphora	M/T	Melian/Theran
AM	Argive Minyan	Mth	mouth
Bk	beaked	OM	oval-mouthed
BSp/HM	bridge-spouted/hole-mouthed	Ped	pedestaled
Burn	burnished	Perf	perforated
Car	carinated	Pir	piriform
Cl	closed	PO	Pink-Orange
CW	Cycladic White	Poly	Polychrome
Cycl	Cycladic	Ptd	painted
E Aeg	east Aegean	RC	Red Coated
Glob	globular	Rd	rounded
GM	Gray Minyan	RM	round-mouthed
Gr/Bl	Gray/Black	S&B	Slipped and Burnished
Hdl	handle	Sm	small
HM	hole-mouthed	SMP	Standard Matt Painted
Lent	lentoid	Spread	spreading
Lg	large	Spt	spouted
Loc	local	Strt-sided	straight-sided
LP	Lustrous Painted	Vaph	Vapheio
Mel	Melian	Var	various
Min	Minoan	Vess	vessel
Min/-izing	Minoan/-izing	WM	wide-mouthed
Min/Myc	Minoan/Mycenaean	WoG	White-on-Gray
Miny	Minyan	WoR	White on Red
Misc	miscellaneous	Unk	Unknown
Mnld	Mainland	YM	Yellow Minyan
MP	Matt Painted	YS	Yellow Slipped

I. INTRODUCTION

Political, economic, and social changes in the Aegean Bronze Age were tied to shifts in maritime interaction, whether the result of novel sailing technologies, communication with new regions or peoples, or better or more diversified access to agricultural, mineral, or other resources. The Cyclades played an important role in Aegean interaction networks. The islands were rich in metal and stone resources, and the geography of the Cycladic archipelago, with its closely spaced islands and numerous harbors, enabled and encouraged travel between the islands and the surrounding landmasses of Anatolia, mainland Greece, and Crete.

During the Bronze Age, the site of Ayia Irini, located on the northwestern coast of Kea on the sheltered natural harbor of Ayios Nikolaos, was a major hub on trade and communication routes that linked the different regions of the Aegean to each other as well as to the nearby metal resources of Lavrion on the Attic coast (Figs. 1, 2). It is a key location for investigating long-term patterns of exchange, interaction, and culture change.

The excavation of Ayia Irini took place in the 1960s and 70s, under the direction of John L. Caskey of the University of Cincinnati. Excavation revealed a settlement occupied off and on from the Final Neolithic through much of the LBA (Table 1.1, Fig. 3). This study provides an analysis of the stratigraphy, architecture, and artifacts, especially ceramics, from Area B (Fig. 4), which date from the EBA to the LBA (Periods III–VII). Analysis of ceramics from Area B, supplemented with published information from other parts of the site, demonstrates that, in every period, Ayia Irini was remarkably multicultural in the variety of goods that were produced, imported, and used by local inhabitants.

A BRIEF HISTORY OF AYIA IRINI

The first settlement at Ayia Irini dates to the very last part of the Neolithic (Period I; Table 1.1). No architecture is known, and artifacts are few (Coleman 1977, 99; Wilson 1999). Rare imported ceramics suggest that, even in this phase, residents of the site were interacting with other areas. Only a few non-ceramic objects that might date to this period were found, and it is unclear how long this settlement may have endured. The site was abandoned before the beginning of the EBA (Wilson 1999, 6–20).

The subsequent phases of occupation, Periods II and III, date to the middle part of the EBA, contemporary with a phase of extensive exchange and interaction in the Cyclades. Ayia Irini was one of a few large sites in the Cyclades of this period (Broodbank 2000, 2008), with good evidence for interaction especially with Cycladic and Attic communities (Wilson 1987; 1999, 20–143). The second EBA phase, Period III, was contemporary with a shift in trade patterns (the Kastri phase), as Cycladic islanders began to interact more regularly with the northeastern Aegean and Euboea (Broodbank 2000; Wilson 1999, 90–143; 2013). During the same period, many Cycladic communities, including Ayia Irini, adopted new Anatolianizing eating, drinking, and pouring ceramic shapes into local repertoires (Wilson 1999, 94–101). At the end of Period III, Ayia Irini was abandoned (Overbeck 1984, 109; Wilson 1999, 2013).

After the MBA had begun elsewhere in the Aegean, Ayia Irini was resettled (Abell 2014a; Crego 2010; Overbeck 1984, 109; Overbeck and Crego 2008). A fortification wall with at least one horseshoe-shaped tower was built. Houses seem to have been freestanding but are poorly preserved (J. C. Overbeck 1989a; Overbeck and Crego 2008). A small ritual structure, the Temple, was built in the southeastern part of the site (Caskey 1986; J. C. Overbeck 1989a, 176). Evidence for metalworking and imported objects were found in the earliest deposits, which suggests that the town was founded deliberately to take advantage of the position of the site at an intersection of trade routes probably oriented especially toward the metal resources of Lavrion (Crego 2010; Overbeck 1982; Overbeck and Crego 2008). Some graves of this period contained objects in exotic stones, imported ceramics, and precious metals, which attest to the relative wealth of at least some members of the community (G. F. Overbeck 1974, 1989). In Period IV, the closest cultural connections of Ayia Irini seem to have been with Aegina, mainland Greece, and the Cyclades, although imports from Crete and the adoption of a few Cretan technologies suggest that residents of Ayia Irini also engaged in exchange relationships with Cretan communities (Caskey 1972; Crego 2010; J. C. Overbeck 1989a; Overbeck and Crego 2008).

In Period V, a new fortification wall was built, which doubled the size of the settlement. Period V was the first phase of the so-called Minoanization phenomenon, in which Cycladic communities began to adopt and adapt Cretan ways of doing things, imitating aspects of Cretan material culture, symbolic imagery, and technological practices on a large scale (Abell 2016; Davis 1984, 1986, 2008). At Ayia Irini, Minoan (i.e., Cretan) and Minoanizing (i.e., Cretan-style) objects from outside of Crete were common imports while local potters began to produce many Minoanizing vessels. Mainland and Cycladic ceramics also continued to form

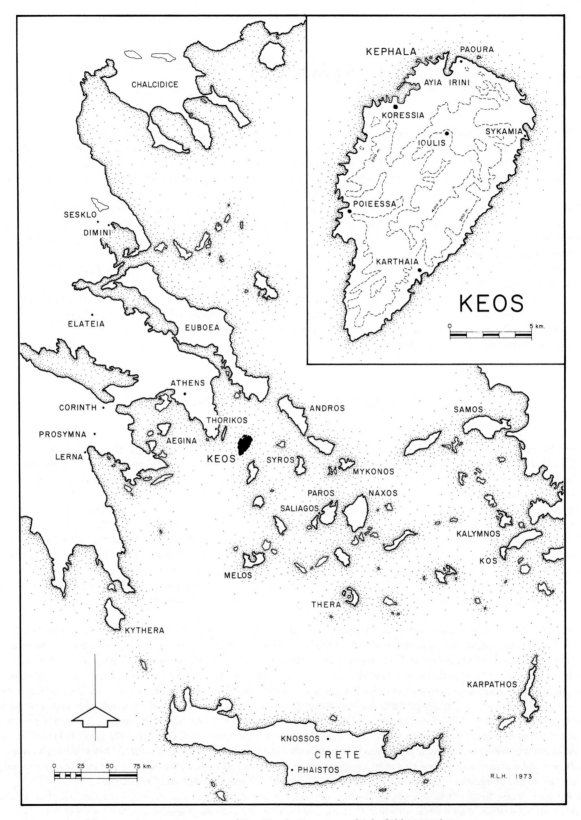

Fig. 1. Map of the central Aegean; inset map of Kea (Keos). Cummer and Schofield 1984, pl. 1.

I. INTRODUCTION

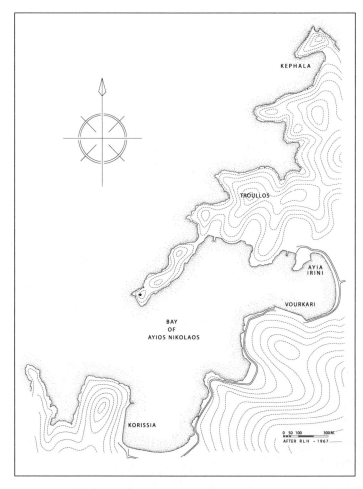

Fig. 2. Map of the northwestern coast of Kea. Cummer and Schofield 1984, pl. 2.

TABLE 1.1. SCHEMATIC CHRONOLOGY OF AYIA IRINI

For a more detailed relative chronology, see Fig. 3. Note that Period III ended before the end of the EBA, while Period IV started after the beginning of the MBA elsewhere.

Aegean	Cyclades	Ayia Irini
Final Neolithic		Period I
EBA	EC II (Keros-Syros)	Period II
	EC II (Kastri)	Period III
MBA	Earlier MC	Period IV
	Later MC	Period V
LBA	LC I	Period VI
	LC II	Period VII
	LC III	Period VIII

part of the assemblage. An earthquake at the end of Period V damaged parts of the fortification wall, which was repaired and remodeled at the beginning of the next phase (Davis 1986; Fitzsimons and Gorogianni 2017; Schofield 2011).

During Period VI, the first phase of the LBA, large buildings were constructed in different parts of the site, including Houses F and C in the Western Sector (Schofield 2011), the Northeast Bastion in the Northern Sector (Fitzsimons and Gorogianni 2017; Gorogianni and Fitzsimons, forthcoming), as well as House B and the first iteration of House A (Cummer and Schofield 1984) in the southeastern part of the site. The Temple continued to be used (Caskey 1986, 2009). Residents of the site engaged in a variety of crafts, processing metals, pigments, and aromatics, as well as producing textiles and ceramics (Schofield 1990). Much local craft production relied on Minoanizing technologies and industrial equipment, like the potter's wheel, warp-weighted loom, and fireboxes (Georgiou 1986). Across the site, Minoanizing objects and imagery were prevalent. Nevertheless, local production and consumption patterns also reflect ongoing interaction with mainland and Cycladic communities.

Period VII followed the eruption of the Theran volcano, which caused shifts in intra-Cycladic exchange networks. House A was expanded and for the first time dwarfed other houses in size (Cummer and Schofield 1984, pl. 4). Throughout this era, Ayia Irini seems to have been a bustling exchange hub, until a major earthquake near the end of the period seriously damaged most buildings in the settlement. Minoan and Minoanizing objects continued to be locally produced and imported, many from mainland Greece (Cummer and Schofield 1984; Gorogianni and Abell, forthcoming; Mountjoy and Ponting 2000).

After the earthquake, and the development of the Mycenaean palaces shortly thereafter, Ayia Irini experienced a decline in prosperity and perhaps population. The peninsula was abandoned as a place of residence in LH IIIB, although the area of the Temple continued to be visited into the Hellenistic period (J. L. Caskey 1979, 1982; M. E. Caskey 1986, 1998, 2009; Gorogianni 2011; Morris and Jones 1998).

EXCAVATION OF AREA B

Preliminary excavation began at Ayia Irini in 1960 (Pl. 1:a). In 1961, several trenches were laid out across the southeastern part of the promontory, just east of the already promising Area A. Excavation there was overseen by Aliki Bikaki. Trenches 1 and 2 (B01T, B02T, respectively) were dug alongside Trench 3 (B03T), until it was clear that two buildings were present in the area (Figs. 4, 5). Large parts of the Temple were found in Trenches B01T and B02T. A Late Bronze Age house, designated House B, was found in Trench B03T. Although the Temple was nominally excavated as part of Area B, it has been separated from the rest of Area B in the excavation records and its publication program. This study considers only remains from Trench B03T—House B, Alley AB, and the deposits below these LBA features—as Area B. Although the southeastern part of Temple Lane was excavated in B03T, it has been studied as part of the Temple area and will be presented in that *Keos* volume.

Most excavation of LBA House B and the mixed EBA and MBA deposits below it took place in 1961. During the same season, LBA deposits in Alley AB were excavated, as was a small test pit at the northern end of the alley. No further excavation took place in the area until 1975 when a second test pit was opened in Alley AB, to the southwest of the original test pit (Fig. 6). The publication of House A incorrectly located these test pits outside of Room A.39 (Cummer and Schofield 1984, 5, pl. 19); the test pits were, instead, excavated outside of Room A.36. Subsequent tests in 1976 were focused on deposits below Rooms B.1 and B.2.

Bikaki's meticulous notes offer clear, straightforward descriptions of the excavation, although her recording techniques changed over time. Descriptions of the soil matrices from 1961 are limited to the relative stoniness and moisture of the soil, which sometimes makes it difficult to understand why she saw some excavation units as part of similar or different deposits. Photos of excavation in progress during the 1961 season also were taken relatively rarely (Pls. 1–8). Her account of soil matrices excavated in test pits in 1975 and 1976 is more comprehensive. The sequence of strata that she observed is fully described in her written notes and drawings, and it is documented in many photos (Pls. 9–18). Apart from a few problems in the transcription of numbers, and rare illegible or confusing sections of text, the only significant problem with the records of Area B is that the total amount of pottery discarded during papsing (below) was not always recorded. In general (and in many specifics), Bikaki's careful techniques and detailed notes distinguish Area B as one of the best excavated and best documented parts of Ayia Irini.

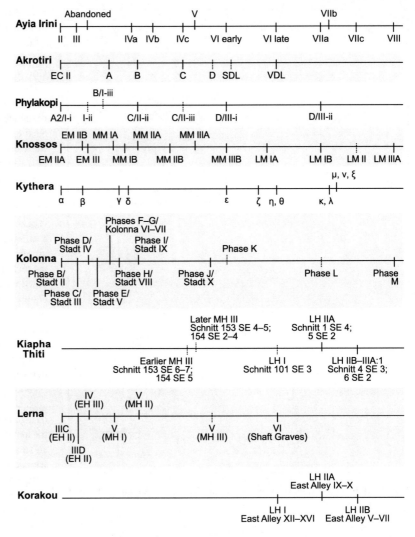

Fig. 3. Comparison of chronological phases at Ayia Irini with other Aegean sites.

TERMINOLOGY

Some notes about terminology are warranted. A "deposit" in this volume follows Schiffer's (1996, 265–266) definition: a "three-dimensional segment of a site (or other area of analytical interest) that is distinguished in the field on the basis of observable changes in sediments and artifacts." Deposits differ from "excavation units," which were the three dimensional areas excavated as part of a particular numbered unit (e.g., B03-72), but which were not always coterminous with observed deposits. For example, the Period III destruction deposit below House B contained many ceramic cross-joins and little evidence for change in sediments or artifacts. It is considered therefore to be a single deposit, formed by a distinct episode of destruction and architectural collapse. Nevertheless, the deposit was dug in several excavation units. A "lot" refers to the pottery from an excavation unit. Ceramic lots have the same number as the excavation unit; i.e., pottery excavated in unit B03-72 belongs to lot B03-72.

I. INTRODUCTION

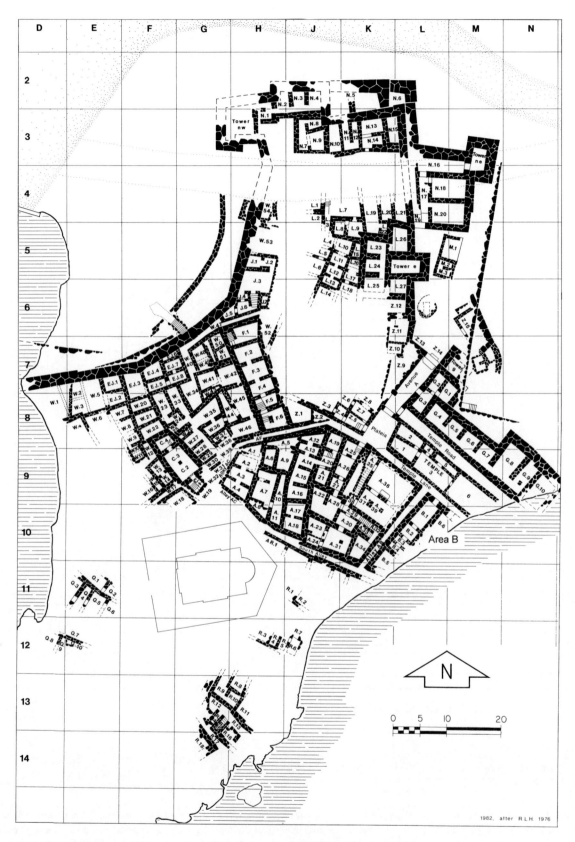

Fig. 4. Plan of LBA Ayia Irini showing location of Area B. After drawing by R. L. Holzen.

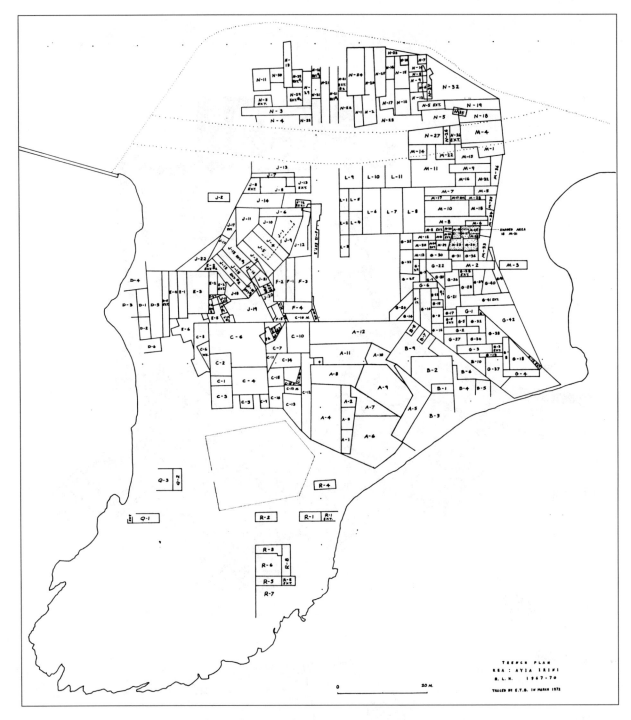

Fig. 5. Trench plan of Ayia Irini. After drawing by R. L. Holzen.

FORMATION PROCESSES

Some deposits in Area B have been disturbed by later human activity, most of which is tied to continued occupation and construction in the area during the Bronze Age. Different visual perspectives on deposits, architectural features, and associated excavation units are presented in stratigraphic sections (Figs. 7–15), Harris matrices (Figs. 16–18), and phase plans (Figs. 19–25).

A large Period III destruction deposit below House B was mostly undisturbed, but upper levels contained some Period IV–VII ceramics. A series of stratified Period IV and V deposits were found in the test pits below Alley AB. Inside and below House B,

I. INTRODUCTION

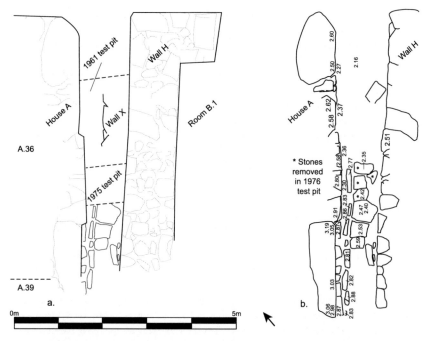

Fig. 6. a. Plan showing location of test pits in Alley AB and Period IV Wall X. After architects' field sheets. b. Plan of Alley AB. The narrow stones along House A Wall E (L) are uprights for Drain 1. After architect's drawing.

Period IV and V pottery was mixed with earlier and later ceramics and cannot be associated with architectural remains. Much of the mixing of ceramics of different periods in these deposits was probably caused by the construction of House B during which much earth must have been moved in order to lay the deep foundations for the house walls. Period VI deposits in House B are primarily represented by accumulated debris and continuously occupied surfaces, while Period VII is represented by surfaces and large destruction deposits. Although Bikaki referred to "floors" in her initial excavation notes, over the course of her study she began to suspect that most of the LBA "floors" were not, in fact, distinct floor levels that had been intentionally laid, but rather that they had accumulated gradually over time. In her initial excavation notes, she also labeled several other "floors" that subsequent research has revealed were not floors at all (e.g., Surface c and Surface i, which seem to have been ground level—but not interior floors—in early Period IV). Thus, all strata that Bikaki recorded as "floors" are called "surfaces" in this volume. Period VII destruction deposits contained some later ceramics, especially at upper elevations, probably the result of erosion down slope into Area B, as well as the postexcavation process of combining ceramic lots from different excavation units (below). However, despite the construction of an Archaic wall—Wall Q—over Room B.2/B.3, Area B was little disturbed by post–Bronze Age anthropogenic processes.

Rising sea levels and erosion since the Bronze Age have resulted in the destruction of the southeastern part of the house, which is evident in photos (Plate 1:b). Most excavation units that recovered EBA and MBA ceramics were located at or below sea level; pumps ran continuously during excavation to keep water from flooding the trench, leaving the soil matrix muddy and sometimes difficult to interpret, especially in the lowest units. Nevertheless, despite these issues, Area B suffered less destruction and disturbance than many other areas of the site (Cummer and Schofield 1984; Gorogianni 2008, 117–359; Schofield 2011).

RECOVERY AND SELECTION

The recovery and processing of artifacts from Area B followed the standards of the site (Gorogianni 2008, 2009–2010). The total amount of pottery and other objects from each excavation unit was usually recorded. However, through two postexcavation practices—papsing and combining lots—some information has been lost.

Papsing was a process by which, on multiple occasions in the study of pottery, sherds that were seen as uninteresting and/or undiagnostic were discarded (Gorogianni 2008, 64–65, 102–105). This often happened at least twice (Gorogianni 2008, 102–105, 350); several lots from Area B were papsed three or four times. In order to determine how significant this problem might be in Area B, I collected discard information for every lot and compared what was described in the pottery notebooks with the preserved ceramics. Pottery notebook descriptions existed for almost all lots, except for the 1976 test pit below Room B.2.

The specific reasons why sherds were deemed uninteresting or undiagnostic is not spelled out in the records. The most common characteristic cited for discarded pottery is its coarseness, although finer ceramics were also discarded, especially from Period VII lots (see also Gorogianni 2008, 102–105, 349–352, table 77). For example, in the Period VII lot B608CL, only 60% of the pottery was coarse, but 90% of the lot was discarded. Since local pottery ranges from moderately fine to, more often, moderately coarse or coarse, much discarded pottery—but certainly not all of it—was probably of local manufacture.

Most imported sherds that were diagnostic enough to be described by ware in the pottery notebooks are still present in Area B lots, with the exception of small Gray Minyan sherds found in LBA deposits, which seem to have been considered to be MBA contamination. Similarly, local sherds that are described in the pottery notebooks are still present, other than pithoi, handleless cups, and tripods, many of which were discarded. Extant pottery includes mainly feature sherds (e.g., rims, bases, handles, spouts) of both plain and decorated vessels in local and imported fabrics. Body sherds from local and imported vessels, plain and decorated, fine and coarse, also exist, although the high proportion of feature and decorated sherds suggests that many body sherds, especially plain, coarse ones, have been discarded. The existence of some plain, coarse body sherds in the extant lots, however, in addition to a wider array of decorated and feature sherds, suggests that the preserved pottery provides a representative sample of the variety of imports that existed during excavation, as well as the majority of local pottery shapes and decorated wares. The existence of plain coarse body sherds in imported fabrics in Area B, and the prevalence of coarse imported vessels in Period III and IV deposits (Chs. 4, 5) suggest that discard practices especially discriminated against local products. The ratio of tablewares to larger coarse vessels must also have been impacted, since sherds from coarse vessels were more likely to be discarded than those from finer tableware shapes.

The major category of missing evidence—plain, coarse local sherds with few distinctive shape or decorative characteristics—is a ceramic category that is unlikely to be as sensitive to changes in ceramic fashions as finer, decorated wares. The preserved dataset, which is made up primarily of feature and decorated sherds in imported and local ceramic fabrics, is therefore reasonably well suited to discussions of chronology and intra-Aegean cultural contact. Nevertheless, in all cases, conclusions based on the preserved ceramics must take into consideration the selected nature of the assemblage in order to determine whether a particular pattern is more likely to be the result of activity in the Bronze Age or the 20th century.

A second postexcavation process has affected the existing assemblage. Ceramic lots at Ayia Irini were often physically combined on the basis of stylistic or perceived chronological similarities, or a belief in the stratigraphic unity of the associated excavation units (Gorogianni 2008, 102–105). Combining of lots was sometimes done by someone other than the excavator (Gorogianni 2008, 102 n. 228). Through this process, artifacts from discrete archaeological contexts (e.g., surfaces, destruction deposits) have been muddled together, sometimes making it impossible to compare how the extant ceramics relate to stratigraphy observed during excavation. Bikaki (pers. comm.) became uneasy about the process of combining lots when she was excavating Area B, so combined lots are not ubiquitous in the area. Because Bikaki left Kea before the end of the 1961 season, lots from Area B, including nearly all of those dating to Periods VI and VII, were combined by someone else that year. When Bikaki returned to study the ceramics, she recorded as much information about the original composition of lots as she could recall (pers. comm.). Most lots from the tests in the 1970s were left uncombined.

GOALS AND METHODOLOGY

Area B has produced evidence of occupation from nearly every phase of the site's history, from Period III–VII. Although LBA construction resulted in some mixing of earlier deposits, the area was almost completely undisturbed by human activity between the destruction of House B and 1961. In addition, Bikaki's skilled direction of excavation in the area, her extensive and meticulous records, and her distaste for combining lots make Area B a distinctive and productive focus of investigation, both for addressing the site history of Ayia Irini and for reconsidering Ayia Irini in an Aegean-wide framework of cultural contact over time.

The nature of deposits in Area B enables a detailed, diachronic analysis of how residents of Ayia Irini participated in and were affected by developments in the broader Aegean. I have focused on the largest dataset—the ceramics. Pottery is a major indicator for the orientation and extent of exchange networks, since import patterns reveal shifts in trade partners and preferred products over time. In addition, analyses of technical, stylistic, and functional aspects of local pottery provide insights into when and how new production and consumption practices were adopted, as well as how traditional practices developed or were abandoned over time.

In order to clarify the impacts of changing patterns of interaction over the long-term, this volume includes the following components. First, the sequence of deposits in Area B is established, artifacts are catalogued, and the occupational history of the space from Period III–VII is summarized (Ch. 2). Ceramic shapes and wares in Area B are then compared to published deposits from the rest of the site (Chs. 4–7). Ceramic synchronisms are summarized in order to establish a chronological framework for regional comparisons. The relative proportions of shapes and wares from Area B are assessed in relation to published deposits in order to evaluate how patterns in Area B compare with the rest of the site and to consider if differences between Area B and published deposits are owed to variation in ancient depositional patterns or modern excavation, processing, and publication practices.

Wares provide a major basis for comparison of local and imported ceramics between Area B, previous *Keos* volumes, and published pottery from other sites. Ware terminology follows conventions established in *Keos* publications (for a summary, see Appendix III). Ware-based classifications, however, can be and often are problematic, in part because wares are not always used to refer to the same thing and may be used to designate functional, textural, or decorative groups (e.g., cookwares, tablewares, coarse wares, painted wares). In addition, ware designations historically have privileged unifying decorative styles as the main basis for classification, rather than distinguishing between different sources or production traditions (Burke, Day, and Kossyva 2020, 24; Mathioudaki 2010; Rice 1976; Sarri 2010a). Even when ware designations take fabric into account, as at Ayia Irini, the defining characteristics may be conceived quite broadly. For example, hard-fired fabrics associated with Cretan imports are lumped together in "Minoan" wares that are further defined only by decorative style, despite differences in color, inclusions, and texture. Likewise, a variety of micaceous fabrics suspected to be from the Cyclades have sometimes been subsumed in a single classificatory group:

I. INTRODUCTION

Cycladic Painted ware. Such ware designations are very useful for addressing broad regional patterns, but they are less helpful for identifying import patterns in relation to specific production centers.

In Area B, therefore, I also classified pottery according to macroscopic fabric groups in order (1) to determine whether there was meaningful variability in the use of local raw materials for different kinds of products over time, in relation to other changes in the local *chaîne opératoire*, and (2) to clarify importation patterns from particular production centers or micro-regions, in addition to the broad regions represented by established ware groups. This volume supersedes a previous analysis (Abell 2014b). Fabrics were examined macroscopically with the aid of a 14× hand lens, and groups were assigned based on color, hardness, texture, and the type and frequency of inclusions. Macroscopic fabric groups were compared with ceramic fabrics in study collections and museums in mainland Greece, Crete, the Cyclades, and the Dodecanese. Samples of ceramics from Area B were selected for petrographic analysis and wave-dispersive X-ray fluorescence (WD-XRF). Results of the petrographic study and preliminary interpretations of the WD-XRF data were used to clarify the coherence, potential provenance, and technical features of the macroscopic fabric groups. An overview of macroscopic and petrographic groups is provided in Chapter 3, together with a discussion of long-term trends in local pottery production techniques, based on analysis of fabrics and forming methods. Detailed macroscopic and petrographic fabric-group descriptions are provided in Appendices IV and V (Color Pls. 1–4); raw WD-XRF data are provided in Appendix VII. Preliminary observations on the relationship between chemical groups, petrographic groups, and potential provenances are included in Appendices IV and V. A complete report on the WD-XRF analysis will be published elsewhere in the future. Raw data were generated at the Fitch Laboratory using their documented methodological set-up (Georgakopoulou et al. 2017; Müller et al. 2018).

Ceramics from unmixed deposits in Area B were quantified according to minimum number of individual vessels in order to establish some empirical basis through which relative proportions of wares, shapes, and import regions could be evaluated over time and in comparison with other parts of the site. Individual vessels were assessed holistically on the basis of feature sherds and distinctive fabric or decorative characteristics, so that even two body sherds, if they belonged to different fabrics, would be counted as different vessels. All quantifications of archaeological material are impacted by depositional and postdepositional processes that generate a "death assemblage" different from the "life assemblage" of artifacts that were in use at any one time (for the concept as applied to ceramic assemblages, see Orton and Hughes 2013, 203–204). Postexcavation processes at Ayia Irini have significantly impacted the "death assemblage" at the site, and interpretation of quantifications in the assemblage must be undertaken cautiously. It nevertheless should be possible to compare relative proportions of different kinds of pottery across periods in Area B and between Area B and different parts of the site with some degree of security, since generally similar patterns of discard were employed everywhere. In addition, even if the numbers are not perfectly comparable between Ayia Irini and other sites, they provide a useful starting point for comparison (with the acknowledgment that no assemblage perfectly encapsulates the total range of ceramic artifacts in circulation at a site at any given time).

The integration of evidence from ceramic fabrics and wares to clarify local production and importation patterns enables a more robust analysis of shifting patterns of engagement and interaction between Ayia Irini and other parts of the Aegean through time. Although I considered changes in consumption patterns broadly, I also paid particular attention to drinking and eating practices. Tablewares are well represented in the extant ceramic assemblage, as noted above. Major shifts in the ceramic repertoire were closely related to developments in eating and drinking practices elsewhere, probably including both everyday consumption patterns as well as periodic communal events like feasts, which afford opportunities for social distinction, and which act as fora for establishing community solidarity or group identity (Dietler 2001; Hayden 2001; Joyce and Henderson 2007). Thus, although many comparisons of local and imported ceramics in this volume are concerned with a subset of the total assemblage, tablewares offer particularly useful insights into changing aspects of social practice and interaction in the town.

PRESENTATION OF FINDS

This volume follows the format of previous *Keos* publications. All excavation data are described by architectural unit. The standard of reference for trenches, excavation units, lots, and combined lots that was developed for the Northern Sector has been employed here (Table 1.2).

Most objects that were inventoried in the field or the apotheke either during or shortly after excavation were given "K" numbers, which are included in parentheses (e.g., K.1608) in the corresponding catalogue entry. For those few objects never given "K" numbers, field numbers are included in the catalogue (Ch. 2). Additional ceramics inventoried by Bikaki or myself were given numbers on the basis of lot or combined lot (e.g., B601: 5, or B70: 2). "B" numbers assigned by me in the apotheke follow this formula: B(lot/CL number): (inventory number), e.g., B601: 1. Appendix II provides a concordance of catalogue numbers to "K" and "B" numbers. Field numbers given to objects as they were excavated are distinctive from "B" numbers assigned by me in the apotheke. Although field numbers are preceded with a "B," that letter is followed by a hyphen, a number keyed to the year of excavation, a period, and a sequence number, e.g., B-1.12.

In the catalogue (Ch. 2), ceramics are presented after each architectural unit (e.g., Room B.1, Alley AB) and are divided by deposit and lot or combined lot. Within each lot or combined lot, a description of uncatalogued ceramics, including any discard

TABLE 1.2. SYSTEM OF NOTATION USED IN THIS VOLUME
After Gorogianni 2008, 137, table 4.

Category	Description	Example
Original excavation units	Area, trench number-sequential number of original uncombined unit	B03-97
Combined lots	Area, combined lot number, CL	B610CL
Trenches	Area, trench number, T	B03T
Rooms	Area –.– room number designation following *Keos* volumes	B.1

information from the first sort and papsing of the lot, precedes the numbered objects. For each lot/combined lot, ceramics are grouped by general provenance (local, Cyclades, Aegina, mainland, Crete), then by ware, following the most recent publication of ceramics from Ayia Irini (Schofield 2011).

Most ceramic shape names conform to the conventions used in previous *Keos* publications. There are two exceptions. The term "Keftiu cup" has been abandoned in favor of the more specific "straight-sided cup," versus Type I–III "Vapheio cups." Since paneled cups do not always preserve paneled decoration, the term "piriform cup" is used for this shape, in accordance with recent descriptions of Cycladic ceramics (e.g., Nikolakopoulou 2019, 163–164). The typology of "handleless cups" at Ayia Irini was developed by Caskey (Davis and Lewis 1985, fig. 5.3) and modified slightly by Schofield (1999; Cummer and Schofield 1984, pl. 47). The majority of handleless-cup types (Schofield's Types 1, 3, 4, and 5) are comparable with shapes generally described as "conical" cups on Crete, although several of these (especially Types 4 and 5) are not strictly conical in profile (Schofield 1999, 758). Indeed, some Type 4 handleless cups might also be called ogival cups, including the example of the type illustrated by Cummer and Schofield (1984, pl. 47:n). Nevertheless, the term "handleless cups" is maintained here, as it is the usual term in previous *Keos* volumes (Davis 1986; Cummer and Schofield 1984; Schofield 2011). Furumark Shape (FS) and Furumark Motif (FM) numbers are given when possible for LBA Lustrous Painted imports probably from the mainland (see Furumark 1941).

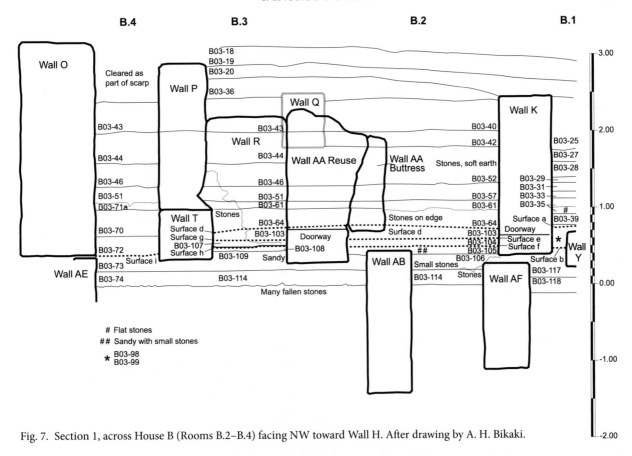

Fig. 7. Section 1, across House B (Rooms B.2–B.4) facing NW toward Wall H. After drawing by A. H. Bikaki.

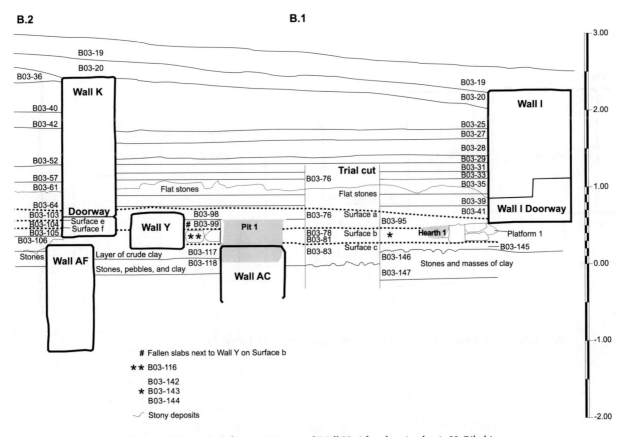

Fig. 8. Section 2, across House B (Room B.1) facing NW toward Wall H. After drawing by A. H. Bikaki.

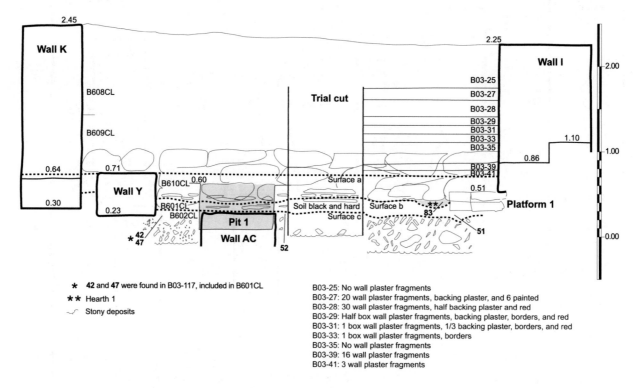

Fig. 9. Section 3, Room B.1, facing NW toward Wall H. After drawing by A. H. Bikaki.

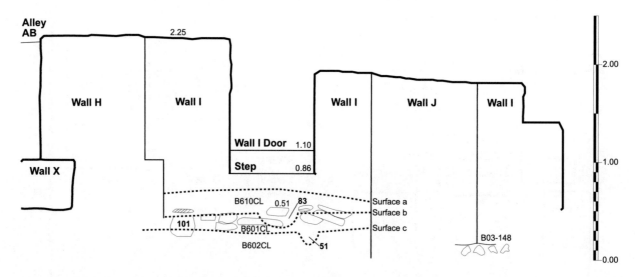

Fig. 10. Section 4, Room B.1, facing NE toward Wall I. After drawing by A. H. Bikaki.

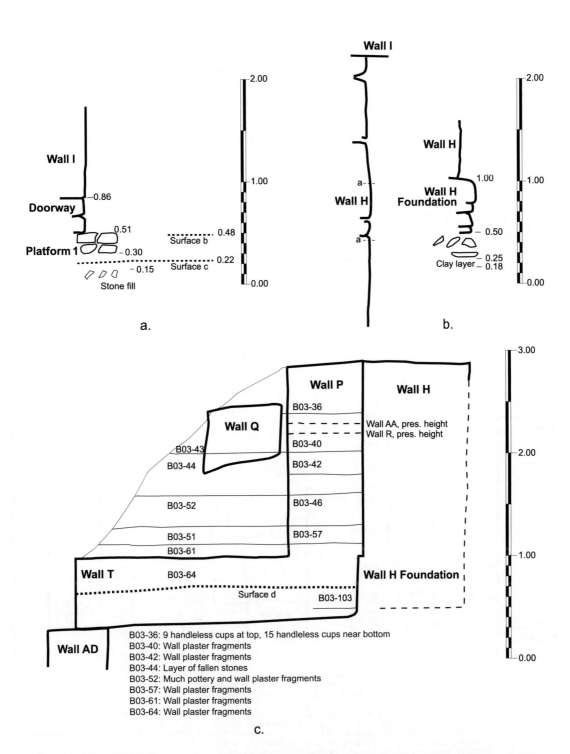

Fig. 11. a. Section 5, test pit in Room B.1 below Wall I, facing SE toward Wall J. After drawing by A. H. Bikaki. b. Plan (L) and section (R) of test pit below the Wall H foundation in Room B.1, facing NE toward Wall I. After drawing by A. H. Bikaki. c. Section 6, Room B.2/B.3, facing SW, toward Wall O. After drawing by A. H. Bikaki.

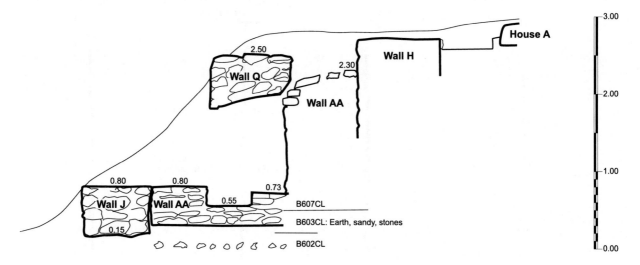

Fig. 12. Section 7, Room B.2, facing SW toward Wall O. After drawing by A. H. Bikaki.

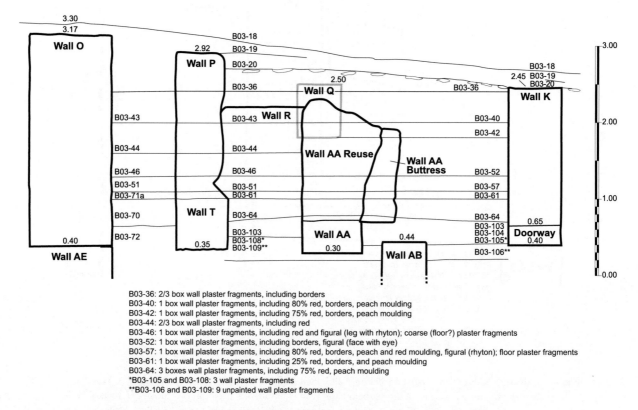

Fig. 13. Section 8, Rooms B.2–B.4, facing NW toward Wall H. After drawing by A. H. Bikaki.

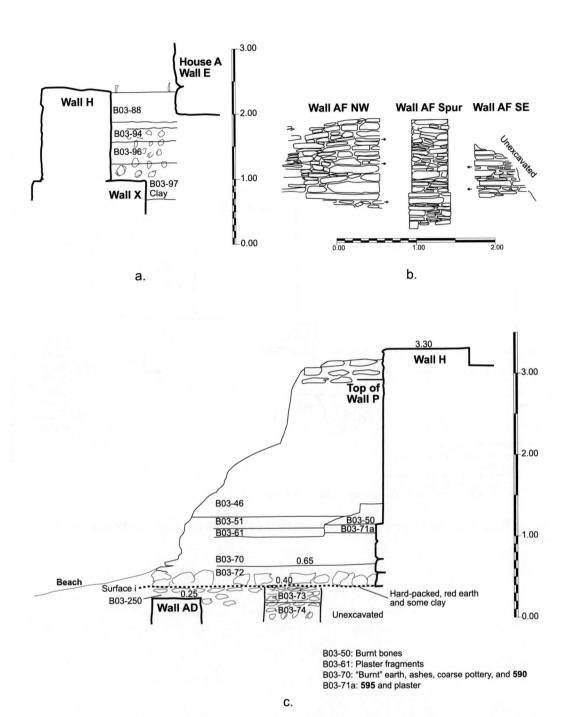

Fig. 14. a. Section 9, 1961 test pit in Alley AB, facing SW toward South Alley. After drawing by A. H. Bikaki. b. Section 10, Wall AF in the Room B.2 test pit, facing NE toward Wall I. After architect's drawing. c. Section 11, Room B.4, facing SW toward Wall O. After drawing by A. H. Bikaki.

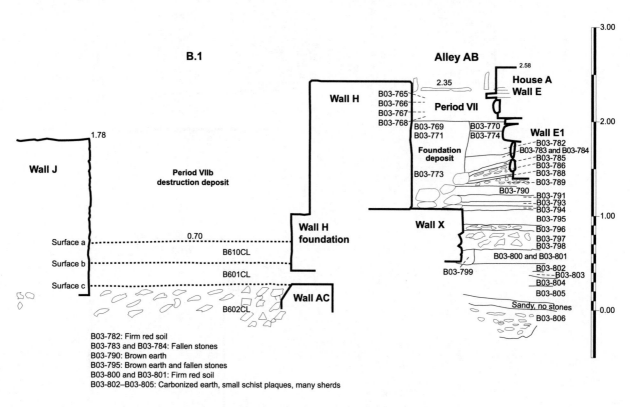

Fig. 15. Section 12, Room B.1 and 1975 test pit in Alley AB, facing SW toward Wall O and South Alley. After drawing by A. H. Bikaki.

I. INTRODUCTION

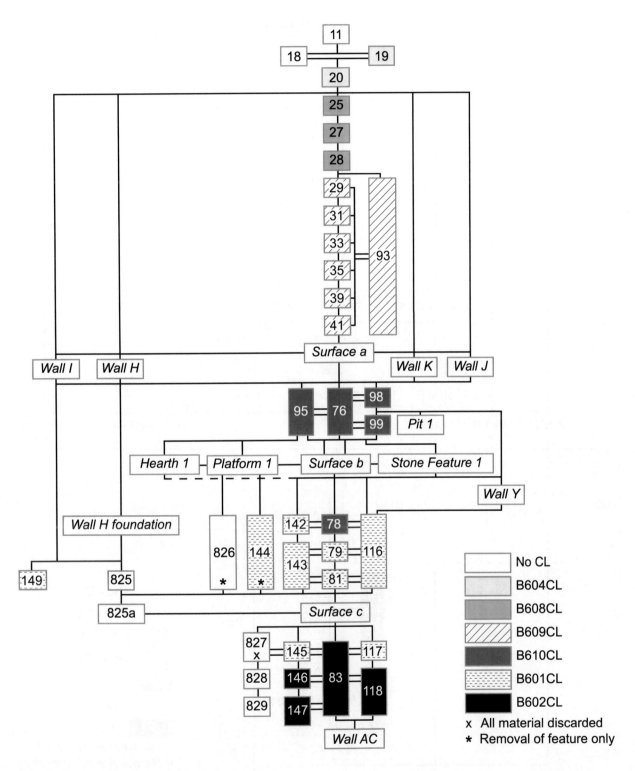

Fig. 16. Harris matrix of excavation units in Room B.1.

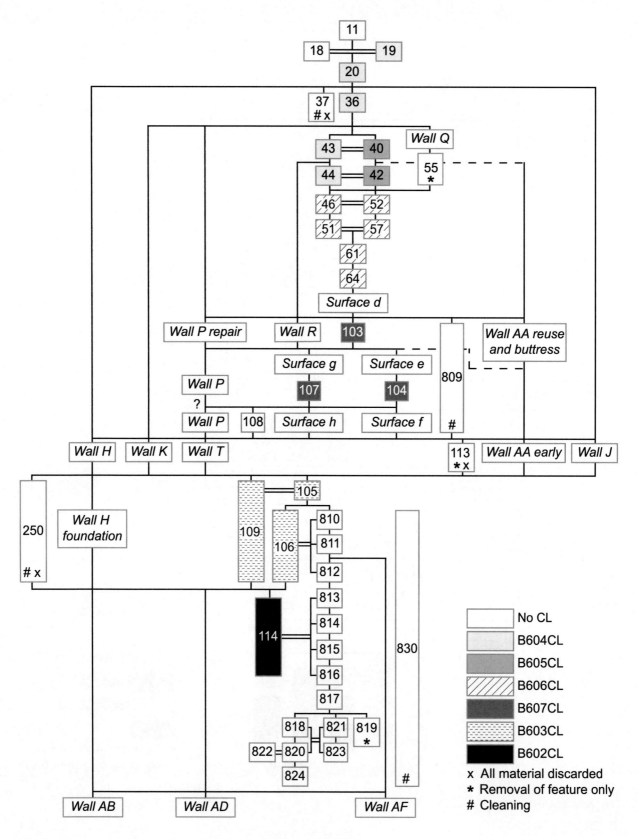

Fig. 17. Harris matrix of excavation units in Rooms B.2, B.3, and B.2/B.3.

I. INTRODUCTION

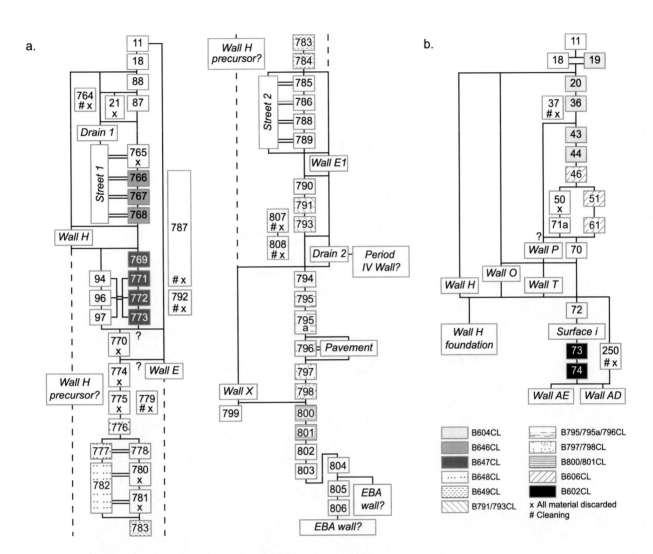

Fig. 18. Harris matrix of excavation units in (a) Alley AB and (b) Room B.4.

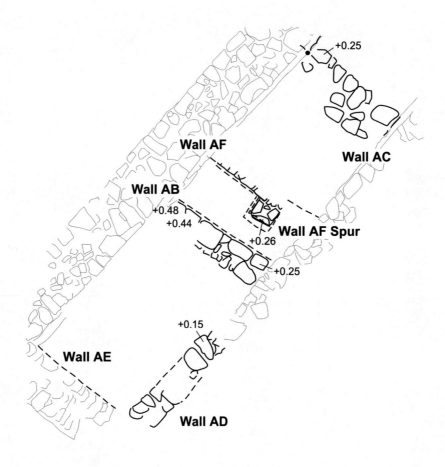

Fig. 19. Plan of Period III architecture in Area B. LBA architecture is shown in gray for reference. Black lines are used for EBA architecture. After architects' field sheets.

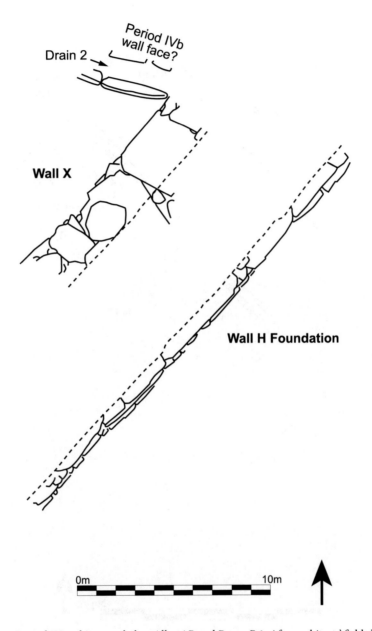

Fig. 20. Period IV architecture below Alley AB and Room B.1. After architects' field sheets.

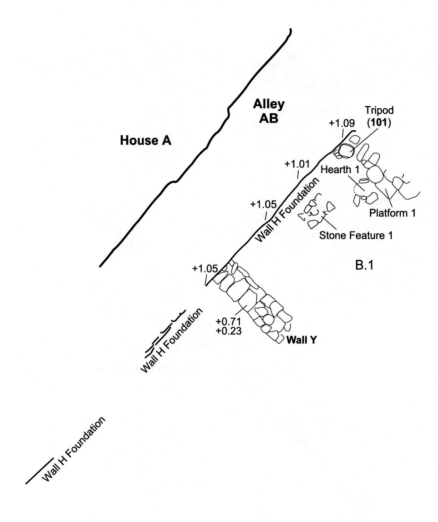

Fig. 21. House B: Phase 1 (Period VI). After architects' field sheets.

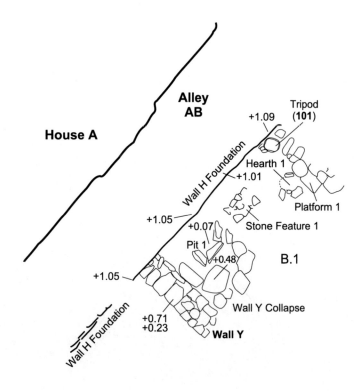

Fig. 22. House B: Phase 2 (Period VI). After architects' field sheets.

Fig. 23. House B: Phase 3 (Period VII). After architects' field sheets.

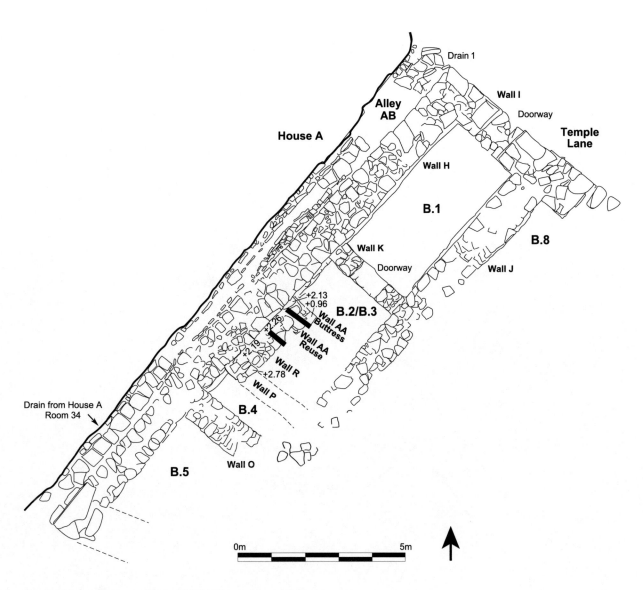

Fig. 24. House B: Phase 4 (Period VII). After architects' field sheets.

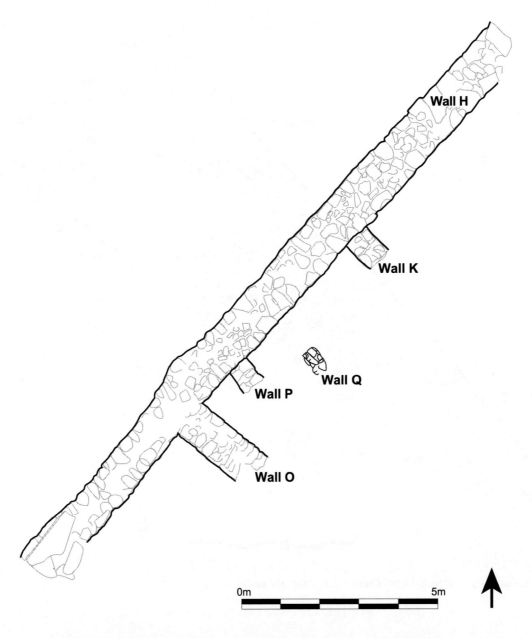

Fig. 25. Walls that continued to be visible (H, K, P, and O) and new construction (Wall Q) that postdate the Period VII destruction of House B. After architects' field sheets.

II. STRATIGRAPHY, ARCHITECTURE, AND POTTERY

This chapter provides a comprehensive examination of the stratigraphy and architectural sequence of Area B, in order to clarify the nature of deposits. This chapter follows the format of previous *Keos* volumes. Features are discussed within the confines of the Period VII architectural unit in which they were found, including earlier and later remains. First, the architectural unit is defined, and a brief summary of the history of the space is provided. Then, architectural features, ceramics, and small finds—organized by deposit and excavation unit—are discussed in detail.

A catalogue of ceramics and small finds follows the narrative presentation of each architectural unit. The catalogue is organized by lot and artifact type. Measurements in catalogue entries are either in meters (m) or grams (g). The volume of ceramics originally collected is given either by tin (17 liters) or by bag for each lot, according to the pottery notebooks or Bikaki's records. Bag sizes were not entirely standardized; in cases where volume was recorded with respect to bags rather than tins, therefore, it is sometimes impossible to estimate precisely how much pottery was collected. A brief description of uncatalogued ceramics (i.e., those that have never been assigned inventory or field numbers), based on excavation records and the pottery that currently exists in the apotheke, precedes numbered catalogue entries for each lot. "K" numbers given to objects by excavation staff are included after the catalogue number. "B" numbers assigned by me are not included in catalogue entries, but can be found in Appendix II. Ceramics are presented in groups organized by probable region of production, then by ware (see Appendix III). Macroscopic and petrographic fabric groups are discussed in Chapter 3, as is the terminology for forming methods (handmade, coil-built, wheel-coiled, and wheelmade). Detailed descriptions of fabrics are presented in Appendices IV and V; see also Color Pls. 1–4.

Previously published objects are noted in the catalogue. Typological categories of spindle whorls, loom weights and bone objects follow Davis (1986, pl. 38). Handleless cup types follow Cummer and Schofield (1984, pl. 47).

With the exception of some handleless cups, nearly all ceramics are illustrated in either the plates or the figures. The standardization of handleless cups renders illustration of all of them unnecessary. There are very few other objects for which it was impossible to obtain an image. The sherds that formed the basis for my interpretations of forming processes and changing import and production patterns are not always well preserved or of high value with respect to typo-stylistic comparisons based on morphology or decorative analysis. Nevertheless, illustrations provide the reader with a clear understanding of the size and state of preservation of the vessels described in the catalogue. Including such images also ensures that catalogued objects may be readily identified by future researchers, should they wish to reexamine some or all of the remains from Area B.

A plan of the southeastern part of Ayia Irini showing showing major features and Bronze Age walls of all phases in Area B is provided on Color Pl. 5. This chapter should also be read in conjunction with the excavation photos (Pls. 1–18), stratigraphic section drawings (Figs. 7–15), Harris matrices (Figs. 16–18), and phase plans (Figs. 19–25). A few sketches from the excavation notebooks are also illustrated (Pls. 19, 20). Harris matrices were drawn based on Bikaki's notes regarding soil type and variation during excavation. Although surfaces and other features were seldom excavated as separate units, they are included in the Harris matrices in order to show more accurately the observed stratigraphic associations of each deposit. The description of each architectural unit and the catalogues that follow are organized by period from earliest to latest, that is, EBA to LBA. Details of elevation and documentation for each excavation unit are provided in Appendix VIII.

OVERVIEW OF REMAINS IN AREA B

Area B is a small, nearly rectangular space, approximately 8 × 18 m, bounded in the north by House A and the Temple and in the south by the sea (Fig. 4). The earliest architecture consists of several EBA walls below House B and Alley AB (Fig. 19). These walls collapsed in Period III, but whether they were built in Period II or Period III cannot be determined.

The most significant architectural remains of Period IV in Area B are Wall X and perhaps the Wall H foundation, which may be two faces of a fortification wall (Fig. 20). Wall X was published as part of J. C. Overbeck's (1989a, 174) study of Period IV stratigraphy and architecture as Wall 58. Other Period IV architecture includes Wall E1 beneath the eastern wall of House A (Wall E), which is mentioned here owing to its discovery in a test pit excavated by Bikaki below Alley AB. Another possible Period IV wall associated with a drain (Drain 2) was found beneath Wall E1. No Period V architecture was found, which is unsurprising since architecture from that period, apart from the fortifications, is rarely preserved (Davis 1986, 1).

TABLE 2.1. ROOM B.1 COMBINED LOTS (CL)

B602CL also includes ceramics from units in Rooms B.2 and B.4.

CL	Excavation units, B03-	↑ elevation	↓ elevation
B601CL	79, 81, 116, 117, 142–145, 149	+0.48	+0.10
B602CL	73, 74, 83, 114, 118, 146, 147	+0.40	-0.20
B608CL	19, 25, 27, 28	+2.45S, +2.00/+1.75N	+1.40
B609CL	19, 29, 31, 33, 35, 39, 41, 93	+1.40	+0.59NE/+0.67NW/ +0.69SE/+0.75SW
B610CL	76, 78, 95, 98, 99	+0.70	+0.40

The most prominent architectural remains in the area are those of the LBA House B, which is not fully preserved, having eroded into the sea on its southeastern side. The first phases of the house were constructed in Period VI (Figs. 21, 22); subsequent phases belong to Period VII (Figs. 23, 24). Alley AB runs along the northwestern edge of the house, while South Alley (Cummer and Schofield 1984, 4) extends beyond House A along the southwestern wall of House B. The only preserved doorway leading into the house is on Temple Lane, which separates House B from the Temple. Six rooms are preserved: Rooms B.1–B.5 and Room B.8. Room B.5 was defined after surface excavation revealed that the northwestern wall of the house (Wall H) continued southward beyond Room B.4, but the space was never excavated more fully.

A small wall (Wall Q) was found in the upper layers of the Period VII destruction deposits (Fig. 25); it may be associated with continuing use of the Temple in the Archaic period.

ROOM B.1

In its final phase (Period VII), Room B.1 was bounded by Walls H, I, J, and K (Fig. 24, Table 2.1). In addition to the Period VII destruction deposit that preserved parts of these walls, earlier LBA surfaces were present, while EBA and MBA remains were found below the LBA room. A summary of deposits is presented in Table 2.2.

EARLY BRONZE AGE

Wall AC and the Associated Period III Destruction Deposit

The earliest feature is Wall AC; its foundation was not reached during excavation. No contemporary use horizon was found. Wall AC was surrounded by a destruction deposit made up of many pebbles, small and moderately sized stones, obsidian fragments, some large animal teeth, and clayey, red, carbon-rich soil (B03-83, B03-118, B03-146, B03-147, B03-829; Kea Excavation Notebook III, 90, 118–119, 139–141; Kea Excavation Notebook LVIII, 54).

With the exception of one lot (B03-829), ceramics from the destruction deposit were combined in B602CL with pottery from similar elevations in Rooms B.1, B.2, and B.4. No ceramics were inventoried before the lots were combined. Ceramics from B602CL date, for the most part, to Period III, although some MBA and LBA sherds were present. The wall was probably destroyed in Period III, but no evidence for its construction date was recovered. A Period III destruction date is supported by the fact that ceramics from B03-829 date exclusively to Period III. MBA and LBA pottery in B602CL is probably the result of combining lots, particularly those from Surface c (below), with the Period III destruction deposit.

MIDDLE BRONZE AGE

A test pit beneath Platform 1, excavated in units B03-827–B03-829, revealed a lens of several shallow strata above the Period III destruction deposit (B03-829) and below Surface c (Fig. 11:a; Kea Excavation Notebook LVIII, 53). The surface was excavated in

TABLE 2.2. ROOM B.1 DEPOSIT SUMMARY

Deposit:	Period III destruction deposit
Contemporary Features:	Wall AC
Date of Deposit Above:	Mixed EBA–MBA (Surface c)
Date of Deposit:	Period III
Date of Deposit Below:	Not excavated
Lots/Combined Lots:	B03-829, B602CL (partial)
Catalogue Numbers:	**1, 2**
Deposit:	Mixed EBA–MBA deposit below Platform 1
Contemporary Features:	None
Date of Deposit Above:	Mixed EBA–MBA
Date of Deposit:	Mixed EBA–MBA
Date of Deposit Below:	Period III
Lots/Combined Lots:	B03-828
Catalogue Numbers:	**3, 4**
Deposit:	Surface c
Contemporary Features:	None
Date of Deposit Above:	Mixed EBA–MBA
Date of Deposit:	Mixed EBA–MBA
Date of Deposit Below:	Period III
Lots/Combined Lots:	B03-825a, B03-827, B601CL (partial), B602CL (partial)
Catalogue Numbers:	**5, 9–28**
Deposit:	Packing beneath Wall H foundation
Contemporary Features:	None
Date of Deposit Above:	None (Wall H foundation)
Date of Deposit:	MBA (Period IV?)
Date of Deposit Below:	Mixed EBA–MBA
Lots/Combined Lots:	B03-825
Catalogue Numbers:	**6–8**
Deposit:	MBA–early Period VI accumulation stratum
Contemporary Features:	Wall H foundation(?)
Date of Deposit Above:	Early Period VI
Date of Deposit:	MBA–early Period VI
Date of Deposit Below:	Mixed EBA–MBA
Lots/Combined Lots:	B601CL (partial)
Catalogue Numbers:	**39–45, 47, 48, 50–78**

TABLE 2.2. (CONT.)

Deposit:	House B: First Phase
Contemporary Features:	Wall Y, Wall H foundation, Surface b, Platform 1, Stone Feature 1, Hearth 1
Date of Deposit Above:	Later Period VI
Date of Deposit:	Early Period VI
Date of Deposit Below:	Mixed MBA–early Period VI
Lots/Combined Lots:	B03-826, B601CL (partial), B610CL (partial)
Catalogue Numbers:	**29–38, 46, 49, 79–90, 101, 122–132, 134**
Deposit:	House B: Second Phase
Contemporary Features:	Pit 1
Date of Deposit Above:	Period VII
Date of Deposit:	Later Period VI
Date of Deposit Below:	Early Period VI
Lots/Combined Lots:	B610CL (partial)
Catalogue Numbers:	**91–100, 102–111, 113–117, 119–121, 133**
Deposit:	House B: Third–Fourth Phase
Contemporary Features:	Walls H, I, J, K, Surface a
Date of Deposit Above:	Period VIIb
Date of Deposit:	Period VIIa–b
Date of Deposit Below:	Later Period VI
Lots/Combined Lots:	B609CL (partial), B610CL (partial)
Catalogue Numbers:	**112(?), 118(?), 140–143, 166, 178**
Deposit:	Period VIIb Destruction Deposit (lower)
Contemporary Features:	Walls H, I, J, K
Date of Deposit Above:	Period VIIb, some Period VIIc–VIII contamination
Date of Deposit:	Period VIIb
Date of Deposit Below:	Period VIIa–b
Lots/Combined Lots:	B609CL (partial)
Catalogue Numbers:	**135–139, 144–165, 167–177, 179–183**
Deposit:	Period VIIb Destruction Deposit (upper)
Contemporary Features:	Walls H, I, J, K
Date of Deposit Above:	None
Date of Deposit:	Period VIIb, some Period VIIc–VIII contamination
Date of Deposit Below:	Period VIIb
Lots/Combined Lots:	B608CL
Catalogue Numbers:	**184–210**

unit B03-827, while the shallow strata were excavated in unit B03-828. The shallow strata were made of one cm of gray soil that ran directly above a 3 cm thick layer of red soil; the red soil was above an average 3 cm thick layer of brown soil and small stones. Pottery from B03-827 was discarded; ceramics from unit B03-828 date to Period III and the MBA. It is unclear what process was responsible for the formation of this lens.

Surface C

In most parts of the room, above the Period III destruction deposit, Bikaki and her workmen found an extremely hard-packed, clayey level—Surface c—at an elevation of ca. +0.25 to +0.28 m above sea level (Figs. 8–11:a). Surface c was more compact than later surfaces (Surfaces a and b; below) and contained much more carbonized material. The surface postdated the destruction of the EBA building associated with Wall AC, and is earlier than the LBA house, the walls of which cut through the surface. No architecture could be associated with Surface c.

Most ceramics from Surface c were included in B601CL (units B03-81, B03-116, B03-117, B03-143, B03-145). Ceramics from B03-83 were incorporated into B602CL. Ceramics from B03-825a remained uncombined and those from B03-827 were discarded. The mixed nature of the ceramics from the combined lots does not allow close dating of the surface. As discussed above, B602CL, from units below and including Surface c, contained primarily Period III ceramics with some Period IV–VII types. Sherds in B601CL derive from excavation units under and including Surface c, between Surface c and the later Surface b, and on top of Surface b (Figs. 8, 16). B601CL included mainly early Period VI ceramics, which should probably be associated primarily with the accumulation of Surface b (below). The only uncombined lot, B03-825a is described as "sherds on 'floor' at 0.25," and contained Period III pottery with one certain Period IV sherd (5; Kea Excavation Notebook LVIII, 52). It is possible that the red stratum formed in Period III, but, if so, it was disturbed by Period IV and later construction in the area.

During Periods IV, V, and earlier Period VI, soil and some cultural material accumulated on top of Surface c. The soil in this accumulation stratum was compact and contained much carbon; it was also moist, owing to its proximity to sea level (B03-78, B03-79, B03-81, B03-116, B03-142, B03-143, and B03-825; Kea Excavation Notebook III, 85, 88–89, 118, 138). No architecture could be directly associated with this horizon, but it is possible that the Wall H foundation, which predates the Late Bronze Age house, might be contemporary with the accumulation stratum (below).

Most ceramics from the upper part of Surface c and those from the subsequent accumulation stratum were combined into B601CL, along with ceramics from Surface b (below). B601CL contains mainly earlier Period VI ceramics. One lot from the accumulation stratum, B03-78, was combined in B610CL with pottery from above Surface b; B610CL contains mainly Period VI ceramics, with a few Period VII sherds. The existence of these few Period VII sherds in B610CL is probably the result of combining lots. Ceramics from unit B03-825, from a test pit beneath the Wall H foundation, remained uncombined; ceramics from this unit are not very chronologically diagnostic, but the latest sherds seem to be compatible with a Period IV date.

LATE BRONZE AGE

House B: First Phase

The first phase of use of House B seems to be restricted to Room B.1. In this phase, Room B.1 was bounded by Wall Y and the Wall H foundation (Fig. 21). One surface (Surface b) and several built constructions can be associated with this phase.

Wall Y and the Wall H Foundation

Wall Y, which cut through Surface c, should be associated with the first phase of House B. In the subsequent phase of the room, Wall Y was covered by Surface a and replaced by Wall K, parallel to it, but set slightly farther to the southwest (Figs. 22, 23).

The Wall H foundation might have been constructed for the first phase of use of House B, although some evidence suggests that this foundation would be better described as a wall predating the house, perhaps the exterior face of Period IVa Wall X, found below Alley AB (below). The Wall H foundation was standing before Wall Y was constructed. Unlike Wall Y, the Wall H foundation did not cut through Surface c or levels earlier than Surface b. A test pit (B03-825) revealed that, unlike other walls of the LBA house (Walls I, J, K, or Y), the Wall H foundation was built on a packing of stone and soil like Wall X and at a similar elevation (Figs. 11:b, 15). This construction practice, different from that used in the LBA Walls I, J, K, and Y, may be owed to a difference in date between the Wall H foundation and the LBA walls. Surface b did not continue under the Wall H foundation, although it did exist at depths 0.02–0.03 m above and below the level of the bottom of the wall, presumably because the wall already existed when the surface was formed. The shallowness of the foundation in comparison with Wall Y and Surface b also suggests that the Wall H foundation was not originally built as part of the first phase of the house but rather was reused in this phase. Furthermore, the Wall H foundation extended into Rooms B.2 and B.4, where no Period VI surfaces or constructions were found (Fig. 21); this also supports the hypothesis that it is an earlier wall that was reused as part of Room B.1. The large size of the stones compared with other walls of the LBA house is remarkable; they are most comparable to the size of stones in the Period IVa Wall X in Alley AB

(Pls. 6:a, 8:a, 13:b, 15:c, d). Unfortunately, the exact relationship between Wall X and the Wall H foundation cannot be evaluated, since the test (B03-825) beneath Wall H and the Wall H foundation did not extend all the way to Wall X (Figs. 11:b, 20). No matter how much earlier the wall, the contemporaneity of Surface b and the preserved height of the Wall H foundation show that at least the lower part of the wall would have been visible and functional while Wall Y was in use in the Period VI room. Although the Wall H foundation was in use in the first phase of Room B.1, Wall H, built on top of the Wall H foundation, must have been built in Period VII, together with Walls J and I (below).

Surface B

Surface b was found approximately 20 cm above Surface c at depths of ca. +0.40 to +0.50 m above sea level (B03-76, B03-78, B03-95, B03-99, B03-116, and B03-142; Kea Excavation Notebook III, 85, 103, 106–107, 118, 138). Surface b was the first preserved floor deposit of Room B.1, and was in use at the same time as Wall Y and the Wall H foundation.

The soil of Surface b was compact and contained much carbon and ash, especially in the vicinity of Hearth 1 (Kea Excavation Notebook III, 104). In places, the surface seemed to be made up of successive layers of ashes, red and yellow soil, and patches of clay (Kea Excavation Notebook III, 138). Ceramics from the surface were included in B610CL (B03-76, B03-78, B03-99) and B601CL (B03-116, B03-142). In addition to pottery from Surface b, B601CL included ceramics from the accumulation stratum between Surface c and Surface b. B610CL was made up of pottery from the stratum between Surface b and Surface a. The latest ceramics from B601CL date to earlier Period VI, while the latest from B610CL date to Period VII. The absence of Period VII ceramics in B601CL suggests that Surface b can be dated no later than Period VI. The few Period VII ceramics from B610CL probably should be associated with Surface a above Surface b, and with accumulation between the two.

Several nearly intact vessels and other artifacts were recovered on and just above Surface b. Some wall plaster had fallen onto Surface b (Kea Excavation Notebook III, 85). A tripod jar (**101**) was in a secondary use as a storage container while Surface b was in use, with its mouth found at floor level in excavation unit B03-95. A floor in Room F.3 in the Western Sector also contained an embedded tripod jar (Schofield 2011, 6). Several handleless cups were found on Surface b (**80–82, 84–90**), above a lens of carbonized material (B03-95). One handleless cup was discovered within Hearth 1 (**83**). Additional handleless cups were excavated just above Surface b (**91–95**). A loom weight was recovered beneath Platform 1 (**127**); three additional loom weights (**130–132**) were found just above Surface b. Stone objects on the surface included a marble mortar (**125**) and a marble or flint denticulate (**124**), as well as an uninventoried flint fragment, millstone, obsidian chips, and an obsidian blade. A bone awl (**123**), perforated terracotta disk (**133**), spindle whorl (**134**), and marble tool(?) (**126**) were also recovered.

Built Features

A small, flat stone construction covered with burned clay (Stone Feature 1, 0.75 × 0.45 × 0.08 m) near the center of the room (Figs. 21, 22; Pl. 3:b) was excavated in units B03-78 and B03-116. It probably functioned as a platform or work surface. Hearth 1 and the abutting Platform 1 were also constructed and used during this phase (Figs. 21, 22). Part of Platform 1 was removed in B03-144 (Kea Excavation Notebook III, 138–139); the rest was taken out in B03-826 (Kea Excavation Notebook LVIII, 53). Sherds from B03-144 were incorporated into B601CL. Lot B03-826 included sherds of Periods IV and V; some of the vessels, especially **30–35**, seem to date to an early phase of Period VI. Together with the chronological evidence from B601CL, the pottery from B03-826 suggests that the first phase of use of Room B.1 dates to the initial part of Period VI (see also Abell, forthcoming).

House B: Second Phase

Large stones were discovered lying flat on Surface b, particularly near Wall Y (Fig. 22; Pl. 3:b; Kea Excavation Notebook III, 106–107). These probably fell when Wall Y collapsed. At some point after this destruction, a small pit lined with stones was dug through Surface b (Pit 1) and disturbed the upper part of Wall AC (Figs. 8, 9, 22). Some of the pit was excavated in B03-99, but the rest may have been excavated in either B03-116 or B03-117 (Kea Excavation Notebook III, 107, 118). The excavation notebook is not clear on this point, and examination of the sections cannot resolve the problem (Figs. 8, 9). The pit belongs to the continuing use of the room between the collapse or demolition of Wall Y and the construction of the walls of Period VII. Although Bikaki called the pit a possible cist grave in the excavation notebooks (Kea Excavation Notebook III, 107, 118), it had no evidence for a burial, and she later decided that it must have been a pit for another purpose (pers. comm.).

The soil between Surface b and Surface a was damp and compact, with a significant amount of carbon and occasional patches of compact, red clay (Kea Excavation Notebook III, 85, 103, 106–107). This stratum probably formed by the accumulation of debris during the use of the room (Kea Excavation Notebook III, 85). Pottery from this level was included in B610CL (B03-76, B03-98, B03-99) along with ceramics from Surface b and Surface a. A few sherds in B610CL date to Period VII and probably result from the combination of ceramics from the lower to the upper parts of the deposit, as well as some from Surface a.

II. STRATIGRAPHY, ARCHITECTURE, AND POTTERY

House B: Third–Fourth Phase

Walls H, I, J, and K

In the next phase, probably early in Period VII, Room B.1 was expanded southward, with the construction of Wall K (Fig. 23; Pls. 3:b, 8:b). Wall H was built above the Wall H foundation, and Walls I and J defined the northeast and southeast limits of the room, respectively; these walls bond together (Kea Excavation Notebook III, 145). An effort seems to have been made to ensure the stability of Walls I and J by founding them at a great depth. Wall K cut through Surfaces b and c. Wall I cut through Surface b and rested on Surface c, while Wall J cut through both surfaces and was founded at the level of the Period III destruction debris.

A fourth phase of House B is apparent in Rooms B.2–B.4, but no corresponding change in the arrangement of the room or use of space is attested in Room B.1.

Surface A

Surface a was in use at the same time as Walls H, I, J, and K, at an elevation between +0.59 m above sea level in the northeast and +0.75 m above sea level in the southwest (Fig. 8–10). Ceramics from the upper part of the surface were incorporated into B609CL along with lots from the bottom layer of destruction debris (B03-41); pottery from the lower part of the surface was included in B610CL (B03-76 and B03-98). Surface a lay directly beneath a layer of stones that had fallen flat during the destruction of the room (Kea Excavation Notebook III, 55, 59); the surface was made up of packed earth with traces of carbon (Kea Excavation Notebook III, 59, 85, 103, 106). A thin lens of ash in the center of the room probably was deposited during the destruction (Kea Excavation Notebook III, 59). No built features were associated with Surface a. It is unclear whether all vessels from B609CL can be associated with the use of Room B.1 since some may have fallen from a second story room, or even from House A, farther upslope.

Period VIIb Destruction Deposit

The layer of flat stones fallen onto Surface a, which resulted from the collapse of the building, was excavated in units B03-39 and B03-41. Above the layer of flat stones was a thick destruction deposit. A compact lens (excavated in B03-27) seems to have separated the lower and upper parts of the destruction deposit. The ceramic evidence, however, suggests that the entire destruction deposit probably formed as part of a single event (below).

The lower part of the destruction deposit contained rather soft soil, some red clay, wall-plaster fragments, and jumbled large stones (Kea Excavation Notebook III, 40, 42, 46, 55, 102). Ceramics from the lower part of the destruction deposit were included in B609CL (B03-29, B03-31, B03-33, B03-35, B03-39, B03-41, B03-93) and B608CL (B03-28). Monochrome red and banded wall-plaster fragments were present (Coleman 1970, 47–49; Kea Excavation Notebook III, 42, 46). The fragments were decorated with parallel white, dark yellow, dark red, and black bands (Fig. 9; Coleman 1970, 48–49). Fragments of wall plaster from some of the excavation units in the lower part of the destruction deposit joined (B03-31 to B03-33, B03-33 to B609CL; Coleman 1970, 49). Banded wall-plaster fragments were also found in the compact lens that separated the lower and upper parts of the destruction deposit (B03-27), but none joined to fragments from the lower part of the destruction deposit.

The upper part of the destruction deposit was characterized by red soil that was less compact than that excavated in B03-27; it was excavated in units B03-20 and B03-25 (Pl. 2). Large stones were common, although less so than in the surface strata, which were excavated in units B03-11, B03-18, and B03-19. Pottery from the upper part of the destruction deposit was included in B604CL (B03-20) and B608CL (B03-25, B03-27). More plain goblets and a few LH IIB–LH IIIA:1 imports were present in B608CL (upper part of the destruction deposit) than in B609CL (lower part of the destruction deposit). The presence of later ceramics in the upper part of the destruction deposit may be the result of post–Period VIIb activity related to the nearby Temple or of erosion down the steep slope into Area B.

Although the collapse was probably not instantaneous, the presence of sherds from the same vessel scattered between the upper and lower levels of the destruction deposit—including in the destruction debris inside the doorway of Wall I—suggests that it probably happened quite quickly and caused substantial dispersal of objects in both horizontal and vertical space. Sherds from one goblet (**166**), for example, were found beneath the layer of flat stones (B03-41) on Surface a; a joining fragment was discovered in the destruction debris within the doorway of Wall I (B03-93), nearly 0.50 m higher than the first, while two more joining fragments were found in B03-90 from Temple Lane. Sherds from a Palace Style jar (**173**) were found in the lower part of the Room B.1 destruction deposit (B609CL); nonjoining sherds possibly from the same vessel were found in the upper part of the destruction deposit in Room B.1 (B03-20) and in Room B.2 (B604CL). More nonjoining sherds, potentially also from the same jar, were found in Room B.8 (B03-148). The widespread scatter of sherds from these vessels suggests that the collapse of Room B.1 was rapid and turbulent. The fact that a sherd joining **166** was found within the destruction debris of the Wall I doorway indicates that the debris was not cleared out so that people could get back into the room. In addition, as debris fell from House A, located at the top of a steep slope above House B, stones and other heavy objects probably collapsed into House B, contributing to its apparently rapid destruction.

ROOM B.1 CATALOGUE

PERIOD III DESTRUCTION DEPOSIT

B03-829.
Destruction deposit associated with Wall AC, underneath LBA Platform 1. Period III.

Pottery

Unknown quantity collected; 14 sherds remain. No discard information. Uncatalogued ceramics include local (RBMa, RBMb), plain, moderately coarse jars, pithoi, closed vessels, and large open(?) vessels.

Local

1 Basin. (Pl. 21)
Body. Moderately coarse, reddish-brown fabric with 10–15% inclusions. Interior and exterior smoothed. Exterior discolored to pale brown in large area. EBA Red-Brown Semifine to Semicoarse. RBMd.

2 One-handled cup. (Fig. 26, Pl. 21)
Short, everted rim and upper body. D. rim est. 0.10. Moderately coarse, reddish-brown fabric with 5–10% inclusions. EBA Red-Brown Semifine to Semicoarse. Interior coated with thin black wash. RBMa, very micaceous.

Bone

One uninventoried long bone, probably ovicaprid.

MIXED EBA–MBA DEPOSITS BELOW HOUSE B

B03-828.
Series of shallow strata excavated in a test pit beneath Platform 1. Period III and MBA.

Pottery

Unknown quantity collected; 42 sherds remain. No discard information. Uncatalogued ceramics include a Period III pedestal foot, perhaps from a deep bowl/open jar (RBMa); a Burnished pedestal foot, probably Period IV (RBMa) (Fig. 26:a); and a slightly raised base from a saucer(?) (RBMc) (Fig. 26:b). Uncatalogued imports include an eroded Period IV krater or basin, probably from Aegina (DVe) (Fig. 26:c); several, plain Cycladic closed vessels (DVc, MxMg); a Melian/Theran closed vessel coated with white slip (DVc); a Cycladic White open vessel body fragment (DVa); and a fine (Urfirnis?) open vessel (FVg).

Attica/Cyclades

3 Jug. (Pl. 21)
Neck and pinched spout. D. neck (max.) 0.08. Coarse, gritty, reddish-brown fabric turning dark gray at exterior margin, with 15–20% inclusions. Handmade. Surfaces rough. Plain. CSWc. PFG 2D (Southeast Attica/Cyclades).

Cyclades

4 Closed vessel. (Pl. 21)
Body. Coarse, gritty, dark red fabric with dark-gray core, turning dark gray to black in places at surface, with 15–20% inclusions. EBA Red-Brown Coarse. Interior and exterior smoothed. CSWe.

B03-825A.
Lower part of test pit beneath Wall H; included the part of Surface c that continued below Wall H. Period III and Period IV (**5**).

Pottery

Unknown quantity collected; 15 sherds remain, belonging to three vessels. No discard information. Uncatalogued ceramics include an EBA Red-Brown Semifine to Semicoarse jar (RBMc) and a large, open, Slipped vessel (RBMb).

Local

5 Globular(?) jar. (Pl. 21)
Neck and upper body. H. pres. 0.05. Moderately coarse, reddish-brown fabric with 5–10% inclusions. Interior: well-smoothed. Handmade. Yellow Slipped. Neck interior coated with matt-black and dripped yellow slip. Exterior coated with yellow slip. Wide band in matt black along neck; upper body preserves fugitive curving band (spiral or circle?). RBMa.

B03-825.
Packing beneath Wall H. Periods III–IV.

Pottery

Unknown quantity collected; 38 sherds remain. No discard information. Uncatalogued ceramics include plain local (RBMa, RBMb) vessels, including a tripod leg and an EBA saucer with mat impression; Yellow Slipped (RBMa, RBMc) open vessels; moderately coarse, closed Melian/Theran vessels, both Painted (DVa) and Yellow Slipped (DVc); and a moderately coarse, closed, plain Cretan(?) vessel (FSTc).

Local

6 Rubber/polisher. (Pl. 21)
90% preserved, broken at edge. W. 0.04. L. 0.10. Moderately coarse, reddish-brown fabric turning gray at one side, with 10–15% inclusions. All edges rounded and smoothed. RBMa.

Melos/Thera

7 Piriform cup. (Fig. 26, Pl. 21)
Slightly concave, torus base and lower body. H. pres. 0.03. D. base 0.05. Moderately fine, porous, white fabric with 5–10% inclusions. Cycladic White. Interior and exterior well-smoothed. Exterior: paneled decoration; wide, vertical band and horizontal band above base; paint now fugitive. DVa.

Stone

8 Rubber/polisher. (Pl. 21)
Intact, with a few chips. H. 0.03. W. 0.03. L. 0.04. Wt. 50 g. Rounded, trapezoidal, mottled dark-gray and green stone. All surfaces well-smoothed.

B602CL (INCLUDES ROOMS B.1, B.2 AND B.4).
Ceramics from Surfaces c and i and destruction stratum associated with Walls AB, AC, AD, AE, and AF below House B. Mixed Period III–VII.

Pottery

2 tins (ca. 34 liters) collected; 2/3 bag remains. 98% coarse, 1% plain; ca. 50% discarded in initial papsing. Uncatalogued ceramics include EBA Red-Brown Semifine to Semicoarse ware (RBMa, RBMb) vessels, including a bowl, saucer with mat impression, and deep bowls/open jars; an EBA Red-Brown Coarse (RBMb) pithos, an EBA Black Burnished (RBMa) sauceboat; a Yellow Slipped (RBMa) jug; a Slipped (RBMa) open vessel; and local, plain (RBMa, RBMb) open and closed vessels. Uncatalogued imports include an EBA Talc ware (PBS) jar; EBA Orange-Buff Semifine to Coarse (MxMd, CSWe) shallow bowls; Burnished (MxMc, CSWd) bowl and open vessel; Cycladic and/or Aeginetan Painted (DVb, DVe) jars; Slipped (CSWe) open vessel; a pseudo-Gray Minyan (MFVb) goblet; a plain, LBA goblet from the mainland (FVd); an MBA or LBA coarse, Lustrous Painted (Monochrome) Cretan jar (FSTf); as well a variety of plain imports (DVb, CSWe, MxMa, MxMd), including a rounded cup, small open jar, rim-handled jar, and stick-handled lamp. Several Gray Minyan sherds have been discarded, including three stems, of which two were perhaps ring stems, and a thickened rim sherd (Kea Pottery Notebook B, 25). Several Cretan imports; a coarse, local tripod leg; and several plain ware (imported?) sherds (pedestal base, high neck and globular body, and a plain rim) were also apparently discarded (Kea Pottery Notebook B, 27).

Local and Local Region

9 Shallow bowl. (Fig. 26)
Slightly incurving rim and upper body. D. rim est. 0.32. Moderately fine, reddish-orange fabric with 1–5% inclusions. EBA Red-Brown Burnished. Exterior surface is worn; interior preserves some traces of burnishing. RBMa, with common mica and shiny, black particles. PFG 1C (Local). For profile, see also J. L. Caskey 1972, 370–371, no. C6, fig. 6.

10 Basin. (Fig. 26, Pl. 21)
Rim and horizontal lug. D. max. ca. 0.20, but difficult to estimate. Moderately fine, brittle, reddish-brown fabric with 5–10% inclusions. EBA Red-Brown Semifine to Semicoarse. Surfaces well-smoothed. RBMd, with shiny, black particles.

11 Deep bowl/open jar. (Fig. 26, Pl. 21)
Incurving rim and upper body. D. rim est. 0.26. Moderately coarse, reddish-brown fabric with black core and interior margin and with 15–20% inclusions. Surface smoothed. EBA Red-Brown Semifine to Semicoarse. RBMb. For shape, see J. L. Caskey 1972, 372, no. C18, fig. 6; Wilson 1999, 32, 107, nos. II-125, III-99, pls. 8, 25, 48, 76.

12 Deep bowl/open jar. (Fig. 26, Pl. 21)
Incurving rim and upper body. D. rim est. 0.40. Moderately fine fabric with black core and brownish-red surface and 1–5% inclusions. EBA Red-Brown Semifine to Semicoarse. Interior and exterior surface well-smoothed; plastic disk applied at rim. RBMa, dark. For profile, see J. L. Caskey 1972, 372, no. C19, fig. 6; Wilson 1999, 107, no. III-99, pls. 25, 76.

13 Deep bowl/open jar. (Fig. 26, Pl. 21)
Rounded rim and upper body. D. rim est. 0.28. Moderately coarse, reddish-brown fabric with thin, dark-gray core and dark, reddish-brown exterior surface and with 15–20% inclusions. EBA Red-Brown Semifine to Semicoarse. Interior and exterior smoothed. RBMa. For shape, see Wilson 1999, 107, no. III-99, pls. 25, 76.

14 Deep bowl/open jar. (Fig. 26, Pl. 21)
Incurving flattened rim. D. rim est. 0.40. Moderately coarse, reddish-brown fabric turning darker at core, with 10–15% inclusions. Coil-built. EBA Red-Brown Semifine to Semicoarse. Exterior somewhat smoothed. RBMa. Similar to Wilson 1999, 107, no. III-103, pl. 26.

15 Saucer. (Fig. 26, Pl. 21)
Rounded rim and upper body. D. rim est. 0.11. Moderately coarse, reddish-brown fabric with thick, dark-brown core and 15–20% inclusions. EBA Red-Brown Semifine to Semicoarse. Exterior surface eroded; interior surface smoothed. RBMa. For shape, see Wilson 1999, 104, no. III-49, pls. 23, 74.

16 Shallow saucer or lid(?). (Fig. 26, Pl. 21)
Rim and body. D. rim est. 0.08. Moderately coarse, brittle, reddish-brown fabric with 15–20% inclusions. Interior and exterior smoothed. Handmade. EBA Red-Brown Semifine to Semicoarse. RBMb, with overfired(?) white schist. PFG 1Bv

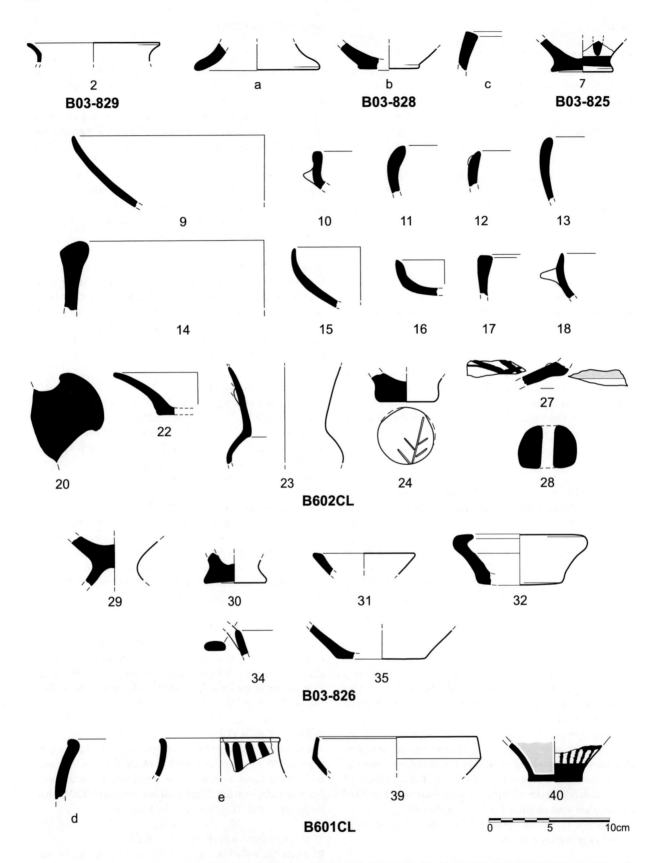

Fig. 26. Pottery from B03-829 (**2**), B03-828 (a–c), B03-825 (**7**), B602CL (**9–18, 20, 22–24, 27, 28**), B03-826 (**29–32, 34, 35**), and B601CL (d, e, **39, 40**). Drawings by Mary-Jane Schumacher (**2**, a, b, **7, 29–32, 34, 35**), Alison Rittershaus (c), Aliki Bikaki (**9–18, 20, 22, 28, 40**), and Lily Bonga (**23, 24, 27,** d, e, **39**).

(Local). For similar, see J. L. Caskey 1972, 366, no. B35, fig. 3; Wilson 1999, 112, nos. III-160, III-162, pls. 28, 78.

17 Small basin or deep bowl/open jar. (Fig. 26, Pl. 21)
Flat, incurving rim and upper body. D. rim est. 0.22. Moderately coarse, brittle, reddish-brown fabric with 15–20% inclusions. EBA Red-Brown Semifine to Semicoarse. Exterior coated with non-lustrous black slip. RBMa. The shape of the rim is similar to basins published by Wilson (e.g., 1999, no. III-112, pl. 26), but the diameter is much smaller than those (Wilson 1999, 108).

18 Bowl. (Fig. 26, Pl. 21)
Incurving rim and horned lug. D. rim est. 0.20. Moderately coarse, reddish-brown fabric with 10–15% inclusions. EBA Red-Brown Semifine to Semicoarse. Interior and exterior coated with pale, pinkish-gray slip; worn. RBMa. For similar, see J. L. Caskey 1972, 372, no. C12, pl. 81; Wilson 1999, 105, no. III-70, pls. 23, 74.

19 Pithos. (Pl. 21)
Body. Moderately coarse, dark reddish-brown fabric with 5–10% inclusions. Handmade. Interior: scoring. EBA Red-Brown Coarse. Three applied bands with diagonal slashes oriented in opposite directions. RBMd. For similar, see J. L. Caskey 1972, 358, no. S7, pl. 76; Wilson 1999, 116, no. III-213, pl. 81.

20 Pithos. (Fig. 26, Pl. 21)
Knob. D. 0.05–0.06. Moderately coarse, reddish-brown fabric with 10–15% inclusions. EBA Red-Brown Coarse. RBMa, with phyllite and shiny, black particles. For similar, see **251**.

21 Bridge-spouted jar. (Pl. 21)
Slightly collared rim and spout rising above rim. D. rim est. 0.15–0.17. Moderately coarse, somewhat compact, orange fabric with well-defined, dark blue-gray core and 15–20% inclusions. Very thin-walled. Handmade(?). Plain. RBMa, with rare calcareous(?) inclusions.

22 Saucer. (Fig. 26, Pl. 21)
Approximately 40% preserved, including entire profile. H. 0.04. D. rim est. 0.14. D. base est. 0.06. Moderately coarse reddish-brown fabric with 10–15% inclusions. Exterior surface and base are eroded. Clay darkened at rim. Wheel-coiled. Plain. RBMa, with rare calcareous(?) inclusions.

Central Cyclades

23 Tankard. (Fig. 26, Pl. 21)
Neck with handle attachment and upper shoulder. Moderately coarse, reddish-brown fabric with dark-gray core and 10–15% inclusions. EBA Red-Brown Burnished. Interior and exterior surfaces eroded and worn; some traces of burnishing remain. CSWe.

Cyclades/Attica/Euboea

24 K.1211. Deep saucer. (Fig. 26, Pl. 21)
Raised, solid, disk base and lower body. H. pres. 0.02. D. base 0.05. From B03-114. Moderately coarse, reddish-brown fabric with gray core and 15–20% inclusions. EBA Red-Brown Semifine to Semicoarse. Leaf impression on base. CSWb.

25 Pithos. (Pl. 21)
Body. Moderately coarse, gritty, dark orange fabric with paler orange surface and dark-gray core, with 10–15% inclusions. Handmade. Plain. Exterior: applied band of disks. RBMe. PFG 2Av (Local region).

Melos/Thera

26 Closed vessel. (Pl. 21)
Body. Moderately coarse, pale pink to pale-gray, brittle, porous fabric with 5–10% inclusions. Forming method indeterminable. Painted. Two faded, flaking matt brown bands. DVa. PFG 5Bv (Melos/Thera).

Unknown

27 Jug(?). (Fig. 26, Pl. 21)
Shoulder and plastic ridge at neck (or rim?) attachment. Moderately coarse, gritty, porous, dull orange fabric with distinct, pale-gray core, brown surface, and 5–10% inclusions. Handmade. EBA Orange-Buff Painted(?). Interior: semi-lustrous black paint overlapping from rim/neck. Exterior: cross-hatching in same. DVe, with gray core, brown surface. PFG 5Dv (Melos?). Decoration and fabric might be compatible with Thin Line Painted ware at Phylakopi, which appears in Phase A2 and, rarely, in Phase B (Renfrew and Evans 2007, 146, 165).

Bone

One fragment of a bovine humerus was discarded.

Stone

Uninventoried:
B03-73: obsidian chip (B-1.209, D. max. 0.02).
B03-83: obsidian blades (B-1.227, L. 0.03, D. max. 0.01; B-1.230, L. 0.04, W. 0.01); obsidian chips (B-1.228, D. max. 0.03; B-1.229, D. max. 0.02).
B03-114: obsidian chips (B-1.288, D. max. 0.04; B-1.291, D. max. 0.02); obsidian blades (B-1.289, L. 0.05, D. max. 0.02; B-1.290, L. 0.02, D. max. 0.01).
B03-118: obsidian fragments (B-1.300, D. max. 0.04; B-1.301, D. max. 0.04; B-1.302, D. max. 0.03; B-1.303, D. max. 0.02).

One fragment of pumice was discarded.

Terracotta

28 K1.389. Spindle whorl. (Fig. 26, Pl. 21)
Type M1. H. 0.03. D. 0.05. D. perf. 0.01. Wt. 82 g. From B03-147. Moderately coarse, pale orange fabric turning gray at center, with 15–20% inclusions. Surface smoothed; now worn and pitted. Broken area at bottom. Breakage around both ends of perforation, especially at narrower, rounded end. DVe (Aegina?).

HOUSE B: PHASE 1

B03-826.
Removal of Platform 1. Period IV, V, probably earlier VI, rare EBA.

Pottery

Unknown quantity collected; 55 sherds remain, mostly plain and coarse. No discard information. Uncatalogued ceramics include local, moderately coarse, plain, Yellow Slipped, and Slipped closed (and some possibly open) vessels (RBMa, RBMb); an EBA Red-Brown Semifine to Semicoarse basin or pithos sherd (RBMb); a Burnished open vessel (RBMa); plain (MxMa, MxMc, CSWa, CSWe) and Yellow Slipped (MxMd, CSWe) Cycladic vessels.

Local

29 Goblet. (Fig. 26, Pl. 21)
Stem and conical lower body. Moderately coarse, rather compact, pale reddish-brown fabric with 10–15% inclusions. Forming method unknown. Burnished. Interior and exterior lightly burnished. Period IV. RBMa, with shiny, black particles.

30 Cycladic cup. (Fig. 26, Pl. 21)
Slightly concave, torus base and lower body. D. base 0.05. Moderately coarse, compact, reddish-orange fabric with pale-gray core and 5–10% inclusions. Handmade(?). Yellow Slipped. RBMa, with rare calcareous(?) inclusions and shiny, black particles.

31 Handleless cup. (Fig. 26, Pl. 21)
Type 1(?). Flattened rim. D. rim est. 0.08. Moderately coarse, reddish-brown fabric with 5–10% inclusions. Wheelmade. Plain. RBMa, with shiny, black particles. Compare with Davis 1986, 41, 57, nos. U-28, AA-53, pls. 27, 32, 53.

32 Lamp. (Fig. 26, Pl. 21)
Full profile, including flat base and sharply incurving rim, folded into body and pinched down at one side. H. 0.04. D. rim est. 0.10. Moderately coarse, reddish-brown fabric with 10–15% inclusions. Wheelmade. Plain. RBMa, with rare calcareous(?) inclusions.

Cyclades

33 Handleless cup or bowl. (Pl. 21)
Flattened rim and upper body. D. rim est. 0.15. Moderately coarse, gritty, orange fabric with thick, brownish-gray core and 5–10% inclusions. Forming method unknown. Slipped(?). Exterior coated with dull red slip(?). MxMc, with probable metamorphics. PFG 3A (Cyclades). Compare with Davis 1986, 41, no. U-28, pls. 27, 53.

34 Straight-sided cup. (Fig. 26, Pl. 21)
Straight rim and high-swung handle with metallicizing attachment. D. rim est. 0.11. Moderately coarse, dark pinkish-orange fabric turning paler orange at surface, with 5–10% inclusions. Forming method unknown. Plain. Interior and exterior smoothed. MxMa, gritty, pinkish-orange. PFG 3Cv (Cyclades [Syros?]).

Melos/Thera

35 Bowl(?). (Fig. 26, Pl. 21)
Flat base and flaring lower body. D. base est. 0.07. Moderately fine, gritty, dusty, pale orange-brown fabric with distinct, dark bluish-gray core and 10–15% inclusions. Handmade. Plain. Two incised lines on base, one overlapping to lower body, possible potter's mark? DVc. For similar potter's marks, see Bailey 2007, 445–452, nos. 010, 013, 028, 042, 044, 074, 115, 201, 203; Cherry and Davis 2007, 436, fig. 10.12:a; Lindblom 2001, 55, no. 124 (K.4629).

Central Mainland

36 Goblet(?). (Pl. 21)
Foot(?). Fine, slightly dusty, gray fabric with fewer than 1% inclusions. Gray Minyan. All surfaces burnished. FVa.

Bone

Uninventoried: four animal bones (ovicaprid?).

Stone

37 K76.3. Weight. (Pl. 21)
Morphologically similar to Type O loom weights. L. 0.06. W. 0.05. Th. 0.01–0.02. D. perf. 0.01. Wt. 89 g. Marble (Whitbread). Flattened, elliptical shape with rounded edges. Large chip at bottom. Off-center perforation.

Uninventoried: obsidian fragment.

Terracotta

38 K76.8. Spindle whorl. (Pl. 21)
Type like M3H, but rounded. H. 0.02. D. 0.03. D. perf. <0.01. Wt. 18 g. Fine, reddish-brown fabric with 1–5% inclusions. Burnished. Breakage around perforation at narrow, non-hollowed side. RBMa. (Local)

B601CL.
Below Surface b. Early Period VI, some may be earlier.

Pottery

2 ¾ tins (ca. 46.8 liters) collected; 1 bag (ca. 0.5 tin or 8.5 liters) remains. 20–25% fine, ca. 5% Matt Painted, ca. 8% plain. Approximately 60% discarded in original papsing, including 39 handleless cups. Uncatalogued ceramics include local (RBMa), plain, coarse, closed vessels, and an open jar or cook-pot (Fig. 26:d); a Burnished open vessel; and Yellow Slipped closed vessels, including a small jar (Fig. 26:e). Imports include an

Aeginetan(?) Painted small, closed vessel (DVe); Melian/Theran plain vessels (DVa), and a Cycladic plain closed vessel (DVg); a fine, open vessel (FSTj) and Lustrous Painted (Monochrome), closed vessel (FSTd) from Crete or the mainland; and several Gray Minyan open vessels (FVa). Three tripod legs and one large fragment of unbaked clay were discarded (Kea Pottery Notebook B, 21).

Local and Local Region

39 Cycladic cup. (Fig. 26, Pl. 22)
Rim and carinated body. H. pres. 0.03. D. rim est. 0.13. Moderately coarse, dark gray fabric turning dark red toward exterior margin, with 10–30% inclusions. Handmade(?). Surface heavily encrusted with salt. Burnished. RBMa.

40 Rounded cup. (Fig. 26, Pl. 22)
Flat base and lower body. H. pres. 0.03. D. base 0.04. From B03-145. Moderately coarse, hard-fired, dark purplish-brown fabric with 5–10% inclusions. Wheelmade(?). Yellow Slipped. Interior probably fully coated with lustrous black; base and extreme lower body also black. Black ripple pattern in two zones, separated by horizontal bands. Thick, vertical band preserved, probably at same line as handle. Well-burnished. Black paint now flaking. RBMa, purplish brown. PFG 1D (Local).

41 Straight-sided cup. (Fig. 27, Pl. 22)
Flat base and lower body, with one nonjoining sherd. Partially restored in plaster. H. pres. 0.06. D. base rest. 0.06. From B03-81. Moderately fine, orange fabric with 1–5% inclusions. Thin-walled. Wheelmade. Yellow Slipped. Decoration nearly entirely missing; matt(?) orange band above base; traces of ripple pattern around lower body, most evident on nonjoining sherd. RBMa. PFG 1A (Local).

42 K.1214.Handleless cup. (Fig. 27, Pl. 22)
Type 1. 90% preserved; broken at rim. H. 0.04. D. base 0.04. D. rim 0.10. From B03-117. Wheel-coiled. Groove on base. Slipped(?). Coated with pale brown slip(?). RBMa.

43 Small, open vessel. (Fig. 27, Pl. 22)
Body. Moderately coarse, moderately hard-fired, gritty, dark-brown fabric turning black at interior margin, with 5–10% inclusions. Wheel-coiled(?). Yellow Painted. Two horizontal bands in pale yellow on plain, dark ground. RBMa, with rare calcareous(?) inclusions.

44 Tripod jar(?). (Fig. 27, Pl. 22)
Published, Gorogianni, Abell, and Hilditch 2017, 68, no. 7. Pinched spout, incurving rim, two ledge handles, and upper body. H. pres. 0.08. D. rim est. 0.16. Moderately coarse, dark reddish-brown fabric with 5–10% inclusions. Wheel-coiled. Plain. Surface blackened in some areas. RBMa.

45 Tripod jar. (Pl. 22)
Published, Gorogianni, Abell, and Hilditch 2017, 68, no. 8. Flat base, broken at leg attachment. D. pres. 0.11. Moderately coarse, reddish-brown fabric with black core and 10–15% inclusions. Coil-built. Exterior surface is grayish brown; interior surface is red, owing to burning. Plain. RBMd. PFG 2Cv (Local [region]).

46 K.1097. Handleless cup. (Fig. 27)
Type 1. Intact, with small chip at rim. H. 0.04. D. base 0.04. D. rim 0.09. From B03-116. Wheel-coiled(?). Burning on one side and interior. Plain. RBMa.

47 K.1372. Handleless cup. (Fig. 27)
Type 1. 90% preserved, broken at rim. H. 0.04. D. base 0.04. D. rim 0.10. From B03-117. Wheel-coiled(?). Plain. RBMa.

48 K.1441. Handleless cup. (Fig. 27)
Type 1. Intact; mended from 3 fragments, with chip at rim. H. 0.04. D. base 0.05. D. rim 0.11. From B03-117. Wheel-coiled. Plain. RBMa.

49 K.1375. Handleless cup. (Fig. 27)
Type 1. 90% preserved, with chips at rim. H. 0.04. D. base 0.04. D. rim 0.09. From B03-142. Wheel-coiled. Burning at rim. Plain. RBMa.

50 K.2108. Handleless cup. (Fig. 27)
Type 1. 90% preserved, restored in plaster. H. 0.04. D. base 0.04. D. rim est. 0.09. Wheel-coiled(?). Plain. RBMa.

51 K.1265. Handleless cup. (Fig. 27)
Type 1. Intact, with small chip at rim. H. 0.04. D. base 0.05. D. rim 0.10. From B03-145. Wheel-coiled(?). Heavily burned at interior; some traces of burning on exterior. Plain. RBMa.

52 K.1274. Handleless cup. (Fig. 27)
Type 1. Intact, with small chips at rim. H. 0.04. D. base 0.04. D. rim 0.09. From B03-145. Wheel-coiled. Traces of burning at interior and exterior upper body. Plain. RBMa.

53 Handleless cup. (Fig. 27, Pl. 22)
Type 2. 80% preserved, including entire profile. H. 0.06. D. base 0.05. D. rim max. 0.12. Coarse, pale, reddish-brown fabric with 15–20% inclusions. Wheelmade(?). Plain. RBMa.

54 Flaring saucer. (Fig. 27, Pl. 22)
80% of vessel, entire profile preserved. H. 0.04. D. base 0.05. D. rim est. 0.15. Coarse, reddish-orange fabric with 15–20% inclusions. Handmade. Plain. RBMa. For similar, see Cummer and Schofield 1984, no. 596, pl. 58.

55 Goblet (Minyanizing). (Fig. 27, Pl. 22)
Thickened rim, flaring neck, shoulder, and conical body. H. pres. 0.17. D. rim est. 0.24. Coarse, reddish-brown fabric with 15–20% inclusions. Wheel-coiled. Plain. RBMa, with rare calcareous(?) inclusions. PFG 1Cv (Local). For similar shape (but smaller), see Schofield 2011, 121, no. 1334, pl. 63.

56 Plug or lid(?) (Pl. 22)
One large fragment, flat at bottom, somewhat rounded at top. H. pres. 0.05. L. pres. 0.12. Coarse, reddish-brown fabric with 15–20% inclusions. Blackened at bottom. Plain. RBMa.

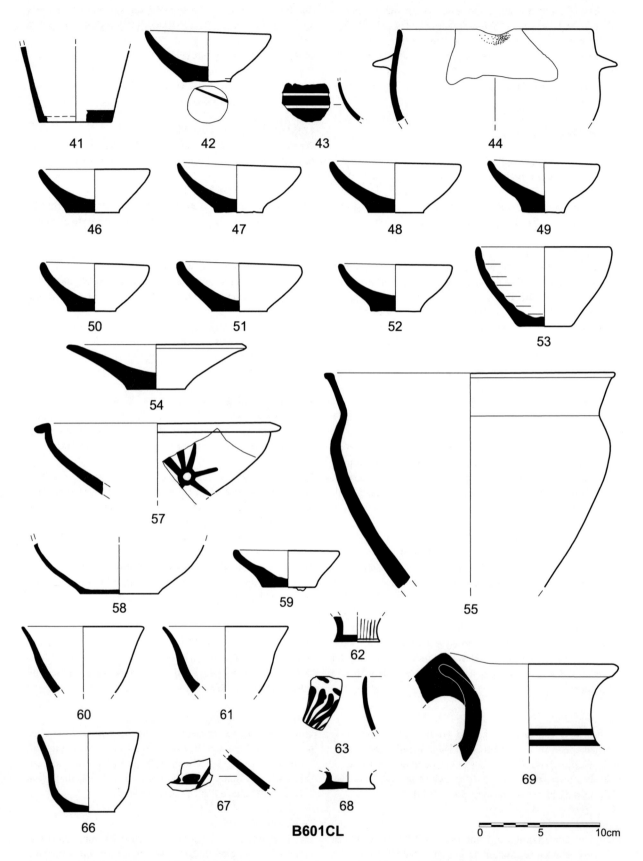

Fig. 27. Pottery from B601CL (**41–44, 46–55, 57–63, 66–69**). Drawings by Aliki Bikaki (**41, 42, 44, 46, 52, 54, 55, 57, 58, 60–62, 66, 68, 69**) and Lily Bonga (**43, 53, 59, 63, 67**).

Cyclades

57 Bowl. (Fig. 27, Pl. 22)
Ledge rim and upper body, partially restored in plaster. H. pres. 0.06. D. rim est. 0.20. Fine, porous, somewhat sandy, pale yellow fabric with fewer than 1% inclusions. Wheel-coiled. Painted. Interior and exterior surfaces smoothed, decorated with faded and flaking matt-brown paint. Rim band; two rosettes with unpainted centers. DVg. PFG 10 (Unknown). Similar in profile but not decoration to ledge-rim bowls on Crete and at Akrotiri (Rethemiotakis and Warren 2014, 14, "Bowl-Everted rim, low, shallow"; Nikolakopoulou 2019, p. 166, "A19 Ledge-Rim Bowl" with references). The profile is similar to larger basins from Kythera (e.g., Coldstream and Huxley 1972, 247, no. E29, fig. 88).

58 Closed vessel. (Fig. 27, Pl. 22)
Flat base and lower body. H. 0.04. D. base 0.06. Moderately fine, slightly gritty, orange fabric with 1–5% inclusions. Wheelmade. Plain. MxMd, with no glassy black particles. PFG 3D (Cyclades [Syros?]).

59 Handleless cup. (Fig. 27, Pl. 22)
Type 1. 80% preserved, including entire profile. H. 0.03. D. base 0.05. D. rim 0.09. Coarse, reddish-brown fabric with 15–20% inclusions. Wheel-coiled. Large, angular, white stone protruding from base causes vessel to sit unevenly. Plain. CSWe. PFG 4A (Naxos).

60 Tumbler. (Fig. 27, Pl. 22)
25% slightly flaring rim and double-curved upper body. D. rim est. 0.10. Moderately coarse, hard-fired, slightly gritty, purplish-brown fabric turning darker at margins and surface, with 10–15% inclusions. Wheel-coiled(?). Plain. MxMf. PFG 5H (Melos/Thera?). For similar, see Coldstream and Huxley 1972, 108, no. 34, fig. 39.

61 Tumbler. (Fig. 27, Pl. 22)
40% slightly flaring rim and double-curved upper body. D. rim est. 0.10. Moderately coarse, hard-fired, slightly gritty, pale brown fabric with thin, gray core and 5–10% inclusions. Wheel-coiled(?). Plain. MxMf, pinkish, with no haloes. PFG 3C (Cyclades [Syros?]). For similar, see Coldstream and Huxley 1972, 108, no. 34, fig. 39.

Melos/Thera

62 Piriform cup. (Fig. 27, Pl. 22)
Base and lower body. H. pres. 0.02. D. base 0.04. Fine, dusty, very pale brown fabric with fewer than 1% inclusions. Wheel-coiled(?). Painted. Exterior: well-smoothed, paneled decoration. One half of lower body painted with narrow vertical rays, ending at base band with points, in matt-brown paint. DVa. For nearly exact parallel, see Marinatos 1972, 62, pl. 62.

63 Piriform cup. (Fig. 27, Pl. 22)
Slightly incurving rim and part of upper body. D. rim est. ca. 0.15. Moderately fine, porous, greenish-yellow fabric with 1–5% inclusions. Construction method unknown. Painted. Interior and exterior well-smoothed. Loop pendant from rim; rosette in matt-brown paint. DVa.

64 Large, closed vessel. (Pl. 22)
Body. Moderately coarse, porous, pinkish-gray fabric with 10–15% inclusions. Handmade. Painted. Exterior: parts of two large, filled disks in matt dark-brown. DVa. PFG 5A (Melos/Thera)

65 Large, closed vessel. (Pl. 22)
Body (two nonjoining fragments). Moderately coarse, porous fabric turning pale gray at interior and pink at exterior margin, with 10–15% inclusions. Coil-built. Slipped and Burnished. Exterior coated with streaky red paint and burnished. DVc. PFG 5D (Melos?).

66 K.2083. Handleless cup. (Fig. 27)
Type 3. 90% preserved; restored in plaster. H. 0.06. D. base 0.04. D. rim 0.08. From B03-81. Wheel-coiled. Plain. DVa. For a very similar cup from Melos, see Davis and Cherry 2007, 273–274, no. P441, fig. 7.5.

Melos/Thera(?)

67 Piriform cup. (Fig. 27, Pl. 22)
Body. Moderately fine, porous, greenish-yellow fabric with 1–5% inclusions. Handmade(?). Painted. Paneled decoration; vertical line; curving horizontal line below filled circles in matt-black paint. DVd, with inclusions that are somewhat more varied in color than usual, but only gold mica. PFG 5Av (Melos/Thera). For similar decoration, see Davis and Cherry 2007, 268, no. 9e.

Aegina(?)

68 Open. (Fig. 27, Pl. 22)
Base and lower body. H. pres. 0.02. D. base 0.05. Fine, dusty, orange fabric with fewer than 1% inclusions. Handmade(?). Painted. Matt red band around base; possible(?) vertical band in same. DVe.

Aegina

69 Hydria. (Fig. 27, Pl. 22)
Most of rim, neck, and part of vertical handle preserved. H. pres. 0.08. D. rim est. 0.15. Moderately fine, pinkish-orange fabric with gray core and greenish-yellow surface and 1–5% inclusions. Handmade. Standard Matt Painted. Part of two bands preserved at bottom of neck, in faded, flaking matt dark-brown paint. DVd.

Central Mainland

70 Goblet. (Pl. 22)
Approximately 10% foot. D. est. 0.15. Fine, hard-fired, gray fabric with fewer than 1% inclusions. Wheelmade. Gray Minyan. FVa.

71 Goblet. (Pl. 22)
Approximately 8% rim. D. rim est. 0.30. Fine, hard-fired, gray fabric with fewer than 1% inclusions. Wheelmade. Surface salt-encrusted. Gray Minyan. FVa.

Kythera/Crete(?)

72 Straight-sided/Vapheio cup. (Fig. 28, Pl. 22)
Rim, very pitted and worn. D. rim indeterminable. From B03-143. Fine, dusty, yellowish-green fabric with fewer than 1% inclusions, primarily rounded, white (calcareous?); tiny, black particles, and rare silver mica. Wheelmade. Lustrous Decorated or Lustrous Painted (DOL); the fabric is unusual for both wares. Exterior: narrow band(?) below rim, naturalistic foliate band (FM 64) in lustrous dark-brown paint. FSTg/FSTj(?).

Crete(?)

73 Ogival bowl or bell cup(?). (Fig. 28)
Rim sherd, slightly flaring. D. est. 0.10. From B03-144. Fine, yellow fabric with fewer than 1% inclusions. Wheelmade. Lustrous Painted (LOD). Coated with lustrous metallic black paint, now flaking; traces of decoration in white. FSTj.

Crete

74 Closed vessel. (Pl. 22)
Body. Moderately fine, compact, gray fabric with pinkish-orange margins and 1–5% inclusions. Handmade. Non-Lustrous Painted (LOD). Exterior coated with dark slip(?), white curving band(?). FSTf, gray, with predominately white inclusions.

75 Lamp. (Fig. 28, Pl. 23)
Spout, rim, and upper body. D. rim est. 0.10. Moderately coarse, compact, purplish-brown fabric with 5–10% inclusions. Handmade. Non-Lustrous Painted (Monochrome). Surface coated in thick, flaking, non-lustrous black paint. FSTc, overfired(?) to purple-brown. For similar shape, see Coldstream and Huxley 1972, 111, no. 87, fig. 39.

76 Large, closed vessel. (Pl. 23)
Body. Moderately coarse, sandy, compact, brown fabric with 15–20% inclusions. Manufacture method unknown. Plain. FSTc.

Shell and Bone

Four limpet shells and a few bone fragments discarded.

Stone

77 K1.635. Obsidian flake
W. 0.02. L. 0.08. Th. 0.01. Wt. 15 g. Torrence no. 8011.

Uninventoried:
B03-79: obsidian blade fragment (B-1.216, D. max. 0.02).
B03-81: obsidian flakes (B-1.220, D. max. 0.03; B-1.222, D. max. 0.02).
B03-116: obsidian flake (B-1.293, D. max. 0.03).
B03-117: obsidian flakes (B-1.297, D. max. 0.03; B-1.298, D. max. 0.02).
B03-142: obsidian flake (B-1.326, D. max. 0.04).

Terracotta

78 K1.217. Spindle whorl.
Type S2H. H. 0.03. D. 0.02. D. perf. 0.01. Wt. 18 g. From B03-81. Moderately coarse, reddish-brown fabric turning gray at core, with 5–10% inclusions. Surface smoothed. Breakage at bottom around perforation. RBMa, with phyllite (Local).

79 K1.437. Spindle whorl.
Type M4, but rounded. H. 0.02. D. 0.03. D. perf. 0.01. Wt. 24 g. From B03-142. Moderately coarse, reddish-brown fabric with 15–20% inclusions. Surface smoothed; broken away in one area and extremely pitted on another. Upper surface: impressed lines radiating from perforation. Breakage around perforation at bottom. RBMa (Local).

HOUSE B: PHASE 2

B610CL.
Upper Surface b and accumulation between Surfaces b and a. Most pottery in this combined lot is clearly Period VI and dates the intermediate use phase of the room. A few sherds, which probably date to Period VII (**112, 118**[?]), suggest the date for the second building phase of Room B.1, associated with Surface a.

Pottery

1 1/2 tins (ca. 25.5 liters) collected; 3/4 bag (ca. 0.4 tin or 6.8 liters) kept. 18% fine. Uncatalogued ceramics include fine, open, possibly Cretan Lustrous Painted (DOL and Monochrome) vessels (FSTj), including a spout from a spouted jar; Non-Lustrous Painted (DOL and LOD) vessels (FSTa, FSTk); a Melian/Theran Painted closed vessel, plain lid(?) and plain Cycladic cup (DVa); a Cycladic Painted closed vessel (CSWb) and plain, strap handle (MxMa); a Painted, vertical handle (from a jug?), perhaps from Aegina (DVe); and fine, open, Burnished and Red Coated vessels, probably from the mainland (FVd, FVe). Several Gray Minyan sherds were discarded, as were eight handleless cups and a coarse lug (Kea Pottery Notebook B, 75).

ON SURFACE B:

Local

80 K.1435. Handleless cup. (Fig. 28)
Type 1. 80% preserved; broken at rim. H. 0.04. D. base 0.05. D. rim est. 0.11. From B03-95. Wheel-coiled. Completely blackened in interior and around rim. Plain. RBMa.

81 K.1483. Handleless cup. (Fig. 28)
Type 1. 90% intact; broken at rim. H. 0.04. D. base 0.04. D. rim est. 0.10. From B03-95. Wheel-coiled. Plain. RBMa.

82 K.1115. Handleless cup. (Fig. 28)
Type 1. 95% intact; chips at rim. H. 0.04. D. base 0.04. D. rim 0.10. From B03-95. Wheel-coiled(?). Plain. RBMa, with well-defined gray core.

83 K.1149. Handleless cup. (Fig. 28)
Type 1. Intact. H. 0.04. D. base 0.03. D. rim 0.09. From B03-95. Wheel-coiled. Blackened in several places. From within Hearth 1. Plain. RBMa.

84 K.1078. Handleless cup. (Fig. 28)
Type 1. Nearly intact, with small chips at rim. H. 0.04. D. base 0.04. D. rim 0.10. From B03-95. Wheel-coiled. Plain. RBMa.

85 K.1064. Handleless cup. (Fig. 28)
Type 1. 90% preserved, broken at rim. H. 0.04. D. base 0.05. D. rim 0.10. From B03-99. Wheel-coiled(?). Plain. RBMa.

86 K.1216. Handleless cup. (Fig. 28)
Type 1. Nearly intact, with chips at rim. H. 0.04. D. base 0.04. D. rim 0.10. From B03-99. Wheel-coiled. Blackened at rim. Plain. RBMa.

87 K.1085. Handleless cup. (Fig. 28)
Type 1. Nearly intact, with small chips at rim. H. 0.04. D. base 0.04. D. rim 0.11. From B03-99. Wheel-coiled. Plain. RBMa.

88 K.1096. Handleless cup. (Pl. 23)
Type 3. 95% preserved; chips at rim. H. 0.09. D. base 0.06. D. rim 0.10. From B03-99. Wheel-coiled(?). Plain. RBMa.

89 K.1355. Handleless cup. (Fig. 28)
Type 5. Nearly intact; broken at base. H. 0.03–0.04. D. base 0.04. D. rim 0.10. From B03-99. Wheel-coiled. Plain. RBMa.

90 K.1350. Handleless cup. (Fig. 28)
Type 6. 90% preserved; broken at rim. H. 0.03. D. base 0.04. D. rim 0.10. From B03-99. Uneven base. Wheel-coiled(?). Plain. RBMa.

First 10 cm above Surface b:

Local

91 K.1426. Handleless cup. (Pl. 23)
Type 1. 95% preserved; chips at rim. H. 0.04. D. base 0.04. D. rim 0.09. From B03-99. Wheel-coiled. Plain. RBMa.

92 K.1294. Handleless cup. (Pl. 23)
Type 1. Intact, with small chip at rim. H. 0.04. D. base 0.04. D. rim 0.09. From B03-99. Wheel-coiled. Plain. RBMa.

93 K.1269. Handleless cup. (Pl. 23)
Type 1. Intact. H. 0.04. D. base 0.03. D. rim 0.09. From B03-99. Wheelmade(?). Plain. RBMa.

Cyclades

94 K.1445. Handleless cup. (Fig. 28, Pl. 23)
Type 3. 95% intact, with some chips at rim. H. 0.07. D. base 0.04. D. rim 0.09. From B03-99. Wheel-coiled(?). Plain. MxMa, no visible metamorphics.

Melos/Thera

95 K.1425. Handleless cup. (Pl. 23)
Type 1. Nearly intact, with chip at rim. H. 0.03. D. base 0.05. D. rim 0.09. From B03-99. Wheel-coiled. Plain. DVb.

Additional vessels from the combined lot:

Local And Local Region

96 Cycladic cup. (Fig. 28, Pl. 23)
Splaying base. H. pres. 0.02. D. base est. 0.05. Moderately coarse, compact, dark reddish-brown fabric with pale-gray core and purple tinge, and with 5–10% inclusions. Wheelmade or wheel-coiled. Slipped and Burnished. Interior and exterior of base coated in dark-brown paint, burnished(?). RBMa, compact, with common mica and rounded, green particles.

97 Closed(?) vessel. (Pl. 23)
Body. Moderately fine, sandy, orange-red fabric with 1–5% inclusions. Coil-built(?). Yellow Slipped. Exterior coated in yellow slip, indecipherable decoration in flaking, reddish-brown paint. RBMa, with common mica. PFG 1A (Local).

98 Large, closed vessel. (Fig. 28, Pl. 23)
Large body, with two additional nonjoining fragments from B609CL. Moderately fine, reddish-brown fabric with purple tinge, dark-gray core, and 1–5% inclusions. Handmade. Yellow Slipped. Exterior slipped yellow, decorated in matt-black paint. Loops or circles above two horizontal bands, with possible traces of spirals(?) below the bands. RBMa, with rare calcareous (some biogenic?) inclusions, perhaps nonlocal(?). PFG 2Bv (Local region).

99 Pedestaled bowl. (Fig. 28, Pl. 23)
Approximately 10% projecting rim and upper body. D. rim est. 0.15. Moderately coarse, dark orange fabric with 5–10% inclusions. Handmade. Yellow Slipped. Slipped in and out, decorated with matt brown paint. Exterior: bands at rim, shoulder, and body. Interior: barred rim between horizontal bands. Radiating line(?) from interior of bowl. RBMa, with rare calcareous inclusions. Shape exists in Period V and later deposits, often with similar decoration: Cummer and Schofield 1984, nos. 362, 418, 510, 824, 1578; Davis 1986, nos. P-2, AA-12, AA-13; Schofield 2011, nos. 239, 913, 1205, 1427, 1519, 1869.

100 Straight-sided/Vapheio cup. (Fig. 28, Pl. 23)
Body. Moderately fine, reddish-brown fabric with paler core and 1–5% inclusions. Handmade. Yellow Slipped. Slipped in and out; traces of semi-lustrous orange-brown paint on interior; flaked. Exterior: horizontal band; thick, vertical band; and ripple pattern in semi-lustrous red paint; burnished(?). RBMa.

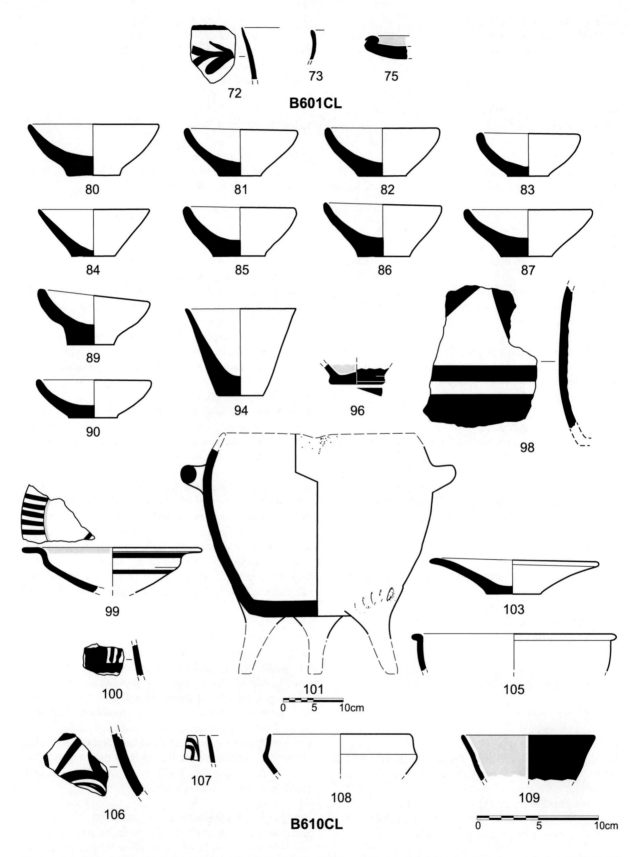

Fig. 28. Pottery from B601CL (**72, 73, 75**) and B610CL (**80–87, 89, 90, 94, 96, 98–101, 103, 105–109**). Drawings by Aliki Bikaki (**72, 73, 75, 80–87, 89, 90, 94**), Lily Bonga (**96, 98–100, 103, 105–109**), and John M. Bouda (**101**).

101 K.1824. Tripod jar. (Fig. 28)
Published, Gorogianni, Abell, and Hilditch 2017, 68, no. 11. Approximately 80% preserved, including upper parts of two flattened-section legs; flat base; two round, horizontal handles; and small, pulled spout. H. est. 0.39. D. rim est. 0.31. From B03-95. Coarse, reddish-brown fabric with 15–20% inclusions. Blackened at bottom. Handmade, probably coil-built. Plain. RBMa.

102 Cycladic cup. (Pl. 23)
Carinated body. Moderately coarse, dark reddish-brown fabric with gray core, gray surface, and 5–10% inclusions. Handmade(?). Plain. Two uneven grooves along upper exterior, one groove in interior at carination. RBMa, with common mica. PFG 1Bv (Local).

103 Flaring saucer. (Fig. 28, Pl. 23)
80% preserved, including entire profile. Slightly sloping rim, raised base. H. 0.03. D. base 0.04. D. rim est. 0.15. Coarse, orange-red fabric with 15–20% inclusions. Wheel-coiled. Plain. Shallow, incised band below rim in interior. RBMa. For similar, see Schofield 2011, 45, 151, 154, nos. 425, 1842, 1885, pls. 46, 74, 75.

Cyclades

104 Small, closed vessel. (Pl. 23)
Body. Moderately coarse, dusty, porous, pinkish-brown fabric with 10–15% inclusions. Wheelmade(?). Painted. Exterior: horizontal, matt brown bands and indistinguishable motif. MxMa. PFG 9A (Cyclades [Tenos?]).

105 Bowl. (Fig. 28, Pl. 23)
Approximately 12% rolled rim and upper body. H. pres. 0.03. D. rim est. 0.17. Moderately fine, pale orange fabric with 1–5% inclusions. Wheel-coiled(?). Plain. MxMa, very dusty, with obvious metamorphics. PFG 3Cv (Cyclades [Syros?]). For similar shape, see Schofield 2011, 70, no. 799, pl. 51.

Melos/Thera

106 Closed vessel. (Fig. 28, Pl. 23)
Body. Moderately coarse, pale orange fabric with 10–15% inclusions. Handmade. Painted. Linked concentric circles or spirals in zones, separated by a band running at a diagonal, all in semi-lustrous red. Surface burnished. DVb. PFG 5D (Melos?).

107 Piriform cup. (Fig. 28, Pl. 23)
Straight rim. Too small to determine diameter. Fine, coarse-grained, dusty, pale brown fabric with fewer than 1% inclusions. Forming method indeterminable. Painted. Exterior: curving lines in matt brown paint. DVb, fine.

108 Melian bowl. (Fig. 28, Pl. 23)
Approximately 8% rim and upper body. H. pres. 0.03. D. rim est. 0.12. Moderately coarse, pale brown fabric with 10–15% inclusions. Forming method indeterminable. Plain. DVb.

Melos/Thera or Aegina(?)

109 Cup or tumbler. (Fig. 28, Pl. 23)
Approximately 8% rim and upper body. H. pres. 0.06. D. rim est. 0.11. Fine, somewhat dusty, orange fabric with fewer than 1% inclusions. Wheelmade. Red Coated. Interior and exterior coated with streaky matt red-brown paint. DVe. PFG 5Hv (Melos/Thera?).

Aegina

110 Hydria. (Fig. 29, Pl. 23)
Rim and vertical handle attachment. Rim distorted by handle attachment. Fine, pale greenish-gray fabric with fewer than 1% inclusions. Wheelmade(?). Standard Matt Painted. Matt dark-brown band at rim and around handle. DVd. Shape similar to Mylonas 1972–1973, no. Γ-17, which was dated by Dietz (1991, 225, 227, no. KB-3, fig. 71) to his LH IB.

111 Narrow-necked jar. (Fig. 29)
Rim, neck, and part of shoulder. Four, nonjoining body fragments in same fabric were also found; all probably belong to same vessel. H. pres. 0.05. D. rim 0.13. Moderately fine, dusty, orange fabric with 1–5% inclusions. Handmade(?). Standard Matt Painted. Exterior coated with faded, pale yellow slip; matt dark-gray band at base of neck. DVe. PFG 5G (Aegina). Shape similar to Mylonas 1972–1973, no. Υ-236, which was dated by Dietz (1991, 224, 226, fig. 71, no. KB-1) to his MH IIIB, although the type continues into the LBA (Zerner 1988, 4, fig. 18, no. 46).

Mainland

112 Straight-sided alabastron. (Fig. 29, Pl. 23)
FS 90. Base and lower body. H. pres. 0.01. D. base est. 0.05. Fine, slightly dusty, pink fabric turning yellow at surfaces, with fewer than 1% inclusions. Wheelmade. Lustrous Painted. Bottom preserves part of wheel in semi-lustrous brown paint. FVc. For similar decoration on an alabastron base, see Mountjoy 1999, 858, fig. 349:1.

113 Vapheio cup. (Fig. 29, Pl. 23)
Kythera type III. Part of base, lower body, and midrib. H. pres. 0.05. D. base 0.05. Fine, slightly dusty orange-pink fabric turning yellow at core and at surfaces, with fewer than 1% inclusions. Wheelmade(?). Lustrous Painted. Exterior: ripple pattern (FM 78) in lustrous brown–black paint, with wide band around midrib and above base in same. FVd.

114 Rounded cup. (Pl. 23)
FS 211. Part of rim and upper body. D. rim est. 0.13. Fine, hard-fired, orange-pink fabric turning paler at surface, with fewer than 1% inclusions. Wheelmade. Lustrous Painted. Rim band in brownish-orange paint; upper body preserves part of spiral that overlaps the rim band. FVd. PFG 3F (Unknown).

115 Hydria. (Fig. 29, Pl. 23)
Part of rim, neck, and round vertical handle attachment at neck. H. pres. 0.08. D. rim est. 0.13. Fine, hard-fired, dark pinkish-purple fabric with pale pinkish-yellow surface and fewer

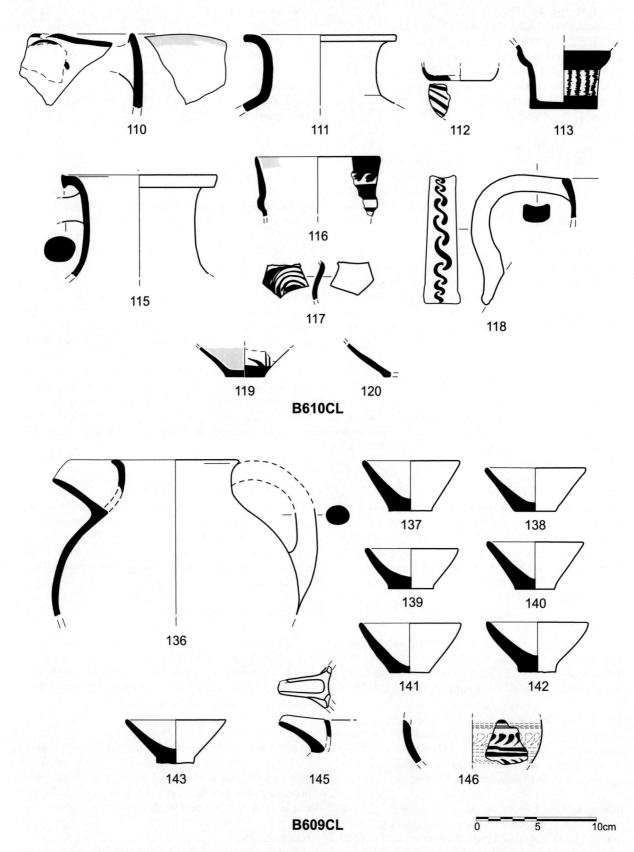

Fig. 29. Pottery from B610CL (**110–113, 115–120**) and B609CL (**136–143, 145, 146**). Drawings by Lily Bonga (**110, 112, 117, 119, 120**), Aliki Bikaki (**111, 113, 115, 116, 118, 136–143**), and Mary-Jane Schumacher (**145, 146**).

than 1% inclusions. Wheelmade. Plain. For shape, see Mylonas 1972–1973, no. E-78, pl. 225; similar rims exist on jars with other handle configurations, e.g., no. Δ-63, pl. 221. FVf. PFG 13Av (Attica?).

Mainland/Kythera

116 Vapheio cup. (Fig. 29, Pl. 23)
Kythera type II. Part of midrib and upper body, including the rim. D. rim est. 0.10. Fine, hard-fired, pinkish brown fabric with greenish surface and fewer than 1% inclusions. Wheelmade. Lustrous Painted. Interior: wide rim band in lustrous black paint. Exterior: black bands below and above midrib, with added white bands over and above midrib. Below rim band: row of schematic blooms. FSTh. PFG 7G (Mainland/Kythera?). For similar, Coldstream and Huxley 1972, 121, pl. 31:2; Lindblom and Manning 2011, 142, fig. 1:P318.

117 Rounded cup. (Fig. 29, Pl. 23)
Shoulder fragment. Fine, pale brown fabric with fewer than 1% inclusions. Wheelmade. Lustrous Painted. Interior: lower part of rim band in lustrous dark-brown paint. Exterior: spiral in same. FSTh.

Crete(?)

118 Bridge-spouted jug. (Fig. 29, Pl. 23)
Fine, hard-fired, pale pinkish brown fabric turning pale green at surface. Fewer than 1% inclusions. Vertical, grooved, strap handle at attachment to rim. H. pres. 0.11. From B03-99. Forming method indeterminable. Lustrous Painted. Interior of neck, bottom and sides of handle painted gray-brown; running quirk within groove of handle (FM 48). FSTj. PFG 7Gv (Mainland/Kythera?).

119 Rounded cup. (Fig. 29, Pl. 23)
Base and part of lower body. H. pres. 0.04. D. base 0.03. Fine, hard-fired, pale orange fabric with fewer than 1% inclusions. Wheelmade. Lustrous Painted. Interior coated with flaking, lustrous red paint. Exterior preserves decoration in same: widely-spaced reeds above a band that extends to underneath the base. FSTk. PFG 7Gv (Mainland/Kythera?).

120 Rounded cup. (Fig. 29, Pl. 23)
Part of lower body and base. H. pres. 0.04. Fine, hard-fired, pale orange-yellow fabric with fewer than 1% inclusions. Wheelmade. Lustrous Painted. Interior: monochrome, lustrous red. Exterior: coated with yellow slip, decorated in red. Thick band above base. Above thick band is another narrow band and the bottom of a spiral. FSTj.

121 Closed vessel. (Pl. 23)
Body. Moderately coarse, hard-fired, pink fabric with pale yellow core and 10–15% inclusions. Forming method unknown. Non-Lustrous Painted. Exterior coated with yellow slip, decorated with non-lustrous brown trickle (or messy band). FSTa, with unusual core and subrounded inclusions.

Unknown

122 K.1154. Handleless cup.
H. 0.03. D. base 0.03. D. rim 0.09. From B03-95. Now missing.

Bone and Shell

A murex shell and a few scraps of bone were discarded from lot B03-99.

123 K1.455. Bone awl.
W. 0.01. L. 0.08. From B03-99. Intact white bone with polished pale brown surface. Socket at one end, point at other. Groove along entire length. Description from notecard; awl now lost.

Stone

124 K1.446. Denticulate. (Pl. 24)
W. 0.05. L. 0.10. Th. 0.09. Wt. 53 g. From B03-99, on Surface b. Marble or flint (Rapp). Chipped and missing one corner. Surface coated with thick encrustation, white on one side, pink on the other.

125 K1.341. Mortar. (Pl. 24)
H. 0.06. W. 0.14. L. 0.10. Wt. 935 g. Approximately 60% preserved, chipped and broken. From B03-99, on Surface b. White marble with some dark-brown areas (Rapp). Slightly convex, elliptical base. Hollowed center. Slightly flaring sides. Evidence of spout.

126 K1.367. Tool or figurine. (Pl. 24)
W. 0.02. L. 0.04. Th. 0.01. Wt. 15 g. From B03-95. Yellowish marble, chipped. Tapered, ovoid section, rounded edges. Rounded and smooth at narrow, unbroken end.

Uninventoried:
B03-98: obsidian flake (B-1.242, from within Surface a).
B03-99: obsidian blade (B-1.264, L. 0.03); obsidian chips (B-1.243, B-1.252, B-1.253, B-1.254, B-1.256); two pieces of white stone (flint(?), no field number); millstone (B-1.267, from above Surface b).

Terracotta

127 K1.188. Loom weight. (Pl. 24)
Type RF. D. 0.08. Th. 0.02. D. perf. 0.01. Wt. 170 g. From B03-78, below Platform 1. Flattened body with very narrow, flattened top. Surface smoothed, now somewhat worn, pitted. RBMa, with common mica. (Local).

128 K1.211. Loom weight. (Pl. 24)
Type RG. D. 0.06. Th. 0.02. D. perf. 0.01. Wt. 62 g. From B03-76. Round, flattened body with grooved top. Moderately fine, dark-brownish gray fabric, turning black at surface, with 1–5% inclusions. Surface black, burnished. RBMa, dark. (Local).

129 K1.186. Loom weight. (Pl. 24)
Type RG. D. 0.08. D. perf. 0.01. Th. 0.03. Wt. 188 g. From B03-76. Round, flattened body, with grooved top. Moderately fine,

orange-brown fabric with 1–5% inclusions. Surface smoothed, somewhat worn. RBMa, with very common mica. (Local).

130 K1.292. Loom weight. (Pl. 24)
Type OG. H. 0.10. W. 0.09. Th. 0.03. D. perf. 0.01. Wt. 260 g. From B03-99, just above Surface b. Flattened body. Surface smoothed. DVa. (Melos/Thera).

131 K1.294. Loom weight. (Pl. 24)
Type RFG. H. 0.08. W. 0.09. Th. 0.03. D. perf. 0.01. Wt. 168 g. From B03-99, just above Surface b. Round, flattened body with flat, grooved top. Moderately coarse, smooth, compact, pink fabric with pale-gray core and 15–20% inclusions. One side well preserved with few chips; opposite side broken. FSTa, with unusual core. (Crete).

132 K1.291. Loom weight. (Pl. 24)
Type RF. D. 0.08. Th. 0.02. D. perf. <0.01. Wt. 100 g. From B03-95, just above Surface b. Flattened body; two perforations. Moderately fine, compact, orange-red fabric with 1–5% inclusions, primarily small–moderately sized shiny white and gray; spalling friable white (calcareous?); elongated red-brown and gray; and rare black inclusions, with few voids at the surface, both elongate and irregular. Surface smoothed. Unknown fabric, probably imported.

133 K1.533. Perforated disk. (Pl. 24)
D. 0.04. Th. 0.01. Wt. 18 g. From B03-98. Intact. Moderately coarse, reddish-brown fabric with 5–10% inclusions. Uneven thickness. Four perforations placed off-center in rough diamond formation. Extensive wear and some breakage around holes. RBMa. (Local).

134 K1.310. Spindle whorl. (Pl. 24)
Type M2; somewhat rounded. H. 0.02. D. 0.03. D. perf. 0.01. Wt. 20 g. From B03-95. Moderately fine, reddish-tan fabric with fewer than 1% inclusions, primarily small, angular, gray schist; shiny, white particles; and small vughs. Minor breakage around perforation at both ends. Slanting incised lines over shoulder and sides. Fabric unknown, probably imported.

Metal

Uninventoried: mass of metal (B-1.239). Gossan-concentration liminitic weathered ore deposit (Bullard). Limonite was sometimes used as a pigment in Aegean painting (Morgan 2020, 343), but the function, if any, of this object is unclear, since this is an abundant, locally available material (Georgakopoulou).

HOUSE B: PHASES 3–4 AND DESTRUCTION DEPOSIT

B609CL.
Surface a and lower part of destruction deposit. Period VIIb, some possibly later. Fragments from a goblet (**166**) were found underneath fallen slabs and just above Surface a (B03-41), in the destruction debris in the Wall I doorway (B03-93), and in Temple Lane (B03-90).

Pottery

4 tins (ca. 68 liters) collected; 0.7 tin (ca. 11.9 liters) remains. 12% fine, about 30% of which was sherds from plain, Lustrous Painted (Monochrome), Slipped, or Burnished goblets. Uncatalogued ceramics include a Lustrous Painted bridge-spouted jar (FSTk), several alabastra (FVb, FVd), a ring-handled cup (FVb); sherds from Lustrous and Non-Lustrous Painted vessels of unknown profile (FSTa, FSTj, FSTk, FVb, FVc, FVd); a Non-Lustrous Painted bell(?) cup, perhaps from Kythera or the mainland (FSTh); a plain hole-mouthed jar and a Lustrous Painted bell cup, perhaps Aeginetan (DVe); Melian/Theran and other Cycladic Painted closed vessels and a rounded cup (DVa, DVb, MxMc); Burnished and Red Coated open vessels, including goblets and a basin/bowl (FVd). Fragments of 8–10 handleless cups, a tripod leg, several pithoi, and burned body fragments probably from a cooking vessel were discarded, as were small Gray Minyan and Matt Painted sherds (Kea Pottery Notebook B, 69).

Local

135 Jar(?). (Pl. 24)
Body. Coarse, dark red fabric with gray core and 15–20% inclusions. Interior surface worn. Forming method indeterminable. Yellow Slipped. Exterior surface preserves faded yellow slip and dark-brown paint. One straight thin band that intersects nine curving thin bands. RBMa, with rare calcareous(?) inclusions.

136 Bridge-spouted jug. (Fig. 29, Pl. 24)
Upper third of vessel; approximately 80% preserved. Globular body, one vertical round handle, bridge spout, slightly flaring rim. H. pres. 0.12. D. rim 0.11. Moderately coarse, reddish-brown fabric with 5–10% inclusions. Wheel-coiled. Yellow Slipped. Traces of pale yellow slip preserved around base and interior of spout, handle, interior of neck, and in patches of exterior body. Horizontal dark bands (?) around handle. RBMa, with blue and gray schist, rare mica, and rare calcareous(?) inclusions. PFG 1Cv (Local). For a similar shape in the Red and Black style, see Cummer and Schofield 1984, 59, no. 218, pl. 50.

137 K.416. Handleless cup. (Fig. 29)
Type 1. 80% preserved; broken rim and chipped base. H. 0.04. D. base 0.04. D. rim 0.08. From B03-29. Uneven base. Wheel-coiled. Plain. RBMa, with common mica.

138 K.184. Handleless cup. (Fig. 29)
Type 1. 80% preserved; broken at rim and chipped at base. H. 0.04. D. base 0.03. D. rim 0.08. From B03-39. Dark-gray core. Wheel-coiled. Surface discolored to dark reddish gray on one side, from firing(?). Plain. RBMa.

139 K.792. Handleless cup. (Fig. 29)
Type 1. 90% preserved; broken and chipped at rim. H. 0.03. D. base 0.04. D. rim 0.08. From B03-39. Wheel-coiled. Plain. RBMa.

140 K.635. Handleless cup. (Fig. 29)
Type 1. 80% preserved; broken at rim. H. 0.04. D. base 0.04. D. rim 0.08. From B03-41. Wheel-coiled. Part of rim and upper body burned. Plain. RBMa.

141 K.775. Handleless cup. (Fig. 29)
Type 1. 90% preserved; broken and chipped at rim. H. 0.04. D. base 0.03. D. rim 0.08. From B03-41. Wheel-coiled. Exterior surface eroded. Plain. RBMa.

142 K.808. Handleless cup. (Fig. 29)
Type 1. 90% preserved; chipped. H. 0.04. D. base 0.03. D. rim 0.08. From B03-41. Thick walls. Uneven base. Wheel-coiled(?). One part of rim burned. Plain. RBMa.

143 K.710. Handleless cup. (Fig. 29)
Type 1. 90% preserved. Chipped at rim; broken at mid-body. H. 0.04. D. base 0.03. D. rim 0.08. From B03-41. Uneven base. Wheelmade(?). Plain. RBMa.

144 Firebox. (Pl. 24)
Published, Georgiou 1986, 20, no. 71. Fragment of capsule at join to rim; two perforations, parts of four other perforations. H. pres. 0.04. W. pres. 0.08. D. est. 0.15. Coarse, reddish-brown fabric with 15–20% inclusions. Surface smoothed; interior blackened. Handmade. Plain. RBMa, with rare calcareous(?) inclusions.

Cyclades

145 Bridge-spouted jug. (Fig. 29, Pl. 24)
Spout. D. rim est. 0.07. L. 0.05. Moderately fine, dusty, greenish-gray fabric with pink core and 1–5% inclusions. Forming method indeterminable. Painted. Flaking matt brown paint preserved around spout and at rim. MxMa, with less common mica than usual. PFG 3G (Cyclades?).

146 Fine closed vessel. (Fig. 29, Pl. 24)
Body. Moderately fine, hard-fired, greenish-gray fabric turning paler at surface, with 1–5% inclusions. Wheelmade or wheel-coiled. Painted. Brown band(s) and double foliate band. MxMc.

147 Jug/jar. (Fig. 30, Pl. 24)
Upper body and neck (three nonjoining fragments). Moderately coarse orange-red fabric with 10–15% inclusions. Wheelmade or wheel-coiled. Painted (Polychrome, Red and Black). Exterior smoothed, with one applied, flat disk. Wide, red bands around neck and upper body. Dark-brown, wavy line between red bands. Below bands are dark-brown pendant loops filled with parallel lines. Below loops is a wavy, dark-brown line between two bands, and a solid, red disk outlined with black. MxMa. PFG 3C (Cyclades [Syros?]).

148 Closed vessel. (Fig. 30, Pl. 24)
Body (four nonjoining fragments). Moderately fine, dusty, pale brown fabric turning to pale gray at interior, with 10–15% inclusions. Wheelmade. Yellow Slipped (Polychrome, Red and Black). Exterior coated with pale yellow slip. Red horizontal bands and dark-brown foliate band above(?) chevrons(?); the foliate band and a red band intersect with solid red circle outlined with dark brown. MxMa.

149 Small jug. (Fig. 30)
Two nonjoining fragments, approximately 40% of vessel, full profile. Neck and handle from B610CL. Flat base, globular body, round vertical handle, narrow neck, slightly flaring rim. H. 0.14. D. base 0.06. D. rim est. 0.05. Moderately fine, orange-brown fabric with well-defined blue-gray core and 1–5% inclusions. Wheelmade(?). Yellow Slipped(?). Possible traces of pale yellow slip. Exterior smoothed and worn. MxMa, with no visible metamorphics. PFG 5C (Melos/Thera).

150 Basket-handled vessel. (Fig. 30, Pl. 24)
Round, arched handle, straight rim, and slightly convex upper body. H. pres. 0.08. Moderately coarse, pale brown fabric with 15–20% inclusions. Wheelmade(?). Plain. Three shallow grooves along body under handle. MxMa, coarse.

151 K.2157. Handleless cup (perforated). (Fig. 30, Pl. 24)
Type 1. 40% preserved. H. pres. 0.03. D. base 0.03. D. rim 0.07. D. perf. 0.01. Moderately coarse, pale pinkish-brown fabric with 15–20% inclusions. Possibly wheel-coiled. Hole pierced through center of base after firing. Plain. MxMf.

152 K.2193. Industrial vessel(?). (Fig. 30, Pl. 24)
Nearly intact, with a few chips. Cracked into two halves. Nonsymmetrical, off-center, flat base; slightly convex body; nonsymmetrical, slightly incurving rim. H. 0.09. D. base 0.05. D. rim 0.06. Coarse, heavy fabric turning from pinkish orange at base and exterior lower body to light gray interior and exterior upper body, probably as a result of heat, with 15–20% inclusions. Handmade. Unsmoothed interior preserves deep finger impressions. Exterior surface is rough and uneven. Cast of interior is amorphous blob (Pl. 24). Plain. Unknown fabric, possibly a variant of MxMa or DVb(?).

Melos/Thera

153 Straight-sided closed(?) vessel (pyxis?). (Fig. 30, Pl. 24)
Lower body and base. H. pres. 0.05. D. est. 0.08. Moderately fine, dusty pink fabric, with gray core and pale green surface and with 5–10% inclusions. Wheelmade(?). Painted. Exterior: two bands at base, with two closely-spaced, solid-center spirals above in matt dark-brown paint. Paint now faded and chipped. DVb, with possible ash temper; I thank Jill Hilditch for this suggestion. For possibly similar shape (but larger), see Cummer and Schofield 1984, 124, no. 1532, pl. 83.

154 Jug. (Fig. 30, Pl. 24)
Shoulder broken at neck attachment. Moderately coarse, gritty, yellowish-brown fabric with 15–20% inclusions. Thickening at neck attachment is a possible coil join. Body is probably

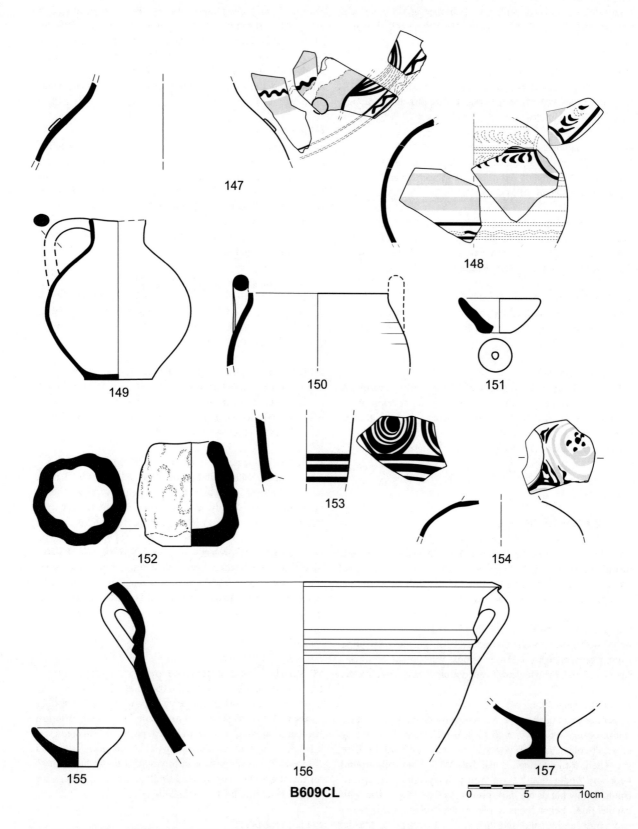

Fig. 30. Pottery from B609CL (**147–157**). Drawings by Mary-Jane Schumacher (**147, 148, 150, 153, 154**), Aliki Bikaki (**149, 155–157**), and Lily Bonga (**151, 152**).

wheelmade. Yellow Slipped (Polychrome, Red and Black). Coated with white slip; decorated with matt brown and red paint. Red spiral with six brown dots at center. Above spiral are wavy, brown bands and a straight, red band. DVb.

155 K.702. Handleless cup. (Fig. 30)
Type 1. 80% preserved; broken at rim. H. 0.03. D. base 0.04. D. rim 0.08. From B03-39. Thick walls and base. Moderately fine fabric. Uneven base. Wheel-coiled. Part of rim blackened. Plain. DVb.

Cyclades/Attica(?)

156 Minyanizing goblet/jar. (Fig. 30, Pl. 25)
Upper body, handle, and ca. 25% of rim of very large goblet-shaped vessel, partially restored in plaster. H. pres. 0.14. D. rim est. 0.34. Moderately coarse, reddish-brown fabric with 5–10% inclusions. Wheel-coiled(?). Plain. Three horizontal ridges below flaring rim. RBMc. PFG 2B (Local region).

Aegina(?)

157 Goblet. (Fig. 30, Pl. 25)
FS 270. Foot, stem, and part of lower body. H. pres. 0.05. D. base 0.05. Moderately fine, gritty, orange-red fabric with fewer than 1% inclusions. Wheelmade(?). Clay is flaky and brittle, probably from action of salt. Burnished. DVe. Similar to Mountjoy 1981, 23, 37, nos. 55, 235, figs. 8, 19.

158 Jug. (Fig. 31, Pl. 25)
Round, slightly flattened, vertical handle with attachment to rim; neck; and neck molding. H. 0.05. Moderately coarse, orange-pink fabric with gray core and 10–15% inclusions. Breakage of fragment shows that neck was attached separately and joined to body with overlying coil. Yellow Slipped. Yellow slip preserved in patches. Decoration is fugitive. Horizontal solid band below ledge; horizontal solid band and band of dots above neck molding. DVf. PFG 5E (Unknown; does not seem compatible with an Aeginetan provenance).

Aegina

159 K.2164. Cooking jar. (Fig. 31, Pl. 25)
Published, Bikaki 1984, 33, no. VII-12, pl. 47; Gorogianni, Abell, and Hilditch 2017, 70, no. 13; Lindblom 2001, 87, no. 1036, pl. 50. Round vertical handle. H. pres. 0.13. Th. 0.02. Moderately coarse, pinkish brown fabric with gray core and 10–15% inclusions. Handmade. Interior and exterior smoothed. Plain. Two incised parallel lines at base of handle. DVf. Parallels for mark at Tiryns and Eleusis (Lindblom 2001, 87).

Attica(?)

160 Goblet. (Fig. 31, Pl. 25)
Approximately 17% rim, upper body. H. pres. 0.08. D. rim est. 0.20. Fine, hard-fired, red fabric with fewer than 1% inclusions. Wheelmade. Red Coated. Slip pinkish; burnished. MFVc. PFG 13A (Attica?). Similar to Maran 1992, 11, nos. 11, 12, pl. 1.

161 Goblet. (Fig. 31, Pl. 25)
Stem and part of lower body. H. pres. 0.04. Th. stem 0.02. H. stem 0.02. Fine, red fabric with fewer than 1% inclusions. Wheelmade. Red Coated. Slip pinkish; burnished. MFVc.

162 Goblet. (Fig. 31, Pl. 25)
Strap handle attached at rim; upper body. H. pres. 0.11. D. rim est. 0.19. Fine, hard-fired, somewhat dusty, red fabric with fewer than 1% inclusions. Wheelmade. Red Coated. Red slip is thick and flaking. MFVc. Similar to Maran 1992, 11, nos. 11, 12, pl. 1.

163 Goblet. (Fig. 31, Pl. 25)
Base, stem, and part of lower body. H. pres. 0.05. H. est. 0.18. D. base 0.02. Fine, hard-fired, red fabric with fewer than 1% inclusions. Wheelmade. Burnished. Although a slip is not completely obvious on the surface, refiring suggests the vessel was coated. MFVc. PFG 13A (Attica?).

Mainland

164 Large, fine, closed vessel. (Pl. 25)
Shoulder. Fine, hard-fired, yellowish-green fabric with fewer than 1% inclusions. Interior: prominent wheel marks; probable join at shoulder. Probably wheelmade in parts and assembled. Lustrous Painted. Ogival canopy (FM 13), band of small dots, two thin bands, band of small dots, and a wide band in lustrous black paint, now almost entirely fugitive. FVb, overfired.

165 Vapheio cup. (Fig. 31, Pl. 25)
Kythera Type III. Approximately 30% preserved, almost full profile, with very bottom missing. H. pres. 0.09. D. rim est. 0.12. Fine, pink fabric with fewer than 1% inclusions. Wheelmade. Lustrous Painted. Interior and exterior surface coated with yellow slip. Band around rim interior and exterior in flaking, lustrous reddish-brown paint. Another band around central rib, overlapping to body. Ripple pattern (FM 78) along upper and lower body. Possible thin band in added white over midrib. FVd.

166 K.334, K.1122. Goblet. (Fig. 31, Pl. 25)
FS 262. Part of rim, upper body, high-swung handle, and lead clamp. Much restored in plaster (K.334). Nonjoining: fragments of lower body, short stem, and hollowed foot probably part of same vessel (K.1122). H. pres. 0.11 (upper body), 0.05 (lower body). D. base 0.08. D. rim est. 0.13. L. clamp 0.03. Th. clamp 0.01. From B03-41. Fine, dusty, orange fabric turning yellow at surface. Fewer than 1% inclusions. Upper body is probably wheelmade; goblet base appears to be coil-built, and must have been added separately. Lustrous Painted. Interior: coated with flaking, lustrous dark-brown paint. Exterior: coated in yellow slip. Solid band along rim and upper part of shoulder in flaking, lustrous red to dark-brown paint. Solid loop connects at rim band and encircles handle attachment at shoulder. Solid, curving band painted down handle. Large palm (FM 14) on each side of handle. There is enough space for a third palm on the side opposite the handle. Two bands along lower body; wide band around stem; band around edge of foot. Interior and

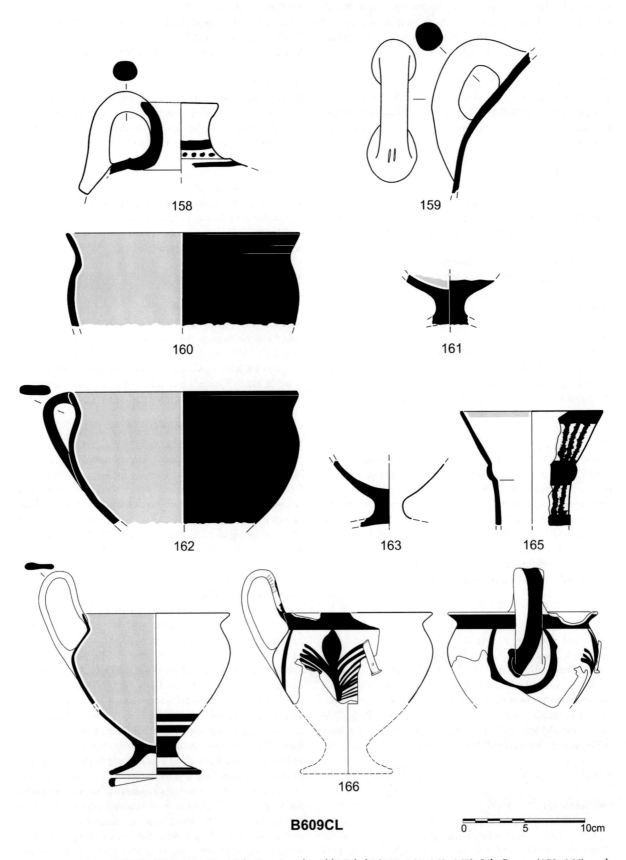

Fig. 31. Pottery from B609CL (**158**–**163**, **165**, **166**). Drawings by Aliki Bikaki (**158**, **161**, **163**, **165**), Lily Bonga (**159**, **166**), and Mary-Jane Schumacher (**160**, **162**).

exterior: burnished. Lead clamp attached to one sherd; rectangular, with flattened projection at one end and a small perforation. FVd. The presence of bands and a possibly repeating motif suggests this is not a proper Ephyraean goblet (Mountjoy 1983). Stylistically, it appears to be transitional between LH IIA and IIB.

167 (Ephyraean?) goblet. (Fig. 32, Pl. 25)
Stem, slightly concave domed foot, and small part of bowl. H. pres. 0.06. H. stem 0.04. D. base est. 0.09. Fine, pale yellow fabric with pale-gray core and some areas with pink margins, with fewer than 1% inclusions. Wheelmade. Lustrous Painted or Burnished. Poorly preserved dash of lustrous red paint within hollow of base, possible potter's mark? If not, the presence of such limited evidence for paint could suggest that this was a small version of an Ephyraean goblet (e.g., Mountjoy 1988, 48–49, no. 2, fig. 54). FVc/FVe. PFG 14Bv (Unknown).

168 Goblet. (Fig. 32, Pl. 25)
FS 263. Strap handle, approximately 12% of rim, and part of upper body. H. pres. 0.08. D. rim est. 0.16. Fine, dark gray fabric with fewer than 1% inclusions. Overfired? Wheelmade. Lustrous Painted (Monochrome). Surface coated in darkbrown slip, burnished(?). FVd, overfired.

169 Goblet. (Pl. 25)
Short, narrow stem. H. stem 0.02. Fine, gray fabric with pink margins and fewer than 1% inclusions. Forming method unknown. Burnished(?). FVc/FVe, with pink margins.

170 Goblet. (Fig. 32, Pl. 25)
Foot. D. base est. 0.05. Fine, dusty, bluish-gray fabric with pale yellow-brown margins and no inclusions. Wheelmade(?). Plain. FVe. PFG 14D (Central Greece?).

171 Goblet. (Fig. 32, Pl. 25)
Outer disk of base, approximately 50% preserved. D. base est. 0.09. Fine, dusty, pale yellow fabric discolored to gray at one side. Fewer than 1% inclusions. Wheelmade. Plain. Surface smoothed. Horizontal groove runs around outside of base. FVb.

Mainland/Kythera

172 Vapheio cup. (Pl. 25)
Approximately 10% of rim. H. pres. 0.04. D. rim est. 0.09. Fine, hard-fired, pale pinkish-brown fabric with fewer than 1% inclusions. Wheelmade. Lustrous Painted. Wide band in lustrous dark-brown paint along rim interior. Narrow band in same along rim exterior. Wide, vertical band and ripple pattern. Burnished. FSTh. PFG 7Gv (Mainland/Kythera?).

Crete/Mainland(?)

173 Palace Style jar. (Fig. 32, Pl. 25)
Nonjoining fragments: rim, neck with molding, and body. Neck fragments from B03-20, others from B604CL. Coarse, dark pink fabric turning pale brown at core and paler brown at surface, with 10–15% inclusions. Handmade. Lustrous Painted. Exterior coated with pale, yellow slip; decorated with flaking lustrous brown paint that turns red in places. Interior of neck painted red; exterior is dark brown. On shoulder: row of dots and wavy line(s). On body: curving, wavy lines between rows of dots; possible floral motif. Horizontal bands from lower body. FSTd. PFG 7H (Argolid/Corinthia?). For similar, see Müller 1909, pl. XVIII:1.

Crete(?)

174 K.2115. Flaring cup-rhyton. (Fig. 32, Pl. 26)
Full profile preserved, including ring handle. Approximately half restored in plaster. Torus base and short, everted rim. Base pierced before firing near edge, opposite handle. H. 0.14. D. base 0.08. D. rim est. 0.19. D. perf. <0.01. Fine, dusty, pale orange fabric with fewer than 1% inclusions. Wheel-coiled. Lustrous Painted. Interior: monochrome, reddish-brown; bottom and sides of base coated with same paint. Wavy band above base, above which reed pattern occupies entire body to top of rim. Paint everywhere is badly preserved and flaking. FSTk.

175 Flaring cup-rhyton(?). (Fig. 32, Pl. 26)
Body. Fine, dusty, grayish-green fabric with fewer than 1% inclusions. Wheelmade. Lustrous Painted. Rock pattern with reeds in black, lustrous paint, now flaking. Plain interior. FSTj, with rounded brown particles. PFG 14A (Unknown).

176 Bell cup. (Fig. 32, Pl. 26)
Two nonjoining fragments: approximately 20% rim and vertical strap handle with metallic attachment. H. pres. 0.05. D. rim est. 0.08. Fine, dusty, pale pinkish-brown fabric with fewer than 1% inclusions. Wheelmade. Lustrous Painted. Interior coated with flaking, lustrous dark-brown paint; handle coated in same. Wide band around handle from rim to lower attachment. Rim band. FSTj.

Unknown

177 Paneled jug(?). (Fig. 32, Pl. 26)
Splaying base and conical lower body. H. pres. 0.09. D. base 0.06. Moderately fine, hard-fired, compact, orange fabric with well-defined gray core and pale brown interior surface, and with 1–5% inclusions. Wheelmade in parts and assembled(?). A partial fingerprint is preserved above the base. Yellow Slipped (Polychrome, Red and Black). Exterior surface, very worn and pitted, coated with yellow slip. Decorated in style similar to paneled cups. Horizontal band above base in purplish-brown paint; above solid band are two vertical bands in same. Within panel, six uneven horizontal bands in purplish-brown. Above bands, two wider gray bands separated by wavy line in purplish-brown. Opposite side, isolated ornament in purplish brown formed by a "v" surrounding two parallel, semicircular bands, perhaps curving around lower handle attachment(?). I thank Jerry Rutter for this suggestion. MxMe. PFG 9A (Cyclades [Tenos?]). For the only other paneled jug so far known in the Aegean, from Argos: Schachermeyr 1976, pl. 41:a; Rutter and Lindblom forthcoming.

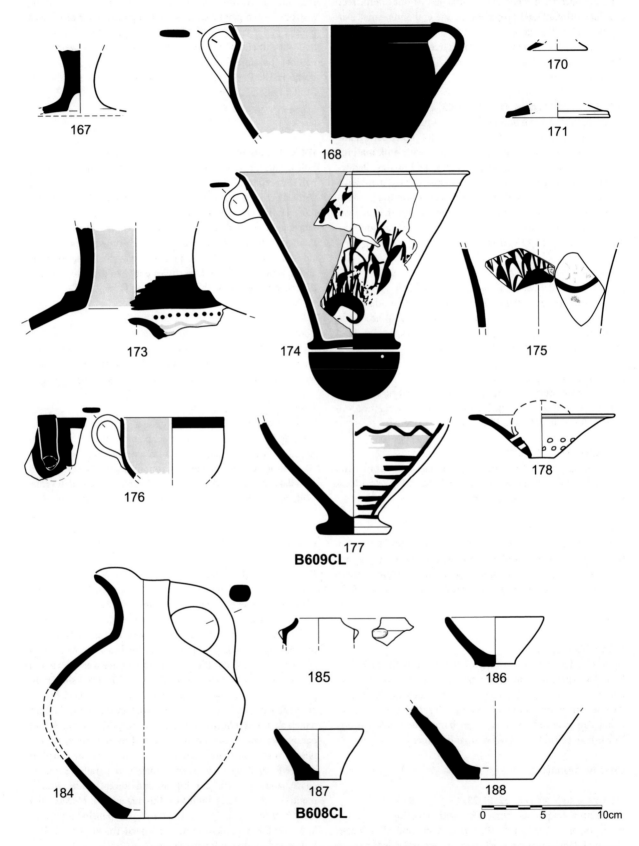

Fig. 32. Pottery from B609CL (**167, 168, 170, 171, 173–178**) and B608CL (**184–188**). Drawings by Mary-Jane Schumacher (**167, 168, 170, 171, 175, 176, 185, 188**), Aliki Bikaki (**173, 177, 178, 184, 186, 187**), and Lily Bonga (**174**).

178 K.2181. Firebox. (Fig. 32, Pl. 26)
Published, Georgiou 1986, 14, no. 9. From B03-41. Lower part of capsule with central hole; part of rim, one tab handle. H. rim 0.3. D. est. 0.11. D. large hole 0.02. Moderately coarse, compact, reddish-brown fabric with 15–20% inclusions, primarily small–moderate subrounded–subangular shiny white, yellow, and gray; lenticular brown and gray (metamorphic?); subrounded, black particles; coarse fraction silver and rarer gold mica; fine fraction gold (and some silver?) mica; and common, small vughs and round voids. Discolored to dark gray in channel between rim and capsule; interior blackened. Unknown fabric, probably nonlocal. Imported fireboxes are rare (e.g., Cummer and Schofield 1984, nos. 1477, 1531, pls. 82, 83).

Bone

179 K1.39. Peg. (Pl. 26)
W. 0.01. L. pres. 0.10. Wt. 4 g. From B03-35. Period VII (Krzyszkowska). Two fragments, point missing. Polished. Proximal end is wider than shaft. Incisions near top. Made from a bone with a thick wall, such as bovid cannon bone (J. L. Caskey).

Stone

180 K1.61. Core, reused as a pestle. (Pl. 26)
H. 0.05. D. 0.05. Wt. 198 g. From B03-31. Off-white marble (Rapp). Cylindrical; fluted in three places (from removal of other cores?). Edges rounded from use. Chipped and encrusted.

Uninventoried:
B03-39: obsidian (B-1.79a).

Metal

181 K1.581. Copper-based object (punch?). (Pl. 26)
Two joining fragments. L. 0.07. Th. 0.01. Wt. 12 g. From B03-39. Square section, elongated object. On one end thins to a thick pointed tip. The other end is broken. Heavily corroded (bronze disease?) (Georgakopoulou).

Terracotta

182 K1.58. Loom weight. (Pl. 26)
Type RG. D 0.07. Th. 0.03. Wt. 135 g. From B03-35. Round, lentoid body with flattened, grooved top. Angled perforation. Coarse, gritty, dark gray fabric turning orange-brown at surfaces, with 20–25% inclusions. Surface smoothed; now extremely worn. RBMa, with overfired schist and calcareous(?) inclusions. (Local).

183 Loom weight.
D. 0.09. From B03-31. Now lost.

Plaster

Uninventoried:
B03-33: wall-plaster fragments, some red, some decorated in zones of black and red, yellow, and white (Kea Excavation Notebook III, 42; Coleman 1970, 48–49).

B03-35: uninventoried fragments of plaster with traces of burning (Kea Excavation Notebook III, 46).

B608CL.
Upper part of destruction deposit. Period VIIb–c, and some later.

Pottery

Of 2 tins (ca. 34 liters), 1 bag (ca. 0.4 tin or 6.8 liters) kept. 40% fine, ca. 25% of which was plain. About 90% discarded in original papsing. Joins to B609CL in lots B03-19 and B03-20. Although many vessels are typical for Period VIIb, there is a larger percentage of plain wares than B609CL, and a few probable LH IIB or later vessels, including a stippled(?) cup (**194**) and an uninventoried goblet with net pattern, as well as two Attic Black Gloss sherds (discarded, Kea Pottery Notebook B, 61). These sherds are evidence that the upper part of the destruction fill was disturbed in Period VIIc and later. Uncatalogued local ceramics include a handle made of two joined coils, a plain torus base, and Painted and Yellow Slipped closed vessels (RBMa). Uncatalogued imports include sherds from Cretan Slipped, Non-Lustrous Painted, and Lustrous Painted vessels of unknown profile (FSTa, FSTc, FSTh, FSTi, FSTj, FSTk); a mainland/Kytheran(?) Lustrous Painted, closed vessel (FSTh); Melian/Theran plain and Painted closed vessels (DVa); a Cycladic Painted straight-sided or Vapheio cup (MxMa) and plain, Painted, and Yellow Slipped closed vessels in similar fabrics; coarser, plain, closed vessels (CSWa, CSWc), probably from the central Cyclades; one or more Standard Matt Painted, Aeginetan hydrias (DVd), an Aeginetan Red Coated krater (DVe), and several other fragments of fine Lustrous Painted, Red Coated, Slipped and plain Aeginetan(?) vessels, including a handleless cup and a straight-sided or bell cup (DVe). Fine, plain, Red Coated, and Lustrous Painted vessels, including many goblets, a shallow cup, a krater, and rounded and straight-sided alabastra probably came from the mainland (FVb–FVf). A Palace Style jar decorated with hatched loops was discarded (Kea Pottery Notebook B, 57). Several fragments of Gray Minyan and Matt Painted vessels were also discarded, as were a spreading saucer, a rim and pinched spout of a cooking pot, and pithos sherds with applied disks, applied bands, and rope decoration (Kea Pottery Notebook B, 61).

Local and Local Region

184 Spouted jug. (Fig. 32, Pl. 26)
Globular upper body, spout, slightly flattened handle, part of flat base, and lower body. H. est. 0.20. D. rim est. 0.05. Moderately coarse, orange-brown fabric with gray core and patches of gray at interior, and with 15–20% inclusions. Coil-built. Yellow Slipped. Exterior coated with yellow slip, continues within neck. RBMa, somewhat unusual, with blue and gray schist, rare mica, and rare calcareous(?) inclusions. PFG 2B (Local region).

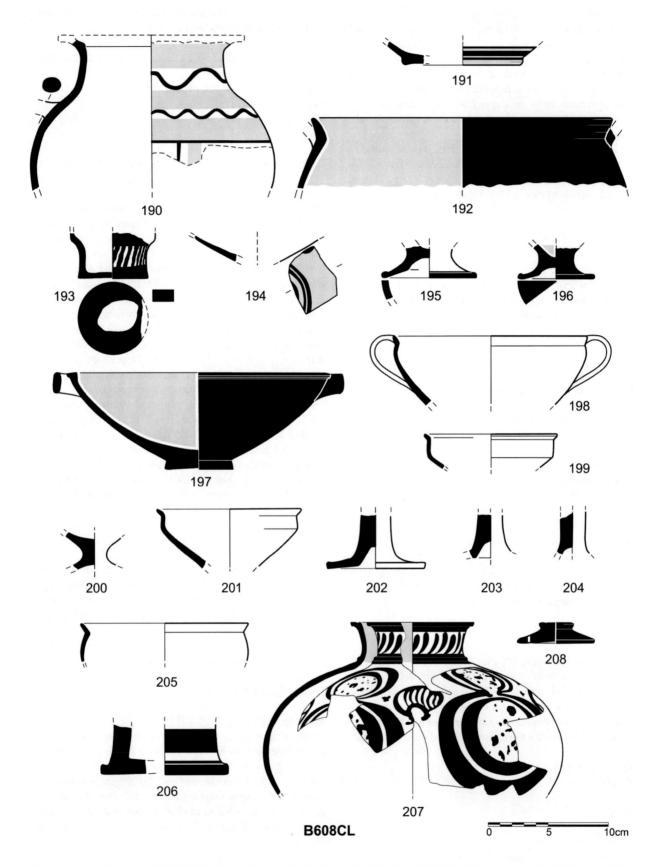

Fig. 33. Pottery from B608CL (**190–208**). Drawings by Aliki Bikaki (**190, 195–205, 208**), Mary-Jane Schumacher (**191–194, 206**), and Lily Bonga (**207**).

185 Miniature pyxis. (Fig. 32, Pl. 26)
Approximately 30% rim, lug handle, and part of carinated upper body. H. pres. 0.03, D. rim est. 0.03. Moderately coarse, reddish-brown fabric with 10–15% inclusions. Forming method indeterminable. Plain. RBMa, with common mica and shiny black particles. PFG 1A (Local).

186 K.330. Handleless cup. (Fig. 32)
Type 1. 80% preserved, broken at rim. H. 0.04. D. base 0.03. D. rim 0.08. From B03-28. Wheel-coiled(?). Part of rim burned. Half of exterior surface eroded. Plain. RBMa, with common mica.

187 K.426. Handleless cup. (Fig. 32)
Type 1. 80% preserved; broken at rim. H. 0.04. D. base 0.04. D. rim 0.07. From B03-28. Walls smoothed. Uneven base. Wheel-coiled. Plain. RBMa.

Cyclades

188 Closed vessel. (Fig. 32, Pl. 26)
Flat base and lower body. H. pres. 0.06. D. base est. 0.07. Moderately coarse, dusty, reddish-brown to pale brown fabric with 5–10% inclusions. Coil-built or wheel-coiled. Yellow Slipped. Exterior coated in yellow slip; possible traces of curvilinear decoration, now fugitive. MxMf.

189 Rounded cup. (Pl. 26)
Approximately 20% rim and body with strap handle attachment. D. rim est. 0.13. Moderately coarse orange fabric turning gray at margins, with 15–20% inclusions. Wheelmade(?). Yellow Slipped. Interior and exterior coated with faded yellow slip. Exterior: narrow band beneath rim, part of curvilinear(?) decoration in faded dark gray paint. MxMa.

190 Jar. (Fig. 33, Pl. 26)
Half of neck, shoulder; part of mid-body. Handle attachment or lug. Collar neck, wide shoulder, interior ledge for lid. H. pres. 0.12. D. rim est. 0.13. Moderately coarse, orange fabric turning gray at core, with 15–20% small inclusions. Exterior smoothed. Wheel-coiled, or wheelmade lower body, with neck and rim attached separately. Yellow Slipped (Polychrome, Red and Black). Interior of neck and exterior surface coated with badly preserved yellow slip. Horizontal, wide bands in reddish-brown, separated by wavy, dark-brown lines. Horizontal, thin, dark-brown band below lowest reddish-brown band. Two vertical, wide, reddish-brown bands and one parallel, thin, black line preserved at mid-body. MxMa. PFG 9Av (Cyclades [Tenos?]). For similar shape, but larger, see Hadjianastasiou 1989, no. 3, fig. 2:a.

Melos/Thera

191 Bowl(?). (Fig. 33, Pl. 26)
Slightly concave, raised base and flaring lower body. H. pres. 0.02. D. base est. 0.10. Moderately fine, rather hard-fired, somewhat dusty, greenish-yellow fabric, with 5–10% inclusions. Handmade. Painted. Interior: plain. Exterior: three bands above base in lustrous reddish-brown, painted over red stipple(?) or paler red slip. DVa, with large, rounded, gray-brown particles.

Aegina

192 Krater. (Fig. 33, Pl. 26)
Everted rim and arched handle attachment. H. pres. 0.06. D. rim est. 0.26. Fine, dusty, red fabric with 1–5% inclusions. Forming method indeterminable. Red Coated(?). Nonlustrous red paint around rim at interior and exterior. DVe.

Mainland

193 Vapheio cup. (Fig. 33, Pl. 26)
Kythera Type II. Midrib, lower body, and base. H. pres. 0.04. D. base 0.06. Fine, dusty, pink fabric with 1–5% inclusions. Wheelmade. Lustrous Painted. Ripple pattern (FM 78) in lustrous paint, fading from dark brown to red. Solid bands along rib and above base. Paint around the outside edge of the bottom of the base, with central uneven circle reserved (ca. 0.03–0.04). Exterior probably burnished. Dripped paint in interior. FVb/FVc.

194 Cup(?). (Fig. 33, Pl. 26)
FS 219(?). Lower body. Fine, hard-fired, pale yellow fabric turning pink at margins. Fewer than 1% inclusions. Wheelmade. Lustrous Painted. Interior: unpainted. Exterior: red stipple (FM 77). Three dark-brown bands above base, curvilinear decoration on lower body. LH IIB–IIIA:1. FVb/FVc.

195 Goblet. (Fig. 33, Pl. 26)
FS 254. Domed foot, stem, and bottom surface of bowl. H. pres. 0.03. H. stem 0.01. D. base 0.08. Fine, dusty, greenish-yellow fabric, with fewer than 1% inclusions. Wheelmade. Lustrous Painted. Lustrous black band above and below edge of foot. FVb, with a gray core. PFG 14C (Unknown). For somewhat similar in an LH IIA deposit at Tsoungiza, see Rutter 1993a, 66, no. 23, fig. 7, pl. 14.

196 Goblet. (Fig. 33, Pl. 26)
FS 263/FS 270. Chipped, domed foot, stem, and bottom surface of bowl. H. pres. 0.03. H. stem 0.01. D. 0.06. Fine, dusty, pale green fabric with fewer than 1% inclusions. Wheelmade. Lustrous Painted (Monochrome). All surfaces coated with flaking, lustrous dark-brown paint. FVb. For similar in an LH IIA deposit at Tsoungiza, see Rutter 1993a, 66, no. 23, fig. 7, pl. 14; see also Maran 1992, 11, no. 13, pl. 1 (LH IIA/IIB).

197 K.4346. Basin. (Fig. 33, Pl. 26)
Full profile preserved; much restored in plaster. Raised disk base; slightly flaring, flattened rim. Attachment for one horizontal strap handle preserved at rim. H. 0.07. D. base 0.06. D. rim est. 0.22. Fragments from B03-20 and several lots in B608CL. Fine, orange fabric with fewer than 1% inclusions. Wheelmade. Red Coated. Coated with orange-red slip; burnished. FVd/FVf. Compare with Cummer and Schofield 1984, 66, no. 340, pl. 52 (Period VIII).

198 Goblet. (Fig. 33, Pl. 26)
FS 263. Rim, strap handle, and shoulder. H. pres. 0.06. D. rim est. 0.16. From B03-25. Fine, very hard-fired, yellow fabric with fewer than 1% inclusions. Wheelmade. Burnished. Interior and exterior surfaces burnished. FVb. For similar profiles, see Frizell 1980, 32–33, 90, nos. 53, 54, pl. 4; Mountjoy 1999, 515–516, no. 79, fig. 183; Rutter 2020, 679–680, no. G92, fig. 9.60.

199 Angular kylix(?). (Fig. 33, Pl. 26)
FS 267(?). Approximately 25% rim and angular shoulder. D. rim est. 0.11. Fine, hard-fired, orange-pink fabric with fewer than 1% inclusions. Wheelmade. Burnished. FVd. For a similar shape in an LH IIB–IIIA1 deposit at Asine, see Frizell 1980, 33, 90, no. 56, pl. 4; see also Rutter 2020, 681–682, 704–705, no. G116, fig. 9.61.

200 Goblet. (Fig. 33, Pl. 27)
Lower part of bowl, stem, and upper part of foot. H. pres. 0.03. Fine, dusty, red fabric with fewer than 1% inclusions. Wheelmade. Burnished. FVd. Similar to Mountjoy 2008b, 329–330, no. 3285, fig. 6.17 (unburnished), from an LH IIB context with much LH IIA.

201 Angular kylix(?). (Fig. 33, Pl. 27)
FS 267(?). Approximately 20% rim and part of shoulder. H. pres. 0.05. D. rim est. 0.12. Fine, dusty, orange-pink fabric with fewer than 1% inclusions. Wheelmade. Slipped. Surface smoothed, coated with faded yellow slip. FVd, with black particles. For similar profile in a LH IIB–IIIA1 deposit, see Frizell 1980, 33, 90, no. 55, pl. 4; see also Rutter 2020, 681–682, 704–705, no. G120, fig. 9.61.

202 Goblet. (Fig. 33, Pl. 27)
FS 263/FS 270. Lower part of stem and part of foot. H. pres. 0.04. Fine, hard-fired, pale yellow fabric with fewer than 1% inclusions. Wheelmade. Slipped. Coated with yellow slip. FVb, with a pale-gray core. For similar shape, see Mountjoy 1981, 23–24, nos. 53 (FS 270), 85 (FS 263), figs. 8, 10 (LH IIB–IIIA:1).

203 Goblet. (Fig. 33, Pl. 27)
FS 263/FS 270. Lower part of stem and upper curve of foot. H. pres. 0.03. Fine, somewhat dusty, pale yellow fabric with fewer than 1% inclusions. Wheelmade. Plain. FVb. For similar shape, see Mountjoy 1981, 23–24, nos. 53 (FS 270), 85 (FS 263), figs. 8, 10 (LH IIB–IIIA:1).

204 Goblet. (Fig. 33, Pl. 27)
FS 263/FS 270. Lower part of stem. H. pres. 0.03. Fine, hard-fired, pink fabric with pale brown core, pinkish-yellow surface, and fewer than 1% inclusions. Wheelmade. Plain. FVb/FVc. For similar shape, see Mountjoy 1981, 23–24, nos. 53 (FS 270), 85 (FS 263), figs. 8, 10 (LH IIB–IIIA:1).

205 Goblet. (Fig. 33, Pl. 27)
FS 263/FS 270. Approximately 15% of rim. D. rim est. 0.14. Fine, dusty, orange-pink clay with fewer than 1% inclusions. Wheelmade. Plain. Surface worn. FVd. Similar to Mountjoy 1981, 24, no. 85, fig. 10 (LH IIB–IIIA:1).

Crete(?)

206 Ewer/jug. (Fig. 33, Pl. 27)
Torus base. H. pres. 0.04. D. base est. 0.11. Moderately coarse, pink fabric with pale brown core and 10–15% inclusions. Lustrous Painted. Exterior coated with yellow slip. Band at base and above base in lustrous dark-brown paint. FSTa, with unusual core and round, brown inclusions. For a similar shape from a Period VII destruction deposit, see Cummer and Schofield 1984, 101, no. 1141, pl. 73.

207 K.4399. Bridge-spouted jug. (Fig. 33, Pl. 27)
Approximately 1/3 preserved, including part of rim, neck, and upper and lower body. Base missing. Many nonjoining sherds. Horizontal rim. Straight neck, with ledge molding at attachment to body. H. pres. 0.15. D. rim est. 0.10. Fragments from lots B03-19, B03-20, and B03-25. Fine, slightly dusty, hard-fired, pale pink fabric with fewer than 1% inclusions. Wheelmade. Lustrous Painted. Surface smoothed and decorated with lustrous dark-brown paint, now cracked and flaking. Interior and upper exterior of neck are coated. Barred rim; foliate band along neck. Ledge molding possibly reserved between horizontal bands. Body decorated with figure-eight shields painted with double outline around uneven blobs. Between shields are unknown ornaments. FSTj. For similar decoration, see Cummer and Schofield 1984, 125, no. 1552, pl. 85; Bikaki suggested that the jug from House A and **207** were painted by the same artist (B608CL Pottery Notes, 2). Similar Marine Style shields on closed shapes are illustrated by Mountjoy (1984, 197, 201, nos. Zakro 14, Kastri 8, figs. 7, 19).

Unknown

208 K.2159. Lid. (Fig. 33, Pl. 27)
Slightly more than half preserved. Small perforation through edge of lid; flat knob handle. H. pres. 0.02. D. est. 0.06. D. perf. <0.01. Fine, soft, gray fabric with fewer than 1% inclusions. Gray/Black Burnished. Traces of black paint across upper surface. MFVb.

Terracotta

209 K1.51. Spindle whorl. (Pl. 27)
Type S1. H. 0.01. D. 0.03. Wt. 12 g. From B03-25. Moderately coarse, reddish-brown fabric with 10–15% inclusions. Surface smoothed, chipped on one side. Perforation at slight angle. Breakage around one end of perforation. RBMa. (Local).

210 K1.661. Spool. (Pl. 27)
D. 0.02. L. pres. 0.03. Wt. 10 g. Moderately coarse, orange-brown to gray fabric with 10–15% inclusions. Surface smoothed. Both ends broken. RBMa, with common mica. (Local).

ROOM B.2 (+ B.3 AND B.4)

In its latest Period VII form, Room B.2 was bounded by Walls H, K, J, and P (Fig. 24); in this phase, it is called Room B.2/B.3 in order to clarify the architectural change that took place during Period VII, when the earlier, smaller Rooms B.2 and B.3 were united into one larger architectural space.

In the earlier phase, Room B.2 was bounded by Walls H, K, J, and AA, while the more southerly space bounded by Walls H, AA, J, and P/T formed a separate room, B.3 (Fig. 23). Nevertheless, just as Room B.2/B.3 had been excavated as a single space, Rooms B.2 and B.3 continued to be excavated as one architectural unit even at lower levels, where the deposits were from two separate architectural spaces (Figs. 7, 13, Table 2.3; see also Appendix VIII). The combined lot from the floor deposits associated with that earlier Period VII phase of the building (B607CL, House B: Phase 3) includes ceramics from both spaces.

The space southwest of Wall P was excavated as part of Room B.2 in its upper levels (Figs. 7, 13), since Wall P did not extend more than 0.70 m. from Wall H (Kea Excavation Notebook III, 52). In lower levels, where it became clear that Wall P was actually a wall, the space to the southwest was excavated as a separate room, Room B.4, also called the "kitchen."

All upper excavation units from Rooms B.3 and B.4 that were excavated as part of Room B.2 will be described in detail in this section. Excavation units specific to Room B.3 will be discussed in the next section; those specific to Room B.4 will be in the section after that.

After the Period VII destruction, the space above Room B.2 was reused and divided by Wall Q. Wall Q was founded on the Period VII destruction debris; the preserved heights of several other walls (Walls H, K, P, and O) suggest that they would have been visible when Wall Q was built and in use (Figs. 7, 12, 13, 25).

Earlier remains were found below the LBA Rooms B.2 and B.3, including three EBA walls, and mixed MBA strata. A summary of deposits is presented in Table 2.4.

EARLY BRONZE AGE

Walls AB, AD, and AF

Below LBA Room B.2, Bikaki found EBA Walls AB and AF (Figs. 7, 13, 14:b, 19; Pls. 16–18; Kea Excavation Notebook III, 112; Kea Excavation Notebook LVIII, 31). A short spur extended southward from the southeastern end of Wall AF. Below LBA Room B.3, a third wall, Wall AD, was recognized (Kea Excavation Notebook III, 148). Wall AD continued to the southwest, below LBA Room B.4 (Figs. 11:c, 14:c, 19; Pl. 4:b). Jogs in the profiles of Walls AF and AB suggest that each had been rebuilt at least once (Figs. 14:b, 19; Pl. 18:b, c).

These walls were associated with a deep destruction deposit from Period III (Figs. 7, 13; Pls. 16–18; Kea Excavation Notebook III, 112; Kea Excavation Notebook LVIII, 31). The lowest elevation of Walls AB and AF was found at the bottom of a deep test pit within Room B.2 (B03-824), at –1.42 m. and –1.09 m below sea level respectively (Kea Excavation Notebook LVIII, 46). An *in situ* pithos was standing upright with its base at ca. –1.00 m below sea level (**232**), probably the approximate level of the floor. Small schist plaques uncovered at a similar elevation could have belonged to floor paving (Kea Excavation Notebook III, 48). Flat schist plaques were also used as paving stones in Period III House D (Wilson and Eliot 1984, 85).

Conditions in these deep excavation units were not ideal. A pump was used to remove water, but the soil was extremely muddy and had to be shoveled indiscriminately out of the trench as Bikaki searched for the bottom courses of the walls (Pls. 17, 18:a, b; Kea Excavation Notebook LVIII, 43, 45–46). Pottery found in the mud that had been shoveled out of the trench during the excavation of units B03-816–B03-824 is included in lot B03-830.

The destruction deposit associated with these walls was made up of soil, small stones, and ceramics; fragments of vessels joined from the top to the bottom of the deposit, which was excavated in units B03-114 and B03-813–B03-824. B03-114 was the only excavation unit to include the area of Room B.3 with Room B.2; units B03-813–B03-824 were excavated in a deep test pit in Room B.2 during 1976. The destruction deposit, which seemed to contain two distinct strata, was produced by the collapse of the EBA building(s) associated with walls AB, AD, and AF, probably at the end of Period III. The lower stratum observed in the test trench (B03-820, B03-823, B03-824) contained fewer stones than the upper stratum, below the level of a long, flat stone slab (0.80 × 0.40 m), which was found resting horizontally at ca. –0.42 m below sea level (B03-821) (Kea Excavation Notebook LVIII, 41–43); Bikaki suggested that this slab might have been a floor slab from an upper story of the EBA building (Kea Excavation Notebook LVIII, 42). Above this slab, the deposit contained larger (0.10–0.30 m) stones, probably fallen from the superstructure of the building (B03-114, B03-812–B03-819, B03-821).

Despite Bikaki's observation of two distinct strata, joins between fragments of pottery found in the highest and lowest parts of the test trench suggest that all of the recovered artifacts must be considered as part of one destruction deposit. A few, small fragments of Period IV pottery in lots from the upper part of the deposit (B03-812, B03-813, B03-816, B03-817) suggest that there was some disturbance to the upper part of the deposit during the earlier part of the MBA. The uppermost unit of the test pit, B03-810, contained ceramics dating to Period III, Period IV, and perhaps Period VI; this part of the deposit was probably also disturbed by construction associated with House B. Ceramics from another upper excavation unit, B03-114, were included in B602CL (above),

TABLE 2.3. ROOMS B.2, B.2/B.3, B.3, AND B.4 COMBINED LOTS (CL)

CL	Excavation units, B03-	Location	↑ elevation	↓ elevation
B602CL	73, 74, 83, 114, 118, 146, 147	B.1, B.2, B.4	+0.40	-0.20
B603CL	105, 106, 109	B.2	+0.50	+0.20
B604CL	19, 20, 36, 43, 44	B.2/B.3 and B.4	+3.20	+1.60
B605CL	40, 42	B.2	+2.40	+1.80
B606CL	46, 51, 52, 57, 61, 64	B.2/B.3 and B.4.	+1.80	+1.00
B607CL	103, 104, 107	B.2 and B.3	+0.70	+0.50

which contained mixed Period III–VII ceramics. Uncombined ceramic lots from the lower part of the destruction deposit date exclusively to Period III.

MIDDLE BRONZE AGE

Immediately above the EBA destruction debris was a stratum of soil and small stones that contained primarily EBA sherds with a few Period IV and probably Period V or VI ceramics. This stratum was excavated in units B03-106, B03-114, B03-810, and B03-811. No surface of compact red clay, like that found below Rooms B.1 (Surface c) and B.4 (Surface i), was discovered below Rooms B.2 or B.3. It is possible that such a surface in these rooms was removed in the course of extensive construction in this space during the LBA.

Ceramics from unit B03-810 and B03-811 are uncombined, but pottery from lot B03-106 was included in B603CL with lots B03-105 and B03-109 from the next highest stratum. B603CL is part of J. C. Overbeck's Group CP (1989a, 174). Ceramics from unit B03-114 were combined with pottery from the upper part of the EBA destruction deposit and Surfaces c and i in B602CL.

Above the stratum of small stones was a shallow stratum of sandy soil that contained Period III, IV, and V ceramics and fewer stones than the previous deposit (B03-105). This stratum continued beneath Room B.3 (B03-109). Ceramics from these excavation units were combined with pottery from the next lowest stratum (B03-106) in B603CL. The range of periods represented in the ceramics from this and the next lowest stratum are probably the result of combining lots as well as, possibly, some disturbance by LBA construction.

The Wall H foundation continues from Room B.1 into Rooms B.2–B.4 (Figs. 20–22; Kea Excavation Notebook III, 78). As noted above, the Wall H foundation may be the outer face of Period IVa Wall X. In Room B.2, the Wall H foundation was built directly on top of EBA Wall AB at a lower elevation of +0.50 m above sea level (Kea Excavation Notebook LVIII, 32).

LATE BRONZE AGE

A series of use surfaces and walls belong to Phases 3 and 4 of House B. After the initial construction of Room B.2, probably early in Period VII, the space was extensively modified. This part of the house was built in two main phases, which postdate the first two phases of use of Room B.1.

HOUSE B: THIRD PHASE

Surface f and Walls H, K, J, and AA

In its earliest form, Room B.2 was bounded by Walls H, K, J, and AA (Fig. 23). Period VII floor levels all abut the Wall H foundation, which must have been visible above ancient ground level when Room B.2 was in use. Wall H was built on the Wall H foundation above ancient ground level; strata associated with its construction in Room B.2 do not exist. Walls H, I, and J were bonded together in Room B.1 and must have been contemporary. Wall J bonded with Wall K (Kea Excavation Notebook III, 145), so Wall K must have been part of the original design of Room B.2. Wall AA does not bond with the other walls but was probably

TABLE 2.4. ROOMS B.2, B.3, AND B.2/B.3 DEPOSIT SUMMARY

Deposit:	Period III Destruction Deposit
Contemporary Features:	Walls AB, AD, AF
Date of Deposit Above:	Period III + IV
Date of Deposit:	Period III
Date of Deposit Below:	Not excavated
Lots/Combined Lots:	B03-818–B03-824, B03-830, B602CL (partial)
Catalogue Numbers:	**9–28** (above), **211–258**
Deposit:	Disturbed Period III Destruction Deposit
Contemporary Features:	None
Date of Deposit Above:	Mixed Period III–VI
Date of Deposit:	Period III with some Period IV disturbance
Date of Deposit Below:	Period III
Lots/Combined Lots:	B03-812–B03-817
Catalogue Numbers:	**259–274**
Deposit:	MBA Mixed Deposits
Contemporary Features:	None
Date of Deposit Above:	Period VIIa
Date of Deposit:	MBA, plus LBA disturbance(?)
Date of Deposit Below:	Period III with some Period IV disturbance
Lots/Combined Lots:	B03-810–B03-811, B602CL (partial), B603CL (J. C. Overbeck's Group CP [1989a, 174])
Catalogue Numbers:	**275–318**
Deposit:	House B: Third Phase
Contemporary Features:	Surfaces e, f, g, h, Walls H, K, J, AA, T
Date of Deposit Above:	Period VIIb
Date of Deposit:	Period VIIa
Date of Deposit Below:	MBA, plus LBA disturbance(?)
Lots/Combined Lots:	B03-108, B03-809, B607CL
Catalogue Numbers:	**319–343**
Deposit:	House B: Fourth Phase
Contemporary Features:	Surface d, Wall AA reuse and buttress, Walls H, K, J, P, R
Date of Deposit Above:	Period VIIb
Date of Deposit:	Period VIIb
Date of Deposit Below:	Period VIIa
Lots/Combined Lots:	B606CL (partial)
Catalogue Numbers:	**385–388**

TABLE 2.4. (CONT.)

Deposit:	Period VIIb Destruction Deposit (lower)
Contemporary Features:	Wall AA reuse and buttress, Walls H, K, J, P, R
Date of Deposit Above:	Period VIIb, some Period VIIc–VIII and Archaic contamination
Date of Deposit:	Period VIIb
Date of Deposit Below:	Period VIIb
Lots/Combined Lots:	B606CL (partial) (includes also Room B.4)
Catalogue Numbers:	**344–384, 389–439**

Deposit:	Period VIIb Destruction Deposit (upper)
Contemporary Features:	Wall AA reuse and buttress, Walls H, K, J, P, R
Date of Deposit Above:	Archaic or later
Date of Deposit:	Period VIIb, some Period VIIc–VIII and Archaic contamination
Date of Deposit Below:	Period VIIb
Lots/Combined Lots:	B605CL, B604CL (includes also Room B.4)
Catalogue Numbers:	**440–559**

Deposit:	Wall Q
Contemporary Features:	Walls H, K, P, O
Date of Deposit Above:	None
Date of Deposit:	Archaic or later
Date of Deposit Below:	Period VIIb, some Period VIIc–VIII and Archaic contamination
Lots/Combined Lots:	B03-55
Catalogue Numbers:	None (discarded)

contemporary with them. The threshold of Wall AA is at +0.55 m, the same elevation of the earliest surface in Room B.2, Surface f (Kea Excavation Notebook III, 111). Part of Wall AA was removed in unit B03-113; all finds were discarded.

The excavation notebook is contradictory about the surfaces in Rooms B.2 and B.3. A "floor" is defined at +0.70, +0.60, and +0.50 m above sea level (B03-64, B03-103, B03-104, B03-105, and B03-107) in each room. However, in one section of the notebook, the space between +0.60–+0.70 is described as "Floor a" (Kea Excavation Notebook III, 111), while the space between +0.50–+0.60 is called "Floor b," in both rooms (Kea Excavation Notebook III, 111, 113). Drawn sections are similarly contradictory (Fig. 7; Pl. 19:a). Because three extremely compact surfaces are described separately at each of the 0.10 m intervals, I have labeled three surfaces in each room, Surfaces d, e, and f (top to bottom) in Room B.2, and Surfaces d, g, and h (top to bottom) in Room B.3. Whether two or three surfaces are defined, the space clearly was used continuously over the course of the LBA; these compact levels probably were created by the accumulation of debris owing to continuous use of the space.

Unlike Room B.1, Room B.2 does not have a Period VI phase. The earliest preserved surface, Surface f, dates to Period VII; it is associated with Period VII Walls H and J. If a Period VI stratum ever existed, it must have been completely removed, since almost no clear Period VI ceramics were found below, in, or on top of Surface f.

Surface f was made up of compact soil and carbon (B03-104); it is probably contemporary with Surface h in Room B.3 and the first use of the southwestern part of House B. Immediately above Surface f was a stratum composed of brown soil and small stones (Kea Excavation Notebook III, 111). Three handleless cups (**324–326**) and a loom weight (**339**) were found on Surface f. Ceramics from Surface f and the stratum of brown soil were combined into B607CL with pottery from Surfaces d and e in Room B.2 and Surfaces g and h in Room B.3.

Surface E

Surface e was identified at an elevation of ca. +0.60 m; it was excavated in units B03-103 and B03-104. The surface was composed of extremely compact soil and carbon. No architectural changes can be linked with Surface e. Walls H, K, J, and AA continued in use. Ceramics from Surface e were combined into B607CL with pottery from Surface d and f in Room B.2, and from Surfaces g and h in Room B.3; the combined lot dates to Period VIIa.

HOUSE B: FOURTH PHASE

Room B.2/B.3: Combination of Rooms B.2 and B.3 between use of Surface E and Surface D

The accumulated debris between Surface e and Surface d in Room B.2 was made up of compact soil and some carbon (B03-103; Kea Excavation Notebook III, 111). At some point during the accumulation of soil above Surface e, Wall AA went out of use. The majority of Wall AA was covered by Surface d (Figs. 7, 12, 13, 24; Kea Excavation Notebook III, 111). No destruction debris can be associated with the destruction or demolition of Wall AA. The northern part of Wall AA was reused and incorporated into the repair of Wall P and construction of Wall R (below). With the demolition or collapse of Wall AA, the spaces of Rooms B.2 and B.3 were combined; thereafter, the space is better named Room B.2/B.3. Wall P was the southwestern boundary of the room after Wall AA went out of use.

Not long before Wall AA was demolished, several walls were added in the southwestern part of Room B.3 (Figs. 13, 24; Pls. 5:a, b, 6:b, c, 19:a; Kea Excavation Notebook III, 142–145). These walls probably were built when Rooms B.2 and B.3 were combined into one space. Wall P, the southwestern wall of Room B.3, must have suffered some damage. Since Wall P was built on top of Wall T, above ancient ground level, it cannot be related to surfaces within Room B.3 or B.4; neither its original construction date (sometime between the use of Surface h and Surface g) nor the date of the damage can be precisely determined. A buttress (Wall R) was added to Wall P. This buttress must have been planned before Surface d covered the majority of Wall AA since the section of Wall AA abutting Wall H was incorporated into the buttress, while the rest of AA was either demolished or not reconstructed after a destruction. This part of Wall AA, the Wall AA "reuse," continued to stand and was itself buttressed by a small stone construction to its north, which also abutted Wall H.

Surface D

After the modification of Walls P and AA and the construction of Wall R, a new surface came into use. Surface d was found across Room B.2/B.3 at an elevation of +0.68 m above sea level in the SE, +0.70 m above sea level in the SW, +0.73 m above sea level in the NE, +0.73 m above sea level in the NW, and +0.78 m above sea level in the middle (Kea Excavation Notebook III, 78). The surface consisted of compact earth and clay with areas of carbonization; it was excavated in units B03-64 and B03-103. Surface d was in use at the time of the Period VIIb destruction. Ceramics from the surface were combined into B607CL (B03-103) with ceramics from earlier surfaces and into B606CL (B03-64) with pottery from the destruction deposit. Ceramics from one excavation unit, B03-809, which removed a 0.02 m. strip of soil along Wall K from Surface d down to Surface f, were not combined and date to Period VII (a and/or b). Bikaki found four handleless cups resting on Surface d (**385–388**).

Period VIIb Destruction Deposit

Immediately above Surface d was a destruction deposit formed by the collapse of the LBA House B during Period VIIb. It was composed of soft brown soil, jumbled large stones, wall-plaster fragments, many pottery fragments, and some carbon. The lower part of the deposit was excavated in units B03-46, B03-51, B03-52, B03-57, B03-61, and B03-64. Although disturbed by later building activity (Wall Q, below), the upper part of the destruction deposit was much like that below, composed of soft brown soil and small fallen stones; it was excavated in units B03-36, B03-37, B03-40, B03-42, B03-43, and B03-44. Surface levels, excavated in units B03-11, B03-18, B03-19, and B03-20, contained mixed debris like that found across the site.

Units B03-36, B03-37, B03-43, B03-44, B03-46, B03-51, B03-57, and B03-61 of the destruction debris comprised the area of B.2/B.3 and B.4. Ceramics from the lower part of the destruction deposit (B03-46, B03-51, B03-52, B03-57, B03-61, and B03-64) were included in B606CL with pottery from destruction debris in Room B.4. Pottery from the upper part of the destruction deposit to the southwest of Wall Q (B03-36, B03-43, B03-44) was included in B604CL, as were most ceramics from the surface strata (B03-19, B03-20).

Pottery from the upper part of the destruction deposit to the northeast of Wall Q (B03-40, B03-42) was combined into B605CL. The upper part of the destruction deposit in Room B.2/B.3 and B.4, B604CL, contained many plain goblets and some LH III imports, unlike the lower part of the destruction deposit (B606CL). Both B604CL and B605CL contained at least one Archaic sherd. It is probable that the upper part of the destruction deposit was disturbed by the construction of Wall Q in the Archaic period (below) and probably also erosion. Bikaki suggested that plowing between Walls P and O, from +3.17–2.40 m above sea level, also may have disturbed the destruction debris (Notecards, 60).

As in Room B.1, although Bikaki noted some stratigraphical differences between the lower and upper parts of the destruction deposit, sherds from the same vessels were found widely scattered in both horizontal and vertical space. For example, sherds from the same bell cup (**534**) were found in B604CL and in lot B03-61, from the lower part of the destruction deposit (B606CL) (Notecards, 64). Several sherds found just above the floor in Room B.2/B.3 could be from a ewer found in the lower part of the Period VIIb destruction deposit in the Temple (**406**), although they do not join (B03-64; B606CL Pottery Notes, 15); these fragments could also derive from look-alikes rather than a single vessel. Nevertheless, the room probably collapsed relatively rapidly.

Wall plaster from Room B.2/B.3 was relatively abundant in comparison to Rooms B.1 and B.4 (Fig. 13). Most fragments were plain red, and Coleman (1970, 154) hypothesized that at least one of the walls was fully painted that color. A banded design, also found in Room B.1, consisted of parallel horizontal bands of white, dark yellow, dark red, and black (**431–435**; Coleman 1970, 48–49, nos. F.45, F.46, F.51–53). Fragments of this motif came from units B03-40, B03-42, B03-46, B03-52, B03-57, and B03-61. Although Coleman's (1970, 211–212) dissertation does not include them, she suggested in notes (Coleman, 1970 Notes) that border fragments were found in unit B03-36. Fragments of a peach-colored molding (from B03-40, B03-42, B03-57, B03-61, and B03-64) may have surrounded a door or window-frame (Coleman 1970, 140). Two fragments (**437**, **438**) preserve curving red areas next to white ones (Coleman 1970, nos. F.48, F.49); pieces of these fragments came from B03-46, B03-52, and B03-57. Three figural fragments were recovered, as well. A miniature male (red-painted) figure on an unpainted white background was identified; the fragment depicts the knee of the figure and the tip of a stone rhyton crossing it (**436** from B03-46; Coleman 1970, 49–50, no. F.47). A second fragment depicts part of a man's body with clothing in black and added white (from B03-043; Coleman 1970, 50, no. F.97). A third fragment represents part of the face and eye of a male figure (**439** from B3-52; Coleman 1970, 50, no. F.50; Abramowitz 1980, no. 130). Painted floor-plaster fragments were found; the floor was painted either in zones or in a grid pattern (Morgan, n.d., 93). Floor plaster, regularly painted red, was also found in Period VII deposits in House A (Cummer and Schofield 1984, 88, 93, 109, 131, 134; see also Coleman 1970, 142–143).

More fragments of wall plaster (three boxes) were found in the lowest excavation unit of the destruction deposit (B03-64), just above the latest floor, than were found at higher elevations (Fig. 13). This disparity suggests that at least some of the painted wall-plaster fragments found in the room derive from this space. Nevertheless, objects seem to have been significantly displaced in the course of the destruction. It is possible that some of the painted wall-plaster fragments, along with other objects, fell from an upper floor of House B. House A also sits on top of a steep slope above House B, and it is possible that some of the objects found within House B were actually originally located in House A. A use context from House A for at least some of the wall painting seems as plausible as one from House B, since fragments of painted wall plaster in House A were found almost exclusively in the eastern rooms—the ones nearest House B (Cummer and Schofield 1984, 38).

ARCHAIC REMAINS

In the upper part of the LBA destruction debris, Wall Q was constructed (Figs. 7, 12, 13, 25; Kea Excavation Notebook III, 52, 70). Wall Q was removed in excavation unit B03-55. An early seventh-century B.C. sherd from within the wall (now discarded) provides a *terminus post quem* for its construction (Kea Excavation Notebook III, 195). Some LBA walls—Walls H, K, P, and O—are preserved to a height that suggests they would have been visible when Wall Q was in use. The alignment of Wall Q is similar to that of the LBA walls, which suggests that these earlier walls could have been reused in the Archaic period, but no other evidence for reuse was found. No Archaic use surface was identified. Only one area of the excavation units with destruction debris was described differently than the rest: the soil removed in unit B03-43, to the southwest of Wall Q, was more compact than elsewhere (Kea Excavation Notebook III, 61). It is impossible to determine whether this compact lens is related to the construction or use of Wall Q.

ROOM B.3

Room B.3 was an architectural unit solely during the third architectural phase of House B. It was dug as a separate architectural unit in only two excavation units (B03-107, B03-108). Only remains associated with the LBA Room B.3 will be discussed below. The EBA and MBA strata beneath Room B.3, as well as the strata from the final phase above Room B.3 (as part of Room B.2/B.3), have been described above. A summary of deposits is presented in Table 2.4.

LATE BRONZE AGE

HOUSE B: THIRD PHASE

Walls H, AA, J, and T

In its first phase as an independent space, Room B.3 was delineated by Walls H, AA, J, and T (Fig. 23), which were contemporary with Surface h in Room B.3 and Surface f in Room B.2. Walls H and J bonded with Wall I in Room B.1; Wall T bonded with Wall J. These walls date to the third phase of construction in House B.

Surface h

Surface h was found at an elevation of ca. +0.50 m above sea level; it was excavated in units B03-107 and B03-108. The surface was compact. It contained two fragments of wall plaster and much carbonized material (Kea Excavation Notebook III, 113), and two handleless cups rested on it (**327, 328**). Ceramics from unit B03-108 were uncombined and provide a *terminus post quem* of Period VIIa for the use of Surface h. However, several sherds belong to a cup (**340**) that may be part of the same cup found in B604CL (**536**), a combined lot consisting of ceramics from the upper part of the Period VIIb destruction deposit (Kea Pottery Notebook B, 55). The presence of fragments of the same vessel in both strata suggests that Surface h had been disturbed. Whatever the nature of the disturbance, it was not of great extent, since no anomalies in the stratum were noticed during excavation. Nonetheless, all strata between Surface h and the upper part of the destruction deposit in this area must also have been affected.

Immediately above Surface h, the next higher stratum was composed of compact accumulated debris and carbon (B03-107). It probably resulted from continuous occupation in Room B.3. Pottery from B03-107 was combined in B607CL with ceramics from B03-103 and B03-104; these ceramics date to Period VIIa.

Surface g

In Room B.3 a second surface, Surface g, was found at an elevation of ca. +0.60 m above sea level; it was excavated in units B03-103 and B03-107. The surface was made up of extremely compact soil that contained traces of carbonized material, including some fragments of burnt wood (Kea Excavation Notebook III, 111). This surface was probably contemporary with Surface e in Room B.2 and the reuse of Wall AA. Walls H and J were also still in use. However, since Surface h, below Surface g, seems to have been affected by a disturbance after the final destruction of the house, Surface g also must have been disturbed at that time.

It is unclear when Wall P replaced Wall T because it was built above Wall T and is not directly associated with either Surface g or Surface d.

The stratum above Surface g was excavated as part of Room B.2 and was probably created by the gradual accumulation of use debris. It consisted of compact soil, carbonized material, and some sherds (B03-103). During this period of accumulation, Room B.3 and Room B.2 were merged, after the majority of Wall AA was destroyed and Wall R was constructed to buttress Wall P. Higher strata within this space have been discussed above.

ROOMS B.2, B.3, AND B.2/B.3 CATALOGUE

EBA DESTRUCTION DEPOSIT

B03-830.
Pottery found in mud shoveled out of Room B.2 test trench, from excavation units below sea level. Period III.

Pottery

No discard information available. Joins with B03-810, B03-812, B03-814, B03-816, B03-817, B03-818, B03-820, B03-821, B03-822, B03-823, and B03-824. Uncatalogued ceramics include EBA Red-Brown Semifine to Semicoarse (RBMa–RBMd) vessels, including saucers, bowls, a shallow bowl, possible pyxides, an askos or jug, jugs, jars, deep bowl/open jars, basins, and a pithos. A Red-Brown Coarse closed vessel (RBMb) was present. Several sherds from Red-Brown Burnished vessels, as well as Black Burnished closed vessels (RBMa, RBMb) are probably local. Uncatalogued imports include Orange-Buff Semifine to Coarse closed (DVd) and open vessels (DVa, DVc, MxMe); a fine, open Urfirnis vessel (FVh) and a Black Burnished sauceboat (MxMc); a Pinkish Buff(?) shallow bowl (FVg); and a Talc ware jug (PBS).

Local(?)

211 Reworked sherd. (Pl. 27)
Rounded sherd, probably from an open vessel. D. max. pres. 0.04. Moderately coarse, rather gritty, reddish-orange fabric with 10–15% inclusions. Smoothed. Edges rough. Hole partially drilled into center of disk. RBMd.

Euboea

212 Shallow bowl. (Pl. 27)
Rim and upper body. D. rim est. 0.29. Fine, dusty, moderately hard-fired, pale pink fabric with thick, dark-gray core and fewer than 1% inclusions. Handmade. EBA Pinkish Buff. Surface worn; some traces of burnishing. FVg. PFG 14Bv (Unknown). For similar, see Wilson 1999, 142, no. III-543, pls. 37, 92.

Stone

213 K76.12. Elliptical object (weight?). (Pl. 27)
H. 0.05. W. 0.09. L. 0.10. Wt. 785 g. Marble (Whitbread). Flattened ellipse. Somewhat chipped; encrusted. Surface smoothed.

214 K76.14. Palette. (Pl. 27)
W. 0.18. L. 0.20. Th. 0.02–0.03. Dark greenish-blue stone (schist). Broken in half. Slightly raised rim; center hollowed through use. Surface smooth, but not polished. Bottom slightly convex.

215 K76.13. Perforated stone. (Pl. 27)
W. 0.12. L. 0.15. Th. 0.02. Wt. 611 g. Irregular schist slab. Surface chipped; some brown discoloration. Two perforations preserved; possibly part of another perforation at break. One perforation is small (D. 0.01); the other is larger (D. 0.02).

216 K76.11. Pestle. (Pl. 27)
H. 0.03. D. 0.02. Wt. 28 g. Steatite (Whitbread). Chipped. Convex profile; surfaces very smooth, with rounded and worn edges. Chips also worn, which suggests continued use after ancient breakage.

Metal

K76.34. Lead clamp.
L. 0.07. Wt. 31 g. Ridged bar and parts of two roughly round-section crossbars (Georgakopoulou).

Uninventoried: five small copper-based fragments (B-76.30). Completely corroded (Georgakopoulou).

B03-824.
Lowest part of the test pit in Room B.2. Period III.

Pottery

No discard information available. Joins with B03-821. Uncatalogued local (RBMa, RBMb, RBMd) ceramics include a Red-Brown Semifine to Semicoarse jug(?), deep bowl/open jar, and a plate or pan. Several closed vessels and a sauceboat in Red-Brown Burnished ware (RBMa, RBMd) were also present.

Local

217 K.4574. Shallow bowl. (Fig. 34, Pl. 27)
Published, Wilson 1999, 122, no. III-279, pl. 84. Profile preserved. H. rest. 0.07. D. rim est. 0.29. D. base 0.09. Fragments from B03-824 and B03-830. Moderately fine, dark reddish-brown fabric with 10–15% inclusions. EBA Red-Brown Burnished. Exterior burnished. RBMb, with rare calcareous(?) inclusions.

218 One-handled cup. (Pl. 27)
Everted rim and rounded upper body. D. rim est. 0.08. Moderately fine, somewhat gritty, reddish-orange fabric with 5–10% inclusions. EBA Red-Brown Semifine to Semicoarse. RBMb, with rare, dark blue particles.

Stone

219 K76.24. Polisher/rubber. (Pl. 27)
W. 0.09. L. pres. 0.08. Th. 0.04. Wt. 353 g. Probably diorite (Whitbread). Broken, probably near middle of object. Flattened, elliptical shape. Flat upper and lower surface are relatively smooth; rounded edges are rough.

220 K76.23. Stone object. (Pl. 27)
L. 0.06. Th. 0.03. Wt. 142 g. Quartzite, somewhat pitted (Whitbread). Trapezoidal section. Smooth surfaces; rounded edges. Possibly natural.

221 K76.30. Stone tool (whetstone?). (Pl. 27)
W. 0.05–0.07. L. pres. 0.09. Th. 0.01–0.02. Wt. 178 g. Fine sandstone or coarse siltstone with flecks of fine white mica (Whitbread). Trapezoidal section. Broken on two long sides. Narrowest edge beveled to sharp edge. Both broad sides smooth.

B03-823.
EBA destruction deposit from test pit below Room B.2. Period III.

Pottery

No discard information available. Joins with B03-812, B03-814, B03-816, B03-818, B03-820, B03-821, B03-822, and B03-830. Uncatalogued ceramics are most common in Red-Brown Semifine to Semicoarse ware (RBMa–RBMd), including saucers, shallow bowls, deep bowls/open jars, jars, basins, pedestal bases, and an askos/jug similar to one published by Wilson (1999, no. II-177). Shallow bowls and closed vessels in Red-Brown Burnished ware (RBMa–RBMd) were also present, as was one Red-Brown Yellow Slipped closed vessel (RBMc) and a body sherd in fabric group MxMc.

Local

222 K.4576. Shallow bowl. (Fig. 34, Pl. 28)
Published, Wilson 1999, 122, no. III-277, pl. 84. Profile preserved. H. 0.06, D. rim est. 0.25. Fragments from B03-823 and B03-830. Moderately coarse, reddish-brown fabric with 15–20% inclusions. EBA Red-Brown Burnished. RBMb, with rare calcareous(?) inclusions.

223 K.4415. Shallow bowl. (Fig. 34, Pl. 28)
Published, Wilson 1999, 104, no. III-60, pl. 74. Nearly intact, chipped. H. 0.04, D. rim ca. 0.09. Moderately coarse, dark gray fabric with 10-15% inclusions. RBMa, dark. EBA Red-Brown Semifine to Semicoarse.

Bone

224 K76.33. Awl. (Pl. 28)
W. 0.02. L. pres. 0.08. Th. <0.01. Wt. 4 g. Type VI (Krzyszkowska). Lower part preserved; tip chipped. Smoothed. From bovid rib, split longitudinally. Distinctive type of the EBA, common in

both the northeast Aegean and on the mainland (Wilson 1999, 157).

Stone

225 K76.20. Palette(?). (Pl. 28)
W. pres. 0.16. L. pres. 0.22. Th. pres. 0.03. Wt. 2364 g. Fine, bluish-gray limestone. Roughly rectangular. Smoothed upper face and two sides; broken on two sides. Upper surface: an incised line runs along shortest side, 0.01 from edge, perhaps remnant of a raised border(?).

226 K76.26. Polisher/rubber or whetstone. (Pl. 28)
W. 0.07–0.08. L. pres. 0.15. Th. 0.03. Wt. 430 g. Greenish schist. Broken at one narrow end; split at the other. Flat surfaces somewhat smoothed; edges smooth and rounded.

227 K76.32. Polisher/rubber(?). (Pl. 28)
W. 0.07. L. 0.12. Th. 0.04. Wt. 585 g. Heavy gray stone with white veins, possibly quartzite (Whitbread). Intact, with some small chips. Trapezoidal in section, narrowing at one end. Smooth surfaces, rounded edges (from use?).

228 K76.19. Pounder/grinder. (Pl. 28)
W. 0.11–0.12. L. 0.18. Wt. 3340 g. Heavy, light gray, pocked stone with small to quite large inclusions (0.02), including purplish, black, and dark gray particles. Also includes euhedral gold mica, although gold color might come from oxidation (Whitbread). Lopsided oval; smoothed. Some large chips broken away. One of narrower ends rough and chipped, perhaps from use.

229 K76.18. Hammer stone. (Pl. 28)
W. 0.11. L. 0.18. Th. 0.09. Wt. 2390 g. Coarse, pocked, volcanic stone (Whitbread). Ovoid, with groove around middle, slightly nearer the flattened end. Both rounded and flatter ends chipped, perhaps from use. For LBA parallels from Akrotiri, see Michailidou 1995, 175, pl. 25.

230 K76.29. Pounder/grinder(?). (Pl. 28)
W. pres. 0.06. L. pres. 0.07. Th. pres. 0.05. Wt. 383 g. Fine, greenish-gray stone. Broken at bottom and along two sides. Rounded trapezoidal shape. Unbroken surfaces are smoothed.

Uninventoried: obsidian blade (B-76.12).

Metal

231 K76.31. Slag tool. (Pl. 28)
L. 0.07. Wt. 840 g. Rounded, cube-shaped object. Surface smooth in places, rough in others. Large depressions on all sides. Magnetic. The shape and impressions are appropriate for holding by hand as a tool for grinding (Georgakopoulou).

B03-822.
EBA destruction deposit, from test pit below Room B.2. Period III.

Pottery

No discard information available. Joins with B03-817, B03-818, B03-820, and B03-823. Uncatalogued ceramics in Red-Brown Semifine to Semicoarse ware (RBMa–RBMd) include fragments from a saucer, shallow bowl, deep bowl/open jar, and several jars. A pithos knob in Red-Brown Coarse ware (RBMd) was also found.

Siphnos(?)

232 K.4420. Pithos. (Fig. 34, Pl. 29)
Published, Wilson 1999, 133, no. III-428, pl. 89. H. pres. 0.58. D. pres. 0.51. D. base 0.13. D. rim pres. 0.27. Entire profile preserved. Biconical body with thickened ledge rim, pedestal foot, and tubular spout above foot. Four horizontal trumpet handles around upper part of shoulder. Body covered with applied pellets; applied rope-band around top of pedestal and shoulder at level of handles; two additional applied rope-bands around upper body and another just below rim. Disks worn off around lower body. Polisher/rubber **235** was found inside the pithos. Talc ware. PBS (based on visual analysis from outside of museum case, and Wilson's ware assessment). Soil from inside the pithos was saved by the excavation team, but flotation by Nikos Kounadis in collaboration with Evi Margaritis revealed that no ancient botanical or zoological remains were present inside.

Stone

233 K76.15. Disk. (Pl. 30)
H. 0.04. D. 0.10. Wt. 720 g. Banded, blue-gray marble. Large chips on each flat face. All preserved surfaces are very smooth; four–five incised grooves encircle one edge. Same size as large drill cores, but very smooth. Reused(?). For similar, see Wilson 1999, 156, no. SF-232, pl. 99.

234 K76.22. Pestle. (Pl. 30)
H. 0.07. D. 0.04. Wt. 190 g. Fine, white marble (Whitbread). Intact. Hourglass profile. Edges rounded and chipped. One third of surface covered with a black encrustation.

235 K76.25. Polisher/rubber. (Pl. 30)
W. 0.09. L. 0.12. Th. 0.05. Wt. 854 g. Greenish-gray stone, possibly chlorite schist (Whitbread). Intact. Flattened ellipse. Surface somewhat pitted. Found inside pithos **232**.

236 K76.16. Saddle quern. (Pl. 30)
H. 0.03–0.08. W. 0.10–0.12. L. pres. 0.15. Wt. 1531 g. Pale, greenish-gray stone with small, shiny, pale-gray and white inclusions. Some white encrustation. All surfaces somewhat smoothed.

Uninventoried: stone lid (B-76.24); millstones (B-76.25, B-76.26).

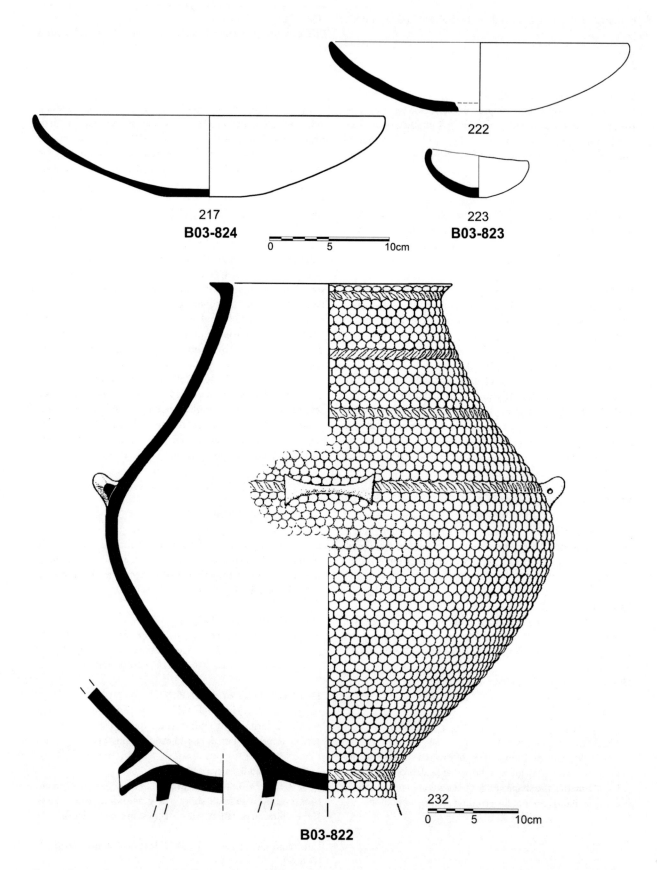

Fig. 34. Pottery from B03-824 (**217**), B03-823 (**222**, **223**), and B03-822 (**232**). Drawings by Lily Bonga (**217**, **222**, **223**) and Alice Fäthke (**232**).

B03-821.

EBA destruction deposit from test pit below Room B.2. Period III.

Pottery

No discard information available. Joins with B03-814, B03-818, B03-819, B03-820, B03-823, B03-824, and B03-830. Most uncatalogued ceramics were sherds in Red-Brown Semifine to Semicoarse ware (RBMb–RBMd). A sherd from a large closed vessel in Orange-Buff Semifine to Coarse ware was also present (CSWe).

Local

237 Large deep bowl/open jar. (Fig. 35, Pl. 30)
Incurving rim and shoulder. D. rim est. 0.30. Coarse, reddish-brown fabric, blackened in places, with 15–20% inclusions. EBA Red-Brown Semifine to Semicoarse. Interior smoothed; exterior covered with rounded and conical pellets. RBMb, with rare, dark blue particles. PFG 1D. (Local).

238 Pithos. (Fig. 35, Pl. 30)
Thickened, flattened rim and upper body. D. rim est. 0.42. Moderately coarse, reddish-brown fabric with thick, dark-gray core and 10–15% inclusions. Interior and exterior surfaces smoothed. EBA Red-Brown Coarse. Three applied rope bands with diagonal slashes oriented in opposite directions. RBMd. PFG 1D (Local)

Stone

239 K76.27. Mortar. (Pl. 30)
H. 0.16. W. 0.25. D. max. 0.34. Marble (Whitbread). Surface of bowl smoothed, undulating. Saw mark on bottom. Now lost.

240 K76.4. Palette. (Pl. 30)
H. 0.04–0.05. W. 0.30. L. 0.52. Coarse, micaceous, blue-gray stone, with white veins on underside. Smoothed upper surface. A bone fragment was found stuck to the upper surface.

241 K76.21. Weight. (Pl. 30)
H. pres. 0.16. W. 0.13. Th. 0.04. Wt. 1278 g. White marble (Whitbread). Flattened ovoid, narrower at top. Hole drilled through top from both sides (diameter 0.02–0.04). Edges are chipped; some yellowish discoloration. The heaviness of this weight in comparison with those published by Wilson (1999, 154–155) suggests that it is unlikely the weight was used in textile production.

242 K76.17. Stone object. (Pl. 30)
H. 0.08. W. 0.08–0.10. L. 0.19. Wt. 2221 g. Dark greenish-gray, micaceous stone. Roughly trapezoidal, pyramidal section. Two long sides are smoothed; one side is rough. One of the smoothed sides has sharp corners at the two long edges. All other edges rounded and/or broken. The two small, trapezoidal sides are uneven: one is incurved and smoothed, but the other is out-rounded and rough. Long narrow side is smoothed and slightly incurving in center.

B03-821 ETC.

EBA destruction deposit from test pit below Room B.2. Sherds probably disassociated from excavation units because of multiple joins between them. Period III.

Pottery

No discard information available. Joins with B03-817, B03-818, B03-820, B03-821, B03-822, B03-830. Uncatalogued sherds are entirely large jar and/or pithos fragments in Red-Brown Semifine to Semicoarse and Red-Brown Coarse ware (RBMa–RBMc).

Local

243 K.4569. Shallow bowl. (Fig. 35, Pl. 31)
Published, Wilson 1999, 122, no. III-272, pl. 84. Entire profile preserved. H. 0.05. D. rim 0.25. Fragments from B03-821, B03-823, and B03-830. Moderately coarse, reddish-orange fabric turning dark red to gray in some areas of rim, with 10–15% inclusions. EBA Red-Brown Burnished. RBMb, with rare calcareous(?) inclusions.

244 K.4582. Large globular jar. (Fig. 35, Pl. 31)
Published, Wilson 1999, 111, no. III-144, pl. 77. Approximately 30% preserved, including part of body; low, straight, collar neck; rounded rim; horizontal, semi-squared (in section) handle at lower shoulder. Smaller horizontal handle at upper shoulder with round section. H. pres. 0.34. D. rim est. 0.19. Fragments from B03-821, B03-823, and B03-830. Moderately coarse, reddish-brown fabric with 15–20% inclusions. Handles attached by a plug pushed through vessel walls. Interior: dark brown, scored. Exterior surface smoothed. EBA Red-Brown Semifine to Semicoarse. Exterior coated in streaky black slip/wash. RBMb, with rare calcareous(?) inclusions. For similar at Mt. Kynthos on Delos, see MacGillivray 1980, 41, no. 392, fig. 15.

245 K.4583. Deep bowl/open jar. (Fig. 35, Pl. 31)
Published, Wilson 1999, 107, no. III-98, pl. 76. Entire profile preserved. Pedestal base, incurving rim with rounded top. H. 0.32. D. rim 0.37. Restored. Fragments from B03-821 and B03-824. Moderately coarse, reddish-brown fabric with 10–15% inclusions. Surface worn in places. EBA Red-Brown Semifine to Semicoarse. RBMb, with rare calcareous(?) inclusions.

B03-820.

EBA destruction deposit from test pit below Room B.2. Period III.

Pottery

No discard information available. Joins with B03-812, B03-815, B03-816, B03-817, B03-818, B03-819, B03-821, B03-822, B03-823, and B03-830. Uncatalogued ceramics all came from Red-Brown wares, include Semifine to Semicoarse (RBMa, RBMb, RBMd) closed vessels, a Burnished (RBMa) open(?) vessel, and Coarse (RBMd) pithos fragments.

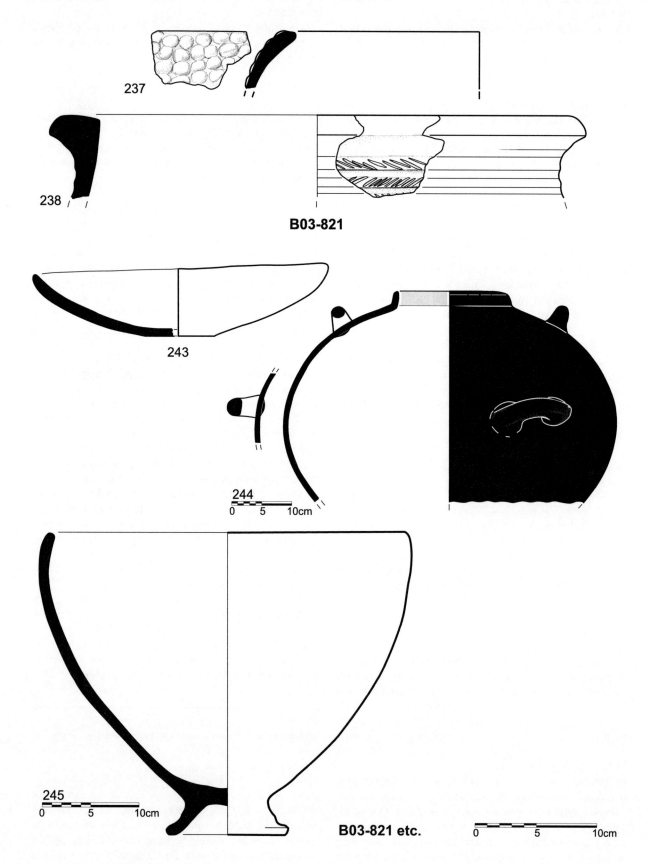

Fig. 35. Pottery from B03-821 (**237**, **238**) and B03-821 etc. (**243**–**245**). Drawings by Mary-Jane Schumacher (**237**, **238**, **244**) and Lily Bonga (**243**, **245**).

Local

246 K.4575. Shallow bowl. (Fig. 36, Pl. 32)
Published, Wilson 1999, 122, no. III-269, pl. 83. Upper profile preserved, base and much of rim missing; restored. H. rest. 0.05. D. rim rest. 0.18. Fragments from B03-820 and B03-830. Moderately coarse, reddish-brown fabric with 10–15% inclusions. A few surface voids, probably from burned-out organics. EBA Red-Brown Burnished. RBMb.

247 Large open jar, perforated. (Fig. 36, Pl. 32)
Thickened, flattened rim; conical body; horizontal lug; and flat base. H. 0.42. D. base est. 0.14. D. rim est. 0.37. D. perf. 0.08. Fragments from B03-820, B03-822, B03-823, and B03-830. Coarse, gray fabric with mottled, dark reddish-brown to orange surfaces and 15–20% inclusions. Clay lumps visible in interior where lug pushed through vessel walls. Interior: shallow scoring. Exterior: scoring and uneven lumps around lug, from attachment. Large hole cut through center of base after firing. EBA Red-Brown Coarse. RBMb, dark, with overfired(?) white schist. PFG 1Dv (Local).

248 Large jar. (Fig. 36, Pl. 32)
Flat base and flaring lower body. D. base est. 0.2. Coarse, reddish-brown fabric with 10–15% inclusions. Base thickness very uneven. Exterior smoothed. Interior preserves irregular incisions, which are much more widely spaced than the usual shallow scraping/scoring marks. They do not, however, seem compatible with the deliberate interior incisions that appear on MBA and LBA beehives from Ayia Irini (J. C. Overbeck 1989a, nos. AT-32, AU-6, AV-11, CE-151) or Crete (D'Agata and De Angelis 2014). EBA Red-Brown Coarse. RBMb, with rare calcareous(?) inclusions.

Stone

249 K76.28. Polisher/rubber. (Pl. 32)
W. 0.05. L. 0.11. Th. 0.03. Wt. 403 g. Steatite (Whitbread). Rounded rectangular shape. Chipped.

250 K76.9. Stone. (Pl. 32)
H. 0.05. W. 0.04–0.05. Wt. 138 g. Dark greenish-gray stone, possibly serpentine (Whitbread). Roughly pyramidal, with two flat sides and two curved sides. Surface chipped. Smooth, chipped, grinding surface at flat bottom. Abraded upper tip from hammering (J. L. Caskey).

B03-819.
EBA destruction deposit from test pit below Room B.2; removal of pithos (**251**). Period III.

Pottery

Joins with lots B03-818, B03-820, and B03-821. The only object is the catalogued pithos.

Local

251 K.4588. Pithos. (Fig. 37, Pl. 32)
Published, Wilson 1999, 115, no. III-191, pl. 79. Approximately 30% preserved; partially restored in plaster. Thickened, everted rim; two knob handles preserved and two restored. H. pres. ca. 0.60. Fragments from B03-819, B03-818, B03-820, and B03-821. Moderately coarse, reddish-brown fabric with 30–50% inclusions. Surface dark gray. EBA Red-Brown Coarse. Band of applied disks below neck; second band at level of knob handles. RBMb, dark, with overfired(?) white schist.

B03-818.
EBA destruction deposit from test pit below Room B.2. Period III.

Pottery

No discard information available. Joins with lots B03-810, B03-812, B03-814, B03-816, B03-817, B03-819, B03-820, B03-821, B03-823, and B03-830. Uncatalogued ceramics include Red-Brown Semifine to Semicoarse (RBMa–RBMd) vessels, including saucers, a shallow bowl(?), deep bowls/open jars, and a basin(?). A pithos in Red-Brown Coarse ware (RBMa) was also present. An open vessel, tankard, and bell-shaped cup in Red-Brown Burnished ware (RBMa, RBMb) were found. A Black Burnished open vessel (RBMa) is probably local, although a Black Burnished saucer and Red-Brown Semifine to Semicoarse deep bowl/open jar (CSWd) may be imported. Also present were Urfirnis(?) and Pinkish Buff (FVg) open vessels, Orange-Buff Semifine to Coarse (DVa, MxMa, MxMg) closed vessels and a shallow bowl, an Orange-Buff Painted (DVd) open vessel, and a Talc ware (PBS) closed(?) vessel.

Local

252 Bowl. (Fig. 37, Pl. 33)
Ring base and chipped lower body. D. base est. 0.05. Moderately coarse, reddish-brown fabric with 10–15% inclusions. EBA Red-Brown Burnished. RBMb, with rare, dark blue particles.

253 K.4581. Footed bowl. (Fig. 37, Pl. 33)
Most of profile preserved, including incurving rim, rounded body, and part of chipped foot. Approximately 50% of entire vessel preserved; restored with plaster. H. pres. 0.13. D. rim est. 0.17. Fragments from B03-818 and B03-823. Moderately coarse, reddish-brown fabric with 15–20% inclusions. EBA Red-Brown Burnished. Exterior surface burnished; interior blackened. RBMa, very micaceous.

254 Jar. (Fig. 37, Pl. 33)
Flat base, slightly flaring lower body. H. pres. 0.16, D. base est. 0.09. Moderately coarse, reddish-brown fabric with 10–15% inclusions. Base interior is very uneven. Interior walls are lightly scored. Exterior is somewhat smoothed, but eroded. EBA Red-Brown Semifine to Semicoarse. RBMb.

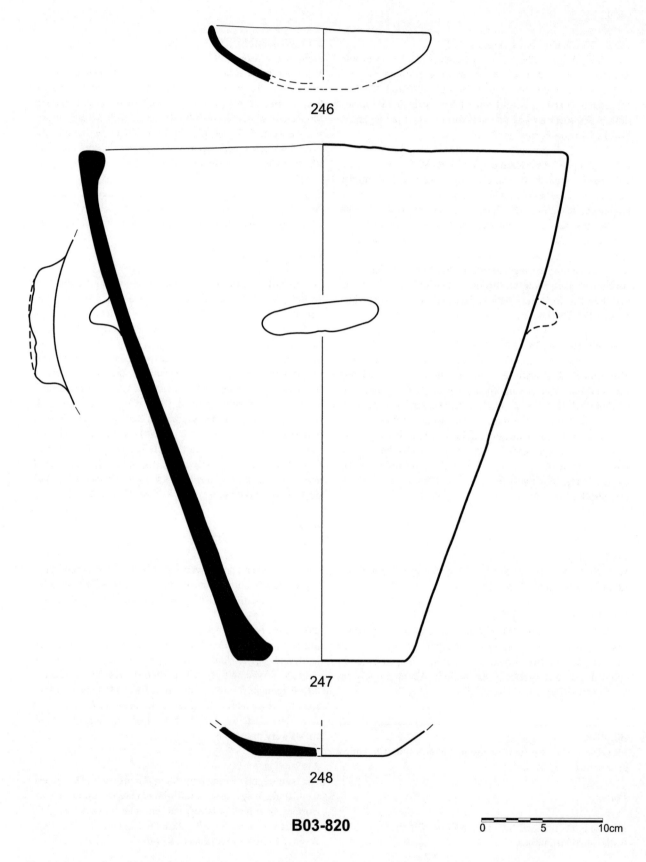

Fig. 36. Pottery from B03-820 (**246**–**248**). Drawings by Lily Bonga (**246**, **247**) and Mary-Jane Schumacher (**248**).

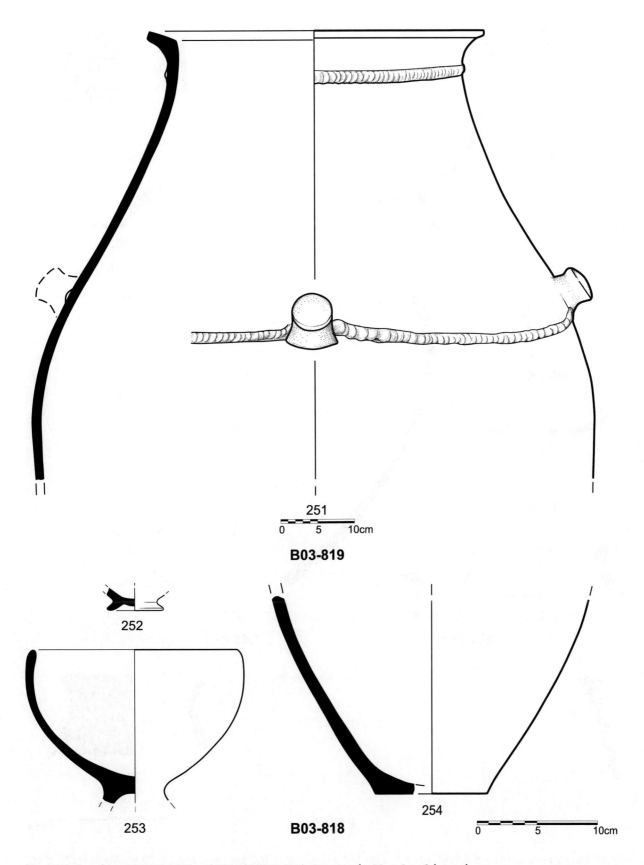

Fig. 37. Pottery from B03-819 (**251**) and B03-818 (**252–254**). Drawings by Mary-Jane Schumacher.

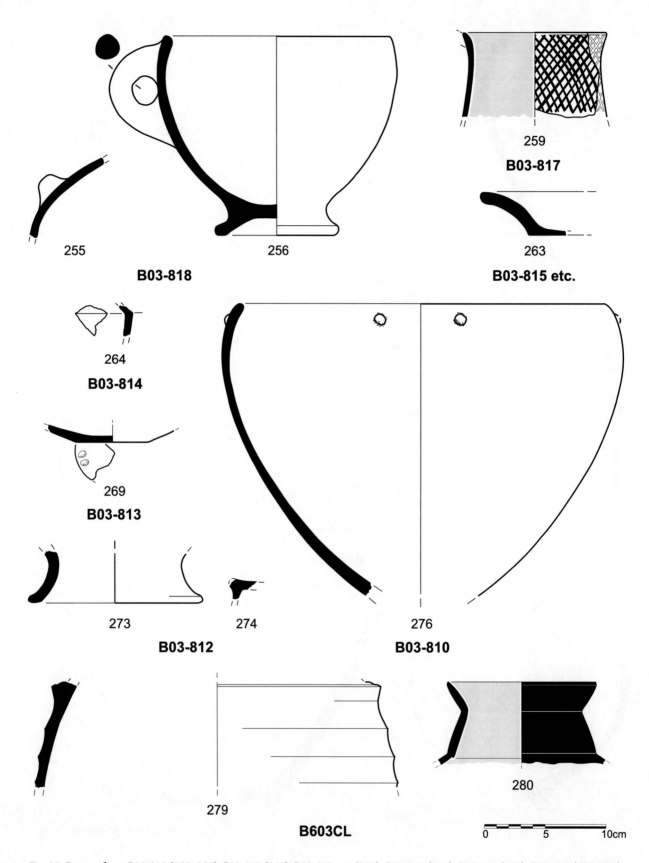

Fig. 38. Pottery from B03-818 (**255**, **256**), B03-817 (**259**), B03-815 etc. (**263**), B03-814 (**264**), B03-813 (**269**), B03-812 (**273**, **274**), B03-810 (**276**), and B603CL (**279**, **280**). Drawings by Lily Bonga (**255**, **256**, **269**, **276**), Mary-Jane Schumacher (**259**, **263**, **273**, **274**), Alison Rittershaus (**264**), and Aliki Bikaki (**279**, **280**).

255 K.4691B. Jar. (Fig. 38, Pl. 33)
Body fragment with conical lug. Fragments from B03-818 and B03-823. Moderately coarse, reddish-brown fabric with 10–15% inclusions. Interior blackened in places. EBA Red-Brown Semifine to Semicoarse. RBMb, with rare blue particles.

Melos

256 K.4691A. Deep bowl. (Fig. 38, Pl. 33)
Entire profile. Ca. 30% preserved, including pedestal foot, incurving rounded rim, and round vertical handle. Partially restored in plaster. H. 0.16. D. base 0.11. D. rim est. 0.19. Fragments from B03-818 and B03-823. Coarse, orange fabric with 15–20% inclusions. Interior surface is paler orange, turning to dark gray and black in places, probably from burning. EBA Orange-Buff Semifine to Coarse. Surface smoothed. DVc, dark orange.

Cyclades(?)

257 Cup(?). (Pl. 33)
Slightly incurving rim. D. rim est. 0.08. Fine, dusty, orange fabric with bluish-gray core and fewer than 1% inclusions. EBA Orange-Buff Painted. Exterior preserves traces of semi-lustrous red paint; cross-hatched net(?). MxMc, fine. PFG 13A (Attica?).

Euboea(?)

258 Fine jar or pyxis. (Pl. 33)
Curved body and round, arched or horizontal handle attachment. Fine, slightly dusty, pinkish-orange fabric turning pale purple-gray at interior, with fewer than 1% inclusions. Interior preserves lump from pushed-through handle. EBA Pinkish Buff. Exterior coated with lustrous red and burnished. FVh, with mica. PFG 12A (S Euboea/NW Cyclades?).

B03-817.
EBA destruction deposit from test pit below Room B.2. Period III, a few possibly Period IV.

Pottery

No discard information available. Joins with lots B03-816, B03-818, B03-820, B03-822, and B03-830. Uncatalogued ceramics include Red-Brown Semifine to Semicoarse (RBMa, RBMb) vessels, including saucers (one of which has a mat impression on its base), a shallow bowl, and a pithos. Small body sherds in imported fabrics (FSTc, FSTi) may be later intrusions, as these fabrics are nonexistent in other Period III lots, but do exist in Period IV lots, at least in Area B.

Melos

259 Pedestaled cup. (Fig. 38, Pl. 33)
Slightly flaring rim and upper body, broken at handle attachment (two nonjoining fragments). D. rim est. 0.13. Moderately fine, pinkish-orange fabric turning bluish gray toward interior, with 1–5% inclusions. Interior surface mostly eroded; traces of brown slip. EBA Orange-Buff Painted. Exterior decorated with semi-lustrous red cross-hatched net pattern; paint almost entirely faded or fugitive. DVa, bluish gray. For similar, see Wilson 1999, 136, nos. III-455, III-457, pls. 35, 90.

Cyclades(?)

260 Rubber/polisher. (Pl. 33)
Trapezoidal lump of clay; worn smooth at all edges. L. 0.04. Fine, porous, orange fabric with fewer than 1% inclusions. MxMc(?).

B03-816.
EBA destruction deposit from test pit below Room B.2. Period III, with one possible Period IV sherd (**261**).

Pottery

No discard information available. Joins with B03-812, B03-815, B03-817, B03-818, B03-820, B03-823, and B03-830. Uncatalogued ceramics in Red-Brown Semifine to Semicoarse ware (RBMb, RBMc) include a saucer, shallow bowl, deep bowl/open jar, and a jar. An Orange-Buff Semifine to Coarse ware bowl(?) was also present (DVc). A plain body sherd in an imported fabric cannot be assigned to a known ware (FVg?).

Melos(?)

261 Closed vessel. (Pl. 33)
Body. Moderately fine, porous, slightly gritty, white fabric turning to very pale pink at core, with 1–5% inclusions. Handmade. Painted. Exterior: large band(?) in matt black. Period IV? DVa, coarse, with glassy inclusions.

B03-815.
EBA destruction deposit from test pit below Room B.2. Period III.

Pottery

No discard information available. Joins with B03-816 and B03-820. Uncatalogued ceramics in Red-Brown Semifine to Semicoarse ware (RBMa, RBMb) include a basin, lid, deep bowl/open jar, and jar. A closed vessel in Orange-Buff Semifine to Coarse ware (MxMa) was also present.

B03-815 ETC.
EBA destruction deposit from test pit below Room B.2. Lot probably disassociated from excavation units because of multiple joins between them. Period III.

Pottery

No discard information available. Joins with B03-816, B03-818, B03-820, B03-823, and B03-830. Uncatalogued ceramics include a large pan or (pedestaled?) plate in Red-Brown

Burnished ware (RBMb) and a small askos or jug in Red-Brown Semifine to Semicoarse ware (RBMa).

Local

262 Jar. (Pl. 33)
Globular body and horizontal, round handle. Fragments from B03-818 and B03-823. Moderately coarse, with orange interior, dark reddish-brown exterior with orange patches, and well-defined dark-gray core, and with 10–15% inclusions. Interior: light scoring. Attachment of handle by pushing through body wall. EBA Red-Brown Semifine to Semicoarse. RBMb, dark, with overfired(?) white schist. PFG 1D (Local).

263 Pan. (Fig. 38, Pl. 33)
Flaring rim and shallow, thin-walled bowl. D. rim est. 0.63(?). Fragments from B03-823 and B03-830. Moderately coarse, reddish-brown fabric with 10–15% inclusions. Interior and exterior: smoothed, now eroded. Exterior: traces of burning. EBA Red-Brown Semifine to Semicoarse. RBMb, with phyllite, rare calcareous(?) inclusions, and common mica. PFG 1Bv (Local).

B03-814.
EBA destruction deposit from test pit below Room B.2. Period III.

Pottery

No discard information available. Joins with B03-818, B03-821, B03-823, and B03-830. Uncatalogued ceramics in Red-Brown Semifine to Semicoarse ware (RBMb–RBMd) include a tankard, deep bowl/open jar, and a pan or pedestaled(?) plate.

Local

264 Pyxis(?). (Fig. 38, Pl. 33)
Shoulder at sharply everted, neck attachment. D. neck ca. 0.08. Moderately fine, reddish-brown fabric with 5–10% inclusions. Burned after breakage. Coil join at neck. EBA Red-Brown Burnished. Interior: smoothed. Exterior: burnished. RBMa, compact, with common mica. PFG 1A (Local).

B03-814 etc.
EBA destruction deposit from test pit below Room B.2. Sherds probably disassociated from original lots because of multiple joins between them. Period III.

Pottery

No discard information available. Joins with B03-818, B03-821, B03-823, and B03-830. Uncatalogued ceramics in Red-Brown Semifine to Semicoarse ware (RBMa, RBMb), including a shallow bowl, deep bowl/open jars, and a pedestal base. A Black Burnished (RBMb) shallow bowl was also present.

Local

265 Large, closed vessel. (Pl. 34)
Flat base and lower body. D. base est. 0.13. Fragments from B03-814, B03-818, B03-821, B03-823, and B03-830. Moderately coarse, orange fabric with well-defined, thick, blue-gray core and 10–15% inclusions. Interior: much scoring. Exterior: mottled orange and dark gray. EBA Red-Brown Semifine to Semicoarse. RBMb, with rare calcareous(?) inclusions.

266 Pithos. (Pl. 34)
Rim and upper body in two, large, nonjoining fragments, plus several nonjoining body sherds. D. rim est. 0.32. Fragments from B03-814, B03-818, B03-821, B03-823, and B03-830. Moderately coarse, orange fabric with well-defined, thick, blue-gray core and 10–15% inclusions. Interior and exterior smoothed and mottled orange and dark gray. EBA Red-Brown Coarse. Band of applied disks below rim. RBMb, with overfired(?) white schist, and rare calcareous(?) inclusions.

B03-813.
EBA destruction deposit from test pit below Room B.2. Period III, with a few MBA intrusions (including probably **269**).

Pottery

No discard information available. Joins with B03-812. Uncatalogued ceramics in Red-Brown Semifine to Semicoarse ware (RBMb, RBMc) include basins, a shallow bowl, and a pedestal base. An open (MxMc) and closed vessel (MxMa) in Orange-Buff Semifine to Coarse ware were also present. A Cycladic White open vessel (DVa) dates to Period IV or V.

Cyclades

267 Shallow bowl(?). (Pl. 34)
Body (two nonjoining fragments). Fine, somewhat dusty, orange-brown fabric with well-defined, gray core and 1–5% inclusions. EBA Orange-Buff Painted. Interior: coated with semi-lustrous red slip. Exterior: well-smoothed. MxMc. PFG 3Cv (Cyclades [Syros?]). For similar, see Wilson 1999, 136, no. III-465, pl. 35.

268 Large, closed vessel. (Pl. 34)
Thick-walled body fragment. Moderately coarse, gritty, porous, pinkish-tan fabric with 10–15% inclusions. Interior: shallow wiping marks. EBA Orange-Buff Semifine to Coarse. Exterior coated with semi-lustrous red slip. DVc (Melos?)

269 K.4600. Large bowl. (Fig. 38, Pl. 34)
Part of flat base and lower body. D. base est. 0.06. Fine, compact, moderately hard-fired, orange-tan fabric with dark-gray core and 1–5% inclusions. Handmade. Burnished. Interior and exterior burnished. Two oval indentations applied to base before firing. MxMc, compact, with silver mica. For similar, see Lindblom 2001, 52–53, nos. 19, 22, 23, 27, pl. 3 (dated to EH III/MH I–II).

Terracotta

270 Spoon. (Pl. 34)
Pronged handle and part of shallow bowl. H. pres. 0.02. L. 0.04. Moderately fine, reddish-brown fabric with 5–10% inclusions. RBMb, with rare, dark blue particles. (Local). For similar, see Wilson 1999, 164, nos. SF-378, SF-381, pls. 39, 102.

B03-812 ETC.
EBA destruction deposit from test pit below Room B.2. Lot probably disassociated from excavation unit because of multiple joins with sherds in other lots. Period III, with a few MBA intrusions.

Pottery

No discard information available. Joins with B03-816, B03-817, B03-818, B03-820, B03-823, and B03-830. Uncatalogued ceramics in Red-Brown Semifine to Semicoarse ware (RBMa–RBMc) include a basin, deep bowl/open jar, and a jar with a low collar rim. A Red-Brown Burnished (RBMa) closed vessel was present, as were several sherds in Talc ware, probably from multiple vessels (PBS).

Local(?)

271 Large jar. (Pl. 34)
Body and horizontal handle attachment (nonjoining fragments). Sherds from lots B03-812, B03-816, B03-818, B03-820, and B03-830. Moderately coarse, reddish-orange fabric with gray core and 10–15% inclusions. Interior: scoring. EBA Red-Brown Burnished. Exterior burnished. Several rope bands with incisions oriented in opposite directions. Shallow grooves run along both sides of applied bands, well-smoothed. RBMb/RBMc, orange, with rare calcareous(?) inclusions. PFG 2Av (Local [region]).

Amorgos

272 Closed vessel. (Pl. 34)
Body (three nonjoining fragments). Fragments from B03-816, B03-817, B03-818, and B03-830. Coarse, brittle, orange-brown fabric with mottled gray exterior and 10–15% inclusions. Interior: light scoring. Interior and exterior rough. Plain. MxMb. PFG 3I (Amorgos).

B03-812.
Upper part of EBA destruction deposit from test pit below Room B.2. Period III, with a few MBA sherds.

Pottery

No discard information available. Joins with B03-813, B03-816, B03-818, B03-820, B03-823, and B03-830. Uncatalogued local ceramics (RBMa–RBMc), most probably dating to Period III, include plain deep bowls/open jars, a shallow bowl, saucer, pedestal base, and basins. Shallow bowls and a tankard in Red-Brown Burnished ware (RBMa, RBMc) were present, as was an open vessel in Black Burnished ware (RBMa) and a pithos in Red-Brown Coarse ware (RBMa). An Orange-Buff Semifine to Coarse saucer (MxMc) and closed vessel (MxMg) may have been imported from the Cyclades; a plain closed vessel (CSWd) is perhaps from the local region. A Slipped closed vessel in an unusual fabric for EBA deposits (MxMf) may be a later intrusion.

Local

273 Deep bowl/open jar(?). (Fig. 38, Pl. 35)
Pedestal base. D. base est. 0.14. Moderately coarse, reddish-brown fabric turning darker at core, with 5–10% inclusions. EBA Red-Brown Semifine to Semicoarse. RBMd.

274 Lid. (Fig. 38, Pl. 35)
Slightly concave, upper body and lower flange; broken at corner. D. ca. 0.10. Coarse, gritty, reddish-brown fabric with dark-gray core and 10–15% inclusions. EBA Black Burnished(?). Traces of thick, black slip. RBMa, dark. For similar, see Wilson 1999, 112, no. III-159, pl. 28.

MIXED STRATA BELOW HOUSE B

B03-811.
Upper part of EBA destruction deposit with MBA intrusions, from test pit below Room B.2. Period III, with some MBA sherds.

Pottery

No discard information available. Uncatalogued ceramics in local fabrics (RBMa–RBMd), most of which may be EBA, include a saucer, basin, and pedestal base (RBMb). Fragments from a pithos in Red-Brown Coarse ware (RBMa); open vessels and a shallow bowl in Red-Brown Burnished ware (RBMa, RBMb); a fine open vessel in Pinkish Buff ware (FVe), and imported Cycladic closed vessels (CSWe, MxMb, MxMg, PBS) were also present. Probable later vessels include a Yellow Slipped, wheel-coiled bowl (RBMd), a Slipped open vessel (FVd/DVe), and a Burnished open vessel (MFVa), as well as two fragments of plain Melian/Theran closed vessels (DVa).

Bone and Shell

Uninventoried: murex shell, ovicaprid tooth, flat bone fragments, and a long bone with joint from an unknown animal.

B03-810.
Upper part of EBA destruction deposit with some MBA intrusions, from test pit below Room B.2. Period III, with MBA and possible Period VI intrusions.

Pottery

No discard information available. Joins with B03-818 and B03-830. Uncatalogued ceramics in local fabrics (RBMa–RBMd), many probably dating to Period III, include shallow bowls, saucers, deep bowls/open jars, jars, and a pedestal foot. Fragments of a shallow bowl in Red-Brown Burnished ware (RBMa), a Black Burnished open vessel (RBMa), a Yellow Mottled sauceboat (FVh), a Pinkish Buff(?) closed vessel (FVe), and imported closed vessels (CSWe, MxMb) were also present. Among later sherds, a handleless cup (RBMa), a piriform cup base (DVe), and a plain, closed Melian/Theran vessel (DVb) were present.

Local And Local Region

275 Jar with two-stage neck. (Pl. 35)
Neck. Moderately coarse, gritty, orange fabric with 10–15% inclusions. EBA Red-Brown Semifine to Semicoarse. RBMe, coarse. PFG 2Av (Local [region]).

276 Deep bowl/open jar. (Fig. 38, Pl. 35)
Incurving rim and body, ca. 40% preserved. D. rim est. 0.30. Fragments from B03-810, B03-818, and B03-830. Moderately coarse, reddish-brown fabric with 5–10% inclusions. Interior: shallow scoring. Exterior: well-smoothed. Traces of burning along rim. EBA Red-Brown Semifine to Semicoarse. Two applied pellets below rim. RBMa, with common mica. For similar, see Wilson 1999, 107, no. III-99, pls. 25, 76.

277 Rounded(?) cup. (Pl. 35)
Slightly flaring rim and upper body. Rim fragment too small to estimate diameter. Moderately fine, gritty, reddish-orange fabric with 10–15% inclusions. Wheel-coiled or wheelmade. Yellow Slipped. Interior and exterior coated in pale, yellow slip. Below rim: festoon or pendent semicircle in matt red to brown paint. RBMd. PFG 2Cv (Local [region]).

278 Reworked sherd. (Pl. 35)
Body. L. pres. 0.03–0.04. Moderately coarse, reddish-brown fabric with 10–15% inclusions. Plain. Edges worn and rounded, probably from use as polisher or other tool. RBMb.

B603CL.
Deposit of sandy soil beneath earliest use levels of Rooms B.2 and B.3. Period III mixed with Periods IV–V; some possible LBA (**304**).

Pottery

1 3/4 tins (ca. 29.8 liters) collected; 1 bag (ca. 0.4 tin or 6.8 liters) remains. 97% coarse, 25% discarded in original papsing. Uncatalogued local ceramics include mainly Period III shapes, such as shallow bowls, bell-shaped cups, deep bowls/open jars, basins, and jars with two-stage necks (RBMa–RBMc). A Cycladic(?) basin coated with yellow slip (MxMd) and a plain vessel (RBMd) are of unknown date. Probable MBA pottery includes a Burnished open vessel (RBMa); a local Burnished Cycladic cup or carinated bowl (RBMd); Melian/Theran imported vessels (DVa); a Cycladic closed vessel (MxMf); coarse, closed, Lustrous Painted (monochrome) and Non-Lustrous Painted vessels (FSTf; FSTi); and Gray Minyan open vessels (FVa). Six handleless cups, two tripod legs, rim and body sherds from an EBA baking pan, and nine sauceboat sherds were discarded (Kea Pottery Notebook B, 33).

Local(?)

279 Open jar(?). (Fig. 38, Pl. 35)
Body, near rim or flange(?). D. at top break est. 0.23. Moderately coarse, moderately compact, reddish-brown fabric with 5–10% inclusions. Handmade. Burnished. Three plastic ridges below rim. Surface worn. Exterior: burnishing marks. Interior: burnished near rim(?). RBMd. PFG 2Cv (Local [region]). Compare with Wilson 1999, 129, nos. III-374, III-375, pls. 34, 88. See also Sotirakopoulou (2016, 274), for comprehensive references to jars with similar ridges/fluting from EC and earlier MC contexts; she argues that such decoration is most common in EC III and early MC.

280 Jar. (Fig. 38, Pl. 35)
Two-stage neck and rim. D. rim est. 0.12. Moderately fine, somewhat sandy, orange fabric with 1–5% inclusions. EBA Red-Brown Semifine to Semicoarse. Exterior and interior coated with thin black slip. RBMd.

Local

281 Deep bowl/open jar. (Fig. 39, Pl. 35)
Flattened, slightly incurving rim. Diameter indeterminable. Moderately coarse, dark gray fabric turning orange at interior, with 10–15% inclusions. Interior: surface worn. Exterior: wiping marks. EBA Red-Brown Semifine to Semicoarse. RBMb, with rare, dark blue particles.

282 Deep bowl/open jar. (Fig. 39, Pl. 35)
Pedestal base. D. base est. 0.10. Moderately coarse, reddish-brown fabric with 10–15% inclusions. EBA Red-Brown Semifine to Semicoarse. RBMb. PFG 1B (Local).

283 Sauceboat(?). (Fig. 39, Pl. 35)
Arched handle. L. 0.04. Moderately fine, orange fabric with blue-gray core and 5–10% inclusions. EBA Red-Brown Semifine to Semicoarse. RBMa.

284 Jar. (Fig. 39, Pl. 35)
Round, horizontal handle at attachment to body. L. 0.08. Moderately coarse, reddish-brown fabric with gray core; ca. 15–20% inclusions in handle and 10–15% inclusions in body. EBA Red-Brown Semifine to Semicoarse. Five incised lines radiating from body of vessel; coated with thin black slip. RBMb, with overfired(?) white schist and rare calcareous(?) inclusions. See J. L. Caskey 1972, 366, no. B44, pl. 79; Wilson 1999, 39, 111–112, nos. II-215–221, III-155–157, pls. 10, 50, 78.

285 Pithos. (Fig. 39, Pl. 35)
Rim. D. rim est. 0.44. Moderately coarse, reddish-orange fabric with slightly darker, reddish-gray core and 5–10% inclusions.

EBA Red-Brown Coarse. Band of overlapping disks below rim. RBMa.

286 Tankard or bell-shaped cup(?). (Fig. 39, Pl. 35)
Round, vertical handle (two nonjoining fragments). Moderately fine, dark reddish-brown fabric with 5–10% inclusions. EBA Black Burnished. RBMa, compact, dark, with common mica. PFG 1B (Local).

287 Goblet. (Fig. 39, Pl. 35)
Rim and carinated body. D. rim est. 0.19. Fine, reddish-brown fabric with 1–5% inclusions. Handmade(?). Burnished. RBMa, with very common mica and sparkling break. For shape, see J. L. Caskey 1972, 378, no. D128, fig. 9.

288 Cycladic cup/carinated bowl. (Fig. 39, Pl. 35)
Carinated rim sherd. D. rim est. 0.15. Moderately fine, reddish-brown fabric turning gray at core, with 1–5% inclusions. Handmade(?). Burnished. Surface worn. RBMa, with rare calcareous(?) inclusions.

289 Jar. (Pl. 35)
Body and shoulder at neck attachment (three nonjoining fragments). Moderately coarse, dark red fabric with thick, dark-gray core and 10–15% inclusions. Coil-built. Yellow Slipped (Polychrome). Exterior coated in yellow slip, decorated in matt black and red. Indecipherable motif(s). RBMa.

290 Jug. (Pl. 35)
Upper body and narrow neck. Moderately fine, reddish-brown fabric with 5–10% inclusions. Break at neck shows scoring for coil attachment. Entire neck probably coil built. Slipped. Exterior partially coated with thin black slip. RBMa.

291 K.713. Handleless cup. (Fig. 39, Pl. 35)
Published, J. C. Overbeck 1989a, 174. Type 3 (Overbeck Type H4). 95% preserved, including entire profile. Chips at rim. H. 0.08. D. base 0.05. D. rim 0.11. From B03-105 (Group CP). Uneven base. Wheel-coiled. Plain. RBMa, with common mica.

292 K.1213. Deep saucer. (Fig. 39, Pl. 35)
Published, J. C. Overbeck 1989a, 174; Wilson 1999, 29, no. II-56. Disk base with leaf impression. H. pres. 0.02. D. base 0.04. From B03-109 (Group CP). RBMb, with rare, dark blue particles.

293 Cycladic cup/carinated bowl. (Fig. 39, Pl. 35)
Arched handle and slightly incurving rim; body sharply curved, but not truly carinated. D. rim est. 0.10. Moderately coarse, orange fabric with 10–15% inclusions. Handmade(?). Plain. RBMa.

294 Large, closed vessel. (Fig. 39, Pl. 35)
Body and arched round handle. Moderately coarse, orange fabric with gray core and interior margin, and with 10–15% inclusions. Interior preserves paring marks. Coil-built. Plain. Exterior smoothed. RBMb, with rare calcareous(?) inclusions.

295 Vessel. (Pl. 36)
Vertical(?) handle, narrowing from wide oval at attachment to body to round section. L. 0.04. Moderately coarse, orange fabric with 5–10% inclusions. Plain. RBMa, with rare calcareous(?) inclusions.

Cyclades

296 Collared jug. (Pl. 36)
Neck and rim (two nonjoining fragments). D. rim est. 0.09. Moderately coarse, compact, brittle, pinkish-orange fabric with well-defined, dark bluish-gray core and 10–15% inclusions. Rim slightly deformed (near handle attachment?). EBA Red-Brown Semifine to Semicoarse. Interior and exterior coated with thin, matt-black slip, mostly worn away. CSWe. PFG 4Av (Naxos). For slightly less flaring example, see Wilson 1999, 110, no. III-133, pls. 27, 77.

297 Bowl. (Pl. 36)
Rim and flaring body. D. rim est. 0.14. Moderately coarse, gray fabric with pink margins and 5–10% inclusions. Handmade. Slipped. Coated in and out with thick, white slip. Possible fugitive decoration on exterior. Pendant semicircles(?). MxMg. PFG 4Cv (Naxos).

298 Closed vessel. (Pl. 36)
Flat base and flaring lower body. D. base 0.08. Moderately fine, somewhat dusty, pale brown fabric that turns pinkish at exterior surface and uneven pale gray at core and interior margin, with 1–5% inclusions. Handmade. Plain. MxMc.

Cyclades/Attica(?)

299 Large jar or pithos. (Fig. 39, Pl. 36)
Body. Moderately coarse, orange-red fabric turning gray at core in places, with 5–10% inclusions. Handmade. EBA Red-Brown Burnished. Three plastic ridges. RBMc. PFG 1Cv (Local).

Melos/Thera(?)

300 Jar. (Fig. 39, Pl. 36)
Broad strap handle. W. 0.08 max. Moderately fine, dusty, pale orange fabric with 1–5% inclusions. EBA Orange-Buff Semifine to Coarse. Coated with streaky, matt black. MxMc, pink-orange tinged.

301 Large jar or pithos. (Fig. 39, Pl. 36)
Broad, tubular, strap handle. W. 0.06. Moderately fine, orange-brown fabric turning slightly grayer at core, with 1–5% inclusions. EBA Orange-Buff Semifine to Coarse. MxMd, fine, dusty. For similar, see J. L. Caskey 1972, 375, no. C51:b, pl. 81; Wilson 1999, 87, 115, nos. II-774, III-203, III-204, pls. 22, 71, 80. See Sotirakopoulou (2016, 255) for a discussion of tubular strap handles on barrel jars from Phase C at Dhaskalio; similar handles appear to occur rarely also on other shapes there (e.g., Sotirakopoulou 2016, 251).

302 Bell-shaped cup(?). (Fig. 39, Pl. 36)
Slightly flaring rim and round handle attachment. D. rim est. 0.07(?). Moderately fine, pale orange-brown fabric with 5–10% inclusions. EBA Orange-Buff Semifine to Coarse. Traces of

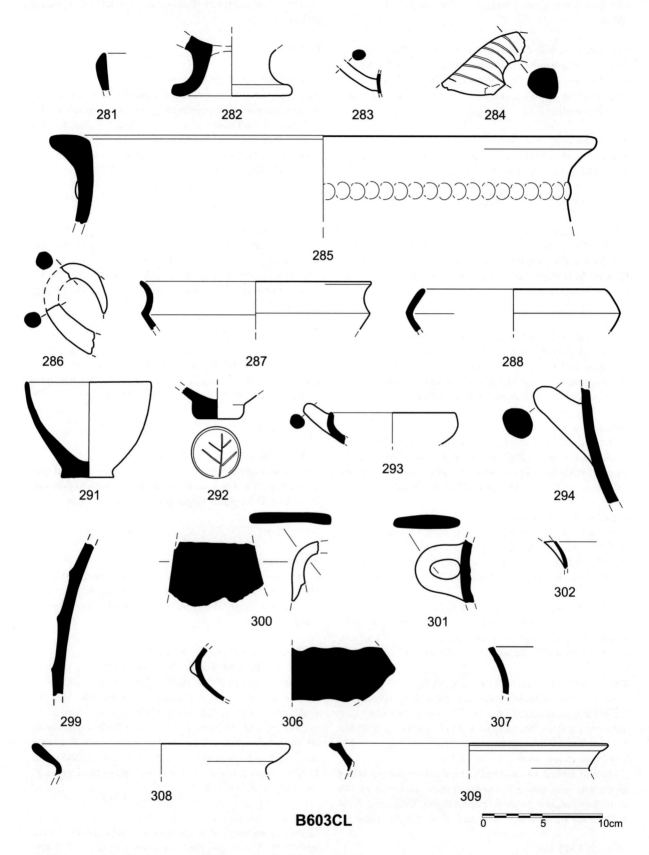

Fig. 39. Pottery from B603CL (**281–288, 291–294, 299–302, 306–309**). Drawings by Aliki Bikaki (**281–288, 291, 293, 294, 299, 302, 306, 308, 309**), Lily Bonga (**292**), and Mary-Jane Schumacher (**300, 301, 307**).

orange slip, probably burnished. MxMc. For shape, see J. L. Caskey 1972, 370, no. C2, fig. 6.

303 Vessel.
Long, round-section, vertical handle. L. 0.07. Moderately coarse, pale orange fabric with pale-gray core and 10–15% inclusions. EBA Orange-Buff Semifine to Coarse. Probable traces of black paint. DVc, with schist/phyllite(?).

Melos/Thera

304 Straight-sided cup. (Pl. 36)
Beveled base and thick-walled lower body. Moderately fine, porous, pale greenish-yellow fabric with 1–5% inclusions. Underside of base has many deep indentations, probably from fingertip and nail. Coil-built. Painted. Three incised bands above base. Decoration in matt brown. Three vertical bands (one now fugitive) between which are narrow, vertical lines. DVa. Period V or perhaps Period VI.

305 Rounded cup. (Pl. 36)
Everted rim and semi-globular upper body. D. rim est. 0.11. Moderately fine, porous, pale yellow fabric with 5–10% inclusions. Handmade. Surfaces smoothed. Plain. DVa, with common, small, white inclusions.

Mainland

306 Pyxis(?). (Fig. 39, Pl. 36)
Globular body and horned lug. D. est. 0.16(?). Fine, pale pinkish-brown fabric with fewer than 1% inclusions. EBA Pinkish Buff. Exterior coated with thick, semi-lustrous red slip. FVg, with no core. PFG 14Bv (Unknown).

307 Bowl(?). (Fig. 39, Pl. 36)
Flaring rim. Diameter indeterminable. Moderately fine, slightly dusty, pale-gray fabric with fewer than 1% inclusions. Handmade(?). Gray Minyan. Surface worn, but probably originally burnished. FVa. For somewhat similar profile, see Sarri 2010b, 323, pl. 36:10.

308 Goblet. (Fig. 39)
Everted, plain rim, slightly thickened at exterior, but not hollowed. D. rim est. 0.21. Fine, gray fabric with no inclusions. Wheelmade. Gray Minyan. FVa. Compare with Davis 1986, nos. E-8, AI-19; Sarri 2010b, 279, pl. 17:10.

309 Goblet. (Fig. 39)
Everted, thickened, flattened, and hollowed rim. D. rim est. 0.23. Fine, hard-fired, gray fabric with no inclusions. Wheelmade. Gray Minyan. FVa. For shape, see Davis 1986, nos. C-28, AI-20; Sarri 2010b, 283, pl. 19:7. At Mitrou, broadly similar rims occur from Phases 4–7 (Hale 2016, figs. 7, 16).

310 Goblet or bowl. (Fig. 40, Pl. 36)
Everted, plain rim and grooved shoulder. D. rim est. 0.21. Fine, gray fabric with fewer than 1% inclusions. Wheelmade. Gray Minyan. FVa. Compare with Davis 1986, nos. G-7, S-12.

Mainland/Kythera(?)

311 Large, closed vessel. (Pl. 36)
Body. Moderately coarse, hard-fired, relatively compact, pale pinkish-brown fabric, turning pale purple at core, with 15–20% inclusions. Handmade. Lustrous Decorated (LOD). Exterior coated in semi-lustrous black. Two diagonal bands in white paint; narrow incised band (possibly result of construction?). FSTg. PFG 8A (Unknown).

Unknown

312 Closed vessel (Pyxis? Duck vase?). (Pl. 36)
Body. Moderately coarse, gray fabric with 10–15% inclusions. Interior: scoring. Handmade. Burnished. Exterior burnished. Incised triangle, with each side made of four lines. CSWd. PFG 2Cv (Local [region]).

313 Sauceboat. (Pl. 36)
Incurving rim. H. pres. 0.03. Moderately coarse, hard-fired, very dark-gray fabric with 15–20% inclusions. Very thin walls; thickening near rim. EBA Black Burnished(?). Interior and exterior coated with lustrous black slip, now flaking. CSWd. PFG 2Cv (Local [region]).

314 Sauceboat. (Pl. 36)
Arched strap handle and attachment to body. Fine, pale, pink fabric with pale-gray core and yellow surface. Fewer than 1% inclusions. Interior smoothed. EBA Urfirnis. Outer surface and exterior of handle coated with lustrous dark-brown to black slip. Underside of handle plain; reserved unpainted area beneath handle. FVg. PFG 14B (Argolid?). For similar, see Wilson 1999, 74, no. II-632, pl. 67.

315 Bowl(?). (Fig. 40, Pl. 36)
Lower body. Moderately fine, slightly dusty, gray fabric with 5–10% inclusions. Handmade(?). Gray Minyan. Interior and exterior burnished. Exterior: five grooves. MFVb, moderately coarse. PFG 11A (Unknown).

Stone

Uninventoried:
B03-106: obsidian flake (B-1.282, D. max. 0.02); obsidian blade (B-1.81, D. max. 0.02).

Terracotta

316 K1.308. Spindle whorl. (Pl. 36)
Published, J. C. Overbeck 1989a, 174, no. CP-2. Similar to type M2, but rounded. H. 0.02. D. 0.03. D. perf. <0.01–0.01. Wt. 22 g. From B03-109 (Group CP). Moderately coarse, orange-red fabric with 15–20% inclusions. Surface lightly burnished; somewhat pitted. Broken around both ends of perforation, especially at narrow end. RBMb, with rare, dark blue particles. (Local).

317 K1.441. Spindle whorl. (Pl. 36)
Published, J. C. Overbeck 1989a, 174. Type S3. H. 0.03. D. 0.05. D. perf. 0.01. Wt. 76 g. From B03-109 (Group CP). Coarse, red-

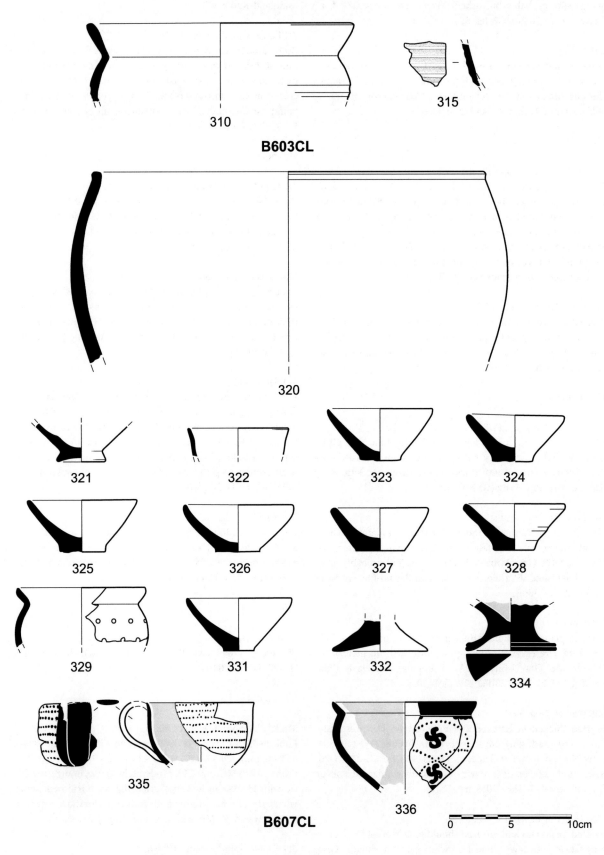

Fig. 40. Pottery from B603CL (**310**, **315**) and B607CL (**320–329**, **331**, **332**, **334–336**). Drawings by Aliki Bikaki (**310**, **320**, **323–329**, **331**, **332**, **334**, **336**) and Mary-Jane Schumacher (**315**, **321**, **322**, **335**).

brown fabric with 20–25% inclusions. Significant breakage around both ends of perforation. RBMa, with phyllite and rare calcareous inclusions. (Local).

318 K1.285. Loom weight. (Pl. 36)
Published, J. C. Overbeck 1989a, 174. Type RG. D. 0.09. Th. 0.03. D. perf. 0.01. Wt. 215 g. From B03-106 (Group CP). Round, flattened body with grooved top. Moderately coarse, red to brown fabric with gray core and 10–15% inclusions. Surface smoothed, covered with pale brown wash, turning to red at top. RBMb, with very rare dark blue-gray and rare calcareous(?) inclusions. (Local).

ROOMS B.2 AND B.3: USE PHASES
(HOUSE B: THIRD PHASE)

B607CL.
Surfaces d and e in Room B.2, Surfaces g and f in Room B.3, and stratum of brown soil above Surface f. Period VIIa.

Pottery

3/4 tin (around 12.75 liters) collected; 1/3 bag (ca. 0.1 tin or 1.7 liters) remains. Few sherds in lots B03-104, B03-107. 98% coarse wares. About 25 handleless cups have been discarded of which one was probably imported. At least six large tripods were present but have also been discarded, including one leg with a large thumb impression at the top. Many jars or plain pithoi, a half of a very coarse and rough miniature jug, and a marked sherd have been either discarded or lost. Two Gray Minyan sherds, three Matt Painted sherds, and a MM Lustrous Painted (LOD) sherd were also discarded, as were two later roof tile fragments (Kea Pottery Notebook B, 53). Uncatalogued sherds in local fabrics (RBMa, RBMc) include a small, plain, bridge-spout; a Burnished Period IV goblet stem; a Burnished open vessel; a Yellow Slipped jar with a wide, ledge rim, and a Yellow Slipped closed vessel. Uncatalogued sherds in imported fabrics include a Lustrous Painted (Monochrome) beaked jug and Lustrous Painted, spouted, bell cup that is almost identical to **337** (Fig. 41:a), both perhaps from Crete (FSTj); a Melian/Theran Painted, closed vessel (DVa); a fine, Cycladic(?) Painted closed vessel (MxMc); a Red Coated open jar or krater (MxMc); an Aeginetan Painted shallow bowl/cup (DVd); and a mainland Slipped jug or jar handle, perforated at one end (FVd).

Local

319 Closed vessel. (Pl. 36)
Body. H. pres. 0.05. Coarse, hard-fired, gray fabric, turning red at surface, with 10–15% inclusions. Coil-built. Plain. Exterior smoothed. Three horizontal, incised lines, filled with white paint(?). RBMa.

320 Open jar, possible cook-pot (tripod jar?). (Fig. 40, Pl. 36)
Rounded rim and upper body. D. rim est. 0.32. Coarse, somewhat porous, relatively hard-fired, reddish-brown fabric with gray core and 15–20% inclusions. Coil-built. Patchy gray in places, fire-clouding. Plain. Three narrow grooves at mid-body. RBMa, with rare calcareous inclusions.

321 Small, closed vessel. (Fig. 40, Pl. 36)
Hollowed disk base and lower body. H. 0.03. D. base 0.04. Moderately fine, hard-fired, dark orange fabric, turning gray at exterior margin, with 5–10% inclusions. Coil-built or wheel-coiled. Plain. RBMa, orange, with blue and gray schist, rare mica, and rare calcareous(?) inclusions.

322 Bell(?) cup. (Fig. 40, Pl. 36)
Rim fragment. H. pres. 0.02. D. rim est. 0.08. Moderately fine, hard-fired, red-orange fabric with well-defined, inky, bluish-black core, and 5–10% inclusions. Wheelmade(?). Plain. RBMd.

323 K.989. Handleless cup. (Fig. 40)
Type 1. 90% intact; broken at rim. H. 0.04. D. base 0.03. D. rim 0.09. From B03-103. Uneven base. Wheel-coiled(?). Plain. RBMa.

324 K.947. Handleless cup. (Fig. 40)
Type 1. 90% preserved; broken at rim and base. H. 0.04. D. base 0.04. D. rim 0.08. From B03-104. Thick, uneven base. Wheel-coiled. Half of rim and upper body burned. Plain. RBMa.

325 K.1392. Handleless cup. (Fig. 40)
Type 1. 90% preserved; chips at rim. H. 0.04. D. base 0.04. D. rim 0.09. From B03-104. Lopsided. Badly bonded coil visible at interior near rim. Uneven base. Wheel-coiled(?). Plain. RBMa.

326 K.708. Handleless cup. (Fig. 40)
Type 1. Nearly intact, with a chip at rim. H. 0.04. D. base 0.04. D. rim 0.09. From B03-104. Wheel-coiled. Plain. RBMa.

327 K.1235. Handleless cup. (Fig. 40)
Type 1. Nearly intact, with chip at base. H. 0.04. D. base 0.03. D. rim 0.08. From B03-107. Coarse. Elliptical rim. Flat base. Wheel-coiled. Plain. RBMa.

328 K.1224. Handleless cup. (Fig. 40)
Type 1. Nearly intact, with chips at rim. H. 0.04. D. base 0.04. D. rim 0.08. From B03-107. Wheel-coiled. Plain. RBMa.

329 Incense burner. (Fig. 40, Pl. 36)
Published, Georgiou 1986, 41, no. 160. Everted rim and upper body; eight perforations partially or wholly preserved. H. pres. 0.04. D. rim est. 0.11. Moderately coarse, reddish-brown fabric with 5–10% inclusions. Wheelmade or wheel-coiled. Plain. RBMd. PFG 1A (Local).

Aegina/Mainland(?)

330 Open jar(?). (Pl. 36)
Raised, splaying base. H. pres. 0.04, D. base est. 0.05. Fine, dusty, orange fabric turning paler at interior surface, with fewer than 1% inclusions. Handmade(?). Lustrous Painted. Exterior coated with yellow slip, decorated with lustrous(?) red. Band(?) above base. DVe. The base appears comparable to Lindblom's (2001, 30–31, fig. 8:FB-15) high cylindrical base, which is

often—although not always—associated with Aeginetan Kitchen Ware (Lindblom 2001, no. 475 is an exception in a fine fabric). Similar bases from the Acropolis Wells, also associated with cooking jars, were in coarse fabrics (e.g., Mountjoy 1981, 22, nos. 27–29, 33–37, fig. 6), although several are slipped and show no sign of burning (Mountjoy 1981, 22, nos. 32, 33, fig. 6).

331 Handleless cup. (Fig. 40, Pl. 36)
Type 1. 90% preserved. H. pres. 0.04. D. base 0.03. D. rim 0.09. Moderately fine, pale green fabric with 1–5% inclusions. Uneven, slightly concave base. Wheel-coiled(?). Interior pinker than exterior. Plain. Exterior smoothed. DVd.

332 Goblet. (Fig. 40, Pl. 36)
Slightly concave, heavy foot, and stem attachment. H. pres. 0.03. D. base 0.08. Moderately fine, rather hard-fired, orange fabric with 1–5% inclusions. Forming method indeterminable. Slipped. Exterior coated in yellow slip; burnished. MFVc/DVe (color and texture similar to DVe, but with probable silver mica). PFG 13B (Euboea). Profile is similar to a goblet from Deposit ξ at Kythera, although earlier parallels from the mainland are also cited by Coldstream and Huxley (1972, 145, no. 110, fig. 44); a goblet from the Acropolis Wells also has a similar foot (Mountjoy 1981, no. 129, fig. 12).

Mainland

333 Rounded cup or goblet. (Pl. 36)
Approximately 12% everted rim and upper body. H. pres. 0.04. D. rim est. 0.12. From B03-103. Very fine, somewhat dusty, orange fabric with 1–5% inclusions. Wheelmade. Lustrous Painted. Surface extremely worn. Interior: plain(?). Exterior coated with yellow slip; lustrous red rim band(?) and spiral on shoulder. MFVc. PFG 11B (Unknown). Similar shape in painted goblets of Period IV at Ayios Stephanos (Rutter and Rutter 1976, nos. 787–790).

334 Goblet. (Fig. 40, Pl. 36)
Concave foot, stem, and lower body. H. pres. 0.04. D. base 0.07. Fine, pinkish-orange fabric with fewer than 1% inclusions. Wheel-coiled(?). Red Coated. Coated in and out with lustrous reddish-brown paint of uneven thickness. FVd. PFG 14Bv (Unknown).

Crete(?)

335 Bell cup. (Fig. 40, Pl. 36)
Rim, handle, and upper-mid body (two nonjoining fragments). H. pres. 0.05. D. rim est. 0.09. Fine, hard-fired, pink fabric turning yellow at surface, with fewer than 1% inclusions. Wheelmade. Lustrous Painted. Interior: monochrome lustrous reddish brown. Exterior: stone pattern in same. Handle: solid-painted and encircled by a wide loop, painted on body. FSTk.

336 Rounded cup. (Fig. 40, Pl. 36)
Rim and body (three nonjoining fragments). H. pres. 0.07. D. rim 0.12. Fine, hard-fired, pale pink fabric with fewer than 1% inclusions. Wheelmade. Lustrous Painted. Interior monochrome, lustrous black. Exterior: rim band, dotted scale pattern with swastika infill, band above base in same. FSTj.

337 Spouted bell cup. (Fig. 41, Pl. 36)
Rim, pulled spout, and upper body. H. pres. 0.05. D. rim est. 0.09. Fine, pale yellow-pink fabric with no inclusions. Wheelmade. Lustrous Painted. Interior: monochrome, lustrous black. Exterior: scale pattern in same. FSTj.

Unknown

338 K.2668. Marked sherd. (Pl. 36)
W. pres. 0.07. L. 0.09. Th. 0.01. Lost. Mark seems unusual, perhaps post-firing, based on excavation photo (KA.48.7).

Terracotta

339 K1.297. Loom weight. (Pl. 36)
Type R, with somewhat flattened top. D. 0.08. Th. 0.02. D. perf. <0.01–0.01. Wt. 110 g. From B03-104. Broken at one corner. Flattened body; two perforations. Smoothed, worn surface. RBMa. (Local).

B03-108.
Surface h in Room B.3. Period VIIa(?).

Pottery

11 sherds collected; 3 sherds remain. Discarded sherds include a Gray Minyan fruit stand, a Matt Painted sherd, a handleless cup rim, the rim of a tripod vessel, the rim of a spreading bowl, and three coarse body sherds, possibly also from tripod vessels (Kea Pottery Notebook B, 55). Uncatalogued sherds include a body fragment (FSTj), which may belong to **340** and/or **536**.

Crete(?)

340 Cup. (Pl. 37)
Body and nonjoining part of strap handle with metallicizing attachment. Possibly the same vessel as **536** (Kea Pottery Notebook B, 55)? Fine, hard-fired, pale pink fabric with no inclusions. Wheelmade. Lustrous Painted. Interior coated in thick, brown paint; exterior decorated in flaking, lustrous black. Wavy, horizontal bands and irises (FM 10a). Handle monochrome, unpainted underneath. FSTj.

B03-809.
Strip of soil against Wall K and under Surface d; consisted of material between Surfaces d, e, and f. Period VII.

Pottery

No discard information. All extant sherds catalogued.

Local

341 Handleless cup. (Pl. 37)
Type 1. 75% preserved. H. pres. 0.04, D. rim 0.10, D. base 0.03. Moderately coarse, reddish-brown fabric with 15–20% inclusions. Uneven base. Wheelmade(?). Painted. Surface extremely worn. Interior preserves two matt-black lines radiating from center. RBMa, with rare calcareous inclusions.

342 Bell cup. (Pl. 37)
Rim, strap handle, and upper body. H. pres. 0.04. D. rim est. 0.10(?). Moderately fine, hard-fired, reddish-brown fabric with 5–10% inclusions. Wheel-coiled(?). Yellow Slipped. Interior plain; heavily encrusted. Exterior coated in yellow slip, matt-black bars along handle. RBMa.

Mainland

343 Goblet. (Pl. 37)
Foot. D. base est. 0.11. Fine, hard-fired, pale yellow fabric turning orange at lower margin. Fewer than 1% inclusions. Wheelmade. Lustrous Painted (Monochrome). Upper and lower sides coated with lustrous red-brown paint. FVc, orange margin. PFG 14B (Argolid?).

ROOM B.2: DESTRUCTION DEPOSIT

B606CL.
Lower part of destruction deposit, Rooms B.2/B.3 and B.4. Ceramics date the deposit to Period VIIb, with some probably Period VI and VIIa sherds as well. Fragments that appear similar to ewer (**406**) were found in the Temple, but they do not join; it is possible that these sherds might belong to similar vessels rather than the same one. Joins exist between B606CL, B03-29, and B609CL (Notecards, 69).

Pottery

6 1/2 tins (ca. 110.5 liters) collected; 1 bag (ca. 0.6 tin or 10.2 liters) plus inventoried objects remain. 13% fineware. Forty handleless cups are inventoried; an additional 86 handleless cups and six tripod legs were discarded (Kea Pottery Notebook B, 45). The hollow stem of a fruit stand in moderately coarse (local?) fabric was discarded, as were about 10 Gray Minyan and Matt Painted sherds. Fragments of two pithoi with applied decoration have been discarded or lost (Kea Pottery Notebook B, 41). Uncatalogued are sherds from local (RBMa) Yellow Slipped and Yellow Painted closed vessels; possibly Cretan (FSTj, FSTk), mainly Lustrous Painted vessels, including a jug and an alabastron(?); Melian/Theran Painted open and closed vessels (DVa); Melian/Theran (DVc) and Cycladic (MxMa, MxMc, MxMf) Painted (including Polychrome, Red and Black) and Slipped closed vessels; possibly Aeginetan (DVd, DVe) vessels including Painted, Bichrome, Slipped, and plain vessels, as well as a Red Coated bridge-spouted jar; mainland imports (FVb, FVc, FVd, one variant classed as FSTk/FVd) in Burnished, plain, Lustrous Painted, and Red Coated wares, including several goblets and a few closed vessels. Several sherds are probably Period IV or V intrusions, including a Period IV Burnished goblet fragment (RBMa), a Period V(?) Painted Cycladic cup rim (DVa), a Slipped, closed vessel (FSTf), and a Slipped and Burnished cup/bowl (CSWc).

Local And Local Region

344 Jar. (Fig. 41, Pl. 37)
Projecting rim. D. rim est. 0.18. Moderately fine, orange-brown fabric turning gray toward outer surface, with 1–5% inclusions. Wheelmade or wheel-coiled. Yellow Slipped. Surface coated in yellow slip; petaloid decoration in matt black along rim. RBMa(?) or perhaps MxMd(?). It is difficult to see the fabric, and although metamorphic rocks appear, there is more coarse fraction silver mica than usual and very small black inclusions that are somewhat atypical among local fabrics.

345 Collar-necked jug(?). (Fig. 41, Pl. 37)
Two nonjoining fragments mended from four sherds; flattened rim, collar neck and shoulder. D. rim est. 0.09. Moderately fine, brittle, bright orange-red fabric with 5–10% inclusions. Wheelmade or wheel-coiled. Yellow Slipped. Interior and exterior coated with faded, lustrous dark gray paint, overpainted with yellow in places, with some traces of decoration over the yellow slip in dark-brown paint. Interior preserves sporadic, elongated, yellow blobs, with a possible yellow band at lower part of neck. Coated in yellow, brown bands with (double?) foliate band along shoulder. RBMa, compact, bright red, with common mica. Somewhat similar in profile to a Mycenaean spouted jug from House A (Cummer and Schofield 1984, 56, no. 174, pl. 49) and a jug from Phylakopi (Barber 2008, 136, no. 622, fig. 36), but no trace of a handle or spout is preserved on **345**.

346 Cup-rhyton. (Fig. 41, Pl. 37)
Base fragment. H. pres. 0.02. D. base 0.05. D. perf. 0.01. Moderately fine, reddish-brown fabric with 5–10% inclusions. Handmade. Perforated near edge of base before firing. Yellow Slipped. Interior and exterior coated with faded, flaking yellow slip. RBMa, compact, with very micaceous break.

347 Rounded cup. (Fig. 41, Pl. 37)
Rim and body. H. pres. 0.04. D. rim est. 0.13. Moderately fine, moderately hard-fired, reddish-orange fabric with gray core in places and with 10–15% inclusions. Wheelmade(?). Yellow Slipped. Surface very worn and coated in yellow slip(?). Interior smoothed. Rim band in and out in matt black. Indistinguishable shoulder decoration. RBMa, with rare calcareous(?) inclusions.

348 K.292. Handleless cup. (Pl. 37)
Type 1. 90% preserved; broken at rim and base. H. 0.04. D. base 0.04. D. rim 0.08. From B03-46. Coarse. Uneven base. Wheel-coiled. Yellow Slipped. Coated with pale orange slip. RBMa.

349 Rounded cup. (Fig. 41, Pl. 37)
Two overlapping but nonjoining fragments, preserving full profile, including hollowed, splaying base and everted rim. H. 0.10. D. base 0.05. D. rim est. 0.15. Fragments from B03-46

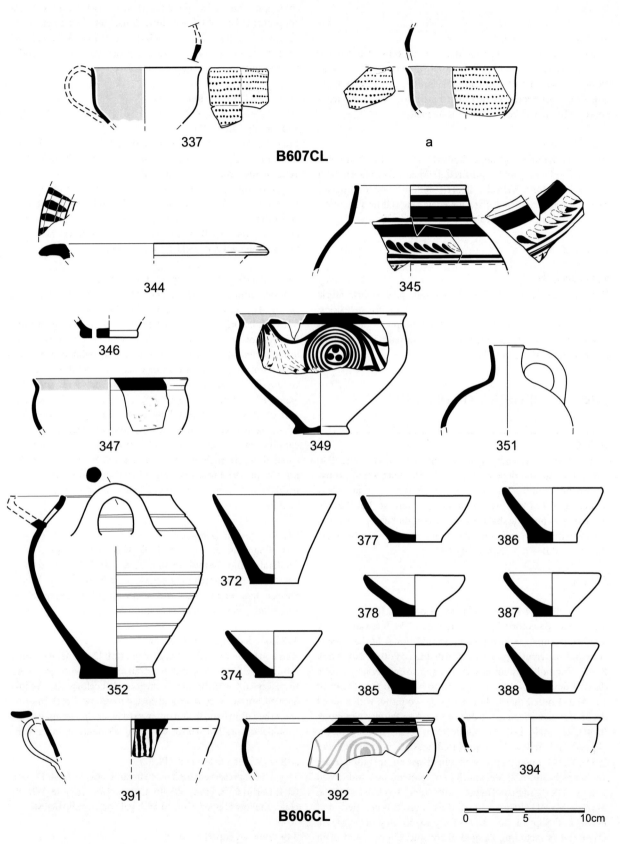

Fig. 41. Pottery from B607CL (**337**, a) and B606CL (**344**–**347**, **349**, **351**, **352**, **372**, **374**, **377**, **378**, **385**–**388**, **391**, **392**, **394**). Drawings by Mary-Jane Schumacher (**337**, a, **344**, **345**, **347**, **349**, **391**, **392**, **394**) and Aliki Bikaki (**346**, **351**, **352**, **372**, **374**, **377**, **378**, **385**–**388**).

and B03-51. Moderately coarse, brittle, reddish-brown fabric with 5–10% inclusions. Wheel-coiled. Surface is worn and pitted. Yellow Slipped (Polychrome, Red and Black). Interior and exterior coated with thick, yellow slip. Rim band in and out. Shoulder: black framed spirals with three dots at center. Below spirals are two narrow black bands above and below a red band, an isolated wide red band, two narrow black bands, and a narrow black band above a wide red band. RBMa, compact, bright red, with common mica.

350 K.1212. Handleless cup. (Pl. 37)
Type 2. 90% preserved. H. 0.03. D. base 0.03. D. rim 0.08. From B03-57. Moderately coarse, compact, reddish-brown fabric, turning gray at core, with 5–10% inclusions. Uneven base. Wheel-coiled(?). Yellow Painted. Exterior coated in yellow slip; interior yellow bands radiating from center. RBMd.

351 Small jug. (Fig. 41, Pl. 37)
Approximately half of upper body preserved, including part of neck, possibly including part of the rim, and round-section, vertical handle. H. pres. 0.06. D. max. pres. 0.11. D. rim 0.03. Moderately fine, moderately hard-fired, dark gray fabric with 5–10% inclusions. Wheel-coiled(?). Burnished(?). RBMa, dark.

352 K.2104. Bridge-spouted jar. (Fig. 41, Pl. 37)
Approximately 75% preserved; restored in plaster. Surface is extremely worn. Raised base, round arched handles, rounded rim. H. 0.15. D. base 0.06. D. rim 0.09. Coarse, dark red fabric turning dark gray at core, with 10–15% inclusions. Coil-built or wheel-coiled. Plain (incised). Two horizontal, shallow, incised bands in shoulder zone, six from mid- to lower body. RBMa, with rare calcareous(?) inclusions.

353 Stirrup jar(?). (Pl. 37)
False spout. W. 0.04. L. 0.05. Moderately coarse, reddish-brown fabric with gray core and 10–15% inclusions. Underside preserves scoring for attachment. Plain. RBMa, with rare calcareous(?) inclusions.

354 K.290. Handleless cup. (Pl. 37)
Type 1. 80% preserved, broken at rim and base. H. 0.03. D. base 0.04. D. rim 0.08. From B03-46. Thin base and walls. Wheel-coiled(?). Plain. RBMa.

355 K.287. Handleless cup. (Pl. 37)
Type 1. 90% preserved; broken and chipped at rim. H. 0.04. D. base 0.03. D. rim 0.09. From B03-46. Wheel-coiled(?). Plain. RBMa, with common mica.

356 K.284. Handleless cup. (Pl. 37)
Type 1. 90% preserved; broken and chipped at rim. H. 0.04. D. base 0.04. D. rim 0.09. From B03-46. Wheel-coiled(?). Plain. RBMa.

357 K.291. Handleless cup. (Pl. 37)
Type 1. 90% preserved; broken and chipped at rim. H. 0.04. D. base 0.04. D. rim 0.09. From B03-46. Wheel-coiled(?). Plain. RBMa, with common mica.

358 K.293. Handleless cup. (Pl. 37)
Type 1. 90% preserved; broken and chipped at rim. H. 0.04. D. base 0.03. D. rim 0.08. From B03-46. Wheel-coiled. Plain. RBMa.

359 K.294. Handleless cup. (Pl. 37)
Type 1. 90% preserved; broken at rim and base. H. 0.04. D. base 0.04. D. rim 0.08. From B03-46. Thick base and walls. Wheel-coiled(?). Plain. RBMa, with common mica.

360 K.281. Handleless cup. (Pl. 37)
Type 1. 90% preserved; broken at rim. H. 0.03. D. base 0.03. D. rim 0.08. From B03-46. Wheel-coiled(?). Plain. RBMa, with common mica.

361 K.283. Handleless cup. (Pl. 37)
Type 1. 90% preserved; broken at rim. H. 0.04. D. base 0.04. D. rim 0.07. From B03-46. Thin walls. Uneven base. Wheelmade(?). Plain. RBMa, with common mica.

362 K.296. Handleless cup. (Pl. 37)
Type 1. 90% preserved; broken at rim. H. 0.33. D. base 0.04. D. rim 0.08. From B03-46. Gray core. Wheelmade(?). Surface crumbly and encrusted with salt. Plain. RBMa.

363 K.299. Handleless cup. (Pl. 37)
Type 1. 90% preserved. Rim chipped; surface broken and pocked. H. 0.03. D. base 0.03. D. rim 0.08. From B03-46. Wheelmade(?). Plain. RBMa, with common mica.

364 K.279. Handleless cup. (Pl. 37)
Type 1. Intact, with tiny chips at base. H. 0.04. D. base 0.04. D. rim 0.08. From B03-46. Rim deformed. Slightly uneven base. Wheel-coiled(?). Exterior encrusted with salt. Plain. RBMa.

365 K.297. Handleless cup. (Pl. 37)
Type 1. Intact. H. 0.04. D. base 0.04. D. rim 0.08. From B03-46. Wheelmade(?). Surface crumbly and salt encrusted. Black encrustation in interior. Plain. RBMa.

366 K.286. Handleless cup. (Pl. 37)
Type 1. Nearly intact, with large chip at rim. H. 0.04. D. base 0.04. D. rim 0.08. From B03-46. Coarse. Uneven base. Wheel-coiled(?). Plain. RBMa.

367 K.280. Handleless cup. (Pl. 37)
Type 1. Nearly intact, with small chips at rim. H. 0.04. D. base 0.04. D. rim 0.08. From B03-46. Wheel-coiled(?). Surface partially eroded and crumbly. Plain. RBMa.

368 K.300. Handleless cup. (Pl. 37)
Type 1. Nearly intact; chipped at rim and base. H. 0.04. D. base 0.04. D. rim 0.08. From B03-46. Thick base. Wheel-coiled. Plain. RBMa.

369 K.298. Handleless cup. (Pl. 37)
Type 1. Nearly intact; chipped at rim and base. H. 0.04. D. base 0.03. D. rim 0.08. From B03-46. Wheelmade(?). Plain. RBMa, with common mica.

370 K.295. Handleless cup. (Pl. 37)
Type 3. 80% preserved; broken at rim. H. 0.06. D. base 0.04. D. rim 0.09. From B03-46. Wheel-coiled(?). Surface pocked. Plain. RBMd.

371 K.288. Handleless cup. (Pl. 37)
Type 3. 90% intact, with many chips at rim. H. 0.07. D. base 0.04. D. rim 0.08. From B03-46. Thin walls. Wheelmade(?). Plain. RBMa.

372 K.282. Handleless cup. (Fig. 41, Pl. 37)
Type 3. 90% preserved; broken at rim. H. 0.07. D. base 0.04. D. rim 0.10. From B03-46. Thin walls. Wheel-coiled. Discolored to dark red to gray at lower body, possibly result of firing. Plain. RBMa.

373 Handleless cup. (Pl. 38)
Type 1. 90% preserved. H. 0.04. D. rim 0.09. D. base 0.04. Moderately coarse, reddish-brown fabric with 5–10% inclusions. Wheel-coiled. Rim burned. Plain. RBMd.

374 K.378. Handleless cup. (Fig. 41)
Type 1. 80% preserved; broken at rim. H. 0.04. D. base 0.03. D. rim est. 0.08. From B03-61. Wheelmade(?). Plain. RBMd.

375 K.358. Handleless cup. (Pl. 38)
Type 1. 90% preserved; broken at rim and base. H. 0.04. D. base 0.04. D. rim 0.08. From B03-61. Wheelmade(?). Plain. RBMd.

376 K.367. Handleless cup. (Pl. 38)
Type 1. 90% preserved; broken at rim and base. H. 0.03. D. base 0.04. D. rim 0.07. From B03-61. Wheel-coiled(?). Plain. RBMd.

377 K.357. Handleless cup. (Fig. 41, Pl. 38)
Type 1. 90% preserved; broken at rim and base. H. 0.04. D. base 0.04. D. rim 0.09. From B03-61. Wheel-coiled(?). Blackened at rim. Plain. RBMd.

378 K.348. Handleless cup. (Fig. 41, Pl. 38)
Type 1. 90% preserved; broken at rim. H. 0.03. D. base 0.03. D. rim 0.08. From B03-61. Wiping in and out. Wheel-coiled(?). Plain. RBMa, with common mica.

379 K.362. Handleless cup. (Pl. 38)
Type 1. Intact, chipped at rim and base. H. 0.04. D. base 0.04. D. rim 0.08. From B03-61. Coarse. Uneven base. Wheelmade(?). Plain. RBMa.

380 K.380. Handleless cup. (Pl. 38)
Type 1. Nearly intact with chipped rim. H. 0.04. D. base 0.04. D. rim 0.08. From B03-61. Wheel-coiled. Plain. RBMa, with common mica.

381 K.385. Handleless cup. (Pl. 38)
Type 1. Nearly intact, with small chips at rim. H. 0.04. D. base 0.04. D. rim 0.08. From B03-61. Thick base and walls. Wheel-coiled(?). Plain. RBMa.

382 K.341. Handleless cup. (Pl. 38)
Type 1. Nearly intact; chipped at rim and base. H. 0.04. D. base 0.03. D. rim 0.08. From B03-61. Coarse. Wheel-coiled(?). Exterior eroded. Plain. RBMa.

383 K.349. Handleless cup. (Pl. 38)
Type 3. 90% preserved; broken base and chipped rim. H. 0.07. D. base 0.04. D. rim 0.09. From B03-61. Wheel-coiled(?). Plain. RBMa, with common mica.

384 K.364. Handleless cup. (Pl. 38)
Type 3. 90% preserved; chipped at rim. H. 0.07. D. base 0.04. D. rim 0.09. From B03-61. Coarse. Exterior: wiping. Fingerprint above base. Wheelmade(?). Interior surface eroded. Plain. RBMa.

385 K.490. Handleless cup. (Fig. 41)
Type 1. 60% preserved. H. 0.04. D. base 0.03. D. rim est. 0.08. From B03-64. Thick walls. Interior: wiping marks. Hole through base, barely pierces outer surface, probably accidental. Exterior surface eroded. Plain. RBMa, with common mica.

386 K.504. Handleless cup. (Fig. 41)
Type 1. 70% preserved; broken at rim. H. 0.05. D. base 0.04. D. rim 0.08. From B03-64. Wheel-coiled(?). Half burned, inside and out. Plain. RBMa.

387 K.478. Handleless cup. (Fig. 41)
Type 1. 90% preserved; broken at rim. H. 0.04. D. base 0.03. D. rim 0.08. From B03-64. Wheel-coiled(?). Plain. RBMa, with common mica.

388 K.734. Handleless cup. (Fig. 41)
Type 1. Nearly intact; chipped at rim and base. H. 0.04. D. base 0.04. D. rim 0.08. From B03-64. Thick base. Wheel-coiled. Surface smoothed. Interior: white encrustation. Plain. RBMa.

389 K.264. Firebox. (Pl. 38)
Published, Georgiou 1986, 14, no. 11. H. pres. 0.05. W. pres. 0.10. D. central hole 0.02. From B03-46. Rounded capsule with large central hole, much of rim broken away. Finger impressions, especially around rim channel; surface eroded. Coarse reddish-brown fabric with 30–50% inclusions. Interior blackened; surface of underside discolored. Handmade(?). Plain. RBMa.

390 K.361. Firebox. (Pl. 38)
Published, Georgiou 1986, 14, no. 10. H. rim 0.03. D. est. 0.11. D. large hole 0.02. From B03-61. Rounded capsule with large central hole; rim missing. Surface at top of capsule eroded. Coarse reddish-brown fabric with 30–50% inclusions, turning gray at top of capsule and rim channel; blackened at top of interior and around holes. Handmade. Plain. RBMa.

Cyclades

391 Vapheio/straight-sided cup. (Fig. 41, Pl. 38)
Rim and nonjoining handle. D. rim est. 0.15. Moderately fine, pale brown fabric with 5–10% inclusions. Wheelmade or wheel-coiled. Yellow Slipped. Interior and exterior surface

coated with yellow slip. Ripple pattern in non-lustrous black; handle diagonally barred. MxMa.

392 Rounded cup or goblet. (Fig. 41, Pl. 38)
Approximately 15% of rim preserved. D. rim est. 0.16. Moderately fine, hard-fired, pale pinkish-brown fabric with well-defined, dark bluish-gray core and 5–10% inclusions. Wheelmade(?). Polychrome Painted (Red and Black). Interior plain; exterior decorated with faded, matt-black rim band and faded, purplish-brown running spirals with blob centers. MxMf.

393 K.285. Handleless cup. (Pl. 38)
Type 1. 90% preserved; broken at rim. H. 0.04. D. base 0.04. D. rim 0.08. From B03-46. Dented on one side. Thick base and walls. Wiping marks in and out. Wheel-coiled(?). Plain. MxMa.

394 Rounded cup. (Fig. 41, Pl. 38)
Small everted rim and upper body. H. pres. 0.03. D. rim est. 0.12. Fine, reddish-brown fabric with 10–15% inclusions. Wiping along interior and exterior surfaces. Wheelmade(?). Plain. MxMc. PFG 3C (Cylades [Syros?]).

Melos/Thera

395 K.2147. Perforated piriform jar. (Fig. 42, Pl. 38)
Approximately 50% preserved including profile from base to neck and one round, vertical handle. Flat base, perforated near edge before firing. H. pres. 0.13. D. base 0.05. D. perf. 0.01. Fine, dusty, pale green fabric with 5–10% inclusions. Wheel-coiled. Surface very worn. Painted. Surface burnished(?). Eleven horizontal bands around lower and mid-body in flaking lustrous dark-brown paint. Shoulder zone preserves running spirals in same; added white dots along diagonal tangent. Neck molding painted with slanting bars; above and below neck molding are horizontal bands with added white dots. DVa. Broadly similar to a Cretan import at Akrotiri (Marinatos 1971, pl. 66:b, cited in Koehl 2006, no. 1131).

396 Bell cup. (Pl. 38)
Rim and upper body (two nonjoining fragments). D. rim est. 0.10. Fine, pale greenish-yellow fabric with fewer than 1% inclusions. Wheelmade. Painted. Decorated flaking, lustrous black paint, now almost entirely fugitive. Interior: monochrome. Exterior: trace of rim band, other indistinguishable decoration. DVa.

397 Piriform cup or stemmed jar. (Fig. 42, Pl. 38)
High, splaying base and part of lower body. H. pres. 0.06. D. base 0.05. Moderately coarse, pale yellow fabric with 10–15% inclusions. Coil-built. Exterior smoothed. Plain. DVc.

398 K.289. Handleless cup. (Fig. 42)
Type 2. Almost intact, with a few chips. H. 0.05. D. base 0.04. D. rim 0.10. From B03-46. Fine, dusty, pale orange fabric with 1–5% inclusions. Thin walls. Wheelmade. Interior and exterior smoothed. Plain. DVa (extremely fine).

Cyclades/Attica(?)

399 Bowl(?). (Fig. 42, Pl. 38)
Hollowed, splaying disk base with beveled edge, part of lower body. D. base 0.05. Moderately coarse, rather compact, orange fabric with well-defined, blue-gray core at lower body, and 10–15% inclusions. Wheel-coiled(?). Yellow Slipped (Polychrome, Red and Black). Interior and exterior coated with faded yellow slip. Lustrous, black band around base. Black festoons(?) outlined(?) with reddish-brown, linear motif in matt purplish brown. RBMc. PFG 2Bv (Local [region]).

400 K.2120. Flaring saucer. (Fig. 42, Pl. 38)
Full profile, approximately 60% preserved. H. 0.03. D. base 0.05. D. rim est. 0.12. Moderately coarse, brittle, dark red fabric turning gray at core, with 10–15% inclusions. Wheelmade(?). One side blackened, as though burned. Yellow Painted. Interior painted with matt yellow lines radiating from center. RBMc.

Aegina(?)

401 Open jar(?). (Fig. 42)
High, splaying base and lower body. H. pres. 0.08. D. base 0.05. Moderately fine, dusty, orange fabric with 5–10% inclusions. Inclusions more frequent in base. Handmade. Thick base cracked at exterior. Interior and exterior surfaces preserve paring marks. Lustrous Painted. Traces of lustrous brown paint on exterior surface. DVe. In shape, the base seems similar to Lindblom's (2001, 30–31, fig. 8:FB-13) low conical foot, which is only associated with Aeginetan Kitchen Ware in that publication. Similar bases from the Acropolis Wells, also associated with cooking jars, were in coarse fabrics (e.g., Mountjoy 1981, 22, nos. 27, 35, 39, fig. 6), although some such vessels are slipped and show no sign of burning (Mountjoy 1981, 22, nos. 32, 33, fig. 6).

Melos/Thera or Western Cyclades(?)

402 K.2093. Rounded cup. (Fig. 42, Pl. 38)
Approximately 80% preserved; restored in plaster. Profile preserved except handle. H. 0.07. D. base 0.04. D. rim 0.10. Moderately fine, pale orange fabric with 5–10% inclusions. Lower body and base are eroded. Wheel-coiled(?). Yellow Slipped. Interior and exterior coated with yellow slip. Interior and exterior rim band in faded, lustrous reddish-brown paint. Three horizontal bands in same along lower body. Along upper body are running spirals connected by double tangent; single dot above and below tangents. Exterior originally burnished(?). MxMa, very dusty, orange, with obvious metamorphics.

403 Bridge-spouted jug. (Fig. 42, Pl. 38)
Approximately 40% of upper body preserved, probably to beginning of foot. Mended from seven pieces. H. pres. 0.12. D. rim est. 0.12–0.15. Moderately coarse, porous, pale, pinkish-gray fabric with greenish-yellow surface and 5–10% inclusions. Wheel-coiled. Plain. DVb, with common mica.

Fig. 42. Pottery from B606CL (**395**, **397–405**, **407**). Drawings by Aliki Bikaki (**395**, **397**, **398**, **401–405**), Mary-Jane Schumacher (**399**), and Lily Bonga (**400**, **407**).

Attica(?)

404 Jar-shaped rhyton. (Fig. 42, Pl. 38)
Raised splaying base (two nonjoining fragments). H. pres. 0.10. D. base 0.06. D. max. est. 0.17. D. perf. 0.01. From B03-57. Fine, hard-fired, orange fabric with 1–5% inclusions. Wheel-coiled. Perforated near edge of base before firing. Lustrous Painted. Interior: plain. Exterior: highly burnished. Band around base in lustrous orange-brown paint. Five bands above base; bottom part of spiral above bands. Possible trace of white paint preserved on one band. MFVc.

405 Goblet. (Fig. 42, Pl. 38)
Foot and short stem preserved. Foot edge flattened. H. pres. 0.03. D. base est. 0.08. Fine, hard-fired, red fabric with fewer than 1% inclusions. Wheelmade. Burnished. Surface burnished(?), eroded (by salt?). MFVc.

Mainland

406 K.2049. Ewer.
Fragments from B03-51, B03-57, B03-64; matching (but not joining) fragments from Temple lots 291 and 318. Fine, reddish-orange fabric with pale brown interior surface and core (only at base). No inclusions. Wheel-coiled. Lustrous Painted. Surface coated in yellow slip. Base/lower body coated with lustrous brown to red paint. Above this are zones of tricurved rock pattern (FM 33) enclosing dots. Wavy line of dots runs above and below tricurved rock pattern. FVd.

407 K.1802. Rounded alabastron. (Fig. 42, Pl. 39)
FS 82. Full profile, 45%, preserved, including one round-section, arched handle. Restored with plaster. Some fragments well preserved, but join to others that are badly weathered. H. 0.10. D. base 0.14. D. rim 0.12. Fragments from B03-61 and B03-64. Fine, pale yellow fabric with no inclusions. Wheelmade. Lustrous Painted. Exterior and interior of neck and rim coated with yellow slip(?) and painted with lustrous black paint, now flaking. Base painted with wavy, spoked double wheel. Two horizontal bands around lower body. Rock pattern outlined with dots around mid-body (FM 32). Above: narrow, solid band and band of dots. Between handles, rock pattern rises to band of dots. Between rock pattern and handles, two short parallel horizontal dotted lines (ten dots each). Handles solid black. FVb. Similar vessels are common in the Argolid, Laconia, Achaea, Boetia, Euboea, all dated to LH IIB (Mountjoy 1999, 98–99, 259–260, 322, 324, 405–406, 654, 699–701, figs. 17:73, 74, 85:42, 108:30, 142:2, 248:24, 268:10). One from Thorikos is very similar in both shape and decoration (Mountjoy 1999, 510–511, fig. 181:54); another from Aegina preserves short, parallel rows of dots beside the handles, present also on **407** (Hiller 1975, 88, no. 219, fig. 34, pl. 22).

408 Closed vessel. (Pl. 39)
Body. Fine, hard-fired, orange-pink fabric turning pale brown at exterior margin, with fewer than 1% inclusions. Wheelmade. Lustrous Painted. Exterior coated with thick, off-white slip, burnished(?). Three rows of dots arranged in triangles in lustrous dark-brown paint. FVb/FVc.

409 Fine, closed vessel, probably piriform jar. (Fig. 43, Pl. 39)
Body (five non-joining fragments). D. max. est. 0.29. Fragments from B03-51 and B03-64. Fine, hard-fired orange-pink fabric with purplish-gray core and 1–5% inclusions. Wheelmade. Lustrous Painted. Exterior coated with thin, pale yellow slip. Lower body: broad bands in lustrous black paint. Shoulder zone: retorted spirals (FM 46) and rock pattern (FM 33) above and below tangent in the same paint. FVf(?), with pink exterior, silver mica.

410 K.2092. Bowl. (Fig. 43, Pl. 39)
Full profile preserved; more than half restored in plaster. Slightly convex base, incurving rim. H. 0.05. D. base 0.04. D. rim 0.10. Fragments from lots B03-46 and B03-57. Fine, hard-fired fabric, turning from pink at base to greenish-yellow at upper body and interior. No inclusions. Wheelmade. Lustrous Painted. Interior coated with lustrous flaking dark-brown paint. Exterior: band around base in dark reddish-brown paint. Above band: stone pattern in same paint, turning from reddish brown to dark brown at upper body, due to firing. Burnished(?). FVb. Similar shape in the Western Sector (Schofield 2011, 73, no. 842, pl. 52); also at Ayios Stephanos (Mountjoy 2008b, 355–356, no. 3525, fig. 6.30). An in-and-out bowl from Phylakopi with a very similar profile may also be a mainland product (Mountjoy 2007, 331–332, no. 367, fig. 8.17).

411 Vapheio cup. (Pl. 39)
One rim fragment mended from two sherds, approximately 10% preserved. D. rim est. 0.10. Fine, pink fabric turning yellow at surface, with fewer than 1% inclusions. Wheelmade. Lustrous Painted. Interior: rim band with lustrous reddish-brown paint. Exterior: very narrow (0.002 m) rim band and running spirals with blob center (FM 46) in same paint. FVc.

412 Vapheio/straight-sided cup. (Pl. 39)
Body. Fine, orange fabric with fewer than 1% inclusions. Lustrous Painted. Interior: rim band in flaking, orange-brown paint. Exterior: decorated in same paint over yellow slip(?). Part of spiral and filled disk (FM 46) preserved. FVc.

413 Goblet. (Fig. 43)
Approximately 25% of rim and upper part of ridged handle. H. pres. 0.04. D. rim est. 0.16. Fine, hard-fired orange fabric with fewer than 1% inclusions. Wheelmade. Red Coated. Exterior and interior coated with thick, lustrous dark reddish-brown paint. FVd.

414 Goblet. (Fig. 43, Pl. 39)
Concave base, part of lower body preserved. H. pres. 0.03. D. base 0.05. Fine, hard-fired, pale pink fabric turning yellow at surfaces, with fewer than 1% inclusions. Handmade(?). Slipped. Coated with pale yellow slip. FVb/FVc, with a pale-gray core.

415 Goblet. (Fig. 43, Pl. 39)
Concave foot, stem, and part of lower body preserved. H. pres. 0.03. D. base est. 0.06. Fine, somewhat dusty, dark gray fabric with 1–5% inclusions. Wheelmade. Gray Minyan. FVa/MFVb.

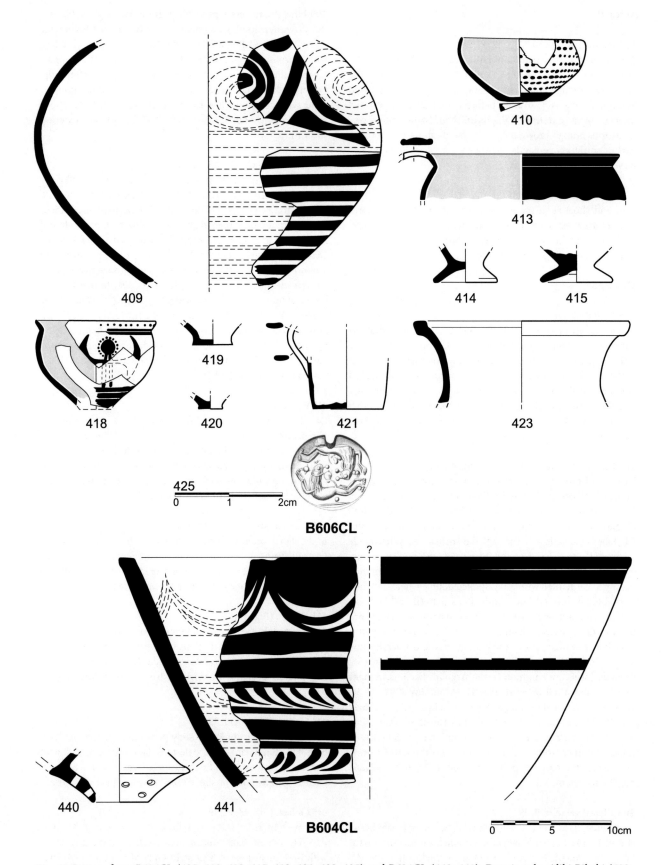

Fig. 43. Pottery from B606CL (**409, 410, 413–415, 418–421, 423, 425**) and B604CL (**440, 441**). Drawings by Aliki Bikaki (**409, 413–415, 418, 419**), Lily Bonga (**410, 423**), Mary-Jane Schumacher (**420, 421, 440, 441**), and Alice Fäthke (**425**).

416 Jar. (Pl. 39)
Fragment of neck, preserving part of flat, rectangular-section rim. H. pres. 0.05. Moderately fine, purplish-red fabric with pale brown surface and 1–5% inclusions. Handmade. Surface chipped and worn, coated with salt. Plain. FVf, with large, white, calcareous(?) particles.

Mainland/Kythera

417 Large, closed vessel. (Pl. 39)
Body (three nonjoining fragments). D. max. est. 0.29. Fragments from B03-57 and B03-103. Fine, hard-fired, pale pink fabric with 1–5% inclusions. Wheel-coiled(?). Lustrous Painted. Exterior burnished. Two horizontal bands in lustrous black paint. Above bands is ogival canopy (FM 13). FSTh.

Crete(?)

418 Rounded cup. (Fig. 43, Pl. 39)
Flaring rim and lower body (three nonjoining fragments, mended from five sherds). H. est. 0.07. D. est. 0.10. Fine, hard-fired, pale brown fabric with 1–5% inclusions. Wheelmade. Lustrous Painted. Exterior probably burnished. Interior: monochrome, lustrous black, now flaking. Exterior: three solid bands above base in same paint; double axes around body; shaft of double axe framed by semicircle of dots. One solid band below rim, band of dots along rim. FSTj. For a nearly exact parallel at Mycenae, see Wace 1932, pl. XXXIII:1 (LH I).

419 Small, closed vessel. (Fig. 43, Pl. 39)
Raised base and part of lower body preserved. H. pres. 0.02. D. base 0.03. Fine, hard-fired pink fabric with 1–5% inclusions. Spiraliform string mark and clay lump at base from removal from wheel. Wheelmade(?). Slipped. Coated with yellow slip. FSTb, fine.

Unknown

420 Miniature open vessel. (Fig. 43, Pl. 39)
Raised disk base and lower body. H. pres. 0.01. D. base 0.02. Fine, slightly dusty, gray fabric with fewer than 1% inclusions, primarily fine silver mica. Handmade. Gray/Black Burnished. Interior and exterior surface burnished, but much damaged by salt. Unknown fabric, possible variant of MFVb(?). PFG 12B (Unknown).

421 Straight-sided cup. (Fig. 43, Pl. 39)
Part of base, lower body, and handle preserved. H. pres. 0.07. D. base 0.06. Fine, hard-fired, dark gray fabric with 1–5% inclusions. Wheelmade. Gray/Black Burnished. Exterior surface worn. MFVb. PFG 3H (Attica/Euboea/Cyclades).

422 K.2084. Handleless cup.
H. 0.04. D. base 0.04. D. rim 0.10. Imported fabric. Lost.

423 K.1635. Jar. (Fig. 43, Pl. 39)
H. pres. 0.07. D. rim est. 0.19. From B03-61. Squared rim and wide neck. Wheel-coiled. Plain. Three corroded lead clamps, which appear to be made up of two round posts through body of vessel, with flattened bar connecting them, with two passing across interior of neck, and one along exterior. The preserved interior cross-bar flares slightly above posts; the exterior cross-bar does not. FVf. (Central Greece?). Compare to **115** (B606CL Pottery Notes, 14).

Bone and Shell

A conical shell, two limpets, a clam shell, and a tooth (bovid?) were discarded (Kea Pottery Notebook B, 37).

Stone

424 K1.118. Marble core/pestle. (Pl. 39)
H. 0.05. D. 0.04. Wt. 15 g. From B03-52. Cylindrical, banded white and blue marble core, reused as pestle (Rapp). Chipped, with some encrustation. Edges worn.

425 K1.159. Sealstone. (Fig. 43)
Published, Caskey, Caskey, and Younger 1975, 388, no. 493. Lentoid seal. Purplish-red stone, perhaps fine-grained limestone (Krzyszkowska 2018, 10–14). Two lions in flying gallop, head-to-tail, heads turned backwards. Groundline, two stars(?) also depicted.

Uninventoried:
B03-52: obsidian blade fragment (B-1.171, W. 0.01, L. 0.02).
B03-64: obsidian flake (B-1.193, W. 0.01, L. <0.01); obsidian blade fragment (B-1.194, W. 0.01, L. 0.03).

Metal

Uninventoried:
B03-64: Copper fragment (B-1.190, D. 0.04). Broken into three pieces; completely corroded (Georgakopoulou).

Terracotta

426 K1.537. Button or attachment. (Pl. 39)
D. 0.04. Th. 0.01. D. perf. <0.01. Wt. 10 g. From B03-51. Approximately 75% preserved. Flat disk with two perforations. Fine, brown fabric turning to dark bluish gray around upper edge of disk, with 1–5% inclusions. Evidence for wear on both sides of both perforations. MFVa, semicoarse. (Cyclades?).

427 K1.282. Loom weight. (Pl. 39)
Type OG. L. 0.10. Th. 0.04. D. perf. 0.01. Wt. 275 g. From B03-64. Ovoid and flattened, with flat, grooved top. Moderately coarse red fabric turning slightly browner at surface, with 15–20% inclusions. Pitted, worn surface. RBMa. (Local).

428 K1.248. Loom weight. (Pl. 39)
Type R. D. 0.09. Th. 0.03. D. perf. 0.01. Wt. 288 g. From B03-64. Irregular, round, flattened body; flattened edge at top. Moderately fine red fabric with 5–10% inclusions, primarily small-large blue-gray and shiny silvery-gray to pink schist, shiny white or semi-translucent white inclusions; with very common fine silver mica. Surface smoothed; somewhat pitted.

Two curving, shallow grooves at one side, incised before firing. Unknown fabric. (Local/local region?).

429 K1.571. Spindle whorl. (Pl. 39)
Type M1. H. 0.03. D. 0.04. D. perf. 0.01. Wt. 32 g. From B03-61. Moderately coarse, reddish-brown fabric turning dark gray at surface, with 15–20% inclusions. Surface smoothed, somewhat chipped. Slanted, off-center perforation. Breakage around both ends of perforation. RBMa. (Local).

430 K1.435. Spindle whorl. (Pl. 39)
Type M4. H. 0.02. D. 0.02. D. perf. <0.01. Wt. 8 g. From B03-61. Fine, dark gray fabric with fewer than 1% inclusions. Radiating, incised lines around perforation at top. Some breakage around bottom. RBMa, with common mica. (Local).

Plaster

Joins with B605CL.

431 Fragment of painted wall plaster. (Pl. 39)
Published, Abramowitz 1980, 78, no. 181; Coleman 1970, 48, no. F.45. Pieces from B03-40, B03-42, B03-46, B03-52, B03-57, and B03-61. Parallel bands of white, black, and yellow, separated by string marks.

432 Fragment of painted wall plaster. (Pl. 39)
Published, Abramowitz 1980, 78, no. 179; Coleman 1970, 48, no. F.46. Pieces from B03-40, B03-42, B03-46, B03-52, B03-57, and B03-61. Parallel bands of red and yellow, separated by string mark.

433 Fragment of painted wall plaster. (Pl. 39)
Published, Abramowitz 1980, 77, no. 177, pl. 10:b; Coleman 1970, 49, no. F.51, fig. 24. Pieces from B03-40, B03-42, B03-46, B03-52, B03-57, and B03-61. Parallel bands of white, yellow, and red, separated by string marks.

434 Fragment of painted wall plaster. (Pl. 39)
Published, Abramowitz 1980, 78, no. 178; Coleman 1970, 49, no. F.53, fig. 26. Fragments from B03-40, B03-42, B03-46, B03-52, B03-57, and B03-61. Parallel bands of yellow and red, separated by string mark.

435 Fragment of painted wall plaster. (Pl. 40)
Published, Abramowitz 1980, 78, no. 180; Coleman 1970, 49, no. F.52, fig. 25. Pieces from lots B03-40, B03-42, B03-46, B03-52, B03-57, and B03-61. Parallel bands of white, black, and yellow, separated by string marks.

436 Fragment of painted wall plaster. (Pl. 40)
Published, Abramowitz 1980, 67, no. 129, pl. 7:c; Coleman 1970, 50, no. F.47, fig. 27. From B03-46. Left leg of male (red) figure carrying a stone rhyton.

437 Fragment of painted wall plaster. (Pl. 40)
Published, Abramowitz 1980, 67, no. 131, pl. 7:c; Coleman 1970, 51, no. F.48. Fragments from B03-46, B03-52, and B03-57. Curving red beside white.

438 Fragment of painted wall plaster. (Pl. 40)
Published, Abramowitz 1980, 67, no. 132, pl. 7:c; Coleman 1970, 51, no. F.49. Fragments from B03-46, B03-52, and B03-57. Curving red beside white (unpainted).

439 Fragment of painted wall plaster. (Pl. 40)
Published, Abramowitz 1980, 67, no. 133, pl. 7:d; Coleman 1970, 51, no. F.50, figs. 27, 28. From B03-52. Left profile of male figure, showing frontal eye.

B604CL.
Upper part of the destruction deposit over Rooms B.2/B.3 and B.4, probably disturbed by the construction of Wall Q, plowing, and perhaps by erosion downslope. Period VIIb–c, with a few later sherds.

Pottery

3 tins (ca. 51 liters) collected; 3/4 bag (ca. 0.3 tin or 5.1 liters) plus inventoried objects remain. Fifty-seven handleless cups and two tripod legs discarded (Kea Pottery Notebook B, 37). Although most ceramics could date to Period VIIb or earlier, the presence of many plain or Burnished goblets, as well as clear LH IIB types, like an LH IIB Ephyraean jug (**526**) and LH IIB goblets with monochrome interiors and plain exteriors, make it impossible to date this deposit more closely than Period VIIb–c. Later intrusions include at least two LH IIIC deep-bowl fragments from lot B03-20; another sherd in the combined lot seems to be Archaic/Classical Black Gloss, and a large body sherd may be part of a roof tile (Uncatalogued, B-1.69). Many sherds from lots B03-19 and B03-20 joined ceramics from 604CL (B604CL Pottery Notes, 1). Sherds from B03-19 and B03-20 also joined to **207** in B608CL (Notecards, 56), additional fragments of which were found in B608CL and B609CL (B604CL Pottery Notes, 7). Sherds from lot B03-20, which included the space over Room B.1 as well as B.2/B.3, join **173** from the lower part of the Period VIIb destruction deposit in Room B.1. A fragment from **534** was found in B03-61 in the lower part of the destruction deposit in Room B.2/B.3. Uncatalogued local (RBMa) ceramics include a plain, spouted jar, and Painted and Yellow Slipped closed vessels. Many imports are uncatalogued. Two Cycladic White sherds (DVa) are probably earlier. Several fine, open and closed vessels, many with indecipherable decoration in non- or semi-lustrous paint may have been imported from Aegina (DVe), including at least one Red Coated open vessel (DVe). A Melian/Theran Painted bowl (DVa), and sherds from several Melian/Theran (DVa) and Cycladic Painted (including Polychrome, Red and Black) (MxMc, MFVa) open vessels were present. A Lustrous Painted (Monochrome) closed vessel might be from the mainland or Kythera (FSTh). Many plain or Burnished goblets probably were produced on the mainland (FVb–FVe). Red Coated (FVc) open vessels probably derive from the mainland. Uncatalogued Lustrous Painted (FSTb, FSTd, FSTf, FSTj, FSTk, MFVc, FVb, FVc, FVf) vessels include several fine jugs and probably come from both the mainland and Crete. Lustrous Painted, Burnished, and Plain (FVb–FVe) goblets were present, as were fine, Burnished or plain (FVc, FVf) closed vessels, all probably from the mainland.

Local

440 Firebox. (Fig. 43, Pl. 40)
Fragment of capsule with three perforations, attachment to rim, and finished edge for central hole. Moderately coarse, reddish-brown fabric with 10–15% inclusions. Interior blackened. Handmade. Yellow Painted. Exterior, yellow band at join between dome and rim. RBMa.

441 Large basin. (Fig. 43, Pl. 40)
Flat, slightly bulging elliptical rim and part of upper body (two nonjoining fragments). Not possible to estimate rim diameter. Moderately coarse, brittle, dark red fabric with well-defined, thick, gray core and 10–15% inclusions. Handmade. Yellow Slipped. Interior and exterior surface coated with yellow slip. Interior: band at rim, double festoons, two wide horizontal bands, foliate bands, and wide horizontal bands in matt-black paint. RBMa. For similar, see Atkinson et al. 1904, pls. XIX:1, 2; XXX:2–6, 9a–c; Davis 1986, 60, no. AA-90, pl. 33; Barber 2008, 124, no. 541, fig. 27.

442 K.448. Handleless cup. (Pl. 40)
Type 1. 90% preserved; broken at rim. H. 0.04. D. base 0.04. D. rim 0.08. From B03-20. White encrustation near bottom interior. Coarse. Thin, dark-gray core. Wheel-coiled. Yellow Slipped. Coated in and out with pale brown slip. RBMa.

443 K.159. Handleless cup. (Pl. 40)
Type 1. Nearly intact, with a few chips at rim. H. 0.03. D. base 0.03. D. rim 0.08. From B03-36. Wheel-coiled(?). Yellow Slipped. Coated with pale brown slip(?). RBMa, with common mica.

444 K.175. Juglet. (Fig. 44, Pl. 40)
Flat base, globular body, and lower part of neck. H. pres. 0.07. D. base 0.03. From B03-36. Moderately coarse, red fabric with 10–15% inclusions. One side fired to gray. Smoothed surface, now pitted. Coil-built(?). Plain. RBMa.

445 K.176. Squat juglet. (Fig. 44, Pl. 40)
Whole profile preserved, rim and neck chipped. Slightly raised, uneven, flat base and squat globular body. H. 0.08. D. base 0.04. From B03-36. Moderately coarse, reddish-brown fabric with 10–15% inclusions. Wiping marks. Surface is pitted. Wheelmade(?). Plain. RBMa, with rare calcareous(?) inclusions.

446 Basin. (Fig. 44, Pl. 40)
Flattened rim, upper body, crescent lug. D. rim est. 0.30(?). Moderately coarse, dark red fabric with dark-gray core and 15–20% inclusions. Wiping marks on exterior surface. Handmade. Plain. RBMa, with rare calcareous(?) inclusions. For similar at Phylakopi, though pattern-painted and without the lug handles, see Barber 2008, 124–125, nos. 538, 544, figs. 27, 28.

447 K.2155. Deep saucer. (Pl. 40)
Solid raised disk base and inner surface of bowl preserved. H. pres. 0.03. D. base 0.04. Moderately coarse, pale reddish-brown fabric with 15–20% inclusions. Base preserves leaf impression.

EBA Red-Brown Semifine to Semicoarse. RBMb, with rare calcareous inclusions.

448 K.2082. Straight-sided cup. (Fig. 44, Pl. 40)
Profile preserved except for handle; restored in plaster. H. 0.09. D. base 0.06. D. rim 0.11. Moderately coarse, reddish-brown fabric turning gray at core, with 15–20% inclusions. Wheelmade. Surface smoothed and blackened in parts (from firing?). Plain. RBMa, with overfired schist.

449 K.697. Handleless cup. (Pl. 40)
Type 1. 80% preserved; broken at rim and base. H. 0.04. D. base 0.04. D. rim est. 0.09. From B03-36. Wheel-coiled. Brown surface discolored to dark red in places, probably due to firing. Plain. RBMa, with common mica.

450 K.421. Handleless cup. (Pl. 40)
Type 1. 60% preserved. H. 0.04. D. base 0.03. D. rim est. 0.08. From B03-20. Coarse. Slightly uneven base. Wheel-coiled(?). Plain. RBMa.

451 K.497. Handleless cup. (Pl. 40)
Type 1. 90% preserved; broken at rim and base. H. 0.04. D. base 0.04. D. 0.08. From B03-20. Wheelmade(?). Plain. RBMa.

452 K.498. Handleless cup. (Pl. 40)
Type 1. Nearly intact, with chips at rim and base. H. 0.04. D. base 0.03. D. rim 0.08. From B03-20. Coarse. Wheelmade(?). Interior surface is red; exterior surface is pale brown. Plain. RBMa.

453 K.446. Handleless cup. (Pl. 40)
Type 1. Nearly intact, with small chips at rim. H. 0.04. D. base 0.03. D. rim 0.08. From B03-20. Thin walls. Wheelmade. Plain. RBMa, with common mica.

454 K.138. Handleless cup. (Pl. 40)
Type 1. 70% preserved. H. 0.03. D. base 0.03. D. rim 0.08. From B03-36. Wheel-coiled(?). Plain. RBMa, with common mica.

455 K.188. Handleless cup. (Pl. 40)
Type 1. 80% preserved, broken at rim. H. 0.04. D. base 0.04. D. rim 0.09. From B03-36. Wheel-coiled(?). Surface eroded. Blackened from fire in most places. Plain. RBMa, with overfired schist.

456 K.139. Handleless cup. (Pl. 40)
Type 1. 80% preserved; broken at rim. H. 0.04. D. base 0.04. D. rim est. 0.09. From B03-36. Wheel-coiled. Plain. RBMa, with common mica.

457 K.180. Handleless cup. (Pl. 40)
Type 1. 80% preserved; broken at rim. H. 0.04. D. base 0.03. D. rim 0.08. From B03-36. Thick base. Fabric is unusually gritty, slightly pinkish, perhaps affected by salt(?). Walls smoothed. Coil-built or wheel-coiled. Plain. RBMa, gritty, pink.

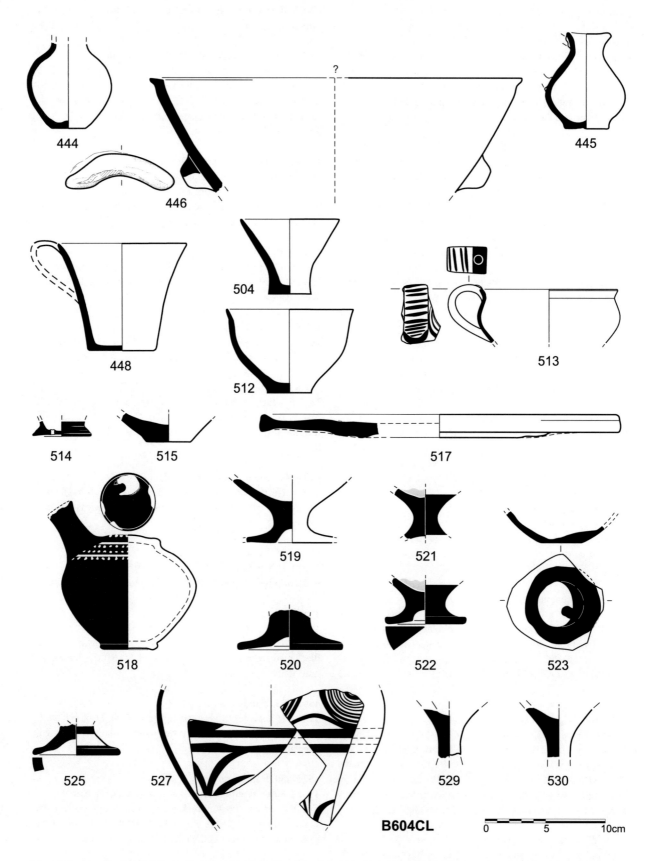

Fig. 44. Pottery from B604CL (**444–446**, **448**, **504**, **512–515**, **517–523**, **525**, **527**, **529**, **530**). Drawings by Lily Bonga (**444**, **445**, **518**), Mary-Jane Schumacher (**446**, **513–515**, **517**, **519–523**, **525**, **527**, **530**), and Aliki Bikaki (**448**, **504**, **512**, **529**).

458 K.134. Handleless cup. (Pl. 40)
Type 1. 90% intact; broken at rim. H. 0.03. D. base 0.04. D. rim 0.08. From B03-36. Surface unsmoothed. Wheel-coiled(?). Plain. RBMa.

459 K.154. Handleless cup. (Pl. 40)
Type 1. 90% preserved, broken at rim. H. 0.04. D. base 0.03. D. rim 0.08. From B03-36. Lopsided. Wheel-coiled. Plain. RBMa, with common mica.

460 K.140. Handleless cup. (Pl. 40)
Type 1. 90% preserved, broken at rim. H. 0.03. D. base 0.03. D. rim 0.08. From B03-36. Moderately fine; not heavy. Wheel-coiled(?). Plain. RBMd.

461 K.167. Handleless cup. (Pl. 40)
Type 1. 90% preserved; broken and chipped at rim. H. 0.04. D. base 0.04. D. rim 0.08. From B03-36. Thick base and walls. Wheel-coiled. Plain. RBMa.

462 K.157. Handleless cup. (Pl. 40)
Type 1. 90% preserved; broken and chipped at rim. H. 0.04. D. base 0.04. D. rim 0.08. From B03-36. Wheel-coiled(?). Plain. RBMa.

463 K.333. Handleless cup.
Type 1. 90% preserved; broken and chipped rim. H. 0.04. D. base 0.03. D. rim 0.08. From B03-36. Coarse. Wheel-coiled. Texture of clay at base suggests cup was too dry when cut from wheel. Discolored to dark pinkish gray in parts, probably as a result of firing. Plain. RBMa.

464 K.143. Handleless cup. (Pl. 40)
Type 1. 90% preserved; broken and chipped rim. H. 0.04. D. base 0.04. D. rim 0.09. From B03-36. Wheel-coiled(?). Part of rim burned. Exterior surface discolored to dark reddish gray. Plain. RBMa.

465 K.169. Handleless cup. (Pl. 41)
Type 1. 90% preserved; broken at rim. H. 0.03. D. base 0.04. D. rim 0.08. From B03-36. Walls smoothed. Wheel-coiled. Plain. RBMa.

466 K.166. Handleless cup. (Pl. 41)
Type 1. 90% preserved; broken at rim. H. 0.03. D. base 0.04. D. rim 0.08. From B03-36. Thick walls. Wheel-coiled. Plain. RBMa.

467 K.182. Handleless cup.
Type 1. 90% preserved; broken at rim. H. 0.04. D. base 0.04. D. rim 0.08. From B03-36. Thick base and walls. Wheel-coiled. Plain. RBMa, with common mica.

468 K.147. Handleless cup. (Pl. 41)
Type 1. 90% preserved; chipped rim, base, and exterior surface. H. 0.03. D. base 0.03. D. rim 0.08. From B03-36. Coarse. Thick base and walls. Uneven base. Wheel-coiled(?). Plain. RBMa.

469 K.206. Handleless cup.
Type 1. Intact, with tiny chip at rim. H. 0.03. D. base 0.04. D. rim 0.07. From B03-36. Wheel-coiled(?). Plain. RBMa, with common mica.

470 K.151. Handleless cup. (Pl. 41)
Type 1. Intact, with tiny chips at rim and base. H. 0.03. D. base 0.04. D. rim 0.08. From B03-36. Lopsided. Wheel-coiled. Plain. RBMa, with common mica.

471 K.171. Handleless cup. (Pl. 41)
Type 1. Intact, with tiny chips at rim. H. 0.04. D. base 0.04. D. rim 0.08. From B03-36. Wheel-coiled. Plain. RBMa.

472 K.163. Handleless cup.
Type 1. Intact, with tiny chips at rim. H. 0.04. D. base 0.03. D. rim 0.08. From B03-36. Thick walls. Wheel-coiled. Plain. RBMa.

473 K.178. Handleless cup. (Pl. 41)
Type 1. Intact, with tiny chips at rim. H. 0.04. D. base 0.04. D. rim 0.08. From B03-36. Walls smoothed. Wheel-coiled(?). Plain. RBMa, with common mica.

474 K.190. Handleless cup.
Type 1. Intact, with tiny chips at rim. H. 0.04. D. base 0.04. D. rim 0.09. From B03-36. Coarse. Wheel-coiled(?). Plain. RBMa, with common mica.

475 K.165. Handleless cup. (Pl. 41)
Type 1. Intact, with tiny chips at rim. H. 0.04. D. base 0.03. D. rim 0.09. From B03-36. Very thin walls. Wheel-coiled. Discolored to gray around parts of rim (burned?). Plain. RBMa.

476 K.267. Handleless cup.
Type 1. Intact. H. 0.03. D. base 0.04. D. rim 0.07. From B03-36. Thick walls and base. Wheel-coiled(?). Plain. RBMa, with common mica.

477 K.195. Handleless cup.
Type 1. Intact. H. 0.03. D. base 0.04. D. rim 0.09. From B03-36. Thin walls, smoothed. Fabric is red in interior and pale brown at exterior. Wheelmade(?). Plain. RBMa, with common mica.

478 K.155. Handleless cup. (Pl. 41)
Type 1. Intact. H. 0.03. D. base 0.04. D. rim 0.07. From B03-36. Wheel-coiled(?). Plain. RBMa, with common mica.

479 K.152. Handleless cup. (Pl. 41)
Type 1. Intact. H. 0.04. D. base 0.03. D. rim 0.08. From B03-36. Lopsided. Wheel-coiled. Plain. RBMa, with common mica.

480 K.173. Handleless cup.
Type 1. Intact. H. 0.04. D. base 0.04. D. rim 0.09. From B03-36. Lopsided. Wheel-coiled. Plain. RBMa, with common mica.

481 K.189. Handleless cup.
Type 1. Intact. H. 0.04. D. base 0.04. D. rim 0.09. From B03-36. Wheel-coiled(?). Plain. RBMa, with common mica.

482 K.181. Handleless cup.
Type 1. Intact. H. 0.04. D. base 0.04. D. rim 0.09. From B03-36. Coarse. Wheel-coiled(?). Plain. RBMa.

483 K.202. Handleless cup.
Type 1. Intact. H. 0.04. D. base 0.04. D. rim 0.08. From B03-36. Walls smoothed. Wheel-coiled. Plain. RBMa, with common mica.

484 K.164. Handleless cup.
Type 1. Nearly intact with a tiny chip at rim. H. 0.04. D. base 0.03. D. rim 0.08. From B03-36. Thick walls and base. Wheel-coiled. Plain. RBMa.

485 K.158. Handleless cup. (Pl. 41)
Type 1. Nearly intact, with a few small chips at rim. H. 0.04. D. base 0.04. D. 0.08. From B03-36. Lopsided. Wheel-coiled. Plain. RBMa, with common mica.

486 K.162. Handleless cup.
Type 1. Nearly intact, with a tiny chip at rim. H. 0.04. D. base 0.03. D. rim 0.08. From B03-36. Wheel-coiled. Plain. RBMa, with common mica.

487 K.137. Handleless cup. (Pl. 41)
Type 1. Nearly intact, with chips at rim. H. 0.04. D. base 0.03. D. 0.08. From B03-36. Wheel-coiled(?). Half of body and all of rim burned. Plain. RBMa.

488 K.185. Handleless cup.
Type 1. Nearly intact, with small chips at rim. H. 0.03. D. base 0.03. D. rim 0.09. From B03-36. Wheel-coiled. Plain. RBMa, with common mica.

489 K.201. Handleless cup.
Type 1. Nearly intact, with small chips at rim. H. 0.04. D. base 0.03. D. rim 0.08. From B03-36. Wheel-coiled(?). Plain. RBMa, with common mica.

490 K.136. Handleless cup.
Type 1. Nearly intact, with small chips at rim. H. 0.04. D. base 0.03. D. rim 0.08. From B03-36. Coarse. Uneven base. Wheel-coiled(?). Plain. RBMa.

491 K.193. Handleless cup.
Type 1. Nearly intact, with small chips at rim. H. 0.04. D. base 0.04. D. rim 0.08. From B03-36. Coarse. Wheel-coiled(?). Plain. RBMa.

492 K.672. Handleless cup. (Pl. 41)
Type 1. 90% preserved; broken at rim. H. 0.04. D. base 0.03. D. rim 0.08. From B03-43. Wheelmade. Surfaces unsmoothed. Plain. RBMa.

493 K.795. Handleless cup.
Type 1. 90% preserved; broken rim and chipped base. H. 0.04. D. base 0.04. D. rim 0.07. From B03-43. Wheel-coiled. Plain. RBMa, with common mica.

494 K.135. Handleless cup. (Pl. 41)
Type 1. 90% preserved, broken at rim. H. 0.03. D. base 0.04. D. rim 0.07. From B03-36. Lopsided. Thin walls. Wheel-coiled(?). Unevenly blackened in and out. Plain. RBMa.

495 K.661. Handleless cup. (Pl. 41)
Type 1. 90% preserved; broken at rim. H. 0.04. D. base 0.03. D. rim est. 0.08. From B03-44. Wheel-coiled(?). Surface crumbling, perhaps from action of salt. One side discolored to dark gray. Plain. RBMa.

496 K.807. Handleless cup.
Type 1. 90% preserved; broken rim and chipped base. H. 0.04. D. base 0.04. D. rim 0.084. From B03-44. Wheelmade(?). Exterior encrusted with salt. Plain. RBMa.

497 K.845. Handleless cup.
Type 1. Intact, with tiny chips at rim. H. 0.04. D. base 0.04. D. rim 0.08. From B03-44. Wheel-coiled. Plain. RBMa.

498 K.677. Handleless cup.
Type 1. Intact. H. 0.03. D. base 0.04. D. rim 0.09. From B03-44. Wheel-coiled(?). Plain. RBMa.

499 K.796. Handleless cup.
Type 1. Nearly intact, with small chips at rim and base. H. 0.03. D. base 0.04. D. rim 0.08. From B03-44. Thick base and walls. Wheel-coiled. Plain. RBMa.

500 K.673. Handleless cup.
Type 1. Nearly intact, with small chips at rim. H. 0.04. D. base 0.03. D. rim 0.08. From B03-44. Wheel-coiled(?). Plain. RBMa.

501 K.453. Handleless cup. (Pl. 41)
Type 1(?). 70% preserved; upper body missing. H. pres. 0.04. D. base 0.04. D. pres. max. 0.09. From B03-20. Wheel-coiled. Plain. RBMa.

502 K.168. Handleless cup. (Pl. 41)
Type 3. 90% preserved; broken and chipped at rim. H. 0.07. D. base 0.04. D. rim 0.10. From B03-36. Wheel-coiled. Plain. RBMa, with common mica.

503 K.261. Handleless cup.
Type 3. 90% preserved; broken at rim, with chipped surface. H. 0.07. D. base 0.04. D. rim 0.09. From B03-36. Coarse. Lopsided. Wheel-coiled. Discolored to dark gray on one side, from firing(?). Plain. RBMa.

504 K.174. Handleless cup. (Fig. 44)
Type 3. 90% preserved; broken at rim. H. 0.06. D. base 0.04. D. rim 0.08. From B03-36. Uneven base. Wheel-coiled(?). Plain. RBMa.

505 K.186. Handleless cup.
Type 3. 90% preserved; broken at rim. H. 0.07. D. base 0.04. D. rim 0.09. From B03-36. Walls smoothed. Wheel-coiled(?). Part of interior discolored to dark red, from firing(?). Plain. RBMd.

506 K.179. Handleless cup.
Type 3. Nearly intact, with chips at rim and base. H. 0.07. D. base 0.04. D. rim 0.09. From B03-36. Brittle, sandy fabric. Wheel-coiled(?). Dark discoloration in and out. Plain. RBMa, sandy texture.

507 K.209. Handleless cup.
Type 3. Nearly intact, with small chips at rim. H. 0.06. D. base 0.03. D. rim 0.08. From B03-36. Coarse. Uneven walls. Base uneven. Wheel-coiled(?). Plain. RBMa.

508 K.172. Handleless cup.
Type 3. Nearly intact, with small chips at rim. H. 0.07. D. base 0.04. D. rim 0.09. From B03-36. Wheel-coiled. Surface crumbly and encrusted by salt. Plain. RBMa.

509 K.265. Handleless cup.
Type 3. Nearly intact, with small chips at rim. H. 0.07. D. base 0.04. D. rim 0.10. From B03-36. Wheel-coiled(?). Plain. RBMa, with common mica.

510 K.160. Handleless cup.
Type 3. 80% preserved; broken at rim. H. 0.07. D. base 0.04. D. rim 0.09. From B03-36. Exterior surface eroded. Wheel-coiled(?). Surface pale brown, from firing(?). Plain. RBMd.

511 K.765. Handleless cup.
Type 3. 90% preserved; broken at rim and base. H. 0.06. D. base 0.04. D. rim 0.10. From B03-43. Thick base and walls. Wheel-coiled. Blackened in many places, in and out, especially upper body. Plain. RBMa.

512 K.670. Handleless cup. (Fig. 44, Pl. 41)
Type 4 (which also might be called an ogival cup). 80% preserved; broken at rim. H. 0.07. D. base 0.04. D. rim est. 0.11. From B03-44. Wheel-coiled. Surface flaking and crumbling, probably from action of salt. Plain. RBMa.

Cyclades

513 Rounded cup. (Fig. 44, Pl. 41)
One sherd from upper body with strap handle. Fine, sandy, grayish-tan fabric turning orange at surface, with 1–5% inclusions. Wheelmade. Yellow Slipped. Interior and exterior coated with yellow slip(?). Interior and exterior rim band(?) in lustrous black paint. Barred handle, outlined by semicircular band at shoulder attachment; spiral on body in same paint. Flat plastic disk applied at upper handle attachment. MxMc.

514 Cup-rhyton. (Fig. 44, Pl. 41)
Perforated, conical, slightly concave base with off-center perforation, pierced from exterior while clay was wet. H. pres. 0.01. D. base 0.05. D. perf. <0.01. Fine, dusty, pale orange-brown fabric with 1–5% inclusions. Very thin walls and regular, interior wiping marks. Wheelmade(?). Red Coated(?). Exterior: coated with lustrous red paint, now nearly entirely gone. MxMa/MxMc.

515 Open(?) vessel. (Fig. 44, Pl. 41)
Extremely thick base and lower body. H. pres. 0.02. D. base 0.04. Fine, dusty, pale orange fabric with 1–5% inclusions. Wheel-coiled(?). Plain. MxMc, compact. PFG 3E (Attica/Euboea/Cyclades).

516 K.779. Handleless cup.
Type 1. Nearly intact, with small chips at rim and base. H. 0.04. D. base 0.04. D. rim 0.08. From B03-44. Wheel-coiled. Plain. DVb. (Melos/Thera).

517 Baking tray. (Fig. 44, Pl. 41)
Published, Gorogianni, Abell, and Hilditch 2017, 70, no. 36. Bulging rim and flat body. Much of the surface is eroded. D. rim est. 0.33. Coarse, pale orange-brown fabric with blue-gray core and 10–15% inclusions. Plain. DVa, with unusual core. (Melos/Thera).

Naxos(?)

518 K.177. Askos. (Fig. 44, Pl. 41)
Almost completely preserved. Missing small fragments of spout, base, and top. Slightly raised base; top closed with flat, thin (0.003) disk. Short narrow spout with slightly flaring end. H. without spout 0.10. D. base 0.05. From B03-36. Moderately coarse, pale orange fabric with 10–15% inclusions. Coil-built or wheel-coiled. Surface pitted. Painted. White band around disk at top; below band are two rows of white dots and a white band, very faded. CSWe, pale, with possible metamorphic inclusions.

Attica(?)

519 Goblet. (Fig. 44, Pl. 41)
Foot with high, articulated dome, stem, and part of lower body. H. pres. 0.05. H. stem 0.02. Fine, dusty red fabric with gray core and 5–10% inclusions. Wheelmade. Burnished. MFVc.

520 Goblet. (Fig. 44, Pl. 41)
Foot with shallow dome, stem, and bottom surface of bowl. H. pres. 0.03. D. base 0.09. H. stem 0.02. Moderately fine, hard-fired red-orange fabric with purple-tinged interior and 1–5% inclusions. Wheelmade. Surface degraded by salt. Red Coated. Underside of foot plain; interior and exterior coated with flaking red slip. MFVc.

521 Goblet. (Fig. 44, Pl. 41)
Foot, narrow stem, lower body. H. pres. 0.04. Fine, somewhat dusty, red fabric with fewer than 1% inclusions. Voids are more common at join between stem and bowl. Wheelmade. Red Coated. Interior and exterior coated with lustrous red slip. MFVc.

522 Goblet. (Fig. 44, Pl. 41)
Foot with high, articulated dome, thick stem, and lower body. H. pres. 0.04. D. base est. 0.07. Fine, dusty, orange-red fabric with fewer than 1% inclusions. Wheelmade. Red Coated. Interior, exterior, and underside of foot coated with flaking, red slip. MFVc.

Mainland

523 Askos. (Fig. 44, Pl. 41)
Flat base and globular body; thick-walled on one side and thin-walled on the other. H. pres. 0.05. D. base 0.04. Fine, pale orange-pink fabric with pale-gray core and fewer than 1% inclusions. Interior uneven. Handmade. Lustrous Painted. Band above base and band around lower body in semi-lustrous dark brown-black paint. FVe. PFG 14D (Central Greece?).

524 Flaring cup-rhyton(?). (Pl. 41)
Body. Fine, dusty, pale yellow fabric with fewer than 1% inclusions. Wheel-coiled. Lustrous Painted. Interior: plain. Exterior: closely-spaced reeds (FM 16) above wavy band in lustrous black. FVb.

525 Goblet. (Fig. 44, Pl. 41)
Foot with shallow dome, stem, and bottom surface of bowl. H. pres. 0.03. D. base 0.08. Fine, dusty, pale green fabric with pale, purplish-gray core and 1–5% inclusions. Wheelmade. Lustrous Painted. Band around outer edge of foot in flaking lustrous black; band overlaps to underside of foot. Band around stem and monochrome-painted interior in same paint. FVb.

526 Jug. (Pl. 41)
Body with metallic handle attachment. Fine, hard-fired, purplish-tan fabric with pinkish-red exterior margin and fewer than 1% inclusions. Wheel-coiled(?). Lustrous Painted. Exterior decorated with flaking, lustrous red paint; burnished. Solidly painted over and around handle attachment; three wavy lines descend from handle. Probably LH IIB, Ephyraean style. FVf.

527 Jug(?). (Fig. 44, Pl. 41)
Body (three nonjoining fragments). Fine, hard-fired, pink fabric with pale brown margins and fewer than 1% inclusions. Wheelmade. Lustrous Painted. Lower register, reeds (FM 16) in lustrous black paint; upper register, framed spirals (FM 46) in same paint. Registers separated by two parallel bands. Exterior burnished. FVc. For similar, see Mountjoy 1986, 28–29, fig. 26:1.

528 Paneled cup. (Pl. 41)
One fragment mended from three sherds, preserving part of foot, stem, and lower body. H. pres. 0.05. D. base est. 0.05(?). Fine, hard-fired, pink fabric with blue-gray core and fewer than 1% inclusions. Manufacture method unclear. Matt Painted. Surface burnished(?), causing paint to look semi-lustrous. Band around edge of foot in dark-brown paint. Band overlaps to underside of foot. Uneven wide band around lower body, below radiating vertical and slanting lines. One isolated vertical band. Although the shape is more typical of mainland rather than Cycladic paneled cups, the decoration is not paralleled on the mainland (Davis 1978; Rutter and Lindblom forthcoming). FVe.

529 Goblet. (Fig. 44, Pl. 41)
Narrow stem and lower body. H. 0.04. Moderately fine, somewhat dusty, red fabric with fewer than 1% inclusions. Wheelmade. Slipped. Exterior and interior coated with faded, pale, yellow-gray slip; burnished. FVd.

530 Goblet. (Fig. 44, Pl. 41)
Narrow stem and lower body. H. pres. 0.04. Fine, dusty, pinkish-orange fabric with no inclusions. Wheelmade. Slipped(?). Interior and exterior surface coated with faded, yellow slip(?). Burnished, but now worn. FVc.

531 Goblet or cup. (Fig. 45, Pl. 41)
One short, sharply everted rim fragment. H. 0.02. D. rim est. 0.10. Fine, hard-fired, pink fabric with fewer than 1% inclusions. Wheelmade. Slipped. Coated with yellow slip. FVd.

532 Angular kylix(?). (Fig. 45, Pl. 41)
FS 267(?). One rim fragment. H. 0.03. D. rim est. 0.11. Fine, hard-fired orange-brown fabric with fewer than 1% inclusions. Wheelmade. Burnished. FVd. For similar profile, see Rutter 2020, 681–682, no. G120, fig. 9.61.

Mainland/Kythera

533 Vapheio cup. (Fig. 45, Pl. 41)
Mended from two sherds. Rim, upper body, and shallow midrib. D. rim est. 0.09. Fine, overfired pale brown fabric turning greenish at surface, with 1–5% inclusions. Interior preserves very slight hollow behind midrib. Wheel-coiled(?). Lustrous Painted. Interior and exterior: rim band in lustrous black. Exterior: band along midrib. Ripple pattern along upper and lower body. FSTh.

Crete

534 K.2091. Bell cup. (Fig. 45, Pl. 41)
Published, J. L. Caskey 1972, 396, no. H18, pl. 95. Full profile; slightly over half of cup preserved. Restored with plaster. H. 0.07. D. base 0.04. D. rim rest. 0.08. Fine, hard-fired, pale brown fabric with fewer than 1% inclusions. Wheel-coiled. Lustrous Painted. Interior: monochrome, lustrous reddish-brown, now flaking. Exterior: two horizontal bands around base and lower body in same paint. Above bands are repeating crocuses (six preserved, FM 10). Handle: monochrome. Exterior probably burnished. FSTj. Similar to Cummer and Schofield 1984, 116, 126–127, no. 1564, pls. 80:s, 85.

535 Bell cup. (Fig. 45, Pl. 41)
Rim and part of upper body. D. rim est. 0.09. Fine, dusty fabric with pink core and pale yellow exterior margin, with fewer than 1% inclusions. Wheelmade. Lustrous Painted. Interior: coated with lustrous orange paint, turning dark brown at rim. Exterior: tricurved rock pattern (FM 33) alternating with crocuses in same paint. FSTk. The decoration is very similar to rounded and bell cups from House A, as well as from Deposit ξ at Kastri on Kythera (Coldstream and Huxley 1972, 140–142, nos. ξ-23, 78, 79, pl. 38; Cummer and Schofield 1984, 57, 126, nos. 182, 1562, pls. 48, 86).

536 Bell cup. (Fig. 45, Pl. 41)
Rim and upper body. D. rim est. 0.10. Possibly the same vessel as **340**. Fine, hard-fired, pale pinkish-brown fabric with fewer than 1% inclusions. Wheelmade. Lustrous Painted. Interior: monochrome, lustrous black with darker rim band. Exterior:

solid festoons in black at rim. Below festoons are a row of dots, a row of irises, and intersecting, wavy lines. Surface probably burnished. FSTj.

Crete/Mainland(?)

537 Jar. (Pl. 41)
Body. Moderately fine, hard-fired fabric with bright pink core and pale brown margins, with 1–5% inclusions. Wheel-coiled or assembled from wheelmade sections(?). Lustrous Painted. Interior: plain. Exterior: two vertical bands with hatched loops (FM 63) on either side in lustrous black; burnished. A Palace Style jar decorated with hatched loops was discarded from B608CL (above); it is possible that this might be part of the same vessel, although it is impossible to verify that. FSTd. PFG 7Hv (Argolid/Corinthia?).

538 Large, open vessel (rhyton?). (Pl. 41)
Body. Fine, dusty, pale pink fabric with fewer than 1% inclusions. Wheelmade. Lustrous Painted. Interior: monochrome, lustrous black, now faded. Exterior: fugitive, closely-spaced reeds. FSTj.

539 K.2101. Rounded cup. (Fig. 45, Pl. 42)
Approximately 80% preserved, including full profile except strap handle; restored in plaster. H. 0.08. D. base 0.05. D. rim rest. 0.12–0.13. Fine, pink fabric with fewer than 1% inclusions. Wheel-coiled(?). Body deformed to elliptical by application of handle. Lustrous Painted. Interior: coated in lustrous red to dark-brown paint, now flaking. Exterior: band around base that overlaps unevenly to bottom in same paint; two horizontal bands around lower body. Shoulder to lower body, alternating trefoil and tricurved rock pattern (FM 33). Band around base of rim, short oblique blobs around rim. Surface burnished. FSTk. For similar at Kastri on Kythera, see Coldstream and Huxley 1972, no. ξ-19.

540 Bowl. (Fig. 45, Pl. 42)
Slightly flaring rim. D. rim est. 0.08. Wheelmade. Lustrous Painted. Interior: coated with lustrous reddish-orange paint, now flaking. Exterior: band at rim; ripple pattern along upper body in same paint. FSTj.

541 Handleless cup. (Pl. 42)
Type 1. 60% preserved, including entire profile. H. 0.03. D. rim est. 0.08. D. base 0.04. Moderately fine, hard-fired pink fabric with yellow margins and 5–10% inclusions. Interior: uneven and disassociating texture suggests clay was too dry while forming. Very light. Wheel-coiled. Plain. FSTb, fine.

542 Handleless cup. (Pl. 42)
Type 1. Rim fragment. D. rim est. 0.10. Fine, pale orange-brown fabric with fewer than 1% inclusions. Wheel-coiled. Plain. FSTb, fine.

Unknown

543 K.266. Handleless cup.
H. 0.03. D. base 0.03. D. rim 0.07. From B03-36. Lost.

Stone

544 K1.31. Curved object. (Pl. 42)
W. 0.08–0.09. Th. 0.05. L. pres. 0.16. Wt. 814 g. From B03-19. White marble (Rapp). One side broken away; both edges missing. Surface is uneven. Curved perforation at one end; at other, tapering channel runs toward broken edge.

545 K1.70. Pounder/grinder. (Pl. 42)
Intact. H. 0.07. D. 0.07. Wt. 418 g. From B03-36. Green-gray stone (Rapp). Some chips, one vertical crack. Slightly hollowed on top, worn on bottom.

546 K1.56. Drill-core. (Pl. 42)
H. pres. 0.04. D. 0.08. Wt. 464 g. From B03-36. Banded blue, gray, and white marble (Rapp). Half(?)-preserved. Chipped; abraded. One end rounded; one broken.

547 K1.113. Pestle. (Pl. 42)
H. 0.06. D. 0.04. Wt. 146 g. From B03-44. Cylindrical, red-purple stone (Rapp). Intact. Some encrustation. Shallow depression at one end, deep at other. Edges rounded.

Uninventoried:
B03-20: obsidian blade fragments (B-1.14, B-1.21).
B03-36: stone basin fragment (B-1.45).

Plaster

Uninventoried painted wall-plaster fragments in lots B03-36 and B03-43.

B605CL.
Upper part of Period VII destruction deposit, northeast of Wall Q. Probably disturbed by construction of Wall Q and erosion downslope. Mixed VI–VIII.

Pottery

2 bags collected; 0.2 bag remains. 95% coarse, 10 handleless cup bases discarded, as were one Gray Minyan and several Matt Painted sherds (Kea Pottery Notebook B, 43). Uncatalogued local (RBMa) ceramics include a Yellow Slipped bell cup and rounded(?) cup; a Burnished, fine, open vessel; and a Painted collar-neck jar. Uncatalogued imports include Melian/Theran Painted open and closed vessels (DVa) and a Cycladic Painted (Polychrome, Red and Black) cup/bowl (MxMa), an Aeginetan(?) Painted (or Bichrome) (DVe) open vessel, Lustrous and Non-Lustrous Painted (FSTa, FSTj, FSTj/FVf, FSTh, FVb, FVc, FVf) closed vessels and alabastra, a Lustrous Painted Vapheio cup (FSTj), a Burnished goblet (FVc). At least two LH IIIA kylikes or goblets were present (FVb).

Local

548 K.194. Handleless cup. (Pl. 42)
Type 1. 90% preserved, broken at rim. H. 0.03. D. base 0.04. D. rim 0.08. From B03-40. Lopsided. Wheel-coiled(?). Plain. RBMa.

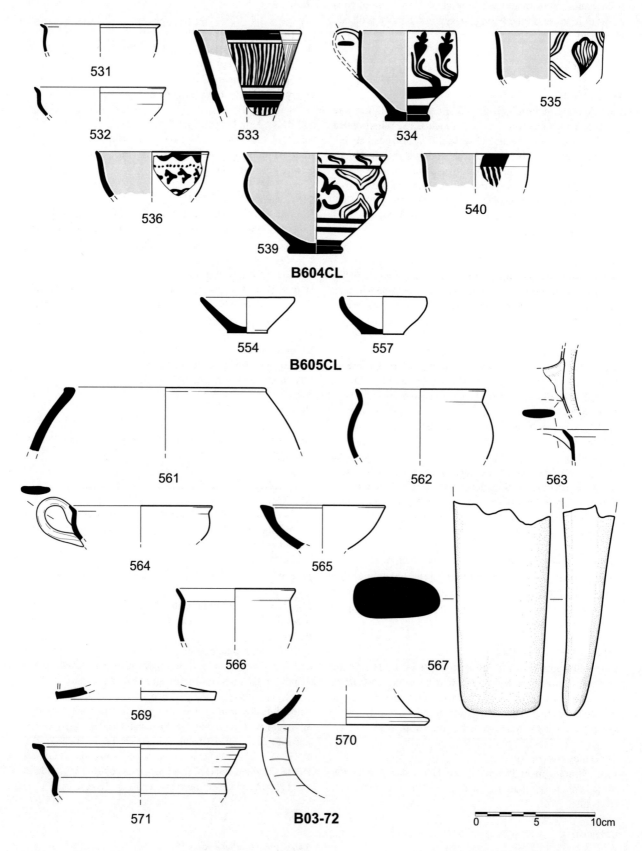

Fig. 45. Pottery from B604CL (**531–536, 539, 540**), B605CL (**554, 557**), and B03-72 (**561–567, 569–571**). Drawings by Mary-Jane Schumacher (**531–533, 536, 540, 561–567, 569, 571**), Aliki Bikaki (**534, 535, 539, 554, 557**), and Lily Bonga (**570**).

549 K.187. Handleless cup. (Pl. 42)
Type 1. 90% preserved; broken and chipped at rim. H. 0.05. D. base 0.04. D. rim 0.09. From B03-40. Wheel-coiled. Half discolored to dark purple. Much of rim blackened. Plain. RBMa.

550 K.161. Handleless cup.
Type 1. 90% preserved; broken at rim. H. 0.03. D. base 0.04. D. rim 0.08. From B03-40. Thick base. Wheel-coiled(?). One side discolored to purple. Plain. RBMa.

551 K.153. Handleless cup.
Type 1. 90% preserved; broken at rim. H. 0.04. D. base 0.04. D. rim 0.09. From B03-40. Wheel-coiled. Surface almost entirely blackened. Plain. RBMa.

552 K.170. Handleless cup. (Pl. 42)
Type 1. Intact, tiny chips at rim. H. 0.03. D. base 0.04. D. rim 0.09. From B03-40. Wheel-coiled(?). Plain. RBMa.

553 K.203. Handleless cup. (Pl. 42)
Type 1. Intact, with tiny chips at rim. H. 0.04. D. base 0.04. D. rim 0.08. From B03-40. Wheel-coiled(?). Plain. RBMa.

554 K.205. Handleless cup. (Fig. 45, Pl. 42)
Type 1. Intact. H. 0.03. D. base 0.03. D. rim 0.08. From B03-40. Thin walls. Wheelmade(?). Parts of rim blackened. Plain. RBMa, with common mica.

555 K.183. Handleless cup. (Pl. 42)
Type 1. Nearly intact, with chip at rim. H. 0.04. D. base 0.04. D. rim 0.07. From B03-40. Wheel-coiled(?). Plain. RBMd.

Local(?)

556 K.150. Handleless cup.
Type 3. 90% preserved; broken at rim. H. 0.07. D. base 0.03. D. rim 0.09. From B03-40. Dark-gray core. Wheel-coiled. Lower body discolored to dark purple-black. Plain. RBMc.

Melos/Thera

557 K.790. Handleless cup. (Fig. 45, Pl. 42)
Type 1. Intact, with small chips at base. H. 0.03. D. base 0.04. D. rim 0.07. From B03-40. Slightly uneven base. Wheel-coiled(?). Plain. DVb.

Unknown

558 K.268. Handleless cup.
H. 0.03. D. base 0.04. D. rim 0.07. From B03-40. Lost.

Stone

559 K1.50. Core. (Pl. 42)
H. pres. 0.03. D. 0.04. Wt. 137 g. From B03-40. Cylindrical, pale to dark gray, banded, marble (Rapp). Intact, chipped, encrusted.

Uninventoried:
B03-40: obsidian fragments (B-1.97, B-1.109).

Plaster

Joins with wall-plaster fragments from B606CL.

ROOM B.4

Room B.4 was called the "kitchen" during excavation. It is bounded by Walls O, H, P/T, and J (Figs. 7, 13, 14:c, 18:b, 23, 24; Pl. 19:a). In upper strata, particularly of the Period VIIb destruction deposit, the area of Room B.4 was excavated as part of Room B.2/B.3. All excavation units related to these upper levels have been described above. Room B.2/B.3 is so named because it was an independent architectural unit in the last phase of the house. B.4 has not been added (i.e., "B.2/B.3/B.4") since it was always a room separated from the rest of the house by Wall P/T. A summary of deposits is presented in Table 2.5.

EARLY BRONZE AGE

Walls AD and AE and Associated Destruction Debris

The earliest architectural features below LBA Room B.4 were Walls AD and AE (Figs. 7, 13, 14:c, 19; Kea Excavation Notebook III, 148, 151). Wall AD, perpendicular to Wall AE, extended northward beneath LBA Wall T into Room B.3 (Fig. 19; Pl. 4:b). LBA Wall O was built over Wall AE; both Walls AD and AE were covered by MBA Surface i (below).

Excavation did not reach the foundations of either wall, nor was any contemporary use surface found. The two walls were enveloped in a stratum of EBA destruction debris, which was excavated in units B03-73, B03-74, and B03-250. This stratum was comparable in its character to that of EBA destruction debris found elsewhere below House B (above). A concentration of stones was found near Wall T at an elevation of +0.20 m above sea level (Kea Excavation Notebook III, 84). Ceramics from excavation units B03-73 and B03-74 were combined into B602CL, along with ceramics from all other areas of EBA destruction debris below House B; everything from unit B03-250 was discarded.

MIDDLE BRONZE AGE

Surface i

Above the EBA destruction deposit was Surface i, composed of packed, red, clayey soil (Kea Excavation Notebook III, 84); it was excavated in units B03-72 and B03-73. Ceramics from B03-73, from Surface i and the stratum below it, were combined into B602CL. Pottery from unit B03-72, from Surface i and the stratum just above it, remained uncombined. Pottery from unit B03-72 and from combined lot B603CL made up J. C. Overbeck's Group CP (1989a, 174).

Pottery from both B602CL (above) and B03-72 was rather mixed. Ceramics from B602CL dated mostly to Period III, with some MBA and LBA sherds as well; pottery from B03-72 dated to Periods IV and V, with a few LBA sherds.

The surface probably was created through the disintegration of mudbricks collapsed from the Period III structure(s) of which Walls AD and AE were a part. The top of this stratum was probably at ground level when the area was reoccupied in Period IV, given the presence of MBA sherds. Immediately above Surface i was a stratum that contained bone and flecks of carbonized material (Kea Excavation Notebook III, 84). It was excavated in unit B03-72, together with the upper part of Surface i. The stratum cannot be clearly associated with any architectural features. Given the presence of mainly late Period IV and Period V ceramics, the stratum seems to represent accumulated debris from MBA activity in the area; LBA construction in the area probably disturbed parts of this deposit, resulting in the presence of a few LBA sherds in the lot.

The Wall H foundation extends into Room B.4 from Rooms B.1–B.3 (Fig. 21), but there is no evidence from Room B.4 that can clarify its original construction date.

LATE BRONZE AGE

Walls H, T, J, and O

A foundation trench for Wall O cut through the Period IV accumulation (Kea Excavation Notebook III, 84). The foundation trench was excavated along with the Period IV accumulation in unit B03-72; the mixing of two contexts explains the presence of some Period VII sherds among the primarily Period IV ceramics of the lot (Kea Pottery Notebook B, 23).

Wall T is bonded with Wall J; Wall O abutted Wall H and was built partially on the Wall H foundation (Kea Excavation Notebook III, 145; Figs. 23, 24). These walls must have been constructed at the same time as Walls H, I, and J, during the third phase of House B. Wall P was built above Wall T (at ca. +1.00 m above sea level), but, because it cannot be linked to any use strata, its precise date of construction is impossible to determine (above).

TABLE 2.5. ROOM B.4 DEPOSIT SUMMARY

Deposit:	Period III Destruction Deposit
Contemporary Features:	Walls AD and AE
Date of Deposit Above:	MBA
Date of Deposit:	Probably Period III
Date of Deposit Below:	Not excavated
Lots/Combined Lots:	B602CL (partial)
Catalogue Numbers:	**9–28** (above)

Deposit:	Surface i
Contemporary Features:	None
Date of Deposit Above:	Period VII
Date of Deposit:	Probably MBA
Date of Deposit Below:	Period III
Lots/Combined Lots:	B03-72 (partial), B602CL (partial)
Catalogue Numbers:	**560–574** (includes also Wall O foundation trench)

Deposit:	Wall O Foundation Trench
Contemporary Features:	None
Date of Deposit Above:	Period VII
Date of Deposit:	Period VII
Date of Deposit Below:	Probably MBA
Lots/Combined Lots:	B03-72 (partial)
Catalogue Numbers:	**560–574** (includes also Surface i) (above)

Deposit:	Carbon-Rich Stratum (House B: Third or Fourth Phase)
Contemporary Features:	Walls O, T
Date of Deposit Above:	Period VIIb
Date of Deposit:	Period VIIb
Date of Deposit Below:	Period VII
Lots/Combined Lots:	B03-70
Catalogue Numbers:	**575–593**

Deposit:	Period VIIb Destruction Deposit (lower)
Contemporary Features:	Walls O, P
Date of Deposit Above:	Period VIIb, some Period VIIc–VIII and Archaic contamination
Date of Deposit:	Period VIIb
Date of Deposit Below:	Period VIIb
Lots/Combined Lots:	B606CL (partial) (includes also Room B.2/B.3)
Catalogue Numbers:	**344–384, 389–439** (above)

TABLE 2.5. (CONT.)

Deposit:	Compact Lens in Period VIIb Destruction Deposit
Contemporary Features:	Period VIIb destruction deposit
Date of Deposit Above:	Period VIIb
Date of Deposit:	Period VIIb
Date of Deposit Below:	Period VIIb
Lots/Combined Lots:	B03-50, B03-71a, B606CL (partial)
Catalogue Numbers:	**594–600**
Deposit:	Period VIIb Destruction Deposit (upper)
Contemporary Features:	Walls O, P
Date of Deposit Above:	Archaic
Date of Deposit:	Period VIIb, some Period VIIc–VIII and Archaic contamination
Date of Deposit Below:	Period VIIb
Lots/Combined Lots:	B604CL (includes also Room B.2/B.3)
Catalogue Numbers:	**440–559** (above)

The Carbon-Rich Stratum

Above the Period IV accumulation was a thick, carbon-rich stratum (0.35 m-thick) that abutted Walls O and T (Fig. 14:c). The compact soil contained carbonized material, ashes, cooking pot fragments, a burned bone awl (**592**; Kea Excavation Notebook III, 80, 82), and three handleless cups (**580–582**). The ceramics, excavated in unit B03-70, date to Period VIIb.

Despite significant evidence for the effects of fire, not all objects in the room were burned (Kea Excavation Notebook III, 82); it is, therefore, probable that the room itself did not burn. Many of the objects were stained to orange or brown in places, perhaps a result of oil or some other substance having been contained in one of the vessels in the room (B03-70 Pottery Notes, 4). No clear floor or use surface was found. The presence of the compact soil, carbonized material, and coarse cooking vessels might suggest that this was a cooking space. However, although the soil was compact and carbon-rich, no hearth was discovered. The lack of a hearth, the absence of a clear floor level, and the small size of the room (ca. 0.75 × 2.50 m) could suggest that it was used as a dumping space, rather than a kitchen. If so, however, it is unclear whether the stratum represented a single dumping episode or accumulated over time. If the former, it is impossible to decide if the dumping occurred when Wall T or when Wall P was the northeastern wall of the room, owing to the ambiguous construction date of Wall P. In at least its upper part, the stratum must have been contemporary with Surfaces a and d, since it lay directly beneath the Period VIIb destruction debris found elsewhere in the house.

Period VIIb Destruction Debris

In most of the room, immediately above the compact, carbon-rich stratum, there was a destruction deposit typical of Period VIIb destruction debris elsewhere in the house. It contained soft soil, a jumble of large stones, and wall-plaster fragments (Kea Excavation Notebook III, 75). Apart from the northwestern part of Room B.4, this destruction debris was apparently more or less uniform between surface levels and unit B03-61. The lower part of the destruction debris was excavated in units B03-46, B03-51, and B03-61; the upper part was excavated in B03-36, B03-37, B03-43, and B03-44. Ceramics from the lower part of the destruction debris were combined into B606CL along with pottery from Room B.2/B.3. Ceramics from the upper part of the destruction debris were combined with pottery from Room B.2/B.3 in B604CL.

In the northwestern part of the room, two unusual lenses were found in the destruction debris. At the corner of Walls O, H, and P, there was a ca. 0.05 m thick lens of compact soil, disintegrated plaster, and coarse vessels, which was excavated in unit B03-71a (Fig. 14:c; Kea Excavation Notebook III, 75, 78). The presence of plaster suggests that this lens is part of the Period VIIb destruction debris, despite its slightly different composition. Above this lens was a second lens containing soft soil, carbonized material, ash, and burnt animal bones, which was excavated in units B03-46 and B03-50 (Fig. 14:c). It was thicker against Wall H and sloped downward from Wall H toward the sea. The lens was surrounded by Period VIIb destruction debris, which suggests that this lens, too, was created during the destruction of the house.

ROOM B.4 CATALOGUE

SURFACE I AND MBA ACCUMULATION

B03-72.
Surface i and MBA accumulation above it; some LBA disturbance, probably from Wall O foundation trench.

Pottery

3/4 tin (ca. 12.8 liters) collected; 1/3 bag (ca. 0.2 tin or 3.4 liters) remains. 95% coarse; 30% discarded in original papsing. Six LBA sherds. Uncatalogued ceramics include an EBA Red-Brown Semifine to Semicoarse deep bowl/open jar (RBMc) and a Yellow Slipped closed vessel (RBMa); Cretan(?) Lustrous and Non-Lustrous Painted vessels, as well as a plain bowl (FSTj); Aeginetan(?) (DVe, DVf) Painted and plain closed vessels; Melian/Theran (DVa, DVc, DVg) plain, Slipped, Painted, and Red Coated vessels, including Cycladic cups and a jug; a central Mainland(?) plain closed vessel (FVf); a Red Coated closed vessel (MFVc), and a Gray Minyan goblet and bowl (FVa). Two handleless cups, a coarse bowl with everted rim, and a pithos rim with applied disk decoration were discarded (Kea Pottery Notebook B, 23).

Local

560 Goblet (Minyanizing). (Pl. 42)
Slightly flaring rim; short, strap handle; and upper body. D. rim est. 0.24. Moderately coarse, dark reddish-brown fabric with 10–15% inclusions. Handmade. Rim slightly distorted by handle attachment. Burnished. Surfaces highly burnished; now worn or eroded in most places. Period IVc or V. RBMa, with shiny, black particles. For similar, see Dietz 1991, 63, 226, figs. 15:83, 71:KA-2; Wohlmayr 2007, 53, fig. 14.

561 Hole-mouthed jar. (Fig. 45, Pl. 42)
Slightly raised, flat rim and rounded, upper body. D. rim est. 0.15. Moderately fine, reddish-brown fabric with 5–10% inclusions. Coil-built(?). Yellow Slipped. Exterior and top of rim coated with thick, yellow slip. RBMa, with common mica.

562 Rounded cup or bowl. (Fig. 45, Pl. 42)
Short, everted rim and rounded body. D. rim est. 0.11. Moderately coarse, dark gray fabric with 10–15% inclusions. Handmade(?). Interior: wiping marks along rim. Plain. RBMa, dark.

Attica/Cyclades(?)

563 Rounded cup. (Fig. 45, Pl. 42)
Short, everted rim; strap handle; and rounded, upper body. Moderately fine, gritty, pinkish-orange fabric with 1–5% inclusions. Very thin walls. Handmade(?). Rim distorted by handle attachment. Plain. Surface darkened, possibly from firing. RBMd, with calcareous(?) inclusions and possible sponge spicules.

Cyclades

564 Rounded cup. (Fig. 45, Pl. 42)
Short, everted rim; strap handle; and globular, upper body. H. pres. 0.03. D. rim est. 0.12(?). Moderately coarse, gritty, pale brown fabric with 5-10% inclusions. Very thin walls. Coil-built or wheel-coiled. Metallicizing lower handle attachment. Plain. MxMa. For similar shape, but with somewhat different handle attachment, see Davis 1986, 34, no. P-6, pl. 25.

565 Handleless cup. (Fig. 45, Pl. 42)
Type 1. Flattened rim and body. H. pres. 0.04. D. rim est. 0.11. Moderately coarse, gritty, orange fabric with 5–10% inclusions. Probable coil joins are visible in interior and exterior; possibly wheel-coiled. Plain(?). Upper body exterior discolored to dark red. Fugitive paint, burning, or action of salt? CSWb. PFG 2C (Local [region]). For shape, see Davis 1986, 71, no. AK-8, pl. 35.

Melos/Thera

566 Rounded cup. (Fig. 45, Pl. 42)
Flaring rim and slightly rounded, upper body. H. pres. 0.04. D. rim est. 0.10. Moderately fine, hard-fired, gritty, pale greenish-yellow fabric with 5–10% inclusions. Extremely thin walls. Wheel-coiled(?). Plain. DVa. Compare with Barber 2007, 198, 208, figs. 6.5:86; 6.8:159, 160.

Aegina(?)

567 Tripod tray. (Fig. 45, Pl. 42)
Published, Gorogianni, Abell, and Hilditch 2017, 69, no. 30. Flattened, ovoid leg. L. pres. 0.18. Moderately coarse, dark orange fabric with 10–15% inclusions. Plain. DVf. PFG 5F (Aegina).

Mainland

568 Goblet. (Pl. 42)
Published, J. C. Overbeck 1989a, 174, no. CP-1a. Everted rim to mid-lower body, with strap handle. D. rim est. 0.20. Fine, hard-fired, gray fabric with fewer than 1% inclusions. Wheel-coiled. Slightly distorted by handle attachment. Gray Minyan. Two horizontal shallow narrow grooves, at level of handle attachment. FVa. Profile similar to Davis 1986, 68, nos. E-8, AI-19.

569 Goblet. (Fig. 45, Pl. 42)
Foot. D. base est. 0.14. Fine, hard-fired, gray fabric with no inclusions. Wheelmade. Gray Minyan. FVa.

570 K.4561. Goblet. (Fig. 45, Pl. 42)
Published, J. C. Overbeck 1989a, 174, no. CP-1b. Foot. D. base est. 0.14. Fine, hard-fired, gray fabric with fewer than 1% inclusions. Manufacture method unclear. Four vertical lines inside foot; incised after firing. Gray Minyan. FVa. No close parallels for the mark have been located (e.g., Crouwel 1973; it is not clear if any marks described by Crouwel were made after firing).

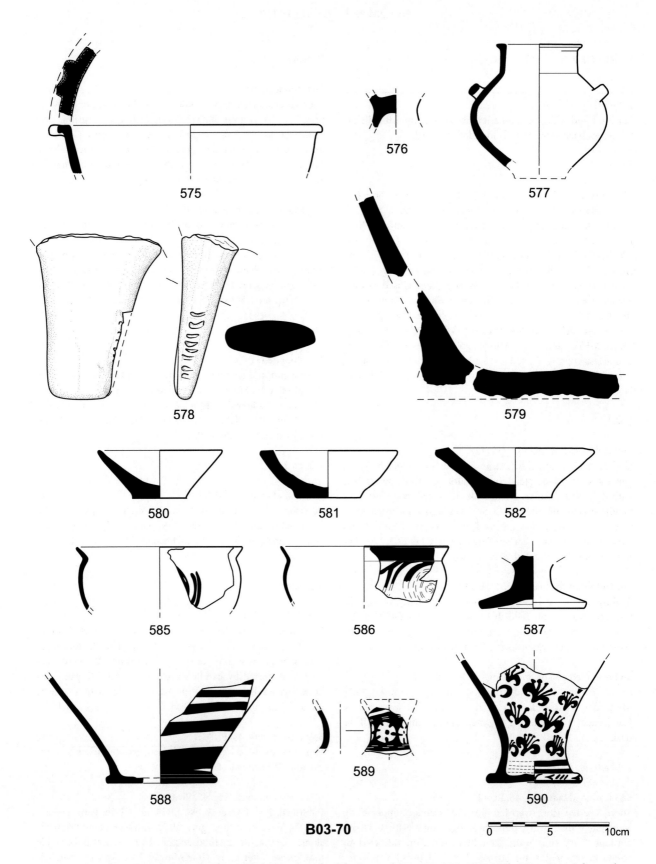

Fig. 46. Pottery from B03-70 (**575–582, 585–590**). Drawings by Lily Bonga (**575, 585, 586, 588, 590**), Mary-Jane Schumacher (**576, 578, 579, 589**), and Aliki Bikaki (**577, 580–582, 587**).

571 Goblet. (Fig. 45, Pl. 42)
Rim and upper body. D. rim est. 0.19. Fine, hard-fired, gray fabric with fewer than 1% inclusions. Wheel-coiled(?). Gray Minyan. Highly burnished. FVa. For profile: Sarri 2010b, 287, pl. 21:11–13.

Crete

572 Straight-sided cup. (Pl. 42)
Body. Fine, very hard-fired, dark pinkish-orange fabric with no inclusions. Interior rough. Wheelmade. Exterior: smoothed. Lustrous Painted (Monochrome). Coated in and out with thick, semi-lustrous dark-brown to reddish-orange slip. FSTk.

573 Open vessel. (Pl. 42)
Body. Fine, hard-fired, pale brown fabric with no inclusions. Forming method indeterminable. Lustrous Painted (Monochrome). Interior and exterior coated with highly lustrous dark-brown to black slip; pitted. FSTk.

Terracotta

574 K1.398. Spindle whorl. (Pl. 42)
Type S2. H. 0.02. D. 0.03. D. perf. <0.01. Wt. 26 g. Moderately coarse, reddish-brown to gray fabric with 10–15% inclusions. Smoothed surface, somewhat worn and chipped. Significant breakage around both ends of perforation, particularly at bottom. RBMd. (Local or local region).

CARBON-RICH DEPOSIT

B03-70.
Period VIIb. Deposit of carbonized soil and cooking pots.

Pottery

2/3 tins (ca. 11.3 liters) recovered; 2/3 bag (ca. 0.3 tin or 5.1 liters) kept, including all finewares and 10% coarsewares. Two sherds may belong to a large Lustrous Painted bridge-spouted jug from Room B.1 (**207**). Although Bikaki noted that the deposit was characterized by many cooking vessels, only a few remain; it is probable that others have been discarded. Uncatalogued sherds include local plain vessels (RBMa), including a possible cooking vessel; Cretan(?) Lustrous Painted (FSTj) vessels, including an askos(?); Melian/Theran (DVa, DVc) plain closed vessels; an Aeginetan(?) Painted (DVe) closed vessel; mainland(?) (FVc) Lustrous Painted open vessels, and a Red Coated closed vessel. A pedestal base, possibly from a fruit stand, and eleven handleless cups (one perforated) were discarded (Kea Pottery Notebook B, 35).

Local

575 Hemispherical deep bowl. (Fig. 46, Pl. 42)
Short, flattened rim, horned lug, and upper body. D. rim est. 0.22. Moderately coarse, dark-brown fabric with 10–15% inclusions. EBA Black Burnished. RBMa. For shape, see Wilson 1999, 128, no. III-357, pls. 33, 87.

576 Goblet or pedestaled bowl. (Fig. 46, Pl. 42)
Hollow pedestal and attachment to lower body. H. pres. 0.02. Moderately coarse, compact, purplish-brown fabric with 1–5% inclusions. Manufacturing method unknown. Yellow Slipped(?). Yellow slip(?) in and out. RBMa, with rare calcareous(?) inclusions.

577 Small jar (cooking vessel?). (Fig. 46, Pl. 42)
Thickened ledge rim, collar neck, globular body, and small, horizontal strap handle at shoulder. H. pres. 0.10. D. rim est. 0.07. Coarse, reddish-brown fabric turning gray at core, with 10–15% inclusions. Blackened in some parts from burning. Wheel-coiled. Plain(?). Interior: spattered and streaked thin yellow slip(?). Exterior smoothed. RBMa, with rare calcareous(?) inclusions.

578 Tripod tray. (Fig. 46, Pl. 42)
Published, Gorogianni, Abell, and Hilditch 2017, 70, no. 35. Large, flattened leg; broken at lower half on one edge. H. pres. 0.14. Moderately coarse, reddish-brown fabric with 10–15% inclusions. Broken part of lower leg preserves fingernail impressions, probably made during vessel forming before additional clay was added to both edges of the leg. Such enlargement of the leg is also indicated by badly smoothed attachment joins on both sides. Plain. RBMa.

579 Unfired or very low-fired vessel. (Fig. 46, Pl. 43)
Nonjoining base and lower body. D. base est. 0.12(?). Coarse, very low-fired, reddish-brown fabric with 15–20% inclusions. Exterior surface is rough and unfinished, perhaps formed directly in the ground. Interior surface smoothed at side, rough at bottom. Rough clay at bottom is spiraliform, probably from construction with large coil. Coil-built. Plain. RBMb.

580 K.459. Handleless cup. (Fig. 46)
Type 1. 90% preserved; broken and chipped at rim. H. 0.04. D. base 0.04. D. rim 0.10. Thick base. Wheel-coiled. Plain. RBMa.

581 K.462. Handleless cup. (Fig. 46)
Type 1. Nearly intact, with chipped, flattened rim. H. 0.04. D. base 0.05. D. rim 0.11. Thick walls; heavy. Wheel-coiled(?). Surface discolored to dark gray in places. Plain. RBMa.

582 K.566. Handleless cup. (Fig. 46)
Type 1. Nearly intact; chipped at flattened rim and base. H. 0.04. D. base 0.06. D. rim est. 0.13. Thick walls and base; heavy. Wheel-coiled(?). After removal from wheel, the base was damaged while still wet (deep scars preserved). Plain. RBMa.

Melos/Thera

583 Shallow cup. (Pl. 43)
Approximately 8% short, sharply everted, hollow rim and upper body. H. pres. 0.02. D. rim est. 0.10. Fine, soft, somewhat sandy fabric with fewer than 1% inclusions. Wheelmade(?). Painted. Interior plain. Rim band (possible traces also in interior?); framed(?) spiral in faded, matt brown paint. DVa.

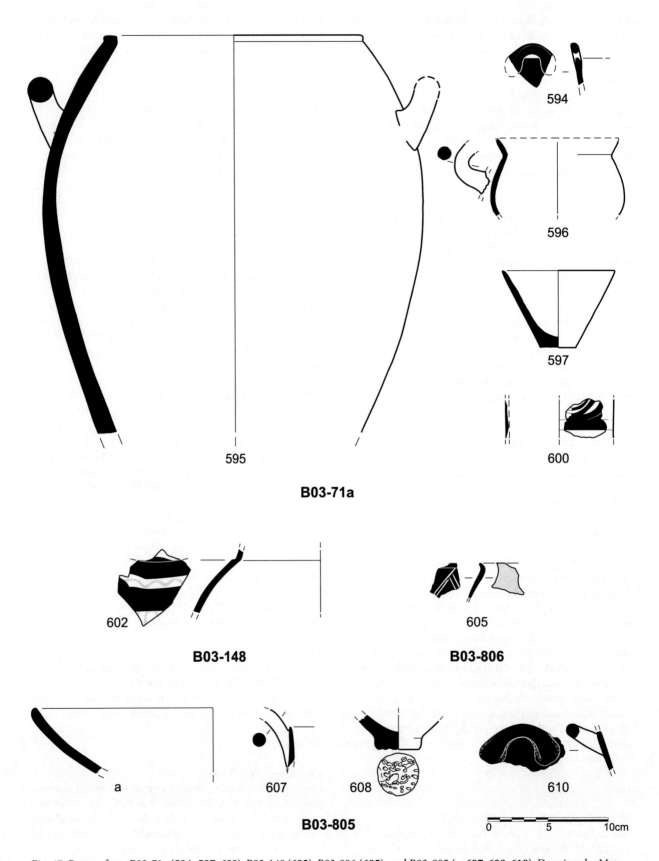

Fig. 47. Pottery from B03-71a (**594–597, 600**), B03-148 (**602**), B03-806 (**605**), and B03-805 (a, **607, 608, 610**). Drawings by Mary-Jane Schumacher (**594, 595, 597, 600, 602**), Alison Rittershaus (**596**), Lily Bonga (**605, 607, 608, 610**), and Aliki Bikaki (a).

584 K.496. Handleless cup. (Pl. 43)
Type 1. Intact, with tiny chips at base. H. 0.03. D. base 0.04. D. rim 0.08. Fine. Wheel-coiled(?). Plain. DVb.

Mainland

585 Ephyraean goblet. (Fig. 46, Pl. 43)
FS 254. Rim and upper body. H. pres. 0.06. D. rim est. 0.14. Fine, hard-fired, yellow fabric with pink core and fewer than 1% inclusions. Wheelmade. Lustrous Painted. Interior and exterior surfaces highly burnished, possibly coated with yellow slip, now stained orange. Exterior surface decorated with palm(?) (FM 14) in lustrous black paint, nearly entirely fugitive. FVc. PFG 14B (Argolid?).

586 Rounded cup. (Fig. 46, Pl. 43)
Rim and upper body. H. pres. 0.06. D. rim est. 0.14. Fine, hard-fired pinkish-orange fabric with fewer than 1% inclusions. Wheelmade. Surface stained orange-brown in some places. Lustrous Painted. Decorated with lustrous red to dark-brown paint, now cracked and flaking. Possible traces of paint at interior; rim band? Exterior: rim band, framed spirals (FM 46), band below shoulder. Mountjoy (1986, 32, 34) associates framed spirals with cups rather than goblets. FVc.

587 Goblet. (Fig. 46, Pl. 43)
Concave foot, stem, and interior surface of bowl. H. pres. 0.04. D. base 0.09. Fine, pale purplish-brown fabric turning paler at surface. Fewer than 1% inclusions. Surface stained dark brown in places. Forming method indeterminable. Burnished. FVf. PFG 13B (Euboea).

Mainland/Kythera

588 Jar. (Fig. 46, Pl. 43)
Flaring lower body and slightly concave torus base. H. pres. 0.09. D. base 0.10. Fine, hard-fired, pale brown fabric with green-tinged surface. Fewer than 1% inclusions. Wheelmade. Surface stained orange-brown in some places. Lustrous Painted. Base and lower body coated with lustrous black paint; three narrow bands above. Paint now cracked and flaking. FSTh. PFG 7G (Mainland/Kythera?).

Crete/Mainland

589 Ewer or jug. (Fig. 46, Pl. 43)
Narrow neck preserved. H. pres. 0.04. Fine, soft, pale pink fabric with fewer than 1% inclusions. Wheelmade. Lustrous Painted. Exterior coated in lustrous black. Reserved rosettes with small, central dots; reserved, short, horizontal lines and bands above and below rosettes. Paint now cracked, flaking, and missing on one side. FSTj.

590 Jug or ewer. (Fig. 46, Pl. 43)
Slightly concave torus base and lower body. Groove where base meets body. H. pres. 0.10. D. base 0.08. Fine, soft, pale pink fabric with greenish-tinge at surface and fewer than 1% inclusions. Wheelmade. Interior and exterior stained dark orange. Lustrous Painted. Chevrons around base; two bands around bottom of lower body in flaking, lustrous red to brown paint. Lower body: four rows of lilies with four or five stamens. FSTj.

591 Large jar. (Pl. 43)
FS 17(?). Body. Moderately fine, hard-fired pinkish brown fabric with purplish gray core and 5–10% inclusions. Wheelmade. Lustrous Painted. Exterior: double arcade (or very large version of scale pattern, FM 70) in red to dark-brown paint. FSTg/FSTh. PFG 7F (Mainland/Kythera?). Mountjoy (1986, 20, 22, 38–39) cites scale pattern as a motif used for large jars in LH IIB but not LH IIA.

Bone

592 K1.233. Awl. (Pl. 43)
W. 0.02. L. pres. 0.12. Wt. 14 g. Type IIIb, Period VII (Krzyszkowska). Cow or deer metaphalanx (Coy). Point missing. Polished, flat, from large splinter; burned.

Terracotta

593 K1.167. Loom weight. (Pl. 43)
Type RG. D. 0.08. Th. 0.03. D. perf. 0.01. Wt. 170 g. Round, flattened body with off-center perforation below groove near top. Smoothed surface, now somewhat pitted. RBMa, with phyllite. (Local).

COMPACT LENS IN PERIOD VIIB DESTRUCTION DEPOSIT

B03-71A.
Lens of compact earth, plaster, and coarse vessels below lens of burned bones, ashes, and soft earth in Period VIIb destruction deposit. Period VIIb.

Pottery

1/2 tin (ca. 8.5 liters) recovered, 8 sherds kept. Three or four handleless cups; a rim of a large (D. est. 0.22) spreading bowl; and handle, feet, and rim sherds from several probable tripod jars were discarded (Kea Pottery Notebook B, 77). All vessels inventoried.

Local

594 Small basket-handled vessel. (Fig. 47, Pl. 43)
Straight rim with flattened, ovoid section basket handle. Moderately coarse, red fabric with gray core and 10–15% inclusions. Handmade(?). Yellow Slipped. Exterior coated with yellow slip. RBMa, with common mica.

595 K.2114. Large jar (probably tripod). (Fig. 47, Pl. 43)
Approximately 50% preserved, including slightly convex body; part of one round, arched handle; and flattened rim. Partially restored in plaster. H. rest. 0.33. D. rim est. 0.21. Coarse, reddish-brown fabric with 15–20% inclusions. Exterior preserves

significant evidence for burning. Surface smoothed; now worn and flaking. Coil-built. Plain. RBMa.

596 Small, cooking(?) vessel. (Fig. 47, Pl. 43)
Two nonjoining fragments, preserving everted lip; globular body; and round, vertical handle. H. pres 0.07. Moderately coarse, dark reddish-brown fabric, with 10–15% inclusions. A few acicular voids in surface probably the result of burnt-out organics. Wheel-coiled. Surfaces blackened, probably result of fire. Plain. RBMa.

597 Handleless cup. (Fig. 47, Pl. 43)
Type 3. 60% preserved. H. 0.06. D. base 0.03. D. rim est. 0.09. Coarse, compact, red fabric with black margins and 15–20% inclusions. Wheel-coiled. Surface blackened in most places from fire. Plain. RBMa, with rare calcareous(?) inclusions and overfired schist.

Cyclades

598 Closed(?) vessel. (Pl. 43)
Body (two nonjoining fragments). Moderately coarse, dark reddish-brown fabric with 15–20% inclusions. Handmade(?). Yellow Slipped. Exterior coated in yellow slip and decorated in faded, matt-black paint; curvilinear motif. CSWa. PFG 4A (Naxos).

599 Bridge-spouted(?) jar. (Pl. 43)
Body and arched, round, handle attachment. Moderately fine, moderately hard-fired, dark pink fabric, turning paler at surface and pale gray at core, with 5–10% inclusions. Wheelmade(?). Plain. MxMf.

Mainland

600 Straight-sided cup. (Fig. 47, Pl. 43)
Body, flake. Fine, pale pinkish-yellow fabric with fewer than 1% inclusions. Forming method indeterminable. Interior surface broken. Lustrous Painted. Exterior: spiral (FM 46) above band in lustrous dark-brown paint. Burnished. FVc.

Stone

Uninventoried: two fragments of obsidian (B-1.207, B-1.208).

B03-50.
Deposit of burned animal bones, ashes, and soft earth.

Pottery

10 coarse sherds recovered; all discarded (Notecards, 94).

ROOM B.8

Room B.8 is bounded by Walls J, I, and the sea (Figs. 23, 24; Pls. 5:c, 8:c). The space was eroded by the sea, and little excavation was possible (B03-148, B03-249, B03-506). At the lowest elevation (+0.20 m above sea level), there was a stratum of stones lying flat and covered with red, compact earth, which was excavated in units B03-249 and B03-506 (Kea Excavation Notebook XXXVIII, 33). Ceramics were mixed and included EBA to LH IIIB pottery (Kea Excavation Notebook XXXVIII, 34).

At their lowest elevation, at +0.15 m above sea level, it was clear that Walls J and I had been built on destruction debris, presumably also of Period III, although no sherds were recovered. At higher elevations, excavated in unit B03-148, no surfaces were found, and pottery seemed to come from an undifferentiated fill.

ROOM B.8 CATALOGUE

MIXED DEPOSITS

B03-148.
Secondary deposit, probably formed by the erosion of ceramics and other objects from further upslope. Above mixed deposits of B03-249 and B03-506, in the corner of Walls I and J. Most decorated pottery can be dated to Period VIIb.

Pottery

1 bag collected; 1/2 bag remains, 25% fine wares. Approximately 50% of the coarse ware was discarded in the original papsing. Among the discards were the lower part of a large, ovoid-shaped jar; the bottom of a spreading bowl; slightly out-turned rim of a large vessel; a pithos rim with rope pattern on the body; sherds from pithoi with plain, plastic bands; and two Matt Painted sherds. Uncatalogued local (RBMa) ceramics were plain, including a pithos handle, ledge-rim bowl, and several goblets or bowls. Uncatalogued imports were mostly Lustrous Painted (FSTd, FSTj, FSTk, FVb, FVd), including an open vessel decorated with reeds; a conical rhyton; a hydria or jar; parts of a Palace Style jar, perhaps the same one as **173** from B609CL. A mainland(?) (FVb) Burnished goblet was also present.

Local

601 Pithos. (Pl. 44)
Body. Moderately coarse, brittle, dark red fabric with 10–15% inclusions. Handmade. Exterior smoothed, blackened. Plain (applied). Half of relief double axe(?). RBMa.

Cyclades

602 Jar. (Fig. 47, Pl. 44)
Shoulder including sharp ledge below neck. Moderately fine, brittle, brown fabric with dark-gray core and 5–10% inclusions. Wheelmade(?). Yellow Slipped (Polychrome, Red and Black). Interior and exterior coated in yellow slip. Exterior: wide black band below and overlapping neck; below this band are a wavy purple band, wide black band, and purple ovals(?). MxMa, with no visible metamorphics.

Aegina

603 K.2156. Open(?) vessel. (Pl. 44)
Published, Bikaki 1984, 35, no. VII-31, pls. 13, 26. Moderately fine, pinkish brown fabric. Plain. DVe. Foot appears comparable to Lindblom's (2001, 30–31, fig. 8:FB-14) high conical foot, which is associated with both cooking and plain wares there. The mark is comparable to Lindblom 2001, 57, no. 182, pl. 10.

B03-506.
Mixed deposit on the shore, just south of Walls I and J. All pottery either discarded or now missing. EBA–LH IIIB (Kea Excavation Notebook XXXVIII, 34).

Terracotta

604 K7.158. Loom weight. (Pl. 44)
Type RFG. D. 0.07. Th. max. 0.24. D. perf. 0.01. Wt. 105 g. Round, lentoid body with flattened, grooved top. Top and one side broken away. Surface smoothed, especially above perforation; worn elsewhere. RBMa. (Local).

Stone

Uninventoried: obsidian fragments (B-7.62).

B03-249.
Mixed deposit on the shore, just south of Walls I and J, beneath unit B03-148. All pottery probably discarded. EBA–LH IIIB (Kea Excavation Notebook XXXVIII, 34).

ALLEY AB

Alley AB is located between Wall H of House B and the southeastern wall of House A, Wall E (Figs. 4, 14:a, 15, 23, 24; Pl. 9:a; Table 2.6). It intersects with Temple Lane in the northeast and South Alley in the southwest. The surface strata of Alley AB and House B were excavated together in upper levels in units B03-11 and B03-18. As soon as Wall H was identified, Alley AB was excavated separately. Alley AB was dug as a whole to an elevation above sea level of approximately +2.20 m in unit B03-21. Two test trenches were then opened in the northeastern end of the alley (Fig. 6). The first, in 1961, was excavated to a depth of ca. +0.70 m above sea level in units B03-88, B03-94, B03-96, and B03-97. The second was excavated in 1975 to a depth of ca. –0.30 m below sea level in units B03-764–B03-806. The test pit from 1961 is incorrectly described by Cummer and Schofield (1984, 5) as being located outside House A Room 39. Both the 1961 and 1975 tests were adjacent to House A Room 36. Alley AB contained strata dating from Period III to Period VII. Table 2.7 presents a summary of deposits.

EARLY BRONZE AGE

Period III Constructions(?) and Destruction Deposit

The earliest strata of Alley AB can be dated to Period III; the lowest of these was excavated in unit B03-806 (Fig. 15). The lowest stratum consisted of an approximately 0.30 m thick layer of soil and many small, flat stones. The stones of the lower stratum were jumbled and the soil was muddy (Kea Excavation Notebook LVIII, 24–25). The lower limit of this stratum was not reached. Despite the significant depth of the excavation unit (approximately 0.45 m), many fewer sherds were collected than in higher strata. The lack of finds other than stones might suggest that the stratum was either a wall or part of a collapsed EBA wall. Above this stratum was an approximately 0.10 m thick layer of soil without stones, also excavated in unit B03-806.

The next higher stratum contained many small (ca. 0.10–0.15 m) flat schist slabs; it was excavated in units B03-802–B03-805. Only Period III ceramics were found in the lowest excavation unit, B03-805. Pottery from excavation units B03-802–B03-804 dates primarily to Period III, but probable Period IV sherds exist (**621, 628**). The upper part of the stratum must have been disturbed by Period IV activity in the area, including the construction of Wall X (below).

TABLE 2.6. ALLEY AB COMBINED LOTS (CL)

CL	Excavation units, B03-	↑ Elevation	↓ Elevation
B646CL	766–768	+2.27	+2.00
B647CL	769, 771–773	+2.00	+1.25
B648CL	776–778, 782	+1.90	+1.60
B649CL	783, 784	+1.70/+1.55	+1.50
B791/793CL	791, 793	+1.23	+1.11
B795/a/796CL	795, 795a, 796	+1.06	+0.85
B797/798CL	797, 798	+0.85	+0.65
B800/801CL	800, 801	+0.65	+0.48

Bikaki suggested that a large stone in the northern part of the test trench, its top at an elevation of ca. +0.43 m above sea level, might be part of a wall (Pl. 15:b; Kea Excavation Notebook LVIII, 21). However, on the basis of the documentary record of the excavation, the stone in the north at +0.43 m cannot be reconstructed convincingly as part of a wall. Photos and section drawings (Pls. 15:b; 20:a) show only earth beneath it; it is as likely to be fallen from a wall as part of one. A stone construction in the southern part of the test trench is more likely to be part of a wall since there appear to be two courses preserved. It is near to, and with an orientation similar to, Period III Wall AC, suggesting that it may be part of either Wall AC or an associated structure. The relationship of the wall to the strata excavated in B03-806 is unclear since its location at the edge of the test pit and beneath Wall X, in addition to the presence of large quantities of loose stones and extremely muddy soil, hindered excavation below its upper courses (Kea Excavation Notebook LVIII, 24–25). Finds of Period III in the lowest stratum in this area suggest that the wall was destroyed during that period.

MIDDLE BRONZE AGE

Compact Red Stratum

Above the probable Period III wall and associated destruction deposit was a thick layer of compact red soil, similar to that of Surface c in Room B.1 and Surface i in Room B.4; it was excavated in units B03-799–B03-801 (Fig. 15). Bikaki did not identify this stratum as a floor or surface in Alley AB, and so it has not been labeled as such here. Excavation units from this stratum contained primarily Period III ceramics with some Period IV sherds, mainly small fragments of Gray Minyan goblets. The red stratum probably was deposited during the final collapse of the EBA architecture on site; it was apparently at or near the surface level when new inhabitants arrived in Period IV. A 0.10–0.15 m foundation trench for Period IVa Wall X cut through the compact red stratum; this or other Period IV construction activity is probably the reason that Period IV ceramics were found in excavation units from the compact red stratum.

Wall X

The foundation trench for Wall X was excavated in unit B03-799, which is part of J. C. Overbeck's Group CQ (1989a, 175). The ceramics from the foundation trench, as well as from the earliest use deposits associated with the wall (below, B03-797, B03-798), date to Period IVa. Wall X was founded on a bedding layer of stones (Fig. 15; AB Stratigraphy, 5).

Wall X, of which only one course is preserved, projected ca. 0.60 m from the exterior face of Wall H, which was founded immediately above it (Figs. 6, 15; Pls. 14:a, 15:a, c). The wall was constructed with large schist slabs and clay mortar (H-E Results, 4). The stones were much larger (ca. 0.30–0.70 × 0.25 × 0.30 m) than those used in nearby EBA and LBA walls.

Wall X may be the northern face of the same wall preserved beneath Room B.1—the Wall H foundation (Fig. 15). The relationship between these two walls (Wall X and the Wall H foundation) is unclear, because excavation beneath Wall H in Room B.1 did not extend fully to Wall X (Figs. 11:b, 15). Nevertheless, the similar size of the stones used in both walls and the fact that both walls

TABLE 2.7. ALLEY AB DEPOSIT SUMMARY

Deposit:	Period III Destruction Deposit (Lower)
Contemporary Features:	Period III wall(?)
Date of Deposit Above:	Period III, plus some Period IV disturbance
Date of Deposit:	Period III
Date of Deposit Below:	Not excavated
Lots/Combined Lots:	B03-805, B03-806
Catalogue Numbers:	**605–616**
Deposit:	Period III Destruction Deposit (Upper)
Contemporary Features:	Period III wall(?)
Date of Deposit Above:	Period III, plus some Period IV disturbance
Date of Deposit:	Period III, plus some Period IV disturbance
Date of Deposit Below:	Period III
Lots/Combined Lots:	B03-802–B03-804
Catalogue Numbers:	**617–628**
Deposit:	Compact Red Stratum
Contemporary Features:	None
Date of Deposit Above:	Period IVa
Date of Deposit:	Period III, plus some Period IV disturbance
Date of Deposit Below:	Period III, plus some Period IV disturbance
Lots/Combined Lots:	B03-799 (partial; J. C. Overbeck's Deposit CQ [1989a, 175]), B800/801CL
Catalogue Numbers:	**629–631**
Deposit:	Wall X Foundation Trench
Contemporary Features:	Wall X
Date of Deposit Above:	Period IVa
Date of Deposit:	Period IVa
Date of Deposit Below:	Period III, plus some Period IV disturbance (both below Wall X Foundation Trench, and cut by it)
Lots/Combined Lots:	B03-799 (partial; J. C. Overbeck's Deposit CQ [1989a, 175])
Catalogue Numbers:	**632–636**
Deposit:	Packing for Pavement Associated with Wall X
Contemporary Features:	Wall X
Date of Deposit Above:	Period IVb
Date of Deposit:	Period IVa
Date of Deposit Below:	Period IVa
Lots/Combined Lots:	B797/798CL (J. C. Overbeck's Deposit CQ [1989a, 175])
Catalogue Numbers:	**637–643**

TABLE 2.7. (CONT.)

Deposit:	Pavement and Use Stratum
Contemporary Features:	Wall X
Date of Deposit Above:	Period IVb
Date of Deposit:	Period IVb
Date of Deposit Below:	Period IVa
Lots/Combined Lots:	B03-97 (partial), B03-794, B795/a/796CL (J. C. Overbeck's Deposit CR [1989a, 175])
Catalogue Numbers:	**644–665, 712–715**

Deposit:	Compact Accumulation (Abell) or Habitation (Bikaki) Stratum
Contemporary Features:	Drain 2, Period IVb wall(?)
Date of Deposit Above:	Period IVb
Date of Deposit:	Period IVb
Date of Deposit Below:	Period IVb
Lots/Combined Lots:	B791/793CL (J. C. Overbeck's Deposit CS [1989a, 175])
Catalogue Numbers:	**666–673**

Deposit:	Accumulation Stratum + Preparative Layer for Construction of Wall E1
Contemporary Features:	Drain 2, Period IVb wall(?)
Date of Deposit Above:	Period IVb
Date of Deposit:	Period IVb
Date of Deposit Below:	Period IVb
Lots/Combined Lots:	B03-790 (J. C. Overbeck's Deposit CS [1989a, 175])
Catalogue Numbers:	**674–685**

Deposit:	Bedding Layer for Street 2
Contemporary Features:	Wall E1
Date of Deposit Above:	Period IVb/c
Date of Deposit:	Period IVb
Date of Deposit Below:	Period IVb
Lots/Combined Lots:	B03-789 (J. C. Overbeck's Deposit CT [1989a, 175])
Catalogue Numbers:	**686**

Deposit:	Street 2: Lowest Paving Level
Contemporary Features:	Wall E1
Date of Deposit Above:	Period IVb/c
Date of Deposit:	Period IVb/c
Date of Deposit Below:	Period IV
Lots/Combined Lots:	B03-788 (J. C. Overbeck's Deposit CT [1989a, 175])
Catalogue Numbers:	**687–691**

TABLE 2.7. (CONT.)

Deposit:	Street 2: Second Paving Level
Contemporary Features:	Wall E1
Date of Deposit Above:	Period IVc–V
Date of Deposit:	Period IVb/c
Date of Deposit Below:	Period IVb/c
Lots/Combined Lots:	B03-786 (J. C. Overbeck's Deposit CT [1989a, 175])
Catalogue Numbers:	**692–697**

Deposit:	Street 2: Upper Level
Contemporary Features:	Wall E1
Date of Deposit Above:	Period V (–VI?)
Date of Deposit:	Period IVc–V
Date of Deposit Below:	Period IVb/c
Lots/Combined Lots:	B03-785 (J. C. Overbeck's Deposit CT [1989a, 175])
Catalogue Numbers:	**698–700**

Deposit:	Period V (–VI?) Destruction Deposit
Contemporary Features:	None
Date of Deposit Above:	Early Period VI
Date of Deposit:	Period V (–VI?)
Date of Deposit Below:	Period IVc–V
Lots/Combined Lots:	B648CL (partial), B649CL
Catalogue Numbers:	**701–703**

Deposit:	Upper Period V (–VI?) Destruction Deposit: Compact Red Soil
Contemporary Features:	None
Date of Deposit Above:	Period VII
Date of Deposit:	Early Period VI
Date of Deposit Below:	Period V (–VI?)
Lots/Combined Lots:	B648CL (partial)
Catalogue Numbers:	**704–711**

Deposit:	Wall H Foundation Trench
Contemporary Features:	Wall H
Date of Deposit Above:	Period VII
Date of Deposit:	Early Period VI (secondary deposition)
Date of Deposit Below:	Period IV (cuts through Period IV and V depoists)
Lots/Combined Lots:	B03-94, B03-96, B03-97 (partial) (J. C. Overbeck's Deposit CR [1989a, 175]), B647CL (partial)
Catalogue Numbers:	**716–743**

TABLE 2.7. (CONT.)

Deposit:	Street 1
Contemporary Features:	Walls H, E
Date of Deposit Above:	Period VII
Date of Deposit:	Period VII
Date of Deposit Below:	Early Period VI (secondary deposition)
Lots/Combined Lots:	B03-88 (partial), B646CL, B647CL (partial)
Catalogue Numbers:	**744–750**

Deposit:	Drain 1
Contemporary Features:	Walls H, E
Date of Deposit Above:	Unknown, probably mixed (surface)
Date of Deposit:	Period VII
Date of Deposit Below:	Period VII
Lots/Combined Lots:	B03-87, B03-88 (partial)
Catalogue Numbers:	**751–758**

follow the same course at approximately the same elevation (+1.00 m) suggests that they are two faces of the same wall. Notes and drawings show that both Wall X and the Wall H foundation rest on a similar stone packing (Figs. 11:b, 15; AB Stratigraphy, 5; Kea Excavation Notebook LVIII, 52). If Wall X is the northern face of the same wall as the Wall H foundation, that wall is extremely thick (up to 1.85 m). Its probable size and Period IVa foundation date make this wall a good candidate for the southeastern section of the first fortifications on the site, founded elsewhere early in Period IVa (J. C. Overbeck 1989a, 175).

Use of Wall X

Abutting Wall X were several strata that were deposited after Wall X was constructed. The earliest was a ca. 0.20 m thick layer of dark-brown earth and level stones, including small, flat marble fragments (Kea Excavation Notebook LVIII, 19–20). This layer was packing for a pavement built immediately above, at ca. +0.90 m above sea level (Pl. 13:c; Kea Excavation Notebook LVIII, 18). The packing was excavated in units B03-797 and B03-798, which were included in J. C. Overbeck's Group CQ (1989a, 175). Sherds from these lots date to Period IVa, which provides the *terminus ante quem* for the construction of Wall X.

The pavement was made up of stones laid flat above the packing (Kea Excavation Notebook LVIII, 18, 29). It was excavated in unit B03-796, which was included in J. C. Overbeck's Group CR (1989a, 175). A stratum above the pavement, made up of soft, brown soil and flat stones, was probably deposited gradually over time (Kea Excavation Notebook LVIII, 16–18; J. C. Overbeck 1989a, 174). The soil above the pavement was excavated in units B03-794, B03-795, and B03-795a, which were included in J. C. Overbeck's Group CR (1989a, 175), together with ceramics from B03-796; lot B03-97 was also included in his Deposit CR, although unit B03-97 also seems to have included the bottom part of the Wall H foundation trench (below; Fig. 14:a). Lot B03-794 contained only one Gray Minyan body sherd and two Cycladic dark burnished body sherds, and, therefore, will not be discussed in more detail. Ceramics were rare in these units, but more sherds were discovered in the southern than the northern part of the test trench (Kea Excavation Notebook LVIII, 7). Ceramic joins were found between lots B03-795, B03-795a, and B03-796; the combined lot dates to Period IVb (B795/a/796CL). The later date of ceramics from the pavement and use stratum in comparison with pottery from the packing probably resulted from the continued use of the space over time from Period IVa to IVb.

Owing to the limited extent of the test trench and the lack of Period IV architecture apart from Wall X, it is impossible to determine if the paving was part of an exterior or interior space. Three fragments of wall plaster, one with traces of red on it, were found on the pavement (Kea Excavation Notebook LVIII, 18; J. C. Overbeck 1989a, 175), as was a lump of clay with traces of burning. White and red-faced plaster also were found in Period IV deposits below Rooms A.26 and A.37 (J. C. Overbeck 1989a, 171, 173). Red-painted plaster from MC deposits at Phylakopi has been noted by Barber (1984, 180 n. 14, referring to Atkinson et al. 1904, 77). A red-painted fragment of plaster, as well as one painted with a red stripe and yellow band, were found in Period V deposits (Davis 1986, nos. U-136, AM-3).

Subsequent MBA Strata

Immediately above the accumulation on the pavement were two lenses of compact soil. The lower lens was grayish-brown and contained flat stones, carbon, and much pottery; the upper lens was brown and contained schist chips, limpet shells, and much carbonized material (Kea Excavation Notebook LVIII, 15–16). These lenses were excavated in units B03-793 (lower) and B03-791 (upper), both of which were included in J. C. Overbeck's Group CS (1989a, 175). A concentration of limpet shells was discovered in the SW corner of the test pit (Test H-E Pottery Notes, 13; Kea Excavation Notebook LVIII, 15). The ceramics from both units were combined into a single lot (B791/793CL), which dates to Period IVb.

The stratum of compact soil covered Wall X, which must have gone out of use by this time (AB Stratigraphy, 6; H-E Results, 5). Elsewhere, the Period IVa fortification wall underwent significant changes in early Period IVb and certainly was destroyed by the end of Period IVb (J. C. Overbeck 1989a, 5–6).

The stratum of compact soil was contemporary with Drain 2, the bottom of which was at +1.12 m above sea level (below; Kea Excavation Notebook LVIII, 16–17, 27, 30). Bikaki interpreted the stratum of compact soil as part of a habitation layer, but it could also have been an exterior accumulation or dumping space, particularly given the presence of the drain. Unfortunately, the small size of the excavated area makes interpretation of the space difficult.

Immediately above the stratum of compact soil was a ca. 0.10 m thick stratum of brown soil and stones (Kea Excavation Notebook LVIII, 14–15, 17). This stratum was excavated in unit B03-790, which was included in J. C. Overbeck's Group CS (1989a, 175). This stratum, like the compact stratum below it, contained Period IVb ceramics and abutted Drain 2. Much of the stratum was destroyed by the deep foundation trench of Wall H (Fig. 15).

Drain 2 was discovered in the space of the 1961 test trench, during cleaning of Wall E1 in the course of 1975. It was built of upright slabs and lacked cover slabs and a slab pavement. The drain was excavated in units B03-790, B03-807, and B03-808. Ceramics from B03-790 were included in J. C. Overbeck's Group CS (1989a, 175). Pottery from lots B03-807 and B03-808 was discarded. Excavation unit B03-790 included ceramics from the drain and the stratum of brown soil that abutted it (above). The soil in the drain (B03-807, B03-808) was compact and contained small stones, sherds, bones, and carbon (Kea Excavation Notebook LVIII, 27). One upright slab extended beneath Wall E1. The northern side of the drain was built with large stones rather than upright slabs, which Bikaki suggested were part of a wall that predated Wall E1 (Kea Excavation Notebook LVIII, 27, 30). The part of the drain that extended beneath Wall E1 was blocked by three stones, probably when Wall E1 was built (Kea Excavation Notebook LVIII, 27).

Wall E1 and Street 2

Above Drain 2 and the stratum of brown soil, Wall E1 was built. This wall is J. C. Overbeck's Wall 57 (1989a, 175). It is also mentioned by Cummer and Schofield (1984, 9). Wall E1 is located beneath the southeastern wall of House A, Wall E. Wall E1 was constructed over a packing layer of small stones; this packing was excavated along with the stratum of brown soil in unit B03-790 (Kea Excavation Notebook LVIII, 15). Wall E1 was constructed of medium-sized to large, somewhat irregularly placed stones (Fig. 15; Pls. 14:b, c, 15:c, 20:b).

A shallow (0.05–0.06 m) layer of small, flat, irregularly placed stones and small sherds was found immediately above the brown stratum southeast of Wall E1; the stratum abutted the more densely packed layer of small stones under Wall E1, as well as the bottom of Wall E1 itself (Pl. 20:b; Kea Excavation Notebook LVIII, 14). Along with the upper 0.02–0.03 m of the brown stratum, the shallow layer of small stones was excavated in unit B03-789 (Test H-E Pottery Notes, 11; Kea Excavation Notebook LVIII, 14). Ceramics dated to Period IVb. The stratum of small stones probably was laid as bedding for a street above (Street 2). Although both Wall E1 and Street 2 were constructed in Period IVb, they seem to have continued in use until Period V, the date of ceramics from the upper (i.e., latest) levels of Street 2.

The bedding layer described above was located beneath a stratum of pebbles that initially served as the paving of Street 2 (Kea Excavation Notebook LVIII, 13). This stratum was excavated in unit B03-788, which was included in J. C. Overbeck's Group CT (1989a, 175). The stratum, which abutted Wall E1, sloped upward from south to north by ca. 0.06 m. Although the bedding level beneath Street 2 contained only Period IVb ceramics, the pottery from the first paving level may be dated to Period IVb/c. Bikaki suggested that the sherds in the stratum may have been intentionally deposited as road fill (Test H-E Pottery Notes, 10).

A second paving stratum lay above the first (Pl. 12:c). The second paving was made of small (ca. 0.07–0.10 m) flat stones and contained pottery and bone (Kea Excavation Notebook LVIII, 12). The stratum was excavated in unit B03-786, which was included in J. C. Overbeck's Group CT (1989a, 175). This stratum sloped upward from southeast to northwest by ca. 0.06–0.07 m. Like the previous stratum, it contained ceramics of Period IVb/c.

Above these two pavements was a third stratum, ca. 0.07 m thick, made of white pebbles and sandy brown soil; it also contained animal bones (Pl. 12:b). The stratum was excavated in unit B03-785, which was included in J. C. Overbeck's Group CT (1989a, 175). This stratum also sloped upward from southeast to northwest ca. 0.07 m (Kea Excavation Notebook LVIII 12). Ceramics from this stratum date mainly to Period IVc, with one probably Period V sherd (**698**). The street may have continued in use into that period. Ceramics from all pavements were small and worn, and joins were found between the ceramics embedded in all three pavements, probably because the strata were thin (ca. 0.05–0.07 m) and the sherds were ground deeply into them.

Period V (–VI?) Destruction Deposit

Above the paving levels of the street was a stratum of irregularly fallen medium-sized stones in brown soil (Fig. 15; Kea Excavation Notebook LVIII, 8–10). It was excavated in units B03-781–B03-784. Ceramics from units B03-783 and B03-784 were combined into B649CL. Pottery from unit B03-782, which also included part of the next higher stratum (below), was combined into B648CL along with ceramics from the stratum just above. All pottery from unit B03-781 was discarded.

The presence of many stones, little soil, and few artifacts in this stratum suggest that it was formed by the collapse of an architectural feature. Although Bikaki assumed that the stones might be the result of the collapse of Wall X (H-E Results, 2), that wall had collapsed before this phase. Wall E1 is a more probable source. Ceramics from B649CL, primarily large body sherds of coarse, closed, local vessels, are difficult to date precisely; the few fine and imported sherds are compatible with a Period V date. A Period V date for this destruction stratum makes sense, given that Street 2 beneath it seems to have continued in use into Period V.

The stony destruction layer was beneath a thick stratum of compact red soil that contained many sherds, small stones, bones, and much carbonized material (Kea Excavation Notebook III, 168–172; Kea Excavation Notebook LVIII, 8–9). This stratum of compact red soil was excavated in units B03-774–B03-778, B03-780, and B03-782. Ceramics from units B03-774, B03-775, and B03-780 were discarded; those from units B03-776–B03-778 and B03-782 were combined into B648CL. Unit B03-782 included both the lower part of this red stratum and the upper part of the stony destruction stratum below. A shallow gray lens appeared in the compact red stratum near Wall E1 (Kea Excavation Notebook LVIII, 8–9). It was excavated along with the red stratum in units B03-775–B03-778, B03-780, and B03-782; the gray lens was excavated with the stony destruction stratum in unit B03-783. This gray lens was, at most, 0.01 m thick, and faded gradually into the compact red stratum as it extended southward from Wall E1 (Kea Excavation Notebook III, 169–172; Kea Excavation Notebook LVIII, 8–9). The compact red stratum and the gray lens probably formed as a result of the same destruction event. The gray lens may have formed either by the burning or decomposition of organic matter. While the stones excavated in units B03-781, B03-783, and B03-784 probably fell from a wall, the compact red stratum may have been created by the collapse of part of a mudbrick superstructure. The destruction strata abut the preserved courses of Wall E1, so at least part of Wall E1 must have been exposed when the collapse occurred.

Chronologically diagnostic ceramics from B648CL (the red stratum) date to an early phase of Period VI. It is unclear how soon the red stratum was formed after the deposition of the stony stratum; ceramics from the lowest excavation units of the red stratum, which might have helped to clarify the situation, were discarded. The lack of any paving or possible street levels between the two strata (and therefore between the two events) suggests that the strata formed around the same time since the main entrance to House A during early Period VI was via Room A.36 (Cummer and Schofield 1984, 31). Wall E1 probably collapsed during Period V, presumably at the same time an earthquake damaged the Great Fortifications (Davis 1986, 106). The Period VI remains in the upper part of the red stratum were probably deposited as a result of subsequent building in the area, which included the construction of Room B.1. Wall E, the southeastern wall of House A, was also constructed early in Period VI, above Wall E1 (Cummer and Schofield 1984, 31). Wall E has been fully discussed by Cummer and Schofield (1984, 7, 9, 31). Since rebuilding on the site and in House A seems to have begun almost immediately after the Period V earthquake (Davis 1986, 8, 106; Cummer and Schofield 1984, 31), it is probable that the Period VI ceramics from B648CL are among the earliest LBA ceramics in Area B.

LATE BRONZE AGE

Above the destruction deposit, there was a 0.10 m thick stratum of firm soil, which was excavated in unit B03-770 (Kea Excavation Notebook III, 167). No ceramics were kept. The stratum must have accumulated after the formation of the destruction deposit discussed above, presumably in Period VI and/or VII. The stratum abutted the uppermost preserved courses of Wall E1. It is possible that this stratum was laid down after Wall E had been built on top of Wall E1, early in Period VI. If this was the case, the debris probably accumulated while Alley AB was being used as a passageway alongside House B and as the main route of entrance to House A.

Wall H Foundation Trench

As discussed above, the northwest wall of House B, Wall H, was built after the first Period VI phase of Room B.1. Unless the Wall H foundation was significantly taller at the beginning of Period VI, another wall must have been built on top of it to delineate the northwest boundary of Room B.1; however, any trace of the wall in use during the first phase of Room B.1 was obliterated by the construction of Wall H. The foundation trench for Wall H in Alley AB is a secondary deposit composed of MBA and earlier Period VI ceramics. It is clear from the construction history of Room B.1, however, that Wall H was constructed in Period VII (above).

The foundation trench cut through all MBA and LBA strata above Wall X (Fig. 15; Pls. 11:c, 12:a). The top (ca. +2.00 m above sea level) of the foundation trench was easily recognized during the 1975 test excavation, owing to its soft soil and high frequency of stones, which contrasted sharply with the nature of the deposit of compact soil along Wall E1 (Kea Excavation Notebook III, 166–168). The lower part of the foundation trench contained several larger stones, probably set as packing against Wall H and/or filler in the bottom of the trench. In the 1961 test pit, such large stones were also found at higher elevations, up to an elevation of

II. STRATIGRAPHY, ARCHITECTURE, AND POTTERY

+1.80 m (Fig. 14:a; Kea Excavation Notebook III, 97). In the 1961 test pit, Bikaki noted that many of the stones in the foundation trench showed traces of burning (Kea Excavation Notebook III, 97). Some of the debris that filled the foundation trench may have derived from an earlier structure that had burned (perhaps associated with Wall E1?).

The foundation trench was excavated in 1975 in units B03-769 and B03-771–B03-773; ceramics from these units were combined into lot B647CL, together with pottery from Street 1 (below). The test excavation within Alley AB in 1961, northeast of the 1975 test pit, recovered ceramics and small finds from the foundation trench in excavation units B03-94 and B03-96 (Kea Excavation Notebook III, 97, 105). Bikaki's notes suggest that the upper portion of unit B03-97 may have included some of the foundation trench deposit (Fig. 14:a; Kea Excavation Notebook III, 105); pottery from unit B03-97 was included in J. C. Overbeck's Group CR (1989a, 175).

Street 1

In the 1975 test pit, Bikaki found a single stratum running across Alley AB above the foundation trench for Wall H and the compact strata abutting Wall E1. This stratum was composed of extremely compact soil and small, horizontally aligned stones (Kea Excavation Notebook III, 166–167); it was excavated in units B03-767–B03-769. Ceramics from lots B03-767 and B03-768 were combined into B646CL; pottery from unit B03-769, which included part of the foundation trench as well as this compact stratum, was combined into B647CL, described above. Only six sherds were kept in B646CL; they are compatible with a Period VII date.

Above this stratum was a layer of small, flat stones in red clayey soil (Pl. 10:b, c; Kea Excavation Notebook III, 165–166). It was excavated in units B03-765 and B03-766. Ceramics from unit B03-765 were discarded, while those from B03-766 were incorporated into B646CL. This and the previous stratum abutted Wall H and Wall E. They probably comprised the original LBA paving of Alley AB and so are designated as Street 1. Neither stratum of the paving was found in the 1961 test pit, where the later drain (Drain 1) had been disturbed; this disturbance apparently also removed the strata of Street 1.

Drain 1

In its final phase of use, Alley AB sloped downward from ca. +3.55 m above sea level in the south to +1.90 m above sea level in the north (Fig. 24). A wide drain (Drain 1) was constructed down the center of the alley, probably in Period VII (Fig. 6:b; Pls. 9, 10:a; Kea Excavation Notebook III, 31). The drain was excavated in units B03-21, B03-87, and B03-88. Drain 1 curved from Alley AB into a subterranean drain beneath Temple Lane (Kea Excavation Notebook III, 97; Kea Excavation Notebook XLIV, 110 [Drain B]). This part of the drain seems to have been excavated as part of B03-88 (Kea Excavation Notebook III, 94–95). An outlet from a bathroom in House A, Room 34, emptied into Drain 1 (Fig. 24; Cummer and Schofield 1984, 5, 17). A terracotta drain from the second story of House A, above Rooms 37 and 39, also probably emptied into Drain 1 (Cummer and Schofield 1984, 5, 8).

Slabs vertically placed against Walls E and H formed the sides of the drain (Fig. 6:b; Pls. 9, 10:a). Paving slabs covering the drain were found in most parts of the alley. The absence of paving slabs in the northeastern part of the alley is probably the result of disturbance. The disturbed part of the drain was excavated along with its northeastern part in unit B03-88, the uppermost unit of the 1961 test pit in Alley A-B (Fig. 14:a; Kea Excavation Notebook III, 94–95, 97). The latest ceramics from these lots belong to Period VII; the disturbance to the paving slabs, therefore, probably happened before the Period VIIb earthquake.

Debris from above the Period VII alley was recovered in two surface excavation units, B03-11 and B03-18 (Kea Excavation Notebook III, 11–12, 28). The excavation notebook is not descriptive enough to permit the strata above the alley to be described as anything but generic "fill." The alley probably went out of use in Period VII, when Houses B and A collapsed.

ALLEY AB CATALOGUE

EBA DESTRUCTION DEPOSIT

B03-806.
Lowest unit of test pit in Alley AB. Period III.

Pottery

1/3 bag collected; 3 sherds remain. A Red-Brown Semifine to Semicoarse basin (RBMe) and deep bowl/open jar (RBMb) were not catalogued.

Local

605 Pyxis. (Fig. 47, Pl. 44)
Slightly everted rim. H. pres. 0.03. D. rim est. 0.05(?). Moderately fine, compact, dark reddish-brown fabric with 1–5% inclusions. EBA Black Burnished. Interior and exterior surface coated with thick, black slip and burnished. Part of incised double or triple zigzag pattern preserved below rim. RBMa, compact, dark, common mica. For similar profile, see Wilson 1999, 130, no. III-382, pl. 34.

B03-805.
Test pit in Alley AB. Period III.

Pottery

1 bag collected; ½ bag remains. Uncatalogued ceramics in Red-Brown Semifine to Semicoarse ware (RBMa, RBMb) include a saucer, shallow bowls (Fig. 47:a), several deep bowl/open jars, a pyxis(?), and a stand(?). Other uncatalogued vessels include Red-Brown Burnished (RBMa, RBMb) shallow bowls; an Orange-Buff Semifine to Coarse closed vessel (CSWe); a Dark-Brown Slipped and Burnished tankard or beaker (DVa); and an Urfirnis open vessel (FVh).

Local

606 Shoulder-handled tankard. (Pl. 44)
Round, vertical handle. H. pres. 0.06. Moderately fine, compact, reddish-brown fabric with a gray core and 1–5% inclusions. EBA Red-Brown Burnished. Surface coated with streaky, thin, black slip; burnished. RBMa. For similar, see Wilson 1999, 102, no. III-12, pls. 23, 72.

607 Neck-handled tankard. (Fig. 47, Pl. 44)
Round, vertical handle and rim. H. pres. 0.05. Moderately fine, moderately compact, reddish-brown fabric with 5–10% inclusions. EBA Red-Brown Semifine to Semicoarse. Surface smoothed. RBMb, with rare, dark blue particles.

608 Saucer. (Fig. 47, Pl. 44)
Solid raised base with mat impression. H. pres. 0.03. D. base 0.04. Coarse, reddish-brown fabric with gray core and 10–15% inclusions. EBA Red-Brown Semifine to Semicoarse. Interior surface smoothed. RBMb, with rare, dark blue particles. PFG 1B (Local). For similar, see Wilson 1999, 103–104.

609 Shallow bowl. (Pl. 44)
Incurving rim, body, and flat base (four nonjoining fragments). H. pres. 0.06. D. rim est. 0.11. D. base est. 0.05. Moderately coarse, reddish-brown fabric with 5–10% inclusions. EBA Red-Brown Semifine to Semicoarse. Surface smoothed, coated with thin, streaky black slip/wash. RBMd. For similar, see Wilson 1999, 105, no. III-62, pl. 23.

Local(?)

610 Sauceboat(?). (Fig. 47, Pl. 44)
Arched trapezoidal-section handle. H. pres. 0.04. D. pres. 0.19. Moderately fine, compact, dark reddish-brown fabric with fewer than 1% inclusions. EBA Black Burnished. Interior and exterior coated with lustrous black slip; burnished. RBMa, unusually fine and compact, dark, with common mica.

Cyclades

611 Small open vessel (pyxis?). (Fig. 48, Pl. 44)
Rim and neck. H. pres. 0.03. D. rim est. 0.09(?). Moderately fine, porous, bluish-gray fabric turning brown at surface. Fewer than 1% inclusions. EBA Dark-Brown Slipped and Burnished. Surface covered with brown slip and burnished; burnishing marks visible. MxMc, blue gray.

612 Tankard. (Fig. 48, Pl. 44)
Flaring rim and upper body. H. pres. 0.05. D. rim est. 0.09. Moderately fine, hard-fired, dusty, bluish-gray fabric with 5–10% inclusions. EBA Black Burnished. Interior and exterior coated with black slip and burnished. MxMa, with no visible metamorphics. PFG 9A (Cyclades [Tenos?]).

613 Pyxis. (Fig. 48, Pl. 44)
Short, everted rim and globular, upper body. D. rim est. 0.11. Moderately fine, compact, orange-brown fabric turning gray at interior with 10–15% inclusions. EBA Red-Brown Burnished(?). Exterior and interior (perhaps only the rim and upper shoulder) are coated in streaky lustrous black slip; burnished. Uneven, curving, vertical groove on upper body. CSWe, with common mica. PFG 2Dc (Southeast Attica/Cyclades).

Euboea(?)

614 K.4414. Sauceboat. (Pl. 44)
Part of neck and spout. L. 0.11. Fine, very hard-fired, orange-pink fabric with distinct dark-gray core and fewer than 1% inclusions. Handmade. EBA Pinkish Buff(?). Coated with streaky dark-brown slip and burnished. The dark color of the slip is unusual for this ware, but the fabric is more like Pinkish Buff than other EBA wares. FVg.

Unknown

615 Open vessel (sauceboat?). (Pl. 44)
Body. Fine, hard-fired, slightly dusty, pinkish-orange fabric with distinct, dark bluish-gray core and fewer than 1% inclusions. EBA Yellow Mottled. Interior and exterior coated with thin, yellow slip and burnished. FVh. PFG 13A (Attica?).

Bone

616 K75.15. Awl. (Pl. 44)
Type II (Krzyszkowska). L. pres. 0.05. Wt. 1 g. Polished point and part of shaft, mended from two fragments. From ovicaprid cannon bone (J. L. Caskey).

B03-804.
Test trench in Alley AB. Period III, with possible Period IV intrusions.

Pottery

25 sherds collected; none discarded. Uncatalogued ceramics include shallow bowls, basins, and deep bowl/open jar fragments in Red-Brown Semifine to Semicoarse ware (RBMa, RBMb, RBMd); a Red-Brown Burnished (RBMa, RBMd) tankard(?) and deep bowl/open jar; Orange-Buff Semifine to Coarse (CSWe) closed vessels; and a Melian/Theran Painted (DVa) sherd, possibly dating to Period IV.

Local

617 Sauceboat(?). (Fig. 48, Pl. 44)
Slightly flaring, uneven rim. D. rim indeterminable. Moderately fine, hard-fired, dark red fabric with 1–5% inclusions. EBA Red-Brown Burnished. Interior and exterior highly burnished. RBMa, with very common mica.

618 Shoulder-handled tankard. (Pl. 44)
Rounded body and vertical handle. H. pres. 0.05. Moderately fine, porous, red fabric with 1–5% inclusions. EBA Red-Brown Burnished. RBMa, porous, with common mica. PFG 1Av (Local). For similar, see J. L. Caskey 1972, 371, 373, no. C46, fig. 6; Wilson 1999, 119, 126, nos. III-244, III-245, III-316, pls. 30, 33, 82, 86.

619 Basin. (Fig. 48, Pl. 44)
Rim, trumpet lug, and upper body. H. pres. 0.07. D. rim est. 0.46. Moderately coarse, compact, reddish-brown fabric with 10–15% inclusions. EBA Red-Brown Semifine to Semicoarse. Below rim: band of applied disks. RBMb.

620 Jar with two-stage neck. (Fig. 48, Pl. 44)
Hollowed, flaring rim and neck. D. rim est. 0.15. Moderately coarse, reddish-brown fabric with 10–30% inclusions. Interior and upper exterior rim darkened, probably from firing. EBA Red-Brown Semifine to Semicoarse. RBMa, with common mica, including more gold than usual. For similar, see Wilson 1999, 37, no. II-198, pls. 9, 50.

621 Hole-mouthed jar. (Fig. 48, Pl. 44)
Flattened, incurving rim and upper body. D. rim est. 0.29. Moderately fine, brittle, reddish-brown fabric with 1–5% inclusions. Plain. Interior and exterior smoothed. Period IV(?). RBMa, with common mica and shiny black particles.

Cyclades

622 Shallow bowl. (Fig. 48, Pl. 44)
Three nonjoining fragments; slightly flattened rim, flat base, and body. H. est. 0.06. D. rim est. 0.18. D. base est. 0.05. Moderately fine, hard-fired, pale orange fabric with thick, pale-gray core and 5–10% inclusions. EBA Orange-Buff Painted. Interior and exterior surface slipped with reddish-orange paint; burnished. MxMc. For similar, see Wilson 1999, 136, nos. III-464 to III-466, pls. 35, 91.

Unknown

623 Open jar (cooking vessel?). (Fig. 48, Pl. 44)
Incurving rim. H. pres. 0.05. D. rim est. 0.31. Moderately coarse, brittle, reddish-brown fabric with 10–15% inclusions. Interior: scoring below rim. Exterior: diagonal wiping(?) marks. Surface blackened in interior and burned patches on exterior. EBA Red-Brown Semifine to Semicoarse. CSWd. PFG 2C (Local [region]).

B03-803.
Test pit in Alley AB. Period III.

Pottery

1/3 bag collected; 6 sherds remain. Uncatalogued ceramics include a Red-Brown Semifine to Semicoarse (RBMa, RBMb) shallow bowl and deep bowl/open jar, as well as a Red-Brown Burnished (RBMc) shallow bowl.

Local(?)

624 Deep saucer. (Pl. 44)
Ring base and lower body. H. pres. 0.03. D. base est. 0.06. Moderately coarse, brittle, reddish-brown fabric with 15–20% inclusions. EBA Red-Brown Semifine to Semicoarse. Somewhat smoothed interior and exterior. RBMe. PFG 2A (Local [region]). For similar, see Wilson 1999, 104, no. III-56, pls. 23, 74.

625 Saucer (lamp?). (Fig. 48, Pl. 44)
Incurving rim and upper body. D. rim est. 0.12. Moderately coarse, reddish-brown fabric with 15–20% inclusions. Interior: wiping marks. Rim interior blackened. EBA Red-Brown Semifine to Semicoarse. RBMe. PFG 2A (Local [region]). For similar, see Wilson 1999, 103–104, nos. III-20, III-49, pls. 23, 72.

Unknown

626 Jar(?). (Pl. 44)
Body. Moderately coarse, hard-fired, relatively fine-grained, reddish-brown fabric with well-defined, gray core and 10–15%

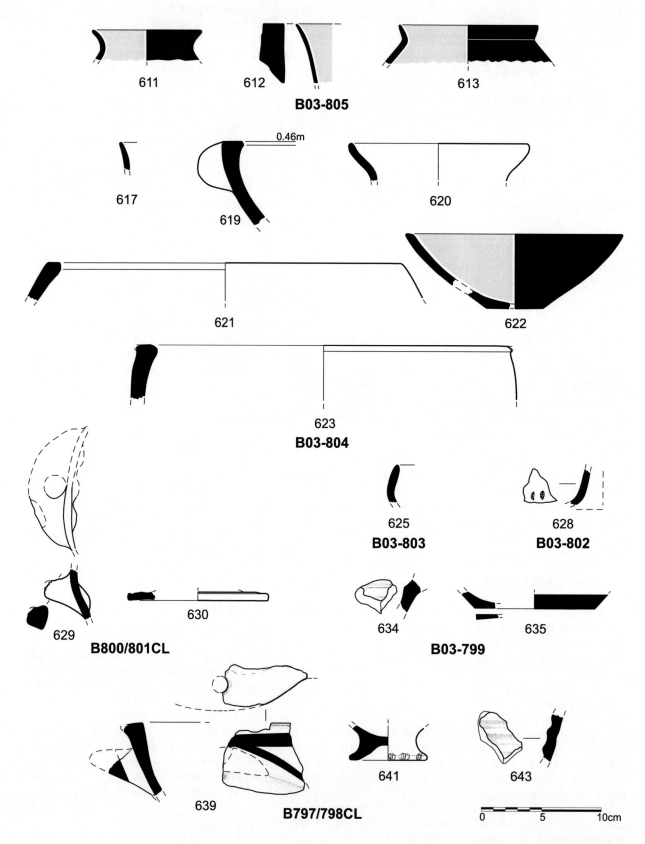

Fig. 48. Pottery from B03-805 (**611–613**), B03-804 (**617, 619–623**), B03-803 (**625**), B03-802 (**628**), B800/801CL (**629, 630**), B03-799 (**634, 635**), and B797/798CL (**639, 641, 643**). Drawings by Lily Bonga (**611, 613, 617, 620, 621, 623, 625, 628–630, 641**), Mary-Jane Schumacher (**612, 634, 635, 639, 643**), and Aliki Bikaki (**619, 622**).

inclusions. Interior: wiping marks. EBA Orange-Buff Semifine to Coarse. Exterior: coated in white slip. CSWe. PFG 4C (Naxos).

B03-802.
Test pit in Alley AB. Period III, plus a Period IV goblet (**628**).

Pottery

1/3 bag collected; 6 sherds remain. Uncatalogued sherds included a Red-Brown Semifine to Semicoarse (RBMb) deep bowl/open jar, and a Red-Brown Burnished (RBMa) saucer and shallow bowl.

Local

627 Shallow bowl. (Pl. 44)
Slightly incurving rim. D. rim est. 0.16. Moderately fine, brittle, reddish-brown fabric with thick, well-defined, dark-gray core and 10–15% inclusions. EBA Red-Brown Burnished. Exterior burnished; interior smoothed. Burnishing now eroded. RBMa, with common mica.

628 K.4599. Tall-stemmed goblet. (Fig. 48, Pl. 44)
Stem fragment near foot. Moderately coarse, compact, red fabric with 10–15% inclusions. Handmade. Burnished. Interior and exterior surface burnished; interior surface preserves two parallel curved grooves, probably made by a fingernail, incised before firing. Third groove possibly preserved at break. Period IV. RBMa, with rare calcareous(?) inclusions. Similar marks have been found on goblets from Period IVa/b deposits elsewhere on site (Bikaki 1984, 11, nos. IV-10, IV-11, pls. 2, 16).

B800/801CL.
Upper unit of Period III destruction deposit in Alley AB test pit. Mixed Period III and Period IV.

Pottery

5/6 bag collected; 17 sherds remain. Uncatalogued vessels in EBA Red-Brown wares (RBMa, RBMb, RBMd) include a sauceboat(?), shallow bowl, basin, open jar, jar, and pithos. A jar/pithos in Orange-Buff Semifine to Coarse ware (MxMf) and Gray Minyan (FVa) sherds were also uncatalogued.

Local

629 Globular(?) jar. (Fig. 48, Pl. 44)
Pierced, crescent lug and attachment to body. Moderately coarse, brittle, slightly porous, dark gray fabric turning to dark orange at interior surface and dark red-brown at exterior surfaces, with 10–15% inclusions. Handmade. Raised clay lumps at interior, probably from attaching the handle by pushing through the vessel wall. Exterior surface smoothed. Plain. RBMa.

Mainland

630 Goblet. (Fig. 48, Pl. 44)
Foot. D. base est. 0.12. Fine, hard-fired, slightly dusty, gray fabric with no inclusions. Wheelmade. Gray Minyan. All surfaces burnished; now eroded, particularly at bottom of base. FVa. For similar profile, see Sarri 2010b, pl. 24:12.

631 Goblet. (Pl. 44)
Foot. D. base est. 0.15. Fine, gray fabric with fewer than 1% inclusions. Wheelmade. Gray Minyan. Upper and lower surfaces of foot are burnished. FVa. For similar profile, see Sarri 2010b, 295, pl. 24:1 and 7.

DEPOSITS ASSOCIATED WITH CONSTRUCTION AND USE OF WALL X

B03-799.
Foundation trench for Wall X. Period IVa.

Pottery

1/3 bag collected; 13 sherds remain. "Scraps" discarded. Uncatalogued ceramics include only an EBA pithos fragment (RBMb) and Gray Minyan (FVa) sherds, most probably goblets.

Aegina

632 Globular jar. (Pl. 44)
Neck just below rim. D. est., at curve to lip, 0.11. Moderately fine, rather gritty, pale yellow fabric with 1–5% inclusions. Handmade. Matt Painted. Decoration in thickly-applied, matt dark-brown paint. Interior: vertical bands, probably overlapping from lip. Exterior: two horizontal bands at curve to lip. DVd. PFG 5Gv (Aegina). For similar shape and decoration in Kolonna, see Siedentopf 1991, pls. 43:188, 44:189 (Stadt IX).

Mainland

633 Pteleon goblet. (Pl. 44)
Handle attachment below rim. Fine, pale-gray fabric with fewer than 1% inclusions. Gray Minyan. Interior and exterior burnished. FVa. For similar, see Pavúk 2007, 299, fig. 3.

634 Goblet. (Fig. 48, Pl. 44)
Ring stem. Fine, hard-fired, gray fabric, slightly paler at core, with fewer than 1% inclusions. Wheelmade. Gray Minyan. Interior: unburnished. Exterior: highly burnished with two ridges. FVa. For similar profile, see Sarri 2010b, 275, 295, pls. 15:1, 24:2.

Unknown

635 Closed vessel. (Fig. 48, Pl. 44)
Flat base and conical lower body. D. base est. 0.09. Moderately fine, hard-fired, pinkish-orange fabric with 5–10% inclusions. Wheelmade. Lustrous Painted (Monochrome). Exterior coated with thick, semi-lustrous orange paint, overlapping and

spattered on base. FSTf, with common calcareous inclusions. PFG 7D (Crete/Peloponnese).

636 Vessel. (Pl. 44)
Body. Moderately coarse, compact, hard-fired, red-orange fabric with 5–10% inclusions. Interior: uneven, with wiping marks. Exterior: vertical paring marks. Handmade. Plain. FSTi. PFG 8D (Unknown).

B797/798CL.
Packing for pavement associated with use of Wall X. Period IVa.

Pottery

1 1/2 bags collected; ½ bag remains. "Scraps" discarded. Uncatalogued vessels include local (RBMa) Yellow-Slipped closed and Burnished open vessels; Lustrous and Non-Lustrous Painted Minoan/-izing (FSTf) closed vessels, including one with trickle decoration and another coated with thin slip; and Gray Minyan (FVa) open vessels.

Local

637 Open vessel. (Pl. 45)
Flaring rim. D. rim est. 0.20. Moderately fine, reddish-brown fabric with dark-gray core and 5–10% inclusions. Forming method indeterminable. Burnished. Highly burnished, dark brown to black. RBMa, with common mica.

638 Large (barrel?) jar. (Pl. 45)
Crescent lug. L. 0.14. Moderately coarse, reddish-brown fabric with gray core and 10–15% inclusions. Interior: four raised clay lumps, from attaching handle by pushing through vessel wall. Yellow Slipped. Exterior coated in thick, yellow slip; traces of matt-black band, probably encircling handle. RBMa, with very common mica.

639 Basin. (Fig. 48, Pl. 45)
Thickened ledge rim, upper body, crescent lug. D. rim est. 0.40. Moderately coarse, reddish-brown fabric with 10–15% inclusions. Interior: clay lump, from attachment of handle by pushing through wall. Handmade. Yellow Slipped. Interior and exterior coated with yellow slip; exterior decorated in matt black. Diagonal bars along rim; band below rim and a band encircling handle. RBMa, with rare calcareous(?) inclusions. PFG 1C (Local). For similar shape, see J. C. Overbeck 1989a, 80, no. AI-5, pl. 54.

640 Large, closed vessel (barrel jar?). (Pl. 45)
Body. Moderately fine, dark-gray fabric turning reddish-brown at surface, with 5–10% inclusions. Handmade. Yellow Slipped (Polychrome). Exterior coated with yellow slip, decorated with matt-black and matt-orange paint. Thick, matt orange band between two, matt-black bands; at oblique angle (intersecting?) is a thin, matt orange band between two, thick, matt-black bands. RBMa, dark. PFG 2B (Local [region]).

641 K.4412. (Wide-mouthed?) Jar. (Fig. 48, Pl. 45)
Pedestal foot. H. pres. 0.03. D. base. 0.07. D. stem 0.05. Published, Bikaki 1984, 14, no. IV-36; J. C. Overbeck 1989a, 175. From B03-797, Group CQ. Moderately coarse, orange to gray fabric, dark reddish brown at interior, discolored to gray in places. Handmade. Plain. RBMc, with phyllite(?). For a similar mark on a different kind of base in Aeginetan fabric, see Lindblom 2001, 69, no. 598, pl. 28.

Melos/Thera

642 Jug(?). (Pl. 45)
Body. Moderately fine, porous, white fabric with 5–10% inclusions. Handmade. Cycladic White. Exterior smoothed. Narrow, horizontal band and three vertical short narrow lines in matt black. DVa. PFG 5A (Melos/Thera).

Mainland

643 Goblet. (Fig. 48, Pl. 45)
Ring stem. Fine, gray fabric with fewer than 1% inclusions. Wheel-coiled. Gray Minyan. Exterior burnished; three ridges. FVa, shiny, white and subrounded, dark gray inclusions.

B795/A/796CL.
Pavement and accumulated soil associated with use of Wall X. Period IVb.

Pottery

1/2 tin (ca. 8.5 liters) and ½ bag collected; ¾ bag remains. No discard information. Uncatalogued ceramics include a local Burnished goblet decorated in white (RBMa), as well as Yellow Slipped and plain closed vessels (RBMa, RBMd); a Cycladic White closed vessel (DVa); an Aeginetan(?) plain closed vessel (DVf); Minoan/-izing plain, Lustrous Painted, and Non-Lustrous Painted closed vessels (FSTa, FSTc, FSTd, FSTf, FSTi); and a Minyan(?)-style open vessel in an unusual fabric (MFVb).

Local

644 Goblet. (Pl. 45)
Flaring rim and carinated body. H. 0.03. D. rim est. 0.19. Moderately fine, dark reddish-brown fabric with 5–10% inclusions. Forming method indeterminable. Burnished. Interior and exterior burnished dark brown. RBMa, with common mica. PFG 1C (Local). For shape, see J. L. Caskey 1972, 379, 383, no. D128, fig. 9.

645 Carinated(?) bowl (shape 1). (Fig. 49, Pl. 45)
Flat base and lower body. D. base est. 0.06. Moderately fine, red fabric with slightly darker, red core and 5–10% inclusions. Handmade(?). Burnished. Interior and exterior highly burnished. RBMa, with very common mica, especially at surface. PFG 1C (Local). For shape, see J. C. Overbeck 1989a, 48, no. S-16, pl. 43.

646 Large (barrel?) jar. (Pl. 45)
Body. Moderately fine, reddish-brown fabric with 5–10% inclusions. Handmade. Yellow Slipped. Exterior: coated with thick, yellow slip. Thick band outlined by two narrow bands, with radiating narrow band, all in matt-black paint. RBMa, compact, with common mica, especially at break. PFG 1C (Local). For similar motifs in various wares, see J. C. Overbeck 1989a, 38, 98, nos. M-18, AQ-17, pls. 41, 59.

647 Wide-mouthed jar. (Fig. 49, Pl. 45)
Flaring rim and upper body. D. rim est. 0.24. Moderately coarse, reddish-brown fabric with thick, gray core and 10–15% inclusions. Handmade. Discolored to dark gray on one side. Plain. RBMa, with rare calcareous(?) inclusions. For shape, see J. L. Caskey 1972, 380, 382, no. D87, fig. 10.

648 Wide-mouthed(?) jar. (Fig. 49, Pl. 45)
Vertical round handle. L. 0.07. Moderately fine, dark orange fabric with well-defined, gray core and 5–10% inclusions. Interior uneven where handle attached. Handmade(?). Plain. RBMd, with rare calcareous(?) inclusions. For possible shape, see J. L. Caskey 1972, 380, 382, no. D87, fig. 10.

649 Jug. (Fig. 49, Pl. 45)
Vertical round handle attached at rim, neck, and shoulder. H. pres. 0.08. Moderately coarse, reddish-brown fabric with thick, pale bluish-gray core and 5–10% inclusions. Handmade. Plain. RBMa, with rare calcareous(?) inclusions. PFG 1D (Local). For similar shape, see J. C. Overbeck 1989a, 63, 69, nos. X-105, AB-30, pls. 49, 51.

650 Baking tray. (Fig. 49, Pl. 45)
Base and triangular-section rim. D. est. 0.32. Moderately fine, reddish-brown fabric with well-defined, dark-gray core and 5–10% inclusions. Exterior: rough. Handmade. Plain. RBMa, with common mica. For similar, although with different rim profile, see J. L. Caskey 1972, 380, 382, nos. D89, D90, fig. 10.

651 Cup. (Fig. 49, Pl. 45)
Flat base and conical lower body. D. base 0.04. Moderately coarse, reddish-brown fabric with 10–15% inclusions. Wheel-coiled. Plain. RBMa, with very common mica. Compare shape with MacGillivray 2007, 132, fig. 4.21:1.

652 Cup. (Fig. 49, Pl. 45)
Slightly raised base and flaring lower body. D. base 0.04. Moderately fine, reddish-brown fabric turning slightly darker at core, with 1–5% inclusions. Wheel-coiled. Plain. RBMa, compact, with common mica and yellow particles. PFG 1Cv (Local). For similar shape, see MacGillivray 2007, 132, fig. 4.21:1.

653 Saucer. (Fig. 49, Pl. 45)
Raised base and wide lower body. D. base 0.05. Moderately coarse, reddish-brown fabric with 5–10% inclusions. Wheel-coiled. Plain. RBMa, with common mica. PFG 1Cv (Local). For similar profile, see J. L. Caskey 1972, 380–381, no. D-74, fig. 10. Shape similar to Cretan vessels (e.g., MacGillivray 2007, 133, Crude Ware bowl type 3, MM IIA–IIIA).

Cyclades

654 Open vessel. (Fig. 49, Pl. 45)
Body, at curve to rim(?). Moderately fine, hard-fired, pale orange-brown fabric with 5–10% inclusions. Forming method indeterminable. Slipped and Burnished(?). Interior and exterior coated with semi-lustrous red slip; exterior burnished(?). MxMc. PFG 4B. (Central Cyclades?).

655 Goblet. (Fig. 49, Pl. 45)
Nonjoining flaring rim and body. D. rim est. 0.17. Fine, slightly dusty, pinkish-brown fabric with 1–5% inclusions. Forming method indeterminable. Slipped and Burnished. Interior and exterior coated with red slip, burnished to high luster. MFVa. PFG 3Cv (Cyclades [Syros?]). For shape, see J. L. Caskey 1972, 379, 383, no. D128, fig. 9; J. C. Overbeck 1989a, 157, no. CE-47, pl. 75.

Aegina(?)

656 Jug. (Fig. 49, Pl. 45)
Rim and thick, ovoid handle attachment. Moderately fine, slightly dusty, orange fabric with 1–5% inclusions. Handle attachment is lumpy. Plain. Short (0.02 m) incised line at top of handle. DVe. PFG 5G (Aegina). No potter's marks of this type have been reported for Aeginetan vessels (Lindblom 2001).

Mainland

657 Jar. (Fig. 49, Pl. 45)
Pierced crescent lug. Fine, hard-fired, red fabric with fewer than 1% inclusions. Forming method indeterminable. Pink-Orange. Interior smoothed; exterior burnished. FVd/FVf. PFG 13B (Euboea). For ware, see Overbeck 2010.

Mainland/Kythera(?)

658 Closed vessel. (Pl. 45)
Body (two nonjoining fragments). Moderately coarse, pale pinkish-brown fabric with greenish tinge at surface and purple tinge at core, and with 5–10% inclusions. Handmade. Lustrous Decorated (Monochrome?). Exterior coated(?) with lustrous black paint, now almost entirely fugitive or faded. FSTg. PFG 7C (Crete/Peloponnese). For ware, see Zerner 2008, 203.

Crete(?)

659 Fine, closed vessel. (Pl. 45)
Body. Fine, hard-fired, dark pink fabric with thin, pale-gray core. No inclusions. Wheelmade. Lustrous Painted (LOD). Exterior coated in semi-lustrous black slip; indecipherable decoration in white and red. FSTk.

660 Small, closed vessel. (Pl. 45)
Body. Moderately fine, hard-fired, pinkish-orange fabric with 1–5% inclusions. Wheelmade. Lustrous Painted (LOD). Exterior: coated with semi-lustrous black; added indecipherable motif in white. FSTk. PFG 6Bv (Central Crete [Mesara?]).

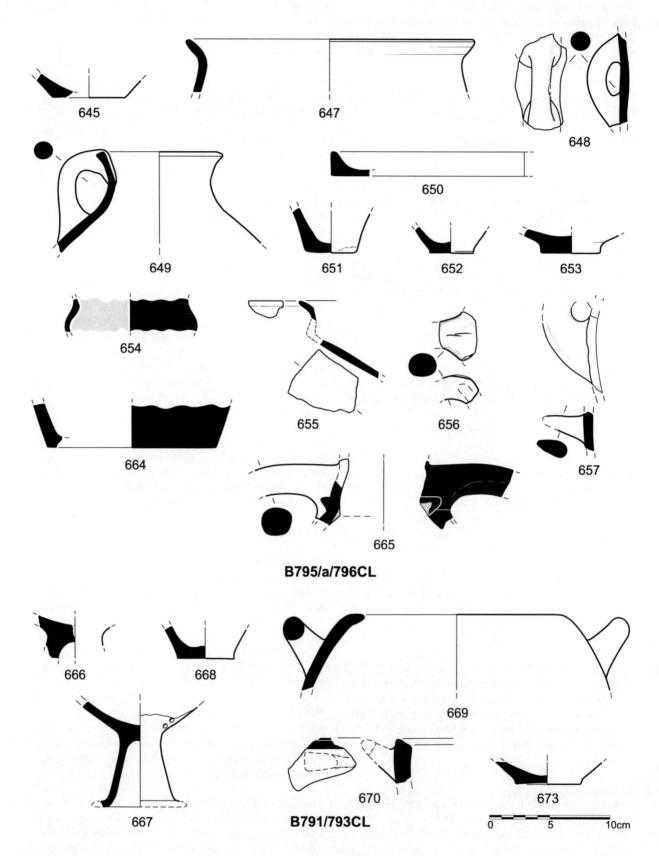

Fig. 49. Pottery from B795/a/796CL (**645, 647–657, 664, 665**) and B791/793CL (**666–670, 673**). Drawings by Mary-Jane Schumacher (**645, 647–657, 664–666, 668, 670, 673**) and Aliki Bikaki (**667, 669**).

661 Jug. (Pl. 45)
Vertical, strap handle at body attachment. Fine, pinkish-brown fabric with 1–5% inclusions. Forming method indeterminable. Lustrous Painted (Monochrome). Surface coated with semi-lustrous black, now flaking. FSTk, with metamorphics(?).

662 Closed vessel. (Pl. 45)
Body. Moderately fine, dark orange fabric turning pale brown at exterior margin, with 5–10% inclusions. Handmade. Non-Lustrous Painted. Exterior: dark-brown trickle. FSTf, with no core. PFG 6C (Crete?).

663 Closed vessel. (Pl. 45)
Body. Moderately fine, pale orange fabric with paler orange exterior margin and 5–10% inclusions. Handmade. Non-Lustrous Painted. Part of filled disk in nonlustrous(?) black, now flaking. FSTc. PFG 7D (Crete/Peloponnese). For somewhat similar decoration, see Betancourt 1985, 86, 88, figs. 61:h, 63:a.

Unknown

664 Large jar. (Fig. 49, Pl. 45)
Base and lower body. D. base est. 0.14. Moderately coarse, slightly gritty, dark pink fabric with thin, pale pink core and 10–15% inclusions. Coil-built. Lustrous Painted (LOD). Exterior: coated in semi-lustrous black, lower part of diagonal red band(?) at edge of base. FSTi, pink-tinged, with microfossils(?). PFG 8B (Unknown).

665 Round-mouthed jug. (Fig. 49, Pl. 45)
Neck with triangular-section molding and round, vertical handle. Moderately fine, dark pink fabric with 5–10% inclusions. Handmade. Broken at coil join to body, not well smoothed. Molding probably made by attaching coil to body and then pinching to form pointed edge; not fully smoothed to body at one side. Non-Lustrous Painted (Monochrome). Surface smoothed, coated in thin, smeary, non-lustrous reddish-brown slip. FSTi, pink-tinged. PFG 8C (Unknown). For shape, see J. C. Overbeck 1989a, 110, nos. AR-9, AR-10, AR-11, AR-12, pl. 62.

Plaster

Uninventoried:
B03-795: wall plaster (B-75.11). Apparently painted, but no additional information exists in records.

Clay

Uninventoried:
B03-795: Lump of clay with traces of burning (B-75.10). Clay is like RBMa; burned at one surface, which bends to form edge. Perhaps a hearth lining or similar?

B03-794.
Accumulation above a pavement associated with the use of Wall X. Period IVb.

Pottery

1/2 bag collected, 3 sherds remain. "Scraps" discarded. Nothing inventoried. Uncatalogued sherds are one Gray Minyan and two Cycladic (local?) burnished sherds from open vessels.

B791/793CL.
Stratum associated with use of Drain 2. Period IVb.

Pottery

1 bag collected, 1/3 bag remains. "Scraps" discarded. Uncatalogued ceramics include local (RBMa) vessels, including a Burnished goblet and carinated bowl, as well as a plain, crescent handle from a jar; two Cycladic White (DVa) closed vessels; Minoan/-izing (FSTc, FSTi) Lustrous Painted, Non-Lustrous Painted, and plain closed vessels.

Local

666 Goblet. (Fig. 49, Pl. 45)
Stem. H. pres. 0.03. Moderately fine, reddish-brown fabric with gray core and 5–10% inclusions. Break shows attachment of stem, but other evidence for forming method is not preserved. Burnished. All surfaces burnished orange-red, except inside stem. RBMa, with common mica. For profile, see J. L. Caskey 1972, 379, 383, no. D128, fig. 9.

667 K.4413. Goblet. (Fig. 49, Pl. 45)
Published, Bikaki 1984, 16, no. IV-58, pl. 19; J. C. Overbeck 1989a, 175, no. CS-1. Tall stem and lower body with two round impressions. H. pres. 0.08. Moderately fine, red fabric. Burnished. RBMa, with a compact, micaceous break.

668 Cup. (Fig. 49, Pl. 45)
Flat base and thick-walled lower body. D. base 0.05. Moderately coarse, orange-red fabric with thin, gray core and 10–15% inclusions. Slightly lumpy texture of clay suggests the vessel was too dry when being worked. Wheel-coiled. Plain. RBMa, with common mica. PFG 1A (Local). For similar vessels, see J. C. Overbeck 1989a, 45, no. Q-46, pl. 43 (Period IVa/b); MacGillivray 2007, fig. 4.30:2.

Cyclades

669 Hole-mouthed jar. (Fig. 49, Pl. 45)
Flattened rim, globular upper body, and slightly arched horizontal handle. H. pres. 0.07. D. rim est. 0.18. Moderately fine, pale brown fabric with 5–10% inclusions. Handmade. Int. lumpy; horizontally oriented wiping marks on top of rim, interior below rim, and exterior around handle attachments. Slightly discolored to pink at one side. Plain. MxMf, with common dark particles. PFG 4Bv (Central Cyclades?). For similar shape, see Barber 2007, 224, fig. 6.14:314, 315.

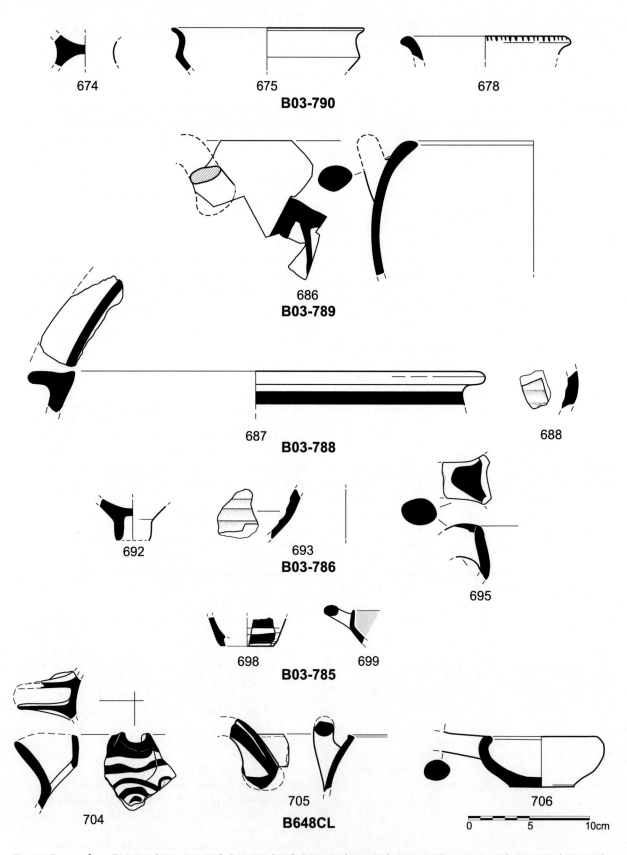

Fig. 50. Pottery from B03-790 (**674, 675, 678**), B03-789 (**686**), B03-788 (**687, 688**), B03-786 (**692, 693, 695**), B03-785 (**698, 699**), and B648CL (**704–706**). Drawings by Mary-Jane Schumacher (**674, 675, 678, 686–688, 692, 693, 695, 698, 704, 705**) and Aliki Bikaki (**699, 706**).

Aegina

670 Basin. (Fig. 49, Pl. 45)
Slightly incurving rim and crescent handle attachment. D. rim est. 0.30. Moderately fine, rather porous, pale orange-brown fabric with 1–5% inclusions. Lump of clay protruding at interior where handle attached by pushing through vessel wall. Forming method indeterminable. Matt Painted. Faded matt brown band below rim. DVe, with sponge spicules. PFG 5G (Aegina). For similar shape, see Philippa-Touchais 2007, 98, fig. 1:4.

Crete(?)

671 Closed vessel. (Pl. 45)
Body. From B03-791. Moderately fine, hard-fired, compact, pale pinkish-orange fabric with 5–10% inclusions. Coil-built. Lustrous Painted (LOD). Exterior: coated with monochrome lustrous black. Fugitive white band(?). FSTe. PFG 7E (Crete/Peloponnese).

Unknown

672 Large, closed vessel. (Pl. 45)
Body. Moderately coarse, compact, hard-fired, purplish-brown fabric with 5–10% inclusions. Handmade. Non-Lustrous Painted. Exterior smoothed, matt-black trickle decoration. FSTi, purple tinged with large, calcareous particles. PFG 8E (Unknown).

673 Bowl(?). (Fig. 49, Pl. 45)
Raised base and flaring lower body. D. base 0.05. Hard-fired, fine, pinkish-orange fabric turning paler at margins. Fewer than 1% inclusions, primarily bright, shiny, white and angular, friable, red particles, common, fine fraction gold mica; and common, small, vughs (and round voids?). Wheelmade. Plain. Unknown fabric. PFG 9B (Unknown).

Stone

Uninventoried:
B03-791: obsidian fragment.
B03-793: flint fragment, obsidian fragment.

B03-790.
Stratum associated with use of Drain 2 and soil within Drain 2. Period IVb.

Pottery

1 bag collected, 1/3 bag remains. "Scraps" discarded. Uncatalogued ceramics include local (RBMa) plain and Burnished open vessels; and Minoan/-izing (FSTf, FSTi) Non-Lustrous Painted closed vessels.

Local

674 Goblet. (Fig. 50, Pl. 46)
Short stem at attachment to body. D. 0.05. Moderately coarse, gritty, reddish-brown fabric, darker at bowl interior and stem exterior, with 5–10% inclusions. Handmade. Burnished. RBMa, with very common mica. For profile, see J. L. Caskey 1972, 379, 383, no. D125, fig. 9.

675 Goblet. (Fig. 50, Pl. 46)
Flaring rim and carinated body. D. rim est. 0.17. Moderately fine, compact, reddish-brown fabric with orange-brown surface and 1–5% inclusions. Forming method indeterminable. Burnished. RBMa, with very common mica.

Cyclades

676 Large, closed vessel. (Pl. 46)
Vertical round handle. Moderately coarse, compact, red fabric with gray core and 10–15% inclusions. Protrusion at lower end from attachment to body by pushing through the wall. Plain. MxMd, with phyllite(?). PFG 3B (Central[?] Cyclades).

677 Closed vessel. (Pl. 46)
Body. Moderately coarse, porous, gritty, pale brown fabric with 15–20% inclusions. Coil-built. Slipped and Burnished. Exterior coated with dark red slip, highly burnished. CSWe. PFG 4Cv (Naxos).

Melos/Thera

678 Jar. (Fig. 50, Pl. 46)
Rim. D. rim est. 0.14. Moderately fine, very pale green fabric with 5–10% inclusions. Handmade(?). Cycladic White. Fugitive bars along rim. DVa.

Aegina

679 Closed vessel.
Body. Moderately coarse, high fired, reddish-brown fabric with 10–15% inclusions. Handmade. Plain. DVf.

Crete(?)

680 Small, closed(?) vessel. (Pl. 46)
Round handle. Fine, pinkish-brown fabric with slightly darker core. Fewer than 1% inclusions. Forming method indeterminable. Lustrous Painted (Monochrome). Exterior coated with thick lustrous black, now flaking. FSTk.

Unknown

681 Hole-mouthed jar(?). (Pl. 46)
Body and ovoid, arched handle attachment. Moderately fine, hard-fired, orange fabric with slightly darker core. Handmade. Handle plug pushed through hole in vessel wall. Non-Lustrous Painted (LOD). Exterior smoothed. Non-lustrous red to dark-brown torsional(?) bands, with added narrow white bands. FSTi. PFG 8C (Unknown). Somewhat similar to reversible decoration like that known in Early and Classical Kamares styles (Walberg 1976, 80–81).

682 Large, closed vessel. (Pl. 46)
Body. Moderately fine, compact, hard-fired, reddish-orange fabric with 5–10% inclusions. Handmade. Non-Lustrous Painted (Monochrome). Exterior coated with streaky non-lustrous brown paint. FSTi, with no core. PFG 8D (Unknown).

683 Fine, closed(?) vessel. (Pl. 46)
Body. Moderately fine, slightly dusty, hard-fired orange fabric with 5–10% inclusions. Handmade. Non-Lustrous Painted (Monochrome). Exterior coated with uneven, thin, red slip. FSTi, with no core. PFG 8D (Unknown).

684 Large, closed(?) vessel. (Pl. 46)
Body (two nonjoining fragments). Coarse, compact, hard-fired fabric turning dark pink at exterior and purplish-gray at interior, with 15–20% inclusions. Handmade. Plain. Exterior: well-smoothed. FSTi. PFG 8Dv (Unknown).

Terracotta

685 K75.11. Spindle whorl. (Pl. 46)
Published, J. C. Overbeck 1989a, 175, Group CS. Type S2. H. 0.02. D. 0.03. D. perf. 0.01. Wt. 16 g. Moderately coarse, reddish-brown fabric with 15–20% inclusions. Surface smoothed; now worn and pitted. Blackened at one edge. Breakage at both ends of perforation, especially at bottom. RBMa (Local).

CONSTRUCTION AND USE OF STREET 2

B03-789.
Packing for Street 2. Period IVb.

Pottery

1/2 bag collected, 5 sherds (4 joining) remain. "Scraps" discarded. Uncatalogued vessel is a body sherd from an Aeginetan vessel (DVd).

Crete

686 Hole-mouthed jar. (Fig. 50, Pl. 46)
Incurving rim; round, horizontal handle; and globular, upper body. Nonjoining body fragment. D. rim est. 0.20. Moderately coarse, pinkish-orange fabric turning paler at surface, with 10–15% inclusions. Uneven interior preserves fingerprints; wiping marks at rim interior. Handmade. Lustrous Painted. Exterior: trickle pattern in semi-lustrous black. FSTe, coarse sand. PFG 6B (Central Crete [Mesara?]).

B03-788.
Lower layer of Street 2 paving. Period IVb/c.

Pottery

1/3 bag collected, 9 sherds remain. "Scraps" discarded. Uncatalogued: 2 Gray Minyan goblet fragments (FVa) and a Minoan/-izing Lustrous Painted (LOD) closed vessel (FSTf).

Local

687 Barrel jar. (Fig. 50, Pl. 46)
Projecting rim with flange and upper body. D. rim est. 0.31. Coarse, reddish-brown fabric with thick, dark-gray core and 15–20% inclusions. Handmade. Yellow Slipped. Interior and exterior coated with yellow slip. Bands in matt-black paint along edge of flange (missing) and below rim. RBMa, very micaceous.

Mainland

688 Goblet. (Fig. 50, Pl. 46)
Ring stem. Fine, hard-fired, gray fabric with no inclusions. Wheelmade. Gray Minyan. Exterior: two ridges preserved. FVa, slightly paler (bluish) at core. PFG 14Dv (Central Greece?).

689 Bowl. (Pl. 46)
Short, everted rim and globular, upper body. D. rim est. 0.17. Fine, hard-fired, gray fabric with fewer than 1% inclusions. Wheelmade. Gray Minyan. FVa.

Crete

690 Closed vessel. (Pl. 46)
Shoulder. Moderately coarse, pinkish-orange fabric turning paler at surface, with 10–15% inclusions. Coil-built. Seam at interior, probably where neck attached. Lustrous Painted (LOD). Exterior coated in semi-lustrous dark-brown paint; indecipherable decoration in white(?). FSTe.

691 Hole-mouthed jar(?). (Pl. 46)
Round, arched handle. Fine, pale, pinkish-orange fabric with no inclusions. Forming method indeterminable. Lustrous Painted (Monochrome). Coated in lustrous black. FSTk.

B03-786.
Second paving stratum of Street 2. Period IVb/c.

Pottery

1/2 bag collected; 7 sherds kept. Chronologically undiagnostic sherds discarded. Uncatalogued ceramics include sherds from a closed, Lustrous Painted (Monochrome) vessel, probably from Crete (FSTf), and a Gray Minyan ring-stemmed goblet (FVa).

Local

692 Vessel. (Fig. 50, Pl. 46)
Stem(?). Moderately coarse, brittle, dark reddish-brown fabric turning dark gray at surface, with 5–10% inclusions. Handmade. Burnished. RBMa, dark.

Mainland

693 Goblet. (Fig. 50, Pl. 46)
Ring stem. Fine, gray fabric with fewer than 1% inclusions. Wheelmade. Gray Minyan. Three ridges preserved. FVa.

Crete

694 Closed vessel. (Pl. 46)
Body. Moderately coarse, hard-fired, pale brown fabric with 10–15% inclusions. Handmade. Lustrous Painted (LOD). Exterior coated in lustrous black; indecipherable decoration in white. FSTa. PFG 7B (Central Crete?).

695 Jug. (Fig. 50, Pl. 46)
Thick, round handle and thin-walled, slightly flaring rim. Moderately coarse, hard-fired, pink fabric. Interior distorted by handle attachment. Forming method indeterminable. Lustrous Painted. Decoration in semi-lustrous black. Blob on top of handle. Interior: diagonal trickle. FSTe. PFG 6C (Crete?).

696 Closed vessel. (Pl. 46)
Body. Moderately coarse, hard-fired, pale pinkish-brown fabric with 10–15% inclusions. Handmade. Lustrous Painted. Exterior: lustrous black band(?) (or trickle?). FSTa. PFG 7A (Central Crete).

Terracotta

697 Loom weight. (Pl. 46)
Approximately 1/3 upper part. H. pres. 0.05. D. perf. 0.01. Wt. 89 g. Moderately coarse, reddish-brown fabric with 10–15% inclusions. Surface well-smoothed. RBMa, very micaceous. (Local).

B03-785.
Upper paving of Street 2. Period IVc–V.

Pottery

1/2 bag collected, 4 sherds kept. Chronologically undiagnostic sherds discarded. Uncatalogued: sherd from a Lustrous Painted (LOD) cup or bowl (FSTk).

Local

698 Straight-sided(?) cup. (Fig. 50, Pl. 46)
Beveled base and lower body. D. base est. 0.05. Moderately fine, reddish-brown fabric with fewer than 1% inclusions. Yellow Slipped. Interior and exterior coated in thick, yellow slip. Exterior: two bands in thick, orange-red paint. Handmade(?). RBMa, with common mica. Period V straight-sided cups often have beveled bases (Davis 1986, 54, 86, nos. AA-1, AA-2, pls. 31, 59), but the bands of this vessel are more similar to those of a straight-sided cup (without a beveled base) from Grave 24, dated to late in Period IV (G. F. Overbeck 1989, 199, no. 24-5, pl. 103; J. C. Overbeck 1989a, 179), a Period V bowl (Davis 1986, 52, no. Y-3, pl. 59), and a straight-sided cup from a Period VIIa deposit in the Western Sector (Schofield 2011, 71–72, no. 821, pl. 51).

Melos/Thera

699 Cycladic cup or carinated bowl (shape 2). (Fig. 50, Pl. 46)
Carinated rim and arched handle. D. rim indeterminable. Moderately fine, hard-fired, yellowish-brown fabric with gray surface and 10–15% inclusions. Forming method indeterminable. Slipped and Burnished. Interior and exterior slipped dark red and burnished. DVc. PFG 5D (Melos?). Similar profile in Period IVc (J. C. Overbeck 1984, 110; 1989a, 105–107, nos. AT-2, AT-8, AT-25, pls. 63, 64) and common in Period V (Davis 1986, 83, 85).

Crete(?)

700 Closed vessel. (Pl. 46)
Body. Moderately coarse, hard-fired, pink fabric with 5–10% inclusions, primarily small–moderate, round to subrounded semitranslucent white, pink, gray, and red particles; rarer red to pink-orange possible phyllite; and small–moderate voids. Coil-built. Lustrous Painted (LOD). Exterior: coated in semi-lustrous red paint; thick, white band. Macroscopic fabric unknown.

PERIOD V (–VI?) DESTRUCTION DEPOSIT

B649CL.
Destruction deposit of stones beneath red soil. Probably Period V. Ca. +1.70–1.50 m above sea level.

Pottery

1/2 bag collected, 15 sherds remain. "Scraps" discarded. Uncatalogued ceramics include several local (RBMa, RBMb) plain and Yellow Slipped, coarse, closed vessels, and a plain (EBA?) Cycladic(?) closed vessel (CSWe).

Crete

701 Closed vessel. (Pl. 46)
Body. Moderately coarse, compact, yellow fabric with 5–10% inclusions. Handmade. Lustrous Painted (LOD). Exterior coated in lustrous black paint; possible traces of white. FSTb, rounded inclusions. PFG 6A (Central Crete [Mesara?]).

Stone

702 K75.13. Purple and white striated stone. (Pl. 46)
W. 0.03. L. pres. 0.04. Wt. 24 g. From B03-784. Elliptical. Broken obliquely at one end. Very smooth.

Terracotta

703 K75.10. Loom weight. (Pl. 46)
Type RF. D. 0.10. Th. 0.04. D. perf. 0.01. Wt. 390 g. Depression near center of each side of object, ca. 0.021 across, 0.003–0.005 deep. From B03-784. Coarse, reddish-brown fabric with 15–20% inclusions. RBMa, with dark blue-gray particles. (Local).

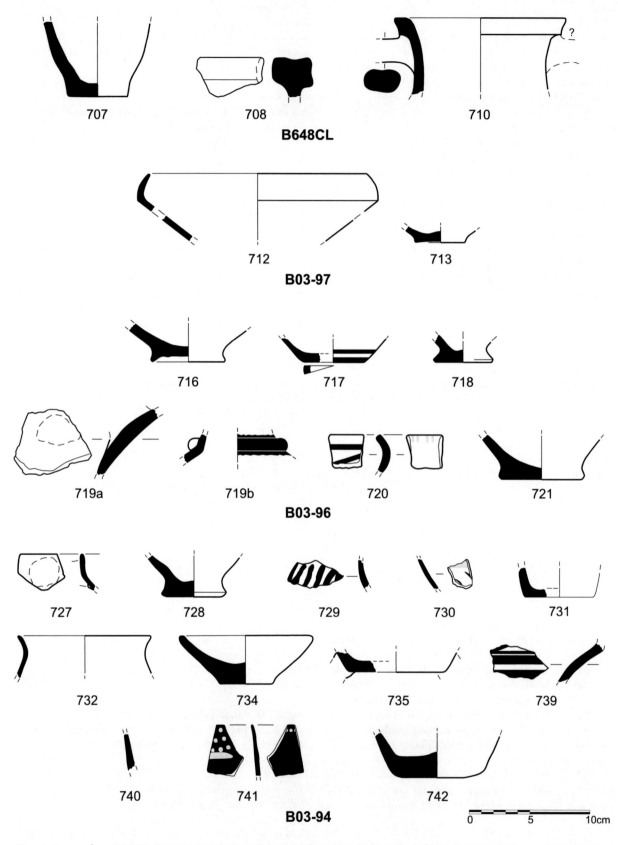

Fig. 51. Pottery from B648CL (**707, 708, 710**), B03-97 (**712, 713**), B03-96 (**716–721**), and B03-94 (**727–730, 732, 734, 735, 739–742**). Drawings by Aliki Bikaki (**707, 710**), Lily Bonga (**708, 716–721, 727–730, 732, 734, 735, 739–742**), and Mary-Jane Schumacher (**712, 713**).

B648CL.
Upper part of red stratum associated with Period V collapse, probably disturbed by building in early Period VI.

Pottery

1 3/4 bag collected, mainly local coarseware; 9 sherds remain. Uncatalogued sherds include a plain, Melian/Theran strap handle (DVc) and base from a local, wheelmade, plain, open vessel (RBMa).

Local

704 Bridge-spouted jar. (Fig. 50, Pl. 46)
Bridge spout preserved. H. pres. 0.06. D. rim est. 0.08. From B03-777. Moderately coarse, reddish-brown fabric with 5–10% inclusions. Handmade. Yellow Slipped. Coated inside spout, inside rim, and on the exterior with yellow slip. Exterior decorated with matt red paint. Curving lines (spirals?) below spout, two curving bands follow curve across spout; uppermost continues to edge of spout. RBMa. Compare with Cummer and Schofield 1984, 136, no. 1707, pl. 88; Schofield 2011, 68, no. 768, pl. 50.

705 Open jar. (Fig. 50, Pl. 46)
Rounded rim and arched handle. H. pres. 0.05. D. rim est. 0.12. From B03-782. Moderately coarse, hard-fired, reddish-brown fabric with 5–10% inclusions. Handmade. Yellow Painted. Traces of yellow slip along rim. Band below and along handle in same. RBMa, with rare calcareous(?) inclusions. For similar profile, see Barber and Hadjianastasiou 1989, 81, no. 73, fig. 10.

706 Stick-handled lamp. (Fig. 50, Pl. 46)
Flat, slightly raised base, incurving rim, and part of long, round, stick-handle. H. pres. 0.04. D. rim est. 0.09. D. base est. 0.05. From B03-776. Moderately coarse, reddish-brown fabric with 10–15% inclusions. Wheelmade or wheel-coiled(?). Burned in interior and at rim. Plain. RBMa, with rare calcareous(?) inclusions. PFG 1C (Local). For similar shape, see Schofield 2011, 120, no. 1299, pl. 62. At Phylakopi, see Davis and Cherry 2007, no. P78 from PLa Layer 77 (earlier LC I, based on fig. 7.19).

Local(?)

707 Juglet(?). (Fig. 51, Pl. 46)
Lower body and flat base. H. pres. 0.06. D. base 0.05. From B03-778. Moderately coarse, reddish-brown fabric with 5–10% inclusions. Wheel-coiled. Plain. RBMd. PFG 2D (SE Attica/Cyclades).

Cyclades(?)

708 Basin(?). (Fig. 51, Pl. 46)
Large, rectangular rim and relatively thin-walled body. D. rim est. >0.60. From B03-782. Moderately coarse, relatively fine-grained, orange fabric with 10–15% inclusions. Yellow Slipped. MxMa, very dusty, less gritty than usual, with obvious metamorphics.

Melos/Thera

709 Closed vessel. (Pl. 46)
Body. From B03-778. Fine, moderately hard-fired, pale brown fabric with fewer than 1% inclusions. Handmade. Painted. Exterior coated with greenish-yellow slip(?), painted with wide, matt brown band. DVa. PFG 5B (Melos/Thera).

Mainland

710 Narrow-necked hydria or jar. (Fig. 51, Pl. 46)
Squared rim, slightly concave neck, and ovoid, vertical handle preserved. H. pres. 0.07. D. rim est. 0.14. From B03-778. Fine, hard-fired, orange-red fabric with fewer than 1% inclusions. Handmade. Slipped. Thick yellow slip coats interior of neck, exterior surface. FVd/FVf. PFG 13B (Euboea).

Bone

711 K75.12. Awl. (Pl. 46)
Type IVa (Krzyszkowska). W. <0.01–0.01. L. 0.05. Wt. 2 g. From B03-782. Chipped at tip and proximal end, cracked. Probably splinter of sheep or goat metatarsal.

Plaster

B03-780: Three fragments of uninventoried wall plaster.

WALL H FOUNDATION TRENCH

B03-97.
Stratum associated with use of Wall X; it is probable that the upper part of the excavation unit included part of Wall H foundation trench (Fig. 14:a), but datable sherds belong to Periods III and IV.

Pottery

Unknown quantity collected; 2/3 bag remains. No discard information. Uncatalogued local (RBMa, RBMb) ceramics include a plain rounded bowl/cup and open or hole-mouthed jar, a pithos with bands of applied disks (RBMa, porous), perhaps LBA(?), as well as Painted, Slipped, and Yellow Slipped (RBMa, RBMc) vessels, mostly closed. Uncatalogued imports include Melian/Theran (DVa) vessels, most plain and closed; Cycladic Slipped (MxMb[?], MxMc, CSWb, MFVa) vessels, including a goblet(?); Aeginetan(?) closed(?) vessels (DVe); a coarse closed, slipped vessel in an unknown fabric; Minoan/-izing vessels, plain, Lustrous or Non-Lustrous Painted (FSTc, FSTe, FSTf, FSTi); and a fine white-painted vessel, possibly EH (FVc).

Local

712 Cycladic cup/carinated bowl. (Fig. 51, Pl. 47)
Carinated rim and nonjoining body. D. rim est. 0.18. Moderately coarse, reddish-brown fabric with well-defined dark-gray core and 1–5% inclusions. Handmade(?). Burnished. RBMa, compact, with rare calcareous(?) inclusions.

713 Open(?) vessel. (Fig. 51, Pl. 47)
Raised base and splaying, lower body. D. base est. 0.04. Moderately fine, reddish-brown fabric with 5–10% inclusions. Wheel-coiled(?). Plain. RBMa, with common mica.

714 K.4540. Wide-mouthed jar(?). (Pl. 47)
Published, J. C. Overbeck 1989a, 175. Pedestal base. D. base est. 0.08. Moderately coarse, reddish-brown fabric, darkened unevenly all around base. Handmade, with two parallel fingernail impressions on underside of base. Plain. RBMa.

Mainland/Kythera

715 Closed vessel. (Pl. 47)
Body (four joining fragments). Moderately coarse, fine-grained, pale pink fabric with purple-tinged core and greenish surface, and with 5–10% inclusions. Handmade. Lustrous Decorated. Exterior: fugitive black bands. FSTg. PFG 7C (Crete/Peloponnese).

Stone

Uninventoried: obsidian fragments (B-1.240, B-1.241).

B03-96.
Lower part of Wall H foundation trench. Early Period VI mixed with EBA and MBA.

Pottery

Unknown quantity collected; 1/2 bag remains. No discard information. Uncatalogued local (RBMa) vessels include a plain, bridge-spouted(?) jar, lid or wide bowl, and an EBA Red-Brown basin and jar. Uncatalogued imports includ a Cycladic White closed vessel (DVa); Melian/Theran Painted and plain (DVa) vessels; Cycladic plain (MxMa, MxMd) vessels; Aeginetan(?) plain and Painted (DVe) vessels, including an open jar or krater; Minoan/-izing Lustrous Painted, Non-Lustrous Painted, and plain (FSTa, FSTb, FSTc, FSTf, FSTi) vessels; a Gray Minyan or Gray/Black Burnished (MFVb) open vessel; Gray Minyan (FVa) goblets or kantharoi; a large Burnished (Mainland Polychrome?) (FVd/FVf) open vessel; mainland(?) Red Coated and plain (FVd, FVe) closed vessels; and plain vessels in unknown fabrics.

Local

716 Open vessel. (Fig. 51, Pl. 47)
Ring base and lower body. H. pres. 0.03. D. base est. 0.06. Moderately fine, dark gray fabric with 5–10% inclusions. Handmade. Burnished. Interior and exterior burnished. RBMa, with common mica.

717 Open vessel. (Fig. 51, Pl. 47)
Flat base and lower body. H. pres. 0.02. D. base 0.05. Moderately coarse, gritty, reddish-brown fabric with 10–15% inclusions. Wheel-coiled(?). Yellow Slipped. Coated in and out with thick, yellow slip. Exterior: two narrow, matt dark-brown bands above base. Interior: splotches in same. RBMa, overfired, purple-tinged.

718 Cycladic cup. (Fig. 51, Pl. 47)
Raised, conical foot and lower body. H. pres. 0.02. D. base 0.05. Moderately fine, reddish-brown fabric with 5–10% inclusions. Handmade. Plain. RBMb.

Cyclades

719 Jug. (Fig. 51, Pl. 47)
Body fragment with vertical handle attachment (a) and non-joining round, neck molding (b). Moderately coarse, gritty, dark reddish-orange fabric with 10–15% inclusions. Handmade. Painted. Neck molding decorated with dull dark reddish-brown paint; body plain. CSWb. PFG 2C (Local [region]).

Melos/Thera(?)

720 Bowl/basin. (Fig. 51, Pl. 47)
Flaring rim and upper body. H. pres. 0.03. D. rim est. 0.25. Moderately fine, porous, pale greenish-yellow fabric with 1–5% inclusions. Painted. Interior: four vertical hashes at rim in matt dark-brown paint. Exterior: horizontal band below rim, with diagonal band underneath in same paint. DVa(?). Although no gold mica was observed, and the inclusions were more colorful than usual for the usual pale-fired Aeginetan fabric (DVd), the shape and decoration of this vessel suggest that it may be more likely from Aegina than Melos/Thera. For similar, see Gauss and Smetana 2007, 78, fig. 10, no. XXXVIII-12; J. C. Overbeck 1989a, 28, no. H-15, pl. 39.

Melos/Thera

721 Open vessel (Cycladic cup?). (Fig. 51, Pl. 47)
Flat, splaying base. D. base 0.07. Moderately fine, porous, pale yellow fabric with pink core and 5–10% inclusions. Interior: vertical finger impressions. Handmade. Plain. DVa.

Mainland

722 Kantharos. (Pl. 47)
Upper body, lower lip, and strap handle attachments. H. pres. 0.06. Fine, hard-fired, gray fabric with 1–5% inclusions. Wheelmade. Gray Minyan. Interior and exterior burnished; four shallow grooves between handle attachments. FVa. For shape, see Davis 1986, 43, no. U-74, pls. 28, 55.

Mainland/Kythera

723 Closed vessel. (Pl. 47)
Body. Moderately coarse, hard-fired, compact, pale pink fabric with 10–15% inclusions. Thin walls. Handmade. Lustrous Decorated. Exterior: narrow band and spiral in lustrous black, now nearly entirely fugitive. FSTg.

Crete(?)

724 Closed vessel. (Pl. 47)
Shoulder. Moderately fine, hard-fired, pale, orange fabric with 1–5% inclusions. Handmade. Lustrous Painted. Exterior yellow-slipped(?) and painted with lustrous reddish-brown, thick,

streaky band. FSTc, with rosy-pink core and probable metamorphic inclusions.

725 Closed vessel. (Pl. 47)
Body. Moderately coarse, gritty, hard-fired, brown fabric with 10–15% inclusions. Handmade. Non-Lustrous Painted. Exterior: narrow, non-lustrous trickle (or band?). FSTc.

Stone

Uninventoried: obsidian fragment (B-1.238).

Terracotta

726 Spool. (Pl. 47)
80% preserved, chipped at ends. L. pres. 0.04. D. perf. 0.01. Wt. 18 g. Fine, somewhat gritty, reddish-brown fabric with dark brownish-gray surface and 1–5% inclusions. Surface smoothed. RBMa, with common mica. (Local).

B03-94.
Upper part of Wall H foundation trench. Early Period VI mixed with EBA and much MBA.

Pottery

Unknown quantity collected; 3/4 bag remains. Uncatalogued local (RBMa) vessels include Burnished Cycladic cups; a plain goblet(?); and plain, Slipped, and Yellow Slipped closed vessels. Uncatalogued imports include Melian/Theran Painted and plain vessels (DVa, DVc); an EBA Orange-Buff Semifine to Coarse jar (DVf); Cycladic Burnished, Painted, and plain open vessels (CSWa, MxMc, MxMf, MFVc); Red Coated closed vessel (MxMd); Aeginetan(?) Painted and Red Coated open vessels (DVe); Cretan and Minoanizing Lustrous Painted, Non-Lustrous Painted, and plain (FSTa, FSTb, FSTd, FSTf, FSTi); a plain mainland/Kytheran closed vessel (FSTg); Burnished (Mainland Polychrome?) open vessel (FVd/FVf); central mainland(?) plain, closed vessel (FVf), and a Gray Minyan closed vessel (FVa).

Local

727 Cycladic cup. (Fig. 51, Pl. 47)
Approximately 8% carinated rim at round handle attachment. D. rim est. 0.14. Moderately fine, reddish-brown fabric with 1–5% inclusions. Wheelmade or wheel-coiled. Burnished. RBMa, with common mica.

728 Cycladic cup. (Fig. 51, Pl. 47)
Base. D. base 0.05. Moderately fine, dark reddish-brown fabric with gray core and 5–10% inclusions. Coil-built. Burnished. RBMa, compact, with shiny, black particles.

729 Small, closed vessel. (Fig. 51, Pl. 47)
Body. Moderately fine, reddish-brown fabric with 1–5% inclusions. Wheelmade or wheel-coiled. Yellow Slipped. Exterior coated with thick, yellow slip. Vertical bars or ripple pattern in semi-lustrous orange paint. RBMa, with common mica.

730 In-and-out bowl. (Fig. 51, Pl. 47)
Body. Moderately fine, reddish-brown fabric with 1–5% inclusions. Very thin walls. Forming method indeterminable. Yellow Slipped (Polychrome, Red and Black). Interior and exterior coated with thick yellow slip. Exterior: possible traces of two curving orange bands (spiral?). Interior: orange band above one curving and one pointed black motif (floral?). RBMa.

731 Small, open vessel (straight-sided cup?). (Fig. 51, Pl. 47)
Flat base and straight walls. D. base est. 0.06. Moderately coarse, orange-brown fabric with well-defined, pale-gray core and 5–10% inclusions. Handmade(?). Painted(?). Two possible fugitive bands above base. RBMa, with common mica.

732 Wide-mouthed jar. (Fig. 51, Pl. 47)
Approximately 10% everted rim and upper body. D. rim est. 0.11. Moderately fine, reddish-brown fabric with darker exterior margin and 10–15% inclusions. Wheelmade(?). Rim interior blackened from fire. Plain. RBMa, with common mica.

733 Flaring bowl. (Pl. 47)
Approximately 20% of large, flattened, flaring rim. D. rim est. 0.20. Moderately coarse, reddish-brown fabric with gray core and 15–20% inclusions. Coil-built. Plain. RBMa, brittle, porous, with phyllite.

734 Handleless cup. (Fig. 51, Pl. 47)
Type 1. 60% preserved, including entire profile. H. 0.04. D. base 0.05. D. rim est. 0.11. Coarse, reddish brown fabric with 15–20% inclusions. Extremely thick base. Wheel-coiled. Plain. RBMa.

735 Small, tripod jar. (Fig. 51, Pl. 47)
Published, Gorogianni, Abell, and Hilditch 2017, 68, no. 13. Flat base and round leg attachment. D. base est. 0.07. Moderately coarse, dark reddish-brown fabric with dark-gray core and 1–5% inclusions. Interior blackened. Plain. RBMa, with common mica and overfired schist.

Cyclades

736 Cycladic cup. (Pl. 47)
Approximately 5% carinated rim and arched, round handle. D. rim est. 0.13. Moderately fine, reddish-brown fabric with gray core and 1–5% inclusions. Well-smoothed. Plain. MxMc.

Melos/Thera

737 Hole-mouthed jar. (Pl. 47)
Flattened rim and upper body. D. rim est. 0.09. Moderately fine, pale yellow fabric with greenish tinge and 5–10% inclusions. Coil-built. Painted. Wide, matt dark-brown band below rim. DVa.

738 Piriform cup. (Pl. 47)
Body. Fine, porous, pale yellow fabric with 1–5% inclusions. Forming method indeterminable. Painted (Polychrome, Red

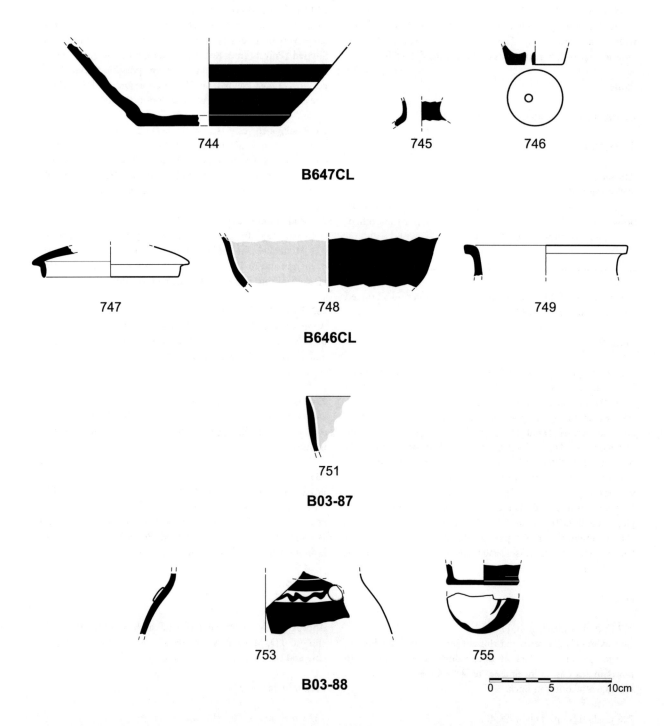

Fig. 52. Pottery from B647CL (**744–746**), B646CL (**747–749**), B03-87 (**751**), and B03-88 (**753, 755**). Drawings by Lily Bonga (**744–746, 748**), Aliki Bikaki (**747, 749**), and Mary-Jane Schumacher (**751, 753, 755**).

and Black). Exterior: thick, vertical, red band(?) and narrow, vertical, dark-brown band, connected by narrow horizontal band and band of chevrons(?). DVa. PFG 5C (Melos/Thera).

Mainland/Kythera

739 Closed vessel. (Fig. 51, Pl. 47)
Shoulder and nonjoining body. Moderately coarse, hard-fired, dark pink fabric with 10–15% inclusions. Handmade. Lustrous Decorated. Exterior coated in yellow slip, burnished(?), decorated in lustrous black paint, now mostly fugitive. Two wide bands and one narrow band. FSTg, with rare spalling.

Crete(?)

740 Fine, closed vessel. (Fig. 51, Pl. 47)
Body. Fine, pink fabric with fewer than 1% inclusions. Wheelmade. Lustrous Painted (DOL?). Exterior: lustrous streaky brown paint (band? Or monochrome?). FSTk.

741 Straight-sided cup. (Fig. 51, Pl. 47)
Rim and upper body. D. rim est. 0.10. Fine, pinkish-brown fabric with fewer than 1% inclusions. Wheelmade. Lustrous Painted (LOD). Interior and exterior coated with thin, semi-lustrous black paint. Exterior: ghost of band below dots in white. Interior: row of dots or band in white below rim. FSTk.

Unknown

742 Closed vessel. (Fig. 51, Pl. 47)
Thick, flat base and thin-walled, lower body. D. base est. 0.08. Moderately coarse, orange fabric with bluish-gray core and interior margin and with 5–10% inclusions. Handmade(?). Exterior is pitted. Painted(?). Possible trace of brown band. FSTi.

743 Closed(?) vessel. (Pl. 47)
Body. Moderately fine, hard-fired, relatively compact, pale purple fabric with 1–5% inclusions, primarily small, black; white, calcareous(?) particles; fine silver and gold mica; and rare, small vughs. Handmade(?). Painted. Two nearly fugitive, narrow, diagonal bands in matt-black paint. Unknown fabric, possibly related to MFVd(?). PFG 12C (Unknown).

B647CL.
Wall H foundation trench and stratum above it. Probably Period VI, but sherds not very chronologically diagnostic.

Pottery

1 1/2 bags collected; 7 sherds remain. "Scraps" discarded. All inventoried.

Crete

744 Open(?) jar. (Fig. 52, Pl. 47)
Flat base and flaring lower body. H. pres. 0.07. D. base est. 0.12. From B03-772. Moderately fine, compact, hard-fired, pale red fabric with 1–5% inclusions. Wheel-coiled. Lustrous Painted. Interior and exterior coated with thick yellow slip; exterior, two wide bands in lustrous red. Exterior burnished(?). FSTb, pink.

Crete(?)

745 Small, closed vessel. (Fig. 52, Pl. 47)
Neck. From B03-771. Fine, pale pink fabric with bluish gray core and fewer than 1% inclusions. Wheelmade. Salt-encrusted. Lustrous Painted (Monochrome). Interior smoothed; exterior coated with lustrous dark-brown slip. FSTj, with unusual core.

746 Cup(?)-rhyton. (Fig. 52, Pl. 47)
Flat base with off-center perforation. D. base 0.05. Moderately fine, hard-fired, dusty, orange fabric with 1–5% inclusions. Probably hand-built or made while wheel moving very slowly. Perforation near middle of base. Plain. FSTj. Similar cup-rhyton from Kythera assigned by Coldstream and Huxley to MM IIIB (1972, 233, pl. 69:35, from Tomb C [MM IIIB/LM IA]); Koehl (2006, 59) noted rare cup-rhyta from MM II–LM IB, but describes their floruit as LM IB.

Plaster

Two uninventoried fragments (B-75.2).

DEPOSITS OF PERIOD VII ALLEY

B646CL.
Upper and lower strata of Street 1. Period VII.

Pottery

1/2 bag collected; 6 sherds remain. Uncatalogued imports include Cretan(?) Lustrous Painted and plain closed vessels (FSTa, FSTj). An uncatalogued white-slipped strap handle from lot B03-768 may be a later intrusion.

Cyclades

747 Lid(?). (Fig. 52, Pl. 47)
Lip and upper body. D. rim est. 0.11. From B03-768. Moderately fine, hard-fired, dark pink fabric with gray core and 5–10% inclusions. Handmade(?). Plain. MxMa, with no visible metamorphics.

Aegina(?)

748 Goblet(?). (Fig. 52, Pl. 47)
Body fragment near rim. From B03-766. Moderately fine, orange fabric with 1–5% inclusions. Forming method indeterminable. Red Coated. DVe.

Mainland

749 Narrow-necked jar. (Fig. 52, Pl. 47)
Rim and neck fragment. D. rim est. 0.13. From B03-767. Fine, somewhat dusty, pale purple fabric with fewer than 1% inclusions. Wheelmade. Plain. FVd.

Terracotta

750 K75.9. Figurine. (Pl. 47)
H. 0.04. W. 0.03. L. 0.04. From B03-767. Head; missing top of hat, tip of nose, left ear, left eye. Moderately coarse red fabric, with smoothed surface preserved about everywhere. Hat or crown made of two concentric circles. Sloping nose-forehead, large round eyeballs, pursed mouth, pointed chin, elongated C-shaped ear, cap of hair at back and sides has slashes and ridges for curls. At back of head just above neck-break is a blob of clay (not hair). Description by Bikaki. On display in the Archaeological Museum of Kea; fabric appears to be RBMa.

B03-87.
Above and inside Drain 1. Probably Period VII.

Pottery

Unknown quantity collected; 16 sherds kept. Possible Period VII sherds among uncatalogued imports include a Lustrous Painted (FSTa) closed vessel decorated with parallel, irregularly curved lines that seem to approximate ripple pattern and a Cretan(?) (FSTf) plain, milk jug(?). Other uncatalogued sherds are small and difficult to categorize apart from by fabric; fabrics represented are RBMa, FSTa, FSTf, MxMa, DVa, FVa, FVc, and FVd. One probably Roman grooved jar fragment is also present.

Cyclades(?)

751 Bowl(?). (Fig. 52, Pl. 47)
Rim and upper body. H. pres. 0.05. Moderately fine, dusty orange fabric with 10–15% inclusions. Wheelmade or wheel-coiled. Red Coated(?). Interior and exterior coated in thick, semi-lustrous red paint. MxMc.

B03-88.
Above and inside Drain 1, along with area of disturbed pavement above Test H-E. Probably Period VII.

Pottery

Unknown quantity collected; ca. 3/4 bag remains. Several of the fine, painted vessels should be dated to Period VIIb, but many of the sherds may come from earlier vessels. Sherds are small, worn, and difficult to categorize apart from by fabric. Fabrics of uncatalogued vessels include RBMa, RBMb, FSTa–FSTc, FSTf, FSTh–FSTk, DVa, DVb, DVe, MxMa, MxMf, CSWb, MFVd, FVb/FVc, FVc, FVf, FVg. One Attic Black Gloss sherd is present.

Local

752 Handleless cup. (Pl. 47)
Type 1. 80% intact; broken at one side and chipped at flattened rim. H. 0.04. D. base 0.06. D. rim est. 0.12. Moderately coarse, orange fabric with gray core and 10–15% inclusions. Heavy. Wheel-coiled. Plain. RBMa, with phyllite. PFG 1Av (Local).

Cyclades

753 Small jar. (Fig. 52, Pl. 47)
Shoulder. Moderately fine, gritty, slightly dusty, orange fabric with 5–10% inclusions. Handmade(?). Yellow Slipped (Polychrome, Red and Black). Exterior coated with yellow slip. Wide black band below neck. Below band are a wavy purple band, wide black band, and running spirals connected by two tangents. Plastic round rivet attached below neck. MxMa.

Mainland

754 Fine, closed vessel. (Pl. 47)
Body. Fine, hard-fired, dusty, pale yellow-brown fabric with pale-gray core and fewer than 1% inclusions. Wheelmade. Lustrous Painted. Exterior: decoration in lustrous brown to black; rock pattern (FM 32), probably with ivy (FM 12) above. FVc.

755 Closed vessel. (Fig. 52, Pl. 47)
Torus base and lower body. D. base est. 0.07. Fine, slightly dusty, pale greenish-yellow fabric, with fewer than 1% inclusions; overfired. Wheelmade. Lustrous Painted. Bands(?) or monochrome(?) above base; paint now fugitive. FVb.

Euboea

756 Fine, closed vessel. (Pl. 47)
Body. Fine, hard-fired, dark pink fabric turning to pale purple at interior, with fewer than 1% inclusions. Wheelmade. Painted. Exterior coated in yellow slip; two fugitive, horizontal bands. MFVd. PFG 13Bv (Euboea).

Terracotta

757 Rubber/polisher(?). (Pl. 47)
90% intact; chipped at edges. Tear-shaped, flattened object. D. pres. 0.04–0.05. Wt. 22 g. Moderately fine, reddish-brown fabric with 10–15% inclusions. Surface and edges well-smoothed. RBMb (Local).

758 Weight. (Pl. 47)
90% intact. Chipped ovoid weight with slightly off-center perforation. D. pres. 0.04–0.05. D. perf. 0.01. Wt. 34 g. Moderately coarse, reddish-brown fabric with 10–15% inclusions. RBMa. (Local).

II. STRATIGRAPHY, ARCHITECTURE, AND POTTERY

SUMMARY OF OCCUPATION IN AREA B

PERIODS I AND II

No deposits of Period I or II were found in Area B. It is possible that such deposits were so far below the modern water level that they were not reached during excavation. Period I and II ceramics were recovered nearby, below House A Courtyard 36 (Wilson 1999, 215–216), which suggests that the settlement extended into the vicinity of Area B during these periods.

PERIOD III

Although there is no evidence for when they were constructed, one or more buildings were used and collapsed during Period III in Area B. The building(s) incorporated Walls AB, AC, AD, AE, and AF; a possible wall beneath Alley AB might be an extension of Wall AC. Walls were made up of small to moderately sized green and gray local schist slabs, like most other EBA architecture at the site (J. L. Caskey 1971, 361). A use surface or floor probably existed under Room B.2 at ca. –1.00 m below sea level. In construction methods and the finds recovered, the house(s) in Area B were similar to published Period III Houses ED and D in the Western Sector, although more evidence of metals and metalworking was found in and around those houses than in Area B (Wilson 1999, 203–208; 2013; Wilson and Eliot 1984).

The ceramic assemblage in Area B consisted of primarily shallow bowls, deep bowls/open jars, and basins, with some tankards, saucers, sauceboats, pyxides, and other shapes. The presence of several pithoi and large, coarse jars suggests that relatively large-scale storage of goods was as important in this house(s) as in other areas of the site (Wilson 1999, 167–226).

The most impressive vessel from these deposits is a large, spouted Talc ware pithos decorated with pellets (**232**). The pithos is without close parallels, but the location of the narrow spout at its bottom suggests that it carried a liquid of some kind, perhaps wine, although oil or some other liquid are also possibilities (for an argument in favor of wine, see M. E. Caskey 2009 n. 9). Residue analysis of four pithoi with perforations near the base at Myrtos Fournou Korifi demonstrated that they had contained resinated wine; residue analysis of two other pithoi suggested the preparation of a mixture of wine and beer as a grog, although it is unclear whether those two pithoi were perforated (McGovern 2009, 184–187). A pithos with a spout near the base from Ayios Kosmas contained grape pips, which may suggest that it, too, was used as a wine container (McGovern 2009, 185; Mylonas 1934, 266; 1959, 39–40, no. 50, fig. 132). No analysis has demonstrated what spouted pithoi from Delos and Aegina may have contained (MacGillivray 1980, 41, no. 288, fig. 22; Walter and Felten 1981, 99, 157, nos. 151, 152, pl. 87). The large size of the Area B pithos, in addition to its elaborate, time-intensive, and apparently unique decoration might be interpreted as evidence that the vessel and its contents were a trade item or gift of substantial value. Moreover, as a possible container for an alcoholic beverage, the pithos may also have had significant social value in the context of the drinking or eating rituals.

The general proportion of ceramic types and percentage of imports were similar to that observed for other areas of the site during Period III (Ch. 4; Wilson 1999, 90–91). Stone tools were probably used for a variety of domestic activities, including the grinding of grain (saddle quern, **236**; uninventoried millstones); processing of coloring agents (pestles and palettes, **214, 216, 225, 234, 240**); polishing, abrading, and sharpening (polishers/rubbers and whetstones, **219, 221, 226, 227, 235, 249**); crushing and hammering (pounders/grinders and hammer stone, **228–230**); and cutting or scraping (uninventoried obsidian objects; Wilson 1999, 147). Bone awls (**224, 616**) were probably used for textile or leather processing, while a perforated stone (**241**) may have been a net weight. An imported spindle whorl (**28**), from unit B03-147, could date to Period III. It is the only evidence in the space for textile production. Imported spindle whorls are unusual in Period III contexts elsewhere at the site (Wilson 1999, 162).

A stratum of Period III destruction debris covered the entirety of Area B. The destruction stratum was made up of soil and small stones like those used in Period III architecture in Area B and elsewhere at the site (J. L. Caskey 1971, 361).

Above the Period III destruction debris in Alley AB, Room B.1, and Room B.4 was a layer of compact, clayey, red soil (Surfaces c and i). A similar stratum has been found in many places across the site, in upper EBA and/or lower MBA levels (J. C. Overbeck 1989a, 3, 6, 31–32, 35, 37, 41–42, 45–46, 54–55, 64–65, 67, 123, 130, 141, 144, 154; Wilson and Eliot 1984, 85). This distinctive stratum probably was made up of disintegrated mudbrick from collapsed Period III buildings, which was then disturbed and redeposited in other places during Period IV (Caskey and Tountas 1998, 696). In Area B, this stratum was disturbed by Period VI and VII building activities related to House B. The layer was completely absent from Rooms B.2 and B.3, where extensive architectural modification took place over the course of Period VII.

PERIOD IV

Finds of Period IV outside Alley AB were rare and generally mixed with EBA, Period V, and/or LBA material. The small 1975 test pit in Alley AB, however, provided well-stratified evidence for Period IV in Area B. The test pit revealed that Wall X was built in early Period IVa. No clear Period IVa architecture was found elsewhere in the area, except perhaps the Wall H foundation, which might be the southeastern face of Wall X. Both Walls X and the Wall H foundation were built of large schist slabs and blocks;

these are the only walls in Area B in which such large schist stones were used. If Wall X was part of the same wall as the Wall H foundation, they probably made up a part of the Period IVa fortification wall and, thus, served as the southeastern boundary of the town. The rarity of Period IVa and early IVb ceramics below House B might support this idea (J. C. Overbeck 1989a, 175), although it is also possible that earlier Period IV ceramics might have been removed by the building of the LBA house. The probable fortification wall was well built with large, squared stones, an indication of the significant labor that must have gone into planning and constructing it.

A pavement was laid against Wall X in Period IVa and continued in use into Period IVb; it is unclear whether this pavement was part of an external or an internal space.

During Period IVb, Wall X went out of use. Afterwards, a drain (Drain 2) and a wall(?) were built to the northeast of Wall X. Two strata of compact grayish-brown soil were probably associated with the use of Drain 2 and the possible Period IVb wall. A thin brown stratum above the compact strata probably is related to a change in use of the space during Period IVb, perhaps after the destruction of Drain 2 and the possible Period IVb wall. A feature like Drain 2 must have resulted from some degree of urban planning. Drainage systems have long been known from Crete, but they exist also by MM IB at Kastri on Kythera (Coldstream and Huxley 1984, 108) and in several MH II and later sites in mainland Greece (Wiersma 2013, 193, 204, 214, with references). Recent excavation has also shown the existence of elaborate drainage works at EC Dhaskalio (Kennedy 2018).

At some point in Period IVb, another wall was constructed along the north side of Alley AB, Wall E1. Wall E1 was located beneath the later Wall E of House A. Associated with Wall E1 was Street 2, which had three construction phases, ranging in date from Period IVb to IVc. Temple Lane, at least that part of it to the northeast of Alley AB, also was used for the first time at some point in Period IV (Cummer and Schofield 1984, 3).

The presence of fine and imported pottery in deposits in Area B and throughout the site (J. C. Overbeck 1989a) demonstrates that access to such objects was not restricted to a single individual or household in this period, although the differential distribution of precious metal objects, imported stones, and pottery in tombs suggests the existence of socioeconomic inequalities within the town (Gorogianni and Fitzsimons 2017; G. F. Overbeck 1989).

PERIOD V

A few sherds of Period V were found with earlier and later ceramics in both Alley AB and beneath the LBA House B. This is unsurprising given that construction in Periods VI and VII stripped away Period V remains in many areas of the site (e.g., Schofield 2011, 1). Pure Period V strata were rare everywhere but especially scarce in the southeastern area (Davis 1986, 1, 73–78). Only one possible Period V stratum, a destruction deposit, was found in Area B, in Alley AB. This deposit may have formed as a result of the earthquake at the end of Period V, which destroyed parts of the fortification wall (Davis 1986, 8–9; Schofield 2011, 1; for a summary of evidence that this destruction was caused by earthquake rather than raiding or some other anthropogenic cause, see Davis 1986, 106).

PERIOD VI

HOUSE B: PHASE 1

In Period VI, the first phase of House B was built. The only room in use during this phase was Room B.1, although only two of its sides can be defined (Wall Y and the Wall H foundation). The Wall H foundation formed the northwestern boundary of the room; it probably was reused following its initial construction in Period IV. While the Wall H foundation continued along the entire length of the Period VII house, no other evidence for Period VI architecture exists in Rooms B.2–B.4 and B.8. It is impossible to determine if the building in this phase continued farther southeastward toward the sea, as the Period VII building did. It is impossible to determine whether or not the house had an upper floor in this phase.

The Period VI floor within Room B.1 (Surface b) contained a round hearth defined by stones (Hearth 1), similar to others in House A and in the Western Sector in Period VI and VII contexts (Cummer and Schofield 1984, 11; Schofield 2011, 32). There is no evidence that the hearth was used for anything other than domestic purposes. A stone platform (Platform 1), and a small stone construction covered with burned clay (Stone Feature 1) were also found in the room; the precise function(s) of these features is unclear. A tripod vessel (**101**) sunk into the floor probably served as a storage container. Ceramics and small finds in the room testify to a variety of domestic activities, including food preparation and consumption, as well as textile production. Plaster fragments found on the floor suggest that the walls of the room were painted.

An accumulated stratum within Alley AB (B03-770) may have been the pathway between Houses A and B during Period VI, although chronologically diagnostic ceramics are lacking. A pathway must have existed, since the main entrance to House A in Period VI was from Alley AB through Room A.36 (Cummer and Schofield 1984, 31).

HOUSE B: PHASE 2

Either later in Period VI or very early in Period VII, Wall Y, the apparent southwestern boundary of the first phase of House B, collapsed. Other evidence for destruction exists during Period VI elsewhere at the site. In House A, for example, the central basements and northwest corner of the house suffered serious damage, including burning, in this period (Cummer and Schofield 1984, 32). Several buildings in the Western Sector preserved evidence for destruction, in some cases accompanied by fire, in Period VI (Schofield 2011, 12, 37, 78, 79, 86, 88–91, 160–161, 167). There is no evidence for human violence, such as weapons, within the debris. It is impossible to know if all of these destructions were exactly contemporaneous, but if some or all of them happened at the same time, it is probable that they were caused by an earthquake, as hypothesized by Cummer and Schofield (1984, 32) and Schofield (1984, 179).

After the collapse of Wall Y, Room B.1 continued to be used. A pit (Pit 1) lined with stones was dug into the area of collapsed stones before the Period VII floor was laid (Surface a). During this phase of reuse, soil covered the platform, stone feature, and hearth of the original Period VI floor, as well as the remains of Wall Y. No new architecture is associated with this phase of use.

Although Temple Lane contained a drainage system further to the northwest during Period VI (Cummer and Schofield 1984, 3), this does not seem to have continued all the way south into Area B. In front of Room B.1, a slab-built pavement of Temple Lane, at an elevation of ca. +0.71 m above sea level, had at least one LM IB sherd between it and the earliest drain in this area (Kea Excavation Notebook XLIV, 123–124). Therefore, until the full study of the material from Temple Lane has been completed, it is impossible to suggest that either the earliest pavement or the earliest drain pre-dated Period VII in this area. These phases of Temple Lane must have been contemporary with the second or third phase of House B.

In the Western Sector, a new street system was planned in Period VI in conjunction with a major, unified construction plan (Schofield 2011, 1). In Area B, however, existing road spaces were reused (Alley AB). Parts of Houses A and B were built immediately above and on the same course as large Period IV walls (Walls X, E1, and perhaps the Wall H foundation). Rather than significantly reorganizing the space in Period VI, the southeastern part of the site was closely tied, architecturally, with earlier periods. This is also true of the Temple, which was damaged at the end of Period IV but repaired and modified during Periods V and VI, following the same orientation as the Period IV building (J. L. Caskey 1964, 326; M. E. Caskey 1998, 124–126).

PERIOD VII

HOUSE B: PHASE 3

In its next phase, probably during Period VIIa, House B underwent a major renovation. It was extended to the southwest to include Rooms B.2–B.5. It was also expanded to the southeast, with Room B.8, although the full extent of the house to the southeast is impossible to assess since it has eroded into the sea. The preserved part of the Period VII house follows an architectural form repeated in many other buildings at Ayia Irini—a long, narrow row of rooms connected by doors along a central axis (Fitzsimons and Gorogianni 2017). In the same period, arguably early in Period VIIa, House A was also expanded (Cummer and Schofield 1984, 32). In Room B.1, the Period VI wall above the Wall H foundation (or the upper part of the Wall H foundation) must have been torn down. A deep foundation trench was dug for the construction of Wall H; similarly, Wall J was founded at an extreme depth (+0.15 to +0.30 m above sea level). Walls J, K, T, and O were built directly above EBA walls. These deep foundations were probably an attempt to find bedrock or a stable surface on which to found the building (Bikaki, pers. comm.). The building must have been planned as a whole, since major walls (H, I, J) bonded together. All walls were built with small to moderately sized local schist slabs, as were most other LBA buildings on site (e.g., Cummer and Schofield 1984, 40). Wall I, the façade of House B, also incorporated larger, squared marble stones, similar to those used along the southeastern facade of House A. The use of large, squared blocks only in the facade of House B was probably intended to create a visual link with House A and perhaps a conceptual link with its residents.

Room B.1 was entered from Temple Lane and gave access to Room B.2. A doorway in Wall AA led from Room B.2 to B.3. Walls T and O were poorly preserved and no evidence exists for the location of doorways.

No clear features could be associated with floors in any of the rooms. Surface f in Room B.2 and Surface h in Room B.3 were probably contemporary with this phase of the building. A second floor level was noted in both rooms at a slightly later phase in Period VII (Surfaces e and g), which cannot be associated with any architectural modifications.

Although Room B.4 existed in this phase of the house, no floor associated with the early floors of Rooms B.2 and B.3 was found. It is unclear how the space was used in this phase.

No stairways or other definitive evidence for an upper floor were found in the preserved part of the house. Since the house was built into the side of the hill, however, it is plausible that there was at least one upper story that shared the same ground level with House A and Alley AB. Most other LBA houses at the site preserve stairs and other evidence for multiple stories (Cummer and Schofield 1984; Schofield 2011). It is possible that stairways were located in the parts of House B that have been eroded by the sea.

After Wall H was built, two paving levels were constructed in Alley AB, presumably linked to two phases of use of the alley. After an unknown period of time, but still in Period VII, a drain (Drain 1) was constructed between Houses A and B, above the previous paving levels. Although Drain 1 probably was covered to create another street surface, those upper levels have been lost to erosion.

Drain 1 curved to the south at the intersection of Alley AB with Temple Lane; the drain there continued southeastward below three steps in the lane at a depth that must have been planned to keep water from entering the doorway through Wall I and into House B (Kea Excavation Notebook XLIV, 120–124).

HOUSE B: PHASE 4

Several major modifications to the house were undertaken during Period VII. Although their exact chronological relationship to each other is unclear, they seem to be connected. First, in either this or the previous phase, Wall P was built on top of Wall T; Wall P must have extended fully to the southeast toward Wall J, based on the stark difference between strata in Room B.4 in comparison with Room B.2/B.3. At about the same time, most of Wall AA collapsed or was dismantled in order to combine the spaces of Rooms B.2 and B.3 (Room B.2/B.3). A spur of Wall AA was left in place against Wall H, supported by a small buttress to its north; between the spur of Wall AA and Wall P, Wall R was built. The whole construction (Wall R and the Wall AA reuse) seems intended to act as an extensive buttress for Wall P and perhaps an upper story. It is possible that some or all of this construction could be related to an early Period VII earthquake that caused significant destruction in House A (Cummer and Schofield 1984, 33), Area G, Tower ne, and the Western Sector (Gorogianni 2008, 313; Schofield 1984b, 179; 2011, 113, 132–134, 135, 167).

The floor surface that formed (Surface d) after the construction of the buttress in Room B.2/B.3 must be contemporary with the final floor in Room B.1 (Surface a) since both were immediately beneath the Period VIIb destruction debris that filled the house. The same is true for the upper level of the dump (carbon-rich stratum) of Room B.4. No built features were found on any of these surfaces.

The use of Room B.4 in this phase of the house is unknown. The space is very small, and the thick, carbon-rich stratum found in it has no parallels elsewhere in House B. It is possible that this was a storage area or dumping space.

In all of its LBA phases, ceramics and small finds from House B were paralleled in other houses, including the largest houses, A and C. These artifacts highlight the variety of domestic industries in which residents of the house participated, including food preparation and consumption, as well as textile production, and, perhaps, aromatic processing using fireboxes (Georgiou 1986, 4–22; for debate about Georgiou's proposed function for these objects, see Abell 2020, 390–393; Poursat 2013, 130; Warren 2014, 28–31, with earlier references). A greater quantity of pithoi in the Northeast Bastion and House A (Gorogianni 2020, 266–268) suggests that House B had less storage capacity than other houses, although it is also possible that the storage rooms are missing from the preserved part of the house. Otherwise, in both its architecture and artifacts, House B was very similar to other houses at Ayia Irini, and there is little evidence that suggests stark differences in domestic or industrial activities, wealth, or status between residents of House B and other published houses.

At the end of Period VIIb, many buildings at Ayia Irini were damaged by a severe earthquake (J. L. Caskey 1971, 363, 376, 383). Many deep destruction deposits were found in House A, where some walls were "twisted" and dislocated, and vessel fragments were widely dispersed in three dimensional space (Cummer and Schofield 1984, 33). Likewise, massive destruction deposits mark most buildings in the Western Sector (Schofield 2011, 34, 87, 137, 163, 164, 168). J. L. Caskey (1971, 374) suggested that the displacement of large blocks from Tower ne might have been caused by this earthquake, although it is impossible to date the destruction precisely in that area (Gorogianni 2008, 313). House B was no exception to these events. All rooms contain deep destruction deposits. Given the steep angle of the slope leading down to House B from House A and the rest of the site, it is probable that the collapse of House B would have happened quickly. The ceramics offer some evidence for a rapid collapse. First, sherds that might be from a single Lustrous Painted ewer (**406**) were found in lower levels of destruction debris in the Temple and in Room B.2. Second, a few joins existed between deposits in Rooms B.1 and B.2/B.3, and between upper and lower parts of the destruction deposit in each room. This pattern of ceramic deposition suggests that the destruction deposit in House B was a mix of debris from the house and its upper floor(s), as well as, probably, debris from further upslope. Bikaki thought it possible that the house stood in ruins for a while before finally collapsing (Summary [Miscellaneous], 2). She seems, however, to have wavered on this idea, telling me in person that she thought the presence of fragments of **166** on the floor and in the doorway of Wall I constituted good evidence that the building was not disturbed after the earthquake.

AFTER THE PERIOD VIIB EARTHQUAKE

The location of Area B on a steep slope at the edge of the sea has also resulted in extensive erosion of cultural deposits at upper elevations. Evidence for activity in the area after the Period VIIb earthquake is limited.

Drain 1 in Alley AB was disturbed, the stones of its paving removed. The uppermost drain in Temple Lane was apparently built on the Period VIIb destruction debris that extended from the Wall I doorway out into the street (Kea Excavation Notebook III, 96, 99, 102). This is significant because it suggests that the inhabitants of Ayia Irini, even after the earthquake, continued to invest time and effort into maintaining the infrastructure of the site and managing the draining of water down through Area B toward the sea.

Although no architecture of Period VIII was found in House B, several Period VIII walls were built above the northeastern corner of House A, and the Temple continued in use in various forms well into the historical period (J. L. Caskey 1962, 280–283;

1979, 412; M. E. Caskey 1998, 126–128). It seems, then, that life continued in this part of the site after the Period VIIb earthquake and destruction of House B.

Wall Q is the only evidence for later activity in Area B. A *terminus post quem* for its construction is provided by a seventh-century sherd found inside the wall (Kea Excavation Notebook III, 195). The wall was probably related to the ongoing use of the Temple in this area, but no deposit could be associated with its construction or use.

III. CERAMIC FABRICS AND FORMING METHODS

This chapter provides an overview of technical aspects of ceramics in Area B, including macroscopic and petrographic fabric groups as well as forming techniques. Chemical analysis using wave-dispersive X-ray fluorescence (WD-XRF) was undertaken by Noémi Müller at the Fitch Laboratory of the British School at Athens. Preliminary interpretations of the WD-XRF results, based on consultation with Müller, are included in this discussion where they impact interpretation of macroscopic or petrographic fabric groupings, especially with regard to possible source locations for imports. The full discussion of WD-XRF results could not be included in this volume, but will be presented in full in the future.

Detailed descriptions of macroscopic and petrographic fabrics are provided in Appendices IV and V respectively. A sample of Munsell color descriptions is included in Appendix VI. The WD-XRF data are provided in Appendix VII.

LOCAL GEOLOGY

Kea is part of the Attic-Cycladic metamorphic complex, in an area where members of the Cycladic Blueschist Unit were overprinted during the Miocene by greenschist facies metamorphism (Rice et al. 2012, 109; Scheffer et al. 2016, 175–176). The following description of local geology relies heavily on the recent studies by Rice, Iglseder, and colleagues (Iglseder et al. 2011; Rice et al. 2012), who have revised the earlier work by Davis (1972, 1982).

The island consists of three tectonostratigraphic layers, the footwall, detachment zone, and the hanging wall. The footwall is dominated by blue-gray calcitic marbles and schists that are probably derived from metabasic or acidic volcanoclastic sediments. Some schists are bright green and rich in minerals such as chlorite, actinolite, and/or epidote, as well as quartz and plagioclase; others have more white mica and quartzofelspathic minerals. Serpentinites, in some cases altered to talc or talc-schists, appear in the upper part of the footwall. Other notable assemblages in the footwall are metalliferous garnet-glaucophane rocks and quartz-feldspar-mica gneisses, both of which occur with greater frequency in the south of the island. Weathered carbonate and graphite sometimes appear in schists, while blue amphiboles and garnet may be locally abundant in gneisses (Rice et al. 2012, 109–111). The detachment zone resulted from ductile to brittle faulting between the footwall and the hanging wall. Ductile stress generated phyllonites from the footwall mica schists, which grade gradually to the "normal" schists of the footwall. Brittle deformation generated coarse cataclasites and foliated pelitic cataclasites from the footwall schists. These are overlain by calcitic marble ultramylonites, which are themselves overlain by dolomitic or calcitic cataclasites, all derived from the hanging wall (Rice et al. 2012, 111–113). Outcrops of the hanging wall are especially visible in the northern part of the island, including at Paouras and Kephala. The hanging wall primarily consists of protocataclasites in its lower sections and dolostone above; some of these rocks are weakly brecciated and are sometimes interleaved with calcitic marbles (Rice et al. 2012, 113–115).

Fluid infiltration caused silicification, dolomitization, or ankeritic alteration of carbonates. Some iron deposits were probably generated by deposition of hot Fe-rich fluids, while the deposition of Fe-Mn-Pb-Au ores may be owed to unexposed magmatic activity (Rice et al. 2012, 115). Younger formations include two minor outcrops of bioclastic sandstone in a valley southwest of Korissia, as well as Holocene alluvial valley-fill and beach deposits, which have not been studied in detail (Rice et al. 2012, 115–117).

The area around Ayia Irini and the northern part of the Ayios Nikolaos harbor is dominated by footwall rocks, especially pelitic greenschists (Rice et al. 2012, fig. 2). Blue-gray calcitic marble is visible in narrow, elongated exposures along the hills to the north of the site, while the valley that runs from the harbor southeast of Ayia Irini toward Otzias is dominated by Holocene valley-fill. Small outcrops of hanging wall rocks and serpentinite are mapped in the hills north of Ayios Nikolaos and west of Otzias, as well as just west of modern Korissia. Outcrops of footwall marbles are exposed to the southwest of Ayios Nikolaos while small marble outcrops also appear to the west and south of Korissia. The wide valley stretching from Korissia through Livadi and along the road to Chora is dominated by Holocene valley-fill. Small outcrops of bioclastic sandstone are found to the southwest of Korissia, as noted above.

Geological sampling was not undertaken as part of this project, but a few fired clay samples from the island exist in the Fitch Laboratory of the British School at Athens. All are iron-rich and red or red-brown in color. There is no evidence in the sherd material, published geological descriptions, or in the geological samples in the Fitch Laboratory for the existence of pale-firing calcareous local clays. The clay samples are generally too fine to be of much help in linking them to the petrographic fabrics (noted also by Hilditch 2004, 12), but small grains of quartz, feldspar, amphibole, mica, and epidote group minerals, as well as rare grains of mica schist are concordant with the range of dominant inclusions in the petrographic fabrics.

MACROSCOPIC FABRICS

OVERVIEW

Macroscopic fabric groupings were initially developed in consultation with Jill Hilditch, who has completed fabric analysis on a variety of Cycladic assemblages, including macroscopic and petrographic analysis of Period V–VII deposits in the Northern Sector at Ayia Irini and petrographic analysis of Period I–III ceramics (Hilditch 2004, 2007, 2008, 2013, 2015, 2019). Our grouping systems have some differences. This project attempted to generate relatively fine subdivisions of fabrics, with a few goals in mind. First, although the local geology is somewhat homogenous, I hoped that it might be possible to detect subtle variation in local production practices that would correlate in meaningful ways with other aspects of the assemblage, either over time or in conjunction with variation in the local *chaîne opératoire* (e.g., between wheel- and hand-formed vessels). Likewise, since there are major geological similarities between Kea and other western Cycladic islands, Attica, and southern Euboea, I hoped this effort could clarify whether imports from within the neighboring region exist in the assemblage. Finally, I considered this an opportunity to examine whether it might be possible to distinguish between imports from other geologically similar areas, like Melos and Thera. The results were somewhat mixed and will be discussed in greater detail below.

MACROSCOPIC FABRIC GROUPS

Eight broad macroscopic fabric categories were defined: Red-Brown Metamorphic (RBM); Fine, Non-Micaceous, Sand-Tempered (FST); Dusty, Volcanic (DV); Mixed Micaceous (MxM); Coarse, with Shiny White Inclusions (CSW); Pink-Brown Soapy (PBS); Micaceous, Fine, Varied (MFV); and Fine, Varied (FV). Each category includes several subgroups (Table 3.1). Detailed descriptions are provided in Appendix IV.

Local and Local Region (RBM)

RBM fabrics, especially RBMa, the main local group, make up the bulk of the assemblage. RBMa fabrics are medium-fine to coarse, red-brown, sometimes turning gray at the core and/or surfaces. Schist, quartz, and mica are the dominant inclusions; phyllite appears occasionally. Both silver and gold mica may be present, although silver is more abundant. Possible calcareous inclusions or spalling may occur, but they are not common. Tiny shiny black or green glassy inclusions occasionally appear and may be amphibole and epidote, respectively. RBMa fabrics were closely associated with the main local petrographic fabric group (PFG) 1 (below). RBMa fabrics were used for all kinds of shapes and both plain and decorated wares.

RBMa encompasses significant variability, especially in terms of fineness vs. coarseness, relative micaceousness, and the appearance of rare inclusions like phyllite, calcareous, and probable amphibole and epidote grains. As part of the initial macroscopic analysis, I defined many additional subgroups in order to investigate whether or not there were meaningful differences in terms of clay choices, processing, or firing over time, across different wares, shapes, or forming methods (cf., Group A in Abell 2014b, 625–667). Fine-grained distinctions in local fabric subgroups, however, are not maintained here. Both the macroscopic and petrographic studies demonstrated that these fine-grained distinctions do not correlate closely with structured differences in local production practices, in terms of different choices being made at different stages of the *chaîne opératoire* for particular kinds of vessels. For example, fineness vs. coarseness is not universally differentiated in terms of vessel size (small or large), forming method (handmade or wheel-coiled), or ware (plain or decorated). That is, even though smaller tableware shapes are often finer than large jars, they are not always so, and medium-fine versions of large jars also exist—the variation appears to be random. There are no obvious differences in fabrics used for particular shapes or decorative wares, including handleless cups, pithoi, and cooking vessels (*pace* Berg 2007b, 94, 117). If such differences had existed, they might have been an indication that potters were making particular choices for the production of different kinds of pots, or that different kinds of pots were made by different people. Rather, most of the variation in fabrics probably derives from naturally occurring variability in clay sources and a long-term pattern of relatively minimal clay processing on the part of local potters.

There is little macroscopic evidence for significant changes in the characteristics of RBMa over time. Such a shift might have been expected at two junctures: between Periods III and IV, when the town was abandoned, and between Periods IV and V–VII, that is, before and after the start of the Minoanization phenomenon. Period III versions of the fabric more regularly have a gray core than Period IV–VII versions, but gray cores also do appear in Periods IV–VII, in all kinds of shapes, from tablewares to basins,

III. CERAMIC FABRICS AND FORMING METHODS

TABLE 3.1. MACROSCOPIC FABRICS WITH THEIR DISTINGUISHING CHARACTERISTICS

Macroscopic group	Distinguishing features
RBM all	Red brown; metamorphic inclusions, mostly schist
RBMa	Multicolored schist, variable
RBMb	Silvery-gray schist, soapy blue-gray particles
RBMc	Obvious calcareous inclusions, spalling
RBMd	Gold schist and/or mica
RBMe	Very common mica and quartz
FST all	Hard-fired, non-micaceous, calcareous, most sand-tempered (except fine FSTj and FSTk)
FSTa	Very compact, yellow or pale pink; hard dark lenticular inclusions
FSTb	Very compact, orange or pink; red and/or red-brown lenticular inclusions
FSTc	Slightly dusty, pale yellow or pink; gray, brown, pink, white inclusions
FSTd	Very compact, dark pink turning pale at surfaces; knobby black inclusions
FSTe	Compact, gritty, pinkish orange; fine sand, mostly pale-colored
FSTf	Very compact, orange to red, sometimes with a dark-gray/black core; various inclusions including dark-colored and/or white particles, possible metamorphics, and/or glassy inclusions
FSTg	Slightly dusty, pale yellow to pinkish brown; dark-brown/black siltstones
FSTh	Moderately fine, brown; dark-brown/black and gray mudstones and/or siltstones
FSTi	Pale brown to orange, usually with a gray core; common spalling, friable off-white inclusions
FSTj	Fine, pale yellow to pink, similar in color/texture to FSTa
FSTk	Fine, pale brown to orange, similar in color/texture to FSTb
DV all	Dusty, with volcanic inclusions
DVa	White, very pale yellow, pink, brown, or gray, porous; few inclusions, mostly small black, brown, red, white, or glassy-clear inclusions, rare silver mica
DVb	Similar to DVa, with larger and more common inclusions, including more common coarse and fine silver and rarely gold mica
DVc	Similar to DVa, with rounded gray and pale bluish-gray inclusions, common fine silver and gold mica
DVd	Pale yellow to pink, porous; mostly white, black, and red (probably volcanic) inclusions with gold mica
DVe	Moderately fine to fine, dusty, orange; inclusions (when visible) as DVd
DVf	Red brown to pinkish orange, gritty; glassy black inclusions and coarse gold mica
DVg	Fine, very pale yellow, porous; sponge spicules, fine silver mica
MxM all	Dusty, micaceous, sandy or gritty, with probable metamorphic inclusions
MxMa	Moderately fine, pale yellow to brown, dusty, sandy; coarse mica, foliated probable metamorphic inclusions, small dark and white particles
MxMb	Red brown; dark purplish brown and dark gray phyllite
MxMc	Moderately fine, pale yellow brown to red brown, very dusty; common silver and/or gold mica
MxMd	Dark red brown; dark and glassy yellow-brown inclusions, possible metamorphics, coarse gold and silver mica
MxMe	Moderately fine, orange brown, gray core, relatively compact and hard-fired; very common coarse and fine silver and gold mica, with possible metamorphic inclusions
MxMf	Gritty, pinkish or purplish brown; common coarse silver mica, some gold, and mostly white inclusions, spalling
MxMg	Pale pinkish brown; mixed inclusions, very common spalling and silver mica

TABLE 3.1. (CONT.)

Macroscopic group	Distinguishing features
CSW all	Coarse, with common pale-colored inclusions
CSWa	Red brown; rare mica
CSWb	Orange; some schist
CSWc	Similar to CSWa; probable calcareous inclusions and spalling
CSWd	Gray to red brown; common silver mica
CSWe	Orange pink to dark red brown, sometimes with a gray core; common coarse gold mica
PBS	Soapy inclusions and clay
MFV all	Fine, micaceous
MFVa	Dusty, pinkish brown; tiny white and gray inclusions, fine gold mica
MFVb	Dusty, dark gray; fine silver mica
MFVc	Dusty, red to orange; large calcareous particles and spalling, coarse and fine fraction silver mica
MFVd	Slightly dusty, fine, purplish brown, gold and/or silver mica
FV all	Fine
FVa	Hard, gray; rare spalling calcareous inclusions
FVb	Hard, yellow
FVc	Hard, pink
FVd	Dusty, orange; sometimes with rare silver mica
FVe	Hard, yellow to pinkish orange with gray core
FVf	Hard, dull purplish brown to brown, sometimes turning to pinkish orange in places
FVd/FVf	Orange, like FVd, but hard-fired like FVf
FVg	Pale pink turning yellow at surface and/or gray at core
FVh	Dusty, pinkish orange, bluish-gray core

large jars, and cooking vessels. Gray cores can be indicative of the presence of organics in the clay and/or the deposition of carbon during firing, or a reduction stage followed by an oxidation stage during firing (Rice 2015, 279–280; Wagner et al. 2000, 439). It is not clear which of these factors might have led to the gray cores in RBMa, or if they might have changed over time. There was also a tendency for a greater frequency of medium-coarse to coarse examples of this fabric in Period III deposits, in comparison with later versions. Nevertheless, similar ranges of coarseness were present in deposits of all periods. A change in local fabrics between Periods III and IV seems linked, instead, to the changing frequency and characteristics of RBMb (below).

Starting in Period V, local potters began to make many vessels in imitation of styles current on Crete. The proportion of Minoanizing pottery in the local assemblage was much higher in Period V than in Period IV, a trend that continued in Periods VI and VII (see Chs. 5–7). In addition, the Minoanizing potter's wheel, which was used rarely in Period IV, was used more frequently in Periods V–VII, especially to make Minoanizing shapes (below; Gorogianni, Abell, and Hilditch 2016, 206–210). Yet, there is no macroscopic evidence that local potters employed new, more Minoanizing kinds of clay processing or firing practices when they started to use the Minoanizing potter's wheel or when they made Minoanizing shapes. Cretan imports (included in macroscopic group FST, below) are easily distinguishable from local pottery, not just because these imports are made from usually pale-firing, calcareous clays, but also because they are hard-fired and sand-tempered. Neither sand-tempering nor consistent high firing was adopted by Keian potters. This observation from the macroscopic analysis is confirmed also by the petrography (PFG 1, below). The characteristics of RBMa, instead, are remarkably stable from Period IV into Periods V–VII, despite other stylistic and technological changes in the local ceramic repertoire.

Variation in the RBM group is represented by subgroups RBMb–e. All of these subgroups are red-brown, medium fine to coarse, and dominated by metamorphic inclusions, but the inclusions differ somewhat from the main (RBMa) group.

Subgroup RBMb has abundant silvery gray and blue-gray schist and silver mica, as well as soapy bluish gray inclusions. It is probable that the group is local, since vessels in this fabric are common in Period III deposits in Area B. A very low-fired vessel

(579) in this fabric from a Period VII context seems too fragile to have been transported over long distances, which also supports the hypothesis that RBMb is a local fabric. RBMb fabrics were closely associated with the main local petrographic group, PFG 1, especially subgroups PFG 1B and 1D (below). Subgroup RBMb is common in Period III deposits in Area B but rare in later deposits. When RBMb appears in MBA and LBA deposits, soapy bluish gray inclusions are typically either absent or extremely rare, while silvery gray schist inclusions are generally much smaller than in the EBA versions. These changes in frequency and appearance in RBMb between Period III and Periods IV–VII strengthen the evidence for a gap in occupation at Ayia Irini between the EBA and MBA. RBMb was associated with all kinds of shapes and both plain and decorated wares.

Subgroups RBMc–e appear to be geologically compatible with a local provenance, but all are rare compared with RBMa and RBMb; these subgroups appear in all periods, in all kinds of shapes and both plain and decorated wares. They are marked by abundant calcareous inclusions (RBMc), gold schist and/or mica (RBMd), and very frequent silver mica (RBMe). The rarity of these subgroups could suggest that they might have been produced elsewhere on Kea or in the broader local region, especially eastern Attica, the northwestern Cyclades, or southern Euboea, which have geological characteristics similar to those of Kea (Scheffer et al. 2016, 176, fig. 1). Petrographic analysis also suggests that these subgroups are atypical, with many petrographic samples from these macroscopic subgroups being classed in PFG 2 instead of PFG 1 (below).

Imports (FST, DV, MxM, CSW, PBS, MFV, FV)

Imports are usually easily distinguished from local products by their difference in clays, firing, and inclusions. Imported fabrics in Area B were abundant and highly varied. Imported fabric groups are made up of several subgroups, which may derive from different locations. The major distinguishing characteristics of each subgroup are summarized in Table 3.1. Coarser imports (FST, DV, MxM, CSW, PBS) are presented before finer ones (MFV), with the finest group, FV, last. Coarse fabrics are ordered roughly from more common to less common groups across the assemblage.

FST fabrics are hard-fired, with fine-grained, non-micaceous, calcareous clays and usually evidence for sand-tempering. They were found primarily in deposits dating from Periods IV–VII. Several FST fabrics seem comparable to fabrics from central Crete, especially FSTa–c, FSTe, and FSTf. These fabrics appeared primarily in association with decorated (Lustrous and Non-Lustrous Painted) wares hypothesized to be from Crete, as well as plain wares. These fabrics were used mostly for medium fine to coarse jugs and jars.

Several FST subgroups probably derive from other parts of the Aegean. FSTi was a relatively common subgroup in Period IV but did not appear in later deposits. It was associated with Minoan and/or Minoanizing plain and decorated wares, mainly medium to large closed shapes. FSTi was closely associated with PFG 8 of unknown origin. Subgroups PFG 8C–E had broad parallels with southeastern Aegean fabrics, although other sources are also possible. Two rare subgroups (FSTg, FSTh) were associated with mainland/Kytheran Lustrous Decorated ware; another rare subgroup (FSTd) was associated with LH Lustrous Painted ware. With the exception of several painted straight-sided/Vapheio cups in FSTh, most vessels in these fabrics were large closed shapes. Two subgroups (FSTj, FSTk) are fine; they were associated primarily with Minoan and/or Minoanizing decorated tablewares. These fabrics were grouped in FST because, macroscopically, the clays are similar in texture and color to coarser, sand-tempered FST fabrics that were hypothesized to be from Crete. Petrographically, however, the two subgroups are not coherent, and some samples do not seem to be compatible with a Cretan origin (Table 3.2, at the end of this chapter).

DV fabrics are dusty, micaceous, and sandy or gritty, with volcanically derived inclusions. They appear in deposits from Periods III–VII. Several pale-firing, calcareous DV fabrics with silver mica probably derive from Melos and/or Thera (DVa–c and perhaps DVg). These subgroups are comparable to pale-firing Thero-Melian fabrics found at both Akrotiri and Phylakopi (Vaughan and Williams 2007, 100–103; Hilditch 2019, 380–383; for the difficulty in distinguishing between Melian and Theran fabrics on the basis of macroscopic, petrographic, and chemical analysis, see also Hilditch 2019, 435–438; Papagiannopoulou, Grimanis, and Kilikoglou 1985; Williams 1981). These subgroups (DVa–c, DVg) were used for all kinds of shapes, both plain and painted. Notably, the two more micaceous subgroups, DVb and DVc, differed petrographically from the main Melian/Theran fabric, being classed in PFG 5D instead of PFG 5A (Table 3.2). This petrographic fabric also has some differences from the main local fabrics defined at Akrotiri, especially in the presence of common nonbiogenic calcite (Day, Müller, and Kilikoglou 2019, 327–340; Hilditch 2019, 404–412). It is possible that these more micaceous fabric groups might derive from Melos, although additional sampling and analysis is needed to confirm such a hypothesis.

One pale-firing subgroup (DVd) is comparable to Aeginetan gold mica fabrics, well known elsewhere in the Aegean, including Kolonna (Gauss and Kiriatzi 2011, 49–50). It is associated with Aeginetan wares, especially Matt Painted, and both tablewares and large closed shapes. The relatively fine, dusty orange fabric DVe is similar to some fabrics at Kolonna, and is associated primarily with plain, Lustrous Painted, and Red Coated wares in a wide variety of shapes. DVf has parallels in cookware fabrics at Kolonna. Petrographic analysis suggests that DVe and DVf are not entirely coherent as macroscopic groups, and it is possible that both may include some imports from other areas.

Group MxM includes micaceous, dusty, fine to medium coarse fabrics, usually with clear metamorphic inclusions. They are associated primarily with Cycladic wares (plain and decorated) and shapes. All probably derive primarily from other Cycladic islands. MxMb is dominated by large phyllite fragments and is comparable to descriptions of Amorgian "Blueschist" pottery from the EBA (Broodbank 2007, 124; Hilditch 2007, 239; Vaughan 2006, 100). Two fabrics (MxMa, MxMc) have similarities to MBA–LBA ceramics from Mikre Vigla in the Naxos Museum, while sherds in fabrics similar to MxMf were present in the assemblage from Paroikia in the Paros Museum. It is not certain, however, whether those fabrics were local on Naxos or Paros, and petrographic analysis (below) suggests that all three subgroups include pots from multiple sources. Several MxM subgroups appeared in deposits of all phases, although MxMa, MxMc, and MxMf were much more common in Period VII deposits than earlier ones in Area B; MxMe was rare and appeared only in Period VII. MxMg appeared only in EBA and mixed deposits, while the rare subgroup MxMb appeared only in the EBA.

CSW fabrics are coarse, red- to orange-brown, with common, shiny, pale inclusions, which probably include quartz, feldspar, calcareous inclusions, and possibly granite. These fabrics were rare in Area B. Subgroups CSWa–c appear only in Period IV–VII deposits, while subgroups CSWd and CSWe seem to be associated mainly with EBA vessels. Shapes and wares (plain and decorated) are varied. Some subgroups (CSWa, CSWe) may come from the central Cyclades, based on similarities to fabrics known elsewhere that are hypothesized to be from Naxos and possibly Paros (e.g., Barber and Hadjianastasiou 1989, 98; Hilditch 2019, 389–391). Other CSW subgroups (CSWb–CSWd) may be local to Kea or the nearby geologically similar region, based on the petrographic analysis.

The PBS fabric contains common soapy particles, while the clay itself also has a soapy feel. It was closely linked to EBA Talc ware, probably from Siphnos (Broodbank 2000, 297; for Melos as a possible origin, see also Vaughan and Wilson 1993; Wilson 1999, 69).

MFV fabrics are fine and micaceous with few or no other inclusions. They were rare in Area B. MFVa and MFVb appeared in Period IV and VII deposits; MFVc and MFVd appeared only in Period VII. MFVa, which was mostly associated with red Slipped and Burnished open vessels, may derive from the Cyclades. MFVb was associated primarily with Gray/Black Burnished ware of unknown origin. Several vessels in MFVc are comparable to Acropolis Burnished ware goblets and could perhaps have come from Attica.

FV fabrics are fine and have very few or no visible inclusions; the main distinguishing characteristics are based on color and hardness (Table 3.1). Many of these fabrics may come from the mainland, although some may have been produced on Crete; the provenance of fine fabrics used for LH/LM I–II Lustrous Painted ware, in particular, is difficult to determine solely on the basis of macroscopic examination of fabrics. Two subgroups (FVb, FVc) appear exclusively in Period VII, when they are associated with LH Lustrous Painted and plain tablewares. These subgroups may be from the Argolid, based on similarities to fine fabrics at Petsas House. FVa, exclusively associated with Gray Minyan ware and most common in Period IV, probably derives from central Greece and/or Euboea, as may FVf and its orange-tinged variant, FVd/FVf, which were associated with Pink-Orange and Mainland Polychrome wares. Two subgroups (FVg and FVh) were extremely rare and appeared only in EBA deposits; FVg was associated with Pinkish Buff and Urfirnis wares, while FVh was associated with Yellow Mottled and Urfirnis wares, with one mica-bearing variant classed as Pinkish Buff.

PETROGRAPHIC ANALYSIS

PREVIOUS STUDIES AND SAMPLING STRATEGIES

Previous studies have defined petrographic fabrics associated with Keian production. Hilditch (2004, esp. 11–18) studied samples of FN–EC II fabrics from Ayia Irini. She defined several possible subgroups among probable local fabrics, although all were defined as being micaceous red-brown primary clays with inclusions derived from greenschists. Likewise, a study of Period V pottery (Davis and Williams 1981, 293–295) generated similar descriptions of ostensibly local fabrics. Petrographic study at Kolonna on Aegina also identified a large group of imports potentially from Kea (FG 3 in Kiriatzi, Georgakopoulou, and Pentedeka 2011, 104–106, 139–140). All previous descriptions are compatible with the proposed local fabrics below (PFG 1).

Some macroscopic fabric groups were not sampled very extensively in Area B. Relatively few samples were taken from import groups that are common in Hilditch's studies of the Northern Sector and EBA pottery. These include DVa (Melian/Theran, associated with Cycladic White and other Melian/Theran wares), DVd (pale Aeginetan, associated with Matt Painted wares), PBS (Talc ware), and FVa ("true" Gray Minyan, probably from central Greece and/or Euboea). Subgroups that were less common or absent from the Northern Sector or which varied slightly from the norm were among the primary targets of sampling in Area B, so that this study might complement rather than replicate Hilditch's fabric study. Finally, FV subgroups were not sampled extensively, given the difficulties of assessing fine fabrics using petrography.

LOCAL FABRICS (PFG 1)

PFG 1 is totally compatible with the local geology. Samples in this group are composed of primary, red-brown, non-calcareous clays. Coarse inclusions are dominated by greenschist-facies metamorphic rock fragments, especially quartz-mica schists and rocks with porphyroblastic feldspars and/or epidote group minerals as well as quartz and mica. White mica and chlorite are common, biotite appears in varying quantities, titanite and tourmaline appear as accessory minerals, and amphibole exists but is rather rare. Quartz in some rock fragments is elongated with undulose extinction; these rocks may be derived from the phyllonitic schists common in association with the detachment footwall, which are observed across much of the north of the island (Rice et al. 2012,

111–112). Calcite may also appear, usually in the form of nonbiogenic micritic lumps that usually show no internal structure and are sometimes altered, with reaction rims and/or opaque patches visible under crossed polars (xpl), probably indicative of recrystallization as a result of firing at moderately high temperatures. Inclusions present in the coarse fraction generally are replicated in the fine fraction, and the size distribution is typically unimodal. These patterns suggest that coarse inclusions were already present in the clay sources rather than being added by the potters. PFG 1 fabrics also all contain common to very few argillaceous textural concentration features (tcfs), probably clay pellets, which appear similar in composition (sometimes with similar inclusions) to the primary fabric.

The micromass is moderately to highly active in nearly every sample across PFG 1A–1C, while those of PFG 1D show moderately high to low optical activity (Table 3.2). Based on analogy with other studies, this suggests a plausible original firing temperature for the majority of these vessels as somewhere between 650° and 900°C, especially given probable recrystallization of micrite in PFG 1C (Kiriatzi, Georgakopoulou, and Pentedeka 2011, 86–90; Quinn 2013, 191). This would be consistent also with the firing temperatures suggested for the Temple statues, samples of which have been analyzed using scanning electron microscopy and infrared spectroscopy. Those analyses suggested that most samples were fired at 650–800°C, although a handful showed lower firing ranges (Maniatis 1986, 111–113; Maniatis, Katsonas, and Caskey 1982).

Refiring tests (to 1050°C in oxidizing conditions) were undertaken for all samples; all refired to red, which is indicative of an iron-rich clay. Where preserved on the samples, yellow slip turned pink, and black paint turned red.

PFG 1 fabrics have been subdivided into four subgroups. The major differences are as follows. PFG 1A has abundant epidote and clinozoisite. PFG 1B has almost no epidote but many porphyroblastic clinozoisite grains in addition to common white mica schist in which the white mica typically shows low (first-order) birefringence colors. There is some streaking in the groundmass of PFG 1B, which might suggest the mixing of two clay sources, or, perhaps, incomplete homogenization of a single somewhat heterogeneous clay source. PFG 1C is differentiated because it contains discrete rounded micritic (or rarely sparitic) lumps in the coarse and fine fractions and may have a weakly bimodal size distribution, perhaps indicative of a difference in processing practices compared with PFG 1A. The groundmass of finer samples in this subgroup typically appears somewhat cleaner (with fewer inclusions and less mica) than is usual in the other subgroups; this is not just an issue of coarseness since many of the PFG 1A samples could be described as moderately fine, and yet have a groundmass that is richer in very fine inclusions than the PFG 1C examples. PFG 1C also displays some streaking in the groundmass, like PFG 1B. PFG 1D represents a possible raw material and/or technical distinction from the other groups, despite having inclusions similar to them. PFG 1D has common voids, including elongate planar/channel voids that are usually parallel to the vessel walls, in conjunction with a gray core. The existence of common voids and a gray core may suggest that the clay was richer in organic material and/or it may indicate differences in drying or firing from the other groups; indeed, this is the only subgroup in which moderately low or low optical activity (indicative of higher firing) appears in more than one sample.

There is gradation between these groups, and similar rock fragments appear in all of them. Nonetheless, some patterns among these subgroups are notable.

PFG 1B is made up nearly entirely of EBA Red-Brown Semifine to Semicoarse wares from Period III (Table 3.2), and it was closely associated with RBMb, also primarily an EBA fabric (above). PFG 1B includes a range of vessel shapes, including small open shapes, a larger deep bowl/open jar (perhaps a cooking vessel, although there is no sooting), and a pan. The only sample (41) from a later vessel that was classed in PFG 1B is a variant from the main group.

The association of PFG 1B and RBMb primarily with the EBA may suggest a break in raw material selection practices between the EBA and MBA. Such a break in manufacturing habits would be consistent with the long-hypothesized period of abandonment at Ayia Irini from late EC II through the earliest MC (Overbeck 1984, 109). This pattern also suggests that discontinuities in the norms of potting practices at Ayia Irini may be detectable, despite what appear to be broad similarities in geological raw materials across the island.

PFG 1D was associated primarily with EBA Semifine to Semicoarse and Coarse wares (Table 3.2), but this may be a bias of sampling. Local (RBMa and more rarely RBMc and RBMd) vessels from later deposits sometimes have gray cores, which seem to be a key distinguishing feature of this group. Unfortunately, few of those pots were sampled as part of this project. In Area B, in all periods, local macroscopic fabrics with gray cores appear in all kinds of shapes, from tablewares, to basins, large jars, and cooking vessels, and include both plain and decorated wares. Among sampled vessels, PFG 1D includes primarily closed vessels, with the exception of a Period VI cup (sample 49) and an EBA deep bowl/open jar (sample 12).

Periods III–VII vessels were associated with both PFG 1A and 1C. There is no correlation between forming technology and petrographic subgroup. Samples from vessels made by hand and those made using a potter's wheel exist in both groups. Wheel-coiled vessels from Period IV, from the earliest phases of wheel-use in the town, were found in each subgroup. There is also no correlation between wares or shapes and either subgroup. Coarser vessels only exist in PFG 1C, but it is possible that this might be a result of the limited number of samples analyzed.

Nearly all samples that were suspected to be local fabrics (RBMa, RBMb) from macroscopic analysis were classed in PFG 1. A handful were classed in PFG 2, which will be discussed below. Very few samples from macro-fabrics RBMc–e and no imports from other macroscopic groups were included in PFG 1.

LOCAL (REGION) FABRICS (PFG 2)

This group of fabrics is, for the most part, geologically compatible with a local source and petrographically very similar to PFG 1. There are, however, some differences that suggest that samples in this group might represent a different production area, whether elsewhere on Kea or in the wider northwestern Cyclades, southeastern Attica, or southern Euboea, which are geologically very similar to each other (Scheffer et al. 2016, 176, fig. 1). This hypothesis is supported also by the macroscopic analysis: several macroscopic fabrics associated with PFG 2 (RBMc–e) were suspected to be possible imports from within the neighboring region, owing to their rarity and deviations from the usual local fabrics. Preliminary interpretation of the WD-XRF results, however, suggests overlap in the chemical signatures of PFG 1 and 2.

PFG 2 includes four subgroups. Similarities between them suggest that some of the subgroups are related, especially PFG 2A and 2B, as well as PFG 2C and 2D. Samples in PFG 2A include metamorphic rock fragments consisting of quartz, feldspar, abundant white mica, opaques, and sometimes talc. Of all of the PFG 2 subgroups, this one is the most likely to be a local product. It has some similarities to PFG 1B (especially in the abundance of white mica and clinozoisite), and its differences from PFG 1 appear relatively minor. Nevertheless, a variant of this group also seems to link it to PFG 2B (samples 10, 115). That variant incorporates coarse metamorphic rocks and tcfs similar to those of PFG 2A together with fine-grained schists and gray cores, similar to those of PFG 2B. PFG 2A was associated with EBA open and closed shapes as well as an MBA or LBA pithos (sample 115); it is closely linked with macroscopic fabric RBMe.

PFG 2B is browner than PFG 1 and other PFG 2 groups; it contains primarily mylonitic(?) fine-grained schists and phyllites; it also lacks the tcfs so common in PFG 1. It incorporates vessels dating from Periods IV to VII, tablewares and large closed vessels and both plain and painted wares. Samples included in PFG 2B belonged to macroscopic groups RBMa and RBMc.

The schists in PFG 2C are relatively amphibole-rich, which is atypical both for PFG 1 and for previous descriptions of Keian fabrics. Samples in this subgroup date from the EBA to the LBA. They include various shapes, including tablewares and cooking vessels, as well as various decorative modes, including plain, painted, and burnished. Macroscopic groups RBMd, CSWb, and CSWd were represented in this petrographic group; all of these macro-fabrics were suspected to be imports.

PFG 2D is similar to PFG 2C, with the addition of rare (meta)granitic rock fragments. Such fragments are incompatible with Keian geology and indicate that this subgroup, and perhaps PFG 2C, might be from a neighboring area with granitic outcrops in association with metamorphic geologies, such as Lavrion, Tenos, Seriphos, Sikinos, or Naxos (Augier et al. 2014; Katzir et al. 2007; Rabillard et al. 2015; Scheffer et al. 2016, 179, fig. 3; Stouraiti et al. 2010). Samples date from Periods III–VI and include a jug, pyxis, and juglet(?), which were plain or burnished. Macroscopic fabric groups represented in this petrographic group include RBMd, CSWc, and CSWe.

IMPORTED FABRICS (PFG 3–14)

The following groups (PFG 3–14) are made up of imports. In many cases, subgroups comprise only one or two samples, and it is hoped that future, more extensive sampling programs may clarify further how these groups and subgroups relate to one another. The discussion below will, therefore, focus on the characteristics and associations of the whole group rather than consider each subgroup in depth. Detailed descriptions can be found in Appendix V.

PFG 3 is made up of nonlocal fabrics that are dominated by micaceous metamorphic inclusions, mainly schists and phyllites. These are probably derived primarily from areas associated with the Aegean/Cycladic Blueschist Unit, including the Cyclades themselves, as well as perhaps Euboea and Attica. There are nine subgroups, but many are represented by only a single sample (PFG 3A, 3B, 3D, 3E, 3F, 3G, 3H, 3I). Most do not have good parallels in published petrographic fabrics from other studies and so it is difficult to confidently associate them with a particular production area. The major exception is PFG 3I, which is compatible with descriptions of Amorgian "Blueschist" fabrics (Hilditch 2007, 239; Vaughan 2006); the associated macroscopic fabric (MxMb) was also hypothesized to be Amorgian. The largest subgroup is PFG 3C, which contained white mica and glaucophane schist (suggestive of a blueschist facies metamorphic environment), as well as microfossils. A sample from a modern whistle from the Ano Manos workshop from Syros, viewed in the collection of the Fitch Laboratory, is remarkably similar, and consequently this subgroup is (very) tentatively associated with Syriote production here. Without additional analysis of prehistoric Syriote fabrics, however, it is impossible to demonstrate such an origin exclusively. PFG 3C included samples from Period III–VII vessels, most of which appear to be tablewares. It was associated primarily with macroscopic fabric groups MxMa and MxMc (Table 3.2). PFG 3D may be related to PFG 3C, being distinguished primarily by the inclusion of possible grog.

A combination of coarse-grained quartzofeldspathic and/or metagranitic and/or granitic inclusions is what distinguishes PFG 4. The group is divided into several subgroups, but all may ultimately derive from Naxos. Subgroups have parallels with the metamorphic and granitic-derived fabrics from Mikre Vigla described by Vaughan (1989, 151–154), as well as proposed Naxian fabrics from Keros and Akrotiri (Hilditch 2013, 475; 2019, 419–422). Vessels range from Periods III–VII and include tablewares and closed vessels in plain, Slipped, and Slipped and Burnished wares. PFG 4A and PFG 4C are relatively closely associated with macroscopic groups CSWa and CSWe, although one MxMg sample (116) was also included in PFG 4C.

The fifth petrographic group is defined by its predominant volcanic inclusions, and includes Melian/Theran (PFG 5A, 5B, 5C, 5H[?]), possible Melian (5D), and Aeginetan (5F, 5G) products. These have close parallels with published descriptions of fabrics from those islands by Williams (1978), Vaughan (1989, 154–155), Kiriatzi, Georgakopoulou, and Pentedeka (2011, 93–104, 112–113, 131–139, 143), Hilditch (2019, 404–412), and Day, Müller, and Kilikoglou (2019, 327–340). For the most part, they correspond well with macroscopic fabrics and wares presumed to derive from each of those regions (DVa–c with Melos and/or Thera; DVd and DVe with Aegina). One subgroup, PFG 5E, does not have close parallels, and its origin is unknown.

Samples from PFG 6 probably derive from Crete. A Cretan origin is also suggested by preliminary interpretation of the WD-XRF analysis. These fabrics are high-fired and sand-tempered, with a mix of metamorphic, sedimentary, and igneous inclusions. Subgroups PFG 6A and 6B are consistent with descriptions of fabrics from central Crete; the presence of fine-grained volcanic rocks may link them with the Mesara in particular (Poursat and Knappett 2005, 21–24; Day 2011, 52–56, 58–60; Nodarou 2015, 347–350). These samples date from Periods IV and V; all were associated with closed shapes in probable Cretan wares and macroscopic fabrics (FSTb, FSTe, FSTf, FSTk).

Like PFG 6, PFG 7 is distinguished by high-firing and sand-tempering. Inclusions in this group are derived from sedimentary sources. As such, in many cases, it is difficult to pinpoint a production location owing to the widespread distribution of sedimentary geological formations in Crete, Kythera, and mainland Greece. This lack of geological distinctiveness is also combined with the intentional imitation of Cretan manufacturing techniques (tempering with sedimentary-derived rock fragments) noted in previous discussions of Minoanizing Lustrous Decorated wares (Kiriatzi 2010; Kiriatzi, Georgakopoulou, and Pentedeka 2011, 141). Lustrous Decorated wares—Minoanizing both technologically and stylistically—were made on Kythera and in at least one location in the Peloponnese; their technological similarities make it difficult to distinguish between products of these two regions and Crete (Kiriatzi 2010; Kiriatzi, Georgakopoulou, and Pentedeka 2011, 141; Whitbread 2001, 372). Two subgroups in PFG 7 are probably central Cretan, based on their similarities with published fabrics associated with that region (PFG 7A, 7B); these are dominated by mudstones and siltstones and a small range of other kinds of metamorphic- and sedimentary-derived inclusions, and they are also linked to a macroscopic fabric group (FSTa) that was hypothesized to be Cretan. Subgroups 7D and 7E are of unknown origin and have no known parallels. Preliminary interpretation of the WD-XRF analysis suggests that they also may be compatible with a Cretan source (Appendix VII). Other subgroups could perhaps be from the mainland or Kythera, owing to relatively close similarities with published fabrics associated with those regions (PFG 7C, 7F, 7G, 7H). Of those, PFG 7C (dominated by gray siltstones with dark rims) is associated exclusively with macroscopic fabric FSTg, which was hypothesized to be from the mainland or Kythera. Petrographically, however, it is impossible to rule out a Cretan origin. Preliminary interpretation of the WD-XRF results also suggests that PFG 7C would be compatible with a Cretan origin (Appendix VII). PFG 7F and 7G are very similar to one another, and both show unusual patterns of cracking in the groundmass. PFG 7G was closely associated with macroscopic group FSTh, which was hypothesized to be of mainland or Kytheran origin; PFG 7F was associated with a macroscopic variant, FSTg/FSTh. PFG 7H, which is red with red mudstone/siltstones, is paralleled in FG 5 at Kolonna, linked to the Argolid or Corinthia (Kiriatzi, Georgakopoulou, and Pentedeka 2011, 141–142). This PFG was associated exclusively with Lustrous Painted jars in macroscopic group FSTd. The preliminary interpretation of the WD-XRF analysis suggests that PFG 7G and 7H differ chemically from PFG 7A, 7C, 7D, and 7E, which may suggest a different, perhaps non-Cretan origin (Appendix VII); it was not possible to sample PFG 7F for WD-XRF analysis. Vessels in PFG 7 dated from Periods IV–VII and belonged to MBA Minoan/-izing and LBA Lustrous Painted wares.

Samples in PFG 8 are high-fired and contain abundant decomposing or altered calcareous rocks. No close parallels are known. All are associated with Period IV Minoan/-izing wares, which may suggest that they derive from somewhere in Crete, the Peloponnese, or the southeastern Aegean. One vessel from PFG 8C is a round-mouthed jug with a rectangular-section ledge at the base of the neck (**665**); the vessel has its closest typological parallels in the southeast Aegean. While the petrography demonstrates that such an origin is possible, it is not certain. PFG 8E, which contains a few acid volcanic rocks, may come from somewhere in the south Aegean volcanic arc. Differences from known Aeginetan, Melian, and Theran fabrics could suggest an eastern Aegean source, like Kos, but no close parallels for the fabric have been located. PFG 8 is closely associated with macroscopic group FSTi.

Samples in PFG 9 are moderately fine, micaceous, and marked by abundant amphibole and birefringent orange inclusions, which in some cases (especially in PFG 9A) are probably serpentinite. Parallels could not be located for either subgroup, although the wares associated with PFG 9A all suggest a Cycladic origin. The existence of major serpentinite outcrops on Tenos (Hinsken et al. 2017; Katzir et al. 2007) may suggest that island as a source, although other possibilities also exist. Three of four samples in PFG 9A were associated with macroscopic group MxMa, also hypothesized to be from the Cyclades.

No parallels for the single sample included in PFG 10 exist. Macroscopically, the sample is very similar to proposed Melian/Theran group DVa; the thin section, however, does not contain volcanic rocks, and the inclusions are not distinctive enough to associate with a particular production region. Preliminary interpretation of the WD-XRF analysis suggests that the sample differs chemically from petrographic groups associated with Melos/Thera (5A, 5B, 5C, 5H). The decoration of the sampled vessel (**57**) strongly suggests a Cycladic provenance.

PFG 11 is moderately fine and contains metamorphic and calcareous inclusions. Attica and Euboea would both be geologically compatible sources, but other possibilities also exist. The two samples date to Periods IV–V and VII and were associated with macroscopic fabrics MFVb and MFVc. The associated wares suggest a source on mainland Greece or Euboea.

PFG 12 is micaceous and moderately fine. One subgroup, PFG 12A, includes both glaucophane and epidote, which suggests it might derive from an area like southern Euboea or the northwestern Cyclades, where greenschist and blueschist facies metamorphic rocks coexist. Other subgroups cannot be linked with a particular provenance on the basis of the petrographic analysis. Samples date from Periods III–VII and include vessels in EBA Pinkish Buff, LBA Gray/Black Burnished, and Painted ware of unknown origin.

PFG 13 is fine, reddish brown, and micaceous, with inclusions of probably metamorphic origin. The two subgroups are very similar to one another but may represent different production areas. Macroscopically, PFG 13A was associated with several rare, fine fabric groups, including MFVc, which was hypothesized to be from Attica. However, only one sample (145), which is a variant to the main group, has good parallels in Gilstrap's (2015; Gilstrap, Day, and Kilikoglou 2016) study of LBA Attic fabrics. Like PFG 13A, PFG 13B was associated with several fine macroscopic fabric groups, including FVf and FVd/FVf, hypothesized to be from central

Greece owing to their connection with Pink-Orange and Mainland Polychrome wares. Preliminary interpretation of the WD-XRF results suggests that PFG 13A and 13B do indeed derive from different areas. PFG 13B appears to be compatible with FG 8 at Eretria, where it is the main local fine fabric associated with clays of the Lelantine plain (Charalambidou et al. 2016).

The final group, PFG 14, is made up of very fine fabrics that are not diagnostic petrographically. More extensive chemical analysis is needed to demonstrate their provenance. The preliminary interpretation of the WD-XRF results suggests that most of the subgroups have similar chemical profiles. Two variants (samples 157, PFG 14Bv, and 148, PFG 14Dv) differ from the rest. One of those (148) is a probable import from central Euboea (Lelantine plain?), based on chemical similarities with FG 8 at Eretria (Charalambidou et al. 2016, table 2). Samples in this group date to all periods and comprise a variety of plain and painted wares, most of which were hypothesized to derive from mainland Greece or Euboea. All but one (71) of the samples in this group were categorized macroscopically as FV fabrics.

SUMMARY

The combination of macroscopic and petrographic analyses clarifies aspects of local production and importation patterns. Local products were remarkably similar through time, especially from Periods IV–VII, after the period of abandonment that separated Periods III and IV. Although some differences in raw materials distinguish EBA products from later ones, there is no evidence for any break in raw material acquisition, processing or firing from Periods IV–VII, that is, before and during different stages of the Minoanization phenomenon.

This study has produced no evidence that different raw materials, processing, or firing practices were associated with local production of particular shapes or wares in any period or over time. It should, however, be acknowledged that very few large storage/transport jars, cooking vessels, and industrial vessels were sampled as part of this project.

Possible imports from neighboring, geologically similar areas have been detected, although additional petrographic and chemical analysis at Ayia Irini as well as in southern Euboea, the western Cyclades, and eastern Attica will be required to further clarify their compositional relationships to local products and their ultimate origins.

Both macroscopic and petrographic analyses hypothesized an array of imports from different parts of the Cyclades, Crete, and mainland Greece, as well as, perhaps, the eastern Aegean. Many groups are of unknown origin, but their presence confirms the general picture of a great deal of variety in imported pottery in the Keian assemblage over the course of the Bronze Age. It is hoped that the origins of such groups may be clarified in future, as more analytical programs of study on Kea, in the Cyclades, and elsewhere in the Aegean are published.

FORMING METHODS

Other aspects of the local pottery-making *chaîne opératoire* also were assessed in Area B, with a particular focus on forming methods. Each vessel was assigned to one of four categories—handmade, coil-built, wheelmade, or wheel-coiled—on the basis of macroscopic evidence of manufacture, such as rilling (wheel marks), wall thickness and consistency, and probable coil joins visible in fractures (see also Abell and Hilditch 2016; Gorogianni, Abell, and Hilditch 2016). Vessels classed as handmade preserved evidence for the use of discontinuous pressures associated with hand-building in their manufacture but no evidence for continuous pressures that are employed when using the potter's wheel. Handmade vessels had no other distinguishing manufacturing characteristics, like coil or slab joins. Vessels described as coil-built had visible coil joins on the surface or in the break. Vessels described as wheel-coiled preserved some evidence of coil joins, as well as rilling, string-cut bases, or other features of wheel manufacture. These vessels were probably roughed out by hand and then finished on a wheel. Vessels described as "wheel-coiled(?)" showed clear signs of wheel manufacture, but the evidence for coils was somewhat ambiguous. Vessels described as "wheelmade" preserved no evidence of coils but instead showed signs of rilling, string-cut bases, or other evidence for the continuous pressures that mark production on a wheel. It is possible that some or all vessels described as wheelmade were, in fact, wheel-coiled since evidence for coils or hand-building may be obscured through modification on a wheel or through finishing activities that mask evidence for forming gestures on vessel walls—even though other evidence, like spiraliform grooves on the base, may be preserved. Assessments about forming methods were based on the criteria set forth by Knappett (1999), Jeffra (2011), Courty and Roux (1995; Roux and Courty 1998), and my own years of experience hand-building and wheel-throwing pottery.

Although all local Period III pottery in Area B was handmade, a wide variety in forming gestures was observed, including variable locations of wiping marks on different kinds of vessels, as well as different methods of handle and neck attachment and base types within and between shape categories, a pattern of variability that also appears in the rest of the published EBA assemblage (Wilson 1999, 101–124). This lack of standardization in manufacturing practices probably suggests that there were multiple potters in the community, making different choices about how to form and finish their vessels. Although Ayia Irini was in communication with wheel-using communities on Euboea during this period, from whom a few wheelmade plates were imported, there is no evidence that the potter's wheel was adopted by contemporary Keian potters (Wilson 1999, 99, 141–143).

The potter's wheel was first used at Ayia Irini in Period IV. Physical potter's wheel disks, including one from a Period IV grave, are clearly Minoanizing in form (Georgiou 1986, 36–39). All pots made with the wheel in Period IV were small Minoanizing cups and bowls. These patterns strongly suggest that wheel technology was adopted as a result of interactions between Keian and Cretan potters, rather than Keian and mainland ones. Learning how to make pottery requires a significant period of apprenticeship; in the case of using a potter's wheel, that apprenticeship is even longer, usually lasting years before an apprentice is considered competent by the rest of the community (Roux 2003; Roux and Corbetta 1989). The adoption of the potter's wheel on Kea, therefore, probably resulted from long-term, intense interaction, probably enabled by the mobility of one or more Cretan potters to Kea (Abell 2014a, 559–561).

Wheel-formed vessels from Period IV deposits in Area B were all probably wheel-coiled rather than wheel-thrown; wheel-coiling was a major method of manufacture on MBA Crete, although there is debate about whether or not true wheel-throwing was also practiced there (Jeffra 2013, 32–33, with references; see also Caloi 2019).

In Period IV, very few pots were made with a potter's wheel (see also Ch. 5). Local potters also did not use this technology to manufacture popular non-Minoanizing shapes. The low-intensity of wheel production over the course of a hundred years (at least), suggests that, at least in this period, the wheel was not strategically employed to scale-up production, either for domestic consumption or for export. Rather, the limited use of the wheel seems to be directly tied to the limited range of shapes made with it: small, Minoanizing cups and bowls.

More and larger vessels, mainly Minoanizing, were made with a potter's wheel during Period V. Even more shapes, including more non-Minoanizing ones, were made with the wheel in Periods VI and VII (Gorogianni, Abell, and Hilditch 2016, 206–212). In these periods, both wheel-coiled and wheelmade vessels have been identified, although, as noted above, it is possible that some or all of the "wheelmade" vessels might be well smoothed versions of wheel-coiled vessels (Gorogianni, Abell, and Hilditch 2016, 206). There is no evidence that any local vessels, including handleless cups, were thrown "off the hump," at least in Area B. Indeed, handleless cups were more frequently wheel-coiled than wheelmade throughout Periods V–VII (Gorogianni, Abell, and Hilditch 2016, 210).

The prevalence of wheel-coiling suggests that the use of the potter's wheel in Periods V–VII cannot be directly linked to an economically motivated intensification of production (i.e., making more pots more quickly in order to meet greater demand; *pace* Davis and Lewis 1985). Wheel-coiling does not offer the same potential for scaling up production as wheel-throwing; it is only slightly less time intensive than coil-building (Roux 2011, 85–87). The increased use of the wheel, instead, appears to be linked to the increased production of Minoanizing shapes in particular (Abell and Hilditch 2016; Gorogianni, Abell, and Hilditch 2016, 206–212).

Different fabrics or clay processing methods were not employed for the local production of Minoanizing vessels made using the wheel, a fact that suggests that people who used this technology after its initial adoption were integrated into the Keian community of practice. Stability in various aspects of local pottery technologies is also apparent in other Cycladic assemblages, namely at Phylakopi and Akrotiri, where the potter's wheel was adopted slightly later than at Ayia Irini, in the later MBA (Phylakopi II-iii and Akrotiri Phase C) (Berg 2007a; Jeffra 2019). Limited sampling of pottery from Phylakopi suggests substantial stability in firing regimes from the EBA–LBA (Maniatis and Tite 2007). Although some possible distinctions in fabrics used for wheel- and hand-forming in the late MBA and early LBA have been noted, wheel-formed vessels, nevertheless, were also manufactured using traditional local fabrics (Berg 2007a, 242–243). At Akrotiri, local clay procurement, processing, and firing practices remained much the same before and after the Minoanizing potter's wheel was introduced (Hilditch 2019, 439–440; Jeffra 2019), with one exception. In the same period that the potter's wheel was adopted at Akrotiri, potters began to introduce phyllite temper to pastes used to make cooking pots (Müller, Kilikoglou, and Day 2015). This new method of tempering did not offer actual practical benefits in terms of toughness, thermal shock resistance, or thermal conductivity, although it may have been perceived to do so. Instead, the technique seems to derive from traditional methods for manufacturing cooking pots on Crete (Müller, Kilikoglou, and Day 2015, 46). At Akrotiri, locally produced tripod jars (Minoanizing) and flat-bottomed, wide-mouthed cooking pots (non-Minoanizing) were phyllite-tempered. The different morphologies of these shapes, which were also fired to different temperatures, suggest that they were utilized to heat foods in different ways (Müller et al. 2013, 6–7). The use of phyllite-tempering for both shapes shows that this technique was strategically incorporated into local traditions, rather than Cretan pot-making and cooking techniques having replaced Theran ones wholesale. This pattern parallels that observed with the introduction of the potter's wheel at both sites: wheel technology was adopted into local practice, but other aspects of the Cretan *chaîne opératoire*, like sand-tempering and high-firing, were not. Some human mobility, probably of Cretan potters to the Cyclades, is implied by the local adoption of Cretan wheel technology and, at Akrotori, phyllite-tempering: both fabric recipes and forming techniques using a potter's wheel are much more likely to be shared through in-person transmission of technical knowledge than on the basis of observation of a finished product. The lack of other changes in local *chaînes opératoires* at Ayia Irini and Akrotiri suggests that such mobile potters were otherwise integrated into local communities of practice. These potters must have adapted many aspects of their manufacturing processes to embrace established parts of Keian and Theran production traditions, from clay selection and processing to firing.

A dynamic pattern of engagement with pottery traditions from other parts of the Aegean is a consistent feature of the Keian ceramic assemblage. In every period, imports came from multiple locations, and local potters manufactured vessels with clear affinities to different regions, whether technologically, morphologically, or stylistically. The ways in which ceramic production, importation, and consumption patterns shifted through time will be examined in greater detail by period in the subsequent chapters.

TABLE 3.2. SUMMARY OF PETROGRAPHIC FABRIC GROUPS (PFG) AND PROPOSED REGIONS OF ORIGIN, IN RELATION TO THEIR OPTICAL ACTIVITY (OPT ACT) AND REFIRING COLOR.

Abbreviations: p: pink; r: red; y: yellow; v: very; mod: moderate; YS: Yellow Slipped. A "v" after the macroscopic or petrographic fabric code (e.g., 1Av, RBMbv) indicates that the sherd or sample is a variant compared with the main fabric group. A "v" after a refiring color means that the color was not homogenous.

PFG	Sample no.	Cat. no.	Region of origin	Opt act	Refiring color	Slip/paint refiring color	Macro fabric group	Shape	Ware	Manufacture	Period
1A	4	264	Local	high	r		RBMa	Pyxis(?)	EBA Red-Brown Burnished	Handmade	III
1A	30	41	Local	mod high	r		RBMa	Straight-sided cup	Local Yellow Slipped	Wheelmade	Early VI
1A	40	668	Local	mod high	r		RBMa	Cup	Local Plain	Wheel-coiled	IV
1A	42	185	Local	mod high	r		RBMa	Miniature pyxis	Local Plain	Unknown	VIIb
1A	44	97	Local	mod low	r	YS to pinkish yellow, nearly gone	RBMa	Closed(?) vessel	Local Yellow Slipped	Coil-built(?)	Later VI
1A	48	329	Local	mod high	r		RBMd	Incense burner	Local(?) Plain	Wheelmade/wheel-coiled	VIIa
1Av	15	618	Local	mod high	r		RBMa	Shoulder-handled tankard	EBA Red-Brown Burnished	Handmade	III
1Av	45	752	Local	mod high	r		RBMa	Handleless cup	Local Plain	Wheel-coiled	VII
1B	9	282	Local	high	r		RBMb	Deep bowl/open jar	EBA Red-Brown Semifine to Semicoarse	Handmade	III
1B	11	608	Local	mod high	r		RBMbv	Saucer	EBA Red-Brown Semifine to Semicoarse	Handmade	III
1Bv	5	286	Local	mod low	r		RBMa, dark	Tankard or bell-shaped cup(?)	EBA Black Burnished	Handmade	III
1Bv	8	16	Local	high	r		RBMb	Shallow saucer or lid(?)	EBA Red-Brown Semifine to Semicoarse	Handmade	III
1Bv	26	263	Local	high	r		RBMbv	Pan	EBA Red-Brown Semifine to Semicoarse	Handmade	III
1Bv	41	102	Local	mod high	r		RBMa	Cycladic cup	Local Plain	Handmade(?)	Later VI
1C	1	639	Local	high	r	YS to pink	RBMa	Basin	Local Yellow Slipped	Handmade	IVa
1C	18	706	Local	high	r		RBMa	Stick-handled lamp	Local Plain	Wheelmade/wheel-coiled(?)	Early VI
1C	35	9	Local	high	r		RBMa	Shallow Bowl	EBA Red-Brown Burnished	Handmade	III
1C	36	644	Local	high	r		RBMa	Goblet	Local Burnished	Unknown	IVb
1C	37	645	Local	mod high	r		RBMav	Carinated(?) bowl	Local Burnished	Handmade(?)	IVb
1C	43	646	Local	high	r		RBMa	Large (barrel?) jar	Local Yellow Slipped	Handmade	IVb
1Cv	2	55	Local	mod high	r		RBMa	Minyanizing goblet	Local Plain	Wheel-coiled	Early VI
1Cv	22	299	Local	high	r		RBMc	Large jar/pithos	EBA Red-Brown Burnished	Handmade	III

PFG	Sample no.	Cat. no.	Region of origin	Opt act	Refiring color	Slip/paint refiring color	Macro fabric group	Shape	Ware	Manufacture	Period
1Cv	27	136	Local	high	r		RBMav	Bridge-spouted jug	Local Yellow Slipped	Wheel-coiled	VIIb
1Cv	38	652	Local	high	r		RBMa	Cup	Local Plain	Wheel-coiled	IVb
1Cv	39	653	Local	mod high	r		RBMa	Saucer	Local Plain	Wheel-coiled	IVb
1D	3	649	Local	mod high	r		RBMa	Jug	Local Plain	Handmade	IVb
1D	7	262	Local	mod low	r		RBMbv	Jar	EBA Red-Brown Semifine to Semicoarse	Handmade	III
1D	12	237	Local	mod low	r		RBMb	Large deep bowl/open jar	EBA Red-Brown Semifine to Semicoarse	Handmade	III
1D	23	238	Local	mod high	r		RBMd	Pithos	EBA Red-Brown Coarse	Handmade	III
1D	49	40	Local	low	r	YS to pinkish yellow; black paint to red-brown	RBMa, dark	Rounded cup	Local Yellow Slipped	Wheelmade(?)	Early VI
1Dv	6	247	Local	mod low	r		RBMbv	Large jar, perforated	EBA Red-Brown Coarse	Handmade	III
2A	33	625	Local (region)	high	r		RBMe	Saucer (lamp?)	EBA Red-Brown Semifine to Semicoarse	Handmade	III
2A	34	624	Local (region)	mod low	r		RBMe	Deep saucer	EBA Red-Brown Semifine to Semicoarse	Handmade	III
2Av	10	271	Local (region)	mod high	r		RBMb/RBMc	Large jar	EBA Red-Brown Burnished	Handmade	III
2Av	32	275	Local (region)	mod high	r		RBMe	Jar with two-stage neck	EBA Red-Brown Semifine to Semicoarse	Handmade	III
2Av	115	25	Local (region)	mod low	r		RBMe	Pithos	Local(?) Plain	Handmade	V–VII
2B	21	156	Local (region)	low	r		RBMc	Minyanizing goblet/jar	Cycladic/Attic(?) Plain	Wheel-coiled(?)	VIIb
2B	28	184	Local (region)	mod low	r		RBMav	Spouted jug	Local(?) Yellow Slipped	Coil-built	VIIb–c
2B	50	640	Local (region)	mod high	r	YS to pinkish yellow	RBMa, dark	Large closed (barrel jar?)	Local Yellow Slipped (Polychrome)	Handmade	IVa
2Bv	19	98	Local (region)	low	r	YS to pink; black paint to red	RBMav	Large, closed	Local(?) Yellow Slipped	Handmade	Later VI
2Bv	20	399	Local (region)	mod low	r	YS gone	RBMc	Bowl(?)	Cycladic/Attic(?) Yellow Slipped (Polychrome)	Wheel-coiled(?)	VIIb
2C	130	719	Local (region)	mod high	r		CSWb	Jug	Cycladic Painted	Handmade	Early VI(?)
2C	131	565	Local (region)	v low	r		CSWb	Handleless cup	Cycladic Plain(?)	Wheel-coiled(?)	IV–VII
2C	139	623	Local (region)	v low	r		CSWd	Open jar (cooking vessel?)	EBA Red-Brown Semifine to Semicoarse	Handmade	III
2Cv	24	45	Local (region)	low	r		RBMd	Tripod jar	Local(?) Plain	Coil-built	Early VI

TABLE 3.2. (CONT.) SUMMARY OF PETROGRAPHIC FABRIC GROUPS (PFG) AND PROPOSED REGIONS OF ORIGIN

PFG	Sample no.	Cat. no.	Region of origin	Opt act	Refiring color	Slip/paint refiring color	Macro fabric group	Shape	Ware	Manufacture	Period
2Cv	25	277	Local (region)	low	r		RBMd	Rounded(?) cup	Local(?) Yellow Slipped	Wheelmade/wheel-coiled	V–VI
2Cv	47	279	Local (region)	mod low	r		RBMd	Open jar(?)	Local(?) Burnished	Handmade	III–IV
2Cv	135	313	Local (region)	v low	r	Paint to red-brown	CSWd	Sauceboat	EBA Black Burnished(?)	Handmade	II–III
2Cv	136	312	Local (region)	v low	r		CSWd	Closed (pyxis or duck vase?)	Unknown Burnished	Handmade	II–IV
2D	16	707	SE Attica/Cyclades	inactive	r		RBMd	Juglet(?)	Local Plain	Wheel-coiled	Early VI
2D	132	3	SE Attica/Cyclades	inactive	r		CSWc	Jug	Attic/Cycladic Plain	Handmade	III–V
2D	137	613	SE Attica/Cyclades	mod low	r		CSWev	Pyxis	EBA Red-Brown Burnished(?)	Handmade	III
3A	102	33	Cyclades	high	r		MxMc	Handleless cup or bowl	Cycladic Slipped	Unknown	Early VI(?)
3B	106	676	Cyclades	high	r		MxMd	Large, closed	Cycladic Plain	Pushed-through	IVb
3C	53	147	Cyclades (Syros?)	mod	p(v)	Paint gone	MxMa	Jug/jar	Cycladic Painted (Polychrome)	Wheelmade/wheel-coiled	VIIb
3C	104	394	Cyclades (Syros?)	high	r		MxMc	Rounded cup	Cycladic Plain	Wheelmade(?)	VIIb
3C	113	61	Cyclades (Syros?)	mod	r		MxMf	Tumbler	Cycladic Plain	Wheel-coiled(?)	Early VI
3Cv	105	267	Cyclades (Syros?)	high	r		MxMc	Shallow bowl(?)	EBA Orange-Buff Painted	Handmade	III
3Cv	117	34	Cyclades (Syros?)	mod	r		MxMa	Straight-sided cup	Cycladic Plain	Unknown	Early VI(?)
3Cv	119	105	Cyclades (Syros?)	mod	r		MxMa	Bowl	Cycladic Plain	Wheel-coiled(?)	Later VI
3Cv	141	655	Cyclades (Syros?)	high	r	Paint to red-brown	MFVa	Goblet	Cycladic Slipped and Burnished	Unknown	IVb
3D	107	58	Cyclades (Syros?)	mod	p(v)		MxMd	Closed	Cycladic Plain	Wheelmade	Early VI
3E	101	515	Attica/Euboea/Cyclades	mod	p		MxMcv	Open(?) vessel	Cycladic Plain	Wheel-coiled(?)	VIIb–c
3F	164	114	Unknown	mod	p	Paint to dark red	FVd	Rounded cup	Lustrous Painted	Wheelmade	Later VI
3G	52	145	Cyclades(?)	low	p		MxMa	Bridge-spouted jug	Cycladic Painted	Unknown	VIIb
3H	142	421	Attica/Euboea/Cyclades	high	r		MFVb	Straight-sided cup	Gray/Black Burnished	Wheelmade	VIIb
3I	14	272	Amorgos	high	r		MxMb	Closed	Cycladic Plain	Handmade	III
4A	17	59	Naxos	low	r		CSWe	Handleless cup	Cycladic Plain	Wheel-coiled	Early VI
4A	129	598	Naxos	low	r		CSWa	Closed(?) vessel	Cycladic Yellow Slipped	Handmade(?)	VIIb

PFG	Sample no.	Cat. no.	Region of origin	Opt act	Refiring color	Slip/paint refiring color	Macro fabric group	Shape	Ware	Manufacture	Period
4Av	138	296	Naxos	mod	r		CSWe	Collared jug	EBA Red-Brown Semifine to Semicoarse	Handmade	II–III
4B	103	654	Central Cyclades(?)	mod low	p(v)	Paint to red-brown	MxMc	Open	Cycladic Slipped and Burnished(?)	Unknown	IVb
4Bv	98	669	Central Cyclades(?)	mod	p(v)		MxMf	Hole-mouthed jar	Cycladic Plain	Handmade	IVb
4C	114	626	Naxos	mod low	r		CSWe	Jar(?)	EBA Orange-Buff Semifine to Coarse	Handmade	III
4Cv	100	677	Naxos	high	dark p	Paint to red	CSWe	Closed	Cycladic Slipped and Burnished	Coil-built	IVb
4Cv	116	297	Naxos	high	p		MxMg	Bowl	Cycladic Slipped	Handmade	III
5A	85	64	Melos/Thera	inactive	p(v)		DVa	Large, closed	Melian/Theran Painted	Handmade	Early VI
5A	86	642	Melos/Thera	inactive	p(v)		DVa	Jug(?)	Cycladic White	Handmade	IVa
5Av	110	67	Melos/Thera	inactive	y		DVdv	Piriform cup	Melian/Theran(?) Painted	Handmade(?)	Early VI
5B	90	709	Melos/Thera	mod low	p		DVa	Closed	Melian/Theran Painted	Handmade	Early VI
5Bv	126	26	Melos/Thera	inactive	p(v)		DVa	Closed	Melian/Theran Painted	Unknown	IV–VII
5C	89	149	Melos/Thera	mod low	r		MxMa	Small jug	Melian/Theran Yellow Slipped(?)	Wheelmade(?)	VIIb
5Cv	91	738	Melos/Thera	high	pale p		DVa	Piriform cup	Melian/Theran Painted (Polychrome)	Unknown	V–early VI
5D	92	65	Melos(?)	v low	y	Paint to red	DVc	Large, closed	Melian/Theran Slipped and Burnished	Coil-built	Early VI
5D	93	699	Melos(?)	mod low	r		DVc	Cycladic cup/carinated bowl	Melian/Theran Slipped and Burnished	Unknown	IVc–V
5D	97	106	Melos(?)	mod	r	Paint to dark red-brown	DVb	Closed	Melian/Theran Painted	Handmade	Later VI
5Dv	124	27	Melos(?)	mod	r		DVev	Jug(?)	EBA Orange-Buff Painted(?)	Handmade	III(?)
5E	96	158	Unknown	v low	p(v)		DVf	Jug	Unknown Yellow Slipped	Unknown	VIIb
5F	95	567	Aegina	mod	r		DVf	Tripod tray	Aeginetan(?) Plain	Unknown	IV–VII
5G	121	656	Aegina	low	p(v)		DVe	Jug	Aeginetan(?) Plain	Unknown	IVb
5G	123	111	Aegina	v low	p(v)		DVe	Narrow-necked jar	Standard Matt Painted	Handmade(?)	Later VI
5G	125	670	Aegina	low	y		DVe	Basin	Aeginetan Matt Painted	Unknown	IVb
5Gv	109	632	Aegina	inactive	p(v)		DVd	Globular jar	Aeginetan Matt Painted	Handmade	IVa
5H	111	60	Melos/Thera(?)	mod low	r		MxMf	Tumbler	Melian/Theran Plain	Wheel-coiled(?)	Early VI
5Hv	120	109	Melos/Thera(?)	v low	p	Paint to red	DVe	Cup	Red Coated	Wheelmade(?)	Later VI
6A	66	701	Central Crete (Mesara?)	inactive	y	Paint to red-brown	FSTb	Closed	Lustrous Painted (LOD)	Handmade	V

TABLE 3.2. (CONT.) SUMMARY OF PETROGRAPHIC FABRIC GROUPS (PFG) AND PROPOSED REGIONS OF ORIGIN

PFG	Sample no.	Cat. no.	Region of origin	Opt act	Refiring color	Slip/paint refiring color	Macro fabric group	Shape	Ware	Manufacture	Period
6B	77	686	Central Crete (Mesara?)	low	p(v)		FSTe	Hole-mouthed jar	Lustrous Painted	Handmade	IVb
6Bv	73	660	Central Crete (Mesara?)	low	p(v)	Paint to dull red-brown	FSTk	Small, closed	Lustrous Painted (LOD)	Wheelmade	IVb
6C	67	695	Crete(?)	low	p(v)	Paint to red-brown	FSTe	Jug	Lustrous Painted	Unknown	IVb/c
6C	81	662	Crete(?)	low	p(v)		FSTf	Closed	Non-Lustrous Painted	Handmade	IVb
7A	56	696	Central Crete	v low	p		FSTa	Closed	Lustrous Painted	Handmade	IVb/c
7B	55	694	Central Crete(?)	inactive	p(v)		FSTa	Closed	Lustrous Painted (LOD)	Handmade	IVb/c
7C	82	658	Crete/Peloponnese(?)	inactive	p(v)		FSTg	Closed	Lustrous Decorated	Handmade	IVb
7C	84	715	Crete/Peloponnese(?)	inactive	p(v)		FSTg	Closed	Lustrous Decorated	Handmade	IV
7D	68	663	Crete/Peloponnese(?)	inactive	p(v)	Paint gone	FSTc	Closed	Non-Lustrous Painted	Handmade	IVb
7D	80	635	Crete/Peloponnese(?)	mod	p(v)	Paint to red-brown	FSTf	Closed	Lustrous Painted (Monochrome)	Wheelmade	IVa
7E	65	671	Crete/Peloponnese(?)	v low	v pale p	Paint to dull red	FSTe	Closed	Lustrous Painted (LOD)	Coil-built	IVb
7F	64	591	Mainland/Kythera(?)	mod	p(v)		FSTg/FSTh	Large jar	Lustrous Painted	Wheelmade	VIIb
7G	61	116	Mainland/Kythera(?)	inactive	p(v)	Paint to crackling red-brown	FSTh	Vapheio cup	Lustrous Painted	Wheelmade	Later VI
7G	62	588	Mainland/Kythera(?)	inactive	p(v)	Paint to dull red	FSTh	Jar	Lustrous Painted	Wheelmade	VIIb
7Gv	63	172	Mainland/Kythera(?)	v low	v pale p	Paint to lustrous red	FSTh	Vapheio cup	Lustrous Painted	Wheelmade	VIIb
7Gv	70	118	Mainland/Kythera(?)	inactive	p(v)	Paint to crackling dark brown	FSTj	Bridge-spouted jug	Lustrous Painted	Unknown	Later VI
7Gv	72	119	Mainland/Kythera(?)	mod	p	Paint to red	FSTk	Rounded cup	Lustrous Painted	Wheelmade	Later VI
7H	75	173	Argolid/Corinthia(?)	inactive	p(v)	Paint to red	FSTd	Palace Style jar	Lustrous Painted	Handmade	VIIb
7Hv	74	537	Argolid/Corinthia(?)	mod low	p(v)	Paint to red-brown	FSTd	Jar	Lustrous Painted	Wheel-coiled or combination technique(?)	VIIb–c
8A	83	311	Unknown	inactive	p(v)	Paint to dull red-brown	FSTg	Large, closed	Lustrous Decorated (LOD)	Handmade	IV
8B	58	664	Unknown	inactive	p(v)		FSTiv	Large jar	Lustrous Painted (LOD)	Coil-built	IVb

PFG	Sample no.	Cat. no.	Region of origin	Opt act	Refiring color	Slip/paint refiring color	Macro fabric group	Shape	Ware	Manufacture	Period
8C	59	665	Unknown	v low	p(v)		FSTiv	Round-mouthed jug	Non-Lustrous Painted (Monochrome)	Handmade	IVb
8C	60	681	Unknown	low	p	Paint to red-brown	FSTi	Hole-mouthed jar(?)	Non-Lustrous Painted (LOD)	Handmade	IVb
8D	76	636	Unknown	low	r		FSTi	Vessel	Unknown Plain	Handmade	IVa
8D	78	682	Unknown	v low	r		FSTi	Large, closed	Non-Lustrous Painted (Monochrome)	Handmade	IVb
8D	79	683	Unknown	mod low	r		FSTi	Fine, closed(?)	Non-Lustrous Painted (Monochrome)	Handmade	IVb
8Dv	57	684	Unknown	mod low	r		FSTi	Large, closed(?)	Unknown Plain	Handmade	IVb
8E	69	672	Unknown	v low	p		FSTiv	Large, closed	Non-Lustrous Painted	Handmade	IVb
9A	51	104	Cyclades (Tenos?)	mod	p		MxMa	Small, closed	Cycladic Painted	Wheelmade(?)	Later VI
9A	87	612	Cyclades (Tenos?)	inactive	r		MxMa	Tankard	EBA Black Burnished	Handmade	III
9A	108	177	Cyclades (Tenos?)	mod	p(v)		MxMe	Paneled jug(?)	Cycladic(?) Yellow Slipped (Polychrome)	Combination technique(?)	VIIb
9Av	54	190	Cyclades (Tenos?)	mod	p(v)		MxMa	Jar	Cycladic Yellow Slipped (Polychrome)	Wheel-coiled or combination technique	VIIb–c
9B	147	673	Unknown	inactive	p		No group	Bowl(?)	Unknown Plain	Wheelmade	IVb
10	128	57	Unknown	inactive	p(v)		DVg	Bowl	Cycladic Painted	Wheel-coiled	Early VI
11A	143	315	Unknown	high	p		MFVbv	Bowl(?)	Gray Minyan	Handmade(?)	IV–V
11B	146	333	Unknown	mod	p	Paint to red-brown	MFVc	Rounded cup or goblet	Lustrous Painted	Wheelmade	VIIa
12A	154	258	S Euboea/ NW Cyclades(?)	mod low	r	Paint to red	FVhv	Fine jar or pyxis	EBA Pinkish Buff	Handmade	III
12B	158	420	Unknown	mod low	pale p		No group	Miniature open	Gray/Black Burnished	Handmade	VIIb
12C	168	743	Unknown	inactive	p		No group	Closed(?) vessel	Unknown Painted	Handmade(?)	IV–early VI
13A	140	257	Attica(?)	mod	p		MxMcv	Cup(?)	EBA Orange-Buff Painted	Handmade	III
13A	144	163	Attica(?)	mod low	p	Paint to red-brown	MFVc	Goblet	Attic(?) Burnished	Wheelmade	VIIb
13A	155	615	Attica(?)	mod	p(v)		FVh	Open vessel	EBA Yellow Mottled	Handmade	III
13Av	145	160	Attica(?)	mod	p	Paint to red	MFVc	Goblet	Red Coated	Wheelmade	VIIb
13Av	151	115	Attica(?)	mod	p		FVf	Hydria	Attic Plain	Wheelmade	Later VI
13B	122	332	Euboea	mod	p(v)		MFVc/ DVe	Goblet	Mainland Slipped	Unknown	VIIa
13B	150	587	Euboea	mod	p		FVf	Goblet	Mainland Burnished	Unknown	VIIb

TABLE 3.2. (CONT.) SUMMARY OF PETROGRAPHIC FABRIC GROUPS (PFG) AND PROPOSED REGIONS OF ORIGIN

PFG	Sample no.	Cat. no.	Region of origin	Opt act	Refiring color	Slip/paint refiring color	Macro fabric group	Shape	Ware	Manufacture	Period
13B	165	710	Euboea	mod low	p		FVd/FVf	Narrow-necked hydria/jar	Mainland Slipped	Handmade	Early VI
13B	166	657	Euboea	mod low	r		FVd/FVf	Jar	Pink-Orange	Unknown	IVb
13Bv	127	756	Euboea	mod low	p(v)		MFVd	Fine, closed	Mainland Painted	Wheelmade	VII
14A	71	175	Unknown	inactive	y	Paint to dark red-brown	FSTjv	Flaring cup-rhyton(?)	Lustrous Painted	Wheelmade	VIIb
14B	152	314	Unknown	low	p(v)		FVg	Sauceboat	EBA Urfirnis	Handmade	II–III
14B	161	585	Unknown	v low	p(v)		FVc	Ephyraean goblet	Lustrous Painted	Wheelmade	VIIb
14B	162	343	Unknown	v low	p(v)		FVc	Goblet	Lustrous Painted (Monochrome)	Wheelmade	VII
14Bv	153	306	Unknown	high	v pale p	Paint to red	FVgv	Pyxis(?)	EBA Pinkish Buff	Handmade	III
14Bv	157	212	Unknown	mod	p		FVg	Shallow Bowl	EBA Pinkish Buff	Handmade	III
14Bv	160	167	Unknown	v low	p(v)		FVc/FVe	Ephyraean(?) goblet	Lustrous Painted	Wheelmade	VIIb
14Bv	167	334	Unknown	low	p(v)	Paint to red-brown	FVd	Goblet	Red Coated	Wheel-coiled(?)	VIIa
14C	159	195	Unknown	inactive	y	Paint to red	FVb	Goblet	Lustrous Painted	Wheelmade	VIIb–c
14D	169	523	Central Greece(?)	inactive	p(v)		FVe	Askos	Lustrous Painted	Handmade	VIIb–c
14D	170	170	Central Greece(?)	high	p(v)		FVe	Goblet	Mainland Plain	Wheelmade(?)	VIIb
14Dv	148	688	Central Greece(?)	mod	p		FVa	Goblet	Gray Minyan	Wheelmade	IVb/c

IV. EARLY BRONZE AGE CERAMIC ANALYSIS

The following chapters (4–7) discuss ceramics from Periods III–VII, based on published deposits and the evidence from Area B. Major wares and shapes of each period are summarized, and ceramic synchronisms are considered. Ceramic fabrics and manufacturing methods in Area B are then discussed, after which broad patterns of importation and consumption are outlined.

This chapter compares Period III pottery from Area B with Wilson's (1999) exhaustive publication of EBA ceramics from the rest of the site, which also included descriptions of inventoried ("K"-numbered) ceramics from Area B. Ware and shape designations follow his conventions. The discussion of synchronisms and import patterns is brief, since the final publication of the EBA settlement is currently in preparation by Wilson. Quantifications of pottery from Area B are based on the following lots: B03-803–806, 814–818, 820–824, 829, 830, 812 etc., 814 etc., 815 etc., and 821 etc.

OVERVIEW OF PERIOD III POTTERY

LOCAL

Wilson defined four red-brown wares that comprise mainly local products: Red-Brown Semifine to Semicoarse, Coarse, Burnished, and Yellow Slipped wares. The proportions of these wares in Area B were similar to those in published deposits. Red-Brown Semifine to Semicoarse vessels were most common by far, making up around 60% of the total (n = 194) vessels in Area B; Coarse ware was rarer, making up only 3% of the total. Wilson (1999, 90, table 3.1) counted Semifine to Semicoarse and Coarse vessels together; these comprised 67% of the total published assemblage. Burnished wares made up around 13% of the total (n = 194) vessels in Area B, and around 7% of published vessels (Wilson 1999, 90, table 3.1). Yellow Slipped ware did not exist in Area B and was represented by one sherd in published deposits (Wilson 1999, 113). Most Red-Brown vessels in Area B had local fabrics. In addition, although most Black Burnished vessels are hypothesized to be imported (below), a few from Area B were probably made locally.

Major shapes in *Red-Brown Semifine to Semicoarse* were shallow bowls, deep bowls/open jars, medium-sized bowls, various other jars, tankards, one-handled cups, basins, various jugs, and saucers (Wilson 1999, 101). Of these, the shallow bowl was extremely common (Wilson 1999, 104). Shallow bowls (**223, 609**) and deep bowls/open jars (**11–14, 237, 245, 273**[?], **276**) were common in Area B. Several deep bowls/open jars from Area B and published deposits were blackened in places and may have been used for cooking (Wilson 1999, 32, 107). One-handled cups (**2, 218**), tankards (**607**), basins (**1, 17**[?], **619**), and saucers (**15, 625**) also appeared. Some saucers (**608**) from Area B had a mat impression on their base, typical for this period at Ayia Irini and a common practice in both mainland Greece and the Cyclades (Wilson 1999, 27, 103). Jars with two-stage necks were the most common jar type in Periods II and III (Wilson 1999, 110) and also were present in Area B (**275, 620**). Some Red-Brown Semifine to Semicoarse vessels, which tended to be of more finely levigated clay than usual, were coated with black wash (Wilson 1999, 101). These were usually new shapes for the period, particularly the one-handled cup and the tankard; it is possible they were meant to imitate Black Burnished ware (Wilson 1999, 101). A shallow bowl (**609**) and a large globular jar (**244**) in Area B were coated in black wash.

Pithoi and pans were common *Red-Brown Coarse* vessels (Wilson 1999, 92, 113–118). Pans, together with deep bowls/open jars, were an important cooking shape; several were found in Area B (e.g., **263**). Pithoi often were decorated with multiple rope-bands on their necks and shoulders (Wilson 1999, 114). Pithoi decorated with multiple rope-bands or bands of applied disks were present also in Area B (**238, 251, 266**). Clay hearths were very popular in Period II but became rare in Period III (Wilson 1999, 117–118); none were found in Area B.

Red-Brown Burnished ware was three times more common in Period III than in Period II (Wilson 1999, 90, table 3.1). The ware included typical shapes of Period II, like deep bowls with flattened rims, as well as new shapes, like shallow bowls, tankards, and rarer bell-shaped and depas cups (Wilson 1999, 92, 119). Most Red-Brown Burnished vessels in Area B were tankards or shallow bowls (**9, 217, 222, 243, 246, 606, 618, 627**), although several other bowls (**252, 253**), a sauceboat (**617**), and a pyxis(?) (**264**) were also found. While most vessels in this ware are probably local, some may be imports (Wilson 1999, 119); two uncatalogued vessels in this ware in Area B had a fabric (RBMc) that may be from the neighboring region rather than Kea.

IMPORTS

The relative proportions of imported wares were somewhat different in Area B than in Wilson's (1999, 93, table 3.4) estimates from elsewhere on site. While a few wares were present in similar proportions in Area B and Wilson's study, most fine wares were less common in Area B (194 total vessels) than elsewhere (4233 total vessels). This pattern included Black Burnished (3% in Area B vs. 7% in published deposits), Urfirnis (2% vs. 8%), and Yellow Mottled wares (0.5% vs. 3%). On the other hand, Orange-Buff Semifine to Coarse ware was more common in Area B than elsewhere (8% vs. 1%).

Several underlying causes may account for these discrepancies in proportions. First, Area B preserved many fewer vessels than the site overall and differences in consumption patterns and/or taphonomic processes in the area may have impacted relative proportions of wares in the assemblage. Variable discard strategies may also have played a role. Wilson (1999, 2) mentioned that most Red-Brown body sherds from published deposits seem to have been discarded. As discussed in Chapter 1, Bikaki had grown skeptical of combining lots and extensive discarding by the 1970s, when the tests below House B took place. The presence of many Red-Brown body sherds in Area B suggests that fewer sherds may have been discarded from Area B than elsewhere, although this cannot be confirmed by excavation records. The greater retention of coarse sherds might explain why a greater proportion of Orange-Buff Semifine to Coarse ware was found in Area B than in Wilson's study, while fine wares were proportionally less significant. If this difference between Area B and other areas published by Wilson is really a discrepancy resulting from differential post-excavation discard practices, it has implications for assessing the Period III assemblage. Imported finewares, primarily used for eating, drinking, and pouring shapes, were more common than jars, pithoi, or other large closed vessels among imported wares in Wilson's (1999) publication; the reverse is true in Area B, where jars and pithoi in possible and probable nonlocal fabrics were more common than imported finewares. The evidence from Area B suggests fine eating, drinking, and pouring shapes could perhaps have made up a somewhat smaller proportion of ceramics at Period III Ayia Irini than is indicated by the extant assemblage from other parts of the site.

Black Burnished ware includes primarily (although not exclusively) imported products, perhaps mainly from the Cyclades (Hilditch 2004, 54–55; Wilson 1999, 67, 125). The ware was more common in Period III than Period II and included new Anatolianizing shapes, especially tankards and bell-shaped cups (Wilson 1999, 93, 125–130). Black Burnished vessels in Area B included an imported Cycladic tankard (**612**) as well as a local sauceboat(?) (**610**) and pyxis (**605**).

Talc ware was twice as common in Period III than Period II. The ware may derive from Siphnos (Broodbank 2000, 297); although Melos has been suggested as a possible origin (Vaughan and Wilson 1993, 179–182), petrographic analysis of Talc ware at Melos suggested that it was an imported product (Vaughan and Williams 2007, 125). Common shapes included deep bowls, deep bowls/open jars, pans, pithoi, and various jugs. Incised decoration was more common in Period III than Period II (Wilson 1999, 130–131). In Area B, vessels were mainly closed, including a spouted pithos covered with pellets (**232**).

Several Period II *Orange-Buff Painted* shapes, like pedestaled cups and jugs continued to be popular in Period III. Other shapes, like sauceboats, shallow bowls, and askoi were also relatively well represented (Wilson 1999, 93, 134–138). Many decorated and monochrome painted vessels in Orange-Buff Painted ware may be Melian, according to stylistic parallels and petrographic analysis (Wilson 1999, 134–135). Rare vessels in this ware in Area B included a pedestaled cup (**259**), shallow bowls (**267, 622**), and a cup(?) (**257**). Of these, **257, 267**, and **622** all seem to derive from non-Melian sources, including possibly Attica and the western Cyclades.

As in Period II, most *Orange-Buff Semifine to Coarse* vessels were jars; other shapes included shallow bowls, askoi, and a single saucer (Wilson 1999, 93, 138). Many may have been Melian, although parallels exist elsewhere in the Cyclades and, rarely, the Peloponnese (Wilson 1999, 138). In Area B, too, most of the vessels in this ware were closed, although a deep bowl (**256**) was also present. Vessels in this ware usually were covered in red or brown paint (Wilson 1999, 138), including a closed vessel from Area B (**268**). A Naxian jar(?) from Area B was white slipped (**626**), a decorative technique attested in other Period II and III deposits (Wilson 1999, 139).

Dark-Brown Slipped and Burnished ware was rare. Most vessels were jars; other shapes include jugs, a shallow bowl, tankard, frying pan, and an askos(?) (Wilson 1999, 93, 140–141). Only one vessel in this ware existed in Area B, a small open vessel (pyxis?) (**611**).

Pinkish Buff ware was new but rare in Period III. It may have been produced in Euboea (Wilson 1999, 141). The most common shapes were shallow bowls, including one from Area B (**212**). Wheelmade plates, bell-shaped cups, jugs, and sauceboats were also relatively well represented (Wilson 1999, 93). Wheelmade plates were only found in this ware (Wilson 1999, 93). Some vessels were coated with red or orange-brown slip, which could be burnished (Wilson 1999, 141), like a fine jar or pyxis (**258**) from Area B.

Urfirnis vessels, most of which were sauceboats, were well represented in published assemblages, despite a significant decline in popularity from Period II (Wilson 1999, 93). The ware was rare in Area B but was represented by a sauceboat handle (**314**). *Yellow Mottled* ware was also made up of primarily sauceboats, including one possible example from Area B (**615**).

SYNCHRONISMS

Two phases in Period III have been defined based on stratified deposits in the Western Sector; the main change is the appearance of wheelmade plates and depas cups in the late phase (Wilson 2013, 405–410). Both of those shapes are rare at the site, and neither appears in Area B. It is therefore impossible to associate deposits from Area B with either phase specifically.

Wilson (1999, esp. 94–101, 229–231; 2013, 410–431) has presented detailed discussions of regional ceramic parallels and synchronisms for Periods I–III. Anatolianizing shapes of Period III link Ayia Irini to the Kastri and Lefkandi I groups, which seem to be contemporary, at least in part, with later EH II deposits at Lerna (IIID), Ayios Kosmas (the final level of occupation of period II), Raphina (House A), Thebes (Group B), Palamari (III), and Kolonna (Phase C) (Wilson 2013, 412–420, with references). The relative dating of Period III (and the Kastri and Lefkandi groups in general) in relation to EC II/III and EH II/III has been much debated (e.g., Broodbank 2000, 333–335; Manning 1995, 51–72; Rutter 1983; Sotirakopoulou 1993; 1996, 113–117; 2016, 351–378; Warren and Hankey 1989, 25–29; Wilson 1999, 229–231; 2013). At Phylakopi, Phase A2 may be connected with Ayia Irini II, but there are no deposits that can be closely linked with Ayia Irini III, since Anatolianizing shapes have not been found there (Renfrew and Evans 2007, 177; Wilson 2013, 421–422). Late EC II deposits from Pillar Pits 7N and 35N at Akrotiri may connect that phase with Ayia Irini III (Wilson 2013, 423, with references; but see also Sotirakopoulou 2016, 355–357, 372–373). The recent publication of ceramics from Dhaskalio (Sotirakopoulou 2016) suggests that Dhaskalio Phase B, the first phase in which Anatolianizing shapes appear, is probably contemporary with Ayia Irini III; the subsequent Phase C, however, may be at least partially contemporary with Phylakopi I (or Phase B; Renfrew and Evans 2007) and probably dates to a time after Ayia Irini III was abandoned. Ayia Irini III also was abandoned before EH III (as defined by Lerna IV; Rutter 1995). Wilson (2013, 425–426, with references) summarized evidence for the overlap of late EM IIA and some of EM IIB with Ayia Irini III.

FABRICS

Discard information for nearly all Period III deposits is missing in the records of Area B. Among extant ceramics, probable local fabrics made up around three-quarters of the assemblage. This percentage must be viewed as a minimum, since discarded pottery probably included mostly local pottery (Ch. 1). Wilson (1999, 90, table 3.1) has estimated that about 75% of the entire Period III assemblage was local. For an overview of the relationship between fabrics, wares, and shapes in Area B, see Table 4.1. A summary of imports according to probable region of production is provided in Table 4.2.

Probable local fabrics RBMa and RBMb were very common in Area B, together making up over 60% of the total assemblage (n = 194), with RBMb being somewhat more common than RBMa. Both fabrics were associated exclusively with Red-Brown wares, apart from a few Black Burnished vessels in RBMa. All kinds of shapes appeared in both fabrics, including tablewares, jars, jugs, pithoi, and deep bowls/open jars, at least some of which were probably cooking vessels. New shapes for Period III, like shallow bowls, bell-shaped cups, and tankards, were found in both fabrics together with traditional shapes like sauceboats, saucers, and deep bowls/open jars. Petrographic analysis also confirms the use of similar clays for Anatolianizing and non-Anatolianizing shapes in Area B (Table 3.2). A range of textures in RBMa and RBMb are attested in Area B, from moderately fine to coarse; there was a general tendency toward coarser fabrics than in Period IV. Finer vessels were mostly tablewares, and included both plain and burnished vessels, which sometimes were coated with black slip or wash.

RBMd made up about 8% of the total (n = 194) assemblage. It was associated with Red-Brown wares and a variety of shapes, including tablewares, deep bowl/open jars, basins, jars, and pithoi. RBMc and RBMe were rare, each making up less than 5% of the assemblage. RBMc was associated with Red-Brown Semifine to Semicoarse and Burnished wares; RBMe was only associated with the former. Tablewares, jars, and a pithos appeared in RBMc; saucers and a basin appeared in RBMe. RBMc–e may include imports from the local region, but all of these fabrics are also geologically compatible with a Keian provenance (Ch. 3). Likewise, fabric CSWd, which made up just over 1% of the total assemblage, may derive from the local region; it was associated with Red-Brown Semifine to Semicoarse and Black Burnished wares.

Among clear imports, Cycladic fabrics were more common than those from other regions and made up over 70% of total (n = 48) imports (not counting "local region" fabrics RBMc–e). PBS was the most common imported group, at around 4% of the total (n = 194) assemblage. The fabric is exclusive to Talc ware and most vessels in Area B were large, closed shapes. Groups DVa (Melian/Theran), MxMc (Cyclades), and CSWe (Naxos) made up 2–3% of the total assemblage. Groups DVa and MxMc were associated with Orange-Buff wares and Dark-Brown Slipped and Burnished ware. One MxMc vessel may be an Urfirnis sauceboat. Tablewares as well as larger closed vessels were represented in these two fabrics. Group CSWe was associated mainly with closed vessels in Orange-Buff Semifine to Coarse ware.

Groups MxMa and DVc made up just under 2% of the total assemblage, while MxMb and MxMg appeared only once each. Most vessels in these fabrics belonged to Orange-Buff Semifine to Coarse ware, including tablewares and larger closed shapes. A Black Burnished tankard also appeared in MxMa. Petrographic analysis suggests a range of origins, including Melos/Thera, Syros(?), Tenos(?), Naxos, and Amorgos (Ch. 3).

The rare group DVd (1% of the total [n = 194] assemblage) also was associated primarily with Orange-Buff wares (open and closed shapes); later versions of this fabric seem to be Aeginetan, but no samples were taken from Period III deposits.

FV fabrics, which probably derive from Euboea, Attica, and elsewhere on the mainland, comprised less than 20% of all imports (total = 48) in Area B. Groups FVh, FVg, and FVe each made up 0.5–2% of the total (n = 194) assemblage, with FVh being most common and FVe being least common. These fabrics were associated with multiple wares, including Pinkish Buff (FVg and a

TABLE 4.1. OVERVIEW OF VESSELS IN PERIOD III LOTS IN AREA B ACCORDING TO MACROSCOPIC FABRIC GROUP

B03-803–806, 814–818, 820–824, 829–830, 812 etc., 814 etc., 815 etc., and 821 etc. The total number of vessels is 194, of which 146 are in RBM fabrics (local and local region) and 48 are in imported fabrics.

Fabric group	No. of vessels	% of total	% of RBM	% of imports	Wares	Shapes
RBMb	69	35.6%	47.3%		EBA Red-Brown Burnished	Bowl (1), shallow bowl (7)
					EBA Red-Brown Semifine to Coarse	Tankard (1), one-handled cup (1), saucer (12), shallow bowl (6), pedestaled(?) plate (2), deep bowl/open jar (17), basin (5), basin(?) (2), jug (1), jar (6), jar/jug (1), globular jar (1), large jar/pithos (1), pithos (2), closed (1), perforated open jar (1), lid (1)
RBMa	51	26.3%	34.9%		EBA Black Burnished	Sauceboat(?) (1), pyxis(?) (1), closed (1)
					EBA Red-Brown Burnished	Bell-shaped cup (1), tankard (2), tankard(?) (1), shallow bowl (4), footed bowl (1), sauceboat (1), sauceboat(?) (1), open (1), pyxis(?) (1)
					EBA Red-Brown Semifine to Coarse	One-handled cup (1), saucer (1), bowl (1), shallow bowl (8), deep bowl/open jar (7), basin (2), pyxis (1), pyxis/small jar (2), askos/jug (1), jar/jug (1), open jar(?) (1), jar (3), jar(?) (1), pithos (2), closed (1), pan (1), stand(?) (1)
RBMd	15	7.7%	10.3%		EBA Red-Brown Burnished	Tankard (1), deep bowl/open jar (1)
					EBA Red-Brown Semifine to Coarse	Tankard (1), saucer (2), shallow bowl (2), deep bowl/open jar (2), basin (2), jar (2), pithos (1), closed(?) (1)
RBMc	7	3.6%	4.8%		EBA Red-Brown Burnished	Shallow bowl (2)
					EBA Red-Brown Semifine to Coarse	Saucer (1), bowl (1), shallow bowl (1), jar (1), pithos (1)
RBMe	4	2.1%	2.7%		EBA Red-Brown Semifine to Coarse	Saucer (1), deep saucer (1), basin (1), jar (1)
PBS	7	3.6%		14.6%	EBA Talc	Large open (1), jug(?) (1), pithos (1), closed (2), closed(?) (2)
CSWe	6	3.1%		12.5%	EBA Orange-Buff Semifine to Coarse	Pyxis (1), jar/jug (1), jar(?) (1), closed (2)
					EBA Red-Brown Semifine to Coarse	Closed (1)
DVa	6	3.1%		12.5%	EBA Dark-Brown Slipped and Burnished	Tankard/bell-shaped cup (1)
					EBA Orange-Buff Painted	Pedestaled cup (1)
					EBA Orange-Buff Semifine to Coarse	Large open (1), closed (1), unknown (1)
					Unknown	Large bowl(?) (1)
MxMc	5	2.6%		10.4%	EBA Dark-Brown Slipped and Burnished	Collared jar(?) (1)
					EBA Orange-Buff Painted	Cup/bowl (1), shallow bowl (1)
					EBA Orange-Buff Semifine to Coarse	Closed (1)
					EBA Urfirnis(?)	Sauceboat (1)
FVh	4	2.1%		8.3%	EBA Pinkish Buff	Jar/pyxis (1)
					EBA Urfirnis	Open (2)
					EBA Yellow Mottled	Open (1)

TABLE 4.1. (CONT.)

Fabric group	No. of vessels	% of total	% of RBM	% of imports	Wares	Shapes
CSWd	3	1.5%		6.3%	EBA Black Burnished	Saucer(?) (1)
					EBA Red-Brown Semifine to Coarse	Basin (1), large open (1)
DVc	3	1.5%		6.3%	Orange-Buff Semifine to Coarse	Bowl(?) (1), pedestaled bowl with handle (1), open (1)
FVg	3	1.5%		6.3%	EBA Pinkish Buff	Shallow bowl (1), sauceboat (1), open (1)
MxMa	3	1.5%		6.3%	EBA Black Burnished	Tankard (1)
					EBA Orange-Buff Semifine to Coarse	Shallow bowl (1), jar/jug (1)
DVd	2	1.0%		4.2%	EBA Orange-Buff Painted	Open(?) (1), closed(?) (1)
FSTc	1	0.5%		2.1%	Unknown	Closed (1)
FSTi	1	0.5%		2.1%	Unknown	Unknown (1)
FVe	1	0.5%		2.1%	EBA Urfirnis(?)	Open (1)
MxMb	1	0.5%		2.1%	Plain (possibly EBA Red-Brown?)	Closed (1)
MxMg	1	0.5%		2.1%	EBA Orange-Buff Semifine to Coarse	Closed (1)
Unk	1	0.5%		2.1%	Unknown	Open (1)

mica-bearing variant of FVh), Yellow Mottled (FVh), and Urfirnis (FVe, FVh). Previous petrographic analysis has demonstrated that Pinkish Buff ware derives more or less exclusively from Euboea (Hilditch 2004, 60; Wilson 1999, 151), which may suggest that there is some overlap in the macroscopic definitions of these rare EBA fine fabrics in Area B. All vessels in these fabrics were fine tablewares or pyxides. Other fabrics were rare and included possible later intrusions (single examples of FSTc and FSTi) and single sherds with fabrics that do not belong to any defined groups.

MANUFACTURE

All EBA pottery in Area B, local and imported, was handmade. The only wheelmade vessels from other EBA deposits are imported Pinkish Buff plates (Wilson 1999, 142–143). In most cases, handmade vessels in Area B probably were coil-built, although the small size of many sherds makes assessments other than "handmade" difficult. While the surfaces of most vessels were smoothed to some degree, some preserve shallow scoring and/or paring marks along either the interior or exterior surface. Wilson (1999, 5) noted that scoring was most usual along the exterior surface in other deposits, but scoring on local vessels in Area B was more common along the interior surface (**19, 244, 247, 254, 262, 265, 271, 276, 623**). Other local vessels from Area B preserved shallow wiping marks along the exterior (**281, 623**) or interior (**625**). A few Orange-Buff Semicoarse to Coarse jars also had wiping marks along the interior (**268, 626**), and a closed Amorgian vessel preserved interior scoring (**272**).

Some EBA vessels, especially saucers, were manufactured with flat bases that preserved a mat or leaf impression. The vessels were probably put on leafs or mats to enable rotation and movement of the vessel during construction (Wilson 1999, 27; see also Cherry and Davis 2007, 405; J. Renfrew et al. 2013, 648–649; Sotirakopoulou 2016, 124, 292). It seems unlikely that there was a significant distinction in the functionality of a leaf versus a mat for this purpose. The usage of mats vs. leafs changed over time, with leaf impressions being more common than mats for saucers in Period II, and mats more common than leafs in Period III. Nevertheless, both kinds of impression appeared in both periods. Despite the association of both kinds of impressions with saucers, mats also appear somewhat frequently on bases associated with other shapes, including hearths and, more rarely, bowls and stands in local wares at Ayia Irini (Wilson 1999, 41, 57–59, 88, 105, 118). At other sites, a wide variety of other shapes with mat-impressed bases have been found (Sotirakopoulou 2016, 124, with references). Leaf impressions, however, do not appear on the bases of other shapes at Ayia Irini in Period III, and they only rarely appear on medium-sized bowls in Period II (Wilson 1999, 29). At other sites, too, leaf impressions were usually associated with small cups and saucers; closed shapes with leaf-impressed bases have been

TABLE 4.2. RELATIVE PROPORTIONS OF IMPORTED VESSELS ACCORDING TO PROBABLE REGIONS OF PRODUCTION IN PERIOD III DEPOSITS IN AREA B

Based on fabric analysis, Ch. 3, and in comparison to the total number of imports (48).

Import region	No. of vessels	% of vessels
Aegina/Cyclades	2	4%
Amorgos	1	2%
Attica/Cyclades	3	6%
Cyclades	9	19%
Mainland	8	17%
Melos/Thera	9	19%
Naxos	6	12%
Siphnos	7	15%
Unknown	3	6%

found only on Amorgos and at Dhaskalio (Sotirakopoulou 2016, 291–292). The association between leaf impressions and small open shapes at Ayia Irini and elsewhere may suggest that these impressions, many of which seem to be from grape vines, held a particular symbolic significance for producers and/or users (Sherratt 2000, 355; J. Renfrew et al. 2013). Since mat impressions have been found more regularly in association with other shapes, this kind of impression may not have been perceived to be symbolically significant in the same way as leaf impressions (but see Sherratt 2000, 355 n. 17).

Handles or lugs on large, local jars from Area B were sometimes attached by being pushed through a hole in the vessel wall (**244, 247, 262**), a phenomenon that appears in association with various kinds of vessels, including a jug, several tankards, and two basins, across the published assemblage (Wilson 1999, nos. II-535, III-12, III-119, III-112, III-119, III-245, III-248, III-259). A Pinkish Buff jar or pyxis from Area B preserved a similar handle attachment (**258**), as did several Black Burnished tankards, depas cups, and a jug published by Wilson (1999, 126–127, 129, nos. III-317, III-320, III-340, III-348, III-369, pls. 33, 34, 86–88).

Wilson noted manufacturing similarities between Red-Brown Semifine to Semicoarse, Red-Brown Burnished, and Black Burnished tankards and bell-shaped cups, which had comparable handle attachments and hollowed bases, while tankards in the different wares often preserved neck ridging (Wilson 1999, 232). Nakou (2000, 35–36) suggested that such hollowed bases were a byproduct of potters imitating Anatolian sheet-metal vessels. In that case, this sort of technical similarity between Red-Brown and Black Burnished vessels might be a result of imitating similar metal prototypes rather than ceramic pots in any particular ware.

The local production of Anatolianizing shapes marks some general changes in forming gestures. Most shapes in Period II and III had relatively wide rim diameters, but several Anatolianizing shapes, especially popular tankards, would have required the development of new forming gestures to overcome the restrictions of the narrower rim diameters. However, other elements of the production sequence seem to have remained much the same, although the forthcoming publication of EBA fabrics by Wilson and Day will clarify this issue.

CERAMIC IMPORTATION PATTERNS

Most Period III imports came from the Cyclades, probably mostly the western Cyclades, in the form of Urfirnis, Black Burnished, Talc, Dark-Brown Slipped and Burnished, and Orange-Buff wares. Most of these wares, apart from Talc (Siphnos?) and perhaps Dark-Brown Slipped and Burnished (Syros?), seem to have been produced in multiple locations, although Melos may have been a particularly important source for imports, especially Orange-Buff wares (Vaughan and Wilson 1993; Wilson 1999, 231–232).

Tablewares were common in Urfirnis, Black Burnished, and Orange-Buff Painted wares. Small closed shapes (askoi and pyxides) appeared in multiple imported wares, although askoi were most common in Orange-Buff wares and pyxides were most common in Black Burnished ware. Jars were common in Orange-Buff Semifine to Coarse, Talc, and Dark-Brown Slipped and Burnished wares. A closed vessel in Area B was imported from Amorgos and a few probably came from Naxos, evidence that some larger vessels also came from the central and eastern Cyclades, as well (see also Wilson 1999, 235). Other large, bulky shapes (pithoi, hearths, pans, and basins) appeared only in Talc ware; deep bowls were also more common in Talc ware than other imported wares (Wilson 1999, 93). It has been suggested that Talc ware cooking vessels such as deep bowls and pans were desirable because this fabric was more resistant to thermal stress (or was perceived to be) than others (Vaughan and Wilson 1993, 176–177; Wilson 1999, 235).

Imports from outside the Cyclades were rarer. Yellow Mottled ware probably came from the mainland and comprised almost entirely sauceboats (Wilson 1999, 76, 134). Some Urfirnis vessels (mainly sauceboats) may have come from the mainland, although Wilson (1999, 72, 231) argued that the bulk are from the western Cyclades. Rare Pinkish Buff vessels probably came from Euboea; almost all shapes are tablewares (Wilson 1999, 141–143).

Analysis in Area B suggests that some vessels (tablewares, basins, jars, and pithoi) could perhaps have been imported from the local region of east Attica, southern Euboea, or elsewhere in the western Cyclades (RBMc–e), although this evidence is not definitive. Certainly, there are strong connections between Kea and eastern Attica in terms of how pottery was made and what kinds of pottery consumers preferred (Wilson 1987).

Some common shapes in the assemblage were more often imported than locally produced; these include sauceboats, bell-shaped cups, askoi, and depas cups (Wilson 1999, 92–93, tables 3:3, 3:4)). Although all of these shapes were found in multiple wares, most depas and bell-shaped cups were Black Burnished, while askoi, as noted above, were mostly in Orange-Buff wares, and sauceboats were most common in Urfirnis and Yellow Mottled wares (Wilson 1999, 92–93, tables 3:3, 3:4). A few shapes that were not locally produced were imported from only one place in Period III: Pinkish Buff wheelmade plates, probably Euboean, and Orange-Buff Painted pedestaled cups, probably Melian (Wilson 1999, 94).

Although wheelmade plates were not locally made, shallow bowls, which probably fulfilled similar functions, were very common in local wares but relatively rare among imports (most were Orange-Buff Semifine to Coarse and Pinkish Buff). Other Anatolianizing shapes (tankards, bell cups, and depas cups) were both locally produced and imported. Among potential imports, these shapes were especially common in Black Burnished ware, although a few versions in Orange-Buff and Pinkish Buff wares exist, as do single examples in Yellow Mottled and Dark-Brown Slipped and Burnished wares (Wilson 1999, 93). The increased proportion of Black Burnished ware in Period III compared with Period II seems connected, in large part, with the growing popularity of Anatolianizing drinking shapes.

In sum, a variety of functions are represented among the abundant Cycladic imports, which include tablewares, small containers for perhaps more highly valued goods, and larger closed vessels, which presumably contained bulk agricultural products. These seem to have derived from multiple locations, especially in the western Cyclades, while the central and eastern Cyclades are represented by fewer imported vessels (Wilson 1999, 235). Imports from the mainland and Euboea were rarer and were comprised almost entirely of tablewares, with the exception of some jars and pithoi from Area B that might be from the local region.

SUMMARY

For the first time in Period III, imports from Euboea form a notable part of the assemblage, and Anatolianizing shapes were used as part of a new drinking set. Cycladic versions of Anatolianizing drinking shapes, at least in some instances, may have been based on similar sheet-metal vessels, and thus, probably were perceived to be of high value (Nakou 2000, 2007). The increased popularity of burnishing among local and imported vessels probably also represents intentional imitation of the shiny surfaces of metal vessels.

The most common new shape in Period III was the shallow bowl. Most were relatively large, which may suggest that they were for sharing or serving rather than individual use. Other new Anatolianizing shapes made up a small proportion of the overall ceramic assemblage (13%; Wilson 1999, 95), and drinking, eating, and pouring forms of Period II continued to be imported and locally produced in Period III (Wilson 1999; 2013, 405–406). Many locally produced shapes did not see a dramatic shift in manufacturing method, morphology, or decorative schemes from Periods II–III. The ongoing local production and importation of traditional shapes like saucers, medium-sized bowls, and sauceboats suggests that older forms of eating and drinking were not entirely eclipsed by drinking practices that incorporated new Anatolianizing shapes.

Several lines of evidence suggest that Ayia Irini was abandoned after Period III, before the end of the EBA. The MBA settlement exhibits different patterns of production and engagement with the wider Aegean, which will be discussed in the next chapter.

V. MIDDLE BRONZE AGE CERAMIC ANALYSIS

This chapter presents an analysis of MBA ceramics from Alley AB in comparison with J. C. Overbeck's (1989a) publication of Period IV stratigraphy and deposits and Davis's (1986) publication of Period V. Overbeck published inventoried ("K"-numbered) ceramics from Area B (1989a, 174–176, Groups CP–CT). Overbeck's Groups included ceramic lots that he considered to be part of discrete strata. Stratigraphic interpretations here differ slightly from Overbeck's publication; the following discussion, therefore, does not follow his Group designations. Only one Period V deposit with very few ceramics existed in Area B (B649CL), although some ceramics from several mixed deposits (especially B603CL and B03-72) also probably date to that era. Nevertheless, Period V is also discussed here in order to update synchronisms of that era in light of recent re-evaluations of mainland and Cretan ceramic sequences and to enable a diachronic evaluation of changing imports and ceramic shapes at Ayia Irini.

Unlike Wilson's (1999) publication of EBA pottery, catalogues of Periods IV–VII pottery (Cummer and Schofield 1984; Davis 1986; J. C. Overbeck 1989a; Schofield 2011) did not include quantifications of ceramics by ware or shape. Thus, in order to aid comparisons with Area B and to investigate how ceramics changed through time, I quantified the ceramics presented in published catalogues for these periods in the following manner. I counted all vessels that belonged to deposits with little or no evidence for chronological mixing or later contamination according to ware and shape. For groups of vessels that were not described individually, I counted the lowest possible number. "Several jars" were counted as two jars, three or fewer tripod legs were counted as a single tripod, and so on. If a vessel was not clearly associated with a ware, I counted it as "Unknown ware," along with any pots catalogued as "Miscellaneous." For Period IV, Overbeck (1989a, 12) stated that most of the plain pottery was probably local; thus, I counted plain vessels as local unless doubts about provenance were given in the catalogue description. Although Overbeck (1989a, 9–10) suggested some vessels in Slipped and Burnished ware might be local, he thought most were imported; in Area B, vessels in this ware were all imported. Slipped and Burnished vessels in Overbeck's catalogue, therefore, were counted as imports. These counts have surely been affected not only by discard processes on site but also the selective nature of the catalogue; it is fortunate that the convention in *Keos* volumes has been to provide brief summaries of the part of the ceramic assemblage that was not individually catalogued, for most deposits. Thus, it is assumed that the catalogues provide a general picture of the wares and shapes present in deposits of each period, and that their relative proportions (especially within similar categories, like imported tablewares) are reasonably reflective of the range that was present after excavation and processing (Ch. 1). The results of the quantification for the Period IV catalogue are presented in Figs. 53 and 54.

Overbeck (1982, 1984, 1989a) did not differentiate between Minoan imports from Crete and Minoanizing imports from elsewhere (see also Crego 2007, 337, fig. 4). Since it is not clear how much of Overbeck's Minoanizing category was produced outside of Crete, I have distinguished this group from other Minoanizing ceramics by using the term "Minoan/-izing" for this category in Period IV.

TIMING OF THE MBA FOUNDATION

Ayia Irini was probably abandoned between Periods III and IV (Overbeck 1984, 109). The town was completely reorganized in Period IV. In Area B, for example, the street and fortification wall are completely unrelated in construction and alignment to the EBA house below House B. Period IV seems to have begun after the start of the MBA elsewhere, since early MH and MM IA wares are absent from the earliest Period IV deposits (Overbeck 1984, 108–109). Vessels that can be dated to the latest EBA are also very rare (Caskey 1964, 320, pl. 49:a; Schofield 2011, 147–148, no. 1739, pl. 72). In Area B, there are no ceramics that date to EH III, MH I, MMIA, or Kolonna Phases E, F, or G.

This period of abandonment at Ayia Irini occurred during an era of disruption in the Cyclades (Rutter 1983) around which there are significant controversies over relative chronologies and ceramic sequences, as well as the causes for discontinuities and culture change (Angelopoulou 2008, 160–162; Brogan 2013; Knappett and Nikolakopoulou 2005, 176–177; Marangou et al. 2008; Momigliano 2007, 94; Nikolakopoulou 2007; Nikolakopoulou et al. 2008, 313; Rutter 2013; Sotirakopoulou 1996; 2008; 2010, 826, fn. 5; Televantou 2008). For recent summaries, see Broodbank (2013), Sotirakopoulou (2016, 354–377), and Nikolakopoulou (2019, 39–52); see Manning (2017) for a discussion of issues associated with radiocarbon dates (see also Bronk Ramsey, Renfrew, and Boyd 2013, 702; Renfrew 2007, 8; Wild et al. 2010, 1020, table 3).

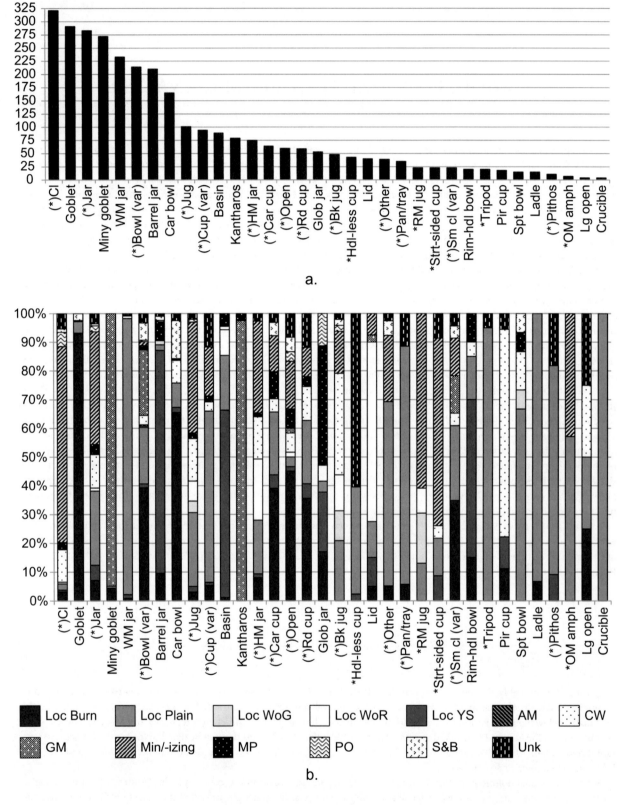

Fig. 53. Number (a) and relative proportions by ware (b) of common shapes in published Period IV deposits, based on a count of vessels reported by J. C. Overbeck (1989a). Total vessels 3051. Shapes marked with "*" are Minoan or Minoanizing; shapes marked "(*)" include some versions that are Minoan or Minoanizing, but others that are not.

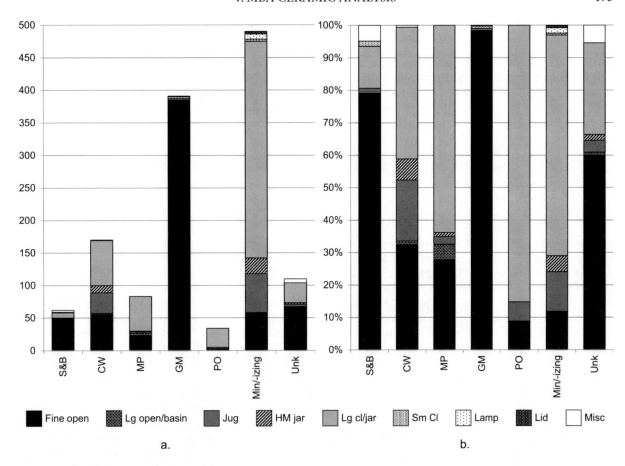

Fig. 54. Number (a) and relative proportions by ware and general shape (b) of imported vessels in published Period IV deposits, based on a count of those reported by J. C. Overbeck (1989a). Total imported vessels 1340. The single Argive Minyan vessel, a bowl in an unusual fabric (Overbeck 1989a, no. BP-2), is omitted from the chart.

Phylakopi I may overlap from the EBA to the earliest MBA, at least as defined outside the Cyclades (Barber 1974, 48–50; 1983, 79; see also Sotirakopoulou 2016, 373). It has long been argued that the existence of incised pottery and duck vases reflects some contemporaneity between at least the earliest part of Period IV and Phylakopi I, but the duration of chronological overlap is contested (Barber 1974, 1983; Overbeck and Overbeck 1979). J. C. Overbeck (1989b, 21–22, 24 n. 19) pointed out similarities between Period IV and the main phase of occupation at Paroikia, Paros, which has, itself, been connected with Phylakopi I and Akrotiri Phase A (Nikolakopoulou 2019, 40). Phylakopi I ceramics and imports in a fabric compatible with a Keian provenance were reported from Kolonna Phase F (later EH III) in a preliminary report (Gauss and Smetana 2008, 329), but no imports in probable Keian or Melian fabric groups (FG 3, FG 7) were noted in association with EH III in a more comprehensive fabric analysis (Gauss and Kiriatzi 2011, 33, 257, table 89; Kiriatzi, Georgakopoulou, and Pentedeka 2011, 139–140, 143). Unfortunately, the two published radiocarbon dates from Period IV deposits (Fishman and Lawn 1978, 217), when recalibrated using OxCal 4.3 (IntCal 13; Bronk Ramsey 2009) produce dates of 2010–1667 BCE (2σ), with a median of 1824 BCE (P.2577), and 1923–1630 BCE (2σ), with a median of 1781 BCE (P.2580). These dates are too broad in range to provide much insight into the absolute dates associated with Period IV, although it is clear that they are situated well after the radiocarbon dates associated with the EBA/MBA (Phase F/G) transition at Kolonna (modeled at 2191–2064 BCE [2σ]) and a set of seeds from the earliest MBA (Phase A) at Akrotiri (2280–2130 [2σ]) (Manning 2008, 59; Wild et al. 2010, 1020, table 3).

OVERVIEW OF PERIOD IV POTTERY

Period IV is divided into three phases, Periods IVa–c (Overbeck 1984, 108; 1989a, 1). Quantifications of Period IV pottery from Area B are based on extant ceramics from unmixed strata in Alley AB: B03-785, 786, 788–790, 799; B791/793CL, B795/a/796CL, B797/798CL. This discussion will need to be updated after publication of a comprehensive study of Period IV pottery from the site, currently in preparation by D. M. Crego and J. C. Overbeck.

LOCAL

In J. C. Overbeck's (1989a) catalogue, plain and coarse wares were most common, followed by Burnished and Yellow Slipped wares. White-on-Red and White-on-Gray wares were rare (see also Overbeck 1982). In Area B, Burnished vessels made up nearly half of all (n = 39) local vessels, while plain vessels made up only around 30% of them. This pattern may have resulted from discard patterns that favored Burnished sherds over plain ones, since Burnished sherds are chronologically diagnostic even when small in size, as sherds from the alley are. Yellow Slipped ware was relatively common in Area B (around 20% of local vessels), while LOD painted wares did not exist.

Across the site, tall- and short-stemmed goblets were common in *Burnished* ware. Tall-stemmed goblets were no longer produced by the end of Period IVb (Overbeck 1984, 110). Several Burnished goblets (**644, 666**), including two with potter's marks (**628, 667**), were found in Area B; one Period IVc or V goblet from a mixed deposit (**560**) had a Minyanizing profile. Two types of carinated bowl, one of which (shape 2) is an early form of Cycladic cup, were also common in this ware (Overbeck 1984, 110; for similarities and differences between carinated bowls and Cycladic cups, see Overbeck 1984, 110). This shape appeared also in Area B (**645, 712**). Carinated cups were similar in profile to Cretan cups (compare Caskey 1972, 380–381, nos. D70, D71, fig. 10, pl. 85, with MacGillivray 2007, 117, fig. 4.9:2, 4). Such cups were less common in Period IVc and very rare in Period V (Davis 1986). Some Burnished vessels, especially cups and jars, were decorated with white paint; burnished barrel jars were sometimes polychrome painted (J. C. Overbeck 1989a, 9). The quality of burnishing was higher for sherds from earlier strata (B797/798CL, B795/a/796CL) in Area B than later ones (B791/793CL, B03-790), a typical pattern at the site (J. C. Overbeck 1989a, 9).

Local *Yellow Slipped* ware imitated MH and MC Matt Painted wares early in Period IV; in Periods IVc and V, however, it imitated Cretan Lustrous Painted pottery (Overbeck 1984, 111; 1989a). The most common shapes in Period IV were barrel jars and basins, both of which are attested in Area B (**638, 639, 646, 687**). Such vessels were more common in the earlier than the later Period IV deposits across the site (Crego 2007, 335, fig. 2). In Period V, Yellow Slipped ware was more regularly used for smaller, open shapes, like a straight-sided cup with a beveled base from Area B, which was found in a Period IVc–V deposit (**698**). Globular jars may have assumed the storage or transport functions previously filled by barrel jars in late Period IV (Overbeck 1984, 111; 2007, 340).

LOD pattern painted pottery, including *White-on-Gray* and *White-on-Red* ware, was more common in Periods IVa–b than IVc deposits (Overbeck 1984, 110; 1989a). Decoration was simple, usually bands, dots, or rosettes, and was painted on the smoothed but unburnished surface of the vessel (Caskey 1972, 381; J. C. Overbeck 1989a, 10). Vessels included many hole-mouthed jars, jugs (especially round-mouthed and beaked), and domed lids. Hole-mouthed jars were sometimes similar in shape to Cretan ones but sometimes had non-Minoanizing tubular spouts and pierced crescent lugs (e.g., J. C. Overbeck 1989a, nos. Q-17 [Minoanizing], CE-53, CE-54 [non-Minoanizing]). By Period V, the Cycladic version of the hole-mouthed jar disappeared, but the Minoanizing version continued to be imported and locally produced.

The most common local *plain* shape was the wide-mouthed jar. Several examples were found in Area B (**647, 648**), including two marked pedestaled bases that might also have been from this shape (**641, 714**). Many wide-mouthed jars were probably cooking vessels. This shape was found in all phases of Period IV but not Period V (Overbeck 1984, 112; Davis 1986). Nevertheless, the shape is found on the mainland in later MBA contexts, contemporary with Period V (Overbeck 1984, 113), and cooking jars with similar profiles exist in LBA contexts at Ayia Irini (Gorogianni, Abell, and Hilditch 2017, 70–71). The absence of wide-mouthed jars in Period V deposits, therefore, is probably a gap in the evidence rather than an indication that cooking in such shapes stopped in Period V. Baking pans and trays, including one from Area B (**650**), were also important cooking shapes. Tripod cooking vessels were first used in Period IVa at Ayia Irini (J. C. Overbeck 1989a, 127), but they were more common in Period IVb and IVc deposits (e.g., J. C. Overbeck 1989a, nos. C-13, E-11, AW-9, BG-32, BH-10, CE-156). Other plain, local, Minoanizing shapes also became more common in later phases of Period IV, especially rounded cups and handleless cups (J. C. Overbeck 1989a; see also Papagiannopoulou 1991, 153); one plain rounded cup or bowl from Area B (**562**) might date to Period IV or V. Small, plain Minoanizing shapes made with the potter's wheel first appeared in Period IVa and became more common later in the period. Fewer than 2% of all published vessels from Overbeck's (1989a) catalogue were noted as having been wheelmade, and only two were Yellow Slipped rather than plain (J. C. Overbeck 1989a, nos. AS-4, AC-5). In Area B, vessels made using the wheel were all plain and wheel-coiled, including cups (**651, 652, 668**) and a saucer (**653**) that seem to imitate Cretan shapes, although the Cretan versions are usually slipped (Macdonald and Knappett 2007, 24, fig. 3.18, pl. 24; MacGillivray 2007, 131, 141, figs. 4.20:1, 4.21:1).

IMPORTS

The most common imported wares in all phases were Gray Minyan, Minoan/-izing, and Cycladic White wares, although their relative proportions changed over the course of the period, as recently summarized by Crego (2007, 337, fig. 4; see also table 5.7). In Period IVa, the most common imported ware was Gray Minyan, followed by Minoan/-izing and Cycladic White wares. From Periods IVa/b–c, Minoan/-izing imports were most common, followed by Gray Minyan and Cycladic White wares. The proportions of imported wares in Area B were somewhat different from those reported for the rest of the site (Crego 2007, 337, fig. 4; J. C. Overbeck 1989a). When all phases are considered together, Minoan/-izing pottery formed a much larger percentage (nearly 60% of total [n = 85] imports) in Area B than elsewhere (ca. 40% of total [n = 1340] imports published by J. C. Overbeck [1989a]). Despite these differences in proportions, in Area B, as elsewhere, Minoan/-izing pottery was the most common imported ware in

Periods IVa/b–c, followed by Gray Minyan and Cycladic White wares. The overrepresentation of Minoan/-izing imports in Area B is probably a result of the small size of the assemblage and the fact that the Minoan/-izing imports were relatively large sherds from coarse closed vessels that seem to have been more resilient to breakage than fine Gray Minyan and Cycladic White sherds from the alley, which were small and worn and so more likely to be discarded.

Those same factors probably lie behind other differences in the relative percentages of wares between Area B and the rest of the site. Gray Minyan ware made up only about 16% of the total number (n = 85) of imports in Area B but was twice as common elsewhere, when all phases are considered together. Similarly, Cycladic White and Matt Painted wares were better represented elsewhere on site (around 15% and 7% of total imports [n = 1340], respectively). In Area B, these wares made up only 6% and 4% of imports, respectively. Other wares (Slipped and Burnished, Pink-Orange, Lustrous Decorated, and imported plain wares from different regions) were all rare, each making up <5% of imports in Area B, similar to the pattern elsewhere on site.

Cycladic White vessels derive from Melos and/or Thera. Beaked jugs, hole-mouthed jars, piriform cups (usually with paneled decoration), carinated bowls, and rarely Melian bowls are typical of the ware; jugs and jars with various profiles also exist (e.g., **642, 678**; see also Overbeck 1984, 111; 1989a). Carinated bowls and piriform cups became more common in the second half of the period. Decoration was usually in matt black, brown, red, or orange paint, and sometimes polychrome; a Cycladic feeding bottle from Period IVc Grave 8 was decorated in the Black and Red style (Overbeck 1984, 111; 1989a, 11, 191, pl. 92).

Slipped and Burnished ware was more common in Periods IVb–c than in Period IVa (J. C. Overbeck 1989a, 9–10). Most vessels seem to be imports from different parts of the Cyclades, although a few may be local products (J. C. Overbeck 1989a, 9–10). The most common shapes were goblets and carinated bowls. Slips were black, brown, or red (e.g., **655, 699**). Slipped and Burnished goblets were rare by Period IVc. Imported Cycladic vessels from Area B also included a *Burnished* bowl with a potter's mark (**269**), which probably dates to Period IV, and several *plain* vessels, including a hole-mouthed jar with a flattened rim (**669**). A few plain vessels might date to Period IV or V, including rounded cups with short everted rims (**305, 564**) and a handleless cup (**565**) with a flattened rim.

Gray Minyan imports may have been produced mainly in central Greece and/or Euboea (Overbeck and Crego 2008, 305–306). Gray Minyan vessels at Ayia Irini were primarily goblets, kantharoi, and bowls. Both plain- and ring-stemmed goblets are attested at the site, with the latter appearing primarily in the first half of Period IV (Overbeck 2007, 340). Only ring stems were found in Area B (**634, 643, 688, 693**), although Pteleon goblets were also present (**633**; for the term "Pteleon" for this type of goblet, see Pavúk 2002, 51; 2007, 300). Pteleon goblets existed in Period IV and, more rarely, Period V deposits (Davis 1986, 43, 84, no. U-76, pl. 28; J. C. Overbeck 1989a, nos. X-46, AO-22, BD-41).

Pink-Orange ware, also probably from central Greece and/or Euboea, was rare (Overbeck 2010, 618). Most identifiable shapes in the ware were closed (e.g., **657**), especially globular jars (J. C. Overbeck 1989a; 2010, 616).

Across the site, MH *Matt Painted* imports were primarily barrel jars and globular jars. Overbeck (2007, 341) suggested that the earliest Matt Painted imports at Ayia Irini might not be Aeginetan, but in Area B, Matt Painted vessels from all phases had fabrics similar to those at Kolonna, including a globular jar (**632**) and a basin (**670**). An imported *plain* jug (**656**) from Area B was also probably Aeginetan.

Minoan/-izing imports were *Lustrous Painted* (e.g., **635, 659–661, 664, 671, 686, 690, 691, 694–696**), *Non-Lustrous Painted* (e.g., **662, 663, 672, 682, 683**), or *plain* (e.g., **684**). The most common Minoan/-izing shapes across the site were closed vessels, including hole-mouthed (e.g., **686, 691**) and other jars, as well as various jugs. A kind of round-mouthed jug with a squared molding at the base of the neck, which also had a round-section handle attached below the rim, was only found in Period IVb deposits, including in Area B (**665**; Overbeck 1984, 112; 1989a, 12). Similar squared moldings existed on jugs with different mouths or different handle placement from MM II deposits in different parts of Crete (Day and Wilson 1998, 355; Evans 1921, 570, no. 415:b; Levi and Carinci 1988, pl. 27:d; Poursat and Knappett 2005, pl. 25:674). However, good parallels for round-mouthed jugs with both this type of molding and round handles attached below the rim have not been located on Crete. Better parallels for jugs with the combination of round mouths, handles placed at mid-neck, and a squared molding at the base of the neck exist in the southeast Aegean (Abell, Crego, and Overbeck, forthcoming; Marketou 2009, fig. 2).

The LOD style was common among Minoan/-izing imports (both Lustrous and Non-Lustrous Painted), although some vessels were painted in the DOL style instead. The light (white and/or red) paint was often poorly preserved on LOD style vessels in Area B (**659, 660, 664, 671, 690, 694**, and perhaps **661** and **691**). Although trickle pattern was a usual form of decoration for the DOL style (e.g., **662, 672, 686, 695**, and perhaps **696**), other designs were also present, including a dark-painted disk on light ground on a closed vessel from Area B (**663**). One Minoan/-izing sherd (**636**) from a Period IVa deposit in Area B had a pared surface. Pared vessels appear to have been more common in the late Prepalatial and early Protopalatial periods than in the later Protopalatial period on Crete (Andreou 1978, 17, 19, 51, 128; MacGillivray 2007, 109; Momigliano 2007, 96).

Lustrous Decorated pottery, produced on the mainland or Kythera, made up a very small proportion of Minoan/-izing imports in Period IV (Overbeck 1982, 41, fn. 21; for the ware, see Kiriatzi 2010; Rutter and Rutter 1976, 10–11 ("Oatmeal Minoanizing"); Zerner 2008, 201–208). Few sherds in this ware were found in Area B; all seem to be from closed vessels (**658, 715**), which seem to have been the most common shape in this ware elsewhere at the site.

AYIA IRINI: AREA B

SYNCHRONISMS

PERIOD IV

An overview of synchronisms can be found in Tables 5.1–5.3. In this and the following sections, I prefer the terms "earlier MC" and "later MC" for Periods IV and V over "MC II" and "MC III," because a tripartite division of MC chronology corresponding to other Aegean regions does not map neatly onto Cycladic ceramic phases (for similar terminology, see also Barber 2007, 183; note that his "later MC" seems to be contemporary both with Period V and early Period VI). As mentioned previously, Period IV began after the start of the MBA elsewhere.

Although there may be some overlap between Period IVa and Phylakopi I, Akrotiri Phase A, Kolonna Phase H, and MM IB, most ceramic parallels for this early phase are with Akrotiri Phase B, Phylakopi II, Kolonna Phase I and MM II (Table 5.1; Nikolakopoulou 2019, 54; Overbeck 2007, 339; Overbeck and Overbeck 1979, 106–107, 110–117). The presence of Cretan imports made using the wheel in Period IVa (**635**; J. C. Overbeck 1989a, 8) demonstrates that this phase did not begin earlier than MM IB (Evely 1988, 125; Jeffra 2013; Knappett 1999, 2004; MacGillivray 2007, 109).

Period IVb was probably synchronous with most of MM II. Carinated cups (J. C. Overbeck 1989a, nos. AQ-34, AR-8) are similar to MacGillivray's Tall-Rimmed Angular Cup (1998, 72) and Macdonald and Knappett's shape 8b (2007, 27, figs. 3.25, 3.37, pls. 28, 38) from MM IB–IIA Knossos; the shape is common throughout Crete (Macdonald and Knappett 2007, 27). A fine, wheelmade tumbler from a Period IVa/b deposit (J. C. Overbeck 1989a, no. CN-6) is similar to MacGillivray's Type 3, dated by him to MM IIA at Knossos (MacGillivray 1998, 68, nos. 663–665, pl. 105; 2007, 126). Local wheel-coiled cups from Area B (**651**, **652**, **668**) were modeled on Cretan forms that were produced from MM IB–MM II (MacGillivray 2007, 141, fig. 4.21:1); similarly, a local, wheel-coiled saucer (**653**) parallels a Cretan shape that was popular throughout MM II and into MM IIIA at Knossos (Macdonald and Knappett 2007, 24, fig. 3.18, pl. 24; MacGillivray 2007, 131, 133, fig. 4.20:1). A jug with protuberances (J. C. Overbeck 1989a, no. X-72) has similarities in profile to MM II and IIIA vessels at Knossos and Phaistos (Levi 1976, pl. XXX:d; Macdonald and Knappett 2007, 100, no. 487, fig. 3.26); the decoration is paralleled at MM II Mallia (Poursat and Knappett 2005, pl. 25:680). MM II polychrome decorated vessels existed in published Period IVb deposits (e.g., J. C. Overbeck 1989a, 61, 85, 102, 161–162). Given the difficulties that defining the division between MM IIB and MM IIIA has caused on Crete (e.g., Rethemiotakis and Warren 2014, 67–85), it is difficult to determine the relationship of Period IVc to either phase. Polychrome decoration exists but is rare, as is white spotted decoration (e.g., J. C. Overbeck 1989a, nos. K.3819, G-15). Although locally produced carinated cups continued into Period IVc, imported Minoan/-izing versions seem to be rather rare (although they do appear; J. C. Overbeck 1989a, 107). Handleless cups are not nearly as abundant in Period IVc as in Period V. Period IVc appears to be broadly contemporary with the Trial KV group at Knossos, which is alternately dated to MM IIB (MacGillivray 2007, 134–144; Knappett, Mathioudaki, and Macdonald 2013, 18) or MM IIIA early (Rethemiotakis and Warren 2014, 83–84).

Period IVb was contemporary with Akrotiri Phase B. Bichrome decoration in matt black and red or orange was more common in Phase B than C at Akrotiri (Nikolakopoulou et al. 2008, 317); matt bichrome decoration was relatively common on Cycladic White vessels of Period IVb and was occasionally present on vessels found in Period IVc deposits (J. C. Overbeck 1989a, nos. D-4, S-45, U-6, X-30, AR-6, BG-14). Similarities in motif also exist between Cycladic White vessels from Period IVb and Akrotiri Phase B (e.g., compare J. C. Overbeck 1989a, nos. AG-10, AR-6, and Nikolakopoulou et al. 2008, 316, fig. 32.3:e, lower right, lower left). A beaked jug with matt bichrome decoration from a Period IVa/b deposit (J. C. Overbeck 1989a, no. CE-92) is a type common in Phase B at Akrotiri (Nikolakopoulou et al. 2008, 317). The existence of Black and Red Style vessels in Period IVc and Akrotiri Phase C deposits suggests that these phases were contemporary (Nikolakopoulou et al. 2008, 317, 323 n. 5; G. F. Overbeck 1989, no. 8-3, pl. 92; J. C. Overbeck 1989a, 79, 131, 135, 139, nos. AH-28, BG-13, BJ-1, pls. 53, 70, 71). Akrotiri Phase C deposits contained early MM IIIA imports (Knappett 2019, 315; Nikolakopoulou et al. 2008, 317; Rethemiotakis and Warren [2014, 86], however, ascribe them to MM IIIA late). Akrotiri Phase C, therefore, was also contemporary with Period V at Ayia Irini. There are few differences between the typical ceramics of Period IVc and Period V. Period IVc was a probably relatively short, transitional phase.

Period IV was contemporary with Phylakopi II-ii (Barber 1974, 48–50; Overbeck and Overbeck 1979, 114–117), which is clear from parallels in Cycladic White and burnished wares, as well as in the presence of MM II imports (Barber 1974, 5; 1983, 77). Phylakopi II-ii is linked with Akrotiri Phase B (Nikolakopoulou et al. 2008, 319). Period IVc may also have been contemporary with the beginning of Phylakopi II-iii since both the Naturalistic and Black and Red styles, typical of Phylakopi II-iii, first appeared in Period IVc (Barber 1974, 5; 1983, 77–78; Davis 1986, 84; Scholes 1956, 24). The earliest MH levels at Kiapha Thiti with Black and Red style imports also may have been contemporary with Period IVc and/or Period V (Schnitt 153 SE 6–7, Schnitt 154 SE 5; Maran 1992, 95–99, 101–106).

The presence of Pteleon and ring-stemmed goblets in Period IVa deposits (e.g., **633**, **634**) confirms the overlap between Period IVa and MH II. The presence of ring-stemmed goblets in Periods IVb and IVc suggests that the whole period was contemporary with some or all of MH II (e.g., J. C. Overbeck 1989a, 82, nos. BD-38, X-47); MH II is usually understood to be a long period (Warren and Hankey 1989, 68). Ring-stemmed goblets appeared first in Phase 5 at Mitrou, while loop handles of the kind used for Pteleon goblets were present in Phases 3–7 (Hale 2016, 277–278, fig. 17). Pteleon goblets were common in MH II and MH III Lerna and in Phase I at Kolonna (Gauss and Smetana 2007, 63–65; Overbeck 2007, 340; Pavúk 2007, 299–300; Walter and Felten 1981, pl. 121, nos. XXV-437–439). While ring-stemmed goblets were present in a few Period IVc and Period V deposits (Davis 1986, no.

TABLE 5.1. PERIOD IVA SYNCHRONISMS

Region	Contemporary phases
Cyclades	Akrotiri Phases A(?)-B (Nikolakopoulou et al. 2008, 313–317)
	Phylakopi I-iii(?)-II-ii (Barber 1974, 4–5; 1983, 77–78; 2007; Renfrew and Evans 2007, 157–176)
Aegina	Kolonna Phase H(?)-I/Stadt VIII-IX (Gauss and Smetana 2007, 61–65; Walter and Felten 1981, 130–136, pls. 117–121)
Mainland	MH II (Mature Minyan, Lerna V) (Dickinson 1977, 21–24; Warren and Hankey 1989, 67–69; Zerner 1988)
Crete	Knossos MM IB(?)-IIA (MacGillivray 2007, 107–134)

TABLE 5.2. PERIOD IVB SYNCHRONISMS

Region	Contemporary phases
Cyclades	Akrotiri Phase B (Nikolakopoulou et al. 2008, 317)
	Paroikia (J. C. Overbeck 1989b)
	Phylakopi II-ii (Barber 1974, 5; 1983, 78; 2007)
Aegina	Kolonna Phase I/Stadt IX (Gauss and Smetana 2007, 63–64; Walter and Felten 1981, 133–136, pls. 119–121)
Mainland	MH II (Mature Minyan, Lerna V) (Dickinson 1977, 21–24; Warren and Hankey 1989, 67–69; Zerner 1988)
Crete	Knossos MM II (MacGillivray 2007, 122–144)

TABLE 5.3. PERIOD IVC SYNCHRONISMS

Region	Contemporary phases
Cyclades	Akrotiri Phase C (Nikolakopoulou et al. 2008, 317–319)
	Phylakopi II-ii–II-iii (Barber 1974, 5; 1983, 77–78; 2007)
Aegina	Kolonna Phase I/Stadt IX (Gauss and Smetana 2007, 63–64; Walter and Felten 1981, 133–136, pls. 119–121)
Mainland	Kiapha Thiti Schnitt 153 SE 6–7, Schnitt 154 SE 5 (Maran 1992, 95–99, 101–106)
	MH II–MH III (Mature–Late Minyan, Lerna V) (Dickinson 1977, 21–24; Warren and Hankey 1989, 67–69; Zerner 1988)
Crete	Knossos Trial KV Group (MacGillivray 2007, 134–144)

AE-3; J. C. Overbeck 1989a, 82), their rarity suggests that Period IVc and perhaps Period V overlapped the last part of MH II at Lerna, when Mature Minyan shapes were beginning to lose popularity (Davis 1986, 85; Dickinson 1977, 21). The later part of MH II Lerna (V.5) has also been linked with MM IIB–MM IIIA on Crete (Girella 2010b, 865–866).

Overbeck (2007, 339) cited parallels between Period IVa/b Deposit CE (1989a, 155) and Kolonna Phase I, which was, itself, synchronous with MH II(–III early?) (Felten, Gauss, and Smetana 2012; Gauss and Smetana 2007, 63–64). Periods IVb, IVc and perhaps part of Period V also seem to have been contemporary with Kolonna Phase I (Overbeck 2007; below).

TABLE 5.4. PERIOD V SYNCHRONISMS

Region	Contemporary phases
Cyclades	Akrotiri Phases C–D (Nikolakopoulou et al. 2008, 317–319)
	Phylakopi II-ii–II-iii (Barber 1974, 5; 1983, 77–78; 2007)
Aegina	Kolonna Phase I/Stadt IX–Phase J/Stadt X (Gauss and Smetana 2007, 63–65; Walter and Felten 1981, 136–138, pls. 122, 123)
Mainland	(?)Kiapha Thiti Schnitt 153 SE 4–7, Schnitt 154 SE 2–5 (Maran 1992, 95–109)
	MH III (Mature Minyan, Lerna V) (Dickinson 1977, 22–24; Warren and Hankey 1989, 67–69; Zerner 1988)
	Tsoungiza Groups A–C (EU2 and EU6; Rutter 1990; 2020, 474–496)
Crete	Knossos Bougadha Metochi Trench A/Baulk II Phases 1–2/Levels 5–7 and 4 (Rethemiotakis and Warren 2014, 26–46)
	Knossos MM (IIB?)–IIIA (Trial KV Group(?)–West and South Polychrome Deposits Group) (MacGillivray 2007, 134–149)

PERIOD V

An overview of synchronisms can be found in Table 5.4.

Period V ceramics are most similar to those dated to MM IIIA on Crete. Although Period V may have been partially contemporary with MM IIIB, it was not totally synchronous with that phase, given similarities between MM IIIB and earlier Period VI (Ch. 6; Abell, forthcoming).

Straight-sided and rounded cups were common, but carinated cups were fragmentary and rare (Davis 1986, 81); carinated cups were rare at Phaistos and Knossos by MM IIIA (Girella 2010a, 393; MacGillivray 1998, 72–74 [Tall- and Short-Rimmed Angular Cups]). At Knossos, carinated cups may have continued in use into only the earliest part of MM IIIA, based on their rarity in stratified MM III deposits in the palace and Southwest Houses (Knappett, Mathioudaki, and Macdonald 2013, 16; Macdonald 2013). Girella (2010b, 864) pointed out that unlike on Crete, carinated cups continued to be popular at Kythera and Lerna in a late stage of MH II, which he associates with MM IIIA. Straight-sided and rounded cups were common in MM IIB–IIIA Group E at Knossos (MacGillivray 1998, 33–34, 135–151, pls. 9–21, 61–90).

Straight-sided cups with clapboarded sides in Period V deposits (e.g., Davis 1986, nos. U-79–U-82) were similar to cups at Knossos, Archanes, and in eastern Crete from MM IIB–IIIA (MacGillivray 1998, 71, fig. 2.10:12; 2007, 147, fig. 4.34:2); the type apparently was not produced in the Mesara (MacGillivray 1998, 71). In deposits from the Acropolis Houses at Knossos, such vessels were found in the lower deposits (Catling et al. 1979, fig. 16:5 [Deposit A]; fig. 18:49, 96–98 [Deposit B]), and they were especially common in later MM IIIA deposits at Bougadha Metochi (Rethemiotakis and Warren 2014, 71). At Akrotiri, such imports belong to Phase C (Knappett and Nikolakopoulou 2008, 10, 14, fig. 6, nos. 10–12).

Local rounded cups (Davis 1986, nos. U-5, U-6) have morphological similarities to MacGillivray's Types 5 and 6, dating from MM II–IIIB (1998, 76, fig. 2.14). At least one local rounded cup (Davis 1986, no. U-4) seems to belong to MacGillivray's Type 7, dated to late MM IIB or early MM IIIA (1998, 76, fig. 2.14).

Lentoid jugs, characteristic of Period V, have parallels with jugs from MM IIA deposits on Crete (Davis 1986, 82). A type of lentoid jug with a globular body has parallels in MM IIA Knossos, in Levi and Carinci's Fase Ib at Phaistos, and at Kommos, where they are dated to MM IIB–III (Davis 1986, no. U-93; Evans 1928, 215, fig. 121a; Levi 1976, pl. 103:b; Levi and Carinci 1988, 91, 320, no. F.1039, pl. 61:f, g; van de Moortel 2006, 355, 357, 363–364, nos. L/15, L/27, pls. 3.14, 3.20; for different perspectives on how Levi and Carinci's revised Phaistian chronology should be synchronized with other Cretan sites, see MacGillivray 2007, 134, table 4.2; van de Moortel 2007, 203–204). A similar lentoid jug, perhaps from the Mesara, was found in a Miletus IIIb deposit (Knappett and Nikolakopoulou 2005, 180; Raymond 2001, 20–22; Raymond et al. 2016, 64). A second type of imported lentoid jug at Ayia Irini had an ovoid body and plastic "eyes" on either side of the spout (Davis 1986, no. C-31). Neither type of lentoid jug was closely comparable with jugs from MM III deposits at Phaistos and Ayia Triada (Girella 2010a, 278–293, figs. 89, 90).

Jugs with truncated bodies were similar to a jug from Phaistos, dated to Fase Ib (Davis 1986, nos. U-89, U-90; Levi and Carinci 1988, 64, no. F.5303, pl. 29). At Phaistos, the jug was described as unusual (Levi and Carinci 1988, 64). Comparable vessels have been found in greater quantities at MM II Mallia (Poursat and Knappett 2005, nos. 676–683, pl. 25). Another jug had a close decorative parallel with Levi and Carinci's Fase Ib at Phaistos (Davis 1986, no. B-1; Levi 1976, pl. 69:a, c; Levi and Carinci 1988, 42, 317, no. F.609). A jar decorated with a "white-bordered dark-painted double ax motif on a buff ground" has been described as typical of the western Mesara (Davis 1986, no. W-5; van de Moortel 2006, 641).

V. MBA CERAMIC ANALYSIS

Hole-mouthed jars (perhaps bridge-spouted) had parallels with MM IIB and MM III shapes (compare Davis 1986, no. C-30 with MacGillivray 1998, 79, fig. 2.16, Type 6 [MM II]; and Catling et al. 1979, no. 128, fig. 20 [MM III]).

Several Minoanizing local cups were decorated with white splashes on dark ground (Davis 1986, nos. U-4–U-6). Close parallels to such decoration appeared at Archanes and Phaistos in MM IIIA (Girella 2010a, 397; Sakellarakis and Sapouna-Sakellaraki 1997, 422, fig. 390, middle row, second and third from left). Similar decoration existed in MM II Knossos and Levi and Carinci's Fase Ia and Ib at Phaistos (Levi 1976, pls. 84:d, e; 127:e; Levi and Carinci 1988, 80, 324, no. F.1589, pl. 37:b; 64, 326, no. F.1954, pl. 30:c; 210, 322, no. F.1370; Macdonald and Knappett 2007, 93, fig. 3.22:426–432), as well as in MM III contexts at Knossos (Popham 1974, 187, fig. 6:21, 25; Rethemiotakis and Warren 2014, Warren 1991, 327–328, nos. J-P1530, F-P1384, figs. 8, 9). Ripple pattern appeared for the first time on imported vessels in Period V deposits (Davis 1986, 82); ripple pattern was initially produced on Crete in MM IIB but was more common in MM IIIA (Evans 1921, 592; Macdonald 2004, 240; MacGillivray 2007, 147). The rarity of ripple pattern in comparison with other decorative motifs on Minoan and Minoanizing pottery is more closely comparable with MM IIIA than IIIB deposits at Knossos.

Akrotiri Phase C deposits contained imports of MM IIIA (Nikolakopoulou et al. 2008, 317; Knappett 2019, 315; Knappett and Nikolakopoulou 2008, 34). The abundance of Cycladic imports painted in the Naturalistic and Black and Red styles in Period V deposits suggests that the period was contemporary with Akrotiri Phase C and Phylakopi II-iii (Nikolakopoulou et al. 2008, 317; Scholes 1956, 24). However, the presence of the Black and Red style already (although rarely) in Period IVc deposits, suggests that both Akrotiri Phase C and Phylakopi II-iii began before Period V (Davis 1986, 84). The presence of the Black and Red style in Akrotiri Phase D might suggest that this phase also overlapped Period V to some degree since the Black and Red style was rare in Period VI (Ch. 6; Cummer and Schofield 1984, 142; Davis 1986, 84; Nikolakopoulou et al. 2008, 319); however, much of the pottery in Phase D deposits might be residual from Phase C (Nikolakopoulou 2019, 57–58). Rare Cretan imports in Akrotiri Phase D deposits were painted with ripple pattern, white dots on dark ground, and a few polychrome schemes, while DOL decoration was slightly more common than in Phase C (Knappett 2019, 314). The Phase D Cretan imports, likewise, are broadly similar to those that appear in Period V, but some overlap with early Period VI cannot be excluded. None of the very rare mainland imports in Phase D Akrotiri are dated later than the MBA (Mathioudaki 2019, 321).

Despite the popularity of Minoanizing ledge-rim bowls at Akrotiri in Phase C as well as on Crete in MM IIIA, they are relatively rare in Period V at Ayia Irini (Davis 1986, nos. U-23, V-9[?], AK-11[?], AL-5[?]; Nikolakopoulou 2019, 55, 166). It is possible that this plain shape may have been particularly discriminated against during papsing, but given other differences in assemblages between Ayia Irini, Akrotiri, and Crete, the disparity may instead reflect real differences in shape preferences.

Period V was contemporary with the later part of the MH period (Davis 1986, 85). A Matt Painted bowl/basin was similar in shape and decoration to vessels from Lerna and the Argolid, dated by Dietz to his MH III (Davis 1986, no. P-5; Dietz 1991, 60–61, no. 77, fig. 14; Zerner 1988, 2, nos. 5–7, fig. 4). Gray Minyan goblets and bowls from Period V had profiles similar to later MH types (e.g., Davis 1986, nos. E-6–E-9; cf. late MH shapes in the Argolid: Dietz 1991, 65, 201–204, no. 99, fig. 16; Rutter 1990, 427, nos. 137–139, fig. 10; 2020, 488). There are also parallels in Phase 7 at Mitrou (Hale 2016, 285, fig. 14:31). The presence of Cycladic Black and Red style pottery in earlier MH III levels at Kiapha Thiti could suggest some chronological overlap with Period V; later MH levels, however, also may have been contemporary with Period V, given similarities in Minyan goblet shapes (Maran 1992, 99–101, 106–109, pls. 28, 30, 31 [Schnitt 153 SE 4–5, Schnitt 154 SE 2–4]). Similarities in goblet shapes, as well as the existence of only LOD decoration among the latest Lustrous Painted imports at Tsoungiza suggests that MH III deposits at that site (groups A–C) were probably contemporary with Period V (Rutter 1990; 2020, 475–496).

Period V has similarities with Kolonna Phase I, particularly among Minoan and Minoanizing vessels, including rounded cups painted with white splashes on a dark ground (compare Davis 1986, nos. U-4–U-6 and Gauss and Smetana 2007, 77, fig. 9: Q3/98-16, Q3/105-2, Q3/181-5, Q3-198-1). Piriform cups, typical of Period V, did not appear at Aegina until Phase J (Davis 1986, 83; Gauss and Smetana 2007, 65). Additional links between Period V and Kolonna Phase J exist (Overbeck 2007, 139; compare Davis 1986, no. P-5 and Walter and Felten 1981, pl. 123:451, 452, or the decoration of Davis 1986, nos. C-13, C-18, U-61, AO-1 with Walter and Felten 1981, pl. 122:446). Period V may have overlapped parts of both Aeginetan phases; Akrotiri Phase C and possibly Phase D have also been linked with Kolonna Phase J (Nikolakopoulou 2019, 56–57).

FABRICS

The amount of preserved pottery in Period IV strata in Area B is too limited to enable diachronic analysis of ceramic fabrics in different phases. The following section, therefore, presents all Period IV ceramics from Area B together. Table 5.5 presents an overview of macroscopic fabrics in relation to wares and shapes in Area B; Table 5.6 is a summary of the percentages of imports by region, based on the macroscopic fabric analysis (Ch. 3). Likewise, the single deposit of Period V pottery in Area B (B649CL) is too small to enable detailed fabric analysis, and so discussion of that period in this section is limited.

The percentage of RBM fabrics in the total preserved Period IV assemblage in Area B is 32%, but this percentage does not take into account discarded ceramics. If the "scraps" mentioned as discards by Bikaki are assumed to be entirely local, a rough estimate

TABLE 5.5. OVERVIEW OF VESSELS IN PERIOD IV LOTS IN AREA B ACCORDING TO MACROSCOPIC FABRIC GROUP

B03-785, 786, 788–790, 799, B791/793CL, B795/a/796CL, and B797/798CL. The total number of vessels is 124, of which 39 are in RBM fabrics (local and local region) and 85 are in imported fabrics.

Fabric group	No. of vessels	% of total	% of RBM	% of imports	Wares	Shapes
RBMa	37	29.8%	94.9%		Burnished	Goblet (9), bowl(?) (1), carinated(?) bowl (1), open (6), jug(?) (2)
					Plain	Cup (2), saucer (1), tumbler (1), large open (1), jug (1), jar (1), wide-mouthed jar (1), pithos (1), pan (1)
					Yellow Slipped	Straight-sided(?) cup (1), basin (1), barrel jar (1), jar (4), closed(?) (1)
RBMc	1	0.8%	2.6%		Plain	Wide-mouthed(?) jar (1)
RBMd	1	0.8%	2.6%		Plain	Wide-mouthed jar (1)
FSTi	14	11.3%		16.5%	Lustrous Painted	Jar (1), closed (4)
					Non-Lustrous Painted	Round-mouthed jug (1), hole-mouthed jar (1), closed (4)
					Plain	Open(?) (1), closed (2)
FVa	14	11.3%		16.5%	Gray Minyan	Goblet (7), bowl (1), open (6)
FSTf	9	7.3%		10.6%	Lustrous Painted	Closed (3)
					Non-Lustrous Painted	Jug (1), closed (5)
FSTe	8	6.5%		9.4%	Lustrous Painted	Bridge-spouted jar (1), jug (1), closed (6)
FSTk	6	4.8%		7.1%	Lustrous Painted	Cup (1), small closed (3), hole-mouthed jar (1), jug (1)
DVa	5	4.0%		5.9%	Cycladic White	Small closed (1), jar (1), closed (3)
FSTc	5	4.0%		5.9%	Lustrous Painted	Closed (3)
					Non-Lustrous Painted	Closed (1)
					Plain	Closed (1)
Unk	4	3.2%		4.7%	Lustrous Painted	Unknown (1)
					Non-Lustrous Painted	Closed (2)
					Plain	Bowl(?) (1)
FSTa	3	2.4%		3.5%	Lustrous Painted	Closed (2)
					Plain	Closed (1)
DVd	2	1.6%		2.4%	Matt Painted	Globular jar (1), closed (1)
DVe	2	1.6%		2.4%	Matt Painted	Basin (1)
					Plain	Jug (1)
DVf	2	1.6%		2.4%	Plain	Closed (2)
FSTb	2	1.6%		2.4%	Lustrous Painted	Closed (2)
CSWe	1	0.8%		1.2%	Cycladic Slipped and Burnished	Closed (1)
DVc	1	0.8%		1.2%	Melian/Theran Slipped and Burnished	Carinated bowl/Cycladic cup (1)
FSTg	1	0.8%		1.2%	Lustrous Decorated	Closed (1)
FVd/FVf	1	0.8%		1.2%	Pink-Orange	Large jar (1)
MFVa	1	0.8%		1.2%	Cycladic Slipped and Burnished	Goblet (1)
MFVb	1	0.8%		1.2%	Minyan	Open (1)
MxMc	1	0.8%		1.2%	Cycladic Slipped and Burnished	Cup/bowl (1)
MxMd	1	0.8%		1.2%	Plain	Large closed (1)
MxMf	1	0.8%		1.2%	Plain	Open (bridge-spouted?) jar (1)

TABLE 5.6. RELATIVE PROPORTIONS OF IMPORTED VESSELS ACCORDING TO PROBABLE REGIONS OF PRODUCTION IN PERIOD IV DEPOSITS IN AREA B

Based on fabric analysis, Ch. 3, and in comparison to the total number of imports (85).

Import region	No. of vessels	% of imports
Aegina	2	2%
Aegina(?)	4	5%
Central Greece/Euboea	15	18%
Crete	26	31%
Crete(?)	10	12%
Cyclades	4	5%
Mainland/Kythera	1	1%
Melos/Thera	6	7%
Naxos	1	1%
Unknown (Minoan/-izing)	14	16%
Unknown	2	2%

for the percentage of RBM vessels in Period IV deposits in Area B is about 75%, at least in those lots for which information exists about the original quantity of ceramics collected (Table 5.7). That estimate was calculated in the following manner. The percentage of imports in the remaining lot was multiplied by the percentage of pottery remaining to yield the percentage of imports in the original lot, assuming that all or nearly all discarded pottery was local. That is: x/100 = (imports/remaining vessels)(remaining volume/original volume). For example, in B797/798CL, 1.5 bags of pottery were collected and 0.5 bag remains in the apotheke, meaning ca. 33% of the original volume is still present. In that 33%, 10 of 17 total vessels are in non-RBM fabrics, thus, 59% of the remaining 33% of vessels are imported. (33%)(59%) = 20%. The calculation of imports in these lots is relatively consistent, mostly falling between 15–25%. The results are also very similar to an estimate for local vs. imported vessels (76% vs. 24%) by Overbeck (1982, 40) in a "typical" lot with 239 pots. Crego (2007, 337, fig. 4) reported that 57% of pottery in Period IV deposits was local; she did not mention whether discarded pottery was taken into account.

Local fabrics in Area B belonged primarily to macroscopic group RBMa, which was used for all wares. Group RBMb was not present. "Local region" fabrics RBMc and RBMd were very rare, appearing only once each, in association with plain, wide-mouthed(?) jars (**641**, **648**). Although a full range of moderately fine to coarse textures existed in RBMa in this period, pastes often had less than 10% inclusions, which were also relatively small (approximately <0.5 cm). This tendency applied especially to Burnished tablewares, but larger jars also sometimes followed a similar pattern (e.g., **640**, **646**). This pattern may reflect some degree of paste processing or different patterns of clay selection in comparison with Period III versions of the fabric, which tended to be somewhat coarser and had a wider range of inclusion sizes.

Petrographic analysis of Period IV samples associated with RBMa, including plain and Burnished tablewares as well as a Yellow Slipped basin and jar, were mostly classed in PFG 1C (Table 3.2). This petrographic group differs from PFG 1A in having (usually very few) calcareous inclusions, as well as a cleaner groundmass. It is possible that the different appearance of the groundmass between PFG 1A and 1C might be linked to a difference in clay source and/or processing. Additional sampling is needed to investigate whether this pattern toward somewhat finer clays is typical of the entire Period IV assemblage.

The most common imported fabrics in Period IV deposits in Area B belonged to group FST, which made up nearly 60% of total (n = 85) imports and was associated with Minoan/-izing wares, primarily closed vessels. Many subgroups were present, with FSTi being most common, followed by FSTf, FSTe, FSTk, and FSTc (in order of decreasing frequency, all with five or more examples). Groups FSTa, FSTb, and FSTg were rare. Most of these subgroups probably derive from Crete, especially FSTa–c, FSTe, FSTf, and perhaps FSTk (Ch. 3). Group FSTi is of unknown origin, although some subgroups have possible parallels in the southeastern Aegean. The majority of these imports were Lustrous Painted, while a few fabrics were also associated with Non-Lustrous Painted

TABLE 5.7. ROUGH ESTIMATE OF THE PROPORTION OF PERIOD IV IMPORTS IN AREA B LOTS.

Calculated on the basis of the volume of pottery collected in comparison with what remains of the original lots and assuming that all discarded pottery was local. Bag calculations were made on the assumption that the current bag is the same one that was used when apotheke staff estimated the volume of pottery collected.

Lot	Collected	Remaining	% discarded	% imports in remaining lot	Rough % imports in original lot
B03-799	0.67 bag	0.05 bag	93%	100%	7%
B797/798CL	1.5 bags	0.5 bags	67%	59%	20%
B795/a/796CL	0.6 tin	0.2 tin	67%	69%	23%
B03-794	0.5 bag	0.1 bag	80%	100%	20%
B791/793CL	1 bag	0.3 bags	70%	58%	17%
B03-790	1 bag	0.3 bags	70%	60%	18%
B03-789	0.5 bag	0.3 bag	40%	100%	60%
B03-788	0.33 bag	0.2 bag	39%	88%	53%
B03-786	0.5 bag	0.2 bag	60%	86%	34%
B03-785	0.5 bag	0.05 bag	90%	75%	8%
Average					26%

(FSTc, FSTf, and FSTi) and plain (FSTa, FSTc, FSTi) vessels. Rare Mainland/Kytheran Lustrous Decorated ware vessels were classed in FSTg. The variety in fabric groups associated with Minoan/-izing wares suggests that several different production areas of Crete, as well as perhaps Minoanizing production centers in the mainland and/or Kythera and potentially elsewhere (e.g., the southeastern Aegean), had access to exchange with Ayia Irini, whether directly or indirectly.

The fabric associated with "true" Gray Minyan ware (FVa) was next most common, after FST fabrics. Group FVa made up over 15% of total (n = 85) imports, of which almost all were goblets or unidentifiable open vessels. This group probably comes from central Greece and/or Euboea. An imported Pink-Orange ware jar (**657**) in FVd/FVf also probably came from Euboea, based on the petrographic and WD-XRF analyses.

Imports in Cycladic and Aeginetan fabrics were rarer. Melian/Theran fabrics DVa and the much rarer DVc made up just over 7% of total (n = 85) imports, with DVa used exclusively for Cycladic White closed vessels, and DVc for a Slipped and Burnished carinated bowl (shape 2) or Cycladic cup. Probable Aeginetan imports in DVd and DVe and Aeginetan(?) imports in DVf also made up around 7% of imports. Group DVd was used for Matt Painted closed vessels, DVf for plain closed vessels, and DVe for a Matt Painted basin and plain jug. Other Cycladic fabrics were represented by singletons associated with Slipped and Burnished and plain vessels.

The only Period V deposit in Area B contained few sherds (B649CL). Local fabrics appear similar to earlier and later ones; group RBMa is best represented, while one example of RBMb was also present. Apart from an EBA intrusion, the single imported sherd (**701**) in this deposit was Lustrous Painted and belonged to FSTb, probably from Crete; petrography suggests an origin in central Crete, perhaps the Mesara. In B649CL, using the same kind of calculation described above to take discards into account, probably around 96% of the original lot was comprised of local products. In the Northern Sector, an estimate that took discards into account suggested that around 18% of the Period V assemblage might have been imported (Gorogianni and Abell, forthcoming, table 2).

MANUFACTURE

Most local pottery from Area B was handmade. Much of it may have been coil-built, but the highly fragmented nature of the sherds makes specific assessments difficult.

Several handles of large, coarse vessels (**638**, **639**) were attached by pushing a plug at the end of the handle through the vessel wall, in much the same way that some local handles had been attached in Period III (Ch. 4). Not all handles of coarse vessels were

TABLE 5.8. RELATIVE PROPORTIONS OF WARES IN PERIOD IV.

After Crego 2007, 337, fig. 4.

Ware	IVa	IVa/b	IVb	IVb/c	IVc	% of total	% of imports
Local	62%	60%	62%	47%	54%	57%	
Gray Minyan	19%	10%	12%	13%	8%	12%	29%
Middle Helladic Matt Painted	3%	3%	3%	4%	3%	3%	7%
Minoan/-izing	8%	20%	14%	26%	24%	18%	42%
Cycladic White	6%	4%	6%	7%	7%	6%	14%
Pink-Orange	2%	1%	1%	0%	1%	1%	3%
Other	0%	2%	2%	4%	3%	2%	5%

attached in this manner (**648, 649**), although it seems to have been quite usual. Pushed-through handles were common among MBA ceramics of Kastri on Kythera and the mainland, and they are also attested on Crete, although they seem to have been rare there (Andreou 1978, 131; Kiriatzi 2010, 694). The fact that handles in local fabrics and wares were not all attached in the same way even on the same kinds of shapes is probably indicative of the existence of several pottery production units, which made different choices about how handles should be attached.

The local use of potter's marks in Period IV also suggests the existence of multiple pottery production units (Bikaki 1984, 7–21; Abell 2020). Ethnographic research suggests that potter's marks tend to be used in the context of specialized production, wherein multiple potters or groups of potters in the community produce ceramics destined for exchange, usually sharing workspace, kiln facilities, or the same space in exchange contexts where the products of different potters may be in danger of being confused (Barley 1994, 128, 159 n. 89; Donnan 1971; Gill 1981; Lewis 1983; 56; Lindblom 2001, 19–21).

The most significant technological development in the local ceramic assemblage of Period IV was the first use of the potter's wheel, which was used exclusively to manufacture Minoanizing cups and bowls. In Area B, the earliest local vessels made on a potter's wheel were found in Period IVb contexts (**651–653, 668**); all have string-cut bases like later handleless cups. That the use of the wheel at Ayia Irini is associated with interaction with Cretan rather than mainland potters is strongly suggested by the fact that the only shapes produced with the wheel were based on Cretan prototypes, not mainland ones, despite the fact that Gray Minyan ware imports from the mainland were very popular and nearly universally wheelmade. Potter's wheel disks at Ayia Irini also are similar to those on Crete (Evely 1988; Georgiou 1986, 36–39).

Local vessels from Area B that were formed using RKE were carefully made. Although the walls were thick in one example (**651**), and a coil join was obvious in another (**653**), walls were well smoothed, and string-cut bases were flat and level. In this respect, they differ from locally made handleless cups in LBA deposits in Area B, which often preserved obvious coils and/or joins, and regularly had uneven, lumpy bases.

Locally produced Minoanizing vessels manufactured using the potter's wheel show no differences in clays or firing from handmade local vessels that belong to different regional traditions. All local vessels in Area B with traces of production through RKE belonged to macroscopic group RBMa (**651–653, 668**). Three of those were sampled, and they were classified as PFG 1A (**668**) and 1C (**652, 653**) alongside handmade vessels of Period IV and later. Both **652** and **653** (petrographic sample nos. 38 and 39) were variants in PFG 1C; each sample had a groundmass that was cleaner and less micaceous than others in that petrographic group. If this dissimilarity in groundmass represents a difference in processing or raw material selection on the part of the potter(s) of these two vessels, it was not adopted more widely. The analysis of **668** (petrographic sample no. 40) placed it firmly within PFG 1A, meaning that it is closely comparable with local fabrics associated with different periods, shapes, wares, and modes of manufacture (including both hand- and wheel-forming).

In Period IV, the wheel was used to make a restricted range of shapes, which were much rarer than handmade goblets and bowls, the main eating and drinking vessels of the period. The rarity of local vessels formed using the wheel and the relative care taken in their manufacture—at least in terms of forming—might suggest that more value was placed on the quality of such objects than their quantity in Period IV, a situation that changed in subsequent periods.

Wheelmade pottery was ubiquitous in mainland fabrics in Area B (for my use of the term "wheelmade," see Ch. 3). Wheelmade vessels from the mainland were nearly all goblets (**634, 688, 693**). None were obviously handmade, and only one Gray Minyan goblet preserved evidence of wheel-coiling (**643**). Nearly all large closed vessels in Minoan/-izing wares were handmade or coil-built. Few, apart from a few small closed vessels (**635, 659, 660**), preserved evidence of the use of the potter's wheel. All Aeginetan, Cycladic, and Melian/Theran imports in Area B for which a method of manufacture was possible to recognize were handmade.

The potter's wheel was used by local potters more regularly in Period V (Davis and Lewis 1985; Gorogianni, Abell, and Hilditch 2016, 206–215; Lewis 1986), when there was also a dramatic increase in the local production of Cretan-style pottery. Local potters in Period V used the wheel to make Minoanizing shapes more often than non-Minoanizing ones (Gorogianni, Abell, and Hilditch 2016, 206–215). Period V also witnessed a major change in the use of potter's marks. The use of traditional potter's marks, like those of Period IV, declined significantly and a new system involving more complex marks was introduced (Bikaki 1984, 22–25). The new system seems to have been somewhat sporadic in its deployment, since far fewer pots were marked in Period V–VII than had been in Period IV (Bikaki 1984, 22–25).

IMPORTATION AND CONSUMPTION PATTERNS

As discussed above, about a quarter of the Period IV ceramic assemblage was probably imported. The most common imports in J. C. Overbeck's publication (1989a) and in Area B were Minoan/-izing wares; by subphase, Minoan/-izing wares were the most common imports from Periods IVa/b–IVc (Table 5.8; Crego 2007, 337, fig. 4). Fabric analyses from Area B suggest that a significant percentage of vessels categorized as Minoan/-izing in Overbeck's publication may, in fact, be Cretan. In Area B and elsewhere, the most common Minoan/-izing shapes were large closed vessels (Figs. 53, 54); of these, most are probably jars, suggesting that bulk agricultural goods—whether foodstuffs, oil, or wine—from Crete were common imports at Ayia Irini in all but the very earliest phase of the period. Fewer fine Cretan cups and pouring shapes were imported, and could, perhaps, have arrived as luxuries or gifts.

Jars and closed shapes were the most common shapes by far in Pink-Orange and Matt Painted wares (Fig. 54). Open shapes were more prevalent in Matt Painted ware than Pink-Orange ware; these included mainly rounded cups. It is possible, however, that some of the Matt Painted wares mentioned in J. C. Overbeck's (1989a) catalogue were Cycladic rather than Aeginetan or mainland products (for the difficulty in distinguishing between them, see J. C. Overbeck 1989a, 11). It is impossible, therefore, to interpret the shape range of this ware in terms of products arriving from a particular region. All nonlocal large, open vessels, mostly basins, belonged to Cycladic White and Matt Painted wares.

In contrast, nearly all Gray Minyan imports were fine open shapes, mainly goblets, kantharoi, and bowls (Figs. 53, 54). Kantharoi were not common in other wares, although bowls (mainly carinated) were found in Slipped and Burnished and Cycladic White wares. Apart from Gray Minyan ware, imported goblets only existed in Slipped and Burnished ware.

Cycladic Slipped and Burnished vessels were mostly carinated bowls, other bowl shapes, and goblets (Figs. 53, 54); Slipped and Burnished imports, therefore, corresponded closely in form and presumably function with local Burnished products, although goblets were more common than bowls in the local Burnished assemblage. Carinated bowls were also common in Cycladic White ware. Beaked jugs and hole-mouthed jars, which were common in Cycladic White ware (especially in the latter half of Period IV), were also common (with somewhat different profiles) in Minoan/-izing wares. Piriform cups, more common in the latter half of the period, were mostly restricted to Cycladic White ware. Jugs were about half as common in Cycladic White ware as in Minoan/-izing wares, but were very rare in other wares; the same is true of jugs in Period V (below; Figs. 55, 56).

In sum, regional differences existed among imports in Period IV. Fine open vessels overwhelmingly came from the Greek mainland, especially central Greece and/or Euboea, where much of the Gray Minyan ware at Ayia Irini was probably produced. Apart from Gray Minyan goblets, kantharoi, and bowls, other imported open vessels were relatively equally represented in Slipped and Burnished, Cycladic White, Minoan/-izing, and unknown wares. Although some Slipped and Burnished open vessels may have been Melian/Theran, fabric analysis in Area B suggests that other Cycladic centers also produced this ware. Fine open vessels in Slipped and Burnished, Matt Painted, and Cycladic White wares were imported in quantities similar to Minoan/-izing ones.

If Pink-Orange ware was produced in the same area as the Gray Minyan ware found at Ayia Irini, then the import pattern from that region seems to be the inverse of the pattern from Crete. Far fewer Gray Minyan or Pink-Orange closed vessels were mentioned in J. C. Overbeck's (1989a) catalogue than Minoan/-izing ones. Both in Area B and in Overbeck's catalogue, the most common imported closed vessels and jars were in Minoan/-izing wares, with far fewer in Cycladic White, Matt Painted, Pink-Orange, and Slipped and Burnished wares (Fig. 54).

This pattern of importation suggests that, although Gray Minyan open vessels probably were commonly used during eating or drinking events at Ayia Irini, some products consumed at those events may have arrived at Ayia Irini in closed containers from Crete. Although the degree to which such bulk products may have been distinguishable from local, Cycladic, or mainland products is unknown, the fact that so much of it seems to have been imported suggests that these products were as desirable as Gray Minyan open vessels in the Keian community.

CHANGES IN PERIOD V

Patterns of local production and consumption shifted significantly in Period V (Abell 2016; Davis 1986). Minoan and Minoanizing vessels became common across the assemblage. Locally produced Minoanizing shapes, including handleless cups, other tablewares,

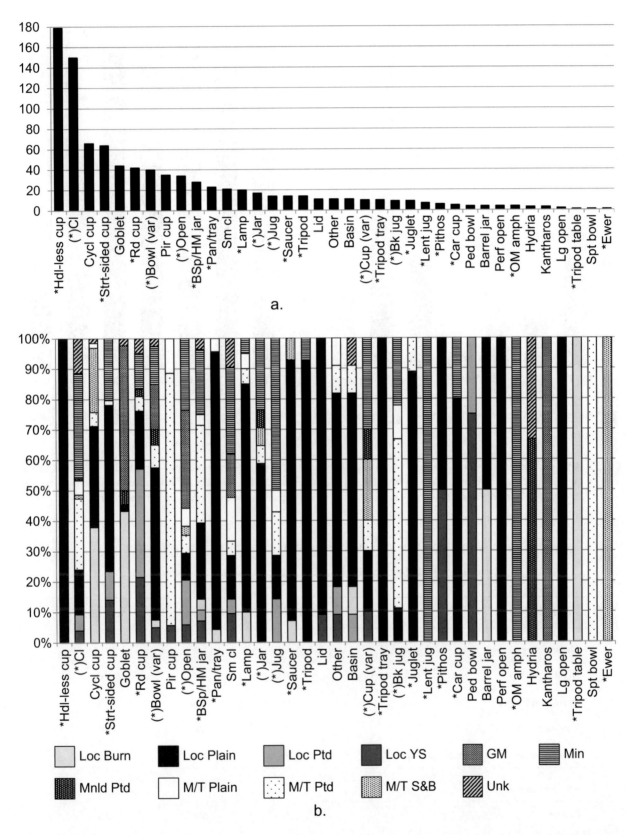

Fig. 55. Number (a) and relative proportions by ware (b) of common shapes in published Period V deposits, based on a count of vessels reported by Davis (1986). Total vessels 921. Davis's Mainland Painted category seems to include mostly Matt Painted wares, although the lustrous character of the paint is not always described in the volume. Shapes marked "*" are Minoan or Minoanizing. Shapes marked "(*)" include some versions that are Minoan or Minoanizing, but others that are not.

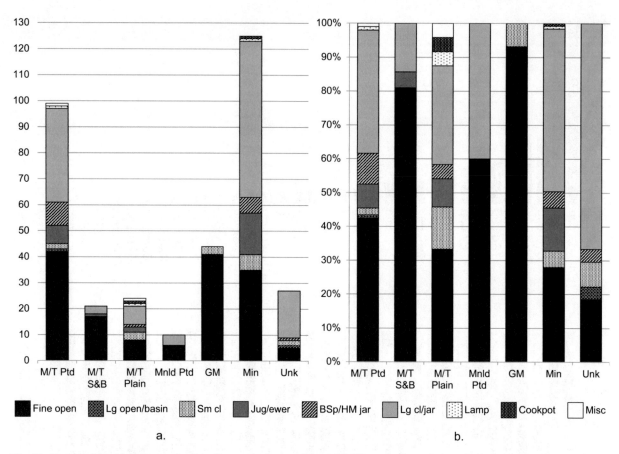

Fig. 56. Number (a) and relative proportions by ware and general shape (b) of imported vessels in published Period V deposits, based on a count of those reported by Davis (1986). Total imported vessels 350. Davis's Mainland Painted category seems to include mostly Matt Painted wares, although the lustrous character of the paint is not always described in the volume.

TABLE 5.9. COMMON TABLEWARES IN PUBLISHED PERIOD V DEPOSITS

After Davis 1986. There are 571 local, 350 imported, and 921 total vessels.

Shape	% of local	% of imports	% of total
Minoanizing			
Handleless cup	31%	0%	19%
Straight-sided cup	9%	4%	7%
Rounded cup	6%	3%	5%
Hole-mouthed/bridge-spouted jar/jug	2%	5%	3%
Non-Minoanizing			
Goblet	4%	9%	5%
Cycladic cup/bowl	8%	5%	4%
Piriform cup	<1%	10%	7%
Pedestaled bowl	1%	0%	<1%

and tripod jars, became much more common (Table 5.9), while Minoan and Minoanizing vessels were imported from Crete and other parts of the Aegean (Figs. 55, 56). Non-Minoanizing shapes continued to be imported and locally produced. Cycladic cups (derived from carinated bowls, shape 2) and goblets continued to be popular among tablewares, while piriform cups—usually imported from Melos and/or Thera—were much more common than in the previous period. The relative popularity of local decorated wares also changed. Yellow Slipped ware became more common, especially for Minoanizing tablewares, and Burnished ware declined in popularity. In addition, plain tablewares were much more plentiful than they had been in the previous period.

Import patterns also shifted. A count of vessels from published Period V deposits (Davis 1986), using the same methodology described above for the Period IV catalogue, suggests that Melian/Theran vessels were slightly more common than Cretan ones in deposits across the site, around 40% vs. 35% of total (n = 350) reported imports (Abell 2016, table 2). This marks a substantial increase in popularity for Melian/Theran imports, which included tablewares like piriform cups, as well as jars and other shapes (Figs. 55, 56). Although Davis (1986) reported imported Cretan wares in nearly the same proportions as Overbeck reported Minoan/-izing ones, mainland imports in Period V dropped off dramatically. In the count of vessels from published deposits, mainland wares made up only around 15% of total (n = 350) reported imports. In a count of imports according to macroscopic fabrics in the Northern Sector, Gorogianni (2008, 443, fig. 92; see also Gorogianni and Abell, forthcoming, table 3) suggested that Cretan imports were more common than other imports in Period V deposits there, with Cycladic imports the next most common, followed by mainland and Aeginetan imports. There was greater variety in the shapes imported from Crete in Period V compared to Period IV; imports included tablewares and miscellaneous vessels alongside jars and larger closed vessels. The result is that the two imported assemblages (Cretan and Melian/Theran) look quite similar to each other in Period V, in terms of the functional variety represented therein. More bulk agricultural goods were probably arriving from Melos/Thera than previously, while more tablewares from both places were being used, replacing a tableware assemblage that had been dominated by mainland-style vessels, at least among imports, in Period IV.

SUMMARY

Period IV deposits in Area B support the hypothesis that Ayia Irini was abandoned in the latest EBA and earliest MBA. Residents of Ayia Irini in Period IV participated in longer-distance interaction networks than had Period III inhabitants of the settlement; those networks linked residents of Ayia Irini to exchange with Aegina, central Greece, other Cycladic islands, perhaps the eastern Aegean, and, for the first time, relatively closely with Crete.

The most common vessels for eating and drinking at Ayia Irini in Period IV parallel shapes in use on the mainland (goblets) and on Aegina and in the Cyclades (carinated bowls). Cups with closer associations to Crete, particularly carinated, rounded, handleless, and straight-sided cups, were also in use, but rarer. Like goblets or carinated bowls, Cretan drinking shapes were not just imported, but were also locally produced, in some cases, using a Minoanizing technology, the potter's wheel. Wide-mouthed jars may have functioned in several ways, with some used as storage and others as cooking jars, given their similarity to cooking shapes on Aegina (Lindblom 2001, 26, fig. 4, S-14, S-15). Some cooking, however, also happened in tripod vessels, a Cretan way of doing things in this period. In all, the Period IV ceramic assemblage of Ayia Irini is suggestive of cooking, drinking, and dining practices that were not wholly part of any one cultural sphere (i.e., Aeginetan, mainland Greek, Cycladic, Cretan) but rather incorporated objects, and perhaps associated practices, from different parts of the Aegean in an assemblage that is distinctive to Ayia Irini. The idiosyncrasy of the Keian ceramic assemblage is not merely a function of the varied imports that arrived at the settlement but also a result of production choices made by local potters. The variety in the local assemblage represents particular choices in how to eat, drink, cook, pour, and store goods. Those choices underwent dramatic changes in Period V and later. Nevertheless, diversity in the regional associations of shapes—both local and imported—continued to be a significant aspect of the ceramic assemblage during the era of Minoanization, Periods V–VII.

VI. PERIOD VI CERAMIC ANALYSIS

Period VI marks the beginning of the LBA at Ayia Irini. Caskey published characteristic ceramics of Period VI from three deposits: from a large building in Area L, Room A.18, and a dump outside the fortifications in Area J (Caskey 1972, 391–394). Additional Period VI deposits were published by Cummer and Schofield (1984) and Schofield (2011). Caskey defined the start of the period with the appearance of LM IA and LH I imports, Cycladic wares like those found in the Shaft Graves at Mycenae, Gray Minyan types like those of mid- to late Troy VI, and "distinctive forms of local red-brown semicoarse fabrics" (Caskey 1972, 391); it ended with the appearance of LM IB and LH II imports (Caskey 1972, 393; see also Cummer and Schofield 1984, 45–48, 140–142; Davis and Cherry 1990, 193–196).

Recent analyses have demonstrated that Period VI can be divided into an earlier and a later phase (Davis and Cherry 1990, 194; Schofield 2011, 10). Deposits from Area B, in comparison with published deposits from the Western Sector, have been used to define the ceramic characteristics and synchronisms of earlier Period VI (Abell, forthcoming), which is probably contemporary with MM IIIB and perhaps the earliest part of LM IA on Crete (below).

Quantifications of Period VI pottery from Area B are based on ceramics from B601CL and B648CL for the early phase and B610CL and B647CL for the later phase. Vessels from published Period VI deposits in House A and the Western Sector (Cummer and Schofield 1984; Schofield 2010) were counted as described in Chapter 5. The results of this quantification are presented in Figs. 57–59. There are a few issues to note about the counts of pottery from these published deposits. Neither volume distinguished routinely between Matt Painted wares from the mainland vs. Aegina. Some Lustrous Painted fine wares were not ascribed to a provenance, and so they were counted as Minoan/Mycenaean Lustrous Painted ware. The House A volume (Cummer and Schofield 1984) described both local and imported Cycladic wares together, which makes it difficult to address the relative proportion of Cycladic imports to those of other regions in some cases. Vessels that were noted as local by the authors or that were discernible as local on the basis of the fabric description were counted as such. The rest were counted as part of Cycladic Painted ware, which is summarized together with other imports; it is, nevertheless, probable that some local vessels from House A may have been included in the count. This problem only impacts discussion of later Period VI and Period VII, since there are no clear deposits of earlier Period VI in House A. Where Melian imports were identified as such, I have counted them as Melian/Theran since macroscopic, microscopic, and chemical analyses have not yet been able to distinguish reliably between imports from those two islands. It is also possible that some Melian/Theran vessels may be included in Cycladic Painted categories if they were not distinguished as specifically "Melian" in the catalogue. Finally, for Period VI and VII deposits, the catalogues record fine imports as "Plain," but plain local vessels as "Coarse." Therefore, plain wares, unless listed as probably being from a particular region, were counted as being of unknown provenance. Coarse wares, however, were counted as local unless otherwise specified since most with descriptions of clays were compatible with local fabrics.

OVERVIEW OF PERIOD VI POTTERY

LOCAL

In both phases of Period VI, plain local vessels were by far the most common in published deposits, primarily because of the large number of handleless cups, over 460 in deposits of the earlier phase and over 2500 in deposits of the later phase. To address the relative percentages of wares in the rest of the assemblage, it is useful to exclude handleless cups from the quantifications. Omitting handleless cups from consideration, plain and painted vessels made up a similar portion of the local assemblage in the early phase, while plain vessels were more common than painted ones in the later phase. In both phases, nearly all painted wares were Yellow Slipped, although some, especially in the earlier phase, were Yellow Painted. Slipped vessels were very rare among local painted wares in both phases. Burnished ware was less common than other local wares in both phases, although it was proportionally more common in the early phase than the later one. Similarly, in Area B, plain ware was the most common local ware in both phases. Local painted wares were also somewhat common, mostly Yellow Slipped (25% of 51 local vessels, or 45% of 29 local vessels other than plain handleless cups). Burnished vessels were rare.

In both phases, published *Yellow Slipped* vessels included mostly tablewares, especially straight-sided/Vapheio cups, pedestaled bowls, bridge-spouted/hole-mouthed jars, and piriform cups. Rounded cups were rather rare in the early phase, but became more

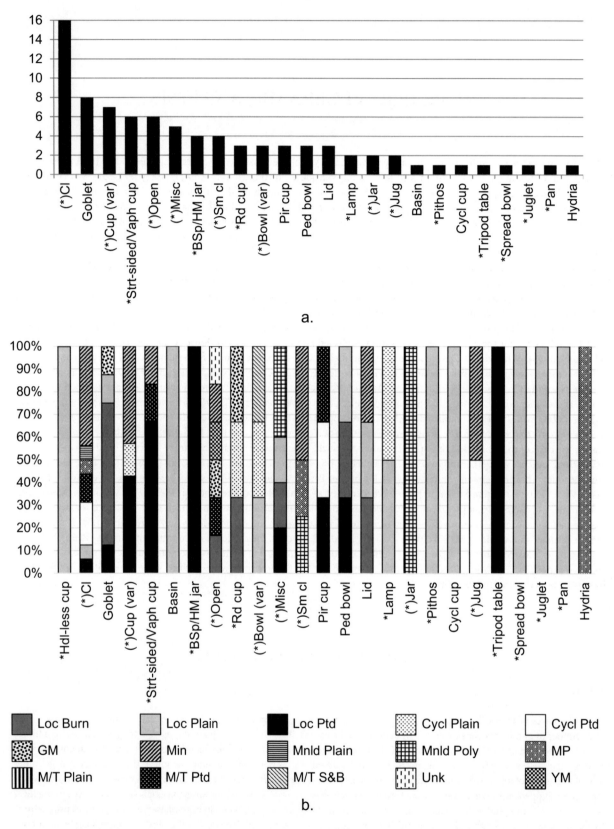

Fig. 57. Number (a) and relative proportions by ware (b) of shapes other than handleless cups (n = 464) in published early Period VI deposits, based on a count of vessels reported by Cummer and Schofield (1984) and Schofield (2011). Total vessels 85. Shapes marked "*" are Minoan or Minoanizing. Shapes marked "(*)" include some versions that are Minoan or Minoanizing, but others that are not.

common in later Period VI. Straight-sided/Vapheio cups (**41**, **100**), rounded cups (**40**), pedestaled bowls (**99**), and bridge-spouted/hole-mouthed jars (**704**) appeared also in Area B. Local vessels decorated with ripple pattern first appeared in early Period VI deposits, including in Area B (**40**, **41**). Ripple pattern and bands were the dominant painted motifs in early Period VI deposits; other motifs were rare and included scallops and, in Area B, a possible floral motif (**730**). Floral motifs and spirals became more common in later Period VI. Painted decoration could be in one color (black, brown, or red) or might be bichrome, with either matt or lustrous paint. Local vessels painted with Minoanizing motifs in the bichrome style included both Minoanizing shapes like rounded cups and non-Minoanizing ones, like a Melian bowl and a goblet (Schofield 2011, nos. 16, 95, 1166). All illustrated piriform cups were decorated in the paneled style (Cummer and Schofield 1984, pl. 62:t, u; Schofield 2011, nos. 537, 1370, 1517).

Yellow Painted vessels were relatively rare, although they were more common in deposits of the earlier phase than the later one. Shapes included a straight-sided/Vapheio cup, bridge-spouted jar, tripod table, and suspension pot, as well as an open jar (**705**) from Area B. Decoration was simple, mostly bands, but also included a spiral (Schofield 2011, no. 205).

Most *Burnished* vessels in both phases were goblets; Cycladic cups were rare but appeared in both phases (e.g., **39**). Other shapes in early Period VI deposits included a rounded cup, pedestaled bowl, lid, and cylindrical vessel; several bowls, bottles, an askos, and a cup were present in later Period VI deposits.

Local *Slipped* vessels were coated with red or brown slip (Cummer and Schofield 1984, no. 818); they were rarely burnished (Schofield 2011, no. 769), including a Cycladic cup (**96**) from Area B. Red slipped and burnished vessels have also been described as a local version of Red Coated ware (Cummer and Schofield 1984, 46).

Handleless cups were the most common *plain* vessels by far in both phases, in published deposits and in Area B (**46–53, 80–93**). Most were Type 1 and are directly comparable to the common conical cup of LM IA Crete, which emerged in MM IIIB (Knappett and Hilditch 2015a, 96–97). Handleless cups of Types 2 (e.g., **53**), 3 (e.g., **88**), 4, 6 (e.g., **90**), and 7, as well as miniature versions appeared in Period VI deposits. Only one Type 5 handleless cup was found in a Period VI deposit, in Area B (**89**). Many handleless cups, mainly of Type 1, were blackened in the interior and/or exterior, suggesting that they were sometimes used as lamps or for industrial purposes; several examples exist in Area B (**46, 49, 51, 52, 80, 86**). Tripod jars were common in published deposits, while straight-sided cups, pithoi, juglets, and crucibles were also relatively well represented. Several of these shapes were also found in Area B deposits (**44, 45, 101, 707**). Tripod jars and baking trays (flat-bottomed and with tripod legs) were the main cooking shapes in Period VI; nevertheless, some traditional cooking shapes, probably related to earlier wide-mouthed jars, were also present in the assemblage, often imported from Aegina (Gorogianni, Abell, and Hilditch 2017, 68–71). Among plain domestic and industrial vessels, spreading bowls, firestands, and, to a lesser degree, fireboxes were relatively common in Period VI (Georgiou 1986, 11–12, 25, 32). Other plain shapes included lamps (e.g., **706**), goblets (e.g., **55**), flaring saucers (e.g., **54, 103**), various bowls, Cycladic cups (e.g., **102**), a krater or jar, a pan, and a plug or lid(?) (**56**).

IMPORTS

In published early Period VI deposits, Cretan and Cycladic wares each made up around a third of total (n = 46) imports. Among Cycladic imports, Melian/Theran Painted vessels were slightly less common than other Cycladic imports, which were both painted and plain. Mainland and Aeginetan vessels made up just under a third of total imports. Most of those were Mainland Polychrome, Matt Painted, and Gray Minyan, with only a couple of Yellow Minyan and plain vessels reported.

In early Period VI deposits in Area B, Cycladic imports were much more common than Cretan ones, which made up just under 10% of total (n = 34) imports. Melian/Theran vessels made up nearly a third and other Cycladic vessels made up around a quarter of total imports. Melian/Theran Painted and plain wares were about equally common, while Slipped and Burnished ware was rare. Most other Cycladic imports were plain; Slipped and other Painted wares were rare. Mainland and Aeginetan wares together made up over a quarter of total imports. Of these, Gray Minyan ware was most common (approximately 12% of total imports) and was about twice as common as Matt Painted wares, which in Area B probably derived from Aegina. Other wares were represented by only a single vessel, including Mainland Slipped, Aeginetan(?) Painted, and Lustrous Decorated, in addition to a few vessels of unknown provenance.

The most common imports in published deposits of later Period VI derived from the mainland and/or Aegina; they made up nearly 40% of the total (n = 233) imported vessels. Matt Painted wares made up nearly 12% of total imports. At least a quarter of these probably came from Aegina since they are classed as Standard Matt Painted ware in the publications. Other common mainland imports were Gray Minyan (12% of total imports), Mainland Polychrome (around 7%), and Lustrous Painted (around 6%) wares. A few Burnished, plain, and Yellow Minyan vessels are represented. Imports from Crete, most of which were Lustrous Painted, made up nearly 20% of total imports. Imports in Melian/Theran Painted wares made up around 15% of total imports; Melian/Theran and other Cycladic plain imports were much rarer (ca. 3%), as were Cycladic Burnished wares (<1%). Cycladic Painted ware made up around 9% of total imported vessels, although, as noted above, some vessels counted in this category from House A may be local products. Red Coated ware, of possibly Cycladic or mainland provenance, as well as Lustrous Painted ware of unknown mainland or Cretan provenance, made up less than 1% of total imports.

In later Period VI deposits in Area B, Cycladic (including Melian/Theran) and mainland (including Aeginetan) imports each made up around 30% of total (n = 39) imports. Melian/Theran wares made up about 20% and other Cycladic wares made up around 10% of total imports. Painted and plain wares were about equally represented among both Melian/Theran and other

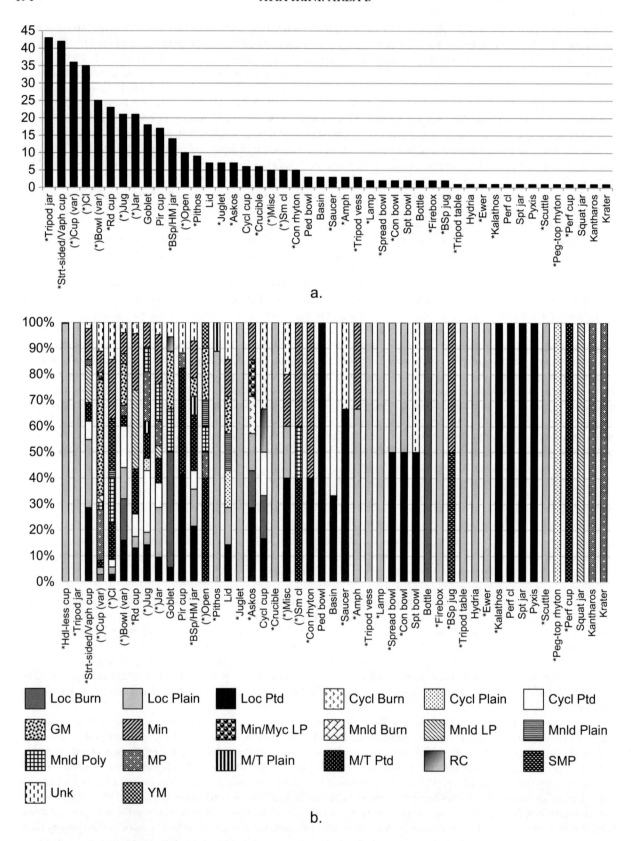

Fig. 58. Number (a) and relative proportions by ware (b) of common shapes other than handleless cups (n = 2609) in published later Period VI deposits, based on a count of vessels reported by Cummer and Schofield (1984) and Schofield (2011). Total vessels 404. Shapes marked "*" are Minoan or Minoanizing. Shapes marked "(*)" include some versions that are Minoan or Minoanizing, but others that are not.

Cycladic imports. Mainland imports were nearly twice as common as Aeginetan ones. Many wares were represented, including Aeginetan Standard Matt Painted and Red Coated wares and mainland Lustrous Painted, Burnished, and plain wares. Cretan wares made up just over 15% of total imports, with Lustrous Painted vessels being more common than Non-Lustrous Painted ones. Fine wares that cannot be definitively associated with a Cretan vs. mainland provenance (mainly in Lustrous Painted ware) made up around 20% of total imports.

In a recent summary of macroscopic fabric analyses in the Northern Sector and Area B (Gorogianni and Abell, forthcoming, table 3), imports from Crete were equally common as those from the Cyclades (including Melos/Thera) and slightly more common than those from the mainland and Aegina (considered separately) during Period VI. Fabrics from the mainland and Aegina were equally represented in the assemblages and, when considered together, made up the largest proportion of imports. Imports from the southeast Aegean were relatively rare (Gorogianni and Abell, forthcoming, table 3; for southeastern Aegean imports from the Northern Sector and Area L, see Davis et al. 1983, 363–364, nos. 2, 7, pl. 70:c; Knappett and Hilditch 2015b, 203).

In sum, different quantifications produce somewhat different proportions of imports in Period VI, which is owed at least in part to differences between assemblages across the site. Nevertheless, according to all of these different quantifications, it is clear that imports from the different regions (Crete, Cyclades, mainland Greece [including Aegina]) are all well represented in Period VI. No one region supplied an outsized proportion of imports to the site.

The majority of *Melian/Theran Painted* imports were piriform cups, straight-sided/Vapheio cups, and various closed vessels (often of uncertain profile). In later Period VI, rounded cups and bridge-spouted/hole-mouthed jars were also relatively common. Although many piriform cups were too fragmented to evaluate the layout of decoration, several were decorated in the paneled style, including some from Area B (**62, 67**). Minoanizing open shapes were often painted with Minoanizing motifs, especially vertical bars or curved stripes made in imitation of ripple pattern; foliate bands and spirals also appeared. Most Melian/Theran Painted vessels were painted with only one color, but some (both Minoanizing and non-Minoanizing) were painted with multiple colors, using red, brown, and/or black. Among the vessels painted in multiple colors was a large pithoid jar with pictorial decoration (the so-called Griffin Jar), which was associated with a series of Period VI floors in Room A.26 (Cummer and Schofield 1984, 111–112, no. 1318, pl. 79); it may have been imported from Akrotiri in earlier LC I (Marthari 1998). One closed vessel was decorated with matt red and black paint (Schofield 2011, no. 244); the use of matt red and black (rather than lustrous red) was typical of Phase D at Akrotiri (Nikolakopoulou et al. 2008, 319), although burnishing of the paint, like that on the pot from Kea, is not.

Melian/Theran *plain* imported shapes were all singletons, including a handleless cup (**66**), Melian bowl (**108**), Cycladic cup, and lid(?) from Area B. Only one Melian/Theran *Slipped and Burnished* import is attested: a large closed vessel from Area B (**65**).

Shapes in *Cycladic Painted* ware in earlier Period VI deposits also were all singletons, with the exception of closed vessels of unknown morphology (e.g., **104**). Vessels classed as Cycladic Painted in later Period VI deposits (which may include some local vessels; above) were mostly jugs, bowls, and straight-sided cups. Several basins are also included in this category (Cummer and Schofield 1984, pl. 62:v–z). At least some of these basins are probably local, since few imported examples are known from deposits where Cycladic and local painted wares are distinguished from one another; nevertheless, an imported Melian version exists in a Period VII deposit (Schofield 2011, no. 2176). Such vessels are often elaborately decorated in their interiors in broadly Minoanizing style (e.g., DOL spirals or floral motifs), but the shape itself does not seem to be typical of LM I Cretan pottery; rather, basins or tubs with similarly elaborate interior decoration are best paralleled on Melos and Thera (Barber 2008, 124–125, 203, fig. 29:544; Nikolakopoulou 2019, 176–177; Scholes 1956, 20). The only Cycladic *Burnished* vessel was an askos. Cycladic *plain* shapes were mostly singletons, including a peg-top rhyton (Koehl's [2006] Type II HL Ovoid), lid, and a jug from published deposits, as well as two Minoanizing tumblers (**60, 61**), handleless cups (**59, 94**), and bowl (**105**) from Area B. Cycladic *Slipped* and *Yellow Slipped* vessels were rare; in Area B, these included closed vessels and a possible basin (**708**) with an unusual rim profile.

Addressing the Minoanizing character of painted Cycladic pottery is complicated in this period, despite the general abundance of Minoanizing shapes and decorative styles represented in local and imported Cycladic ceramics. Non-Minoanizing motifs sometimes appeared on Minoanizing shapes, as for example on an imported Cycladic bowl from Area B (**57**), which is similar in profile to Cretan ledge-rim bowls, but which is painted with Cycladic-style rosettes. The Red and Black style, long recognized as a distinctive phenomenon of the earlier LBA in the Cyclades, has been defined as a Minoanizing style that used semi-lustrous red and matt-black paint (Davis and Cherry 2007, 265–266; Scholes 1956, 24). As at Phylakopi (Davis and Cherry 2007, 267), however, the red paint used for Minoanizing motifs at Ayia Irini was not always lustrous or was sometimes burnished, features more typical of the non-Minoanizing MC Black and Red style (Scholes 1956, 20–21). Moreover, as at Phylakopi (Davis and Cherry 2007, 265–266), vessels in the bichrome or polychrome styles (including both imports and local vessels) at Ayia Irini were sometimes, but not always, Minoanizing in shape and/or motif. For example, a Minoanizing Melian/Theran Painted cup-rhyton was painted with Minoanizing bands and spirals (Koehl 2006, no. 1285 [Type IV Cup: Semiglobular]; Schofield 2011, no. 92), while a non-Minoanizing bichrome painted Melian/Theran piriform cup was decorated with non-Minoanizing bracket pattern and dots (Schofield 2011, no. 1402). Bichrome and polychrome styles of decoration also gained popularity on Aegina and in mainland Greece in this era, particularly in the form of Mainland Polychrome and Aeginetan Bichrome wares (Davis 1979a; Gauss and Smetana 2007; Lindblom 2007; Mathioudaki 2010, 2014). Some Cycladic vessels appear to be decorated in a manner that is more closely affiliated with mainland and Aeginetan styles than those of LM IA Crete. For example, a Melian/Theran miniature beaked jug was painted with red bands framed in black (Schofield 2011, no. 1985; cf. also no. 1404). Such framed bands are relatively common among painted Cycladic (including local) wares of Periods VI and VII, as well as Mainland Polychrome and Aeginetan Bichrome wares, but they are atypical of Cretan painted pottery. The framing of bands in mainland, Aeginetan, and Cycladic bichrome/polychrome styles

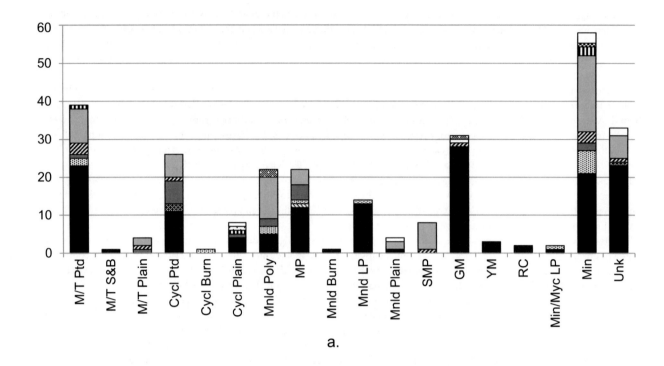

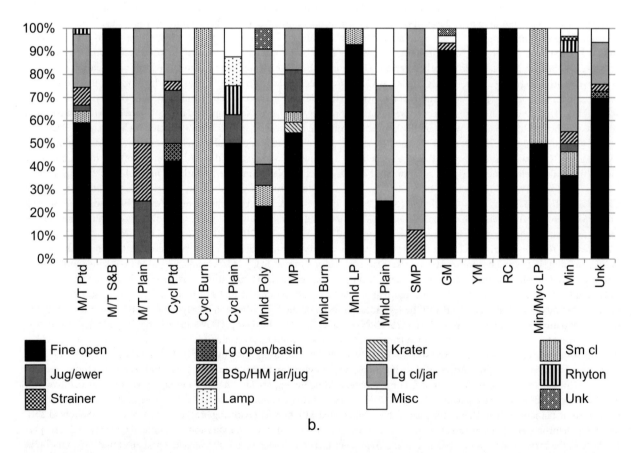

Fig. 59. Number (a) and relative proportions by ware and general shape (b) of imported vessels in published Period VI deposits of both phases, based on a count of those reported by Cummer and Schofield (1984) and Schofield (2011). Total imported vessels 279.

is a syntactical similarity that reflects a closer link between the Cyclades, Aegina and/or the mainland than between the Cyclades and Crete, with respect to at least some bichrome/polychrome painted vessels in this period.

Imports from the mainland and Aegina existed in diverse wares. *Matt Painted* imports from earlier Period VI deposits were entirely closed shapes, including hydrias and jars, as well as smaller closed shapes that are probably tablewares (e.g., Schofield 2011, no. 775). Matt Painted vessels from later Period VI deposits were mostly cups (including rounded, straight-sided/Vapheio, and piriform) and jugs. Examples of this ware in Area B all had Aeginetan fabrics. Hydrias, amphoras, and closed vessels of uncertain profile were present in *Standard Matt Painted* ware in both earlier and later Period VI deposits and include three from Area B (**69, 110, 111**).

Plain and other *Painted* (e.g., **68**) Aeginetan imports were very rare. An amphora/hydria from a later Period VI deposit might belong to *Aeginetan Bichrome* ware (Schofield 2011, nos. 6, 7). *Mainland Polychrome* vessels from early Period VI deposits were probably mostly jars, although many sherds are undiagnostic of shape. Cutaway neck jugs and goblets appeared in later Period VI deposits. Most *Gray Minyan* imports were open vessels, especially rounded cups, goblets, and bowls, including several from Area B (e.g., **70, 71**). *Yellow Minyan* was represented by very few open vessels, including a goblet (or kantharos?) (Schofield 2011, no. 1197); Caskey (1972, 392) also reported sherds from cups and jugs in this ware. Only goblets and a possibly local loop-handled bowl existed in *Red Coated* ware, which appeared only in later Period VI deposits. Fabric analysis in Period VII deposits in Area B suggests that Red Coated ware is made up of products from different regions, including Aegina, mainland Greece, and the Cyclades. Only one mainland *Burnished* vessel has been published, a pedestaled cup; mainland *plain* vessels were all singletons, including a lid and a goblet or krater, as well as a hydria (**115**) from Area B. A narrow-necked hydria or jar from the mainland, found in Area B, was *Slipped* (**710**).

Two tiny fragments of *Burnished Gray/Black* vessels from later Period VI deposits have been published (Cummer and Schofield 1984, 85, 95); it is unclear where this ware was produced. A similar ware is described from Crete, where it first appeared in LM IA; it was apparently also rare there and of unknown origin. The range of shapes on Crete during LM I, which included mainly small cups, jugs, and askoi, is similar to that of Burnished Gray/Black ware found at Ayia Irini (Hallager 2011, 175–176; Hood 2011, 168–170, figs. 39, 44:61 P541 [Black Burnished ware]; Brogan et al. in Brogan and Hallager 2011, 179–181).

A *Lustrous Decorated* (or perhaps Lustrous Painted?) straight-sided/Vapheio cup (**72**) from an earlier Period VI deposit in Area B was the only vessel in that ware; its unusual fabric differs from earlier examples of Lustrous Decorated ware in Area B and from later examples of LH I DOL-style Lustrous Painted ware vessels. Only two *Light-on-Lustrous-Dark Painted* cups, both from a later Period VI deposit, have been published (Cummer and Schofield 1984, 85, pl. 64:f, g).

LH I *Lustrous Painted* ware only appeared in later Period VI deposits. A squat jar and a jug with cutaway neck are the only published early Mycenaean shapes apart from the more common Vapheio and rounded cups (Caskey 1972, no. G10, pl. 92; Mountjoy 1999, 867; Schofield 2011, 47, no. 505, pl. 46). In Area B, rounded cups (**114, 117, 119, 120**) were more common than straight-sided or Vapheio cups (**113, 116**) in Lustrous Painted wares; most Lustrous Painted vessels in Area B seem to have been mainland rather than Cretan products. Vapheio cups of Types II (**116**) and III (**113**) were present in Area B (for the types, Coldstream 1978, 392–396). Straight-sided/Vapheio cups in Area B were decorated with ripple pattern (**113**) or schematic blooms (**116**); rounded cups were painted with widely spaced reeds (**119**) and spirals (**114, 117, 120**).

In early Period VI, Cretan imports were *Lustrous Painted, Non-Lustrous Painted*, and *plain*; painted decoration was usually DOL, but monochrome and LOD painted vessels also appeared (e.g., **73–75**). On most examples, only one color of paint (black, brown, or red) was used, sometimes with added white paint and rarely with black, red, and white used together. Bands and ripple pattern or the related curved stripes pattern were common decorative motifs. A few closed vessels preserved zones of DOL ripple pattern in addition to LOD decoration (Schofield 2011, nos. 214, 635, 1221). Recognizable shapes were mainly singletons, including a tall cup, early bell cup, straight-sided cup with clapboarded sides, jug, and lid from published deposits, as well as an ogival bowl or bell cup (**73**) and lamp (**75**) from Area B.

In later Period VI deposits, most Cretan imports were *Lustrous Painted*, and included primarily straight-sided/Vapheio cups, rounded cups, jars, and closed vessels of unknown profile. A few Cretan Lustrous Painted conical rhyta, bowls, bridge-spouted/hole-mouthed jars, and jugs were also present, and a cup(?)-rhyton (**746**) from Area B might also date to this period. Ripple pattern was common among Lustrous Painted imports from both Crete and the mainland, but other motifs, especially spirals, foliate bands, and curvilinear motifs were also popular; sometimes details were added with white paint (Caskey 1972, 392). True LOD decoration was very rare in later Period VI deposits (Schofield 2011, nos. 261, 803).

SYNCHRONISMS

Period VI synchronisms are summarized by phase in Tables 6.1 and 6.2.

The prevalence of DOL decoration and predominance of straight-sided/Vapheio cups in early Period VI deposits suggests this phase was contemporary with the Cretan Neopalatial period. The rarity of motifs other than ripple pattern or bands and the existence of some LOD decorated vessels suggests that early Period VI overlapped MM IIIB on Crete as defined by the KS 178 group at Knossos (Girella 2007b, 251; Hatzaki 2007b, 162–163). The rare presence of spirals and floral motifs in early Period VI deposits suggests that early Period VI may also have been contemporary with the beginning of LM IA on Crete.

TABLE 6.1. EARLY PERIOD VI SYNCHRONISMS

Region	Contemporary phases
Cyclades	Akrotiri Phase D(?); SDL (Marthari 1984, 1990; Nikolakopoulou 2019, 57–59; Nikolakopoulou et al. 2008, 319)
	Early LC I Phylakopi (Davis and Cherry 2007)
Aegina	Kolonna Phase K/Stadt XI (Gauss and Smetana 2007, 65)
Mainland	(?)Early LH I at Brauron (Kalogeropoulos 2010, 215–216)
	(?)Kiapha Thiti Schnitt 153 SE 4–5, Schnitt 154 SE 2–4 (MH III); Schnitt 101 SE 3 (LH I) (Maran 1992, 79–80, 99–101, 106–109)
	(?)Tsoungiza Group D (Rutter 2020, 496–607, nos. D1–D125, D137–D363).
Kythera	Kastri Deposits ε, ζ (Coldstream and Huxley 1972, 98–114)
Crete	Knossos MM IIIB–LM IA (Hatzaki 2007b, 160–184)

TABLE 6.2. LATER PERIOD VI SYNCHRONISMS

Region	Contemporary phases
Cyclades	Akrotiri VDL (Marthari 1984, 1990)
	Later LC I Phylakopi (Davis and Cherry 2007)
Aegina	Kolonna Phase K/Stadt XI (Gauss and Smetana 2007, 65)
Mainland	LH I Korakou (Davis 1979a)
	LH I Lerna Shaft Graves (Lindblom and Manning 2011)
	Tsoungiza, East Building, later Group E (Rutter 2020, 628–632, 649, nos. E57, E58, E63–E65, E70, E79–E85)
Kythera	Kastri Deposits η, θ (Coldstream and Huxley 1972, 115–123)
Crete	Knossos LM IA (Hatzaki 2007b, 172–184)

Later Period VI, as defined especially by Room A.18 Deposit A, was contemporary with LM IA on Crete (Caskey 1972, 391–392). Warren (1991, 338–339) argued that the Room A.18 deposit should be contemporary with MM IIIB–LM IA, based partly on the absence of reed decoration, which was, however, present in a later Period VI deposit in Area B. Warren's (1991) MM IIIB–LM IA terminology has been redefined by recent studies, as being contemporary with Evans' MM IIIB (Hatzaki 2007a, 279; 2007b, 152–158; Hood 1996, 14). Later Period VI overlaps later LC I/LM IA as represented in the Volcanic Destruction Level (VDL) at Akrotiri, since LH I pottery was found in Room A.18 and the VDL (Davis 1992, 710; Marthari 1990, 63). Hatzaki (2007b, 183–184) argued for the synchronism of the Room A.18 deposit and LM IA, which she also linked with the VDL at Akrotiri. Later Period VI also was probably contemporary with "Mature" LM IA level 11 (or Pelon's Phase IIIA) at Malia, based on the presence of plain straight-sided cups, more variable motifs than the previous period, and plant motifs on small and large vessels (van de Moortel 2011, 537–538).

Ceramics from early Period VI deposits, including tumblers, a lamp, and an in-and-out bowl from Area B (**60, 61, 75, 730**), have parallels with deposits ε and ζ on Kythera. Ceramics from later Period VI deposits are most similar to those of Kythera deposits η and θ, in which LH I Lustrous Painted ware, Type III Vapheio cups, and a greater variety of motifs among Lustrous Decorated or Painted wares appear. A later Period VI Type II Vapheio cup with schematic blooms (**116**) had a close parallel in Deposit θ (Coldstream and Huxley 1972, 121, no. 2, pl. 31), as well as in the Lerna Shaft Graves, which, like later Period VI, can be linked to the VDL at Akrotiri (Lindblom and Manning 2011, 141–145, fig. 1:P318).

LH I Lustrous Painted pottery was not found in earlier Period VI deposits from Area B or the Western Sector, and Davis (1992, 710; Davis and Cherry 1990, 194) noted the absence of LH I Lustrous Painted ware from early Period VI deposits in Area L. The earliest features of LH I Lustrous Painted ware (Type I Vapheio cups and the "metopal spiral"; see Dickinson 2014) do not exist at

Ayia Irini, which suggests that the ware was probably being produced in some parts of the mainland during this time, even if it did not appear at Ayia Irini.

Other mainland wares do not provide precise chronological links between the early and later phases of Period VI and mainland sequences, although broad parallels in Mainland Polychrome and, to some extent, Red Coated wares, suggest that some or all of Period VI was contemporary with LH I deposits at Eleusis, Kiapha Thiti, and Brauron in Attica (Cosmopoulos 2010, 555; Kalogeropoulos 2010, 215–218; Maran 1992, 75–77, 79–80, 204–205). Later Period VI was probably contemporary with the Shaft Graves at Lerna. The presence of LH I vessels in Phase K deposits at Kolonna (Gauss and Smetana 2007, 65–66) suggests that this phase is contemporary with later Period VI at Ayia Irini, although it may also overlap some or all of early Period VI, as well. In 1972, Caskey noted that Period VI Gray Minyan imports were paralleled in later Troy VI (especially the rounded cups, which were more common in the later phase but appeared also in earlier Period VI deposits at Ayia Irini). At the time, later Troy VI was thought to be significantly later than LH I (Caskey 1972, 391, 393), but redating of Troy VI and the identification of similar cups from other Aegean contexts suggests that such vessels are characteristic of LH I Gray Minyan shapes (Davis 1979a, 255; Dietz 1991, 201; Graziadio 1988, 356 n. 65; Maran 1992, 120–121; Pavúk 2007, 301; Rutter 2020, 587).

Early Period VI is probably contemporary with an early LC I phase at Phylakopi and the Seismic Destruction Level (SDL) and possibly Phase D at Akrotiri. All of these phases are characterized by the presence of Cretan Lustrous Painted DOL and LOD pottery but no LH I Lustrous Painted pottery, as well as a limited set of decorative motifs other than ripple pattern among DOL Lustrous Painted and Minoanizing wares (Davis and Cherry 1990, 194; 2007, 296–302; Marthari 1984, 129; 1990, 61–66; Nikolakopoulou et al. 2008, 319). LOD styles are relatively prevalent in Akrotiri Phase D deposits, which also has broad parallels with Period V (Ch. 5). A later LC I phase at Akrotiri (VDL) and Phylakopi was typified by the presence of LH I Lustrous Painted pottery and a wider array of spiraliform and floral motifs in Lustrous Painted and Minoanizing wares, which suggests these phases were contemporary with later Period VI (Davis and Cherry 1984, 157, fig. 5; 2007, 301; Marthari 1984, 129; 1990, 61).

Period VI, like LM IA, probably continued for a short time after the eruption of the Theran volcano (Schofield 1984b, 182). Although no Type III Vapheio cups were found in the VDL at Akrotiri (Hatzaki 2007b, 184; Lolos 1990, 55; Warren 1999, 894–895), this shape was found both in a later Period VI deposit (**113**) and in the LM IA Upper Gypsades Well deposit at Knossos (Hatzaki 2007b, 175; Popham 1967, pl. 76:d; see also Warren 1999, 894–895). Davis and Cherry's seriation analysis of LC I deposits at Phylakopi determined that tephra from the Thera volcano appeared in deposits that contained late—but not the latest—LM IA imports, which suggests that, at Phylakopi, like Ayia Irini, LC I continued after the Theran eruption (Davis and Cherry 1984; 1990, 195–196; 2007, 301–302).

FABRICS

Both Period VI phases are considered together, because the fabrics do not change significantly between them and because the quantity of ceramics is quite small, with only 124 total vessels represented. A summary of macroscopic fabrics and their relationships to wares and shapes is provided in Table 6.3. The relative proportions of imports by region, based on the macroscopic fabric analysis in Area B, is presented in Table 6.4.

Using the methodology described in Chapter 5, a rough estimate suggests that about 87–90% of pottery in Period VI deposits before discard may have been local (Table 6.5). Gorogianni estimated that just over 90% of pottery in Period VI deposits in the Northern Sector was probably local, with discards taken into consideration (Gorogianni and Abell, forthcoming, table 2; see also Gorogianni 2008).

Local fabrics in Period VI were very similar to those discussed in previous chapters. Nearly all vessels belonged to group RBMa. Fabrics RBMb and RBMc did not appear. Fabric RBMd was represented by two vessels, both of which were classed petrographically in PFG 2. Moderately fine versions of RBMa were less common in Period VI than Period IV deposits. This may be because most local Period VI vessels in Area B were handleless cups, which tended to be moderately coarse or coarse, although some moderately fine examples do exist. Although Berg (2007b, 117) suggested that a "semicoarse pale brown clay" was used for the production of handleless cups at Ayia Irini, analysis in Area B suggests that the fabrics associated with handleless cups were typical of those used for other shapes.

Petrographic analysis classed most Period VI samples of RBMa fabrics in PFG 1A and 1C (Table 3.2). There is no clear correlation between PFG and ware, with Yellow Slipped vessels in fabric RBMa, for example, classed in PFG 1A, 1D, and a variant of PFG 2B (sample 19); plain vessels were classed in PFG 1B and 1C. Style of the vessel also was not related to fabric: a Minoanizing lamp and a Minyanizing goblet in RBMa were both classed in PFG 1C. In addition, both wheelmade and coil-built Period VI vessels were classed in PFG 1A.

The majority of clearly imported fabrics in Area B deposits were Melian/Theran. These fabrics made up around 25% of the total (n = 73) imports. As in Period IV, Group DVa was most common by far (ca. 15% of total imports). Groups DVb and DVc were also present. These fabrics were associated with Painted, Slipped and Burnished, and plain vessels, open and closed, small and large, Minoanizing and non-Minoanizing.

TABLE 6.3. OVERVIEW OF VESSELS IN PERIOD VI LOTS IN AREA B ACCORDING TO MACROSCOPIC FABRIC GROUP B601CL, B610CL, B647CL, and B648CL. The total number of vessels is 124, of which 51 are in RBM fabrics (local and local region) and 73 are in imported fabrics.

Fabric group	No. of vessels	% of total	% of RBM	% of imports	Wares	Shapes
RBMa	49	39.5%	96.1%		Burnished	Cycladic cup (1), open (Period IV goblet?) (1)
					Plain	Handleless cup (22), Cycladic cup (1), Minyanizing goblet (1), flaring saucer (2), open (1), closed (2), tripod jar (2), tripod jar(?) (1), lamp (1), plug/lid (1)
					Slipped and Burnished	Cycladic cup (1)
					Yellow Painted	Open (1)
					Yellow Slipped	Rounded cup (1), straight-sided/Vapheio cup (2), handleless cup (1), pedestaled bowl (1), bridge-spouted jar (1), closed (1), closed(?) (1), open jar (2), open jar(?) (1)
RBMd	2	1.6%	3.9%		Plain	Juglet(?) (1), tripod jar (1)
DVa	11	8.9%		15.1%	Melian/Theran Painted	Piriform cup (2), closed (4)
					Plain	Handleless cup (1), Cycladic cup (1), closed (1), lid(?) (1), unknown (1)
FSTj	9	7.3%		12.3%	Lustrous Painted	Rounded cup (1), ogival bowl or bell cup (1), open (2), bridge-spouted jug (1), spouted jar (1), small closed (1)
					Plain	Cup(?)-rhyton (1), unknown (1)
DVe	5	4.0%		6.8%	Aeginetan Painted	Open (1), small closed (1)
					Red Coated	Cup (1), jug(?) (1)
					Standard Matt Painted	Narrow-necked jar (1)
MxMa	5	4.0%		6.8%	Cycladic Painted	Small closed (1)
					Cycladic Yellow Slipped	Basin(?) (1)
					Plain	Handleless cup (1), bowl (1), small open(?) (1)
DVb	4	3.2%		5.5%	Melian/Theran Painted	Piriform cup (1), closed (1)
					Plain	Handleless cup (1), Melian bowl (1)
FVa	4	3.2%		5.5%	Gray Minyan	Goblet (2), open (2)
FVd	4	3.2%		5.5%	Lustrous Painted	Rounded cup (1), Vapheio cup (1)
					Mainland Burnished	Open (1)
					Mainland Slipped	Hydria/jar (1)
DVd	3	2.4%		4.1%	Melian/Theran(?) Painted	Piriform cup (1)
					Standard Matt Painted	Hydria (2)
DVg	3	2.4%		4.1%	Cycladic Painted	Bowl (1)
					Cycladic Slipped	Fine closed(?) (1)
					Plain	Fine closed(?) (1)
FSTa	3	2.4%		4.1%	Lustrous Painted	Closed (1)
					Non-Lustrous Painted	Closed (2)
DVc	2	1.6%		2.7%	Melian/Theran Slipped and Burnished	Closed (1)
					Plain	Open(?) (1)
FSTc	2	1.6%		2.7%	Non-Lustrous Painted	Lamp (1)
					Plain	Closed (1)

TABLE 6.3. (CONT.)

Fabric group	No. of vessels	% of total	% of RBM	% of imports	Wares	Shapes
FSTh	2	1.6%		2.7%	Lustrous Painted	Rounded cup (1), Vapheio cup (1)
FSTk	2	1.6%		2.7%	Lustrous Painted	Rounded cup (1)
					Non-Lustrous Painted	Jug (1)
MxMf	2	1.6%		2.7%	Plain	Tumbler (2)
Unk	2	1.6%		2.7%	Cycladic Painted	Open (1)
					Plain	Handleless cup (1)
CSWb	1	0.8%		1.4%	Cycladic Painted	Closed (1)
CSWe	1	0.8%		1.4%	Plain	Handleless cup (1)
FSTb	1	0.8%		1.4%	Lustrous Painted	Open(?) jar (1)
FSTd	1	0.8%		1.4%	Lustrous Painted	Closed (1)
FSTf	1	0.8%		1.4%	Non-Lustrous Painted	Closed (1)
FSTg/ FSTj(?)	1	0.8%		1.4%	Lustrous Painted or Decorated	Straight-sided/Vapheio cup (1)
FVc	1	0.8%		1.4%	Lustrous Painted	Straight-sided alabastron (1)
FVe	1	0.8%		1.4%	EBA Pinkish Buff	Open (1)
FVf	1	0.8%		1.4%	Plain	Hydria (1)
MxMd	1	0.8%		1.4%	Plain	Closed (jug?) (1)

Other parts Cycladic fabrics made up around 16% of total (n = 73) imports. Group MxMa (western Cyclades?) was most common, with around 7% of total (n = 73) imports, while group DVg (Melos/Thera?) made up around 4% of the total. Groups MxMd and MxMf (unknown Cycladic provenance), as well as CSWe (Naxos), were also represented. There were no obvious patterns of shape or ware distribution in different fabric groups, with painted and plain, Minoanizing and non-Minoanizing, and open and closed vessels represented in multiple fabrics.

Mainland fabrics also made up around 16% of total (n = 73) imports. Most were group FVd (Attica and/or Euboea?) and group FVa (probably from central Greece). Groups FVd and FVa each made up just over 5% of total imports. Group FVd was associated with Lustrous Painted and Burnished open vessels, as well as a Slipped narrow-necked hydria or jar. The only vessels in group FVa, as in Period IV, were Gray Minyan open vessels. Excavation notes suggest that additional Gray Minyan sherds were discarded from Period VI lots in Area B (Ch. 2). Rare mainland fabric groups included FSTd, FVc, FVe, and FVf.

Fine fabric FSTj made up around 12% of total imports, but its origin is unknown. Macroscopically, it was hypothesized to be Cretan, but petrographic analysis and preliminary interpretation of the WD-XRF results suggest it may instead be from the mainland. It was closely associated with tablewares, most of which were Lustrous Painted, although a few were plain. A Lustrous Painted or Decorated straight-sided/Vapheio cup (**72**) in a variant fabric, FSTg/FSTj(?), is also of unknown Cretan or mainland origin.

Fabrics hypothesized to be from Aegina and Crete each made up between 10–13% of total imports, with Cretan fabrics being slightly more common than Aeginetan ones. Most Cretan imports were in FSTa (ca. 4% of total imports), but FSTb, FSTc, FSTf, and FSTk were also represented. Vessels in probable Cretan FST fabrics were Lustrous Painted (FSTa, FSTb, FSTk), Non-Lustrous Painted (FSTa, FSTc, FSTf, FSTk), and plain (FSTc), with coarser fabrics used for larger closed vessels and fine fabrics (especially FSTk) used for a variety of tablewares.

Among hypothesized Aeginetan fabrics, group DVe was more common than group DVd (around 7% vs. 4% total [n = 73] imports), but petrographic analysis suggests that group DVe may include some non-Aeginetan vessels, as well. In addition, a piriform cup (**67**), which was classified in group DVd macroscopically, was shown to be potentially Melian/Theran as part of the petrographic analysis, although it was a variant from the main group (sample 110; PFG 5Av). Both groups DVd and DVe were associated with Standard Matt Painted closed vessels; group DVe was also associated with Red Coated and Painted open vessels. There were a few more vessels in group DVe in later Period VI than early Period VI deposits; in Period VII deposits there were many more vessels of group DVe than DVd.

Group FSTh (from the mainland and/or Kythera?) comprised only two total imports, while there was only one vessel classed in CSWb (local region). Group FSTh was associated only with a Lustrous Painted Vapheio cup and rounded cup (**116, 117**).

To summarize, many of the common imported fabrics of Period VI deposits in Area B seem to be either the same or related to fabrics that were found also in Period IV, although differences in the assemblages exist. Although the main Melian/Theran fabric,

TABLE 6.4. RELATIVE PROPORTIONS OF IMPORTED VESSELS ACCORDING TO PROBABLE REGIONS OF PRODUCTION IN PERIOD VI DEPOSITS IN AREA B

Based on fabric analysis, Ch. 3, and in comparison to the total number of imports (73).

Import region	No. of vessels	% of imports
Aegina	2	3%
Aegina(?)	5	7%
Attica/Cyclades	1	1%
Central Greece/Euboea	5	7%
Crete	7	10%
Crete(?)	2	3%
Crete/Mainland	10	14%
Cyclades	11	15%
Mainland	1	1%
Mainland (Attica/Euboea?)	4	5%
Mainland (Euboea?)	1	1%
Mainland (Peloponnese?)	1	1%
Mainland/Kythera	2	3%
Melos/Thera	18	25%
Naxos	1	1%
Unknown	2	3%

TABLE 6.5. ROUGH ESTIMATE OF THE PROPORTION OF IMPORTED PERIOD VI POTTERY IN AREA B LOTS

Calculated on the basis of the volume of pottery collected in comparison with what remains of the original lots and assuming that all discarded pottery was local.

Lot	Collected	Remaining	% discarded	% imports in remaining lot	Rough % imports in original lot
B601CL	2.75 tins	0.5 tins	82%	56%	10%
B610CL	1.5 tins	0.4 tins	73%	48%	13%
B648CL	1.75 bags	0.5 bag	71%	44%	13%
B647CL	1.5 bag	0.2 bag	87%	100%	13%
Average					*12%*

DVa, was common in both periods, fabrics MxMc and MFVa were rare in Period IV and absent in Period VI, while fabrics MxMa and DVg appeared in Period VI but not Period IV. The newly attested macroscopic fabric MxMa was the most common Cycladic fabric other than Melian/Theran ones in Area B. Cycladic fabrics, including those from Melos and/or Thera, made up a much larger proportion of the imports in Area B (around 40% of total [n = 73] imports) than they had in Period IV (Tables 5.5, 6.3). This may be reflective of a change in import patterns that began in Period V when Melian/Theran wares began to be imported in greater quantities (Abell 2016, 76, 83). The appearance of a variety of Cycladic fabrics that derive from islands other than Melos and/or Thera could suggest that more Cycladic communities were producing ceramics for exchange and/or had better access to longer-distance networks than previously, although further analysis of the full assemblages of Periods IV and VI is necessary to determine how significant these differences are, given the limited quantity of pottery in Area B. Cycladic imports included tablewares, large closed vessels, and miscellaneous other vessels, as in Period IV.

The percentage of probable Cretan imports in Area B was less than half the percentage of Cycladic imports, in stark contrast to the relative proportions in Period IV. The range of Cretan fabrics was also more restricted than it had been in Period IV. Many of the coarser fabrics associated with Minoan/-izing wares in Period IV are rare or absent in Period VI deposits (e.g., FSTc, FSTe, FSTf, FSTi), a significant shift in exchange patterns in comparison with the previous period. In contrast, the main Cretan fabric in Period VI, FSTa, was rare in Period IV. These changes in fabrics could reflect a shift in exchange partners between Ayia Irini and different Cretan communities by Period VI, although additional sampling and analysis is needed to support this hypothesis. Although tablewares were more common among Cretan and Minoanizing Lustrous Painted vessels than among Minoan/-izing imports in Period IV, it is not possible to ascribe many of these Lustrous Painted vessels specifically to a Cretan origin. The largest group of imported Lustrous Painted tablewares was in fine fabric FSTj, and at least some of them may come from the mainland (Ch. 3, Appendix IV).

The range of mainland fabrics was also somewhat different from those that appeared in Period IV. Although FVa continued to be well represented, additional fabrics appeared: FSTd and FVc, although the only FVc vessel was probably a Period VII intrusion (**112**). Group FVd was rare in Period IV but was as common as group FVa in Period VI. Imports from the mainland made up a similar proportion of the Period VI assemblage in Area B in comparison with Period IV, although mainland imports in Period IV deposits in Area B are underrepresented compared to published deposits (Ch. 5). As noted above, at least some fine Lustrous Painted imports in group FSTj may derive from the mainland, as well.

MANUFACTURE

In Period VI deposits, local vessels constructed using the potter's wheel were much more common than in Period IV. Some were clearly wheel-coiled; others were classed as wheelmade (see Ch. 3 for this terminology). There is no evidence that local vessels were thrown "off the hump," including handleless cups, most of which were wheel-coiled (**42, 46–52, 80–92**).

Unlike Period IV, when all wheel-coiled vessels were Minoanizing, by Period VI, there were no clear patterns dictating what vessels were handmade versus wheelmade (see also Gorogianni, Abell, and Hilditch 2016, 208–212). Both Minoanizing and non-Minoanizing vessels were sometimes made with the potter's wheel (e.g., **40–42, 46–53, 55, 80–93, 706**). Several shapes were sometimes made with the wheel but sometimes made by hand, including both Minoanizing shapes like straight-sided/Vapheio cups (**41, 100**) and non-Minoanizing shapes like Cycladic cups (**96, 102**). In addition to tablewares, cooking (**44**) and larger closed vessels also sometimes were made with the potter's wheel in Period VI, a trend that had begun in Period V (Gorogianni, Abell, and Hilditch 2016, 205, 211, tables 3, 4).

Vessels that were handmade, like those made with the potter's wheel, could be small or large, open or closed, painted or plain, Minoanizing or not. The diversity of forming techniques applied to the same kinds of shapes across the assemblage probably reflects the existence of multiple production units that made different choices about how to form particular shapes.

Although the idea of wheel-forming seems to have been closely linked with the production of Minoanizing shapes in Period IV at Ayia Irini, that connection broke down by Period VI, given how many non-Minoanizing vessels were made with it. The use of the potter's wheel over time probably reconfigured local understanding of the cultural connections of this technology, as subsequent generations of potters were trained in the use of this technique within the local community of practice (Abell and Gorogianni 2019, 658). By Period VI, the potter's wheel may have been perceived primarily as a local technology rather than an explicitly Minoanizing one since it had been used at Ayia Irini for well over a century.

Local and imported vessels with push-through handles did not appear in Period VI deposits in Area B, despite the popularity of this method of handle attachment in Periods III and IV. In Period IV, this method of handle attachment was more closely associated with mainland- and Cycladic-style shapes than Cretan-style ones. Likewise, potter's marks like those used in Period IV for non-Minoanizing shapes were not common in the highly Minoanized assemblage of Period VI. Since neither pot-marking nor attaching handles by pushing through were usual in the local *chaînes opératoires* of making Minoanizing shapes in Period IV, the decreased use of these techniques by Period VI may be tied to the increased production of Minoanizing shapes rather than to a dramatic shift in the organization of production or the replacement of local potting traditions by an influx of nonlocal potters.

TABLE 6.6. COMMON TABLEWARES IN PUBLISHED PERIOD VI DEPOSITS.

With respect to the number of local (3282), imported (279), and total (3561) vessels (after Cummer and Schofield 1984; Schofield 2011). Because handleless cups were so numerous in Period VI, a calculation of the relative percentages of other shapes with respect to the number of local (220), and total (499) vessels, not including local handleless cups, was also made in order to demonstrate more clearly the relative proportions of other shapes.

Shape	% of local	% of local (minus handleless cups)	% of imports	% of total	% of total (minus handleless cups)
Minoanizing					
Handleless cup	93%		4%	86%	
Straight-sided/Vapheio cup	1%	12%	8%	1%	10%
Rounded cup	<1%	2%	8%	1%	5%
Hole-mouthed/bridge-spouted jar/jug	<1%	4%	4%	1%	4%
Non-Minoanizing					
Goblet	<1%	7%	4%	1%	5%
Piriform cup	<1%	4%	4%	1%	4%
Cycladic cup	<1%	1%	1%	<1%	1%

Certainly, many other aspects of local production practices, especially with respect to clay selection, paste processing, and firing were very consistent between Periods IV and VI, which suggests that shifts in other aspects of local ceramic manufacture were rooted in choices made by members of the established Keian community of practice (Ch. 3).

With the exception of a few fine, closed vessels, most imported Cycladic (non-Melian/Theran) vessels in Area B seem to have been made using a potter's wheel, including open (**57, 59, 61, 94, 105**) and small closed vessels (**58, 104**). Among Melian/Theran fabrics, open vessels (**60, 62, 66, 95**) were made using RKE, while larger, closed shapes (**64, 65, 106, 709**) and a piriform cup in an unusual fabric (**67**) were probably handmade. All of the shapes above, with the exception of piriform cups (**62, 67**) and sherds from closed vessels of indeterminable profile, were Minoanizing.

About half of the vessels in possible Aeginetan fabrics were handmade, while the other half were probably made using a potter's wheel. Small, open and larger closed vessels existed in both categories, although the closed vessels were more regularly handmade.

Imported vessels in mainland fabrics in Area B, regardless of ware, fabric, or shape, were nearly all wheelmade, when forming method could be determined. The exception was a handmade narrow-necked hydria or jar (**710**).

Fine, open and closed vessels in probable Cretan fabrics in Period VI deposits were, for the most part, wheelmade. Some coarser, closed vessels were made using a potter's wheel, while others were probably handmade (e.g., **75**).

IMPORTATION AND CONSUMPTION PATTERNS

Imports from the mainland and Aegina, Crete, and the Cyclades were all relatively common in Period VI. Although more fabrics (and perhaps more producers) seem to be represented among Cycladic and mainland imports, fewer existed among Cretan ones when compared with Period IV deposits in Area B.

As in Period V, the functional variety of shapes imported from Melos and/or Thera is similar to those imported from Crete, including tablewares like cups and jugs, large and small closed vessels like jars and askoi, or special function vessels like rhyta (Fig. 59). A similarly wide functional range of shape categories was imported in other (non-Melian/Theran) Cycladic wares. Among both Melian/Theran and other Cycladic imports, tablewares were more common than large closed vessels, while tablewares and large closed vessels are more equally represented among Minoan wares in published deposits. It is possible that these patterns have been impacted by discard and/or publication patterns, which might have discriminated more heavily against coarser, plain, or simply decorated sherds in Cycladic wares in comparison with more highly decorated and hard-fired Cretan imports. Yet, similar patterns are also apparent in Area B, where sherds from plain and simply slipped closed vessels in Melian/Theran and other Cycladic fabrics are still present among the extant ceramics, alongside decorated Cretan ones. Some of these vessels (Cretan and Cycladic) are represented only by body sherds. This suggests that the functional differences represented among Cretan vs. Cycladic wares may reflect an actual differentiation in import patterns during Period VI. In any case, it is also significant that there is a wide functional range of shapes represented among imports from both regions.

Standard Matt Painted and some Matt Painted vessels probably were made on Aegina, and Aeginetan fabrics were relatively well represented in Area B. Matt Painted imports were varied, including tablewares and large closed shapes in addition to a krater. Most Standard Matt Painted imports were large closed vessels.

In Period V, imported mainland wares became significantly less popular than they had been in Period IV (Abell 2016, 76, table 2), but this trend reversed in Period VI. Most shapes imported in probable mainland fabrics were open, especially goblets and cups. This pattern is similar to that which had existed in Period IV, when the primary imports from the mainland were drinking shapes. The precise production areas of Mainland Lustrous Painted, Burnished, Yellow Minyan, and plain wares are unclear. Gray Minyan and Mainland Polychrome wares at Ayia Irini were probably produced in central Greece (including Euboea). In Area B, most mainland fabrics also may derive from central Greece, Euboea, and/or Attica. As in Periods IV and V, Gray Minyan ware imports were primarily open shapes, mainly cups (Fig. 59). Similarly, most or all shapes of Mainland Burnished, Yellow Minyan, and Lustrous Painted vessels were open, with the most common shapes being Lustrous Painted straight-sided/Vapheio cups and rounded cups. Jars and other large, closed shapes were only found in Matt Painted, plain, and Mainland Polychrome wares. Despite the abundance of different mainland wares, this seems to be a pattern of importation similar to that which had existed in previous periods, with nearly two-thirds of all mainland imports being fine, open vessels and less than 20% being jars or large, closed shapes, mainly in Mainland Polychrome ware, which might be derived from Pink-Orange ware (Overbeck 2010). Nevertheless, there was significantly more variability in the kinds of shapes being imported from the mainland than there had been in the MBA (Ch. 5).

In general, imported fine, open vessels were most common in mainland wares (Figs. 57–59). After mainland wares, fine, open vessels were nearly equally represented in Melian/Theran, Minoan, and unknown wares. Askoi and other small closed vessels were most common in Minoan, mainland, and Melian/Theran wares. Jugs and ewers were most common in Cycladic and mainland wares, while hole-mouthed/bridge-spouted jars were most common in Melian/Theran and Minoan wares. Jars and large closed vessels, on the other hand, were most common in Minoan wares but existed also in mainland (mainly Mainland Polychrome), Aeginetan, and Melian/Theran wares. Rhyta were most common in Minoan wares, but a few Cycladic and Melian/Theran rhyta were also imported.

All major imported shapes were also locally produced, including the most common drinking shapes in imported wares: rounded cups, straight-sided/Vapheio cups, piriform cups, and goblets (Table 6.6). In addition, all of the most common drinking shapes were imported from multiple regions. The only possible exception is goblets, imported primarily in mainland wares and, very rarely, Red Coated ware, which cannot be closely tied with one region of production.

SUMMARY

Major changes mark the Period VI ceramic assemblage in comparison with Periods IV and V. Different fabrics were imported, and several shapes were better represented in multiple wares, especially from the mainland and Cyclades. Melian/Theran imports, as in Period V, covered a similar functional range as Cretan imports, but other Cycladic and mainland imports were also more varied than they had been in Periods IV and V. In addition to Minoan imports from Crete, Minoanizing pottery was imported from Melos and/or Thera, other Cycladic islands, and the mainland. As in Period V, much locally produced pottery in Period VI was Minoanizing in shape and/or decorative motifs. Yet, among both local and imported Cycladic painted wares, vessels that were Minoanizing in decoration were not always based on Cretan shapes and vice versa, while motifs were not always derivative of Cretan prototypes.

Among drinking shapes, non-Minoanizing goblets and piriform cups continued to make up a significant part of the tableware assemblage, alongside Minoanizing shapes like handleless, rounded, and straight-sided/Vapheio cups (Table 6.6). Cycladic cups, on the other hand, a standard shape of Period IV and V, were much less popular. The decline in importance of this shape, as well as the remarkable increase in the production and use of handleless cups, suggests that drinking and eating practices in Period VI had changed in significant ways from such practices in the MBA. Nevertheless, the ceramic assemblage of Ayia Irini incorporated shapes and wares associated with several regions, and local residents continued to engage in eating, drinking, and cooking practices connected with different parts of the Aegean, despite the clear popularity of those derived from Crete. This pattern continued in Period VII.

VII. PERIOD VII CERAMIC ANALYSIS

Period VII represents, in many ways, the *floruit* of Ayia Irini. Most LBA architecture preserved at the site was in use at this time, and the majority of artifacts, including many imported ceramics from mainland Greece, Crete, and the Aegean islands, were found in destruction deposits of Period VII (Schofield 1984b, 179). The beginning of this period, like Period VI, was primarily defined on the basis of its association with ceramic imports (LM IB/LH II), rather than architectural changes (Caskey 1972, 393–395; 1979; Schofield 1984b, 181–182). Caskey (1979) considered Period VII to have ended with a major earthquake.

Subsequent analyses by Schofield defined three chronological subdivisions. In Schofield's scheme, Period VIIa began after an earthquake at the end of Period VI, which left deposits in House A; that phase ended with a destructive event, perhaps another earthquake, which left deposits in House A, the Western Sector, and other parts of the site (Cummer and Schofield 1984, 32–33, 142; Schofield 1984b, 179; 2011). Most Period VIIa deposits were small, possibly because much of the debris was removed during cleanup and rebuilding after the destruction (Schofield 1984b, 179). Period VIIb started after the Period VIIa destruction and ended with a major earthquake. Period VIIb was distinguished by more variety in ceramic shapes and motifs, especially in Lustrous Painted wares; many ceramics were either imported or have clear connections to LM IB and LH II pottery (Cummer and Schofield 1984, 142–144; Schofield 1984b, 179). Mycenaean imports in Period VIIb deposits mainly dated to LH IIA, with a few early LH IIB types present, as well (Cummer and Schofield 1984, 143–144; Hershenson 1998). Period VIIc postdated the earthquake and was associated with cleanup and reoccupation just after that disaster (Hershenson 1998, 162; Schofield 1984b, 182; 2011). Period VIIc deposits included many LH IIB imports but none of LH IIA (Hershenson 1998).

OVERVIEW OF PERIOD VII POTTERY

Many deposits of Period VII from House A and the Western Sector have been published (Cummer and Schofield 1984; Schofield 2011). Two small Period VIIa deposits exist in House B (B607CL, B03-108). Ceramics from the lower destruction deposits in House B (B606CL, B609CL) date to Period VIIb, although a few later ceramics are also present. Pottery from the upper parts of the destruction deposits dates to Period VIIb–c, probably because these deposits include material that eroded down the slope into Area B after the earthquake.

Quantifications of ceramics from Area B are based on deposits in the house (B03-70, B03-71a, B03-108, B03-809, B604CL–B609CL), as well as B03-148 from Room B.8 and B646CL from Alley AB. Relative proportions of ceramics from published deposits were calculated using the principles outlined in Chapters 5 and 6. Several issues with the way ceramics are presented in the House A and Western Sector catalogues impact the way that I counted and described published pottery. Matt Painted wares from the mainland vs. Aegina were not routinely distinguished from one another in the catalogues. Both local and imported vessels were categorized together as Cycladic Painted ware in the House A catalogue. Although the authors sometimes noted probable local vessels, or they included clay descriptions that enable an assessment provenance, these practices were not universal. Although an effort was made to distinguish between local and imported Cycladic vessels subsumed under "Cycladic Painted" ware, it is possible that some local products may have been included in the count of "Cycladic Painted" vessels, which I otherwise consider to be primarily imports. In both catalogues, vessels categorized as "Plain" appear to be mainly imports, while those categorized as "Coarse" appear to be mostly local. All "Plain" vessels, therefore, were counted as imports of unknown provenance, and "Coarse" vessels were counted as local, unless otherwise specified in the catalogues. The results of the quantifications of published deposits are presented in Figs. 60–63.

LOCAL

In Period VII, the most common ware by far in published deposits of all phases was plain. This pattern is owed partially—but not entirely—to the presence of thousands of plain handleless cups (Figs. 60–62; Cummer and Schofield 1984; Schofield 2011). Even when handleless cups are excluded from the calculations, local painted wares (almost entirely Yellow Slipped) made up only around 5% of total (n = 787) published local vessels, while Burnished wares were extremely rare. This pattern may have changed through time. Painted wares were proportionally somewhat more common in Period VIIa than VIIb deposits, whereas only plain

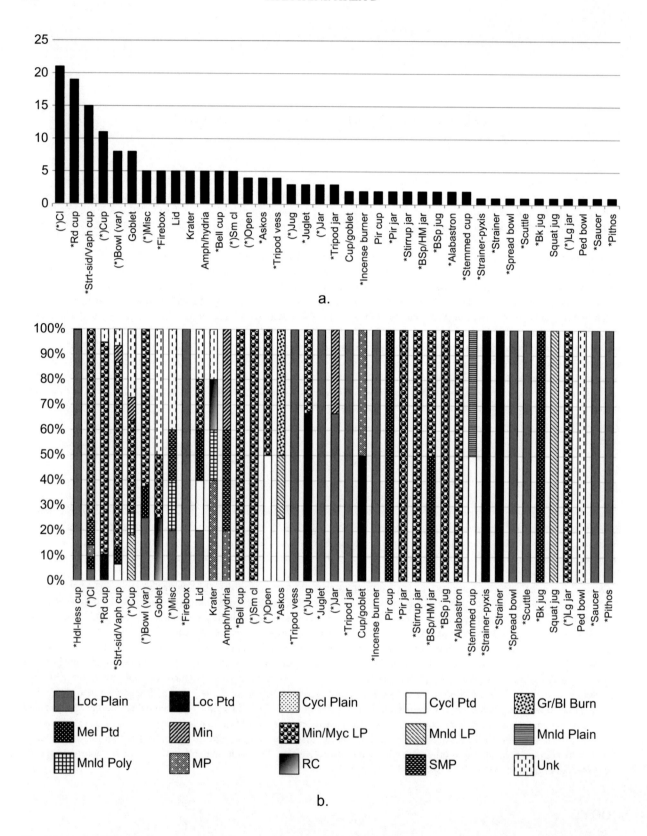

Fig. 60. Number (a) and relative proportions by ware (b) of common shapes other than handleless cups (n = 1445) in published Period VIIa deposits, based on a count of vessels reported by Cummer and Schofield (1984) and Schofield (2011). Total vessels 169. Shapes marked "*" are Minoan or Minoanizing. Shapes marked "(*)" include some versions that are Minoan or Minoanizing, but others that are not.

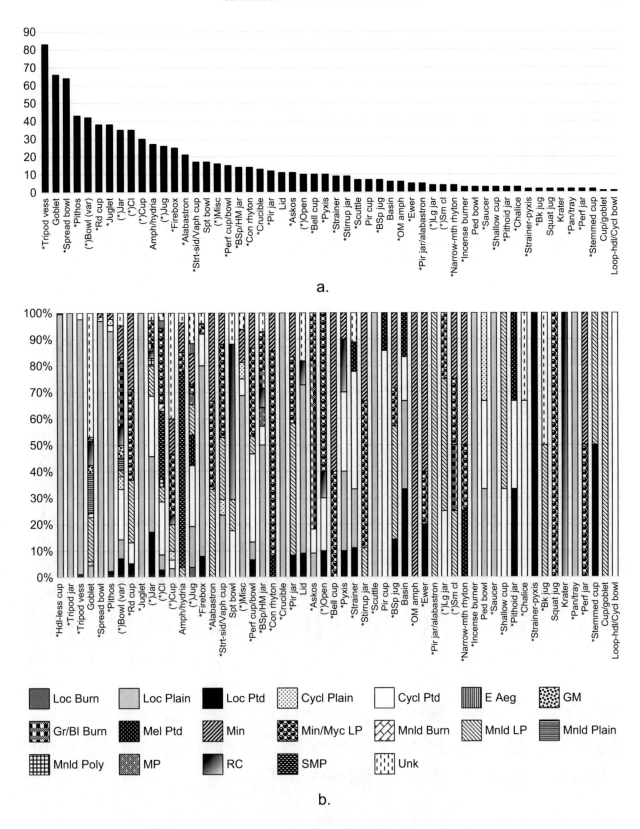

Fig. 61. Number (a) and relative proportions by ware (b) of common shapes other than handleless cups (n = 7150) and tripod jars (n = 326) in published Period VIIb deposits, based on a count of vessels reported by Cummer and Schofield (1984) and Schofield (2011). Tripod vessels included here are those that are reported as having a shape other than canonical tripod cooking jars. Total vessels 850. Shapes marked "*" are Minoan or Minoanizing. Shapes marked "(*)" include some versions that are Minoan or Minoanizing, but others that are not.

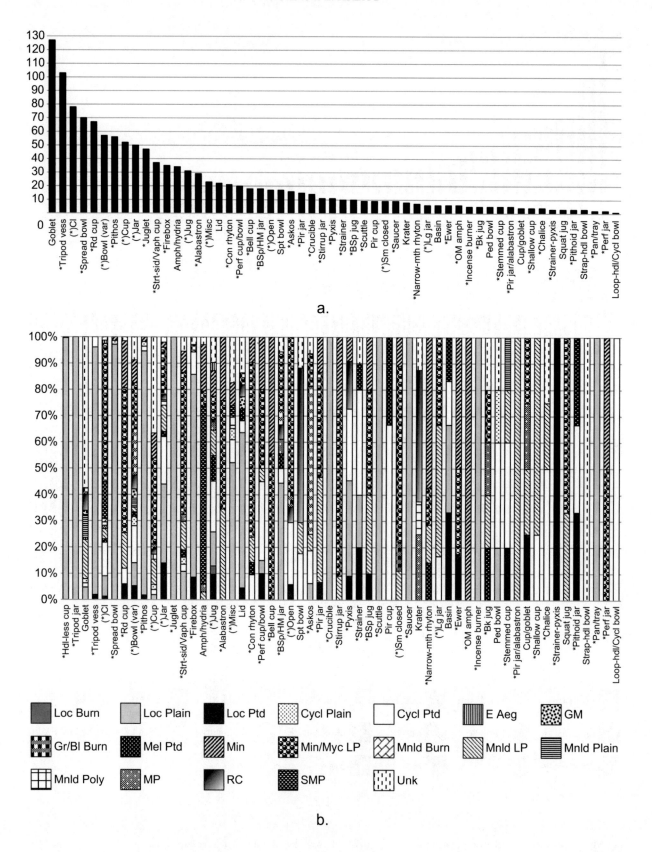

Fig. 62. Number (a) and relative proportions by ware (b) of common shapes other than handleless cups (n = 10,885) and tripod jars (n = 329) in published Period VII deposits of all phases, based on a count of vessels reported by Cummer and Schofield (1984) and Schofield (2011). Total vessels 1245. Shapes marked "*" are Minoan or Minoanizing. Shapes marked "(*)" include some versions that are Minoan or Minoanizing, but others that are not.

wares were reported from Period VIIc deposits. Few Period VIIa and even fewer Period VIIc deposits have been published, however, so additional research on unpublished assemblages is necessary to support this hypothesis. On the basis of the publications, there do not seem to be major changes in the shapes represented across local wares from Period VIIa–c.

The low number of local painted wares counted in published deposits may have been impacted by the fact that local and imported Cycladic Painted vessels were not always distinguished from one another in the House A catalogue, as noted above (Cummer and Schofield 1984). Certainly, in Area B, painted ware is proportionally more common than in published deposits. Over 15% of total (n = 195) local vessels in Area B had painted decoration, including mostly Yellow Slipped, but also Yellow Painted and Painted wares. (All vessels in RBM fabrics are considered local for the purposes of this discussion.) Around 3% of total local vessels in Area B were Burnished, although more than half are probably Period IV intrusions. Plain vessels (including handleless cups) made up just over 80% of the total. Area B also has relatively few handleless cups (only 306 total, including those that have been discarded) in comparison with House A and the Western Sector, where some individual deposits have hundreds of handleless cups. The low number of plain handleless cups in the preserved part of House B means that other local shapes and wares are proportionally better represented in the assemblage. Despite these differences between Area B and published deposits, it is clear that plain ware became proportionally more common, while Painted and Burnished wares became less common in Period VII in comparison with Periods V and VI.

Closed vessels, jugs (e.g., **136, 184, 344, 345**), rounded cups, and various bowls were common shapes in local painted wares; most were *Yellow Slipped*. Many other shapes appeared only one or two times. Some were Minoanizing, while others were not (e.g., Cummer and Schofield 1984, nos. 671, 1645). In Area B, Minoanizing shapes included rounded cups (**347, 349**) and a cup-rhyton (**346**), while a Yellow Slipped(?) goblet or pedestaled bowl (**576**) as well as Yellow Slipped and plain basins (**441, 446**) were non-Minoanizing. Several handleless cups (**348, 442, 443**) were slipped yellow but preserved no evidence for painted decoration. Yellow Painted ware was rare in Area B, as elsewhere, and included only a handleless cup (**350**) and a firebox (**440**).

Yellow Slipped vessels could be painted with one color but many were bichrome or polychrome painted (including the Red and Black style), with black, brown, and/or red motifs. Minoanizing shapes, like rounded cups, were often painted with Minoanizing motifs like spirals (Cummer and Schofield 1984, no. 992; Schofield 2011, no. 822). As in Period VI, however, some painted vessels were not Minoanizing in shape or decoration, such as piriform cups, which were sometimes painted in the paneled style (e.g., Cummer and Schofield 1984, nos. 410, 1112).

Many shapes that appeared in local painted wares were paralleled in the local plain assemblage, as in the previous period. This pattern is true not only of relatively well-represented shapes like rounded cups but also for shapes that were new and unusual in Period VII. For example, a Yellow Slipped bowl with flat, horizontal handles and a deep, rounded profile (Schofield 2011, 133, no. 1551, pl. 67) was paralleled by a plain bowl from House A (Cummer and Schofield 1984, 72, no. 421, pl. 55). New, unusual shapes in the local assemblage also have parallels on Crete and in Minoanized assemblages elsewhere in the Aegean. The bowl with horizontal handles, for example, is similar to Lustrous Painted bowls from Deposit μ at Kastri on Kythera, a Phylakopi III-ii deposit, and LM IA final deposits at Ayia Triada on Crete (Barber 1974, 15, no. 138; Coldstream and Huxley 1972, 130, nos. μ-17, 18, fig. 42, pl. 33; Dawkins and Droop 1910–1911, pl. X:138; Puglisi 2011, 271–272, fig. 4:f for a smaller version without handles). A local bichrome painted double-rimmed jug has an imported parallel from the Temple and also in vessels from Phylakopi and Koukonisi on Lemnos, all of which seem to be modeled on a rare Minoan shape (Atkinson et al. 1904, 136, pl. XXVII:8, 9; Boulotis 2009, 188–189, fig. 11:b; Caskey 1964, 328, pl. 56:d; Schofield 2011, 71, no. 815, pl. 51; Scholes 1956, 25). A local plain pedestaled jar and an imported Cycladic Painted one from House A (Cummer and Schofield 1984, 78, 123, nos. 591, 1522, pls. 58, 83) are similar to a painted high-footed jar and a plain pedestaled jar found in LM IB deposits at Chania (Andreadaki-Vlazaki 2011, 66–69, figs. 16:g, 20:b). Andreadaki-Vlazaki (2011, 67–69) suggested that these jars were based on Egyptian prototypes; the shape is apparently rare or unknown on Crete outside of Chania (Betancourt in Brogan and Hallager 2011, 88).

Perforated shapes of various kinds became common among local (and imported, below) wares in Period VII. Some of these, especially strainer-pyxides and their associated lids, were usually painted, sometimes with one color and sometimes in the Red and Black style (Cummer and Schofield 1984, nos. 983–986; Georgiou 1986, nos. 173, 174, 176; Schofield 2011, no. 311). The shape may have been used for the storage of sponges or the production and use of aromatics (Georgiou 1986, 43–44; Hallager 2011, 175, 179–180; for similar vessels on Crete, see Andreadaki-Vlazaki 1987, fig. 2; pls. 5–8; 2011, 69–70, fig. 21:e; Hood 2011, 165–166, figs. 31, 32; Tsipopoulou and Alberti 2011, 480, fig. 27). The lid for the Cretan versions is more domed than the nearly flat lid from Ayia Irini. The fact that different kinds of perforated vessels were sometimes painted, in some cases quite elaborately, may suggest that some of these painted perforated vessels were used in the course of activities that had social or performative components, rather than in the course of purely practical industrial activities. Painted perforated vessels included various other kinds of strainers, as well as rhyta, which are usually associated with ritual pouring and/or drinking activities. Many were imported (below), and local versions also exist, including cup-rhyta and perforated piriform jars (Cummer and Schofield 1984, no. 672; Schofield 2011, no. 2307).

Rare *Burnished* vessels included a blossom bowl and a neck-handled jug (Cummer and Schofield 1984, no. 1170; Schofield 2011, 179). Ceramic blossom bowl imitations were somewhat common on Kythera but are rare elsewhere, including on Crete (Coldstream and Huxley 1972, 286, pls. 76:20–24, 81:16; Cummer and Schofield 1984, nos. 361, 1170; for a blossom bowl from Tsoungiza that is hypothesized to be a Keian import, Rutter 2020, 556). In Area B, the only Burnished vessels were a goblet and possibly a small jug (**351**) that was fired to dark gray, perhaps in imitation of Gray Minyan or Gray/Black Burnished ware.

Handleless cups were the most common *plain* vessels by far. Types 1–6 and miniature versions were represented in published deposits. Types 1 and 3 were most common throughout Period VII (Cummer and Schofield 1984, 49–138; Schofield 2011, nos.

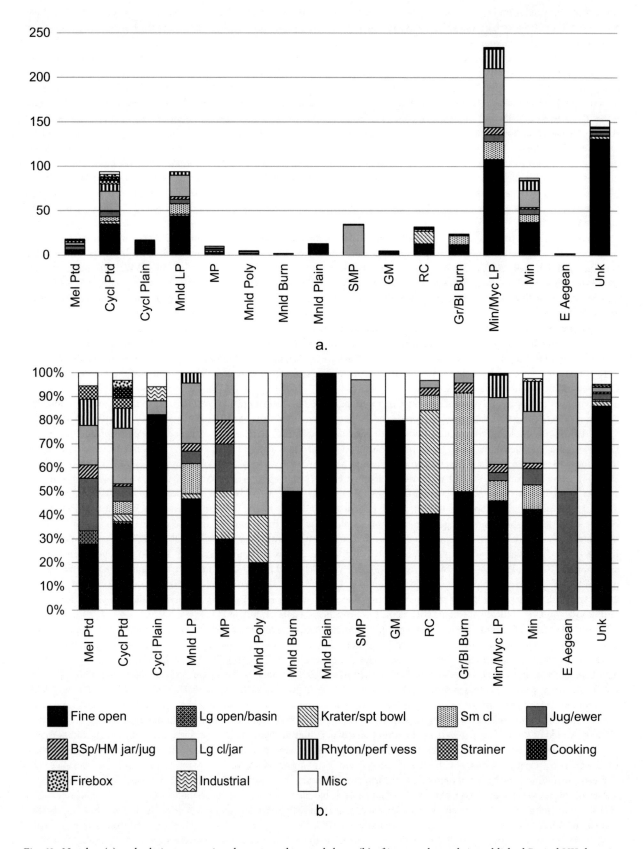

Fig. 63. Number (a) and relative proportions by ware and general shape (b) of imported vessels in published Period VII deposits of all phases, based on a count of those reported by Cummer and Schofield (1984) and Schofield (2011). Total imported vessels 824. Some Cycladic Painted and Plain vessels may be local, as discussed in Chapter 7.

2137, 2138, 2184–2199, 2338–2472). Gillis (1998) noted that, in comparison with Period VI, fewer handleless cups from Period VII deposits showed traces of burning, and there was less variety in shapes. In Area B, most handleless cups belonged to Type 1 (**137–143, 186, 187, 323–328, 354–369, 373–382, 385–388, 449–501, 548–555, 580–582, 752**). A few Type 3 handleless cups (nos. **370–372, 383, 384, 502–511, 556, 597**) and one of Type 4 (**512**) were also present. Several Type 1 handleless cups showed traces of burning (**140, 142, 377, 386**).

Other common plain shapes were tripod jars and other tripod vessels (including, e.g., trays, basins, dishes), spreading bowls, pithoi, juglets, and fireboxes (e.g., **144, 389, 390**), as well as various jars, crucibles, lids, and perforated vessels (including strainers, strainer-pyxides, spreading bowls, and handleless cups). Scuttles, saucers, jugs, bowls, hole-mouthed/bridge-spouted jars, goblets, incense burners (e.g., **329**), and pyxides (e.g., **185**) were also relatively well represented. Some of these shapes are clearly Minoanizing, like tripod jars, spreading bowls, juglets (e.g., **444, 445**), fireboxes, a possible imitation bell cup (**322**), and stirrup jar(?) (**353**) from Area B. Others, like flaring saucers and goblets, were non-Minoanizing. A plain bridge-spouted jar (**352**) was Minoanizing in shape, but the incised bands along the lower body are atypical of the decoration of imported Cretan vessels. A plain, coarse jar, either local or from the neighboring region, was shaped like a very large Minyan goblet (**156**).

Tripod jars and trays (tripod and flat-bottomed) were the main cooking shapes, but cooking jars derived from earlier local and mainland traditions were also present among local plain vessels (Gorogianni, Abell, and Hilditch 2017, 68–71). In Area B, cooking vessels may include several small jars (**577, 596**), a tripod tray (**578**), and a large jar, probably a tripod (**595**).

IMPORTS

In published deposits, Lustrous Painted wares were very common, making up nearly 30% of total (n = 824) imported vessels; this percentage includes both mainland and Cretan products. Mainland and Aeginetan wares made up around 20% of total published imports, with mainland Lustrous Painted ware being most common among these. Standard Matt Painted ware, probably from Aegina, made up a bit less than 5% of total imports, while other mainland and/or Aeginetan wares (Matt Painted, Mainland Polychrome, Burnished, plain, and Gray Minyan) were even rarer. Cycladic wares made up around 15% of total imports, but the largest category was Cycladic Painted ware, which, as noted above, probably includes some local vessels. Melian Painted and Cycladic plain imports were relatively rare. Cretan wares (mostly Lustrous Painted) were less common than in Period VI, making up only around 10% of total imports in published deposits. Vessels of unknown provenance are common, constituting around a quarter of total published imports. Some of these vessels were in wares like Red Coated (which seems to include products from several regions) and Gray/Black Burnished (of unknown origin). The majority, however, were imported plain wares, for which an origin was not given in published catalogues. Given their similarities to plain vessels in Area B, it is probable that many published plain imports came from the mainland. If published plain wares are counted with other mainland wares, the combined group makes up nearly 35% of total (n = 824) imports. It is difficult to consider deposits by phase because few Period VIIa and VIIc deposits have been published. On the basis of current evidence, Melian imports seem to have declined over the course of the period, while mainland imports increased in proportion.

The proportions of imports from different regions in Area B are similar to published deposits. Vessels from the mainland and Aegina were the most common by far, over 50% of the total (n = 380) imports. The majority of these were Lustrous Painted vessels from the mainland. Less common were mainland plain, Slipped, Red Coated, and Burnished imports (some of which might also be classifiable as Acropolis Burnished ware; Mountjoy 1981, 51–56; 1995, 13–14). Gray Minyan and Matt Painted vessels were extremely rare. Most Aeginetan imports were Matt Painted or Standard Matt Painted, although a few plain vessels exist. Imports from the Cyclades made up over 20% of total imports, with fewer Melian than "other Cycladic" vessels, which represent a range of fabrics. Among Melian and other Cycladic imports, Painted imports were twice as common as plain ones, while other wares, like Slipped and Burnished or Red Coated, were extremely rare. Cretan imports made up less than 10% of total imports; nearly all of these were Lustrous Painted, although a few vessels were Slipped or plain. Fine imports that cannot be associated confidently with Cretan or mainland production, almost all of which were Lustrous Painted, made up over 10% of total (n = 380) imports.

In a recent discussion of imports based on macroscopic fabric analysis in the Northern Sector and Area B, mainland imports were much more common than those from the Cyclades (including Melos) or Crete (Gorogianni and Abell, forthcoming, table 3). Cycladic imports were more common than Cretan ones, with "other Cycladic" vessels more common than those from Melos. Aeginetan imports were about as common as those from Melos. Eastern Aegean imports were very rare, as in published deposits.

In sum, every quantification that has been performed on the Period VII assemblage to date suggests that imports from the mainland were more common than imports from other regions. All quantifications also suggest that the proportion of Cretan imports declined from Period VI to Period VII, while analysis by ICP-AES also suggested that substantially more Lustrous Painted ware at Ayia Irini may be Mycenaean than Minoan (Mountjoy and Ponting 2000, esp. 167–169, 173; see also Mountjoy 1999, 865; 2004). Cycladic, and, to a lesser extent, Aeginetan imports also continued to make up an important part of the Period VII assemblage.

The most common shapes in *Cycladic Painted* ware were jars, jugs, various bowls, perforated cups and bowls, and piriform cups. Minoanizing and non-Minoanizing shapes are attested. As noted above, some published Cycladic Painted ware vessels might be local rather than imported. Nevertheless, in Area B, too, imported Cycladic Painted vessels were both Minoanizing (e.g., an askos [**518**] and bridge-spouted jug [**145**]) and non-Minoanizing (e.g., a jug[?] with paneled decoration [**177**]). Most *Melian Painted* imports from published deposits were jugs and piriform cups; a shallow cup (**583**) and bell cup (**396**) were found in Area B. Piriform cups in Melian and other Cycladic painted wares sometimes bore paneled decoration (e.g., Schofield 2011, nos. 820, 1110).

Painted decoration on both Melian and other Cycladic imports could be in one or more colors. Many imported Cycladic (including Melian) vessels imitated Minoan shapes and decorative motifs, especially spirals and foliate bands. These include rounded cups (**189, 402, 513**) decorated with bands and spirals and a Vapheio/straight-sided cup decorated with ripple pattern (**391**) from Area B. Polychrome decoration includes the Red and Black style (e.g., **392**), but not all Red and Black style vessels were Minoanizing. A Melian bathtub or basin, for example, which was painted with black linked spirals and red crescent-shaped fill (Schofield 2011, no. 2176) is similar to local, polychrome painted versions of the shape from Periods VI and VII discussed above, as well as **441** from Area B; the best parallels for these vessels are from Phylakopi and Akrotiri rather than Crete (Ch. 6). Imported Cycladic closed vessels in Area B were often decorated in the Red and Black style (**147, 148, 154, 190, 753**).

As with local wares, perforated vessels were more common among Cycladic and Melian imports (painted and plain) in Period VII than previously; they include both strainers and probable rhyta of different forms (Cummer and Schofield 1984, nos. 129, 1524, 1525; Schofield 2011, 94, nos. 2308, 2309, 2536). In Area B, such rhyta include a Melian Painted perforated piriform jar (**395**) and a Cycladic Red Coated(?) cup-rhyton (**514**). Cycladic Painted tall cups with a flaring profile are probably cup-rhyta, based on their similarities to Lustrous Painted flaring cup-rhyta in shape and the presence of reed decoration, although a perforated base is not always preserved (Cummer and Schofield 1984, nos. 1393, 1527; Schofield 2011, no. 1026).

The majority of *Cycladic plain* vessels were handleless cups. In Area B, imported Cycladic plain vessels included handleless cups (**393**), one of which was perforated (**151**), as well as a rounded cup (**394**), a basket-handled vessel (**150**), and a bridge-spouted(?) jar (**599**). An imported firebox and an unusual, burnt object, perhaps an industrial vessel, from Area B also may be from the Cyclades (**152, 178**). *Melian plain* handleless cups were also found in Area B (**155, 398, 516, 557, 584**), as were a piriform cup or stemmed jar (**397**), bridge-spouted jug (**403**), and baking tray (**517**). A few published nonlocal Cycladic plain or Slipped vessels seemed to imitate Mycenaean shapes, including two goblets and a cup that seem to be modeled on FS 263 and FS 213 (Cummer and Schofield 1984, nos. 183, 1001, 1002).

Most Aeginetan and mainland wares (other than Lustrous Painted) were individually rare, even though imports from these regions overall were common. Nearly all published *Standard Matt Painted* imports, probably from Aegina, were amphoras, hydrias, or closed vessels of unknown morphology, similar to the pattern in Periods V and VI. Possible Aeginetan imports in Area B also included a Lustrous Painted open jar(?) (**401**) and Red Coated(?) krater (**192**), Burnished and Red Coated goblets (**157, 748**), and a plain cooking jar (**159**). Most published *Matt Painted* vessels were kraters, jugs, and closed vessels; drinking shapes like a straight-sided cup and goblet also appeared. A Matt Painted paneled cup from Area B (**528**) might be an earlier intrusion, since this kind of vessel appears to have only been produced on the mainland during the late MH and LH I, at least in the Argolid (Rutter and Lindblom forthcoming). Most motifs were bands, although pendant wavy lines, semicircles, and multiple zigzags are also attested (Schofield 2011, nos. 1442, 1543, 1827, 2057, 2058). *Mainland Polychrome* imports included closed vessels, a krater, and a carinated cup (Schofield 2011, 64, 72, 132, 154, no. 825); the ware seems to have become rarer over the course of Period VII (Cummer and Schofield 1984, 80, pl. 60:a; Schofield 1984b, 181; 2011, no. 1075).

Goblets were by far the most common *plain* mainland imports, when these were designated by provenance in publications. Although closed vessels were not reported among mainland plain imports in published deposits, several narrow-necked jars were found in Area B (**416, 749**). Most published plain imports that were not associated with a region of production were goblets (FS 263). In Area B, all plain goblets were associated with mainland fabrics (**170, 171, 205**). Many Burnished (**169, 198, 200, 587**) and Slipped (**202, 332, 414, 529, 530**[?]**, 531**[?]) goblets from Area B, plus a few possible angular kylikes (**199, 201, 532**), also seem to be from the mainland.

In published deposits and in Area B, goblets (**334, 413**) were also associated with *Red Coated* ware, as were spouted bowls/kraters. (Red Coated spouted bowls/kraters were called spouted bowls by Cummer and Schofield [1984] but kraters or spouted kraters by Schofield [2011]). Red Coated goblets had rounded profiles, similar to Mycenaean Lustrous Painted goblets. The few illustrated Red Coated goblets from Period VIIa seem to have a less rounded shoulder and a less sharply everted rim than illustrated Period VIIb goblets, but too few vessels are illustrated to determine whether this is a meaningful chronological difference between the two phases. Many Red Coated vessels (including several from Area B, e.g., **334, 413, 748**) were probably imported from the mainland and/or Aegina. Macroscopic fabric analysis suggests that some Red Coated ware may also have been produced in the Cyclades, including perhaps a cup-rhyton (**514**) from Area B. Some Burnished and Red Coated goblets from Area B may have been imports from Attica, given their unusual fabric and similarities to vessels from the Acropolis wells (**160–163, 405, 519–522**; Mountjoy 1981). Published mainland *Burnished* shapes included a goblet and a closed vessel. Goblets and bowls were the most common *Gray Minyan* shapes.

The majority of published imports from the mainland were *Lustrous Painted*; over a quarter of total (n = 380) imports in Area B were mainland Lustrous Painted vessels. The most common published shapes were goblets, which were nearly twice as common as other shapes. Mainland Lustrous Painted goblets were also common in Area B (**166, 195, 525**) and include some of Ephyraean type (**167**[?]**, 585**) and some that were monochrome painted (**168, 343**). No goblets in clear Cretan fabrics or decorative styles were present in Area B or published deposits of Period VII (Cummer and Schofield 1984, 143, fn. 9). The presence of Ephyraean goblets imported from the mainland in Period VIIb destruction deposits demonstrates that these vessels were produced on the mainland before Crete (Hatzaki 2007b, 195–196; Hershenson 1998, 163; Schofield 1984b, 181; 2011, nos. 421, 1080). Ephyraean goblets in Period VIIb deposits appear to be early versions of this style; for example, an argonaut body on an Ephyraean goblet from House A resembles those of the Marine Style (Cummer and Schofield 1984, no. 1161; Hershenson 1998, 162; Mountjoy 1983, 266). Alabastra, rounded cups, piriform jars, and piriform jars/alabastra, as well as various other jars were also common in published deposits. Although Vapheio and/or straight-sided cups ascribed to mainland production were not very common in published deposits, they are well represented in mainland and mainland/Kytheran fabrics in Area B (**172, 411, 412, 533, 600**); both probable Type II (**193**) and Type III (**165**) Vapheio cups appeared. A rounded cup (**586**), an askos (**523**), a jug with possible Ephyraean decoration (**526**), and a Palace Style jar (**173**) were also associated with mainland Lustrous Painted ware in Area B. Several alabastra, mainly rounded, also were found in Area B; the best preserved can be dated to LH IIB (**407**).

Most published Cretan imports in Period VII were also *Lustrous Painted*. Common shapes among published Cretan imports were rounded cups, bell cups, alabastra, amphoras, various other cups and bowls, and various rhyta. In Area B, possible Cretan Lustrous Painted imports included a bell cup (**535**) and a rounded cup (**539**). Other possible Cretan imports in Area B included plain handleless cups and a Slipped small, closed vessel (**419, 541, 542**).

Many Lustrous Painted imports cannot be associated with a provenance. The most common shapes (including those of mainland, Cretan, and unknown provenance) were rounded cups (e.g., **418**), straight-sided/Vapheio cups, goblets, bell cups (e.g., **176, 534–536**), rhyta, piriform jars, piriform jars/alabastra, alabastra, stirrup jars, amphoras, bridge-spouted and other jugs, ewers, and various closed vessels, cups, and bowls. Despite their popularity in previous periods, hole-mouthed/bridge-spouted jars were very rare in Period VII, while bridge-spouted jugs (e.g., **207**) became more popular (Cummer and Schofield 1984, 56; Mountjoy 1999, 872). Lustrous Painted shapes and decorative motifs are paralleled in many parts of the southern Aegean, including Crete, mainland Greece, Aegina, and the Cyclades (for a thorough discussion, see Mountjoy 1999, 863–880).

Stylistic changes within Period VIIa–c are most evident in Lustrous Painted ware. A lack of variety in decorative motifs was characteristic of Period VIIa in comparison with Period VIIb (Schofield 1984b, 179–181). Two motifs were common in Period VIIa— stone pattern, either alone or as background for other motifs, and double axes. Typical Period VIIa Lustrous Painted vessels in Area B included a rounded cup (**336**) decorated with dotted scale pattern, a bell cup (**335**) painted with stone pattern, and at least two spouted bell cups painted with stone pattern (**337**). Motifs were more varied among Period VIIb–c Lustrous Painted imports, including ogival canopy, lilies, reserved rosettes, triangular groups of dots, spirals, reeds, rock pattern, and hatched loops (e.g., **164, 408, 409, 417, 524, 527, 537, 589–591, 754**). The Marine and Alternating styles did not appear in Period VIIa but were prevalent in Period VIIb deposits (Schofield 1984b, 181). Straight-sided/Vapheio cups were less common in Period VIIb than previously, while stirrup jars, bell cups, and goblets were more common. Several bell cups were decorated in the Alternating Style, although cups with inverted scale pattern and net pattern were also found (Caskey 1972, 396; Cummer and Schofield 1984, nos. 419, 682, 683, 1157, 1564, 1565; Schofield 1984b, 96, 181).

Lustrous Painted rhyta and perforated vessels also were more common in Period VIIb than in previous periods, a pattern paralleled in local and imported Cycladic wares as discussed above. Flaring cup-rhyta (Koehl's [2006] Type IV Cup: Deep-Flaring) decorated with reeds or grass were common (Caskey 1972, 395–396, no. H8, pl. 95; Cummer and Schofield 1984, 56, no. 1393 [= Koehl 2006, no. 1125, Type IV Jar: Cylindrical]; Schofield 2011, nos. 419, 2314–2316). Caskey (1972, 395–396) suggested that several flaring cup-rhyta might have been painted by the same hand. Similar Lustrous Painted vessels have been found in Deposit ξ at Kastri on Kythera and at LM IB Kato Zakro (Coldstream and Huxley 1972, 145–146, nos. ξ-112–114, fig. 45, pl. 39; Koehl 2006, 229–230). Several versions of this shape, all painted with closely spaced reeds, were found in Area B (**174, 175[?], 538[?]**). Other Lustrous Painted rhyta and perforated shapes include cup-rhyta, perforated jars with different morphologies (e.g., **404**), peg-top, and pear rhyta (Cummer and Schofield 1984, nos. 175–177, 179, 995, 999, 1140, 1221, 1559–1561; Schofield 2011, nos. 2180, 2313, 2318; Koehl [2006] describes most peg-top rhyta as Type II HL Piriform, rarely, Type II HL Ovoid, while the pear rhyton is categorized by Koehl as Type II NH Ovoid). Conical rhyta (including both Koehl's [2006] Type III CV and Type III S Conical), often bearing zones of curved stripes, were common in Period VIIb deposits (Cummer and Schofield 1984, nos. 1049, 1149, 1197, 1440, 1556–1558; Schofield 2011, nos. 645, 646). This may be a mainland rather than Cretan motif, although it is rare even in the mainland (Mountjoy 1999, 876). Mountjoy (1999, 876) hypothesized that these vessels were made by a Mycenaean production center specifically to meet demand in the Cyclades.

In Period VIIc, many open shapes in Lustrous Painted and other fine mainland wares were imported. Acropolis Burnished ware was common, while LH monochrome imports were rare (Hershenson 1998, 165). Cretan imports were also rare (e.g., Cummer and Schofield 1984, 60). Imported *plain* goblets were very common, in two varieties. One had a shape similar to that of the Ephyraean goblet (FS 263), and another was small and shallower (e.g., Cummer and Schofield 1984, 60–62). Goblets of all sorts were more common in the upper part (VIIb–c) than the lower (VIIb) part of the destruction deposits in House B, while possible angular kylikes appeared only in the upper part. In Area B, goblets from both parts of the destruction deposit were similar in shape. By Period VIIc, most fine tablewares were apparently imported from the mainland, while coarser closed imports were primarily in Standard Matt Painted ware (Hershenson 1998, 164–165).

Gray/Black Burnished ware, of unknown origin, included mainly small or miniature shapes, especially bowls and askoi. A Gray/Black Burnished straight-sided cup (**421**), a miniature open vessel (**420**), and a lid (**208**) were found in Area B. *Eastern Aegean* imports were rare in published deposits; all were jugs or closed vessels (Davis et al. 1983, 363; see also Knappett and Hilditch 2015b, 203 for possible Milesian imports).

SYNCHRONISMS

Summaries of Period VII synchronisms by phase can be found in Tables 7.1–7.3.

The earliest LM IB and LH IIA imports were found in Period VIIa deposits (Schofield 1984b, 181). Period VIIa was contemporary with an early stage of LM IB, during which the Marine and Alternating styles were not produced or were produced in limited quantities (Schofield 1984b, 181). An early LM IB phase with little Marine Style pottery has been suggested for several Cretan sites, including Malia and Palaikastro, but the division between the LM IA and LM IB ceramic phases across the island remains unclear (Brogan and Hallager 2011, 629–646; Niemeier 2011; van de Moortel 2011, 538–539). Warren (2007, 498) also has suggested that LH IIA may also have overlapped the very end of LM IA, based especially on the presence of an LH IIA bridge-spouted jug in an LM IA deposit in House B Room 10 at Palaikastro. The presence or absence of ripple pattern has been suggested to be a marker for the division between LM IA (ripple) and LM IB early (no ripple), but this distinction is not helpful for Ayia Irini, given the close ceramic connections with the mainland, where, as at Ayia Irini, ripple decoration continued to be in vogue in LH IIA/Period VII (Mountjoy 1999, 865; Schofield 2011, nos. 1546, 1840).

The presence of the Marine and Alternating Styles demonstrates that Period VIIb was contemporary with LM IB. The precise relation of the end of Period VIIb with the end of LM IB, however, is impossible to establish with confidence. At Chania and Mochlos, there may have been a final stage of LM IB with no Marine Style pottery in circulation (Andreadaki-Vlazaki 2011, 71; Andreadaki-Vlazaki and Brogan in Brogan and Hallager 2011, 633). If such a phase existed in other parts of Crete, it would be possible to suggest that Period VIIb ended before the LM IB phase did, and that Period VIIc (which also lacks these styles) was contemporary with the latest part of LM IB, at least partially. Yet, other evidence suggests that Period VIIb may have ended near the end of LM IB. For example, the vertical separation of decorative elements on some imported vessels in Period VIIb deposits anticipates LM II decoration (Cummer and Schofield 1984, 143). Several elements dated to a late stage of LM IB on Crete exist in Period VIIb deposits, including horizontal-handled bowls, cups with everted rather than flaring rims, and Alternating Style vessels painted with Mountjoy's Type C octopuses (Barnard and Brogan 2011, 436–439; Betancourt 2011, 408–412; Mountjoy 2011; Rutter 2011, 313–324; van de Moortel 2011, 533, 542–543).

There is little evidence that would help associate Period VIIc with the confused chronology of Crete at the LM IB–II transition, apart from the absence of Marine Style in Period VIIc deposits. Period VIIc, with its plethora of goblet shapes, might overlap some or all of LM II, the first period in which goblets and kylikes were used on Crete (Popham 1969, 299; see also Rutter 2011, 320). Although the vast majority of goblets at Ayia Irini were imported from the mainland, connecting Period VIIc with some or all of LM II works well with J. L. Caskey's association of Period VIII with LH/LM IIIA (Caskey 1979; Morris and Jones 1998). A very few Minoan Ephyraean goblets are reported from mixed Period VII–VIII and VIII deposits (Cummer and Schofield 1984, 143, fn. 9, 146), which may suggest, however, that LM II overlaps some of Period VIII instead of, or in addition to, Period VIIc.

Period VIIa probably predated Kythera deposits κ and λ since the Marine and Alternating Styles were present in those Kytheran deposits; Period VIIb was probably contemporary with Kythera deposits κ, λ, μ, ν, and ξ (Coldstream and Huxley 1972, 128–148, 292–303, figs. 42–45, pls. 33–40; Cummer and Schofield 1984, 144; Schofield 1984b, 181; see also Mountjoy 1999, 864 for a more cautious interpretation).

Periods VIIa and VIIb at Ayia Irini have many parallels with Period IV at Ayios Stephanos (Rutter and Rutter 1976, 54–60, nos. 865, 880–884, 894, figs. III.17, III.18), as well as the LH IIA deposit in pit EU-10 (Group F) at Tsoungiza (Rutter 1993a; 2020, 473–474) and Schnitt 4, SE 1 at Kiapha Thiti (Maran 1992, 30–33, pls. 6, 7). Goblets and a few possible angular kylikes from Period VIIb–c destruction deposits from Area B have parallels also among plain and monochrome vessels from Schnitt 1 SE4 at Kiapha Thiti, Room C Stratum 2 at Asine, and Group G from Tsoungiza (Frizell 1980, 32–33, nos. 51–55, pl. 4; Maran 1992, 11, no. 12, pl. 1; Rutter 2020, 657–727).

For the most part, Period VIIb seems earlier than Levels V–VII of the East Alley Pit (LH IIB) at Korakou (Cummer and Schofield 1984, 144; Dickinson 1972, 106–107, pls. 33, 34). However, the presence of a few LH IIB vessels, including those in the Ephyraean style, in Period VIIb deposits suggests that the end of Period VIIb was contemporary with the transition of LH IIA–IIB (Cummer and Schofield 1984, 143; Hershenson 1998, 163; Mountjoy 1999, 865; Schofield 1984b, 181). Ceramics from Area B support this dating. Fragments of an LH IIB rounded alabastron (**407**) were found in lots B03-61 and B03-64, very low in the Period VII destruction deposit of House B. Sherds from a mended goblet (**166**) came from the lowest part of the destruction deposit, just above the floor in Room B.1; this vessel was painted with a palm in a style more like LH IIB than LH IIA, but probably repeating in a fashion more typical of LH IIA than LH IIB; the vessel had time to be made, imported, broken, and repaired before the Period VIIb earthquake occurred. Period VIIc can be associated with LH IIB on the mainland, as exemplified by Korakou East Alley Levels V–VII (Dickinson 1972, 106–107; Hershenson 1998). In a detailed, thorough discussion of LH IIB synchronisms and possible phasing, Rutter (2020, 710–717) argued that the end of Period VIIc may date to a late phase of LH IIB, rather than in LH IIIA:1, as has previously been suggested (Mountjoy 1999, 866).

Period VII was contemporary with Phylakopi III-ii (Barber 1974; Mountjoy 1985, 198–199; 1999, 889–891, 894–901; 2007). At least part of Period VIIb was contemporary with the first phase of occupation at Grotta on Naxos, which was marked by Marine Style and typical LH IIA ceramics (Cosmopoulos 1998, 134). The absence of Ephyraean goblets in the Naxian deposits may suggest that the first phase of occupation there ended before Period VIIb did.

VII. PERIOD VII CERAMIC ANALYSIS

TABLE 7.1. PERIOD VIIA SYNCHRONISMS

Region	Contemporary phases
Cyclades	Phylakopi III-ii (LC II/LH IIA/LM IB) (Barber 1974; Mountjoy 1985, 198–199; 1999, 889–891, 894–901; 2007)
Crete	(?)Malia *Abords Nord-Est*, Level 12 ("LM IB Early") (van de Moortel 2011, 538–532; van de Moortel and Darcque 2006, 182–188)
	(?)Palaikastro, lower deposit of Building 5 (Hemingway, MacGillivray, and Sackett 2011, 528–530, 551–552)
Mainland	Ayios Stephanos Period IV (Rutter and Rutter 1976, 46–60)
	Kiapha Thiti Schnitt 1, SE 4; Schnitt 5 SE 2 (Maran 1992, 10–14, 36–38)
	Korakou East Alley Levels IX–X (Dickinson 1972, 103–106)
	Tsoungiza Group F (Rutter 1993a; 2020, 473–474)

TABLE 7.2. PERIOD VIIB SYNCHRONISMS

Region	Contemporary phases
Cyclades	Grotta, first phase (LC II/LH IIA/LM IB) (Cosmopoulos 1998, 134)
	Phylakopi III-ii (LC II/LH IIA/LM IB) (Barber 1974; Mountjoy 1985, 198–199; 1999, 889–891, 894–901; 2007)
Kythera	Kastri, Deposits κ, λ, μ, ν, ξ (Coldstream and Huxley 1972, 125–148, 291–303)
Crete	Knossos, Royal Road North and North Building LM IB destruction levels (Hood 2011; Wall, Musgrave, and Warren 1986, 335–345; Warren 1980–1981, 77–89; 2011)
Mainland	Asine Room C Stratum 2 (Frizell 1980, 23–33)
	Ayios Stephanos IV (Rutter and Rutter 1976, 46–60)
	Kiapha Thiti Schnitt 1, SE 4; Schnitt 5 SE 2 (Maran 1992, 10–14, 36–38)
	Korakou East Alley Levels IX–X (Dickinson 1972, 103–106)
	Tsoungiza Group F (Rutter 1993a; 2020, 473–474)

TABLE 7.3. PERIOD VIIC SYNCHRONISMS

Region	Contemporary phases
Mainland	Acropolis Well Deposits (Mountjoy 1981)
	Asine, Room F Stratum 3 (Frizell 1980, 60–69)
	Kiapha Thiti Schnitt 4, SE 3; Schnitt 6, SE 2 (Maran 1992, 28–29, 45)
	Korakou East Alley Levels V–VII (Dickinson 1972, 106–107)
	Tiryns, House D1 (Gercke, Gercke, and Hiesel 1975, 18–26)
	Tsoungiza, Group G (Rutter 2020, 657–727)

FABRICS

An overview of macroscopic fabrics in relation to wares and shapes in Area B is provided in Table 7.4. A summary of imports by region is provided in Table 7.5. When discards are taken into consideration, RBM fabrics in Area B seem to have comprised usually about 80–95% of the assemblage, depending on the lot (Table 7.6).

As in previous periods, the most common local fabric was RBMa, which was associated with 90% of total (n = 195) extant local vessels. There are no major changes in the macroscopic characteristics of RBMa between Period VI and VII. As in Period VI, RBMa fabrics ranged between moderately fine to coarse in texture. While smaller tablewares tended to be finer than larger cooking or closed vessels, a few larger closed vessels were moderately fine, while many small vessels were relatively coarse, especially (but not exclusively) handleless cups.

Group RBMd was slightly more common than groups RBMb and RBMc, but all were relatively rare. Although at least one vessel made with fabric RBMb was probably an EBA intrusion, at least one must be contemporary with Period VII. This vessel (**579**) is extremely low fired, and the exterior surface is not finished; the vessel appears to have been built in place and may have been fired incidentally through use. The existence of this fragile vessel, as mentioned in Chapter 3, strongly suggests that RBMb is local.

RBMa was used for all kinds of shapes—large and small, open and closed, Minoanizing and non-Minoanizing—in all local wares. Likewise, the other local and "local region" fabrics groups cannot be associated with a particular ware or shape class. Petrographic samples from Period VII vessels classed macroscopically as RBMa and RBMd were both included in PFG 1A. There are no major differences in the Period VII examples of PFG 1A in comparison with previous periods. The two sampled vessels of RBMc from this period, as well as a variant of RBMa, were classed petrographically in PFG 2B. Additional sampling is needed to determine whether the association of RBMc with PFG 2B is a pattern elsewhere in the Period VII assemblage or the result of the limited number of samples in this fabric from deposits of this period.

The most common imported fabrics in Area B were closely associated with fine Lustrous Painted ware vessels. These fabrics were FSTj, FVd, FVc, FVb, and FVb/FVc, each of which made up 7–10% of total (n = 380) imports in order of decreasing frequency. Except for FSTj, of unknown Cretan or mainland provenance, the other common fabrics are from the mainland, probably including the Argolid (FVb/FVc, FVc). Despite their close association with Lustrous Painted tablewares, all of these fabrics were also associated with plain imports; several were also associated with Burnished (FVb, FVb/FVc, FVc, FVd), Red Coated (FVb/FVc, FVd), and Slipped (FVb, FVb/FVc, FVc, FVd) wares. There were no clear associations between fabrics and shapes in Lustrous Painted ware. Most common shapes were associated with multiple fabrics, with the exception of bell cups, which were all in FSTj.

Group DVe was also occasionally associated with Lustrous Painted ware and was relatively common. This fabric made up around 6% of total (n = 380) imports, but petrographic analysis suggests that the group is not coherent in terms of provenance. In Period VII, the group was composed almost entirely of fine fabrics, which probably include some mainland or Cycladic products, as well as Aeginetan ones (Ch. 3). The group encompassed several different wares, including Aeginetan(?) Bichrome, Burnished, Painted, Red Coated, Yellow Slipped, and plain wares, in addition to Lustrous Painted. Most Red Coated vessels in this fabric were open, while Painted vessels were closed. Lustrous Painted vessels were open jars. There are otherwise no close associations between ware and shape in this fabric.

Other fabrics associated with fine Lustrous Painted imports were less common and include probable mainland (FVe, FVf, MFVc) and possible Cretan (FSTk) products. These fabrics made up between 2–5% of total (n = 380) imports. FVf was most common, followed by MFVc, FSTk, and FVe. FVf (central Greece/Euboea?) was used for Burnished and plain wares, in addition to Lustrous Painted. Small open and larger closed shapes were represented in each ware associated with FVf. Only a couple of Lustrous Painted vessels were associated with MFVc (Attica?): a jar-shaped rhyton and a rounded cup. Red Coated and Burnished wares were more common in MFVc, while Slipped and plain vessels were also represented; nearly all shapes in these wares in this fabric were goblets. FSTk was associated only with Lustrous Painted vessels, most of which are probably tablewares. Plain, Matt Painted, and Lustrous Painted vessels were associated with FVe (central Greece/Euboea?); most were open, including several goblets.

Coarser fabrics associated with Lustrous Painted ware were relatively rare and include FSTh (mainland/Kythera), FSTa and FSTb (Crete), and FSTd (Argolid/Corinthia?), which each accounted for 1–3% of total (n = 380) imports, in order of decreasing frequency. FSTb, FSTd, and FSTh were associated with open and closed vessels; FSTa was associated only with closed vessels. Several other fabrics were associated with Lustrous Painted ware (FSTk/FVc, FVc/FVe, FSTg, FSTg/FSTh, and FVf/FSTj); these were very rare, each making up <1% of imports.

Fabrics DVa and MxMa were the most common Cycladic fabrics. Each represented between 5–6% of total (n = 380) imports, with DVa being somewhat more common. Other Cycladic fabrics were rarer, including MxMc, DVb, MxMf, CSWa, and DVc, each of which made up between 1–3% of total imports, in order of decreasing frequency. Fabrics DVa–c (Melian), MxMa (western Cyclades?), MxMc (Cyclades), and MxMf (Cyclades) were associated with painted and plain wares and both open and closed shapes, which were mainly but not entirely Minoanizing. All CSWa (central Cyclades) examples were closed, whether painted or plain. Other Cycladic fabrics each made up less than 1% of the imported assemblage; they include MxMa/MxMc, CSWe (Naxos), DVa/DVg (Melos?), MFVa, MxMa/DVg, MxMd, and MxMe, and as well as CSWc, hypothesized to be Attic or Cycladic.

Group DVd, probably Aeginetan, was rare (ca. 1% of imports); it was associated with Matt Painted, Standard Matt Painted, and plain vessels, both closed and open. The variant fabric group FVd/FVf, which may be from central Greece, also made up around

TABLE 7.4. OVERVIEW OF VESSELS IN PERIOD VII LOTS IN AREA B ACCORDING TO MACROSCOPIC FABRIC GROUP B03-70, B03-71a, B03-148, B03-148, B604CL–B609CL and B646CL. The total number of vessels is 575, of which 195 are in RBM fabrics (local and local region) and 380 are in imported fabrics.

Fabric group	No. of vessels	% of total	% of RBM	% of imports	Wares	Shapes
RBMa	175	30.4%	89.7%		Burnished	Goblet (1), goblet (Period IV) (1), open (Period IV?) (2), jug (1)
					EBA Black Burnished	Deep bowl (1)
					Painted	Handleless cup (1), closed (1)
					Plain	Straight-sided cup (1), handleless cup (117), goblet/stemmed cup (1), bowl (1), bowl/basin (1), basin (1), spouted jar or bowl (1), bridge-spouted jar (1), hole-mouthed jar (1), juglet (1), squat juglet (1), small closed(?) (2), stirrup jar (1), pithos (2), pithos(?) (1), closed (1), small cooking(?) vessel (1), large jar (tripod?) (1), open jar (cookpot) (1), tripod tray (1), miniature pyxis (1), firebox (3), handle (scoop?) (1)
					Yellow Painted	Firebox (1)
					Yellow Slipped	Rounded cup (3), bell cup (1), handleless cup (3), cup (1), goblet or pedestaled bowl (1), basin or barrel jar (Period IV) (1), bathtub (1), large open(?) (1), bridge-spouted jug (1), spouted jug (1), spouted jug(?) (1), basket jar(?) (1), jar (1), jar(?) (1), closed (3), small jar (cooking vessel) (1), cup-rhyton (1)
RBMd	13	2.3%	6.7%		Plain	Bell(?) cup (1), handleless cup (11), incense burner (1)
RBMc	4	0.7%	2.1%		Plain	Minyanizing goblet-shaped jar (1)
					Yellow Painted	Flaring saucer (1)
					Yellow Slipped	Bowl(?) (1), closed (1)
RBMb	3	0.5%	1.5%		EBA Red-Brown Semifine to Coarse	Deep saucer (1)
					Plain	Low-fired vessel (1)
					Yellow Painted	Closed (1)
FSTj	38	6.6%		10.0%	Lustrous Painted	Rounded cup (2), Vapheio cup (1), bell cup (4), spouted bell cup (2), cup (1), cup (rhyton?) (1), bowl (1), deep bowl (LH III) (1), open (5), large open (1), eyed jug (1), bridge-spouted jug (1), jug (2), bridge-spouted jar (1), bridge-spouted jar/jug (1), askos(?) (1), alabastron (1), alabastron(?) (1), small closed (2), closed (5), closed(?) (1)
					Non-Lustrous Painted	Small closed (1)
					Plain	Closed (1)
FVd	36	6.3%		9.5%	Black Gloss	Open (1)
					Lustrous Painted	Vapheio cup (1), goblet (5), open (5), alabastron (1), three-handled jar (1), closed (1), closed(?) (1)
					Mainland Burnished	Goblet (1), angular kylix(?) (2), basin/bowl (1), open (3)
					Mainland Slipped	Goblet (1), angular kylix(?) (1), goblet/cup (1), open (1)
					Plain	Goblet (2), basin (1), small jar (1), unknown (1)
					Red Coated	Goblet (3), open (1)

TABLE 7.4. (CONT.)

Fabric group	No. of vessels	% of total	% of RBM	% of imports	Wares	Shapes
FVc	30	5.2%		7.9%	Lustrous Painted	Vapheio cup (1), Vapheio/straight-sided cup (1), straight-sided cup (1), goblet (4), goblet or rounded cup (1), open (6), open(?) (1), jug(?) (1), alabastra (2), small closed (5), closed (1)
					Mainland Burnished	Small closed (1)
					Mainland Slipped	Goblet (1)
					Plain	Shallow cup (1), goblet (1), bowl (1), closed (1)
FVb	27	4.7%		7.1%	Lustrous Painted	Ring-handled cup (1), goblet (3), bowl (1), open (4), open (LH III?) (1), jug/jar (1), alabastron (5), closed (2), closed(?) (2)
					Mainland Burnished	Goblet (3)
					Mainland Slipped	Goblet (1)
					Plain	Goblet (3)
FVb/FVc	26	4.5%		6.8%	Lustrous Painted	Vapheio cup (1), cup (1), goblet (2), open (3), alabastron (1), closed (7), conical rhyton (1)
					Mainland Burnished	Goblet (2), goblet/cup (1), deep bowl(?) (LH III) (1)
					Mainland Slipped	Goblet (1), goblet/kylix (1)
					Plain	Rounded cup/goblet (2)
					Red Coated	Goblet (1), basin/krater(?) (1)
DVa	24	4.2%		6.3%	Melian/Theran Painted	Rounded cup (2), straight-sided cup (1), bell cup (1), shallow cup (1), Cycladic cup (1), cup/goblet (1), cup (1), shallow bowl/cup (1), bowl (1), bowl(?) (1), open (3), closed (5), jar-shaped rhyton (1)
					Melian/Theran Plain	Handleless cup (1), open (1), pan (1), vessel (1)
DVe	22	3.8%		5.8%	Aeginetan(?) Bichrome	Large open (1)
					Aeginetan(?) Burnished	Goblet (1)
					Aeginetan(?) Painted	Closed (4), closed(?) (1)
					Aeginetan(?) Yellow Slipped	Closed (1)
					Lustrous Painted	Open jar(?) (2)
					Plain	Handleless cup (1), bowl/krater (1), stemmed vessel (1), vessel (2)
					Red Coated	Goblet(?) (2), open (3), krater (1), spouted krater/basin (1)
FVf	20	3.5%		5.3%	Lustrous Painted	Open(?) (1), jug (1), jar/jug (1), closed (3), closed(?) (alabastron?) (1)
					Mainland Burnished	Goblet (4), large jar (1)
					Plain	Goblet (2), open (1), narrow-necked jar (1), jar (1), closed (2), closed(?) (1)
MxMa	19	3.3%		5.0%	Cycladic Painted	Straight-sided or bell cup (1), cup/bowl (1), bridge-spouted jug (1), jug (1), jug/jar (1), cylindrical jar (1), collar-necked jar (2), closed(?) (1)
					Cycladic Yellow Slipped	Rounded cup (2), Vapheio/straight-sided cup (1), jar (1), closed (1)
					Melian/Theran Yellow Slipped(?)	Small jug (1)
					Plain	Handleless cup (1), basket(?) (1), closed(?) (1), lid (1)

TABLE 7.4. (CONT.)

Fabric group	No. of vessels	% of total	% of RBM	% of imports	Wares	Shapes
MFVc	13	2.3%		3.4%	Lustrous Painted	Rounded cup (1), jar-shaped rhyton (1)
					Mainland Burnished	Goblet (3)
					Mainland Slipped	Open(?) (1)
					Plain	Goblet (1)
					Red Coated	Goblet (6)
MxMc	12	2.1%		3.2%	Cycladic Painted	Rounded cup (1), straight-sided cup (1), open (3), closed (2), closed(?) (1)
					Plain	Goblet/cup (1), open (2), closed (1)
FSTk	11	1.9%		2.9%	Lustrous Painted	Rounded cup (1), bell cup (1), open (4), small closed (3), closed (1), flaring cup-rhyton (1)
Unk	11	1.9%		2.9%	Gray/Black Burnished	Miniature open (1)
					Plain	Handleless cup (3), jar (1), closed (2), firebox (1), industrial vessel (1), vessel (1)
					Unknown Yellow Slipped	Closed (1)
FSTh	10	1.7%		2.6%	Lustrous Painted	Vapheio cup (2), bridge-spouted jug (1), jar (1), closed (5)
					Non-Lustrous Painted	Cup (1)
DVb	8	1.4%		2.1%	Melian/Theran Painted	Pyxis (1), closed (1)
					Melian/Theran Yellow Slipped	Jug(?) (1)
					Plain	Handleless cup (4), bridge-spouted jug (1)
FSTa	8	1.4%		2.1%	Lustrous Painted	Jug (1), jug (ewer?) (1), closed (5)
					Non-Lustrous Painted	Closed (1)
MxMf	7	1.2%		1.8%	Cycladic Painted	Rounded cup/goblet (1), ewer/jug (1), closed (1)
					Cycladic Slipped and Burnished	Small closed (1)
					Plain	Handleless cup (perforated) (1), bridge-spouted(?) jar (1), closed (1)
FVe	6	1.0%		1.6%	Lustrous Painted	Askos (1)
					Matt Painted	Paneled cup (1)
					Plain	Goblet (3), open (goblet?) (1)
FSTb	5	0.9%		1.3%	Cretan Slipped	Small closed(?) (1)
					Lustrous Painted	Jar (1), closed (1)
					Plain	Handleless cup (2)
DVd	4	0.7%		1.1%	Matt Painted	Basin(?) (Period IV) (1), closed (1)
					Plain	Handleless cup (1)
					Standard Matt Painted	Hydria (1)
FVd/FVf	4	0.7%		1.1%	Matt Painted	Hydria/jar (1)
					Plain	Large open (1), closed(?) (1)
					Red Coated	Basin (1)
CSWa	3	0.5%		0.8%	Cycladic Painted	Closed (1)
					Cycladic Yellow Slipped	Closed(?) (1)
					Plain	Closed (1)
DVc	3	0.5%		0.8%	Melian/Theran Painted	Closed (1)
					Plain	Small closed(?) (1), closed (1)

TABLE 7.4. (CONT.)

Fabric group	No. of vessels	% of total	% of RBM	% of imports	Wares	Shapes
FSTd	3	0.5%		0.8%	Lustrous Painted	Open (1), jar (1), closed (1)
CSWc	2	0.3%		0.5%	Cycladic(?) Burnished	Cup/bowl (1)
					Plain	Closed (1)
DVf	2	0.3%		0.5%	Plain	Cooking vessel (1)
					Unknown Yellow Slipped	Jug (1)
FSTf	2	0.3%		0.5%	Cretan Slipped	Closed (2)
FSTk/FVc	2	0.3%		0.5%	Lustrous Painted	Open (2)
FVc/FVe	2	0.3%		0.5%	Lustrous Painted	Goblet (1)
					Mainland Burnished	Goblet (1)
MFVb	2	0.3%		0.5%	Gray/Black Burnished	Straight-sided cup (1), lid (1)
MFVd	2	0.3%		0.5%	Mainland(?) Painted	Closed (1)
					Mainland(?) Slipped	Closed (1)
MxMa/ MxMc	2	0.3%		0.5%	Cycladic Painted	Closed (1)
					Red Coated	Cup-rhyton (1)
CSWe	1	0.2%		0.3%	Cycladic Painted	Askos (1)
DVa/DVg	1	0.2%		0.3%	Plain	Cylindrical jar (1)
DVd/DVe	1	0.2%		0.3%	Plain	Hydria/jar (1)
FSTc	1	0.2%		0.3%	Non-Lustrous Painted	Closed (1)
FSTg	1	0.2%		0.3%	Lustrous Painted	Closed (1)
FSTg/FSTh	1	0.2%		0.3%	Lustrous Painted	Jar/jug (1)
FSTk/FVd	1	0.2%		0.3%	Non-Lustrous Painted	Goblet (1)
FVa/MFVb	1	0.2%		0.3%	Gray Minyan(?)	Goblet (1)
FVf/FSTj	1	0.2%		0.3%	Lustrous Painted	Closed (1)
MFVa	1	0.2%		0.3%	Cycladic Painted	Open (1)
MFVc/DVe	1	0.2%		0.3%	Mainland(?) Slipped	Goblet (1)
MxMa/DVg	1	0.2%		0.3%	Cycladic Painted	Closed (1)
MxMd	1	0.2%		0.3%	Cycladic Yellow Slipped	Jar (1)
MxMe	1	0.2%		0.3%	Cycladic Yellow Slipped	Paneled jug(?) (1)

1% of imports. This fabric was associated with Matt Painted, Red Coated, and plain vessels, all of which were closed vessels except for a basin. Other imported fabrics, including several variants, were rare, each making up less than 1% of imports: DVd/DVe, DVf, FSTc, FSTf, FSTk/FVd, FSTk/FVc, FVf/FSTj, MFVb, MFVd, MFVc/DVe, FVa/MFVb. Of those, MFVb was associated with Gray/Black Burnished ware, but other connections between these fabrics and particular shapes and wares are impossible to determine.

In sum, many more imported fabrics existed in Period VII deposits in Area B than were found in earlier deposits, and more production centers in the mainland and the Cyclades seem to be represented. Non-Melian Cycladic fabrics were more common and more varied than in Period VI, including many rare fabrics as well as fabric MxMc, which was relatively common for the first time. Fabrics among mainland imports were also more varied than in Period VI. Fabrics FVc and FVb/FVc are similar to fabrics observed at Mycenae; their abundance suggests that the Argolid became a newly significant source for pottery in this period. (It is notable that LH II was also when the influential Argive workshop at Berbati began operation; Åkerstrom 1987, 24; Rutter 2015, 221; Schallin 1997, 77–78). Cretan imports were associated with a range of fabrics similar to Period VI. Imported fabrics were not closely associated with only one or two wares but with several. In addition, most fabrics were associated with all kinds of shapes. Apart from goblets, popular imported vessels were often Minoanizing, regardless of fabric, although most seem to have been imported from regions other than Crete.

TABLE 7.5. RELATIVE PROPORTIONS OF IMPORTED VESSELS ACCORDING TO PROBABLE REGIONS OF PRODUCTION IN PERIOD VII DEPOSITS IN AREA B

Based on fabric analysis, Ch. 3, and in comparison to the total number of imports (380).

Import region	No. of vessels	% of imports
Aegina	5	1%
Aegina(?)	24	6%
Attica/Cyclades	2	1%
Attica(?)	15	4%
Central Greece/Euboea	24	6%
Crete	16	4%
Crete(?)	10	3%
Crete/Mainland	43	11%
Cyclades	44	12%
Cyclades (Central)	3	1%
Cyclades(?)	2	1%
Euboea(?)	2	1%
Mainland	9	2%
Mainland(?)	1	<0.5%
Mainland (Attica/Euboea?)	35	9%
Mainland (Peloponnese?)	86	23%
Mainland/Kythera	12	3%
Melos	36	9%
Naxos	1	<0.5%
Unknown	10	3%

MANUFACTURE

Nearly 75% of local vessels in Period VII deposits in Area B were made with the potter's wheel, a slight increase in frequency compared with Period VI. Many more vessels were wheel-coiled than wheelmade (for this terminology, see Ch. 3). This pattern probably results from the large number of handleless cups, which were predominantly wheel-coiled. The increased technical standardization for Type 1 handleless cups in Period VII (i.e., most were clearly wheel-coiled rather than wheelmade or handmade) is paralleled by their very standardized height and rim and base diameters (Davis and Lewis 1985; Gorogianni, Abell, and Hilditch 2016, 210). This increased standardization—both technical and metrical—may suggest a change in the operation of ceramic production in this period, with either a smaller number of producers working at the site or increased specialization in the production of certain shapes by certain producers. In addition to handleless cups, the potter's wheel was used for all kinds of other shapes, small and large, open and closed, and in all local wares; likewise, the range of shapes that were handmade included all sizes and functional classes. Minoanizing shapes were more typically made using RKE than not, but non-Minoanizing shapes, as in the previous period, were also sometimes made with the wheel. This trend has been noted across the site (Gorogianni, Abell, and Hilditch 2016, 206–212).

As with local fabrics, nearly three-quarters of vessels in imported Cycladic (excluding Melian) fabrics were made using the potter's wheel. Handmade shapes were mainly closed vessels (**598, 753**). Vessels that employed rotational kinetic energy (RKE) from the use of the wheel were mainly Minoanizing shapes. Apart from the fact that the use of RKE was more common than hand-building, there does not seem to be a pattern of particular forming techniques being used for certain wares in Cycladic fabrics.

TABLE 7.6. ROUGH ESTIMATE OF THE PROPORTION OF IMPORTED PERIOD VII POTTERY IN AREA B LOTS

Calculated on the basis of the volume of pottery collected in comparison with what remains of the original lots and assuming that all discarded pottery was local.

Lot	Collected	Remaining	% discarded	% imports in remaining lot	Rough % imports in original lot*
B03-70	0.67 tin	0.1 tin	85%	67%	10%
B03-71a	0.5 tin	0.05 tin	90%	43%	4%
B03-108	11 sherds	3 sherds	73%	100%	27%
B604CL	3 tins	0.3 tin	90%	53%	5%
B605CL	2 bags	0.2 bag	90%	58%	6%
B606CL	6.5 tins	0.6 tin	91%	60%	6%
B607CL	0.75 tin	0.1 tin	87%	48%	6%
B608CL	2 tins	0.4 tin	80%	92%	18%
B609CL	4 tins	0.7 tin	83%	87%	15%
B646CL	0.5 bag	0.1 bag	80%	100%	20%
Average					12%

Among Melian imports, about half employed RKE, while the other half were handmade. Those that were produced using RKE were mostly Minoanizing; handmade vessels included non-Minoanizing shapes like a piriform cup or stemmed jar, a Cycladic cup, and vessels of unknown morphology. The use of RKE was not closely associated with any one Melian ware.

More vessels in possible Aeginetan fabrics (DVd, DVe) were handmade than made using RKE. Among the vessels showing evidence of RKE, most were Minoanizing shapes, including a handleless cup (**331**). All Standard Matt Painted vessels were handmade.

Among vessels in mainland fabrics, wheelmade vessels were much more common than handmade or wheel-coiled ones. Wheelmade vessels included all functional classes, as well as all mainland wares. A few Lustrous Painted vessels appeared to be handmade or coil-built, even though other vessels in the same fabrics were made using RKE. A similar pattern holds for Lustrous Painted vessels in fabric FSTj, of unknown mainland or Cretan origin; the majority of those for which forming method could be determined were wheelmade, with single examples of possibly wheel-coiled or handmade vessels.

Among mainland/Kytheran imports in fabric FSTh, all vessels for which forming method could be assessed showed evidence for RKE, both among cups and larger closed vessels. Wheelmade and wheel-coiled vessels were approximately equally represented, but the forming method could not be specified closely for most vessels.

Nearly all vessels in the Attic(?) fabric MFVc were wheelmade, regardless of ware; the exception is a jar-shaped rhyton (**404**) that appears to have been wheel-coiled.

More variability in forming methods existed among Cretan than mainland imports. This pattern probably results from the fact that more large, coarse, closed vessels existed among the Cretan imports (in FSTa and FSTb, for the most part), which were the only shapes that were handmade. Handmade closed vessels were plain (FSTb), Non-Lustrous Painted (FSTa, FSTb), and Slipped (FSTf). All Lustrous Painted vessels, on the other hand, were made using some form of RKE, including open and closed, as well as fine to moderately coarse vessels.

IMPORTATION AND CONSUMPTION PATTERNS

Mainland imports in Lustrous Painted and other wares were most common in the Period VII assemblage. Open shapes were more common than jars, jugs, and other closed vessels among mainland imports. Fabric analysis in Area B suggests that such pottery was arriving from central Greece (including Euboea), Attica, and the Argolid. Laconia is another possible source (Mountjoy 1999, 865). While a variety of different shapes seems to have been imported from both central Greece and the Argolid, nearly all

TABLE 7.7. COMMON TABLEWARES AND RHYTA IN PUBLISHED DEPOSITS OF PERIOD VII

With respect to the number of local (11,635), imported (824), and total (12,459) vessels (after Cummer and Schofield 1984; Schofield 2011). The number of handleless cups is 10,885. A calculation that omits handleless cups among local (787) and total (1,574) vessels was made, in order to clarify the relative percentages of other shapes with respect to each other. Rhyta are included because they may have been utilized in feasting contexts, especially ritualized ones (Girella 2007a; Hamilakis 1999; Koehl 2006).

Shape	% of local	% of local (minus handleless cups)	% of imports	% of total	% of total (minus handleless cups)
Minoanizing					
Handleless cup	93%	0%	5%	87%	0%
Rounded cup	<0.5%	1%	8%	1%	4%
Straight-sided/Vapheio cup	<0.5%	1%	4%	<0.5%	2%
Bell cup	0%	0%	2%	<0.5%	1%
Hole-mouthed/bridge-spouted jar/jug	<0.5%	1%	2%	<0.5%	2%
Cup-rhyta	<0.5%	<0.5%	2%	<0.5%	1%
Conical rhyta	0%	0%	3%	<0.5%	1%
Other rhyta	0%	0%	1%	<0.5%	1%
Non-Minoanizing					
Goblet	<0.5%	1%	15%	1%	8%
Piriform cup	0%	0%	1%	<0.5%	1%
Cycladic cup/bowl	0%	0%	<0.5%	<0.5%	<0.5%
Spouted bowl/krater	0%	0%	3%	<0.5%	2%

vessels in fabric MFVc (Attica?) were goblets. Additional analyses from other parts of the site are needed to clarify whether different import patterns may be associated with particular mainland regions.

Open and closed shapes were more equally represented among Cretan imports than mainland ones. More rhyta/perforated vessels were Cretan than mainland products, but the functional range of vessels imported from both areas was similarly varied. In contrast, more Aeginetan imports were closed than open. A few cooking vessels were probably imported from Aegina, but other special-purpose shapes like rhyta, strainers, or industrial vessels were not.

Although Melian imports were rarer in Period VII than in Period VI, imports from other parts of the Cyclades were relatively common. As in previous periods, most functional categories were represented among Melian and other Cycladic imports. Fine, open vessels were nearly twice as common as larger closed vessels among Melian imports, but closed vessels were more common among other Cycladic imports.

Among all imported wares, most open vessels came from the mainland, but other regions also supplied such shapes. Likewise, other common shape categories like askoi/small closed vessels, jugs/ewers, and jars/closed vessels were imported in different wares (Fig. 63). That is, although more vessels seem to have been imported from the mainland, vessels with the same functional categories were well represented in nearly all common wares and were imported from various regions. This pattern suggests that, during LC II, increasing diversity developed within exchange networks, and more ceramics (which overlapped both stylistically and functionally) from more places were being produced and exchanged.

In previous periods, all common imported shapes were also produced by local potters. In Period VII, for the first time, this pattern was not universal. Many shapes common among imports were produced locally, and both local and imported versions of the same shape are regularly found in the same deposits. Neither alabastra nor rounded goblets typical of LH II Mycenaean pottery (as opposed to Minyanizing goblets) were manufactured by local potters, however, despite the fact that these shapes were common imports from the mainland.

SUMMARY

Like that of Period VI, the Period VII ceramic assemblage as a whole—including local and imported products—was markedly Minoanizing. Nevertheless, as in Period VI, non-Minoanizing shapes continued to form a notable part of the assemblage as well (Table 7.7). Changes in proportions of tableware shapes in comparison with Period VI (Table 6.6) suggest some changes in eating and drinking habits during this phase. Several shapes that were common in the previous period became relatively rare in Period VII, including straight-sided/Vapheio cups, hole-mouthed/bridge-spouted jars, and piriform cups. Handleless cups made up a similar proportion of the overall assemblage in Period VII compared with Period VI, which suggests a continued interest in the consumption events in which such cups were utilized. The large number of rhyta and perforated vessels may suggest that some communal events had become more ritualized, requiring the use of new, specialized equipment (see also Knappett and Hilditch 2015a).

Changes in local ceramic production, importation, and consumption patterns, as well as the expansion of various industries at Ayia Irini in Period VII (Georgiou 1986; Schofield 1990), suggest that exchange in the Aegean was becoming more commercialized in this period, with more goods moving across greater distances, and with more production centers becoming integrated into Aegean exchange networks. The bewildering diversity of imported ceramic fabrics, wares, and shapes is a testament to a significant intensification of regional production and trade within exchange networks, with Ayia Irini serving as a sort of barometer for the growth and development of new production centers and longer-distance exchange networks in this period. At the same time, there are many similarities in ceramic assemblages, especially among tablewares, between Ayia Irini and other Cycladic communities, as well as Cretan, eastern Aegean, and mainland Greek ones. The perpetuation of such similarities suggests that many people across the Aegean were engaged in broadly comparable eating, drinking, and perhaps feasting practices in this era. Possible effects of these changes in production and consumption patterns on the local community will be discussed in greater detail in Chapter 8.

VIII. AREA B, AYIA IRINI, AND THE WIDER AEGEAN

PRODUCTION AND CONSUMPTION PATTERNS AT AYIA IRINI

The excellent preservation and excavation of Area B by Aliki Bikaki have enabled a reconstruction of the history of this part of the site, which was occupied from Period III–VII. Pottery from Area B has been analyzed in combination with published deposits from Ayia Irini in order to clarify patterns of exchange and local production. The ceramic connections of Ayia Irini in the EBA were primarily with Attica and the western Cyclades. In the MBA and LBA, other parts of mainland Greece, Crete, Aegina, and the Cyclades produced vessels that were imported to the town. Local production, especially in Periods IV–VII, is marked by stability in raw-materials selection and processing, as well as firing practices. Yet, there was also long-lived heterogeneity in forming technologies and the kinds of vessels that were made. The ceramic assemblage as a whole, including local and imported vessels, incorporates shapes and decorative styles typical of multiple regions in each period. This chapter considers local production and consumption patterns over time in order to assess changes in the role of Ayia Irini in Aegean networks and the effects of shifts in those networks on local society.

THE EBA

During EC II (Table 1.1), a few large Cycladic centers emerged, e.g., at Ayia Irini, Chalandriani-Kastri on Syros, Grotta-Aplomata on Naxos, and Dhaskaleio-Kavos on Keros, as well as Skarkos on Ios (Broodbank 2000; 2008, 55; Marthari 2008). Other sites, like Phylakopi on Melos and Akrotiri on Thera, may also have been large sites, but the evidence for the size and population density of these settlements during the EBA is somewhat less clear (Broodbank 2000, 220–221; Sotirakopoulou 2008).

Human mobility at different spatial and temporal scales was an important part of EC society. Distribution patterns of metals, obsidian, and ceramics show that raw materials and finished products were exchanged widely. Broodbank (2000, 247–275) argued for the significance of regular raiding and trading by longboat as a strategy for acquiring social prestige. The potential for accruing social benefits by organizing and participating in longboat expeditions may have formed a sort of feedback loop at larger settlements, attracting people to them and enabling additional voyages (Broodbank 2000, 258). Given the relatively small size of insular settlements, exogamy was also probably practiced (Broodbank 2000, 86–89).

Several of these larger settlements are located in places that had high potential for network centrality and maritime connectivity, according to proximal point analyses (Broodbank 2000, 237–246). Ayia Irini was central not within Cycladic networks but on an interregional scale, between Cycladic, Attic, and Euboean ones (Wilson 1987). The geographical position of Ayia Irini would have offered its residents significant potential to interact—and interfere—with paddlers on their way to or from Lavrion, one of several major sources of metal in the EBA Aegean, which included also Siphnos, Kythnos, and Seriphos, as well as Anatolia (Gale 1998; Gale and Stos-Gale 1984; 2008, 387–390; Gale, Stos-Gale, and Davis 1984; Stos and Gale 2006, 313–316; Stos-Gale and Macdonald 1991; for the possible exploitation of metals on Kea during the Bronze Age, see Caskey et al. 1988; Mendoni and Belogiannis 1991, 100–103).

EBA Ayia Irini was relatively well connected, evident from imported stone and metal (Ch. 2; Wilson 1999, 144–157), as well as from the variety of imported ceramics, which made up around 25–30% of the assemblage in Periods II and III (Wilson 1999, 22, 92). By comparison, at both Markiani on Amorgos and Chalandriani on Syros, ceramic imports seem to have been relatively rare (Hekman 2003, 102, 105, 111, 129–130; Renfrew 2006, 251–253; Vaughan 2006). Imports at Skarkos are reported to represent a minor part of the assemblage, despite being wide-ranging in origins (Marthari 2008, 72, 79). Imported fabrics at Korfari ton Amygdalion (Panormos) made up less than 5% of the 389 vessels that were studied in depth for the publication (Angelopoulou 2014, 92–93). In Phase A2 at Phylakopi, likewise, imports seem to have made up less than 10% of the assemblage (Renfrew and Evans 2007, 141). Although Broodbank (2007, 181–183) argued that the imported ceramic assemblage at Ayia Irini was comparable to that at Dhaskalio-Kavos, the percentage of imports at Ayia Irini is much lower than at Dhaskalio or Kavos, where the majority—if not all—of the pottery was imported (Hilditch 2007, 246–249; 2013, 480–482; Sotirakopoulou 2016, esp. 389–391). These exchange patterns suggest that Ayia Irini and Dhaskalio-Kavos had somewhat different roles in Cycladic networks, presumably owing to the ideologically loaded status of Kavos, which was the focus of unusual patterns of deposition of fragmented marble figurines (Renfrew 2015; Renfrew et al. 2015).

At Dhaskalio, most imported pottery came from within the "Keros Triangle," edged by Naxos, Ios, and Amorgos; fewer imports came from southern mainland Greece and other Cycladic islands (Broodbank 2007; Hilditch 2007; 2013, 481, table 23.24;

Sotirakopoulou 2016). At Ayia Irini, too, imports and stylistic connections attest to close connections with the immediately neighboring regions of Attica and the western Cyclades, while imports from further afield were less common (Wilson 1987, 1999). These distribution patterns highlight the economic and social importance of relatively short-distance contacts within Cycladic micro-regions, despite the significance of longer-distance patterns of interaction for the accrual of social capital (Broodbank 2000, 186–210). Micro-regional connections would have been strengthened through human mobility (including marriage patterns) and would have generated social networks that extended beyond the geographical confines of any single insular community. The development of a micro-regional network that connected Kea with the western Cyclades was enabled by the spatial configuration of these islands, which are comparatively close to each other, at distances that would have allowed one-day (ca. 20 km) journeys between islands using canoes (Broodbank 2000, 75, 102–103, figs. 15, 24). Other Cycladic island clusters are more distant and would have required a greater time investment to reach, unless longboats, which have a greater daily range, were employed (Broodbank 2000, 102, table 3). Travel within micro-regional networks, therefore, was probably more frequent and potentially accessible to more people than longboat expeditions (see also Tartaron 2013, 185–188).

The standard dining set in Period II consisted of the sauceboat (pouring), medium-sized bowl (eating/serving), and saucer (drinking) (Wilson 1999, 233). Eating/drinking rituals in which these shapes were used may have been centered on large, stamped-rim hearths (Wilson 1999, 233, 235). In Period III, new Anatolianizing eating and drinking practices were adopted, in which novel drinking (tankard) and eating/serving (shallow bowl) shapes became standard, while the number of sauceboats and other Period II vessels declined (Wilson 1999, 233). In this era, the prestige vocabulary shifted from a focus on Cycladic cultural practice and display to a new one, adopted or adapted from the east, at the same time that Cycladic exchange networks shifted and tin-bronzes began to arrive in the archipelago, probably from the northeast Aegean (Broodbank 2000, 316; Nakou 1997). The forms and dark, shiny surfaces of Anatolianizing ceramic shapes suggest that they were modeled after high-value sheet-metal vessels, which may have added symbolic potency to the use of these ceramic shapes (Nakou 2000, 2007).

The adoption of new forms of material culture, ceramic and otherwise, and the adaptation of those forms in local contexts of production and use could have led to increased tensions in group interactions and social identity in the Cyclades (Broodbank 2000, 276–319). These changes may have destabilized existing social structures that linked people through participation in group actions, including eating, drinking, and feasting activities. However, given the long duration of this period (ca. 2500–2250 B.C.), primary causes for the disruptions of EC III and the abandonment of Ayia Irini must be sought elsewhere.

At Ayia Irini, there is no evidence for different spatial patterning of the various drinking/eating sets (Wilson 1999, 2013). Rather, although sauceboats, saucers, and medium-sized bowls became rarer through time, they were still produced and found in deposits that also contained tankards, bell-shaped cups, and other Anatolianizing shapes, including in Area B (Ch. 2; Wilson 1999, 167–226). This lack of spatial differentiation might be explained in a few ways. Different people within households might have used different vessels. In that case, users of each set might have been linked by similarities in age, gender, social status, or membership in other social groups. Alternatively, it is possible that people chose which vessels to use according to the social context of consumption. That is, perhaps some vessels were used in household contexts and others in communal contexts, or perhaps different kinds of events required different sets. It is not possible to determine which option is more likely on current evidence, and other scenarios also probably exist. Regardless, it is clear that local residents engaged in a complex process of adapting new drinking/eating practices into existing social structures rather than completely swapping out one set of cultural behaviors for another.

Broodbank (2000, 336–341) summarized a range of possible issues that may have affected changes in the settlement patterns and material culture of the late EBA Cyclades. These issues include a possible world-systemic disruption following turbulence in the core areas of the Near East (although the Cyclades seem very marginal to that world-system), land degradation, drought, epidemic, and/or increasing conflict in areas of intense inter-community competition (see also Manning 1997, 2017). A significant factor in changing patterns of settlement and interaction in the late EBA Cyclades was probably also the development of deep-hulled sailing boats, which collapsed the expanses covered in maritime voyages and seriously affected perceived distances within the Cyclades (Broodbank 2000, 341–349).

Whatever the cause(s) of the changes in the late EBA, the disruption of exchange networks and dismantling of Cycladic prestige ideologies—as well as, perhaps, changes in climate (Manning 1997, 2017)—made life at Ayia Irini unsustainable, and the site was abandoned. The growth of maritime power at Kolonna and/or Lefkandi also may have negatively impacted the abilities of residents of the town to control access to Lavrion metals or to manipulate interaction between Cycladic and mainland maritime networks. Ayia Irini was not resettled until after a shift in Aegean exchange networks again made the peninsula appealing.

THE EARLIER MBA

Social structures of the Aegean changed dramatically by the time Ayia Irini was resettled in Period IV. (Note that Ayia Irini was refounded after the start of the MBA elsewhere; for my use of the term "earlier MBA" rather than "MC II" for Period IV, see Ch. 5.) During the earlier MBA, sailing boats traveled more regularly between the Near East and Aegean, a complex, state-level society had developed on Crete, and Kolonna on Aegina had emerged as a major regional power, sometimes referred to as a chiefdom or proto-state (Niemeier 1995; Rutter 1993b). For the first time, Cycladic island life was subject to significant external political and economic influence, a pattern that has persisted into the modern period (Broodbank 2000, 320–321).

Although many things changed after the EBA, some similarities with the earlier period are worth noting. Several major MBA and LBA sites (Ayia Irini, Akrotiri on Thera, Phylakopi on Melos, and Grotta on Naxos) were located on coasts; maritime interaction and mobility must have been as important to economic and social strategies at these sites as they had been for EC communities (see also Sotirakopoulou 2010, 829). In addition, although sailing boats had developed, shorter-distance travel in smaller boats probably continued to take place. Indeed, short-distance maritime interactions could have happened quite frequently, as part of regular provisioning, interaction, and mobility (including through exogamous practices) in this era, as in the EBA (see also Tartaron 2013, 185–188). Smaller boats would have required smaller investments of time and resources for construction, maintenance, and crews, and so could have provided an opportunity for MBA and LBA Cycladic islanders to participate in exchange and interaction networks on their own terms (to some degree and at limited geographic scales), even after sailing boats came into use and maritime travel had lost the particular ideological significance that typified the EBA Cyclades. Lastly, it may be noted that in the EBA, large ceramic shapes like pithoi, jars, basins, and hearths were imported at several sites in Talc and other wares, while building stone from Naxos was used at Dhaskalio (Ch. 4; Dixon 2013; Sotirakopoulou 2016, 15–18, 70–75, 156–163). The transport of these heavy, bulky objects must have relied on oar- or paddle-powered boats. This fact suggests that, in later periods, the movement of cargo may not have been limited to sailing ships alone, even if that was the more usual method of transport.

The foundation of the Period IV town at Ayia Irini was probably targeted to take advantage of the resurgence of north-south movement between Lavrion, the western Cyclades, and, in this period, Crete (Broodbank 2000, 357–358, 361). It has long been hypothesized that Cretan interest in the area was focused on the Lavrion ores, which became a major metal source for the MBA and LBA Aegean (Davis 1979b; 2008, 200–201; Gale, Stos-Gale, and Davis 1984; Schofield 1982; Wiener 1990, 1991, 2007, 2013, 2016). It is surprising, therefore, that although a lead weight from MM II Quartier Mu at Mallia was compatible with a Lavrion source, all of the analyzed copper objects from that site have signatures compatible with other sources, including Anatolia and Cyprus (Poursat and Loubet 2005, 118–119). Nevertheless, residents of Ayia Irini probably played a direct role in accessing and processing Lavrion ores for exchange with other Aegean communities already in Period IVa, since a crucible, slag, and metal fragments have been found in deposits of that era (J. C. Overbeck 1989a, 36, 127, no. K-25; Overbeck and Crego 2008, 306–307; see also Caskey et al. 1988; Mendoni and Belogiannis 1991, 100–103). The deposition of a miniature crucible in the Temple in Period IV, presumably a votive, also attests to the importance of metallurgy in the community (Caskey 2009, 145).

People originally from different parts of the Aegean may have been incorporated into the community during the early years of its foundation. Overbeck and Crego (2008) suggested that the initial Period IV inhabitants came from central Greece, owing to abundant Minyan imports, as well as parallels in town plans. Similarities in the forms of the fortification walls, pottery production and consumption patterns, as well as the use of comparable pot-marking practices at Ayia Irini and Kolonna led Crego (2010) to suggest that Period IV settlers might have come from Aegina. Technical patterns of ceramic production, especially hand-building and handle attachment by pushing a plug through the vessel wall, link potters in Period IVa with established communities of practice across the Cyclades, mainland, and Aegina (Ch. 5), and much locally produced pottery was modeled on shapes that were popular in each of those areas.

In addition, the local adoption of several Cretan technologies in Period IVa—the potter's wheel, vertical loom, and cooking techniques that used tripod vessels—suggests the existence of a few mobile Cretan-trained craft producers at the site (Crego 2010, 843; Cutler 2019; Davis 1984, 160–163; Overbeck and Crego 2008, 308–309). The potter's wheel and the loom are technologies that require long-lasting, intense periods of apprenticeship to master; the adoption of these techniques at Ayia Irini after they had first appeared on Crete strongly suggests the movement to Kea of some potters and weavers trained in Cretan communities of practice (Abell 2014a, 559–561; Cutler 2012, 2019). The use of these techniques was limited, with few wheel-formed local pots, discoid loom weights, and tripod legs recovered from Period IV deposits (J. C. Overbeck 1989a). The mobility of craftspeople trained in Cretan or Minoanizing communities of practice to Ayia Irini, therefore, was probably quite small scale, involving few individuals. The distribution of tripod legs and loom weights (J. C. Overbeck 1989a) suggests that the use of Minoanizing cooking and weaving technologies was not spatially separated from non-Minoanizing ones. For ceramics, raw material selection, processing, and firing practices were closely comparable among vessels that were produced with the potter's wheel and those that were not (Chs. 3, 5). These patterns suggest that the craftspeople who brought Minoanizing techniques to Ayia Irini were integrated into the local community or communities of practice.

The mechanisms by which these mobile craftspeople arrived at Ayia Irini are not entirely clear. There is no reason to assume that they were entirely or even primarily attached palatial specialists sent out to the islands. Although some craft production in the town was specialized (i.e., oriented toward exchange), it seems to have operated primarily in household contexts throughout the MBA and early LBA (Georgiou 1986, 53–54; Schofield 1990). There is no evidence for extra-domestic workshops for the production of pottery or other crafts (Abell 2020). Given the rarity of related objects in the assemblage, Minoanizing technologies do not seem to have been used for higher intensity production than non-Minoanizing ones over the course of Period IV.

Craftspeople trained in Minoanizing weaving practices were probably women, given the long-term link between women and weaving in the eastern Mediterranean (Cutler 2012, 150; 2019). The adoption of all three Minoanizing techniques at the same time suggests that they may have been employed by the same people. It is tempting to associate the presence of mobile female craftspeople at Ayia Irini with patterns of exogamy (whether or not they were elite brides, as hypothesized for Periods V–VII by Gorogianni, Cutler, and Fitzsimons 2015). Women also could have moved as part of family units, as captives or slaves, as elite gifts, or by other means (Cutler 2019, 8–10).

The introduction of new technologies like weaving with a warp-weighted loom or using a potter's wheel are good indicators of mobility at Ayia Irini because these techniques require long periods of direct apprenticeship to master and cannot be imitated only through observation of finished products (Abell 2014a, 556–561; Cutler 2019, 7–8). Yet, other kinds of small-scale mobility also probably existed, even though they are difficult to establish archaeologically (Broodbank 2004, 67–69; Schofield 1984a). Economic opportunities may have attracted individuals to Ayia Irini in periods after its initial foundation. In addition, the town was small, probably housing only a couple of hundred people at most (Broodbank 2000, 218; Gorogianni 2016, 139; Schofield 1998, 119). Exogamy, therefore, probably would have been required at least in some cases to sustain the local population and may have involved more individuals (including non-Cretans) than the craftspeople who initially introduced Minoanizing technologies. Later evidence, from Periods V–VII and contemporary phases at other "Minoanized" sites, suggests that small-scale, multidirectional mobility was also a feature of those eras across the southern Aegean (below; Cutler 2019, 8–9; Nikolakopoulou and Knappett 2016, 111–114).

Ayia Irini was rapidly integrated into Aegean exchange networks during Period IV. Imports included possible prestige items like precious metals, exotic stones, Kamares ware, and Minoan seals, some of which were found in tombs (G. F. Overbeck 1989; J. C. Overbeck 1989a), as well as many ceramic vessels. The proportion of imported ceramics in Period IV is similar to that of Period III, although wider ranging in terms of origins.

Distribution patterns of mainland and Cretan imports in the Cyclades suggest some differences in how objects from the different regions were accessed. Much Gray Minyan ware has been found at Ayia Irini; less pottery in this ware exists at Phylakopi, and very little was found at Akrotiri, while it also seems to be quite rare in the central and eastern Cyclades (Nikolakopoulou 2007; Mathioudaki 2019, 321; Sotirakopoulou 2010, 833–834 with references; Minyan vessels were reported to be relatively common on the surface at Akroterion Ourion on Tenos [Scholes 1956, 13]). This distribution pattern is similar to that noted by Cherry and Davis (1982) for mainland products in the Cyclades during LH I. Cherry and Davis (1982) argued that the linear nature of the LH I distribution pattern suggested the presence of traders or middlemen who engaged in tramping—obtaining cargo at one port of call, exchanging some of that cargo and obtaining new commodities at the next port of call, and so on—along a particular route, the Western String, stretching from the mainland, through Ayia Irini, Phylakopi, and Akrotiri, to Crete (Cherry and Davis 1982; Davis 1979b; Schofield 1982).

MM Cretan imports do not follow a fall-off pattern similar to Gray Minyan ones, in which, hypothetically, MM pottery would be abundant at Akrotiri, rarer at Phylakopi, and even rarer at Ayia Irini. Rather, Cretan imports were common at Period IV Ayia Irini, making up 16% of the total assemblage based on a count of published vessels (Ch. 5), 8% of Overbeck's (1982, 40) "typical lot" of 239 vessels, and probably at least 7% of the total assemblage in Area B, with discards taken into account. MM imports from Phylakopi have not been quantified in relation to the total assemblage, but Hood (2007, 249) reported them to be less common than at Ayia Irini. At Akrotiri, sherds in Minoan fabrics made up between 2–7% of Phase B sherds in Pillar Pit 61N (Hilditch 2019, 400, table 3.14; Knappett 2019, 313–314). This distribution pattern contrasts with the more linear one associated with Gray Minyan ware, and Ayia Irini stands out as having an unusually large proportion of Cretan imports given its geographical distance from Crete. Thus, while exchange of Gray Minyan wares may have operated through mechanisms similar to the later "tramping" hypothesized by Cherry and Davis, exchange between Cretans and Ayia Irini may have been more targeted, presumably owing to Ayia Irini's status as the point of access to Lavrion metals. Notably, other contemporary sites with evidence for intense interaction with Protopalatial Crete—especially Mikro Vouni on Samothrace and Miletus in Anatolia—were also located at key articulation points between regional networks, through which metals could be obtained.

The ways in which earlier MBA exchange operated must have been different from the EBA, at least to some degree, given the development of complex administrative institutions on Crete and the emergence of a regional power at Kolonna. Interactions between residents of Ayia Irini and more highly organized political entities at Kolonna and especially on Crete probably had inherent power imbalances. Nevertheless, the variety of trade goods, their wide dispersal in deposits across the town, as well as idiosyncrasies in the material culture of Ayia Irini compared with other sites in the Cyclades, Aegina, and Crete (below) suggest that local residents maintained significant independence in terms of production and exchange activities.

Oka and Kusimba (2008), citing a vast array of recent archaeological analyses, argued that commercial or market-based trade is a feature of most societies, even preindustrial ones with centralized states; moreover, market-based trade, while often regulated by political elites, is seldom directly controlled by them. This vision of trade and exchange fits reasonably well with the archaeological evidence of Ayia Irini with its large quantity and widespread distribution of imported objects. While Ayia Irini may have had special kinds of relationships with Kolonna or Cretan polities, there is little reason to suggest that residents of the community did not participate more broadly in some form of market-based exchange, as was long ago hypothesized by Overbeck (1982), and which might also be suggested by the similarities in the distribution pattern of Gray Minyan ware to LH I pottery, as noted above.

Ayia Irini is the only site in the area where Cycladic, central Greek, Aeginetan, and Cretan pottery—i.e., pottery from regions with quite different sociocultural traditions in this era—has been found in such abundance (Crego 2007, 2010; Overbeck 1982, 1989a; Overbeck and Crego 2008). Around a quarter of the Period IV assemblage was imported, even when discards are taken into consideration; of this group, across various kinds of quantification (Ch. 5; Overbeck 1982, 40; Crego 2007, 337, fig. 4), mainland and Cretan imports were abundant, Cycladic and Aeginetan imports were somewhat less common, and possible southeastern Aegean imports were rare (Abell, Crego, and Overbeck, forthcoming). For comparison, imports at Akrotiri made up 12–23% of sherds in Phase B deposits in Pillar Pit 61N (Hilditch 2019, 400, table 3.14; Nikolakopoulou 2019, 190; Mathioudaki [2019, 317] suggests that the higher estimate [23%] is unusually elevated compared with the proportion of imports in Phases A and C, perhaps a result of unusual depositional patterns in this space). Cretan imports in Phase B deposits at Akrotiri were discussed above. Mainland and southeast Aegean imports were rare, while Cycladic, especially Naxian, imports were common (Knappett 2019, 313–314; Mathioudaki 2019, 319–322; Nikolakopoulou 2007, 349). I am not aware of quantifications of the earlier MC assemblage at Phylakopi. Dickinson (2007, 238, 244) found fewer than 180 sherds of MBA mainland wares in deposits of Phases C–E at Phylakopi; MM imports were slightly more numerous, but, as noted above, Hood (2007, 248, 253, table 6.2) suggested that MM imports were more common at Ayia Irini than Phylakopi. Overbeck (1989b) did not quantify pottery from Paroikia, but imports are represented by fewer than 30 vessels in his catalogue, including Minoan/Minoanizing, Cycladic White, and other Matt Painted vessels (4–6 in each ware), as well as Gray Minyan (11) ones. Although Cycladic (especially Keian) and Aeginetan imports are often found in assemblages at sites in Attica, "true" Gray Minyan imports from Boeotia and/or Euboea seem to be rare at Attic sites, while Cretan and Minoanizing imports are even rarer (Gorogianni, Abell, and Hilditch 2020, 630–632, with references; Philippa-Touchais and Balitsari 2020). Among surface finds from Ayios Nikolaos Mylon in southern Euboea, approximately 30% of the MBA assemblage was imported, primarily from other parts of Euboea, the Cyclades (especially Kea), and central mainland Greece (Tankosić and Mathioudaki 2011, 124–128).

Given its coastal location, large quantity of imported objects (ceramic and otherwise), and the wide range of origins for those objects, it is probable that Ayia Irini acted as more than just a notional articulation point between different regional exchange networks, one that happened to be located opposite a major metal resource for the Aegean. Rather, it may have acted, to some degree, as an actual exchange center along the lines of emporia or gateway communities, as characterized by Knapp and Cherry (1994, 134–142) for the eastern Mediterranean (for the concept, see also Burghardt 1971; Hirth 1978). Ayia Irini was "strategically situated to exploit factors of supply" in the form of raw materials from Lavrion, as well as "to facilitate the flow of goods within or between regional trade systems" (Knapp and Cherry 1994, 135; see also Crego 2007, 2010; Overbeck 1982; Overbeck and Crego 2008; Schofield 1982). In such a position, traders from different cultural backgrounds would have encountered each other, as well as Keians at Ayia Irini. Yet, while the position of Ayia Irini near Lavrion enabled such interaction, residents of Ayia Irini probably also made efforts to encourage exchange, primarily by making themselves indispensable as middlemen who could ensure access for people from different parts of the Aegean to either Lavrion or the metals that were being processed at Ayia Irini (Crego 2007; Gale and Stos-Gale 1984, 258, fig. 2).

The wide variety of drinking styles at Ayia Irini could be related to such efforts. Period IV pottery displays a mix of ceramic types, including goblets, kantharoi, and bowls imported from the mainland; carinated bowls, beaked jugs, and piriform cups from the Cyclades; and smaller cup shapes in Matt Painted and Minoan/-izing wares. All of these shapes were both imported and locally made, especially goblets and carinated bowls. The diversity of drinking shapes in use in Period IV probably represents varied drinking practices, not just aesthetic differences. Goblets and kantharoi, with their wide mouths and large capacity, presumably were used for the consumption of large quantities of liquids and perhaps for sharing among several individuals. Neither shape was common in Phase B at Akrotiri (Nikolakopoulou 2019, 155–216), and while goblets exist in Dark Burnished ware at Phylakopi, kantharoi seem quite rare, mainly represented by imports (Barber 2007, 2008). Carinated bowls probably served as eating rather than drinking vessels since the sharply incurving rim would have hindered the ability of a person to drink without spilling the contents. Similar bowls also were used on Aegina (Lindblom 2001, 26–27, fig. 4, shape S-1) and in the Cyclades, but they do not seem to be a regular feature of mainland assemblages. Cretan and Minoanizing drinking vessels seem to have served a different function, since these shapes generally were smaller in size and with smaller rim diameters than the mainland or Cycladic shapes. Cretan and Minoanizing vessels, either handleless or with one handle, also would have been held and manipulated in very different ways than stemmed goblets and two-handled kantharoi.

As with Period III, it is impossible to determine precisely how the incorporation of shapes with connections to drinking and eating habits of Crete, the Cyclades, Aegina, and mainland Greece affected local drinking and eating practices, whether by creating varied occasions for drinking and eating that required different shapes, by singling out particular groups through their use of such vessels, or by being used all together in an amalgamation of different drinking styles in a single, distinctively Keian practice. Regardless, the incorporation of all these shapes, whether used separately or together, by different groups or by the same groups on different occasions, is, in many ways, peculiar to Ayia Irini.

As residents of an exchange hub, it would have been advantageous for local residents to tolerate diversity in the local repertoire, since this would have facilitated participation in drinking or eating activities that would have been relatively familiar to sailors and traders who arrived at the town from other parts of the Aegean. The use of such a variety of vessels—and, in general, an openness to many aspects of nonlocal culture—could be interpreted as an active strategy by at least some local residents to create strong, sustained relationships with people from different cultural backgrounds through providing opportunities to participate in notionally shared drinking, eating, or feasting practices. For visitors to the site, participating in events with local residents while using familiar kinds of equipment in familiar kinds of ways would have reinforced perceptions of shared values across other kinds of cultural divides and encouraged the development of trust between potential exchange partners, a requirement in many contexts of premonetary trade. The possibility that some nonlocal craftspeople (and perhaps others as well) were incorporated into the local community also may have bolstered connections with other communities, since residents of Ayia Irini could, at least in some cases, claim shared heritage with people from elsewhere.

In this context, it is also notable that Ayia Irini is the only earlier MBA Cycladic site with a clear, physical ritual structure, the Temple, which was built very early in Period IV (J. C. Overbeck 1989a, 176). Reconsiderations of trading emporia in later Greek contexts have suggested that religious institutions served to create social cohesion within communities that were, to some degree, multiethnic. Moreover, religious institutions may be particularly important in exchange situations where not all traders are connected by personal relationships, since they can minimize the perceived risks of exchange through the implicit threat of supernatural retribution for bad behavior (Demetriou 2011, 268–270; Domínguez Monedero 2001). Of course, the Temple need not have developed specifically to fulfill such a function, but the existence of a visible connection to supernatural forces at Ayia Irini may have helped to facilitate exchange and encourage repeated visits by traders, even in the early stages of the settlement. The Temple, of course, also may have served as a focus for regularly scheduled drinking or eating events that could have been attended by visitors to the site (see also Caskey 2009, 145; for links between periodic markets and ritual events in other cultural and historic contexts, see Hirth 2020, 284–287).

A DIACHRONIC PERSPECTIVE ON PROCESSES OF MINOANIZATION (MBA–LBA)

Residents of Ayia Irini had a long history of interaction with Cretan communities. Abundant Cretan imports, in addition to possible evidence for gift exchange in the form of fine Kamares ware vessels and seals, suggest that personal and perhaps political relationships developed between Keians and Cretans over the course of the century or more of Period IV. The limited adoption of a few technologies derived from Crete also suggests the existence of some mobile craftspeople, probably also from Crete. Nevertheless, local people did not emulate Cretan material culture, styles, or practices in the ways they did in later eras.

During Periods V and VI, the ways in which residents of Ayia Irini interacted with Cretan culture—and probably also Cretan people—changed significantly. The same periods marked significant social shifts across the Aegean. Cycladic sites, including Ayia Irini, grew in size and perhaps population (Davis 1986; Hilditch 2008, 305; Knappett and Nikolakopoulou 2005, 181; Whitelaw 2004). On Crete, Knossos emerged as the key cultural and economic, if not also political, leader (Driessen and Macdonald 1997; Hamilakis 2002; Knappett and Schoep 2000; Macdonald and Knappett 2013; Warren 2002; Wiener 1990, 2007, 2013). At the same time, a new elite was developing on the mainland, members of which, for example, began to be buried in the elaborate Shaft Graves at Mycenae. Across the Cyclades and eastern Aegean, Cretan-derived material culture, styles, and practices became popular as part of the Minoanization phenomenon (recently, see papers in Gorogianni, Pavúk, and Girella 2016; Macdonald, Hallager, and Niemeier 2009).

Early perspectives posited that the changes in material culture associated with the Minoanization phenomenon must have resulted from Minoan palaces either establishing new colonies and/or conquering existing Cycladic populations (e.g., see papers in Hägg and Marinatos 1984; Wiener 1990, 2013). The material record of the southern Aegean, however, is very resistant to Minoan colonization narratives (for extensive discussion, see Broodbank 2004, 54–73). Cycladic settlements preserve little evidence for spatial differentiation between Minoan/Minoanizing and non-Minoanizing forms of material culture, nor is there any "plausible externally imposed elite residence" at these sites (Broodbank 2004, 56). Significant variability exists in the spatial and temporal manifestations of Minoanization among Cycladic communities, and there are clear continuities with previous, pre-Minoanized periods at Ayia Irini, Phylakopi, and Akrotiri (e.g., among many others, Davis 1986, 105–107; Davis and Cherry 1990; Doumas 1982; Earle 2016, 97–102; Gorogianni 2016; Hadjianastasiou 1989, 1993; Knappett 2016, 202–204; Marthari 2009; Nikolakopoulou 2009; Vlachopoulos 2016, 119–124). Throughout the Cyclades, production and consumption practices during these eras also incorporate a mix of Minoanizing and non-Minoanizing forms of material culture.

It is unlikely to be coincidental, however, that the Minoanization phenomenon began at Akrotiri, Phylakopi, and Ayia Irini at around the same time late in the MBA, during a period in which Knossos began to exert new power and influence on Crete (for the idea that Crete itself was "Minoanized" by ideas spreading out from Knossos in MM III, see Knappett 2016, 203). The start of the Minoanization phenomenon in the Cyclades may have been driven at least in part by leaders at Knossos, who seem to have played a key role in initiating new patterns of interaction and perhaps new kinds of relationships with southern Aegean communities in MM III (Knappett 2006; Knappett and Nikolakopoulou 2005). Those relationships certainly may have had unequal power dynamics. Knossos could have exerted direct political control over some parts of the Minoanized Aegean, or its leaders instead may have wielded influence through soft power strategies of alliance-building or generating attraction to ideologies connected with and originating from Knossos, as might be suggested, for example, by widespread participation in Cretan-style ritual practices (Davis 1984, 164–165; Knappett and Hilditch 2015a; for a review of the concept of soft power, see Nye 2021). The existence of palatial tools like Linear A, sealings, and perhaps weight standards in Cycladic communities suggests that formalized relationships may have existed between Cretans and Cycladic communities, even though their extent, duration, and nature are unclear (Karnava 2008, 2018; Michailidou 2008; Petruso 1992). Linking the archaeological record conclusively with particular kinds of political relationships is extremely challenging, and consensus has grown that it may be impossible to fully characterize the political connections between Cretan palaces and Cycladic communities on the basis of material culture alone (Broodbank 2004, 55–73; Davis 1986, 106–107; Karnava 2018, 236–237; Petruso 1992, 67).

Recent analyses have argued that Minoanizing forms of material culture and practice were adopted by Cycladic islanders as part of a "new environment" of intra-regional elite competition that viewed Cretan (perhaps especially Knossian) material culture as particularly high value, as outlined by Davis and Gorogianni (2008; see also Broodbank 2004, 62–65; Whitelaw 2005, 59–61). From this perspective, Cretan ways of doing things were adopted as Cycladic islanders tried to distinguish themselves within and between communities, which could have involved actively trying to develop stronger relationships with Cretans, as well. At the same time, Minoanizing material culture itself also may have played an important role in "colonizing" tastes in the islands and generating widespread interest in Minoanizing styles and practices (Knappett and Nikolakopoulou 2008, 35–39).

VIII. AREA B, AYIA IRINI, AND THE WIDER AEGEAN

At Ayia Irini, engagement with Minoanizing practices and material culture certainly formed part of local competitive strategies. Yet, continued production and consumption of mainland and Cycladic objects, as well as the construction of several large tombs in Periods VI and VII similar to those that exist in Attica, suggest that non-Minoanizing objects and practices were also incorporated into such strategies (Papadimitriou 2001, 132–136; Gorogianni, Abell, and Hilditch 2020, 633–634). Moreover, much of the evidence for Minoanization at the site is derived from ceramics, which are difficult to associate with explicitly elite strategies (see also Whitelaw 2005, 59–61). There is no spatial differentiation in the distribution of Minoan/Minoanizing products and those imported from or imitative of other regions, a pattern evident in House B and elsewhere at the site. Everyone in the community seems to have had access to both imported Cretan (which were not exclusively Knossian, e.g., **701**, from the only Period V deposit in Area B) and imitative Minoanizing products. The holistic perspectives on ceramic assemblages in Chapters 5–7 highlight how complicated and interwoven Cretan and Minoanizing elements were in production and consumption practices over Periods V–VII. Despite a clear new interest in Minoan and Minoanizing ways of doing things, pottery with connections to local traditions and other parts of the Aegean world never disappeared from the assemblage. Likewise, although a few nonlocal craftspeople probably arrived in the community over these periods, local production practices never fully replicated those of Crete.

The use of the Minoanizing potter's wheel, warp-weighted loom, and tripod cooking technologies after Period IV would not have required the movement of new craftspeople to the community (see also Cutler 2016). The appearance of these techniques for the first time at other Cycladic sites in the later MBA and early LBA, however, suggests that potters and weavers trained in Minoan or Minoanizing communities of practice were mobile in the wider Aegean during these eras (Cutler 2019; Gorogianni, Abell, and Hilditch 2016, 2017; Knappett and Hilditch 2015a). The transfer of other techniques, like wall painting, also suggests the movement of some Cretan-trained craftspeople to the islands (Boulotis 2000; Knappett 2018; Morgan 2020; Nikolakopoulou and Knappett 2016). (The presence of some red-painted wall plaster in Period IV deposits [Ch. 2] indicates that plaster-preparation techniques, at least, may have appeared before the era of Minoanization at Ayia Irini, although the technical relationship of these painted plasters to later Minoanizing wall painting has not been analyzed.) The appearance of new Minoanizing technologies, such as aromatic processing practices that used fireboxes, also may provide evidence for the movement of nonlocal craftspeople to Ayia Irini in this era. Although it has been argued that fireboxes might have acted as incense burners (e.g., Warren 1987, 2014), I follow Georgiou's interpretation that they were industrial tools (for discussion and references, see Abell 2020, 390–393, fn. 60). Using fireboxes would have required careful manipulation of ingredients and heat and so may have involved substantial training (Georgiou 1986, 4–22). The appearance of such tools—like the potter's wheel or vertical loom in previous generations—also therefore may have resulted from the movement of one or more trained craftspeople to Kea.

Imported loom weights also provide evidence for the small-scale mobility of weavers in Periods V–VII. Such objects have little value to people other than their owners and are easily replicated in local materials. Thus, imported loom weights have been proposed to represent personal possessions that moved with weavers (Cutler 2012, 2019). At Ayia Irini, imported loom weights came not just from Crete (e.g., **131**) but also from elsewhere in the Cyclades and eastern Aegean (e.g., **130, 132**; Cutler 2012, 149–150; Knappett and Hilditch 2015b, 203; an imported[?] spindle whorl from Area B [**134**] could perhaps be considered part of a similar phenomenon). This variety among imported loom weights suggests that the mobility of craftspeople was multidirectional within the Cyclades and between Aegean regions.

At Ayia Irini, there is no clear evidence for extra-domestic workshops or for the existence of specialists attached to a small group of elites in Periods V–VII. Rather, specialized crafting seems to have been undertaken by multiple production units and, when spatial evidence exists, craft production is associated with multiple houses, including House B (Ch. 2; Abell 2020; Davis 1984; Georgiou 1986; Schofield 1990). Although the status of wall painting specialists is unclear, other craftspeople using Minoanizing technologies probably operated in household contexts.

Despite the probable incorporation of some nonlocal artisans into the community over the course of Periods V–VII, there is no evidence that such people replaced local craftspeople or that local production traditions were abandoned, neither at the start of the Minoanization phenomenon nor thereafter. For example, despite their rarity in Neopalatial Crete (Alberti 2008, 28), spindle whorls continued to be made and used at Ayia Irini throughout these periods, extending a tradition that existed also in Period IV (e.g., **78, 79, 134, 209, 429, 430**). Spools, associated with pre-Minoanizing weaving techniques, did not go out of use until Period VI (Davis 1984, 163). Only a small subsection of Minoan-style loom weight types has been found at Cycladic sites, including Ayia Irini (Cutler 2016), which marks another area of divergence between local practices and Cretan ones. Vakirtzi (2019, 499–500) has argued that this targeted, limited (and early, at both Ayia Irini and Akrotiri) adoption of one kind of warp-weighted weaving from Crete was tied specifically to the production of heavy fabrics used for sails. It is possible that the intensification of interest in this weaving technology in the later MBA and early LBA might also be owed to a desire to produce Cretan-style textiles, especially given the popularity of Minoanizing garment styles in wall paintings at Akrotiri and Ayia Irini (Davis 1984, 162; Cutler 2016, 176–177).

Diversity in crafting techniques and in the output of local artisans is also apparent in the ceramic assemblage. In Period V, potters working with local raw materials began to produce more vessels with functional and stylistic connections to Crete. Yet, they also continued to make vessels with connections to other regions, including Cycladic cups and Minyan-style goblets, a pattern that continued into Periods VI and VII (Chs. 5–7; see also Gorogianni 2016). The continued, though limited, production of burnished vessels reflects ongoing interest in an explicitly non-Minoanizing form of surface treatment. Bichrome styles, although sometimes employing Minoanizing motifs, in other cases seem to reflect closer stylistic connections with imported bichrome- or polychrome-painted products from the mainland, Aegina, and the Cyclades (Chs. 5–7); these styles were also sometimes applied to non-Minoanizing shapes like goblets. Clearly, local potters were open to adapting shapes and motifs with connections to the Minoanizing repertoire in different and sometimes non-Minoanizing ways.

The Minoanizing potter's wheel was used more regularly in Periods V–VII, and it was employed to produce more kinds of shapes than previously (Gorogianni, Abell, and Hilditch 2016). Many shapes made on the wheel were Minoanizing, but some were not. The potter's wheel was not used consistently: some shapes that were often made with the wheel were not always made with the wheel, including even the iconic Type 1 handleless cup, which is comparable to the most common form of conical cups elsewhere in the Aegean (Gorogianni, Abell, and Hilditch 2016; Schofield 1999). This lack of technical patterning suggests that multiple potters in the community were making different choices about how to deploy Minoanizing wheel technology. All members of the pottery-making community of practice, however, seem to have participated in similar raw material selection, processing, and firing practices (Ch. 3). Outside of the use of the potter's wheel, local potters at Ayia Irini did not adopt typical Cretan pottery-manufacturing techniques like sand tempering or high firing. This long-term continuity of practice in the community demonstrates that local potters were selecting which aspects of Cretan manufacturing traditions to adapt, without replicating Cretan production techniques fully.

The cooking assemblage at the site was also diverse (for the importance of cooking practices in the context of Minoanization, see Schofield 1984a; Wiener 1990). Minoanizing tripods and baking trays were very popular at Ayia Irini from Periods V–VIII; most were locally produced, although a few were imported from other Cycladic islands and, more rarely, Crete (Gorogianni, Abell, and Hilditch 2017, 68–70). The long-lived tradition of using flat-bottomed baking trays in the Cyclades (Nikolakopoulou 2019; Sotirakopoulou 2016; Wilson 1999) suggests that the use of such trays in Period V and later may not have been strictly Minoanizing in all cases, despite their similarities in form to Cretan versions. Mainland- and/or Aeginetan-style cooking vessels continued to be imported and locally produced at Ayia Irini, albeit rarely, during Periods VI and VII (Gorogianni, Abell, and Hilditch 2017, 61–63). Davis (1986, 105) noted that a distinctive Cretan cooking dish with a thin rounded bottom has never been found at Ayia Irini, which highlights an additional difference in cooking practices between Keian and Cretan communities.

Deposits across the site incorporate imports from various parts of the Aegean, as well as local objects—especially ceramics—that either functionally or stylistically imitate objects typical of the Cyclades, mainland Greece, Aegina, and Crete. Non-Cretan Minoanizing ceramics were imported throughout these periods, and some had features that were atypical of Cretan products in their shape or decoration. For example, several Melian/Theran hole-mouthed jars that were imported in Period V were made with a basket handle that passed over the main opening of the jar, thus impacting how the vessel would be lidded and how the contents would be accessed or stirred (Davis 1986, 83–84). This form is very rare on Crete (Levi and Carinci 1988, 155) but appears more frequently at Miletus and elsewhere in the eastern Aegean (Heidenreich 1935–1936, 167, fig. F84; Kaiser 2009; Lamb 1936, 141, fig. 41:9, 9a; Marketou et al. 2006, 12, no. 64, fig. 2; Voigtländer 2004, pls. 65.4, 148). The popularity of this Minoanizing-but-not-quite-Minoan shape at Ayia Irini, therefore, may have been spurred by interaction with non-Cretan communities that were also participating in the Minoanization phenomenon (Abell, Crego, and Overbeck, forthcoming; see also Momigliano 2012, 159–170).

Despite local interest in manufacturing Minoanizing objects starting in Period V, there was not a corresponding increase in actual Cretan imports (Gorogianni and Abell, forthcoming). Instead, the proportion of mainland imports declined in Period V while the proportion of Cycladic imports, especially Melian/Theran ones, increased (Ch. 5). The functional similarities of Melian/Theran and Cretan imports and their relative abundance, especially in Period V, may suggest that Melian/Theran objects carried a perceived value similar to Cretan products. In Period VI and especially VII, Cretan imports declined in frequency and eventually became less common than imports coming from the mainland and/or Aegina (Chs. 6, 7; see also below).

The abundance of handleless cups in Period V–VII deposits speaks to the adoption and perhaps adaptation of Cretan-derived ritual feasting or toasting practices (Knappett and Hilditch 2015a; Wiener 2011, 2013). As noted previously, several handleless cup types at Ayia Irini are directly comparable to conical cup types on Crete (Schofield's types 1, 3, 4, and 5) (Cummer and Schofield 1984, pl. 47; Schofield 1999). Burning and perforation on some—especially those of Type 1—indicates that they had multiple uses, including as lamps and industrial objects (Schofield 1999). The majority, however, were probably intended for use in communal eating or drinking events. Such events may have been hosted by different households that provided vessels as well as food and drink to participants, as has been suggested for toasting events using conical cups on Crete (Girella 2007a; Rupp and Tsipopoulou 1999). If different households had to provide equipment for communal events, that might help to explain why thousands of handleless cups were found in destruction deposits of Periods VI and especially VII, when the population of the town was still probably less than 500 people (Schofield 1998, 119; Gorogianni 2016, 139; Wiener 2013, 154). If each household provided cups for events at which residents in the town and perhaps visitors to the site might participate, then the quantity of handleless cups in each house would be a reflection of the anticipated number of participants in such events, or the need to build up a stockpile for distribution at several such events.

Some aspects of Minoanization at Ayia Irini are most apparent in Period VII, in part because of the large, artifact-rich deposits of this phase. The majority of Minoanizing industrial implements were found in Period VII deposits (Georgiou 1986, 11–12, 28–29, 32, 41, 52–53), as were the majority of Temple statues (Caskey 1986) and Minoan and Minoanizing rhyta (Ch. 7). The use of the Minoanizing potter's wheel was more common and more standardized in its application to particular shapes in Period VII than it had been previously (Davis and Lewis 1985; Gorogianni, Abell, and Hilditch 2016). Minoanizing shapes were very common among local products, and imported vessels from the mainland, southeast Aegean, and Cyclades were often—although not always—Minoanizing in shape and decoration.

Yet, by Period VII, Minoan and Minoanizing material culture had been circulating for centuries, and local craftspeople had been using Minoanizing techniques for generations. Use of Minoanizing technologies and interaction with Minoanizing material culture over this long span of time must have impacted how local people understood them in their broader Aegean context. Contact with Minoanizing techniques, objects, and mobile craftspeople from within the Minoanized southern Aegean over time would have blurred the edges around what can appear to archaeologists to be strict categories of "Keian," "Cycladic," or "Cretan" material culture. Regular and, in some cases, daily interactions with such objects and practices would have reshaped the foreign into something that was understood to be embedded in local ways of doing things, with a deep history in the rhythms of life in the community (Abell and Gorogianni 2019).

Even the iconic handleless cups might have been subject to such shifts in meaning for residents of Ayia Irini. The use of handleless cups must have been recognized as being part of a Cretan-derived practice in the initial phases of their adoption, a fact suggested also by the fact that the technology of the Minoanizing potter's wheel seems to have been bound up with ideas of how to make a "correct" version of this vessel during the later MC and LC I (Hilditch 2014; Knappett and Hilditch 2015a). By the later stages of the Minoanizing phenomenon in LC II, however, these toasting or feasting practices could have been understood to form part of common southern Aegean ritual practices rather than ones exclusively connected to Crete, given the widespread—and by then, long-lived—use of the shape across the region. The importation of handleless cups from non-Cretan sources might also suggest that users recognized a wide regional association for the shape. In Area B, Cycladic (including Melian/Theran) imported versions of the shape are more common than Cretan ones in Periods VI and VII. The continued popularity of handleless cups in Period VIII (Morris and Jones 1998), after the decline of Cretan influence in the Aegean and the emergence of the Mycenaean palaces, also indicates that the popularity of the feasting or toasting practices that employed these vessels eventually became untethered from their original associations with Cretan ways of doing things.

Residents of Ayia Irini kept up with fashions across the wider Aegean over the course of Period VII. The very wide-ranging parallels for rare ceramic shapes provide an example (Ch. 7). Yet, by Period VII, those fashions were no longer exclusively being driven by Cretans, at least not at Ayia Irini. Cretan imports were less common than imports from other areas, especially the mainland (Ch. 7; Cummer and Schofield 1984, 146; Mountjoy and Ponting 2000). The reorientation of trade routes following the eruption of the Theran volcano may have contributed to this pattern (Gorogianni and Abell, forthcoming). Beyond trade patterns, the most common drinking shapes in Period VII, apart from handleless cups, were goblets, a mainland shape rather than a Cretan one; likewise, spouted bowls and kraters suggest links to mainland rather than Cretan drinking and consumption practices (Ch. 7). Residents of Period VII Ayia Irini were as, if not more, closely connected to mainland and Cycladic networks as to Cretan ones.

Over the course of Periods V, VI, and VII, residents of Ayia Irini were enmeshed in a material and social context that was not replicated on Crete, nor, indeed, totally comparable with other parts of the Cyclades (below), regardless of what political relationships existed with Cretan or other Aegean polities. Even if there was a period of external political domination, the idiosyncrasies of the Keian assemblage compared with contemporary Cretan ones demonstrate that any potential oversight did not extend into every aspect of local life, and it did not prevent members of the local community from engaging with Minoan and non-Minoanizing people and practices in a variety of different ways. It is, therefore, useful to consider some final points about exchange and consumption patterns at Periods V–VII Ayia Irini more broadly and with less focus on elucidating the complex material correlates of Minoanization in the town.

EXCHANGE AND INTERACTION BEYOND MINOANIZATION IN PERIODS V–VII

Shifts in intra-Cycladic exchange and production patterns occurred over the course of Periods V–VII. Melian/Theran imports became much more common in Period V than they had been previously (Abell 2016, table 2; Gorogianni and Abell, forthcoming, table 3). By contrast, Naxian vessels became more common in Phase C at Akrotiri, being even more numerous than Cretan vessels in some deposits (Hilditch 2019, 400–401, table 3.14, fig. 3.82; Mathioudaki 2019, 319). That is, the earliest phase of Minoanization at these towns saw an increase in evidence for importation of Cycladic, as well as Cretan and Cretan-style objects.

The relative proportions of imports at Cycladic sites also varied in the LBA. As mentioned above, Cherry and Davis (1982) noted a distributional fall-off pattern in mainland imports to the Cyclades during LC I, with many from Ayia Irini, few from Phylakopi, and very few from Akrotiri, a pattern that is consistent with what was presented here (Ch. 6) and recent publications from Akrotiri (Georma, Nikolakopoulou, and Bitis 2017, 481; Marthari 1990, 63; Mathioudaki 2019, 322). Southeastern Aegean imports seem to have been much more common at Akrotiri than Ayia Irini or Phylakopi in LC I, making up around 4% of the total assemblage, at least in sector Delta (Mathioudaki and Nikolakopoulou 2018, 68, chart 1; see also Davis et al. 1983; Gorogianni and Abell forthcoming; Hood 2007, 262). The majority of imports at LC I Akrotiri were Cretan, although Cycladic imports were also relatively common in Sector Delta (Georma, Nikolakopoulou, and Bitis 2017, 481; Knappett et al. 2011, 219–220; Kriga 2018, 59–60; Marthari 1990, 63; Mathioudaki and Nikolakopoulou 2018, 68). At Phylakopi, nonlocal Cycladic imports were about as common as Cretan ones (Cherry and Davis 1982, 337, ill. 2; somewhat different quantifications are provided by Berg 2007b [111, fig. 33], but it is not clear what was being counted there [sherd number, weights, minimum number of vessels], so I follow Cherry and Davis's results here). At Period VI Ayia Irini, most calculations suggest that mainland and Aeginetan imports, when considered together, were somewhat more common than those from Crete or the Cyclades (mainly Melos/Thera), but imports from all three regions were relatively well represented (Ch. 6). Thus, although Ayia Irini was unusual in the earlier MBA in terms of the relative proportion of Cretan imports in the assemblage, that pattern no longer held true by LC I, when Akrotiri was the only Western String site with a preference for imported pottery from Crete over other imported wares.

Intra-Cycladic import patterns also differ somewhat between these LC I sites. Melos and Naxos were the main sources of imported Cycladic pottery at LC I Akrotiri (Knappett et al. 2011, 220; Kriga 2018, 60). At Phylakopi, Cycladic imports are argued to be mostly northern and/or central Cycladic (perhaps Keian and Naxian) (Cherry and Davis 1982, 337, ill. 2; Davis and Cherry 2007, 268). On Kea, Melian/Theran imports form the largest group, although there is a mix of other Cycladic imports, as well (Ch. 6).

Akrotiri was destroyed late in LC I; LC II deposits at Phylakopi are poorly represented (Earle 2018 with references). At Grotta, there were more Cretan imports in LC II than previously (about 10% of imports) (Cosmopoulos 1998, 134–135). Naxos may have taken on a more prominent position in regional Cycladic and Aegean exchange routes in this era. For the first time in LC II, "other Cycladic" fabrics were more common than Melian/Theran ones in Area B. More mainland imports also began to arrive, from new production areas, including the Argolid. The diversity of imported ceramics at Ayia Irini in Period VI and especially VII may have been impacted, at least in part, by the emergence of an increasingly market-oriented Aegean during these centuries in which more communities began to produce more products for exchange, with more traders moving around the Aegean to take advantage of that production and concurrently expanding distribution patterns (for the growth of market-oriented forms of production and exchange in relation to the Minoanization phenomenon, see Davis 1984; Davis and Gorogianni 2008, 342; for a similar pattern of increased quantities and diversity among imports in early LH I Tsoungiza, see Rutter 2015, 217–220).

Much local specialized craft production took place at Ayia Irini during Periods V–VII, especially in the realm of metallurgy and/or metalworking and aromatic processing; more evidence for tools associated with these industries have been found on Kea than at most other Aegean sites (Abell and Georgakopoulou, forthcoming; Georgiou 1986, 4–22, 52–53). Given shifting exchange and production patterns elsewhere in the Aegean, local residents may have pursued more intensive modes of production over the course of these eras in order to compete more effectively not only with Cretan producers (Davis 1984, 160, 162–163; Davis and Lewis 1985, esp. 87–91) but with mainland and Cycladic ones, as well.

There is little evidence for direct regulation over either production or exchange at Ayia Irini, whether from inside the community or beyond it, especially before Period VII. House A has been hypothesized to be the residence of a town administrator, in part owing to its size and position opposite the main gate of the town (Cummer and Schofield 1984, 1). Although the house incorporated some Minoanizing features (Hitchcock 1998), several of the architectural embellishments of House A are also attested elsewhere, such as the Minoan-style banquet hall of the Northeast Bastion (Fitzsimons and Gorogianni 2017), the bathroom suite in House C (Schofield 2011, 195), or even the use of large, squared blocks for the facade of House B (Ch. 2). House A was not expanded to a size that was substantially larger than other houses in the town until Period VII. The assemblage of House A was not very different from other houses in the town in either Period VI or VII, and neither administrative documents nor weights or industrial tools are concentrated exclusively there. As noted above, the community always probably housed under 500 people (Schofield 1998, 119; see also Gorogianni 2016, 139). As such, most decision-making throughout these centuries was probably driven by face-to-face interaction (Johnson and Earle 1987; Kosse 1990). Members of House A, therefore, may not have been substantially elevated in the local social hierarchy before Period VII, and even during that phase, they may not have been able to exert stable or wide-ranging control over the town (see also Gorogianni and Fitzsimons 2017).

In LB I and II, regional networks increasingly became incorporated into a broader Aegean system of trade and interaction. Sharp boundaries between "mainland," "Cycladic," or "Cretan" styles of material culture began to break down as communities throughout the southern Aegean embraced various Minoanizing styles and practices in what can be compared to globalizing phenomena in other geographical and cultural contexts (Knappett 2016; Maran 2011). Some changes associated with the Minoanization phenomenon are most evident at the level of elites, including the more limited manifestations of Minoanization in mainland Greece (Wiener 1990; see also Davis and Gorogianni 2008; Maran 2011). Through competitive social behaviors and emulation, Aegean elites were making themselves ever more recognizable to each other, across a broad geographical area. The globalization of material culture and growing consensus around elite ideologies over the long-term probably had complicated impacts at Ayia Irini. On one hand, these shifts provided a context in which local residents could compete with each other and with other communities on a playing field with broadly similar terms of engagement. On the other hand, globalization of material culture styles and practices also may have begun to undermine the notional status of Ayia Irini as a town that could facilitate interaction across recognizable cultural divides, thus, forcing local residents to reconfigure their attempts to attract traders from different areas and participate in exchange in new ways.

As in Period IV, it would have been advantageous for local people during Periods V–VII to develop strong relationships with traders and visitors to the town in order to encourage stable, regular exchange connections. There were a variety of mechanisms that could have been utilized for this goal. As in previous periods, the incorporation of nonlocal craftspeople (and potentially other people) into the community over the long-term would have meant that families within the town were enmeshed in kinship webs that connected them to both neighboring and faraway communities. It is possible that some memory of such practices may be retained in legends like that of King Minos and the Keian princess Dexitheia, whose son by Minos, according to the myth, eventually ruled over Kea (Bacchylides, *Ode* 1). Claiming kinship connections with people from other areas, especially if such claims were accompanied by knowledge of distant social networks, could have served as a powerful tool for generating trust and encouraging participation in transactions. Abundant lead weights also could have been used to regulate transactions and encourage mutual commensurability of value with respect to commodities, especially as Minoanizing standards of weight became more commonly accepted across the southern Aegean (Petruso 1992).

Investment in communal ritual activities in these periods is attested by the abundance of handleless cups and rhyta, as well as continued use of the Temple (Caskey 1998). Knappett and Hilditch (2015a) suggested that the increased numbers of handleless cups on Crete, starting in MM III, might reflect more frequent participation in formalized and standardized ritual in daily life;

they argued that the development of more formalized rituals might also be suggested by the increase in the use of rhyta during the Neopalatial period, since rhyta probably were used for ritual pouring or libations (Koehl 2006). The increasing popularity of these shapes (handleless cups and rhyta) at Ayia Irini may reflect a similar shift toward more frequent and/or more formalized ritual behaviors in the community. Moreover, it might also reflect increased investment in promoting local ritual activities that were legible—at least to some degree—to communities in the Cyclades and beyond, which were becoming entrenched in an ever more substantially Minoanized southern Aegean over the course of the earlier LBA.

As in Period IV, events focused on the Temple, festivals, and other kinds of drinking, eating, or feasting occasions would have provided excellent opportunities to draw people from other parts of the Aegean to the town on a regular basis. Diversity in drinking shapes continued to be an important feature of the ceramic assemblage at Ayia Irini throughout Periods V, VI, and VII. The drinking assemblage of Periods V and VI Ayia Irini is composed of many Minoanizing shapes—handleless, straight-sided, and rounded cups were particularly common. Handleless cups were mostly, although not entirely, locally made. Although some straight-sided and rounded cups were made on Crete, many were imported from other Cycladic islands, especially from Melos and/or Thera (Chs. 5, 6). A purely Cycladic shape, the piriform cup, was more common among imports than Minoanizing open shapes at Ayia Irini in Period V; the shape continued to be a common import in Period VI. Piriform cups with their usual paneled decoration (common in Periods V and VI) would have been used and viewed differently than typical Cretan shapes (Davis 1978; see also Abell 2016). They were larger, and the paneled decoration was meant to face away from the viewer (assuming the drinker was right-handed), strongly implying that they were intended to be used during social drinking activities, where the decoration could be viewed by other participants. Common Cretan drinking shapes at Ayia Irini are generally smaller with a more limited capacity than piriform cups; they are either undecorated or decorated in horizontal zones. Both visually and practically, therefore, Cretan cups and Cycladic piriform cups would have evoked different behaviors and reactions from participants in drinking events.

Mainland-style goblets, both local and imported, continued to form a part of the assemblage at Ayia Irini during these periods, which suggests some degree of continuity with the earlier MBA in terms of drinking practice. That continuity mirrors the ongoing use of such shapes on the mainland. By Period VII, goblets—mostly rounded Mycenaean-style goblets, which were all imported from the mainland—were the most common drinking shape other than handleless cups in the Keian assemblage. The continued use of goblets and other mainland-derived shapes at Ayia Irini probably speaks to the ongoing importance of relationships between Keians and mainlanders during these periods. The use of goblets also distinguishes drinking practices at Ayia Irini from Crete as well as from Phylakopi and Akrotiri, where Minoanizing and Cycladic shapes seem to have been the major drinking and eating equipment throughout these eras (Barber 1987, 2007; Berg 2007b; Davis and Cherry 2007; Marthari 1980, 1984, 1987, 1990, 1993; Nikolakopoulou 2009; Nikolakopoulou et al. 2008; Papagiannopoulou 1991). The incorporation of all of these kinds of drinking equipment, as in previous periods, distinguishes the assemblage of Ayia Irini as remarkably multicultural in comparison with most neighboring communities, even ones in similar geographical positions that were liminal between cultural zones (coastal sites in Attica or southern Euboea, for example, or even Phylakopi; for detailed comparison between Kea and Attica, see Gorogianni, Abell, and Hilditch 2020, 630–633). It is probable, therefore, that the assemblage was shaped by long-term production and consumption strategies that privileged an openness in material culture and enabled local people to maintain links with ways of doing things across the wider Aegean.

EPILOGUE?

From EC II–LC II, for nearly one thousand years (with some interruption), Ayia Irini was a dynamic hub of exchange, an articulation point in interaction patterns for paddlers, sailors, and traders moving between mainland and Cycladic networks, and a key focus for access to Lavrion for Aegean people. In LC III, that role ended. Local residents continued to acquire pottery from several parts of mainland Greece (Morris and Jones 1998), but connections to other parts of the Cyclades and Crete (at least based on ceramic imports) vanished, suggesting that Ayia Irini had become peripheral to major exchange routes (Gorogianni and Abell, forthcoming). An entire way of life disintegrated—local potters stopped producing fine tablewares and imported such vessels wholesale from the mainland (Morris and Jones 1998). At the same time, many of the industries that had existed in Period VII declined (Georgiou 1986, 52).

These developments were probably impacted by the contemporary rise of Mycenaean palaces in mainland Greece. The centralizing force of Mycenaean palaces on the production of commodities like pottery and worked metals may have undermined local economic strategies, particularly if residents of Ayia Irini lost their ability to facilitate access between different Aegean communities and the metal resources of Lavrion (Gorogianni and Abell, forthcoming). The fact that the major producers and consumers of goods were now not coastal settlements, but inland Mycenaean palaces probably reoriented exchange networks (Mountjoy 2008a), either as a byproduct of the new location of strong consumer hubs, or as a result of new economic and political strategies of Mycenaean elites, or, very likely, both. The reorientation of the metals trade inland, rather than overseas, also would have undermined the role of Ayia Irini as the main point through which Lavrion metals were accessed, contributing to the shrinkage and eventual abandonment of the site as a place of residence in the LC III period.

CONCLUSIONS

Diachronic analysis of production and consumption patterns in Area B and at Ayia Irini has clarified aspects of exchange that shifted in response to changing conditions in the Aegean, and those that did not. The geography of the town in every period was significant in the context of maritime routes that facilitated the movement of metals and other goods within and beyond the Cyclades; knowledge of the possibilities for participation in exchange networks is probably what brought people to the site of Ayia Irini, time and time (and time) again, in the Final Neolithic, EBA, and MBA.

Ayia Irini was multicultural in all periods, incorporating nonlocal people, as well as material culture and practices from different Aegean regions into local contexts. The degree of intra-Aegean connections was significantly different in the EBA, before sailing boats or states appeared, and the MBA and LBA, when exchange intensified along maritime routes that were traversed by traders, as well as agents of Cretan states and the proto-state of Kolonna. The adoption of nonlocal practices in the MBA and LBA, particularly in socially loaded eating and drinking contexts, reflects changes in local internal status negotiations. Furthermore, through participation in eating, drinking, and feasting events with elements that would have been familiar to Cretans, Cycladic islanders, and mainlanders, at least some residents of Ayia Irini promoted notions of shared practices and identity not just with distant elites, but with sailors and traders (whether independent operators or not) from Aegina, Crete, other Cycladic communities, and mainland Greece.

Since economic and social strategies at Ayia Irini developed around the ability of local residents to facilitate access between exchange networks and the metal resources of Lavrion, particularly in the earlier MBA, the town seems to have played a somewhat different role in exchange networks than did other Cycladic settlements. This particular status eroded over the course of the later MBA and LBA, as Cretan polities engaged in new modes of interaction with the Cycladic islanders and as production and exchange intensified within the Cyclades themselves. Moreover, as Cretan, Cycladic, and mainland communities became ever more integrated into the "new environment" of the Minoanized Aegean in LB I and II, cultural or social barriers that had previously differentiated Aegean regions began to break down. The blurring of cultural boundaries probably undermined the status of Ayia Irini as a middle ground, where people from different backgrounds could interact in what previously had been a relatively unusual context of shared values. As the privilege of its position and its unique role between culturally different regions was undercut, especially after the emergence of the Mycenaean palaces in LC III, the settlement at Ayia Irini was again abandoned, echoing the Neolithic and EBA fates of the site.

APPENDICES

APPENDIX I: CONCORDANCE OF ROOM NUMBERS

Room no. in text	Excavation room no.
B.1	B-I
B.2	B-II
B.3	B-III
B.4	"Kitchen"
B.5	n/a
B.8	B-VIII

APPENDIX II: CONCORDANCE OF INVENTORY NUMBERS TO CATALOGUE NUMBERS

For numbering conventions, see p. 9 of this text. *Wall plaster fragment numbers from Coleman 1970.

Inv. No.	Cat. no.	Inv. No.	Cat. no.	Inv. No.	Cat. no.
B-1.32	**183**	B70: 11	**579**	B72: 10	**569**
B70: 1	**590**	B70: 12	**583**	B72: 11	**571**
B70: 2	**588**	B70: 15	**576**	B72: 12	**568**
B70: 3	**589**	B71a: 1	**597**	B72: 13	**573**
B70: 4	**585**	B71a: 2	**599**	B72: 14	**572**
B70: 5	**586**	B71a: 3	**598**	B72: 15	**564**
B70: 6	**591**	B71a: 4	**596**	B72: 16	**565**
B70: 7	**587**	B71a: 5	**594**	B72: 17	**561**
B70: 8	**577**	B71a: 6	**600**	B72: 18	**560**
B70: 9	**575**	B72: 1	**567**	B72: 19	**563**
B70: 10	**578**	B72: 2	**566**	B72: 20	**562**

Inv. No.	Cat. no.	Inv. No.	Cat. no.	Inv. No.	Cat. no.
B87: 1	751	B97: 21	715	B602: 6	10
B88: 6	756	B108: 1	340	B602: 7	17
B88: 8	754	B148: 1	601	B602: 8	9
B88: 11	755	B148: 2	602	B602: 9	16
B88: 20	758	B601: 1	57	B602: 10	12
B88: 22	753	B601: 2	40	B602: 11	11
B88: 23	757	B601: 4	41	B602: 12	13
B88: 24	752	B601: 5	72	B602: 13	15
B94: 1	738	B601: 6	54	B602: 14	23
B94: 2	737	B601: 7	61	B602: 15	19
B94: 4	743	B601: 8	60	B602: 16	25
B94: 10	739	B601: 9	69	B602: 17	21
B94: 12	741	B601: 10	67	B602: 18	26
B94: 13	740	B601: 11	63	B603: 1	279
B94: 16	742	B601: 12	62	B603: 2	299
B94: 21	734	B601: 13	68	B603: 3	301
B94: 22	728	B601: 14	75	B603: 4	300
B94: 24	729	B601: 15	73	B603: 6	286
B94: 25	730	B601: 16	55	B603: 7	295
B94: 26	735	B601: 17	44	B603: 8	283
B94: 27	731	B601: 18	58	B603: 9	303
B94: 28	733	B601: 22	65	B603: 10	314
B94: 29	727	B601: 23	64	B603: 11	294
B94: 30	736	B601: 24	76	B603: 12	306
B94: 31	732	B601: 26	45	B603: 13	284
B96: 1	721	B601: 27	56	B603: 14	293
B96: 2	720	B601: 31	59	B603: 15	302
B96: 8	722	B601: 32	53	B603: 16	312
B96: 12	716	B601: 33	43	B603: 17	290
B96: 14	718	B601: 34	39	B603: 18	285
B96: 15	717	B601: 35	70	B603: 19	281
B96: 16	726	B601: 36	71	B603: 20	280
B96: 18	724	B601: 37	74	B603: 21	310
B96: 21	725	B602: 1	27	B603: 22	308
B96: 24	719	B602: 2	22	B603: 23	309
B96: 28	723	B602: 3	20	B603: 24	287
B97: 13	712	B602: 4	14	B603: 25	288
B97: 16	713	B602: 5	18	B603: 26	282

Inv. No.	Cat. no.	Inv. No.	Cat. no.	Inv. No.	Cat. no.
B603: 27	**304**	B604: 33	**542**	B607: 7	**329**
B603: 28	**296**	B606: 1	**416**	B607: 8	**333**
B603: 30	**298**	B606: 2	**418**	B607: 9	**320**
B603: 31	**297**	B606: 3	**404**	B607: 10	**321**
B603: 34	**311**	B606: 4	**417**	B607: 13	**330**
B603: 35	**305**	B606: 5	**413**	B607: 14	**319**
B603: 36	**289**	B606: 6	**409**	B607: 16	**322**
B603: 37	**315**	B606: 7	**397**	B608: 1	**190**
B603: 38	**307**	B606: 8	**401**	B608: 2	**184**
B603: 39	**313**	B606: 9	**419**	B608: 3	**204**
B604: 1	**441**	B606: 10	**414**	B608: 4	**202**
B604: 2	**513**	B606: 11	**405**	B608: 5	**203**
B604: 3	**528**	B606: 12	**415**	B608: 6	**200**
B604: 4	**536**	B606: 13	**421**	B608: 7	**195**
B604: 5	**533**	B606: 14	**411**	B608: 8	**196**
B604: 6	**540**	B606: 15	**412**	B608: 9	**198**
B604: 7	**535**	B606: 16	**391**	B608: 10	**201**
B604: 8	**538**	B606: 17	**408**	B608: 11	**199**
B604: 9	**524**	B606: 18	**346**	B608: 12	**205**
B604: 10	**537**	B606: 19	**345**	B608: 13	**193**
B604: 11	**526**	B606: 20	**351**	B608: 14	**189**
B604: 12	**527**	B606: 21	**403**	B608: 15	**194**
B604: 13	**525**	B606: 22	**349**	B608: 16	**185**
B604: 14	**520**	B606: 23	**392**	B608: 18	**206**
B604: 15	**522**	B606: 24	**396**	B608: 19	**192**
B604: 16	**519**	B606: 25	**399**	B608: 25	**191**
B604: 17	**521**	B606: 26	**420**	B608: 28	**188**
B604: 18	**529**	B606: 28	**373**	B609: 1	**136**
B604: 19	**530**	B606: 29	**347**	B609: 2	**156**
B604: 21	**531**	B606: 30	**344**	B609: 3	**158**
B604: 22	**532**	B606: 32	**353**	B609: 4	**149**
B604: 23	**446**	B606: 33	**394**	B609: 5	**177**
B604: 24	**440**	B607: 1	**336**	B609: 6	**144**
B604: 25	**541**	B607: 2	**335**	B609: 7	**154**
B604: 26	**515**	B607: 3	**337**	B609: 8	**147**
B604: 27	**514**	B607: 4	**334**	B609: 9	**135**
B604: 31	**517**	B607: 5	**332**	B609: 10	**148**
B604: 32	**523**	B607: 6	**331**	B609: 11	**146**

Inv. No.	Cat. no.	Inv. No.	Cat. no.	Inv. No.	Cat. no.
B609: 12	**153**	B610: 21	**106**	B790: 5	**676**
B609: 13	**150**	B610: 22	**109**	B790: 6	**679**
B609: 14	**145**	B610: 23	**121**	B790: 7	**680**
B609: 15	**165**	B610: 26	**107**	B790: 8	**682**
B609: 16	**172**	B610: 27	**112**	B790: 9	**681**
B609: 17	**176**	B610: 30	**104**	B790: 10	**684**
B609: 18	**175**	B647: 1	**744**	B790: 12	**675**
B609: 19	**164**	B647: 2	**745**	B790: 13	**674**
B609: 20	**173**	B647: 3	**746**	B791/793: 1	**669**
B609: 21	**160**	B649: 1	**701**	B791/793: 2	**670**
B609: 22	**161**	B766: 1	**748**	B791/793: 3	**672**
B609: 23	**162**	B767: 2	**749**	B791/793: 4	**671**
B609: 24	**163**	B768: 1	**747**	B791/793: 5	**666**
B609: 25	**168**	B776: 1	**706**	B791/793: 7	**668**
B609: 26	**167**	B777: 1	**704**	B791/793: 9	**673**
B609: 27	**169**	B778: 1	**710**	B795/a/796: 2	**662**
B609: 28	**171**	B778: 2	**709**	B795/a/796: 3	**656**
B609: 29	**157**	B778: 3	**707**	B795/a/796: 4	**654**
B609: 30	**170**	B782: 1	**705**	B795/a/796: 6	**657**
B610: 1	**118**	B782: 2	**708**	B795/a/796: 7	**655**
B610: 2	**113**	B785: 1	**698**	B795/a/796: 9	**661**
B610: 3	**111**	B785: 2	**700**	B795/a/796: 10	**658**
B610: 4	**115**	B785: 4	**699**	B795/a/796: 11	**663**
B610: 5	**116**	B786: 1	**697**	B795/a/796: 12	**665**
B610: 6	**100**	B786: 2	**692**	B795/a/796: 14	**664**
B610: 7	**119**	B786: 3	**693**	B795/a/796: 15	**645**
B610: 8	**120**	B786: 4	**696**	B795/a/796: 16	**644**
B610: 9	**114**	B786: 5	**695**	B795/a/796: 17	**648**
B610: 10	**117**	B786: 6	**694**	B795/a/796: 18	**647**
B610: 11	**98**	B788: 1	**687**	B795/a/796: 19	**646**
B610: 12	**99**	B788: 2	**689**	B795/a/796: 20	**650**
B610: 13	**97**	B788: 5	**691**	B795/a/796: 22	**649**
B610: 14	**103**	B788: 6	**690**	B795/a/796: 23	**651**
B610: 15	**96**	B788: 7	**688**	B795/a/796: 24	**652**
B610: 16	**102**	B789: 2	**686**	B795/a/796: 25	**653**
B610: 17	**105**	B790: 1	**683**	B795/a/796: 26	**660**
B610: 18	**108**	B790: 2	**678**	B795/a/796: 27	**659**
B610: 19	**110**	B790: 3	**677**	B797/798: 2	**642**

Inv. No.	Cat. no.	Inv. No.	Cat. no.	Inv. No.	Cat. no.
B797/798: 3	643	B810: 3	275	B826: 11	35
B797/798: 5	639	B810: 17	278	B828: 10	3
B797/798: 7	638	B810: 18	276	B828: 9	4
B797/798: 8	637	B812 etc.: 7	271	B829: 1	2
B797/798: 10	640	B812 etc.: 8	272	B829: 2	1
B799: 1	632	B812: 7	273	B830: 3	211
B799: 2	634	B812: 11	274	B830: 5	212
B799: 3	636	B813: 1	270	F.45*	431
B799: 4	635	B813: 3	268	F.46*	432
B799: 6	633	B813: 5	267	F.47*	436
B801: 2	629	B814: 2	264	F.48*	437
B801: 8	631	B814 etc.: 2	265	F.49*	438
B801: 9	630	B814 etc.: 3	266	F.50*	439
B802: 3	627	B815 etc.: 1	262	F.51*	433
B803: 1	624	B815 etc.: 3	263	F.52*	435
B803: 3	625	B816: 1	261	F.53*	434
B803: 5	626	B817: 3	260	K.134	458
B804: 1	620	B817: 6	259	K.135	494
B804: 5	623	B818: 1	254	K.136	490
B804: 9	621	B818: 9	252	K.137	487
B804: 10	618	B818: 12	257	K.138	454
B804: 11	619	B818: 16	258	K.139	456
B804: 14	622	B820: 4	248	K.140	460
B804: 16	617	B820: 5	247	K.143	464
B805: 1	609	B821: 1	238	K.147	468
B805: 3	607	B821: 2	237	K.150	556
B805: 6	608	B824: 4	218	K.151	470
B805: 7	606	B825: 1	6	K.152	479
B805: 8	610	B825: 6	7	K.153	551
B805: 9	611	B825: 9	8	K.154	459
B805: 11	612	B825a: 1	5	K.155	478
B805: 12	615	B826: 1	32	K.157	462
B805: 14	613	B826: 2	31	K.158	485
B806: 3	605	B826: 3	30	K.159	443
B809: 1	341	B826: 5	29	K.160	510
B809: 2	342	B826: 8	36	K.161	550
B809: 3	343	B826: 9	34	K.162	486
B810: 2	277	B826: 10	33	K.163	472

Inv. No.	Cat. no.	Inv. No.	Cat. no.	Inv. No.	Cat. no.
K.164	484	K.265	509	K.367	376
K.165	475	K.266	543	K.378	374
K.166	466	K.267	476	K.385	381
K.167	461	K.268	558	K.416	137
K.168	502	K.279	364	K.421	450
K.169	465	K.280	367	K.426	187
K.170	552	K.281	360	K.446	453
K.171	471	K.282	372	K.448	442
K.172	508	K.283	361	K.453	501
K.173	480	K.284	356	K.459	580
K.174	504	K.285	393	K.462	581
K.175	444	K.286	366	K.478	387
K.176	445	K.287	355	K.490	385
K.177	518	K.288	371	K.496	584
K.178	473	K.289	398	K.497	451
K.179	506	K.290	354	K.498	452
K.180	457	K.291	357	K.504	386
K.181	482	K.292	348	K.566	582
K.182	467	K.293	358	K.635	140
K.183	555	K.294	359	K.661	495
K.184	138	K.295	370	K.670	512
K.185	488	K.296	362	K.672	492
K.186	505	K.297	365	K.673	500
K.187	549	K.298	369	K.677	498
K.188	455	K.299	363	K.697	449
K.189	481	K.300	368	K.702	155
K.190	474	K.330	186	K.708	326
K.193	491	K.333	463	K.710	143
K.194	548	K.334, K.1122	166	K.713	291
K.195	477	K.341	382	K.734	388
K.201	489	K.348	378	K.765	511
K.202	483	K.349	383	K.775	141
K.203	553	K.355	380	K.779	516
K.205	554	K.357	377	K.790	557
K.206	469	K.358	375	K.792	139
K.209	507	K.361	390	K.795	493
K.261	503	K.362	379	K.796	499
K.264	389	K.364	384	K.807	496

Inv. No.	Cat. no.	Inv. No.	Cat. no.	Inv. No.	Cat. no.
K.808	142	K.2049	406	K.4588	251
K.845	497	K.2082	448	K.4599	628
K.947	324	K.2083	66	K.4600	269
K.989	323	K.2084	422	K.4691A	256
K.1064	85	K.2091	534	K.4691B	255
K.1078	84	K.2092	410	K1.31	544
K.1085	87	K.2093	402	K1.39	179
K.1096	88	K.2101	539	K1.50	559
K.1097	46	K.2104	352	K1.51	209
K.1115	82	K.2108	50	K1.56	546
K.1122, K.334	166	K.2114	595	K1.58	182
K.1149	83	K.2115	174	K1.61	180
K.1154	122	K.2120	400	K1.70	545
K.1211	24	K.2147	395	K1.113	547
K.1212	350	K.2155	447	K1.118	424
K.1213	292	K.2156	603	K1.159	425
K.1214	42	K.2157	151	K1.167	593
K.1216	86	K.2159	208	K1.186	129
K.1224	328	K.2164	159	K1.188	127
K.1235	327	K.2181	178	K1.211	128
K.1265	51	K.2193	152	K1.217	78
K.1269	93	K.2668	338	K1.233	592
K.1274	52	K.4346	197	K1.248	428
K.1294	92	K.4399	207	K1.282	427
K.1350	90	K.4412	641	K1.285	318
K.1355	89	K.4413	667	K1.291	132
K.1372	47	K.4414	614	K1.292	130
K.1375	49	K.4415	223	K1.294	131
K.1392	325	K.4420	232	K1.297	339
K.1425	95	K.4540	714	K1.308	316
K.1426	91	K.4561	570	K1.310	134
K.1435	80	K.4569	243	K1.341	125
K.1441	48	K.4574	217	K1.367	126
K.1445	94	K.4575	246	K1.389	28
K.1483	81	K.4576	222	K1.398	574
K.1635	423	K.4581	253	K1.435	430
K.1802	407	K.4582	244	K1.437	79
K.1824	101	K.4583	245	K1.441	317

Inv. No.	Cat. no.	Inv. No.	Cat. no.	Inv. No.	Cat. no.
K1.446	124	K75.15	616	K76.20	225
K1.455	122	K76.3	37	K76.21	241
K1.533	133	K76.4	240	K76.22	234
K1.537	426	K76.8	38	K76.23	220
K1.571	429	K76.9	250	K76.24	219
K1.581	181	K76.11	216	K76.25	235
K1.635	77	K76.12	213	K76.26	226
K1.661	210	K76.13	215	K76.27	239
K7.158	604	K76.14	214	K76.28	249
K75.9	750	K76.15	233	K76.29	230
K75.10	703	K76.16	236	K76.30	221
K75.11	685	K76.17	242	K76.31	231
K75.12	711	K76.18	229	K76.32	227
K75.13	702	K76.19	228	K76.33	224

APPENDIX III: WARE DESIGNATIONS

Ware	Provenance	Main characteristics
EBA Black Burnished	Local, Cyclades	Red-brown, orange, or gray fabric, coated with thick black slip and burnished.
EBA Red-Brown Burnished	Local	Red-brown fabric, burnished, sometimes burnishing marks still visible
EBA Red-Brown Coarse	Local	Red-brown fabric, sometimes with applied or occasionally incised decoration
EBA Red-Brown Semifine to Semicoarse	Local	Red-brown fabric, sometimes coated with black wash or with applied decoration
Local Burnished	Local	Red-brown fabric, burnished
Local Painted	Local	Red-brown fabric, painted with dark paint on unslipped surface
Local Plain	Local	Red-brown fabric, no decoration
Local Slipped	Local	Red-brown fabric, coated with dark slip
Local Slipped and Burnished	Local	Red-brown fabric, coated with dark slip, burnished
Local Yellow Painted	Local	Red-brown fabric, unslipped surface painted with designs in yellow
Local Yellow Slipped	Local	Red-brown fabric, coated with yellow slip, often painted with black, red, and/or brown decoration
White-on-Gray	Local	Gray or gray-brown fabric, decorated with white or yellow paint (Period IV)
White-on-Red	Local	Red-brown fabric, decorated with white or yellow paint (Period IV)
Aeginetan Bichrome	Aegina	Orange or pale brown fabric, sometimes coated with yellow slip, painted with dark brown and red
Aeginetan or Mainland Burnished	Aegina, Mainland	Various hard-fired, fine fabrics, burnished
Aeginetan or Mainland Painted	Aegina, Mainland	Orange, pink, or pale yellow fabric with designs in non-lustrous or semi-lustrous red or brown paint; paint color is variable and not the same dull paint of the MH period
Aeginetan(?) Yellow Slipped	Aegina(?)	Orange or pale brown fabric, coated with yellow slip, painted
Argive Minyan	Northern Peloponnese	Fine red or reddish-brown fabric turning dark gray or black at surfaces, burnished

Ware	Provenance	Main characteristics
Cretan Slipped	Crete	Cretan fabrics, coated with yellow or pale brown slip, no other decoration preserved
Cycladic or Melian/Theran Burnished	Cyclades, Melos/Thera	Nonlocal Cycladic fabrics, burnished
Cycladic or Melian/Theran Painted	Cyclades, Melos/Thera	Nonlocal Cycladic fabrics with unslipped surface, painted with matt or semi-lustrous brown, black, red, and/or white paint, sometimes bichrome or polychrome painted
Cycladic or Melian/Theran Slipped	Cyclades, Melos/Thera	Nonlocal Cycladic fabrics, coated with dark slip or rarely thick white slip, not burnished
Cycladic or Melian/Theran Slipped and Burnished	Cyclades, Melos/Thera	Nonlocal Cycladic fabrics, coated with brown, black, or red slip, burnished
Cycladic or Melian/Theran Yellow Slipped	Cyclades, Melos/Thera	Nonlocal Cycladic fabrics coated with yellow slip, painted with brown, black, red, and/or white paint, sometimes bichrome or polychrome painted
Cycladic White	Melos/Thera	Very pale yellow, gray, or white fabric, sometimes also coated with white slip, decorated with black or brown paint
EBA Dark-Brown Slipped and Burnished	Syros(?), Cyclades	Micaceous pale-gray fabric, coated with thick slip and highly burnished; surface ranges from dark brown, reddish brown, to nearly black
EBA Orange-Buff Painted	Melos(?), Cyclades	Fine, orange or yellow-brown fabric with dark painted decoration
EBA Orange-Buff Semifine to Coarse	Melos(?), Cyclades	Orange or yellow-brown fabric, sometimes painted with dark paint, occasionally white painted
EBA Pinkish Buff	Euboea	Fine, hard-fired, pink or yellowish-pink fabric, often plain, but sometimes slipped or painted with red or brown
EBA Talc	Siphnos (or Melos?)	Soapy, red-brown to mauve fabric, often with grooved or applied decoration
EBA Urfirnis	Mainland, western Cyclades(?)	Fine, pale pink, yellow, or gray, hard-fired fabric, with lustrous, crackly black slip
EBA Yellow Mottled	Mainland	Fine, hard-fired, orange to yellow fabric coated with yellow slip and burnished
Gray/Black Burnished	Unknown	Soft, dusty dark gray to black fabric, burnished
Gray Minyan	Central Greece/Euboea	Fine, dark gray, hard-fired fabric, burnished or well-smoothed
Lustrous Decorated	Mainland/Kythera	Fine, tempered, slightly dusty, pale brown fabric with large, lenticular, very dark-brown or black inclusions, painted with lustrous paint

Ware	Provenance	Main characteristics
Lustrous Painted	Mainland, Attica(?), Aegina, Crete, Mainland/Kythera	Pale fabrics decorated with designs (Minoan/Minoanizing) in lustrous brown or black, can be DOL, LOD, or Monochrome; sometimes painted over yellow slip, sometimes burnished
Mainland Polychrome	Central Greece	Fine, hard-fired dark pink to purplish brown fabric, burnished, painted with matt black and red
Mainland Slipped	Mainland	Fine, compact, hard-fired, pale pink or orange fabric, coated with yellow or very pale brown slip, no other decoration
Matt Painted	Aegina, Mainland	Pale yellow to nearly white fabrics with geometric designs in matt dark-brown to black paint
Minoan	Crete	Published Period V–VII vessels in Cretan fabrics, plain and decorated
Minoan/-izing	Unknown	Period IV vessels of uncertain provenance, with Cretan or Minoanzing shapes and/or decorative styles
Non-Lustrous Painted	Crete, Mainland/Kythera	Sand-tempered fabrics, painted with non-lustrous brown or black paint, can be DOL, LOD, or Monochrome; occasionally painted over yellow slip. Not completely dull like the paint used for MH Matt Painted
Pink-Orange	Central Greece	Fine, hard-fired, pink-orange fabric
Plain	All	Undecorated vessels in various fabrics
Red Coated	Aegina, Attica(?), Cyclades(?)	Fine to moderately fine, orange or pale brown fabrics, coated with red or pinkish-orange slip
Standard Matt Painted	Aegina	Pale yellow or pale orange fabric with sparse designs in matt brown
Yellow Minyan	Mainland	Fine yellow fabric, burnished

APPENDIX IV: DESCRIPTIONS OF MACROSCOPIC FABRIC GROUPS

A summary of the characteristics of each macroscopic fabric subgroup is provided, according to the template below, which is modeled on that developed by Hilditch (2008, 146; 2019, 379). Fabric groups are ordered with local and local region fabrics (RBM) first, followed by imports. Coarse imports (FST, DV, MxM, CSW, PBS) are presented before fine ones (MFV) with the finest group (FV) last. Coarse imports are ordered from generally more common to less common across the assemblage. The relation of each macroscopic group to petrographic groups is described (see also Ch. 3, Appendix V). When possible, reference is made to preliminary interpretation of the results of wave-dispersive X-ray fluorescence (WD-XRF), undertaken by Noémi Müller at the Fitch Laboratory at the British School at Athens (Appendix VII). References to frequency of inclusions follow the terminology of Kemp (1985, 17). Predominant >70%; Dominant 50–70%; Frequent 30–50%; Common 15–30%; Few 5–15%; Very few 2–5%; Rare 0.5–2%; Very Rare <0.5%.

PRESENTATION TEMPLATE

GROUNDMASS
a) degree of firing (roughly determined by hardness of fabric when scratched by a fingernail), i.e., hard is well-fired, soft is low-fired;
b) color of fabric, including any visible variation between core and margins or surface;
c) density of visible inclusions within the overall fabric, i.e., sandy, gritty, sparse, etc.;
d) texture of the sherd break, reflecting clay properties, i.e., smooth, semi-textured, textured, etc.;
e) range of thicknesses observed in vessel walls;
f) feel of sherd between fingers, i.e., dusty, smooth, soapy, etc.;
g) density of visible voids within the overall fabric;
h) other consistent features of sherd exterior or interior surfaces, i.e., spalling, etc.

COARSE FRACTION (CF)
a) size range of visible inclusions;
b) relative frequency of coarse fraction, using terminology from Kemp (1985, 17);
c) inclusion types (in order of abundance, highest first):
   i) color range, optical properties, degree of hardness, habit (rounded [r], subrounded [sr], subangular [sa], or angular [a]) of inclusions

FINE FRACTION (FF)
a) color of visible fine particles

RED-BROWN METAMORPHIC (RBM)

RBM fabrics are reddish brown and gritty. They contain mica and metamorphic inclusions, mainly schist. RBMa and RBMb are almost certainly local. Samples from these fabrics were associated with PFG 1, the main local fabric, in the petrographic analysis. Three subgroups (RBMc–e) are geologically compatible with a local origin but have unusual qualities compared to presumed local products. In petrographic analysis, most samples from those macroscopic subgroups (RBMc–e) were associated with PFG 2, which is broadly compatible with a local origin but has some dissimilarities from PFG 1 that might suggest an origin in the broader local region of eastern Attica, southern Euboea, and/or the western Cyclades. Therefore, RBMa and RBMb are referred to as "local" and RBMc–e are described as "local region."

RBMa: MICACEOUS, RED-BROWN CLAY, SCHIST INCLUSIONS

This group was common in all periods. It corresponds with Hilditch's (forthcoming) main local (A1) group in her study of pottery from the Northern Sector. It is red- or orange-brown with schist inclusions and mica, sometimes turning darker or gray at the core, more rarely turning dark gray at the surfaces or throughout. It ranges from medium-fine to coarse in texture. The fabrics are variable. Common variations include versions that are very micaceous at either the break or surface or contain sparse phyllite or calcareous inclusions. Petrographically, variations of the fabric, with the exception of those that turned gray at the core, do not seem to be related to a patterned difference in clay sources, processing behaviors, or firing strategies. Twenty-four sherds from this group were sampled for petrographic analysis (Table 3.2). The majority were classed in PFG 1A and 1C. Two samples (5, 41) were classed in PFG 1B. Two samples (3, 49), were classed as PFG 1D. Three samples (19, 28, 50), all of which were macroscopic variants, were associated with PFG 2B.

Moderately low- to moderately high-fired, orange- to red-brown fabric, sometimes with gray or darker red-brown core and/or surfaces; gritty paste with textured break; thin- to thick-walled vessels; voids few to common, mainly vughs, more rarely round or obvious spalling

0.5 mm<CF<1 cm, inclusions few to common, in order of abundance:

Gray, green, gold, purple, pink, brown schist inclusions, sr–sa; white, light gray, pink, and pale blue-gray inclusions, hard, sr; semi-translucent white, gray, yellow inclusions, hard, sr–sa; silver particles, platy; shiny black particles, r; purplish red particles, hard, sr; rare gold particles, platy; white to yellow calcareous(?) inclusions, soft, r–sr; brown and greenish gray phyllite(?) inclusions, planar

FF<0.5 mm

Sparkling silver particles; gray–brown inclusions (schist?) (above); white, black inclusions (above); rare gold particles

RBMb: VERY MICACEOUS, SILVERY-BLUE SCHIST, RARE SOAPY INCLUSIONS

This fabric was most common in Period III deposits in Area B. It is characterized by its orange to red or dark red-brown fabric, sometimes with a well-defined gray or blue-gray core and common, lenticular, shiny, silvery blue-gray or sometimes silvery-white (overfired?) platy schist inclusions. Bluish gray soapy inclusions are often present in the EBA version of this fabric; such inclusions are both smaller and more rare in MBA and LBA versions of the fabric. A variant has rare calcareous inclusions. Four petrographic samples (8, 9, 11, 26) of this fabric were classed as PFG 1B, while another three (6, 7, 12) were classed as PFG 1D. A macroscopic variant (RBMb/RBMc) that was sampled (10) was classed as a variant of PFG 2A.

Low- to moderately well-fired, orange to red-brown fabric, sometimes mottled with gray/black or entirely gray/black, often with gray or blue-gray core; gritty paste with textured break; mostly moderately thick-walled vessels; few to common voids, mostly vughs

0.5 mm<CF<7 mm, inclusions common, in order of abundance:

Shiny, silvery gray or white to dark blue-gray inclusions, lenticular, probably schist, sr; shiny white inclusions, hard, r–sr; semi-translucent white, gray, bluish-gray inclusions, hard, sr–sa; dark blue to blue gray inclusions, soapy, sr; brown, gray, purple schist inclusions; silver particles; white inclusions, calcareous(?), soft, sr; shiny dark gray–black inclusions, hard, sr–sa

FF<0.5 mm

Silver particles, common throughout; blue, gray particles, sr–sa (above); pale (white, yellow, pink, gray) particles, r–sr (above); rare gold particles

RBMc: CALCAREOUS INCLUSIONS

This orange to red, brittle fabric is distinguished from other RBM fabrics by its large, obvious calcareous particles and spalled surface; it sometimes appears to have a more compact paste at the break than the typical local fabric, RBMa. It was found in deposits of all periods. A distinctive, moderately fine EBA subgroup is made up of relatively thin-walled vessels with well-smoothed surfaces, sometimes covered with wash. Of three petrographic samples from this subgroup, one (22) was classified in PFG 1C (Local), and two (20, 21) were classified in PFG 2B (Local region). One macroscopic variant (RBMb/RBMc) was sampled (10) and classed as a variant of PFG 2A.

Moderately well-fired, orange to red fabric, sometimes with gray core; brittle paste, textured break; thin- to thick-walled vessels; few to common voids, mostly vughs, spalling at surface

0.5 mm<CF<4 mm, inclusions few to frequent, in order of abundance:

Gray, gold, purple, green schist inclusions, platy, lenticular–sr; semi-translucent white, gray inclusions, hard, sr–sa; off-white or yellow inclusions, friable (calcareous?), sr–r; rare, shiny black inclusions, hard, sr–sa

FF<0.5 mm

Sparkling silver particles; sparkling gold particles; gray particles (schist?) (above); white particles (above)

RBMd: GOLD MICA

This fabric is red-brown, often with a gray or bluish-gray core. It was found in deposits of all periods. It is differentiated from the other RBM fabrics because of its relatively common gold schist and/or gold mica. Petrographic analysis of six samples from this group classed four (16, 24, 25, 47) in PFG 2 (Local region) and two (23, 48) in PFG 1 (Local).

Moderately high-fired, reddish-brown fabric, sometimes with darker red-brown or bluish gray core; gritty paste, textured break; thin- to thick-walled vessels; few to common voids, mostly vughs

0.5 mm<CF<6 mm, inclusions few to common, in order of abundance:

Gold, dark gray, brown, green, silver schist, sa–sr; semi-translucent white–gray or yellow inclusions, hard, sr; white, pink, gray inclusions, hard, sr–r; black inclusions, smooth, hard, r–sr; gold particles, platy
FF<0.5 mm
Gold particles; silver particles; shiny black and fewer shiny gray particles; white, yellow and gray particles (above)

RBMe: FREQUENT FINE SILVER MICA AND QUARTZ

This subgroup is rare and appears only in EBA Red-Brown Semifine to Semicoarse ware in Period III deposits in Area B. The fabric is distinguished by its frequent fine silver mica at the surface, as well as the presence of common knobby, semi-translucent (probably quartz) particles. All four samples (32–34, 115) of this fabric were classed as PFG 2A (Local region).
Moderately well-fired, dark red to red-brown fabric, sometimes with darker core; brittle or gritty paste, textured break; moderately thick-walled vessels; common voids, mostly vughs
0.5 mm<CF<6 mm, common inclusions, in order of abundance:
Gray, green, silver schist particles, sr–sa; semi-translucent, white, particles, knobby and hard, sr–sa
FF<0.5 mm
Silver mica, especially common at surface; gray, green, white, pink, orange particles

FINE-GRAINED, SAND-TEMPERED, NON-MICACEOUS (FST)

These fabrics are non-micaceous and fine-grained, with a sharp, low-textured or flat break. They appear to be quite high-fired, giving off a high-pitched "clinky" sound when tapped. The more-or-less bimodal size distribution of inclusions, combined with their round to subangular habit, suggests that these fabrics were sand-tempered. There is substantial variation in the color of the paste and the characteristic inclusions; nine macroscopic subgroups have been distinguished. These fabrics are closely associated with imported Minoan and Minoanizing wares from Period IV–VII deposits. Petrographic analysis suggests origins on Crete as well as the mainland and/or Kythera for most subgroups, although additional sampling is needed in order to clarify more fully the coherence of macroscopic groups and the possible provenances thereof.

FSTa: COMMON DARK GRAY LENTICULAR INCLUSIONS (MUDSTONES/SILTSTONES)

This pale yellow to pink fabric contains dark, hard, lenticular inclusions, probably mudstones and siltstones (cf. Hilditch 2019, 383, FCSa). Two samples (55, 56) were taken for petrographic analysis. Both were classed in PFG 7 as probable central Cretan fabrics (Table 3.2).
Well-fired, pale yellow to pale pink fabric; slightly gritty paste, semi-textured to low-textured break, smooth feel, moderately thin- to thick-walled vessels; few to common voids, mainly vughs; some spalling at surface
0.5 mm<CF<7 mm, inclusions few to frequent, in order of abundance:
Dark-brown or dark red-brown and gray inclusions, hard, lenticular–sr; pale, matt gray inclusions, lenticular–sr; white or yellow (calcareous?) inclusions, friable, r–sr; semi-translucent white to gray, hard, sr–sa
FF<0.5 mm
Dark-brown, red-brown, and dark-gray inclusions (above); pale-gray inclusions (above); white or yellow inclusions (above); semi-translucent white and gray inclusions (above); silver inclusions, very rare

FSTb: COMMON RED-BROWN LENTICULAR INCLUSIONS

This fabric is usually dark pink or orange, with primarily red and red-brown lenticular particles. Only one sample (66) of this group was taken for petrographic analysis; it was classed in PFG 6, probably Cretan. In that sample, lenticular inclusions are primarily metamorphic rock fragments and siltstones.
Well-fired, pink to pale orange fabric, rare core/margin differentiation; somewhat gritty paste, semi-textured to low-textured break, smooth feel, moderately thin- to thick-walled vessels; few to common voids, mainly vughs; some surface spalling
0.5 mm<CF<7 mm, inclusions few to frequent, in order of abundance:
Red and red-brown inclusions, hard, lenticular–sr; white and yellow (calcareous?) inclusions, friable, sr–r; semi-translucent, white to gray inclusions, hard, sr–sa
FF<0.5 mm
Red, red-brown inclusions (above); white and yellow inclusions (above); semi-translucent, white or gray (above); silver particles, very rare

FSTc: SLIGHTLY DUSTY, MIXED SAND

This fabric is distinguished on the basis of its less densely packed clay, compared with FSTa and FSTb, as well as the wide variety of colors and shapes of inclusions. The only petrographic sample (68) from this group was classed in PFG 7 with a proposed origin in Crete or the Peloponnese; preliminary interpretation of the WD-XRF results suggests that this petrographic group may be compatible with a Cretan origin.

Well-fired, dark-brown/gray to pale brownish-pink fabric; somewhat gritty paste, semi-textured break, slightly dusty feel, moderately thin- to thick-walled vessels; few to common voids, mostly vughs

0.5 mm<CF<5 mm, inclusions few to frequent, in order of abundance:

Black and dark gray inclusions, hard, lenticular-sa; semi-translucent white inclusions, hard, sr-sa; white, yellow, pale pink inclusions, friable, sr-r; shiny, gray, angular inclusions, hard, a-sa; black, porous(?), dull, sr-r; shiny, white inclusions, hard, sr-sa; dark red to orange inclusions, hard, sr-sa; red and brown, hard, planar, sr-sa

FF<0.5 mm

Dark gray, black, red, orange inclusions (above); white, yellow inclusions (above); shiny white and semi-translucent white inclusions (above); silver particles, very rare

FSTd: ROSY PINK WITH KNOBBY BLACK INCLUSIONS

This fabric is distinguished by the inclusion of very few to rare knobby black to red particles in a hard-fired, deep rosy pink fabric, usually turning slightly paler toward the surfaces. The mainland style of a Palace Style jar in this fabric (**173**) could suggest that a mainland production center is possible for some or all vessels categorized in this group. Petrographic analysis classed both samples (74, 75) of this fabric in PFG 7H, tentatively associated with the Argolid or Corinthia; preliminary interpretation of the WD-XRF results also suggests that the group may be incompatible with an origin on Crete.

Well-fired, reddish pink fabric, often with color variation between core and margins, sometimes with yellow margins, turning reddish pink and/or gray at core; somewhat gritty paste, semi-textured break, thick-walled vessels with a smooth feel; few voids, mostly vughs; some spalling

0.5 mm<CF<7 mm, inclusions few to common, in order of abundance:

Red, dark gray, dark-brown, and knobby black and black to red inclusions, hard, porous(?) with uneven texture, sr-sa; black, gray, red-brown inclusions, smooth and hard, a-sa; white and pale yellow inclusions, friable, r-sr; semi-translucent white to pale-gray inclusions, hard, sr-sa

FF<0.5 mm

Red, dark gray, dark-brown, knobby black inclusions (above); white and pale yellow inclusions (above)

FSTe: FINE SAND

This subgroup was only recognized in Period IV contexts. The fabric is orange to pale pink, sometimes with a gray, pale brown, or rosy pink core. It is tempered with fine sand, grains of which are mostly pale in color (perhaps mostly quartz?). A variant has coarser sand inclusions, which also tend to include more dark-colored grains than the main group. Petrographic analysis suggests that the macroscopic group is not completely coherent. Three samples were taken, which were classed as PFG 6B (77), 6C (67), and 7E (65). Preliminary analysis of WD-XRF results of samples 65 and 67 suggests that they are compatible with a Cretan provenance.

Hard-fired, orange to pale pink or pinkish orange fabric, sometimes with a gray, brown, or rosy pink core and/or turning paler at surfaces; sandy texture; low-textured break; thin- to moderately thick-walled vessels; somewhat dusty; very few to common voids, mostly vughs, sometimes oriented parallel to vessel walls, and vesicles, perhaps from loss of rounded fine sand inclusions; spalling rare or absent

0.25 mm<CF<1 mm, inclusions absent to very rare, in order of abundance:

White (calcareous?), rarely spalling, occasionally rounded, shiny, and partially hollow, sr–r; semitranslucent white (quartz?), hard, shiny, sr–sa; dark gray to black, elongate inclusions; matt dark gray to black, sa–sr; shiny pink to gray, elongate inclusions; red-brown, sr or elongate inclusions; shiny black, hard, sr

FF<0.25mm

Semitranslucent white, gray, white, brown, black, red-brown, red, pink inclusions, sr

FSTf: ORANGE TO RED, MIXED INCLUSIONS

This fabric was most common in Period IV deposits and appeared only rarely in Period VI deposits. It was orange-brown to bright orange or red, with a wide variety of inclusion types, including spalling calcareous inclusions and possible metamorphic rocks. No good parallels for this fabric have been found. The group is somewhat broadly defined and contains several variations.

It is difficult to distinguish between variants, owing to overlaps between inclusion types and similarities in color and texture. The first variant may be bright orange to orange brown, sometimes turning paler at the surface or gray at the core. It generally has both pale-colored and dark inclusions and usually less common spalling/calcareous inclusions than the other variants; pale inclusions include primarily shiny white or semitranslucent white and spalling calcareous inclusions, while dark inclusions are varied, including knobby black grains as well as lenticular, foliated, gray and rarely pink (metamorphic?) inclusions. The second variant more regularly has a gray core and ranges in color from orange to sometimes purplish brown. It includes both pale and dark inclusions like those in the first variant, with the addition of rare glassy clear to brown inclusions; it also tends to have more spalling and friable off-white inclusions. A third variant has frequent spalling calcareous inclusions, as well as relatively rare dark inclusions similar to those above and elongated red or brown, compact grains (perhaps mudstones/siltstones?). Petrographic analysis suggests that the macroscopic fabric group is not coherent, which is not that surprising, given the range of variation within it. One sample (81) of this fabric taken for petrographic analysis was classed as PFG 6C and associated with Cretan production; the fabric of the sampled vessel (**662**) belongs to the first fabric variant of FSTf, described above. Another sample (80) was classed as PFG 7D; the fabric of this sampled vessel (**635**) belongs to the third variant of FSTf. Preliminary interpretation of the WD-XRF results suggests that both of these petrographic groups may be compatible with a Cretan provenance.

Well-fired, brownish orange or purplish brown to bright orange or red fabric, sometimes with a dark gray, and/or paler surfaces; gritty paste, semi-textured to flat break, moderately thin- to thick-walled vessels; common voids, mostly vughs

0.5 mm<CF<7 mm, inclusions few to common, often in different proportions and not always all present:

Dark red and gray inclusions, hard, sa–r and sometimes lenticular; gray and rarely pink, foliated, lenticular; dark-brown, black, purplish red inclusions, hard, knobby, sr–sa; white or yellow (calcareous?) inclusions, friable, sr; semi-translucent and milky white inclusions, hard, sr–r; glassy, clear to yellowish brown inclusions, hard, glassy, a–sa

FF<0.5 mm

White or yellow particles (above); dark gray, brown, red inclusions (above); semi-translucent and bright white inclusions (above)

FSTg: PALE PINKISH BROWN WITH DARK SILTSTONES

This fabric was restricted mainly to Period IV in Area B. It is pale yellow to pinkish brown, sometimes with a purplish tinge at the break, and a greenish cast at the surface. Its inclusions are almost exclusively smooth, angular or planar, very dark-brown or black inclusions, probably mostly siltstones. The paste was slightly grainier than FSTa and FSTb, and the surface is somewhat dusty. This fabric was associated primarily with MBA Minoanizing Lustrous Decorated ware and has similarities with some Lustrous Decorated ("Oatmeal") ware vessels from Lerna in the study collection of the American School of Classical Studies at Athens. A similar fabric for Lustrous Decorated ware was described from Ayios Stephanos, where it was considered a possible Kytheran import (Zerner 2008, 201–206). The fabrics of some Middle Helladic Matt Painted (MHMP) vessels from Tsoungiza housed in the Nemea Museum appear to be similar to this group; it is possible that some sherds in Area B that do not bear decoration could belong to MHMP ware rather than Lustrous Decorated ware. Petrographic analysis of two samples (82, 84) from this group classed both in PFG 7C, associated with Crete or the Peloponnese. Preliminary interpretation of the WD-XRF results suggests that the group may be compatible with a Cretan origin. One macroscopic variant that was sampled (83) was associated with PFG 8A of unknown origin; another (64) was associated with PFG 7F, tentatively associated with the mainland or Kythera.

Well-fired, pale yellow to pinkish brown fabric, occasionally with a purplish tinge at the break, and often a greenish cast at the surface; somewhat gritty fabric, semi-textured break, moderately thin- to thick-walled vessels; common voids, mostly vughs; some spalling at surface

0.5 mm<CF<7 mm, inclusions common to frequent, in order of abundance:

Shiny, black or very dark gray inclusions, planar, lenticular–sa; white or pale yellow (calcareous) inclusions, friable, sr–r; shiny white inclusions, very rare, hard, sr–r

FF<0.5 mm

Shiny black or dark gray inclusions (above); white or pale yellow (calcareous?) inclusions (above); silver mica, very rare

FSTh: BROWN WITH SPARSE DARK INCLUSIONS (MUDSTONES, SILTSTONES)

This moderately fine brown fabric has little variety in inclusions, which are mainly small, lenticular, black or very dark gray particles, probably mostly mudstones and siltstones. This fabric appeared primarily in Period VI and VII deposits. Three samples (61–63) from this group were classed in PFG 7G, tentatively associated with the mainland (Corinthia/Argolid?) or Kythera. Preliminary interpretation of the WD-XRF results suggests that the group may be incompatible with a Cretan source. A variant (sample 64) was classed in PFG 7F, also hypothesized to be from mainland Greece or Kythera.

Well-fired, pinkish to purple-brown fabric; fine paste, semi-textured to flat break, thin- to moderately thick-walled vessels; voids few to common, mainly vughs; rare spalling at surface

0.5 mm<CF<3 mm, inclusions rare, in order of abundance:

Black, dark gray, and brown inclusions, hard, shiny, lenticular, sa–sr; white and off-white/pale yellow (calcareous?) inclusions, friable, sr–r
FF<0.5 mm
Dark gray, black, brown inclusions (above); white particles (above)

FSTi: COMMON CALCAREOUS INCLUSIONS AND SPALLING

This fabric was only found in Period IV deposits. It is pale pinkish brown with a gray core; it is marked by frequent spalling and the predominance of pale-colored (white and off-white) probably calcareous inclusions. A variant of the group ranges in color from bright orange (sometimes with no core) to purplish brown with a gray core; this variant usually has rare to few rounded, knobby black and/or lenticular, planar black inclusions in addition to common calcareous and spalling inclusions. Samples of both the main group and the variant (57–60, 69, 76, 78, 79) were all classed in PFG 8 of unknown origin. A few subgroups (PFG 8C–E) have broad parallels with southeastern Aegean fabrics, but other sources are also possible.
Well-fired, pale pinkish brown to pale orange fabric, usually with a bluish-gray core; somewhat gritty paste and dusty at the surface, semi-textured break, moderately thin- to thick-walled vessels; common to frequent voids, mostly vughs; common spalling at surface
0.5 mm<CF<6 mm, inclusions common to frequent, in order of abundance:
White, pale yellow, and pale pink (calcareous?) inclusions, friable and knobby, sr; shiny white inclusions, hard, sr–sa; elongated and/or lenticular gray inclusions (metamorphic?); dark gray and black inclusions, hard, sr–sa
FF<0.5 mm
White and off-white particles (above); shiny and semi-translucent white particles (above); dark gray and black particles (above); silver/gold mica, very rare

FSTj: FINE, PALE YELLOW TO PALE PINK, RARE RED OR DARK-BROWN INCLUSIONS

This slightly dusty, pale yellow to pink to pale brown fabric bears few or no visible inclusions. When inclusions were present, they were usually dark brown or red. Macroscopically, this fabric was hypothesized to be a fine variant of one or more of the FST fabrics, especially given its association with Minoan/-izing and Lustrous Painted wares in Periods IV–VII. The two samples (70, 71) subjected to additional analysis were classed in different petrographic groups (PFG 7G and 14A), both of which were tentatively associated with mainland Greece or Kythera rather than Crete. Preliminary interpretation of the WD-XRF results suggests that PFG 7G may be from a non-Cretan source. Most samples from PFG 14, including 71, were chemically similar to one another, which suggests that they may derive from a similar source. Nearly all the wares and macroscopic fabrics associated with PFG 14 were hypothesized to be from mainland Greece or Euboea.
Well-fired, pale yellow to pale pink to pale brown fabric; fine, densely packed paste, smooth break, thin-walled vessels; few to common voids, mostly vughs but some round
0.5 mm<CF<2 mm, inclusions very rare to rare, in order of abundance:
Round, white particles, friable(?), r–sr; dark-brown, red-brown, gray particles, hard, r–sr
FF<0.5 mm
White particles (above); gray, brown, red particles (above); silver particles, very rare

FSTk: FINE, DARK ORANGE-PINK TO BROWN

This fine fabric is dark orange-pink to brown. Inclusions are rare, but when present they appear similar—at least in color—to those of FSTc. The two petrographic samples (72, 73) were classed in different groups, PFG 6B and a variant of PFG 7G.
Well-fired, dark orange-brown to brown fabric, sometimes with darker core and thin, orange or pink margins; fine, smooth paste with smooth break, thin-walled vessels; few to common voids, mostly vughs
0.5 mm<CF<2 mm, inclusions very rare to rare, in order of abundance:
White, calcareous(?) particles; red, orange, dark-brown, gray particles, hard, sr–r
FF<0.5 mm
White particles (above); red, orange, dark-brown, gray particles (above); silver particles, very rare

DUSTY VOLCANIC (DV)

All fabrics in this group are dusty, sandy or gritty, and micaceous; they contain volcanic inclusions. The majority of these fabrics seem to have come from Melos, Thera, and Aegina.

DVa: PALE, WITH RARE SILVER MICA

This fabric is typically pale yellow to orange-brown with small black and red inclusions and relatively rare silver mica; it was usually paler in Period IV deposits and browner in LBA deposits. It is similar to fabrics from Melos and Thera (compare with Hilditch 2019, 380–382, PCV; Davis and Williams 1981, Group B). A rare variant is pink to gray, and contains large, shiny, glassy fragments. Petrographic samples (85, 86, 90, 126) of this fabric were classed primarily as PFG 5A and 5B, which appear to be compatible with published petrographic descriptions of Melian/Theran fabrics (Table 3.2). One sample (91) was classed as PFG 5C, which may be a fine variant of PFG 5B.

Well-fired, very pale yellow or white to orange brown fabric, sometimes with a greenish tinge, sometimes with a gray core, rarely pale gray turning pale pink in the margins; sandy to gritty paste, semi-textured to textured break, thin- to thick-walled vessels; dusty feel, voids common, mostly round and vughs

0.5 mm<CF<8 mm, inclusions few to frequent, in order of abundance:

Black and gray particles, hard, shiny, a–sa; dark gray, dark-brown, and occasional red or orange (volcanic?) particles, hard, knobby, sr–sa; white and off-white (calcareous?) inclusions, soft, sr–r; pink to pale orange inclusions, r; silver (and some gold?) mica

FF<0.5 mm

Black, gray, and red particles (above); white particles (above); silver and very rare gold(?) mica

DVb: PALE, COMMON SILVER MICA

This fabric is similar in color and inclusions to the previous one but with common mica. It is probably also a Melian and/or Theran fabric. It was found in Period VI and VII deposits in Area B. The only sample (97) of this fabric was classed as PFG 5D, which is hypothesized to be possibly Melian rather than Theran.

Well-fired, pinkish orange fabric, rarely with gray core; gritty paste, semi-textured break, thin- to moderately thick-walled vessels; dusty feel, voids common, mainly round and vughs; some spalling at surface

0.5 mm<CF<7 mm, common to frequent inclusions, in order of abundance:

Black inclusions, shiny, hard, a–sa; gray, orange, dark brown-red inclusions, hard, knobby, sr–sa; white (calcareous?) inclusions, soft, sr–r; milky white to gray inclusions, shiny, hard, sr–sa; silver mica; yellow-brown inclusions, glassy, hard, a–sa

FF<0.5 mm

Silver mica; black, gray, dark brown-red inclusions (above); white inclusions (above); gold mica, rare

DVc: PALE, WITH SUBROUNDED PALE-GRAY (CALCAREOUS?) INCLUSIONS

This group is similar in color and texture to DVa but bears subrounded, pale bluish gray (calcareous?) inclusions and common fine silver and gold mica. A few vessels in similar fabrics were also found among the sherds from Phylakopi in the Archaeological Museum of Melos. Petrographically, both samples (92, 93) of this fabric were classed in the same subgroup (PFG 5D), which is hypothesized to be a possible Melian import, given differences from published petrographic descriptions of Theran fabrics (Appendix V; Day, Müller, and Kilikoglou 2019; Hilditch 2008, 2019).

Well-fired, pale pinkish brown to pale orange fabric, often with pale-gray core; sandy paste, semi-textured break, thin- to thick-walled vessels; dusty feel, voids common, mostly vughs and round; some spalling at surface

0.5 mm<CF<6 mm, inclusions common, in order of abundance:

Black, dark gray, dark red inclusions, hard, knobby, sr–sa; black inclusions, hard, shiny, a–sa; milky and semi-translucent blue-gray particles, hard, r–sr; white or yellow (calcareous?) inclusions, soft, r–sr

FF<0.5 mm

Silver mica, throughout matrix; black, dark gray, red inclusions (above); pale blue-gray particles (above); white particles (above)

DVd: PALE, GOLD MICA

This fabric is similar in color and texture to DVa, but bears exclusively (although few to rare) gold mica, both coarse and fine. No silver mica is present. The fabric is very similar to pale-firing fabrics from Aegina (Gauss and Kiriatzi 2011, 49–50, MG 2). It was present in Period IV–VII deposits. The only petrographic sample (109) of a canonical DVd fabric was classed as PFG 5G and has clear parallels with Aeginetan petrographic fabrics (Kiriatzi, Georgakopoulou, and Pentedeka 2011, FG 2). A variant of this fabric that was sampled (110) had few inclusions, including rare gold mica; it was classed as a variant of PFG 5A and may be a Melian or Theran product instead an Aeginetan one. For the difficulties of distinguishing macroscopically between Melian/Theran and Aeginetan products in the islands, see also J. C. Overbeck 1989a, 11.

Well-fired, pale-yellow fabric, sometimes with a greenish cast; sandy paste, semi-textured break, thin- to thick-walled vessels; dusty feel, voids common, mostly vughs and round

0.5 mm<CF<5 mm, inclusions few to common, in order of abundance:

Dark reddish-brown, orange, black, gray particles, hard, knobby, sr–sa; white and pale-gray particles, matt, porous-looking, sr–r; black and yellow brown particles, shiny, hard, a–sa; gold mica, platy

FF<0.5 mm

Dark-brown, orange, black, gray particles (above); white particles (above); gold mica

DVe: ORANGE, GOLD MICA

This fine to moderately fine, dusty, orange fabric bears few inclusions, usually small black particles and fine mica, usually gold. It is similar to a fine, orange fabric from Aegina (Gauss and Kiriatzi 2011, 49–50, MG 2B). It was present in Period IV deposits but was more common in Period VI and VII deposits, when it was also typically quite fine. Petrographic analysis suggests that this macroscopic group is not coherent. Three samples (121, 123, 125) were classed as PFG 5G and associated with Aegina. Two samples (120, 124) were classed as variants of PFG 5 subgroups (H and D) that instead may be associated with Melos and/or Thera. One variant (MFVc/DVe, sample 122) was classed in PFG 13B, which may be associated with Euboea on the basis of both the petrographic study and preliminary interpretation of the WD-XRF results.

Well-fired, orange to reddish-orange fabric; sandy paste, semi-textured break, thin- to moderately thick-walled vessels; dusty feel, voids common; some spalling at surface

0.5 mm<CF<4 mm, inclusions few to rare, in order of abundance:

Black inclusions, shiny, hard, a–sa; dark gray, darkibrown, black, red inclusions, hard, sr–sa; white inclusions, soft, sr–r; gold mica, rare to absent

FF<0.5 mm

Gold mica, throughout matrix; black, dark-brown, dark-gray, red particles (above)

DVf: RED-BROWN, GLASSY INCLUSIONS AND GOLD MICA

This dark red-brown to pinkish orange fabric bears common glassy and shiny black (volcanic?) inclusions and coarse gold mica. It was found in Period IV to Period VII deposits. The presence of primarily gold mica, and the fact that one of the vessels in this fabric was a tripod cooking vessel (**567**), could suggest that this fabric is the same Aeginetan cooking fabric that is common elsewhere in the Aegean. Other production locations are also possible, especially since the fabric sometimes includes lenticular gray inclusions that might be metamorphic and/or some silver mica. Petrographically, at least two sources are suggested. One sample (95) is comparable to Kiriatzi, Georgakopoulou, and Pentedeka's (2011, 93–99) FG 1 at Aegina (PFG 5F), but the other sample (96) derives from a different, unknown (possibly Koan?) source (PFG 5E).

Well-fired, dark red-brown to pinkish orange fabric, often darker or gray at core; gritty paste, textured break, thin- to thick-walled vessels; dusty feel, voids common, mostly vughs

0.5 mm<CF<8 mm, inclusions common to frequent, in order of abundance:

Dark reddish-brown, brown, black, gray inclusions, hard, knobby, sr–sa; black inclusions, hard, shiny, a–sa; white inclusions, soft, sr–r; yellow-brown inclusions, glassy, a–sa; gray (metamorphic?) inclusions, shiny, lenticular–sr; semi-translucent white inclusions, hard, a–sa; gold mica

FF<0.5 mm

Gold mica; dark-brown, gray, black inclusions (above); white inclusions (above)

DVg: PALE YELLOW, SPONGE SPICULES

This fabric is very similar in color and texture to DVa, but has very rare inclusions; among them were obvious but rare sponge spicules. Few sherds in this fabric were found in Area B. The fabric was present in deposits dating from Period IV to Period VI. Petrographically, the only sample (128) of this fabric was a loner, being classed in PFG 10. Preliminary interpretation of the WD-XRF results also suggests that the fabric differs chemically from other fabrics in this assemblage associated with Melos and/or Thera.

Well-fired, pale yellow fabric; sandy paste, semi-textured break, thin- to moderately thick-walled vessels; dusty feel, voids common, mainly round and vughs

0.5 mm<CF<3 mm, inclusions rare to few, in order of abundance:

Black particles, shiny, hard, r–sr; dark gray, pink particles, hard, r–sr; white particles, soft, r–sr; white particles, shiny, hard, long and acicular (sponge spicules); brown and gray, glassy, hard, a–sa
FF<0.5 mm
Silver mica; black, brown, dark gray, pink particles (above)

MIXED MICACEOUS (MxM)

Fabrics in this group are micaceous, usually with mica-bearing, probable metamorphic inclusions. The majority of these fabrics seem to have come from other parts of the Cyclades.

MxMa: DUSTY, SANDY, PALE YELLOW TO BROWN

This is a dusty, slightly sandy, moderately fine to moderately coarse, pale yellow to brown fabric, occasionally turning gray or pink at core. It contains metamorphic particles (probably mostly schist) and a variety of hard, subrounded, red, gray, and black inclusions as well as fine and coarse mica, mostly silver. It appears in deposits of all periods (III–VII), but was more common in Period VII deposits. It was associated with painted and plain Cycladic wares, and tablewares as well as large open and closed vessels. A few sherds similar to this fabric are present among the sherds from Mikre Vigla in the Archaeological Museum of Naxos, although they may not be local there. Petrographic analysis suggests that the group is not completely coherent, with most samples classed in PFG 3 (samples 52, 53, 117, 119) and PFG 9 (samples 51, 54, 87) associated with different Cycladic production areas, including perhaps Syros and/or Tenos (Table 3.2).

Moderately well-fired, pale yellow to pale orange or pale red-brown fabric, rarely turning pink or gray at core; sandy paste, semi-textured break, thin- and rarely thick-walled vessels; dusty to very dusty feel, voids common, mostly vughs, more rarely round
0.5 mm<CF<6 mm, inclusions very few to common, in order of abundance:
Gray and pink, shiny, foliated, probable metamorphic (schist); black particles, shiny, hard, a–sa; silver mica, platy; pink particles; hard, sr–sa; white particles (calcareous?), sr–r; semi-translucent white particles, hard, sr–sa; gray and red inclusions, hard, sr–sa; gold mica, platy
FF<0.5 mm
Silver mica; sometimes with black, gray, pink inclusions (above); white inclusions (above); gold mica

MxMb: RED-BROWN, PHYLLITE

This group is very rare and exists only in plain, closed vessels in Red-Brown Semifine to Semicoarse ware in Period III deposits. It is a brittle, coarse orange-brown fabric with common, platy, purple and dark gray phyllite and schist particles. It is probably from Amorgos, given its similarity to the "Blueschist" fabric of Amorgos (Vaughan 2006, 100), also found at Dhaskalio-Kavos on Keros (Broodbank 2007, 124; Hilditch 2007, 239); petrographic analysis (sample 14) confirms the association (PFG 3I). I am grateful to Jill Hilditch for this suggestion.

Moderately low-fired fabric, reddish-brown core, dark gray margin, exterior surface patchy orange and gray; brittle paste, linear fracture; thin-walled vessels; frequent voids (predominantly vughs)
0.5 mm<CF< 5 mm, inclusions common to frequent, in order of abundance:
Purple–dark gray (phyllite?) inclusions, platy, shiny, sa–sr; dark gray–dark purple (metamorphic?) inclusions, shiny, lenticular–sr; semi-translucent white-gray inclusions, shiny, a–sa; dark red–black particles, somewhat porous, sr
FF <0.5 mm
Gold particles, sparkling throughout matrix; gray particles (above); white particles (above); red–black particles (above); silver particles, sparkling throughout matrix

MxMc: FINE, DUSTY, SLIGHTLY GRITTY, FF SILVER AND GOLD MICA

This relatively fine pale yellow-brown to orange-brown fabric was distinguished by its very dusty surface and fine silver and/or gold mica. This fabric was found in deposits from Period III–VII; it was hypothesized to be a finer version of one (or more?) of the coarser MxM fabrics and was associated mainly with tablewares, both plain and painted. There are sherds in similar fabrics from Mikre Vigla, stored in the Archaeological Museum of Naxos, although it is not certain that the fabrics were local there. Of six petrographic samples, four (101, 102, 104, 105) were classed in PFG 3 and one (103) in PFG 4B, all of which are associated with the Cyclades. The last sample (140), a macroscopic variant, was classed in PFG 13A, tentatively associated with Attica on the basis of the petrographic analysis.

Moderately well-fired, pale yellow-brown to orange-brown fabric, sometimes turning paler or gray at core; sandy paste, semi-textured break, thin- to moderately thick-walled vessels; very dusty feel, common to frequent voids, mainly vughs, more rarely round.

0.5 mm<CF<5 mm, inclusions rare to few, in order of abundance:

Black, dark gray, rare red inclusions, hard, r–sa; black inclusions, shiny, hard, a–sa; dark gray inclusions, shiny, lenticular–sr; semi-translucent and milky white to pale-gray inclusions, shiny, hard, sr–sa; semi-translucent white inclusions, shiny, hard, sa–sr; white (calcareous?) inclusions, dull, sr–r

FF<0.5 mm

Silver and/or gold mica, throughout matrix; black, dark gray inclusions (above); white inclusions (above)

MxMd: RED-BROWN WITH DARK GLASSY INCLUSIONS

This dark red-brown fabric was found in Period IV and VI deposits. The group differed from other MxM fabrics in its dark color, the presence of common dark, glassy inclusions, and coarse silver mica. It was associated mostly with plain open and closed shapes of unknown profile. Two samples (106, 107) of this fabric were taken, which were classified in PFG 3B (Cyclades) and 3D (Cyclades (Syros?)).

Moderately well-fired, red-brown fabric, sometimes with gray core; gritty paste, textured break, moderately thin- to thick-walled vessels; voids common, mostly vughs

0.5 mm<CF<8 mm, inclusions common to frequent, in order of abundance:

Black, red, dark gray inclusions, hard, knobby, sr–sa; black inclusions, shiny, hard, a–sa; black, yellow-brown inclusions, glassy, hard, a–sa; gray, brown, and purple-silver schist(?) particles, sr–sa; semi-translucent and milky white inclusions, shiny, hard, hackly sr–sa; silver mica; white inclusions, dull, relatively soft, knobby, sr–r; gold mica

FF<0.5 mm

Silver/gold mica, throughout matrix; black, red, gray, brown inclusions (above); shiny white inclusions (above)

MxMe: HARD-FIRED, COMPACT, VERY MICACEOUS

This rare fabric, with common silver and gold mica, was found in Period VII deposits. It is distinguished especially by the texture of its clay, which is more fine-grained and compact than most MxM fabrics. The paneled decoration of 177 suggests a Cycladic production center is possible, although the density and planar breaks of the fabric are unlike any other probable Cycladic fabrics. The few vessels in this fabric were painted and probably tablewares. Petrographically, the only sample (108) of this fabric was classified as PFG 9A, very tentatively associated with Tenos.

Well-fired, orange-brown fabric with a thick gray core; gritty fabric, semi-textured to flat break, moderately thin-walled vessels; slightly dusty feel, voids few to common, mainly vughs, spalled surface

0.5 mm<CF<8 mm, inclusions few, in order of abundance:

Silver mica, platy; gold mica, platy; gray metamorphic(?) inclusions, sa–sr; white (calcareous?) inclusions, dull, soft, sr–r; black inclusions, shiny, hard, a–sa; dark red inclusions, hard, sr–sa

FF<0.5 mm

Silver/gold mica; gray and black inclusions; white inclusions (above)

MxMf: GRITTY PINK-BROWN, COARSE SILVER MICA

This fabric appeared in Period IV, VI, and VII deposits. It is gritty, pink-brown to pale purple fabric with common, coarse silver mica, blocky white inclusions, and spalling, sometimes haloed. The fabric appears rather similar to fabrics represented among sherds from Paroikia, stored at the Archaeological Museum of Paros. Nevertheless, petrographic analysis suggests that this is not a coherent macro-group, with samples (98, 111, 113) that appear to derive from various parts of the Cyclades (PFG 3C [Cyclades, Syros?], 4B [Central Cyclades?], 5H [Melos/Thera?]). It was associated with tablewares and closed vessels, plain and painted.

Well-fired, dull pink to pale brown fabric, sometimes with a purplish cast, often with a thick, gray core; gritty paste, semi-textured break, moderately thin- to thick-walled vessels; dusty feel, voids common to frequent, mainly round and vughs; some spalling at surface, which may preserve haloes

0.5 mm<CF<6 mm, inclusions common, in order of abundance:

Semi-translucent white inclusions, shiny, hard, hackly, a–sa; white (calcareous?) inclusions, dull, sr–r; dark gray, black, rare red inclusions, hard, sr–sa; silver mica, platy; black inclusions, shiny, hard, a–sa

FF<0.5 mm

silver mica; white inclusions (above); dark gray, black inclusions (above); gold mica

MxMg: MIXED INCLUSIONS, FREQUENT SPALLING

This rare fabric was found only in Period III deposits. It was a relatively compact, pale pinkish brown fabric with subrounded inclusions in gray, black, purple-red, and white, as well as frequent spalling. Apart from a bowl (**297**), all vessels were closed and were plain or slipped. The only petrographic sample (116) of this fabric was classified as a variant of PFG 4C, associated with Naxos.
Moderately well-fired, pale pinkish brown to pale purple fabric, sometimes with thick, pale-gray core; sandy paste, textured break, moderately thin- to thick-walled vessels; voids common to frequent, mostly round and vughs; frequent spalling
0.5 mm<CF<4 mm, inclusions few to common, in order of abundance:
Dark gray and black inclusions, hard, sr; off-white to pale yellow (calcareous?) inclusions, friable, r–sr; silver mica, platy; gray, silver-gray, purple-red schist(?), hard, lenticular–platy; semi-translucent white inclusions, hard, sr–sa; gold mica, platy
FF<0.5 mm
Silver mica, sparkling throughout; black, dark gray, purple-red inclusions (above); off-white to pale yellow inclusions (above)

COARSE, WITH SHINY WHITE INCLUSIONS (CSW)

These fabrics contain common shiny pale-colored inclusions, probably primarily quartz, feldspar, marble, limestone, and possibly granitic rocks. All CSW fabrics were rare in Area B.

CSWa: RED-BROWN, RARE MICA

This reddish-brown fabric has common blocky white and gray inclusions, rare small, dark particles, and rare mica, mostly gold. It was found only in mixed and LBA deposits, and it was associated with open and closed shapes of uncertain profile in plain, burnished, and Yellow Slipped wares. Macroscopically, the fabric is hypothesized to be from the central Cyclades based on its similarities to probable Naxian or Parian fabrics at Akrotiri (Hilditch 2008, 172–175; 2019, 389, RBCa); petrographically, the only sample (129) of this fabric was classified in PFG 4A, associated with Naxos (Table 3.2).
Moderately well-fired, reddish-brown fabric, rarely with a gray core; gritty paste, textured break, moderately thick-walled vessels; voids few to common, mostly vughs
0.5 mm<CF<5 mm, inclusions few to common, in order of abundance:
White, pale-gray, and pale blue-gray inclusions, hard, shiny, sr–sa; black and brown inclusions, hard, sr–sa; platy gold mica
FF<0.5 mm
White, pale-gray, pale blue-gray inclusions (above); mica

CSWb: ORANGE-BROWN, METAMORPHIC INCLUSIONS

This rare orange-brown fabric contains probable metamorphic inclusions in addition to blocky, shiny white ones. It appeared mostly in chronologically mixed deposits and was associated mainly with plain vessels, open and closed. The two samples (130, 131) taken for petrographic analysis were classified as PFG 2C (Local region).
Moderately well-fired, orange-brown fabric, rarely with a gray core; gritty paste, textured break, moderately thick-walled vessels; voids few to common, mostly vughs
0.5 mm<CF<8 mm, inclusions few to common, in order of abundance:
White, pale-gray, and pale blue-gray inclusions, hard, shiny, sr–sa; black and brown inclusions, hard, sr–sa; platy gold mica; gray schist(?), sr
FF<0.5 mm
White, pale-gray, pale blue-gray inclusions (above); mica

CSWc: RED-BROWN, SPALLING CALCAREOUS INCLUSIONS

This fabric is very similar in color and inclusions to CSWa, but with the addition of friable, probably calcareous inclusions and spalling. The fabric appeared in mixed and Period VII deposits; it was associated with plain and Slipped and Burnished vessels, open and closed. The only sample (132) of this fabric studied as part of the petrographic analysis was classed as PFG 2D, tentatively suggested to be from southeastern Attica or the Cyclades.
Moderately well-fired, orange-brown fabric, rarely with a gray core; gritty paste, textured break, moderately thick-walled vessels; voids few to common, mostly vughs; common spalling at surface, with some haloes
0.5 mm<CF<6 mm, inclusions few to common, in order of abundance:

White, pale-gray, and pale blue-gray inclusions, hard, shiny, sr–sa; white (calcareous) inclusions, friable, sr–r; gray schist(?), sr
FF<0.5 mm
White, pale-gray, pale blue-gray inclusions (above); mica

CSWd: COMMON SILVER MICA

This fabric was found in EBA and chronologically mixed deposits. One sherd might belong to a Period IV duck vase (**312**). Other shapes were varied and belonged to plain, Slipped, or EBA Black Burnished wares. The fabric is coarse, gritty, gray to red-brown, with common shiny, pale-colored particles, rarer schist and calcareous(?) particles and fine and coarse silver (and, rarely, gold) mica. Petrographic analysis classed three samples (135, 136, 139) of this fabric with PFG 2C (Local region).

Moderately well-fired, brittle, gray to red-brown fabric, sometimes with gray core; gritty paste, textured break, moderately thin- to thick-walled vessels; few to common voids, mostly vughs

0.5 mm<CF<7 mm, inclusions few to common, in order of abundance:

White, pale-gray, and yellow inclusions, hard, shiny, sr–sa; gray, silver, gold, purple schist, sr–sa; white (calcareous?) inclusions, soft, r–sr; black and dark gray inclusions, hard, sr; silver mica, platy

FF<0.5 mm

White and gray inclusions (above); gray schist(?) (above); silver and gold(?) mica

CSWe: ORANGE TO DARK RED-BROWN, COMMON CF GOLD MICA

This fabric is gritty, orange-pink to dark red, sometimes with a dark gray core, and with shiny pale-colored and black inclusions as well as relatively common platy, coarse gold mica. It was found in deposits of Periods III–VI, although most identifiable vessels appear to date to the EBA. It was associated mostly with closed vessels, in a variety of plain and decorated wares. Four of five samples (17, 100, 114, 138) of this fabric were classified in PFG 4, associated with the central Cyclades, especially Naxos; a sample of a macroscopic variant (137) was classified as PFG 2D, tentatively associated with southeast Attica or the Cyclades.

Moderately well-fired, brittle, orange-pink to red-brown fabric, usually with dark gray core; gritty paste, textured break, moderately thick- and rarely moderately thin-walled vessels; voids few to frequent, mostly vughs

0.5 mm<CF<8 mm, inclusions few to frequent, in order of abundance:

Semi-translucent gray and bright white inclusions, shiny, hard, hackly, sa; yellow and pink inclusions, hard, sr–sa; white (calcareous?) inclusions, friable, r–sr; black, dark gray, orange inclusions, hard, sr; gold mica, platy; gray, green, purple schist(?) inclusions, hard, lenticular–sr; yellow to gray inclusions, glassy, hard, sa

FF<0.5 mm

White, gray, and yellow inclusions (above); dark gray, black, orange inclusions (above); silver(?) and gold mica

PINK-BROWN, SOAPY TEXTURE AND INCLUSIONS (PBS)

There is only one fabric with predominant soapy particles in Area B. All examples were Period III Talc ware closed vessels. It is pink- to red-brown, with a very soapy surface. This fabric is probably from Siphnos, although Melos has also been suggested as a source (Vaughan and Wilson 1993). This fabric, well known from other studies, was not sampled for additional analysis.

Moderately well-fired, soapy, pink- to red-brown fabric; soapy paste, semi-textured break, moderately thin- to thick-walled vessels; few voids, mostly vughs

0.5 mm<CF<8 mm, inclusions frequent, in order of abundance:

Pale-gray to dark bluish-gray inclusions, soft and soapy, a–sr; white to yellow inclusions, shiny, sr–sa

FF<0.5 mm

Pale-gray, dark blue-gray inclusions (above); yellow and off-white inclusions (above); silver mica

MICACEOUS, FINE, VARIED (MFV)

These fabrics are fine and micaceous, probably from the Cyclades and perhaps also the mainland, especially Attica and/or Euboea. All were very rare in Area B.

MFVa: DUSTY PINK-BROWN, FF GOLD MICA

This fabric is dusty, pinkish brown with small, white and gray particles and common FF gold mica. It was found only in Period IV and later deposits. It was associated mainly with open vessels, plain, slipped, burnished, or painted. The only sample (141) of this fabric was classified in PFG 3C, tentatively associated with Syros (Table 3.2).

Moderately well-fired, pinkish-brown fabric; smooth paste, smooth break, thin-walled vessels; few voids, mostly vughs
0.5 mm<CF<2 mm, inclusions few, in order of abundance:
White, pale-gray, pink inclusions, hard, shiny, sr–sa; white (calcareous?), friable, sr–r; dark gray and black inclusions, hard, sr
FF<0.5 mm
Gold mica, sparkling throughout matrix; silver(?) mica

MFVb: REDUCED, SILVER MICA

This dark gray fabric contains common fine silver mica. A few Gray Minyan shapes were found in this fabric, but it was more common in the rare Period VII Gray/Black Burnished ware. The two samples (142, 143) of this fabric were classified in different petrographic groups, PFG 3H (Attica/Euboea/Cyclades) and 11A (Unknown).

Moderately well-fired, dusty, dark gray fabric; smooth paste, smooth break, thin-walled vessels; few to common voids, mainly vughs
0.5 mm<CF<4 mm, inclusions rare to very few, in order of abundance:
White inclusions, shiny, hard, a–sa; dark gray, brown, and black, hard, sr–sa
FF<0.5 mm
Silver mica

MFVc: RED TO ORANGE, CALCAREOUS INCLUSIONS

This fine, red to orange fabric bears large, calcareous particles and coarse and fine silver mica; gold mica was sometimes present. It was found almost exclusively in Period VII deposits, especially in association with Burnished and Red Coated goblets, some of which are probably also classifiable as Acropolis Burnished ware (Mountjoy 1981, 51–56; 1995, 13–14). Two of three samples (144, 145) were classified as PFG 13A, tentatively associated with Attica. The third sample (146), a macroscopic variant, was classified in PFG 11B, of unknown origin.

Well-fired, red to orange-red fabric; smooth paste, smooth break, thin-walled vessels; few to common voids, mainly vughs; some spalling
0.5 mm<CF<6 mm, inclusions rare, in order of abundance:
White (probably calcareous) inclusions, friable, sr–r; black inclusions, shiny, hard, sr–sa; silver mica, platy
FF<0.5 mm
Silver mica; gold mica; white inclusions (above)

MFVd: PINK- TO PURPLE-BROWN

This very rare dark pink to purplish-brown fabric contains fine mica. It is of unknown provenance. The fabric was only found in Period VII deposits in Area B. Sherds belonged to plain and painted, open and closed shapes. The single sample of this fabric taken for petrographic analysis was classed in PFG 13B and associated with Euboea; preliminary interpretation of the WD-XRF results also suggests that this sample would be compatible with a provenance in the Lelantine plain.

Well-fired fabric, dark pink, sometimes turning to pale purple at interior margin; sandy paste, semi-textured break, thin-walled vessels; dusty feel, voids common, mainly vughs
0.5 mm<CF<3 mm, inclusions few, in order of abundance:
Gray inclusions, hard, knobby, r–sr
FF<0.5 mm
Gray inclusions (above); gold and/or silver mica

FINE, VARIED (FV)

These fabrics are fine and non-micaceous. Many probably derive from the mainland, including the Peloponnese, Attica, Euboea, and Boeotia, although they are difficult to characterize with certainty either macroscopically or petrographically.

FVa: HARD, GRAY, RARE CALCAREOUS INCLUSIONS

FVa is a hard-fired, gray fabric with rare, large, round calcareous particles and spalling. It was found exclusively in Period IV to Period VII deposits and was the major fabric associated with Gray Minyan ware. It appears to be the same fabric that is associated with "true" Gray Minyan from central Greece and/or Euboea. The only petrographic sample (148) of this fabric was classified as a variant of PFG 14D (Table 3.2); preliminary interpretation of the WD-XRF results suggests that the fabric is comparable to FG 8 at Eretria, hypothesized to be the main local fine fabric for the Lelantine plain (Charalambidou et al. 2016, table 2).

Well-fired, gray to dark gray fabric; smooth or sometimes slightly dusty paste, smooth break, thin-walled vessels; rare to common voids, mainly vughs; rare spalling

0.5 mm<CF<6 mm, rare

White (calcareous?) inclusions, friable, sr–r

FF<0.5 mm, very rare

Silver mica(?)

FVb: HARD, PALE YELLOW

This hard-fired, pale yellow fabric was only found in Period VII deposits. It was used for Mainland Slipped, Burnished, Lustrous Painted, and plain vessels, in a variety of shapes. The only sample (159) was classed as PFG 14C.

Well-fired, pale yellow fabric, sometimes turning pale pink at margins; smooth paste, smooth break, thin-walled vessels; few voids, mainly vughs

0.5 mm<CF<2 mm, very rare

White (calcareous?) inclusions, sr–r; red and dark gray inclusions, hard, sr–sa

FF<0.5 mm, very rare

Silver particles

FVc: HARD, PALE PINK

This hard-fired, pale pink fabric sometimes has a pale brown or yellow core, which is similar in color to fabrics categorized as FVb; sherds with cores are categorized as FVb/FVc. This fabric has parallels at Mycenae, from Petsas House. Vessels in this fabric were usually plain, Burnished, or Lustrous Painted, in a variety of shapes. The fabric is almost entirely restricted to the LBA, being especially common in Period VII. All petrographic samples of this fabric were classified in PFG 14B.

Well-fired, pink fabric, often with a yellow or pale brown core, sometimes with paler pink or yellow margins and/or surface; smooth paste, smooth break, thin-walled vessels; few voids, vughs and round

0.5 mm<CF<2 mm, very rare

White (calcareous?) inclusions, sr–r; red and dark gray inclusions, hard, sr–sa

FF<0.5 mm, very rare

Silver particles

FVd: DUSTY, ORANGE

This dusty, orange fabric bears white, friable, calcareous(?) inclusions and, in some cases, rare silver mica. It has similarities to Classical Black Gloss fabrics, most of which are presumably from Attica. The fabric was rare in Period IV deposits and common in Period VI and (especially) Period VII deposits. It was used for various shapes and plain, Mainland Slipped, Burnished, Lustrous Painted, and Red Coated wares. A less dusty, harder-fired subgroup of this fabric (FVd/FVf) was similar to fabrics used for Mainland Polychrome vessels elsewhere on site. Two samples (164, 167) in this fabric were classified in different petrographic groups: PFG 3F (Unknown) and a variant of PFG 14B (Unknown). Samples of the variant FVd/FVf were classed in PFG 13B (Euboea).

Well-fired, dusty, orange to orange-pink fabric; smooth paste, smooth break, thin-walled vessels; few voids, mostly vughs

0.5 mm<CF<4 mm, very rare

White (calcareous?) inclusions, friable, sr–r

FF<0.5 mm, rare

Silver particles

FVe: PALE YELLOW, GRAY CORE

This hard-fired, pale yellow to orange to pink fabric always has a gray core. It was most common in Period VII deposits, in plain, Burnished, Red Coated, and Lustrous Painted wares. A variant with a darker core was present in Period III lots, in Urfirnis(?) ware. The two petrographic samples (169, 170) of this fabric were classified as PFG 14D, hypothesized to be from Central Greece; preliminary interpretation of the WD-XRF results suggests that at least one of these (sample 169) is incompatible with an origin in the Lelantine plain on the basis of comparison with FG 8 at Eretria (Charalambidou et al. 2016, table 2). A variant (FVc/FVe, sample 160) was classified as a variant of PFG 14B of unknown origin.

Well-fired, dusty, pinkish orange to pinkish yellow fabric with pale-gray to blue-gray core; smooth paste, smooth break, thin-walled vessels; few voids, mostly vughs

0.5 mm<CF<2 mm, very rare

White (calcareous?) inclusions, sr–r; brown, gray brown, and orange inclusions, hard, a–sr; white and dark gray inclusions, hard, sa–sr

FF<0.5 mm, very rare

White inclusions (above); silver mica(?)

FVf: HARD, PURPLISH BROWN TO BROWN

This very hard-fired, dull purplish brown to brown fabric was associated with Burnished, Lustrous Painted and plain wares. It appears to be the same fabric that is used for many Mainland Polychrome vessels found in other areas at Ayia Irini, although no polychrome-painted sherds were found in Area B. One of two samples (151) of this fabric was included in PFG 13A, perhaps from Attica; the other (150) was classified as PFG 13B, probably from Euboea. A macroscopic variant that was orange in color (FVd/FVf) was also sampled (165, 166); these samples were classified as PFG 13B (Euboea) as well.

Well-fired, dull pinkish purple to pale purplish gray or brown fabric, sometimes turning paler or more gray at surface; smooth paste, smooth break, moderately thin- to moderately thick-walled vessels; rare voids, mostly vughs

0.5 mm<CF<2 mm, very rare

White (calcareous?) inclusions, friable, sr–r; brown, black, and gray inclusions, hard, a–sa; red inclusions, hard, sr–r

FF<0.5 mm, very rare

Silver mica(?)

FVg: PINK, COLOR VARIATION

This slightly dusty fabric is pale pink to orange with color variation, sometimes turning yellow at the surface and/or gray at the core. The fabric was very rare. It was only found in Period III deposits, where it was associated with Urfirnis and Pinkish Buff wares. All three samples (152, 153, 157) of this fabric were classified in PFG 14B.

Well-fired, pale pink to orange-pink fabric, sometimes turning yellow at surface and/or gray at core; smooth to slightly dusty feel, smooth break, thin-walled vessels; rare voids, mostly vughs

0.5 mm<CF<2 mm, very rare

Pink, orange, red, pale brown, gray, and black inclusions, hard, sr–r; white (calcareous?) inclusions, smooth, sr–r

FF<0.5 mm, very rare

Silver mica(?)

FVh: PINKISH-ORANGE, DARK-GRAY CORE

This pinkish orange, somewhat dusty fabric may have a bluish gray core. It was very rare. It was associated with Period III Yellow Mottled and Urfirnis wares. A mica-bearing variant in Pinkish Buff ware was also found. Two samples (154, 155) were analyzed petrographically and were classified in different groups, PFG 12A (S Euboea/NW Cyclades) and PFG 13A (Attica?).

Well-fired, pink-orange fabric, usually with blue-gray core; smooth paste, smooth break, thin-walled vessels; rare voids, mostly vughs

0.5 mm<CF<1 mm, very rare

White, black, purplish red inclusions, hard, sr–sa; pinkish-yellow and white (calcareous?), smooth, sr

FF<0.5 mm, very rare

Silver mica(?)

APPENDIX V: PETROGRAPHIC DESCRIPTIONS

Descriptions follow a system modified after Whitbread (1995, 379–388). Images of a sample from each group are provided in Color Pls. 1–4. When possible, preliminary interpretations of the results from the wave-dispersive X-ray fluorescence analysis (WD-XRF) are summarized, when they supply additional insight into the chemical coherence of groups or clarify potential provenance. WD-XRF analysis was undertaken by Noémi Müller at the Fitch Laboratory of the British School at Athens, and all preliminary interpretations are based on discussions with her. The results of the WD-XRF analysis are provided in Appendix VII. For the correlation between sample numbers, catalogue numbers, macroscopic and petrographic groups, and refiring characteristics, see Table 3.2.

GROUP 1: RED-BROWN, METAMORPHIC

The four subgroups that constitute Group 1 are very similar to one another and probably represent local products. The existence of several outliers, listed as variants after each group, suggests even greater heterogeneity is probable across the full local assemblage, which could be investigated further with future sampling programs. Inclusions in all of these subgroups are dominated by metamorphic rock fragments, especially quartz-mica schists and schists composed of quartz, porphyroblastic feldspar ± epidote group minerals ± mica ± chlorite, with accessory minerals like tourmaline, actinolite/tremolite, or titanite appearing more rarely. Quartz is sometimes elongated with undulose extinction, which may suggest that these rocks are derived from the phyllonitic schists common in association with the detachment footwall, visible especially in the north of the island (Rice et al. 2012, 111–112).

Although some possible differences in processing exist, the relative angularity of inclusions, more or less unimodal size distribution, and red to red-brown color of the groundmass suggest the use of primary iron-rich clays. Optical activity ranges from low to high, with the majority of samples having moderately high to high optical activity, especially in subgroups PFG 1A–1C. All refired to red.

SUBGROUP A: MICA SCHIST AND EPIDOTE GROUP MINERALS
Samples: 4, 30, 40, 42, 44, 48

This subgroup is distinguished by a prevalence of white mica (muscovite) and/or biotite schist, sometimes altering to chlorite. Epidote group minerals are common. Clinozoisite (first-order birefringence colors) is equally or more common than epidote (second to third-order birefringence colors). Some schist bears white mica with low (first-order) birefringence colors, extremely strained quartz grains, and talc (40, 48). Biotite is especially common in 48, which also has more porphyroblastic rock fragments than the rest. A narrow band along the exterior wall surface of 40 is darker (red-brown, xpl) clay, perhaps evidence for a briefly reducing environment near the end of firing. Single grains in this fabric strongly resemble those that are common in PFG 2A and 2B, but there is typically more amphibole in those subgroups. All samples (including variants) bear common to few textural concentration features (tcfs), probably clay pellets, red-brown, eq and slightly el, r, often bearing inclusions that are compatible with the rest of those in the groundmass (metamorphic rock fragments and dissociates thereof).

Microstructure
Common–few voids, predominantly micro- to macrovughs and channels; some voids around inclusions in 44 and 48; double- to open-spaced. Voids show either no orientation or very weak orientation parallel to vessel walls (4, 30). Irregular, elongated micro- and meso-channels are more common in 48 and are more strongly oriented parallel to vessel walls; perhaps this cracking is associated with heating, either as part of firing or during use (as an incense burner). Inclusions single- to double-spaced. Inclusions show no orientation or very weak orientation parallel to vessel walls.

Groundmass
Not homogenous; deep yellow brown, orange brown, red brown, or brown (ppl); red to yellow brown to dark brown (xpl) (40x); groundmass typically paler toward one or both surfaces; 40 is paler also at core in places; optically active.

Inclusions
c:f:v$_{0.15\text{ mm}}$, ca. 35:60:5 to 45:30:25. Poorly sorted, mostly el, some eq, a–r, <2.9 mm, mode 0.3–1.8 mm, unimodal size distribution.

Coarse fraction
Predominant: Metamorphic rock fragments and dissociated fragments thereof, mostly el, a–sr, mode 0.3–1.8 mm. Quartz-mica schists, often banded, with white mica and/or biotite (often altering to chlorite), sometimes with oxidized probable mica or other opaques, rarely with possible talc (high birefringence, little apparent crystal structure). Schist fragments composed of porphyroblastic feldspar and quartz ± clinozoisite/epidote ± mica ± chlorite ± opaques. White mica is occasionally very slightly

green in ppl, and birefringence is sometimes very low (first-order). Tourmaline, apatite(?), titanite, possible amphibole (usually pale green in ppl, actinolite?), and birefringent red-brown material (clay?) is rarely present. Quartz usually shows undulose extinction; in some cases, it is very strained. Some feldspars are altered, bearing small mica, epidote/clinozoisite, apatite, titanite(?) inclusions or red-brown (clay?) material; rarely with alteration in fine black bands, particularly in 48. Fine-grained mica schists, micaceous phyllite (occasionally crenulated), and quartzite also appear; fine-grained schists are more common in 40 than in the rest of the samples.

Dissociated fragments include mica aggregates (mostly biotite), el, sr–r, mode 0.3–1.4 mm; quartz (mono- and polycrystalline) and feldspar (rarely showing albite twinning), eq and el, sa–r, mode 0.3–1.4 mm; and clinozoisite/epidote, eq to el, sa–sr, mode 0.3–0.6 mm, some of which appears to be altering after feldspar. Grains (very few) in 40, 44, and 48 of unknown origin perhaps could be altered epidote/clinozoisite? A few of the larger grains appear, in parts, to be more typical of epidote/clinozoisite in relief, color, etc., but the majority of the grains are yellow brown in ppl with anomalous birefringence in xpl, often appearing nearly opaque; these very rarely appear as part of metamorphic rock fragments rather than dissociated grains.

Very rare–absent: Talc, eq and el, sa–r, mode 0.3 mm; birefringent orange-red (iron-rich?) grains.

Very few–very rare: Opaques, mostly el, a–sr, mode 0.3–0.5 mm; 48 has more opaques that are distinctively elongate and rectangular (up to 2.6 mm long).

Fine fraction

Dominant: Quartz, feldspar (many grains indistinguishable as one or the other) and metamorphic rock fragments as above, eq and el, sa–sr.

Frequent–few: Mica laths.

Few–very rare: Epidote/clinozoisite, as above.

Very few–rare: Opaques, eq, sa–sr.

Very rare–absent: Talc, as above; tourmaline, eq, sa; titanite(?), el, sr; birefringent orange-red grains.

Tcfs

Few–rare, red to dark red-brown in ppl, red to almost opaque in xpl, sharp to merging boundaries, high optical density, a (rectangular)–wr, eq to prolate, mode 0.2–0.6 mm, sometimes bearing small quartz/feldspar grains, metamorphic rock inclusions, and/or mica laths; probably clay pellets.

Few–rare, pale brown to brown in ppl, mostly opaque with tiny yellow speckles in xpl, diffuse boundaries, low optical density, irregular in shape, r, sometimes bearing small quartz/feldspar inclusions.

Variant: 15

Metamorphic rocks are primarily biotite-chlorite schist, much quite fine-grained; white mica is rare; epidote/clinozoisite is very rare and primarily in fine fraction. Darker at core. Very few voids, meso- and macro-vughs and channels, no alignment. Preliminary interpretation of the WD-XRF results also suggests this sample is an outlier, with some values (especially chromium) in ranges similar to those seen in PFG 2B, which is also notable for having abundant fine-grained schists.

Variant: 45

Very coarse; common epidote/clinozoisite, some porphyroblastic, with one large coarse-grained metamorphic rock that bears quartz, porphyroblastic feldspar, chlorite, mica, and small garnets. Talc and phyllite (sometimes showing crenulation) also appear. A few feldspar grains display alteration in the form of black banding; feldspars often have mica inclusions, and acicular inclusions of brown amphibole(?) appear more rarely.

SUBGROUP B: VERY MICACEOUS, FREQUENT CLINOZOISITE
Samples: 9, 11

This fabric is distinguished from PFG 1A by very common clinozoisite, as well as abundant white mica schists and white mica aggregates, with much of the white mica showing relatively low (first-order) birefringence. Cloudy feldspars, some with twinning, and some of which are quite large (1–2 mm), are also unusual in comparison with typical inclusions of PFG 1A. White mica aggregates are particularly common in 9, where biotite aggregates are very rare.

Microstructure

Few voids, predominantly meso- and macrovughs and meso-channel, open-spaced, no orientation. The shape of some large voids is suggestive of burned-out organic inclusions, although these are not very common. Inclusions single and double-spaced; no clear orientation. Some patches with few inclusions and much rarer mica, probably a result of incomplete clay homogenization.

Groundmass

Not homogenous, yellow brown to red brown (ppl), red or orange red (xpl) (40x), some streaking, optically active.

Inclusions
c:f:v$_{0.15\text{ mm}}$, 32:65:3. Poorly sorted, mostly el and some eq, a–r, <4.0 mm, mode 0.4–1.4 mm, weakly bimodal size distribution.

Coarse fraction
Dominant: Metamorphic rock fragments, mostly el, sa–r, mode 0.4–1.4 mm. Quartz-mica schists, with white mica ± chlorite ± biotite (occasionally oxidized), with rare possible amphibole; occasionally with crenulation textures and acicular crystals of unknown composition. Fragments composed of quartz, porphyroblastic feldspar and/or clinozoisite (more rarely, epidote), with mica and sometimes small, cloudy, high-relief, inclusions with third-order birefringence colors, which in one case (9) take up a substantial part of a schist grain (altered epidote?). Feldspars sometimes exhibit albite and simple twinning. Quartzite with rare white mica and birefringent red-brown (clay?) material is present. Titanite, tourmaline, and apatite(?) also appear. Quartz usually shows undulose extinction; in some cases, it is strained and deformed. Dissociated fragments from these rocks are common (mode 0.4–0.7 mm), including clinozoisite, sometimes with attached mica, eq and rarely slightly el, a–sr; epidote is much rarer; altered feldspar grains, with small mica, epidote/clinozoisite, or rarely possible amphibole inclusions, most eq, sr–r; mica (white mica and more rarely biotite) laths and aggregates, el, sr–r; quartz (mono- and polycrystalline), eq and el, sa–r.
Rare–very rare: Opaques, eq and el, sa–r, some basically square, mode 0.15–0.6 mm.
Very rare–absent: Serpentinite(?), pale brown in ppl, nearly opaque with faint net-like appearance in xpl, 0.15 mm.

Fine fraction
Dominant: Quartz/feldspar and metamorphic rock fragments as above, eq and el, sa–sr; mica (biotite and white mica) laths.
Common–few: Clinozoisite, eq, a–sa.
Few–very rare: Opaques, mostly eq, sa–sr.
Few–rare: Cloudy, high-relief grains (altered epidote?), as above, el, r.
Rare: Birefringent yellow-orange and orange-red grains, eq and slightly el, r.
Very rare–absent: Chert(?), el, r.

Tcfs
As in PFG 1A.

Variant: 5
Common chlorite, more epidote than in the main group; common voids, meso- and macro-vughs, no alignment, one surrounded by darkened clay.

Variant: 8
Very micaceous; clinozoisite less common than in the main group, but large grains exist and are more common than epidote; frequent mica schists, white mica more common than biotite and often shows low birefringence colors; rare probable talc grains are present. Voids are few, but meso- and macro-channels are more common than vughs; elongate/planar channels exist, there is some cracking around inclusions, and voids are oriented parallel to vessel walls, probably evidence of stress while drying/firing.

Variant: 26, 41
Much less clinozoisite but very common mica and white-mica schist and no obvious epidote.

SUBGROUP C: MICRITE/SPARITE
Samples: 1, 18 (coarse); 35, 36, 37, 43 (moderately coarse)

The groundmass of the moderately coarse examples generally appears cleaner than PFG 1A or 1B, sometimes with weakly bimodal size distribution of inclusions. Red streaks in a few samples are probably owed to poor homogenization of the clay body or perhaps mixing of two clay sources. Fine mica in the groundmass is more common in 36 than the rest of the samples; 36 also has only clinozoisite and no epidote, as well as common white mica, some with low birefringence colors, all of which may link this sample also to PFG 1B. Nonetheless, in the presence of micritic/sparitic grains, a relatively clean groundmass, and weakly bimodal size distribution of inclusions, this sample is also compatible with PFG 1C and so provides a link between the two subgroups. Although very few–very rare micrite lumps appear in the fine fraction, the clay(s) used for this fabric are not calcareous or otherwise significantly different from those of the other subgroups.

Microstructure
Few–very few voids, single- to open-spaced, predominantly micro- and macro-channels and rarer vughs; oriented roughly parallel to vessel walls except in 37, where voids are oriented at oblique NE/SW angle relative to vessel walls. Some elongate planar/channel voids in 1, 18, 35, and 36, filled with secondary calcite in 18 and 35; calcite rims in 1. Some blackening around a few voids and/or calcite inclusions in 1 and 36. Some voids/cracking around inclusions in 1, 18, and 36. Inclusions single- to double-spaced; those

with long axis are weakly to strongly oriented parallel to vessel walls in 1, 35, 36, 43; no orientation in 18, 37. Weakly bimodal size distribution.

Groundmass
Not homogenous; yellow, yellow-brown, orange, red-brown (ppl); yellow, orange, red (xpl) (40x); generally paler toward vessel surfaces; some red clay streaks in 1, 35, and 43; optically active.

Inclusions
c:f:$v_{0.15\,mm}$, ca. 50:30:20 (coarse), 35:55:10–45:30:25 (moderately coarse). Poorly sorted, mostly el and some eq, sa–r, <3.9 mm, mode 0.6–2.3 mm, unimodal to weakly bimodal size distribution.

Coarse Fraction
Predominant: Metamorphic rock fragments and dissociated fragments thereof, el and more rarely eq, sa–r, mode 0.6–2.3 mm. Fine- and medium-grained mica schists, often banded, with quartz, white mica ± biotite ± chlorite (sometimes oxidized) ± calcite; sometimes with red-brown (clay?) material. Tourmaline, calcite, talc/shimmer grains, opaques, and titanite rarely appear. Medium- and coarse-grained fragments composed of quartz, porphyroblastic feldspar ± clinozoisite/epidote (clinozoisite is more common in 1, 37, and 43; epidote is more common in 18, 35, 36) ± biotite ± white mica ± amphibole (mostly pleochroic green, actinolite(?), especially in 1); feldspars very rarely show simple or albite twinning; quartzite. Fine-grained schists and phyllite are relatively common in 18 and 37.
Few–very few: Calcite, most micrite/sparite, sometimes with reaction rims or altered to black, gray, or speckled yellow in xpl, eq, r, mode 0.3–0.7 mm.
Few–very rare: Mica aggregates, el, r, mode 0.3–0.8 mm.

Fine Fraction
Dominant: Quartz/feldspar (small fragments are indistinguishable from one another) and metamorphic rock fragments as above, eq and el, sa–r.
Dominant–few: Mica laths (white mica and less biotite) (dominant in 36).
Common–very rare: Epidote/clinozoisite, eq, sa–r; opaques, eq and el, a and sr.
Very few–very rare: Calcite, mostly micrite, eq and slightly el, r.
Very rare–absent: Tourmaline(?), eq, sa; titanite(?), el, sr; birefringent yellow and orange-red grains, el, sr.

Tcfs
As in PFG 1A.

Variant: 2, 22
Common calcite; epidote/clinozoisite and phyllite are also relatively common in 2. Sample 22 has relatively well-sorted inclusions with weakly bimodal size distribution; inclusions in sample 2 are more poorly sorted.

Variant: 27
Very micaceous and browner in color than the main group, with common opaques, some elongated and rectangular in shape (much like those in sample 48, in PFG 1A). Some probable talc. Relatively common epidote/clinozoisite, including some porphyroblastic; rare possible glaucophane and common white mica in banded mica schists.

Variant: 38, 39
Groundmass quite clean and mica rarer than in the main group; a few large weathered plagioclase grains exist; no calcite in 39 but otherwise very similar to 38, which has micritic (altered) inclusions. Few voids, mostly meso- and macro-vughs and channels, a few elongate planar/channel voids, with some secondary soil/mud(?) infilling (yellow in ppl, anomalous birefringence). Both are slightly paler at core than margins.

SUBGROUP D: COMMON VOIDS
Samples: 3, 7, 12, 23, 49

This group is distinguished by having common voids (including many elongate planar/channel voids) and turning gray to black at the core, at least in places. The core-margin boundary is diffuse in 12, 23, and 49. Samples 12 and 49 are gray at the core only in places rather than across the entire section. The core-margin boundary in 3 and 7 (both closed vessels) is rather sharp and on both is most prominent toward the interior surface, which is paler colored than the exterior. This pattern probably suggests a reducing or partially reducing atmosphere during the last stages of the firing. All are optically active, although 49 is only slightly so. (Sample 49 is also the only Period VI sample in this subgroup.)

All of the samples in this group are very micaceous. Apart from being more micaceous than PFG 1A, samples 3, 7, and 49 are quite similar to that subgroup in terms of inclusions, although rare probable micritic grains also exist, which would be more similar to PFG 1C. Samples 12 and 23 are more similar to PFG 1B, with quite common clinozoisite and white mica showing low birefringence colors; some possible altered calcite grains also exist in 23. Probable amphibole exists, especially in 7, 12, and 23, although this is less common than in PFG 2C. Rare feldspars in 12 show black bands of alteration; brown grains in 3, 7, and 49 with anomalous birefringence may be altered epidote/clinozoisite(?). Schists in 3 are generally finer grained, rather like PFG 2B, although the color of the groundmass is atypical for that subgroup.

The color variation of 49 is not as extreme as the others, and fewer elongate channel/planar voids exist, although voids (mostly meso- and macro-vughs and channels) are still common. This sample also preserves a thick layer of slip, green-brown (ppl); dark greenish gray (xpl), possibly calcareous; bearing quartz (and perhaps some feldspar) inclusions. Metamorphic rock fragments as in the main fabric, mica, epidote/clinozoisite, and amphibole are rare. The clay underneath the slip is dark at the very surface in a thin band. A dark band, probably paint (dark-colored slip), runs along the exterior surface of the thick green-brown slip.

The co-occurrence of common voids and gray cores in these samples could suggest that this subgroup was relatively rich in organic material. Although some voids resemble those hypothesized elsewhere as generated by dung-tempering (e.g., Livingstone Smith 2001, fig. 8.13: 54, 166, 10), most voids are not clearly pseudomorphic of organic remains (cf. Gilstrap, Day, and Kilikoglou 2016, figs. 4, 12; van Doosselaere, Delhon, and Hayes 2014, figs. 4, 6, 7). The large planar/channel voids in particular seem most likely to be cracks that were caused by stress during drying or firing. This is the only PFG 1 subgroup in which more than one sample shows low optical activity, although some samples (3, 23) have moderately high optical activity (visible particularly at the oxidized edges of the slides). It is possible that aspects of the firing regime other than maximum temperature, such as soaking time or rate of temperature increase, might have caused such stresses within the clay matrix. In any case, these samples seem to represent a divergence from the *chaîne opératoire* associated with PFG 1A–C, despite the use of similar raw materials.

Microstructure
Common voids, single- and double-spaced, predominantly meso- and macro-channels, including elongate planar/channel voids and rarer vughs, except in 49, where elongate planar/channel voids are very rare and vughs predominate. One large vugh (1.8 mm long) in 49 is surrounded by blackened clay, probably left by burning out of an organic inclusion. Voids are oriented roughly parallel to vessel walls except in 49, which shows no orientation; very few inclusions show voids/shrinkage cracking around them. Inclusions single- to double-spaced, no orientation (3, 23) or weakly aligned with vessel walls (7, 12, 49); unimodal size distribution.

Groundmass
Not homogenous; red, orange, red brown, gray, very dark brown (ppl); red, orange brown, dark red brown, dark gray (xpl) (40x); darker toward cores; optically active (3, 7, 12, 23) to optically slightly active (49).

Inclusions
c:f:$v_{0.15\,mm}$, ca. 35:40:25–45:30:25. Poorly sorted, el and eq, sa–r, <3.0 mm, mode 0.3–1.5 mm, unimodal size distribution.

Coarse Fraction
Predominant: Metamorphic rock fragments and dissociated fragments thereof, el and more rarely eq, sa–r, mode 0.3–1.5 mm. Fine- and medium-grained mica schists, sometimes banded, with quartz, muscovite ± biotite ± chlorite; sometimes with red-brown (clay?) material or oxidized streaks. Metamorphic rock fragments consisting of porphyroblastic feldspar and/or clinozoisite/epidote and sometimes quartz; cloudy brown grains like those in the previous groups (altered epidote?) also appear. Quartzite. One grain of possible altered calc-schist in 7, with the possible calcareous component turning dark brown-gray in xpl; micaceous phyllite also exists. Quartzes often show undulose extinction and individual grains sometimes are elongated and strained. Feldspars rarely show simple or albite twinning; they may be cloudy and/or bear mica or possible amphibole inclusions. Titanite, tourmaline, and apatite appear as accessory minerals; amphibole (usually brown or green in ppl; very rare probable glaucophane grains in 3 and 7) is generally rare, as are angular opaque grains (most common in 23) and talc/shimmer grains. A few tiny pink grains (piemontite?) are present in 7 and 23.
Few–very few: Mica aggregates, el, sa, mode 0.3–0.6 mm.
Very few–absent: Calcite(?), altered, appears micritic, greenish-brown in ppl, dark brown in xpl, eq and el, sr–r, mode 0.3–1.0 mm; a few grains in 3 are partially unaltered and clearly micritic; opaques, eq and el, sa–sr, mode 0.2 mm.
Very rare–absent: Serpentinite(?), greenish yellow (ppl) grain with probable epidote inclusion, dark with mesh-like texture in xpl, sr, 0.4 mm; chert(?), 0.8 mm.

Fine fraction
Frequent: Mica laths and aggregates; quartz/feldspar (often indistinguishable from each other), eq and el, a–sr.
Common–very few: Metamorphic rock fragments, as above.
Few–very rare: Epidote/clinozoisite, eq, sa–sr; opaques, eq, sa.
Rare–absent: Altered calcite(?), as above.
Very rare–absent: Titanite, el, sa–sr; tourmaline, eq and el, sa.

Tcfs
As in PFG 1A.

Variant: 6
Entirely dark, very coarse; some fine-grained metamorphic rock grains resemble those in PFG 2B, as does the "wispy" appearance of the fabric (although it is possible that this "wispiness" may be related to different firing temperatures rather than a different geological source). With abundant coarse clinozoisite, white micas with low birefringence, and a very micaceous groundmass, this sample also resembles PFG 1B.

GROUP 2: LOCAL OR "LOCAL REGION" MICA SCHISTS

This group comprises fabrics that appear somewhat similar to those above, and they are geologically compatible with a local origin, with the probable exception of PFG 2D. However, all have characteristics that are unusual among the main local fabrics and so could represent production either from another area on Kea or from a geologically similar area, like Attica, southern Euboea, or elsewhere in the western Cyclades (see, e.g., Scheffer et al. 2016, 176, fig. 1). The petrographic analysis supports the macroscopic study, which classed most of these samples in groups that were suspected to be possibly nonlocal on the basis of their rarity in the assemblage and their deviation from the norms of local fabrics. All refired red. Preliminary interpretation of the WD-XRF results suggests that most PFG 2 samples have a similar overall composition (which is also quite variable) to samples from PFG 1.

SUBGROUP A: WHITE MICA SCHIST, TALC
Samples: 33, 34

This subgroup is distinguished by having fine- to coarse-grained metamorphic inclusions, including frequent weathered white mica schists with common opaque material, as well as large feldspars, probably dissociated from coarse-grained metamorphic rocks. Talc grains and talc schists appear, as do large tcfs with common inclusions and clear boundaries. There are similarities with PFG 1B, particularly in the prevalence of clinozoisite in comparison with epidote, prevalence of white-mica schists, and low (first-order) birefringence colors for some of the white mica, although clear talc grains only exist in a variant of that group (8), and mica laths are less common in the groundmass of PFG 2A. A petrographic variant (10, 115), which shares similarities both with PFG 2A and 2B, suggests that these two groups may be related. Preliminary interpretation of the WD-XRF results indicates that, apart from 32 (below), all of the PFG 2A samples have chemical signatures very similar to those of PFG 1.

Microstructure
Few voids, single- to open-spaced, predominantly meso- and macro-vughs and channels; two voids in 33 are surrounded by darkened clay and probably were created by burning organic material. Voids with a long-axis are oriented roughly parallel to vessel walls. Rare inclusions in 34 have shrinkage/cracking at some of their edges. Inclusions single- to double-spaced, no orientation; unimodal size distribution.

Groundmass
Not homogenous; pale brown to red-brown (ppl); orange, red, or red-brown (xpl) (40x); somewhat darker toward core; optically active.

Inclusions
c:f:$v_{0.15\,mm}$, ca. 40:40:20. Poorly sorted, el and eq, sa–r, <3.9 mm, mode 0.3–2.4 mm, unimodal size distribution.

Coarse Fraction
Predominant: Metamorphic rock fragments and dissociated fragments thereof, el and eq, sa–r, mode 0.3–2.4 mm. Fine- and medium-grained quartz-mica schists, often grading between fine- and medium-grained in the same rock fragment, usually banded, composed of quartz, mica (mostly white mica) ± chlorite ± talc/shimmer, often with small patches and large bands of opaque material; red-brown or brown material (clay?) also appears. Medium- and coarse-grained metamorphic rock fragments composed of quartz, mica (mostly white mica), porphyroblastic feldspar ± epidote/clinozoiste ± chlorite ± talc/shimmer. Micaceous phyllite is present and occasionally shows crenulation textures. Probable actinolite appears, sometimes as quite large crystals (up to 0.3 mm). Titanite is present; apatite and tourmaline appear rather rarely. Clinozoisite is more common than epidote. Quartzes regularly show undulose extinction and sometimes elongated shapes. Feldspars sometimes show simple or albite twinning; sometimes with mica, titanite(?), epidote, or amphibole (actinolite?) inclusions, sericitization, or alteration in the form of black bands.
Few–very few: Talc, el, sr, mode 0.3–1.4 mm; birefringent orange/red grains, eq, sa–sr, 0.3–1.0 mm.

Very few: Mica aggregates, el, sr, mode 0.5–1.3 mm.
Rare: Opaques, el, sa–sr, mode 0.3–1.0 mm.
Very few–absent: Calcite (micrite), eq, r, up to 1.0 mm(?), but the single clear grain is mostly surrounded by a void; a few other probable grains exist, but altered, dark in xpl, 0.2–0.3 mm; one of these (33) has a shape that could perhaps be indicative of a burned-out microfossil.

Fine fraction
Dominant: Quartz/feldspar (often indistinguishable from each other), mostly eq, a–sr.
Common–few: Mica laths.
Few–very few: Metamorphic rock fragments as above; opaques, as above; birefringent orange-red grains, as above.
Rare: Epidote/clinozoisite, eq, sa–r.
Rare–absent: Altered calcite(?), as above.
Rare–very rare: Titanite, el, sr.
Very rare–absent: Tourmaline, eq, sa.

Tcfs
As in PFG 1A, plus very few–very rare tcfs that are red-brown to dark red-brown (ppl), red to red-brown (xpl), sharp boundaries, high optical density, eq, r, up to 1.3 mm, bearing inclusions typical of the main fabric.

Variant: 10, 115
These sherds are like a combination of PFG 2A and 2B. Biotite is more common than in PFG 2A, but the coarser schist inclusions are otherwise similar, and large tcfs appear similar to those mentioned above. Fine-grained schist is more common than in PFG 2A, however, and appears very similar to those typical of PFG 2B. The color and the existence of a darker core are also similar to PFG 2B, as is the relative infrequency of mica in the groundmass. The similarities of these sherds to both subgroups, both of which are notable for the existence of talc, could suggest that they derive from a similar origin.

Variant: 32
The groundmass color is more brown than the main group; common opaque and white mica schists, but porphyroblastic feldspar is much rarer, and epidote/clinozoisite exists only in the fine fraction; it is also very micaceous. In color, it is rather similar to PFG 2B, but the metamorphic rock fragments are not particularly fine-grained. Preliminary interpretation of the WD-XRF results suggests that this sample is also chemical variant from the rest of PFG 2A.

SUBGROUP B: CHAOTIC FINE-GRAINED SCHIST, PHYLLITE
Samples: 21, 28, 50

This subgroup is distinguished by a chaotic texture, dominant fine-grained schist or phyllite and relatively common voids. The clay is more brown than red, in contrast with PFG 1 and other subgroups in PFG 2; it has a "wispy" appearance in ppl. The co-occurrence of common voids and gray cores (especially in 21 and 28) could suggest that these clays were rich in organic material; it is notable that these two samples come from vessels dated to the LBA, while the only early sample (50, from Period IV), has fewer voids and is only slightly darker at core. Differences from PFG 1 fabrics, including the absence of tcfs similar to those in nearly all other ostensibly local subgroups, strongly suggest that these samples represent a different raw material source, either on Kea or further afield. Preliminary interpretation of the WD-XRF results suggests that, chemically, samples 28 and 50 are more similar to each other than sample 21, with high chromium and nickel values; these values are also much higher than those associated with PFG 1, except for sample 15, a variant of PFG 1A.

Microstructure
Common–few voids, single- to open-spaced, meso- and macrovughs, micro- to macrochannels, meso-vesicles, and elongated planar/channel voids. In 21 and 28, which have relatively low optical activity, it seems probable that the elongated voids may result from stress/cracking during firing. A macrovugh in 50 is surrounded by darkened clay, probably a result of burning organic material. Oblong voids are oriented parallel to vessel walls. Inclusions close and single-spaced, very roughly oriented parallel to vessel walls (21, 28) or no orientation (50).

Groundmass
Not homogenous; orange-brown, brown, red brown, very dark brown (ppl); dark red brown, brown, dark brown (xpl) (40x); optically slightly active (21, 28) to active (50).

Inclusions
c:f:$v_{0.15\,mm}$, 40:35:25–53:25:22. Poorly sorted, el and more rarely eq, sa–r, <4.5 mm, mode 0.2–2.1 mm, unimodal size distribution.

Coarse fraction
Predominant: Metamorphic rock fragments and dissociated fragments thereof, el and more rarely eq, sa–r, mode 0.2–2.1 mm. Fine-grained usually banded quartz-mica schists with white mica ± biotite ± chlorite and sometimes bands or patches of opaque material, rarely with talc/shimmer grains and sometimes with calcite (? usually altered); occasional porphyroblasts of quartz or feldspar, probably mylonitic. Micaceous brown phyllite, occasionally showing crenulation textures. Medium- and coarse-grained rock fragments composed of quartz, porphyroblastic feldspar, and mica ± epidote/clinozoisite ± opaques. Quartzite, rarely with attached mica. Calc-schist, especially in 50. Quartz often shows undulose extinction, sometimes with elongated, sutured grain boundaries. Feldspars sometimes show simple or albite twinning. White mica often has low birefringence colors. Small garnets sometimes appear; actinolite, tourmaline, and titanite are rare. Brown slightly birefringent to opaque material is common in rock fragments (clay?).
Few–very rare: Mica aggregates, rarely laths, el, sr–r, mode 0.2–0.9 mm.
Very few–very rare: Calcite, mostly altered, dark in xpl but appears micritic in ppl, sometimes with small a–sa quartz inclusions, eq and slightly el, sr–r, mode 0.3–0.4 mm.
Very few–absent: Opaques, eq and el, a–r, mode 0.3 mm; talc/shimmer grains, eq and slightly el, sr–r, mode 0.3–0.5 mm; serpentinite(?), orange with anomalous birefringence, el, sa, 0.3–0.6 mm.
Very rare–absent: Brown siltstone/sandstone(?), with sa–sr quartz ± biotite inclusions, sometimes oxidized, eq, r, 0.3–0.5 mm; chert(?), el, sa, 0.4–1.0 mm; cloudy brown grains, perhaps altered epidote(?), eq, sr, mode 0.2–0.3 mm.

Fine fraction
Dominant: Quartz/feldspar (often indistinguishable from each other) and metamorphic rock fragments as above, eq and el, sa–r.
Common–very rare: Opaques, eq and el, sa–sr.
Few–rare: Mica (biotite and white mica) laths.
Few–very rare: Epidote/clinozoisite, eq, sa–r.
Rare–absent: Calcite, altered, eq, r.
Rare–absent: Talc, el, sr; cloudy brown grains as above.

Tcfs
None.

Variant: 19
This sample is more red- than brown-tinged, but fine-grained metamorphic rocks and micaceous phyllite are common. Voids are common, and the core is gray. Several feldspar grains show fine black bands of alteration. In addition to some altered possibly calcareous grains in schists, microfossils exist. Although microfossils are attested in one sandstone outcrop on Kea, SW of the Ayios Nikolaos harbor (Rice et al. 2012), they are abundant in other parts of the Aegean, and so this sample (if not the whole subgroup) may well be imported.

Variant: 20
Fine-grained metamorphic rocks but little phyllite; otherwise the rock fragments are very similar to those of the main group. Voids are mostly meso- and macro-vughs, rarer channels, and no elongate planar/channel voids; darker at core. Common talc and chlorite, no epidote/clinozoisite, and some large red grains that may be iron pellets. Color at surfaces is more reddish, as PFG 1.

SUBGROUP C: COARSE, AMPHIBOLE-BEARING METAMORPHIC ROCKS
Samples: 130, 131, 139

This subgroup is distinguished by the presence of relatively common metamorphic rocks that bear brown or green amphibole. These samples are geologically compatible with a Keian origin, as amphibole (primarily actinolite) is not unusual in the local greenschists (Rice et al. 2012). Brown amphibole similar in appearance to that which appears in some of the schists of this group exists in fired clay samples from Kea held at the Fitch Laboratory, although it is relatively rare. Amphibole is a minor component in previous descriptions of Keian fabrics (Gauss and Kiriatzi 2011; Hilditch 2004). Preliminary interpretation of the WD-XRF results suggests that this group is chemically quite varied. Samples 136 (a petrographic variant) and 139 both have similar chemical values to those of PFG 1; the rest of the samples (including petrographic variants 24 and 47) fall outside the norm for the main group.

Microstructure
Common voids, macro-vughs and meso- to mega-channels (including elongate planar cracking/channels), especially in 131 and 139, which also show some cracking around inclusions; oriented parallel to vessel walls; the shape of one large void in 139 strongly suggests it formed around an organic inclusion. Inclusions single-spaced or less, weakly oriented parallel to vessel walls, except in 131, which shows no preferred orientation.

Groundmass
Not homogenous; orange, red, dark red-brown (ppl); red to red-brown (xpl) (40x); optically active (130) to only very slightly active (131, 139).

Inclusions
c:f:v$_{0.15\,mm}$, 32:45:23–40:30:30. Poorly sorted, eq and mostly el, sa–r, <4.5 mm, mode 0.3–1.8 mm, unimodal size distribution.

Coarse fraction
Predominant: Metamorphic rock fragments and dissociates thereof, mostly el, sa–r, mode 0.3–1.8 mm. Quartz-mica schist, usually banded, including biotite and/or white mica ± chlorite ± brown material ± opaque material, mostly in bands. Fragments consisting of quartz, porphryoblastic feldspar and/or clinozoisite/epidote ± mica ± chlorite ± brown or green amphibole, ± nearly opaque or dark red-brown material, occasionally with high-relief acicular amphibole(?) inclusions. Micaceous phyllite; mica aggregates, consisting of biotite, chlorite, amphibole, and dark-brown material; quartzite; quartz-garnet-biotite schist, one grain (139). White mica is less common in 130 than 131 and 139; it sometimes is coarse and shows low birefringence colors, as in many of the groups above. Quartz usually shows undulose extinction, sometimes with sutured boundaries; ribbon-textured quartz is also present. Rarely, talc/shimmer grains appear. The epidote (both as part of rock fragments and as dissociated grains) is sometimes bright green in ppl. Titanite, tourmaline rarely appear.
Very few–rare: Birefringent yellow-orange grains, el, r, mode 0.3 mm.
Very few–absent: Altered calcite(?), yellow to pale brown in ppl, speckled yellow/black in xpl, occasionally a fragment that looks more clearly like an altered lump of micrite, eq, r, mode 0.1–0.3 mm.
Rare–absent: Opaques, mostly el, a–sr, mode 0.2–0.3 mm.

Fine fraction
Dominant–frequent: Quartz/feldspar (often indistinguishable from each other), eq and el, a–sr.
Frequent–common: Mica laths.
Common–very few: Metamorphic rock fragments as above; epidote/clinozoisite, eq, sa–sr; amphibole, el, a–sr.
Few–rare: Opaques, as above.
Very rare–absent: Altered calcite(?) as above; tourmaline, eq, sr.

Tcfs
Rare, dark brown to nearly opaque (ppl), dark red-brown to nearly opaque (xpl), sharp to slightly diffuse boundaries, optically dense, eq and slightly el, r, <0.2–0.7 mm, occasionally bearing quartz and/or mica inclusions.

Variant: 24
Extremely micaceous. Rarer probable amphibole; epidote/clinozoisite clear rather than green in ppl, with more fine-grained schists than in the main group. Common voids and gray core.

Variant: 25, 47
Less amphibole; weakly bimodal size distribution. Minor piemontite(?) exists (25); more common tourmaline(?) in 47 than is usual.

Variant: 135, 136
Less amphibole, more and larger opaques, much less mica. Probably subjected to reduced firing, dark greenish gray (ppl), gray to dark reddish gray (xpl), with weakly bimodal size distribution of inclusions. The paint on sample 135 refired to red-brown.

SUBGROUP D: BIOTITE-RICH METAMORPHIC ROCKS WITH RARE IGNEOUS
Samples: 16 (medium); 132, 137 (coarse)

This fabric is very similar to PFG 2C (especially the variant samples 135 and 136) in many respects. Amphibole and large epidote/clinozoisite grains are less common in this subgroup, and there are more fine- and medium-grained metamorphic rocks. Coarse-grained rock fragments with large epidote/clinozoisite grains that appear closely comparable with those of the previous subgroup appear, if rarely. Epidote/clinozoisite grains are occasionally green or, especially in 132, bright yellow in ppl; altered calcite(?) is more common than in the previous subgroup. This subgroup also contains rare grains that appear to be granitic or metagranitic, which would mean that this must be an imported group as there are no such outcrops on Kea. Granitic and metagranitic outcrops in association with metamorphic geologies are known in the area of Lavrion (Scheffer et al. 2016, 179, fig. 3), as well as on various islands, including Sikinos, Paros, and Ios; the largest ones are located on Naxos, Seriphos, Tenos, and Ikaria (Augier et al. 2014; Katzir et al. 2007; Mizera and Behrmann 2016; Rabillard et al. 2015; Stouraiti et al. 2010).

Microstructure
Common–few voids, mostly meso- and macro-vughs and channels, occasional cracking around inclusions in 132 and 137; some infilling in 137. Those with a long-axis are oriented roughly parallel to vessel walls, except in 16, which shows no orientation. Inclusions single (132, 137) to open-spaced (16); those with a long axis are weakly (16) to moderately aligned parallel to vessel walls (132, 137).

Groundmass
Not homogenous; brown, greenish brown, dark brown, red brown (ppl); dark brown or dark red brown (xpl) (40x); moderately optically active (137) to inactive (16, 132).

Inclusions
c:f:v$_{0.15\ mm}$, 33:42:25–45:22:33. Poorly sorted (132, 137) to moderately well-sorted (16), eq and el, a–r, <4.1 mm, mode 0.2–1.3 mm, unimodal (132, 137) to weakly bimodal (16) size distribution.

Coarse fraction
Dominant: Metamorphic rock fragments and dissociated fragments thereof, a–sr, eq and el, mode 0.2–1.3 mm. Quartz-feldspar aggregates ± biotite ± epidote/clinozoisite (sometimes porphyroblastic) ± chlorite ± brown or green amphibole, rarely with large eq, a–sa, opaque grains. Banded quartz-mica schist (usually biotite) ± feldspar (usually untwinned) ± chlorite ± large angular (eq) opaque grains ± brown amphibole, sometimes with red-brown material (clay?), and/or cloudy brown grains with small patches showing second- to third-order birefringence colors (altered epidote?). Quartzite, rarely with small mica inclusions. Micaceous, usually red-brown phyllite, sometimes showing crenulation textures. The majority of disaggregated fragments are quartz or feldspar, usually a–sr. Quartz (as part of rock fragments or dissociated) often shows undulose extinction and sutured grain boundaries, including some fragments with ribbon texture. Feldspars are often cloudy and rarely show simple or albite twinning. Titanite appears. Amphibole is more common in 137 than the others.
Common–rare: Altered calcite(?), appears micritic in ppl but anomalous in xpl, eq and slightly el, r, mode 0.2–0.6 mm.
Very few–very rare: (Meta)granitic rock fragments, very rarely with micrographic textures, eq and el, a–sr, mode 0.3 mm; mica aggregates (white mica appears only very rarely), el, sa–sr, mode 0.3 mm.
Rare–very rare: Glassy, altered volcanic rock fragments(?), yellow to clear in ppl, opaque or cloudy red in xpl, sometimes with possible phenocrysts of quartz and biotite, eq and slightly el, sr–r, mode 0.3 mm.
Very rare–absent: Opaques, el, sa, up to 1.0 mm.

Fine fraction
Predominant–dominant: Quartz/feldspar (often indistinguishable from each other), a–sr, mostly eq.
Frequent–very few: Mica laths.
Few–rare: Cloudy brown grains with anomalous birefringence (altered epidote?), eq, r.
Few–very rare: Altered calcite as above.
Few–absent: Brown and green amphibole, el, sa.
Very few–absent: Titanite, el, sr; birefringent orange grains, el, sr.
Rare–absent: Metamorphic rock fragments as above; opaques, eq and el, sr; tiny epidote/clinozoisite(?) grains, eq, sa.

Tcfs
Very few–very rare; red, red-brown, brown, or nearly black (ppl); red-brown to nearly opaque (xpl); sharp to merging or diffuse boundaries; optically dense or neutral; eq and el, r, <0.15 mm–0.6 mm; sometimes bearing inclusions, mostly quartz.
Rare–very rare, red or brown (ppl), dark in xpl, diffuse boundaries, low optical density, eq and el, r, mostly <0.2 mm.

GROUP 3: NONLOCAL MICACEOUS METAMORPHIC

This and following groups are made up of certain imports at Ayia Irini. Dominant inclusions in this group are micaceous metamorphic rocks. Although parallels for some of the subgroups have been located in publications or in the reference collections of the Fitch Laboratory of the British School at Athens, many of the subgroups have no known comparanda. Metamorphic geologies are widespread in the neighboring northern and western Cyclades, Attica, and southern Euboea; it is probable that much or all of PFG 3 derives from within this broad area.

SUBGROUP A: QUARTZ-RICH ROCKS
Sample: 102

Metamorphic rock fragments in this fabric are rich in quartz, with comparatively rare micas. No clear parallels are known, although the shape of the vessel suggests an origin either on Crete or in the Cyclades. The high optical activity (and, therefore, relatively low firing temperature) seems more typical of firing regimes in the Cyclades than Crete. Given the widespread metamorphic geologies of the Cyclades, it is not possible to narrow down the possible provenance. Refired to red.

Microstructure
Few voids, meso- and macro-vughs and channels; weakly oriented parallel to vessel walls. Inclusions single-spaced; those with a long axis are roughly oriented parallel to vessel walls.

Groundmass
Not homogenous, honey brown to brown with irregular patches and streaks of dark brown in some places (ppl), yellow to yellow brown (xpl) (40x), very optically active.

Inclusions
$c:f:v_{0.2\,mm}$, 20:55:25. Poorly sorted, eq and el, sa–r, <2.1 mm, mode 0.3–1.0 mm, weakly bimodal size distribution.

Coarse fraction
Dominant: Fine- and medium-grained metamorphic rock fragments, el, sa–r, mode 0.3–1.0 mm. Schists, occasionally banded, consist of quartz ± feldspar ± mica (white mica and/or biotite, sometimes altered and nearly opaque) ± chlorite ± green, brown, or rarely blue amphibole ± tourmaline ± epidote/clinozoisite(?) (high relief, mostly dark brown with small patches of second-order birefringence in xpl) ± radiating high-relief acicular inclusions with inclined extinction (amphibole?); sometimes with patches of brown material. Quartzite, sometimes with rare mica laths. Rarely, phyllite. Quartz often shows undulose extinction, grains sometimes strained and elongated.
Frequent: Feldspar grains, rarely showing albite twins, many altered, some with tiny mica or clinozoisite/epidote(?) inclusions, eq and el, sa–sr, 0.3–0.6 mm.
Very few: Micrite/sparite lumps, grains often enclosed by dark rim, in one case with a metamorphic rock inclusion, el and eq, r, 1.8–2.1 mm.
Rare: Mica aggregates, slightly el, r, mode 0.3–0.4 mm.
Very rare: Altered volcanic(?) rock, cloudy red turning mostly black in xpl with quartz and elongate (feldspar?) phenocrysts(?) with low birefringence colors, el, sr, 0.4 mm; unknown rock, yellow in ppl, dark brown (nearly opaque) with tiny birefringent yellow areas in xpl, slightly el, r, 0.4 mm; volcanic rock(?) that appears to have felsitic groundmass and feldspar phenocryst, el, r, 0.8 mm.

Fine fraction
Frequent: Quartz/feldspar (often indistinguishable from each other) and metamorphic rock fragments as above, eq and el, sa–r.
Common: Mica laths.
Few: Opaques, eq and el, sa–r.
Very few: Epidote and more rarely clinozoisite, eq and el, sr.
Rare: Tourmaline, eq, sa.
Very rare: Pyroxene(?), eq, sr; amphibole, el and eq, sa–r.

Tcfs
Very few, red-brown (ppl), red to red-brown (xpl), sharp boundaries, optically dense, eq, sa–r, <0.2 mm.

SUBGROUP B: MICA SCHISTS, PHYLLITE, COARSE FELDSPARS
Sample: 106

The groundmass and rock fragments, especially the frequent phyllite, are somewhat similar to those of sample 14 and to those in Hilditch's Dark Phyllite fabric at Keros, hypothesized to be from Amorgos (Hilditch 2007, 241). Metamorphic deposits elsewhere (even within the Keros triangle) could also be compatible with these inclusions, especially since phyllite is not predominant among rock fragments in the sample. Macroscopically, the vessel was hypothesized to be Cycladic. Refired to red.

Microstructure
Few voids, meso- and macro-vughs; no orientation. Inclusions single-spaced, no orientation.

Groundmass
Not homogenous, honey brown to red brown (ppl), yellow to orange (xpl) (40x), optically active.

Inclusions
c:f:v$_{0.2\,mm}$, 50:30:20. Moderately well-sorted, eq and el, sa–r, <1.8 mm, mode 0.4–1.2 mm, weakly bimodal size distribution.

Coarse fraction
Frequent: Metamorphic rock fragments and dissociated fragments thereof, mostly el, sa–r, mode 0.4–1.2 mm. Fine- and medium-grained quartz-mica schists, sometimes banded, including white mica and/or biotite (sometimes altered or nearly opaque) ± feldspar ± chlorite ± opaques (eq, a–sr) ± titanite(?), tiny garnets very rarely appear, as do bands of red-brown material. Micaceous and in some cases dark-brown phyllite, sometimes with crenulation textures. Quartzite, rarely with sparse mica. Quartz-feldspar aggregates ± mica ± red-brown or nearly opaque material (clay?).
Common: Feldspar grains, often showing albite twinning, eq and el, sa–r, mode 0.6–1.4 mm.
Very few: Mica laths, white mica and biotite, 0.2–0.3 mm. Argillaceous grains, with red-brown matrix, bearing poorly sorted, el, sa–sr sedimentary (quartz arenite with rare mica) and metamorphic rock (quartz-mica schists and phyllites as above) fragments as well as small quartz/feldspar grains and/or mica laths and/or very rare opaques, el, sa–sr, mode 0.6 mm.
Rare: Volcanic rock fragments, altered, including examples with a glassy matrix and phenocrysts of feldspar and possibly quartz; fragments with trachytic texture, rare quartz, and altered pyroxene(?) phenocrysts; and fragments with felsitic texture, eq, sr–r, 0.3–0.4 mm.
Very rare: Shale(?), red-brown, rare mica, el, sr, 0.3–0.4 mm; pale greenish-brown grain, speckled greenish-yellow and opaque in xpl, el, r, 0.3 mm.

Fine fraction
Dominant: Quartz/feldspar (often indistinguishable from each other).
Frequent: Mica laths (mostly white mica).
Few: Metamorphic rock fragments as above.
Very few: Opaques, eq and slightly el, sa–sr.
Rare: Red and orange grains with anomalous birefringence, slightly el, sa–r.
Very rare: Glaucophane(?), slightly el, a.

Tcfs
Few, red-brown to nearly opaque (ppl), red to nearly opaque (xpl), sharp or rarely diffuse boundaries, optically dense, el and eq, r, probably related to argillaceous grains above, mostly <0.2 mm.

SUBGROUP C: WHITE MICA, GLAUCOPHANE SCHIST, MICROFOSSILS
Samples: 53, 104, 113

The existence of glaucophane schist suggests an origin in the Cycladic Blueschist Unit. Syros is one possible origin, since there are prevalent glaucophane schists intercalated with microfossil-bearing marbles in outcrops that are spread out across the island (Schumacher et al. 2008, esp. fig. 1). A parallel (especially for sample 104) exists with a sample in the Fitch Laboratory's collection, Syros (80) Sy 71b, a whistle from the Ano Manas pottery workshop, although that sample is missing glaucophane. In general, the samples in this subgroup are relatively fine, and glaucophane grains are rare, so their absence in the Ano Manas sample may be understandable. However, without additional samples of ancient pottery from Syros with which to compare this subgroup, the association must remain tentative. Apart from Syros, Siphnos also provides a plausible alternative, given the abundance of glaucophane schists there, but blueschists also exist elsewhere, including on southern Tenos and northern Ios (Forster and Lister 2005, Fig. 1), in addition to southern Euboea (Xypolias et al. 2012). All samples refired red, although 53 varies to pink at the core. Preliminary interpretation of the WD-XRF results suggests that this group, including the petrographic variants, as well as PFG 3D (below), is relatively coherent in its chemistry.

Microstructure
Few–rare voids, mostly macro-vughs, some meso- to mega-channels (elongate) and vesicles in 113, some calcite rims and infilling; no orientation. Inclusions open-spaced; those with a long axis are roughly oriented parallel to vessel walls.

Groundmass
Not homogenous; honey brown to pale red brown and greenish brown, with the different colors appearing in either patches or streaks (ppl); yellow, orange, brown, or green-brown (xpl) (40x); optically active.

Inclusions
c:f:v$_{0.3\,mm}$, 20:70:10–13:85:2. Poorly sorted (53) to well-sorted (104, 113), eq and el, sa–r, <4.2 mm, mode 0.4–1.2 mm, unimodal (53) to weakly bimodal (104, 113) size distribution.

Coarse fraction
Dominant–frequent: Mica laths and aggregates (white mica common, biotite rarer), el, mode 0.5–1.0 mm. Metamorphic rock fragments, el, sa–r, mode 0.5–1.2 mm. Quartz-mica schist (biotite and/or white mica), in some cases with titanite, glaucophane, clinozoisite, and/or opaques (eq and el, sa). Quartz-feldspar-mica schist, with white mica and more rarely biotite, porphroblastic clinozoisite/epidote occasionally appears. Polycrystalline quartz with sutured boundaries and undulose extinction.
Common–very few: Calcite. Micrite and more rarely sparite lumps, eq and slightly el, r, mode 0.4–1.0 mm, rarely bearing angular quartz, mica, or epidote/clinozoisite inclusions. Microfossils (including ostracod) and curving shell, mode 0.4–0.7 mm.
Very few–absent: Epidote/clinozoisite, eq, sa, mode 0.4–0.5 mm.
Rare–very rare: Quartz arenite or quartzite, with very rare white mica, el, sa, mode 0.9 mm.
Rare–absent: Argillaceous grains, bearing poorly sorted, a–sa quartz-mica schist fragments, quartz, and/or epidote/clinozoisite in red-brown matrix, el, sa–sr, 0.4–1.4 mm, somewhat similar to those in PFG 3B.
Very rare–absent: Plagioclase with mica inclusions, eq, sa, mode 0.4–0.7 mm.

Fine fraction
Dominant: Mica laths (mostly white mica).
Frequent: Quartz (mono- and polycrystalline), feldspar (including plagioclase), eq and el, sa; metamorphic rock fragments as above.
Common: Epidote/clinozoisite, eq, sa–r.
Common–few: Calcite, micrite/sparite, mostly lumps, although some may be degraded microfossils, occasionally holocrystalline grains, eq and slightly el, r.
Rare–very rare: Opaques, eq, sa–sr.
Very rare: Tourmaline, eq, sa; glaucophane, el, a.
Very rare–absent: Birefringent orange-brown grains, eq, sr; sponge spicules.

Tcfs
Very few, red to red-brown (ppl), red to dark red-brown (xpl), sharp to merging boundaries, optically dense to rarely optically neutral, eq and el, r, <0.3 mm–0.8 mm, occasionally bearing angular quartz, mica, or metamorphic rock fragments.
Few–very few, yellow brown (ppl), speckled orange and black (xpl), sharp to rather diffuse boundaries, low optical density, el and eq, r, usually <0.3 mm, sometimes with small inclusions (quartz? and mica).

Variant: 105
Dominated by a–sr quartz and feldspar grains; metamorphic rock fragments more rare, and glaucophane is only present as individual grains in the fine fraction. Microfossils and tcfs are rare. Refired to red.

Variant: 117
Coarser and darker in color than the main group. No microfossils, but calcite/micrite lumps exist (altered). Red-brown (ppl) to red (xpl) core turning yellow toward surface, very micaceous, mostly mica schists with very rare glaucophane. Refired to red.

Variant: 119
Slightly darker in color than the main group with more fine inclusions; microfossils are predominantly foraminifera and glaucophane is very rare. Otherwise inclusions appear very similar to those of the main group. Refired to red.

Variant: 141
Relatively fine, but the appearance of the fine fraction is very similar to the main group. Most amphiboles are green. Rare possible microfossils. Coarse inclusions are mostly quartz-feldspar aggregates, large grains of quartz (ribbon-textured) and feldspar, including plagioclase. Refired to red; paint refired to red-brown.

SUBGROUP D: GROG(?)
Sample: 107

This fabric is very similar to PFG 3C (especially the variant 119), but it has abundant argillaceous inclusions that may be grog. Refired to pink. Preliminary interpretation of the WD-XRF results suggests that this sample is very similar to PFG 3C in its chemistry, as well.

Microstructure
Very few voids, meso- and macro-vughs, rarer channels; those with a long axis are aligned to vessel walls, for the most part. Inclusions double- to open-spaced; those with a long axis are weakly aligned to vessel walls for the most part, except for one area with inclusions aligned perpendicular to the vessel walls (perhaps a coil join?).

Groundmass
Not homogenous, brown (ppl), yellow-brown (xpl) (40x), with narrow streaks of red, optically active.

Inclusions
$c{:}f{:}v_{0.2\,mm}$, 40:50:10. Poorly sorted, eq and el, sa–r, <2.0 mm, mode 0.3–1.2 mm, weakly bimodal size distribution.

Coarse fraction
Frequent: Argillaceous fragments, probably grog, eq and slightly el, sr–r, mode 0.3–0.6 mm. Red-brown with sharp boundaries, optically dense, slightly optically active, sometimes with one flat edge that may be darker than the rest of the fragment, perhaps suggesting these were original vessel surfaces with slightly different firing effects or added slip. Argillaceous fragments bear inclusions that are usually <0.4 mm, sa–r, including any or all of the following: quartz, feldspar, mica, epidote, and possible amphibole, as well as metamorphic rock fragments like those that appear elsewhere in the fabric. Some rock fragments (including banded schist fragments up to 1.4 mm) are surrounded by a thin layer of similar red-brown clay, suggesting they may ultimately be derived from the same source as the argillaceous grains. Metamorphic rock fragments and dissociates thereof, mostly el, sr, mode 0.4–1.2 mm. Banded quartz-mica-feldspar schist with biotite and/or white mica, sometimes with streaks or patches of red-brown material. Quartz-feldspar aggregates ± mica ± amphibole (green or brown) ± epidote/clinozoisite(?) ± patches of opaque material. Micaceous phyllite, mica aggregates, quartzite all also appear. Quartzes usually show undulose extinction and sometimes sutured, elongated grain boundaries, occasionally ribbon textured. Feldspars are generally untwinned.
Few: Epidote/clinozoisite, eq and slightly el, sa, 0.3–0.7 mm, sometimes with mica inclusions. Feldspar, usually untwinned, sometimes with small mica or epidote(?) inclusions, eq or slightly el, sa–sr, 0.3–0.6 mm.
Very few: Microfossils, mostly foraminifera, micritic, eq, r, 0.3–0.4 mm.
Very rare: Calcite, sparitic lump, slightly el, sr, 0.3 mm; chert(?), el, sr, 0.5 mm.

Fine fraction
Dominant: Quartz/feldspar (often indistinguishable from each other), eq and slightly el, sa–sr.
Frequent: Metamorphic rock fragments as above.
Few: Mica laths; epidote/clinozoisite, eq and slightly el, a–sr; calcite crystals (eq, a) and micritic lumps (eq, r).
Rare: Microfossils, including foraminifera; rarely, shell; green amphibole, el, a.
Very rare: Sponge spicules(?); titanite(?), el, sr.

Tcfs
Few, red (ppl, xpl), sharp to merging or diffuse boundaries, optically dense, eq and el, sometimes stretched, r, <0.3 mm; probably clay pellets.

SUBGROUP E: BIOTITE SCHIST
Sample: 101

Most inclusions are fragments of biotite schist. The origin of this fabric is unknown; Attica, Euboea, or the Cyclades are all plausible production regions. Refired to pink.

Microstructure
Few voids, meso- and macro-vughs and channels, some with secondary calcite infilling; those with a long-axis are roughly oriented parallel to vessel walls. Inclusions open-spaced; those with a long-axis are oriented parallel to vessel walls.

Groundmass
Relatively homogenous, greenish brown (ppl), brown (xpl) (40x), turning slightly paler at margins, optically active, patches and streaks of probably secondary calcite.

Inclusions
$c{:}f{:}v_{0.15\,mm}$, 25:45:30. Poorly sorted, mostly el, sa–r, <3.3 mm, mode 0.3–0.6 mm, weakly bimodal size distribution.

Coarse fraction
Predominant: Metamorphic rock fragments and dissociated fragments thereof, mostly el, sa–r, mode 0.3–0.6 mm. Quartz-feldspar-mica schists, more biotite than white mica, ± brown amphibole ± titanite ± opaques, very rarely with tiny epidote/clinozoisite(?) inclusions; usually banded, grains often elongated and stretched, and sometimes with relatively angular feldspar porphyroclasts in fields of much finer grained material (mylonitic?). Quartz-feldspar aggregates with patches and streaks of red material. Feldspars very rarely show microcline or albite twinning.
Rare: Brown siltstones and sandstones with angular quartz and mica being the major identifiable mineral components, slightly el, r, mode 0.3–0.4 mm; mica aggregates, eq, r, 0.2 mm.
Very rare: Shale(?), foliated red-brown clay-rich grain with small quartz inclusions, slightly el, sr, 0.4 mm.

Fine fraction
Predominant: Quartz/feldspar (often indistinguishable from each other), eq and el, a–sr.
Few: Biotite and white mica laths.
Very few: Metamorphic rock fragments as above; orange grains with anomalous birefringence, eq and el, sa–sr.
Rare: Altered calcite, mostly dark in xpl, eq, r.

Tcfs
Common, red to nearly opaque (ppl), red (xpl), sharp or diffuse boundaries, optically dense, eq, r, most <0.15 mm; probably clay pellets.
Common, yellow brown (ppl), mostly dark in xpl, sharp to rather diffuse boundaries, low optical density, el and eq, r, usually <0.15 mm, sometimes with small inclusions (mostly quartz?).

SUBGROUP F: BIOTITE SCHIST, DENSE MICRITE LUMPS
Sample: 164

This fabric is notable for common micrite lumps (microfossils?) in the fine fraction. It has no known parallels, although an Attic or Euboean provenance seems most likely given the ware and macroscopic fabric associations. Such an origin would be compatible with the metamorphic nature of inclusions, but more information is needed. Refired to pink; slip refired to red.

Microstructure
Rare voids, mostly meso- and macro-vughs and channels, sometimes surrounding larger calcite inclusions. Inclusions open-spaced, prophyric, oriented more or less parallel to vessel walls.

Groundmass
Homogenous, red-brown (ppl), red (xpl) (40x), optically slightly active.

Inclusions
c:f:$v_{0.15\,mm}$, 18:80:2. Moderately well-sorted, eq and el, sr–r, <1.5 mm, mode 0.3–0.5 mm, bimodal size distribution.

Coarse fraction
Predominant: Metamorphic rock fragments, el, sr–r, mode 0.3–0.5 mm. Quartz-mica schist, often banded, with biotite and/or white mica, rarely with green amphibole (actinolite?). Quartz-feldspar-mica aggregates, feldspars untwinned, altered, with fine mica and epidote/clinozoisite(?) inclusions.
Few: Calcite. Micrite lumps, somewhat altered, eq and slightly el, r, mode 0.3–0.5 mm, sometimes with small angular quartz inclusions.
Rare: Biotite and white mica laths and aggregates, mode 0.3 mm.
Very rare: Epidote/clinozoisite(?), eq, a, mode 0.2 mm.

Fine fraction
Dominant: Calcite. Micrite lumps, eq, r, no biogenic structure visible but possibly degraded microfossils(?).
Common: Metamorphic rock fragments as above, quartz/feldspar and polycrystalline quartz, eq and el, sr.
Rare: White mica and biotite laths; opaques, eq and el, sr–r.
Very rare: Tourmaline, eq, sr; green amphibole, eq, a; chert(?), el, a.

Tcfs
Few, red-brown to nearly opaque (ppl), red to dark brown or nearly opaque (xpl), generally sharp boundaries, optically dense, eq and el, r, <0.15 mm–1.2 mm, rarely with quartz and/or mica inclusions.

SUBGROUP G: GREENISH BROWN WITH PHYLLITE
Sample: 52

This subgroup is relatively fine and contains phyllite. The ware suggests a Cycladic provenance. Given the metamorphic geologies of many islands, however, it is impossible to narrow down the origin more specifically. Refired to pink.

Microstructure
Very few voids, mostly macro-vughs, channels, and rarely vesicles, often rimmed with calcite; generally oriented parallel to vessel walls. Inclusions open-spaced, oriented more or less parallel to vessel walls.

Groundmass
Homogenous, greenish brown (ppl, xpl) (40x), common small red round tcfs (probably clay pellets), optically slightly active, streaks of probably secondary calcite.

Inclusions
c:f:$v_{0.15\ mm}$, 20:65:15. Moderately well-sorted, eq and mostly el, sa–r, <1.1 mm, mode 0.3–0.6 mm, bimodal size distribution.

Coarse fraction:
Predominant: Metamorphic rock fragments, el, sa–r, mode 0.3–0.6 mm. Micaceous red-brown phyllite. Rock fragments composed of quartz, feldspar, and mica, both white mica and biotite, with some red-brown material, some with sericite(?), showing minimal alignment/banding.
Few: White mica and biotite laths and aggregates, mode 0.2–0.6 mm. Calcite, mostly micrite, rarely sparite, round lumps, altered, sometimes rimmed with brown, eq, r, mode 0.4 mm; a few elongate micritic inclusions might be shell, 0.3 mm. Quartz (mono- and polycrystalline), eq, sa–sr, mode 0.2–0.3 mm.
Rare: Argillaceous grains with angular metamorphic rock fragments enclosed in red-brown matrix, slightly el, r, 0.6 mm; sandstone, eq, sa, 0.3 mm.

Fine fraction
Dominant: Quartz/feldspar (often indistinguishable from each other), eq and slightly el, sa–r; metamorphic rock fragments as above.
Frequent: White mica and biotite laths.
Few: Calcite, as above; bright yellow grains (ppl) that turn speckled in xpl, mostly eq, sr.
Rare: Chert, eq, a.

Tcfs
Common, red-brown to dark red-brown (ppl), red to dark red-brown (xpl), sharp to merging boundaries, some quite diffuse, optically dense, mostly eq, r, <0.15 mm–0.3 mm, rarely with tiny quartz(?) and mica inclusions.

SUBGROUP H: GREENISH BROWN, VERY MICACEOUS
Sample: 142

Most inclusions are quartz-feldspar-mica schists and white mica. The origin of this petrographic fabric, as well as the ware and macroscopic fabric, are unknown. A provenance from the Cyclades, Attica, or Euboea is plausible. Refired to red.

Microstructure
Common voids, mostly meso-vughs and elongate planar/channel voids, oriented parallel to vessel walls; majority on one side of slide, infilled with secondary calcite. Inclusions double- to open-spaced, oriented more or less parallel to vessel walls.

Groundmass
Not homogenous; brown to dark brown (ppl, xpl) (40x); optically active; massive streaks of calcite concentrated on one half of the sample, presumably secondary.

Inclusions
c:f:$v_{0.1\ mm}$, 25:50:25. Poorly sorted, eq and el, sr–r, <1.2 mm, mode 0.1–1.0 mm, unimodal size distribution.

Coarse fraction
Dominant: Metamorphic rock fragments, eq and mostly el, sr–r, mode 0.2–1.0 mm. Quartz-feldspar-mica schist, mostly white mica, chlorite rather common, occasionally with talc/shimmer grains, opaques, and/or probable amphibole (weakly pleochroic blue-green and rarely violet in ppl; second-order birefringence or anomalous violet in xpl), perhaps glaucophane.
Common: Mica laths, mostly white mica, up to 0.6 mm.
Few: Calcite, micrite lumps, eq and slightly el, r, mode 0.1–0.3 mm, concentrated in areas of calcite streaks, perhaps also secondary. Epidote/clinozoisite, eq, sa–r, mode 0.1–0.2 mm.

Fine fraction
Dominant: Quartz/feldspar (often indistinguishable from each other), eq and el, a–sr.
Common: Mica laths.
Rare: Calcite crystals, eq, sa; opaques, eq, sa.
Very rare: Microfossil(?) (part of a foraminifera?), el, r.

Tcfs
Few; greenish brown, dark brown, and opaque (ppl); dark brown to nearly opaque (xpl); generally sharp boundaries; optically very dense; mostly eq, r, up to 0.4 mm; occasionally with small quartz/feldspar, mica, epidote/clinozoisite, or tiny birefringent inclusions.

SUBGROUP I: PHYLLITE
Sample: 14

Phyllite rock fragments are the dominant inclusions. The fabric is closely comparable with the "Amorgian Blueschist" fabric known from Keros and Amorgos (Hilditch 2007, 239; Vaughan 2006). Refired to red.

Microstructure
Common voids, mostly meso- and macro-channels and elongate planar/channel voids, some meso- and macro-vughs, oriented parallel to vessel walls; some cracking around inclusions. Inclusions single-spaced; those with a long axis oriented parallel to vessel walls.

Groundmass
Not homogenous, yellow to brown (ppl), pale brown to red-brown (xpl) (40x), optically active.

Inclusions
$c{:}f{:}v_{0.15\,mm}$, 45:30:25. Poorly sorted, el and more rarely eq, sa–r, <4.4 mm, mode 0.3–1.2 mm, unimodal size distribution.

Coarse fraction
Predominant: Metamorphic rock fragments and dissociated fragments thereof, mostly el, sa–r, mode 0.3–1.2 mm. Dark-brown phyllite, occasionally grading into schist. Quartz-mica schist, usually banded, with white mica and/or biotite ± chlorite ± feldspar ± opaque or red-brown material in patches or bands. Mica aggregates, polycrystalline quartz, and quartzite all appear. Quartz usually shows undulose extinction, occasionally with sutured, elongated grain boundaries. Feldspars are generally untwinned.
Rare: Calcite(?), altered, cloudy brown to yellow in ppl, gray-brown to nearly opaque in xpl, eq, r, 0.3 mm.
Very rare: Volcanic rock fragment, trachytic, el, r, 0.6 mm; opaque, el, sr and curving (perhaps dissociated from metamorphic rock), 1.0 mm.

Fine fraction
Dominant: Quartz/feldspar (often indistinguishable from each other), eq and el, a–sr; metamorphic rock fragments as above.
Common: Mica laths.
Few: Opaques, eq and el, sa–sr.

Tcfs
None.

AYIA IRINI: AREA B

GROUP 4: METAMORPHIC/GRANITIC

Fabrics in this group include abundant quartzofeldspathic rocks. They have parallels with the metamorphic and granite-derived fabrics from Mikre Vigla, Naxos, in the Fitch Laboratory, as well as published fabrics hypothesized to be from the central Cyclades, especially Naxos.

SUBGROUP A: ANGULAR QUARTZ AND FELDSPAR
Samples: 17, 129

Most inclusions are angular, coarse quartz and feldspar and aggregates, probably derived from granite and/or metagranite; biotite and amphibole are relatively rare. Similarities exist with Vaughan's (1989, 151–154) Metamorphic/Granitic fabric from Mikre Vigla. Refired to red.

Microstructure
Few voids, primarily meso- and macro-channels (some elongate, planar) and macro-vughs; generally oriented parallel to vessel walls. Inclusions single- to double-spaced; those with a long axis are roughly oriented parallel to vessel walls.

Groundmass
Not homogenous, honey brown to red brown (ppl), yellow to orange-brown (xpl) (40x), optically active.

Inclusions
$c:f:v_{0.2\,mm}$, 40:50:10. Moderately well-sorted, eq and el, a–sr, <1.3 mm, mode 0.3–0.9 mm, weakly bimodal size distribution.

Coarse fraction
Dominant: Quartz (mono- and polycrystalline), eq, sa–sr, mode 0.3–0.4 mm. Feldspar (sometimes showing albite twinning), eq and el, a–sr, mode 0.3–0.6 mm. Rock fragments, mostly eq, some slightly el, a–sr, mode 0.4–0.9 mm, primarily consisting of relatively coarse-grained quartz-feldspar aggregates, with small quantities of mica (mostly biotite) and red-brown material, occasionally with epidote/clinozoisite, some feldspars extremely weathered, occasionally bearing acicular medium- to high-relief minerals with high birefringence and/or chlorite, sometimes with sericitization; very rarely showing micrographic textures; epidote sometimes vivid green in ppl.
Very few: Metamorphic rock fragments consisting of weathered feldspar (including plagioclase), quartz, and biotite ± angular opaques (eq and el), ± chlorite, eq and slightly el, sr, mode 0.5–1.0 mm.
Very few–rare: Biotite, el, a–sa, mode 0.5 mm.
Rare: Sandstone (perhaps slightly metamorphosed), quartz arenite, el, sr, mode 0.3–0.5 mm.
Very rare–absent: Chert, eq, r, mode 0.3 mm; unknown rock fragment, streaked with red, opaque apart from the red bands in xpl, eq, sr, 0.4 mm; piemontite(?) (bright pink, pleochroic to yellowish in ppl), el, sa, mode 0.3 mm.

Fine fraction
Common: Quartz/feldspar (often indistinguishable from each other) and quartzofeldspathic rock fragments as above.
Few: Epidote and more rarely clinozoisite, eq, r.
Very few: Birefringent orange-red grains, eq, r; opaques, eq, a–sa.
Very few–rare: Biotite laths.
Rare–absent: Amphibole, brown and green, el, sa.
Very rare: Unknown rock fragment as above; white mica laths.

Tcfs:
Rare, red-brown to dark brown (ppl, xpl), sharp to merging boundaries, optically dense to nearly optically neutral, eq, r, 0.3–0.7 mm, sometimes bearing quartz, feldspar, or quartzofeldspathic rocks as above.
Common, yellow to white (ppl), speckled yellow and gray/black (xpl), rather diffuse boundaries, low optical density, eq, r, mostly <0.2 mm.

Variant: 138
Darker in color than the main group, orange-red to red-brown (ppl), red to red-brown (xpl) (40x), with angular inclusions. The majority of quartz and feldspar grains are smaller (sand/silt-sized); a few granitic grains exist; biotite schist, epidote/clinozoisite, and possible altered volcanic rocks are present; mica is rare in the fine fraction. Refired to red.

SUBGROUP B: CALCITE, MICROFOSSILS
Sample: 103

This fabric differs from PFG 4A in containing calcite inclusions and no coarse epidote/clinozoisite. It is broadly paralleled by Vaughan's (1989, 152) Metamorphic/Granitic Dark Burnished/Plain group at Mikre Vigla, but this fabric has more microfossils and more white mica. A Cycladic provenance seems probable on the basis of the ware. A thin layer of slip at the exterior is visible in thin section: brown in ppl, red-brown in xpl; includes rare tiny mica and quartz/feldspar grains, occasionally with attached mica, and rare tiny red clay pellets; slightly optically active. Refired to pink, turning paler at core; slip refired to red-brown.

Microstructure
Rare–very rare voids, primarily meso- and macro-vughs, rarely with calcite rims; no orientation. Inclusions double- to open-spaced; those with a long axis are roughly oriented parallel to vessel walls.

Groundmass
Not homogenous, honey brown with irregular patches and streaks of dark brown (ppl), yellow to orange to brown (xpl) (40x), optically slightly active.

Inclusions
$c:f:v_{0.2\,mm}$, 33:65:2. Moderately well-sorted, eq and el, a–sr, <2.7 mm, mode 0.3–1.0 mm, bimodal size distribution.

Coarse fraction
Dominant: Quartz (mono- and polycrystalline), feldspar (untwinned), and rock fragments primarily composed of relatively coarse-grained feldspar and quartz-feldspar aggregates, rarely bearing biotite or white mica, occasionally with micrographic textures, eq and el, a–sr, mode 0.4–1.0 mm.
Common: Calcite. A few large (ca. 0.3 mm) crystals exist, but most calcite inclusions are micrite, some sparite, lumps (el, sr, mode 0.3–0.5 mm), rarely with blackened rim; micritic grains occasionally bear quartz, mica, or larger calcite crystals.
Few: Microfossils (including algae(?) and foraminifera) and shell, el, r, mode 0.3–0.6 mm.
Very few: Biotite, white mica, el, mode 0.3–0.5 mm.

Fine fraction
Dominant: Quartz (mono- and polycrystalline), feldspar (untwinned or showing albite twinning), sometimes quartz/feldspar indistinguishable from each other, eq and slightly el, sa–sr.
Common: Calcite as above, including probable foraminifera microfossils; biotite and white mica.
Few: Quartzofeldspathic rock fragments as above.
Rare–very rare: Opaques, eq, sa–r.
Very rare: Chert, eq, sr; brown amphibole, el, sa; epidote/clinozoisite(?), slightly el, sr.

Tcfs:
Very few, red-brown to brown (ppl), red to red-brown (xpl), mostly sharp to rarely merging boundaries, optically dense, eq, r, <0.2–1.1 mm, sometimes bearing quartz/feldspar, calcite, or mica.

Variant: 98
Color different (greenish brown in ppl, brown in xpl). Inclusions are generally similar, but calcareous inclusions are more common, mostly micrite lumps and microfossils. A second type of tcf is present: few, pale brown in ppl, dark and speckled in xpl, low optical density, most <0.2 mm. Refired to pinkish yellow, turning darker and reddish toward surfaces.

SUBGROUP C: GRANITE
Sample: 114

This subgroup contains granite rock fragments. Clear comparisons exist with Hilditch's (2019, 467–469) Group D at Akrotiri, hypothesized to be primarily from Naxos; there are also similarities with Vaughan's (1989, 153) Metamorphic/Granitic Red-Brown Micaceous group at Mikre Vigla and Hilditch's (2007, 240) Felsic Granite + Schist subgroup from Keros. Refired to red.

Microstructure
Few voids, meso- and macro-vughs, micro- to rarely macro-channels; generally oriented parallel to vessel walls. Inclusions single- to double-spaced; no orientation.

Groundmass
Not homogenous, honey brown to red-brown with green-brown core (ppl), yellow to red to dark green-brown (xpl) (40x), optically slightly active.

Inclusions
c:f:v$_{0.4\,mm}$, 30:50:20. Moderately well-sorted, eq and el, a–sr, <2.1 mm, mode 0.6–1.2 mm, bimodal size distribution.

Coarse fraction
Dominant: Granitic and metagranitic rock fragments, composed of altered alkali and plagioclase feldspar, quartz, and biotite, rarely with accessory epidote(?) or titanite(?), occasionally showing micrographic intergrowth, feldspars very weathered, eq and el, sa–sr, mode 0.6–1.2 mm. Quartz-feldspar aggregates and feldspar grains also exist, presumably dissociated from similar rocks. Quartzite, el, sa, mode 0.6 mm.
Very few: Biotite, el, 0.6–1.2 mm.
Rare: Calcite. Micrite lumps, altered to brown in xpl, eq, r, mode 0.6 mm.

Fine fraction
Dominant: Quartz, feldspar, and aggregates thereof, eq and el, a–sr.
Common: Biotite laths; white mica is much rarer.
Few: Calcite, micrite lumps, as above.
Rare: Epidote/clinozoisite, eq and el, sa–r; opaques, eq, sa–r.
Very rare: Tourmaline(?), eq, sa; titanite(?), el, sa; altered volcanic(? glassy yellow with biotite and quartz inclusions, turning speckled black in xpl); amphibole, el, a.

Tcfs
Few; red to dark red-brown to brown (ppl); red, orange-red, or brown (xpl); sharp to merging boundaries; optically dense; eq and el, sr–r, <0.4 mm–0.4 mm, sometimes bearing a–sa quartz, feldspar and/or very fine mica inclusions.

Variant: 100
With much more common calcite (micritic and holocrystalline), more amphibole, very rare serpentinite(?); one possible altered volcanic grain. Refired to dark pink; paint refired to red.

Variant: 116
Darker in color, gray to brown with slightly "wispy" texture (ppl, xpl). Micrite lumps are common, and although possible microfossils exist, they are too degraded to identify with certainty. Rare siltstones/sandstones, banded mica schists, chert, and very rare possible volcanic rock fragments exist. Appears comparable with Hilditch's (2007, 241, 248) Volcanic-bearing Metamorphic Calcareous Rich subgroup. Refired to pink.

GROUP 5: VOLCANIC

Fabrics in this group contain common volcanic inclusions, which suggests that they derive from within the south Aegean volcanic arc. Most subgroups are comparable with the well-known fabrics of Melos, Thera, and Aegina.

SUBGROUP A: ACID–INTERMEDIATE VOLCANIC ROCKS, MICROFOSSILS
Samples: 85, 86

Acid–intermediate volcanic rocks including lava and glass fragments, micrite, and microfossils are common. The fabric is comparable with Hilditch's (2019, 462–436) Group A at Akrotiri and Vaughan's (1989, 154–155) Rhyodacite-Tuffaceous fabric at Mikre Vigla; both fabrics are hypothesized to be Melian/Theran. Refired to pink, turning darker in places.

Microstructure
Very few voids, mostly macro-vughs, rarely channels, one with darkening around void, perhaps a burned-out organic; roughly oriented parallel to vessel walls. Inclusions single- to double-spaced, no clear orientation.

Groundmass
Generally homogenous, yellow-brown (ppl), brown with slightly greenish tinge (xpl) (40x), crystallitic b-fabric, optically inactive.

Inclusions
c:f:v$_{0.1\,mm}$, 40:50:10. Poorly sorted, eq and el, a–r, <1.8 mm, mode 0.3–1.0 mm, unimodal size distribution.

Coarse fraction
Dominant–frequent: Calcite, primarily micrite, round lumps, mode 0.3–0.6 mm; microfossils (mostly foraminifera), eq and el, r, mode 0.2 mm, one large elongated and slightly curving micritic inclusion in 85 may be shell; rarely sparite, probably secondary filling in voids. Volcanic rock fragments, acid-intermediate, eq and slightly el, sa–r, mode 0.3–1.0 mm. Includes abundant glass, in some cases showing flow textures or perlitic cracks; other fragments with porphyritic, trachytic, and felsitic textures, phenocrysts primarily of feldspar (alkali feldspar, plagioclase), one grain showing intergrowth (symplectic texture) of feldspar and groundmass, occasionally with tiny amphibole, or pyroxene; rarely pumice, in one case with calcite filling the vesicles and matrix largely altered to cloudy red; feldspar including plagioclase, eq and el, a, mode 0.15–1.0 mm, sometimes zoned.

Common–very few: Metamorphic rock fragments; el, sr, mode 0.2–0.5 mm. Includes mica schist (mostly biotite), relatively fine-grained, some banded; polycrystalline quartz (sutured boundaries, undulose extinction), sometimes with attached mica; very rare phyllite, brown with abundant white mica.

Few–very few: Amphibole (hornblende), eq, sa, mode 0.15 mm.

Rare: Biotite and white mica laths, mode 0.15 mm; opaques, eq, a, mode 0.3 mm.

Very rare–absent: Pyroxene, eq, a, 0.3 mm; birefringent orange grains, eq, r, 0.15 mm.

Fine fraction
Dominant: Calcite, micrite, mostly probably microfossils, though the structure is not clear in many instances, eq and el, r; rare sparite.

Frequent: Quartz/feldspar, eq and el, sa–sr, rarely with attached mica; plagioclase, eq, sa.

Few–rare: Amphibole (hornblende), eq, sa–sr; biotite and white mica laths.

Very few–rare: Volcanic rock fragments as above, eq and el, sr; bright red-orange birefringent grains, eq, r.

Very rare: Pyroxene(?), eq, sr.

Tcfs
Few–very few, dark brown to nearly opaque (ppl), dark red-brown (xpl), sharp to merging boundaries, optically dense, eq and el, sr, mode 0.15 mm, rarely with tiny quartz or birefringent orange inclusions.

Variant: 110
Less glass and more volcanic rock fragments with trachytic, felsitic, or porphyritic textures. Very rare mica, including almost no white mica and very little biotite, mostly fine; a few larger laths and tabular crystals of biotite exist. Although microfossils exist, some of the micritic grains appear to be nonbiogenic. Refired to yellow.

SUBGROUP B: ABUNDANT GLASS
Sample: 90

This fabric is very similar to PFG 5A, but different in color, with more glass and more mica. Melian/Theran. Refired to pink.

Microstructure
Very rare voids, mostly macro-vughs, rarely channels, mostly where rock fragments have been partially plucked from the fabric during thin-sectioning; no preferred orientation. Inclusions double- to open-spaced; those with a long axis are weakly oriented parallel to vessel walls.

Groundmass
Not homogenous, yellow at edges to brown at core (ppl), yellow to yellow-brown (xpl) (40x), crystallitic b-fabric, optically slightly active.

Inclusions
c:f:v$_{0.2\,mm}$, 45:50:5. Poorly sorted, eq and el, sa–r, <1.4 mm, mode 0.3–0.6 mm, unimodal size distribution.

Coarse fraction
Dominant: Volcanic rock fragments, acid-intermediate, eq and el, sa–r, mode 0.3–0.6 mm. Glass, often with perlitic cracks and/or flow textures; tuff; fragments with felsitic, trachytic, or porphyritic textures are more rare; phenocrysts are typically plagioclase and/or pyroxene, or are so altered (generally clouded with red-brown material) that they are unidentifiable. Glass is sometimes pinkish gray in ppl.

Common: Microfossils (mostly foraminifera), el, r, mode 0.3 mm, occasionally with dark rims; one large shell fragment, el, sr, 0.9 mm long. Feldspar, including plagioclase, eq and el, sa–sr mode 0.3 mm; some feldspar aggregates.

Few: Metamorphic rock fragments, el and rarely eq, sa–sr, mode 0.3–0.5 mm. Fine-grained mica schist (mostly biotite), in some cases with highly strained and elongated quartz grains, rarely with titanite(?) inclusions; rarely brown phyllite, rich in white mica; very rarely calc- or biotite-calc-schist; polycrystalline quartz (sutured boundaries, undulose extinction).

Very few: Calcite lumps, mostly micritic, rarely sparitic, eq and slightly el, r, 0.2–0.4 mm, sometimes with quartz or feldspar inclusions.

Very rare: Chalcedony, possibly infilling voids, el and rather amorphous, r, mode 0.4 mm; serpentinite(?), bright orange, eq, sr, 0.3 mm; opaque grain, el, sa, 0.3 mm.

Fine fraction

Frequent: Quartz/feldspar (often indistinguishable from one another), eq, a.

Common: Biotite and white mica laths and rarely tabular crystals; glass, eq and el, r; plagioclase, eq, a; calcite, micrite and rarely sparite, including some microfossils but mostly lumps, eq, r.

Very few: Metamorphic rock fragments, as above, and polycrystalline quartz with sutured boundaries and undulose extinction, eq and slightly el, sr; birefringent yellow-orange and orange-red grains, eq, r.

Rare: Amphibole (hornblende), eq, sa; opaques, eq and el, sa–r.

Very rare: Pyroxene(?), el and eq, a–sa.

Tcfs

Common, pale orange-brown (ppl), speckled yellow (xpl), sharp to merging boundaries, low optical density, eq and el, r, mode 0.3–0.4 mm.

Rare, with very dark red (nearly opaque) core and pale orange (ppl) to orange (xpl) halo, optically neutral (halo) to dense (core), eq, r, 0.3–0.6 mm, occasionally with plagioclase inclusions; perhaps altered rock fragments, but the grain edges in the halo are diffuse.

Rare, dark brown (ppl), reddish brown (xpl), sharp boundaries, optically dense, eq, r, <0.15 mm.

Variant: 126

Inclusions are similar to above but have weakly bimodal size distribution, voids are more common (mostly meso- and macro-vughs), and mica is less frequent. Refired to pink, with a large yellow patch at the core.

SUBGROUP C: FINE VOLCANIC
Sample: 89

This subgroup is probably related to PFG 5B, but it is quite fine. Melian/Theran. Refired to red.

Microstructure

Rare voids, macro-vughs, some with calcite rims or filled with sparite; roughly oriented parallel to vessel walls. Inclusions open-spaced; those with a long axis are roughly oriented parallel to vessel walls.

Groundmass

Mostly homogenous, though slightly more gray toward core, brown (ppl), honey-brown (xpl) (40x), optically slightly active.

Inclusions

$c:f:v_{0.1\,mm}$, 6:90:4. Well-sorted, eq and el, a–r, <0.4 mm, mode 0.1–0.3 mm, unimodal size distribution.

Coarse fraction

Common: Plagioclase, eq, a, mode 0.2–0.3mm, quite fresh looking in most cases, occasionally with attached biotite; alkali feldspar, eq, a, mode 0.2–0.3 mm; quartz, eq, a, mode 0.2–0.3 mm; some grains exhibit strained extinction.

Very few: Yellow grains with anomalous birefringence, slightly el, r, 0.1–0.2 mm.

Rare: White mica laths, 0.2 mm; microfossils, foraminifera, micritized, el, r, mode 0.3 mm.

Fine fraction

Common: White mica and more rarely biotite laths; quartz/feldspar, eq, sa; clear feldspar with twinning is more rare, eq, sa.

Few: Opaques, eq, sa–r.

Very few: Discrete calcite (micrite) grains, eq, r, some are probably microfossils, but they are small and without internal structure; birefringent orange and orange-red grains, eq, sr–r; polycrystalline quartz, occasionally with attached mica, el, sr; brown and rarely green amphibole, el, sa.

Very rare: Clinozoisite(?), eq, sa.

Tcfs
Few, brown (ppl), red-brown (xpl), sharp to merging boundaries, optically dense, eq and el, sr, <0.1–0.3 mm, sometimes bearing quartz/feldspar, mica, and/or birefringent orange inclusions.
Few, pale brown (ppl) to speckled brown/orange or opaque (xpl), sharp to slightly merging boundaries, optically neutral, eq, r, <0.1–0.3 mm.

Variant: 91
No volcanics preserved, but the calcareous inclusions are very similar to the main group and comparable also to published descriptions and slides available at the Fitch Laboratory associated with fine Melian/Theran wares. Refired to pale pink.

SUBGROUP D: NON-BIOGENIC CALCITE
Samples: 92, 93, 97

This fabric is dominated by acid–intermediate volcanic rocks, which are most distinctive of Melos and Thera. With common non-biogenic calcite, however, this fabric does not seem to be a very close match to Group A fabrics in Hilditch's (2019, 462–463) analysis at Akrotiri, which are presumed to be local there. Perhaps Melian? Sample 92 refired to yellow; 93 and 97 refired to red. Paint on 92 refired to red; on 97, it refired to dark red-brown. Preliminary interpretation of the WD-XRF results suggests that 92 has a much higher calcium value, perhaps indicative of a less mixed clay, which could also be hypothesized on the basis of the difference in firing colors between 92 and the other samples.

Microstructure
Few–rare voids, mostly macro-vughs, rarer macro-channels, meso-vesicles; roughly oriented parallel to vessel walls. In 97, calcite rims and some infilling; central void in 93 is at center of handle section and surrounded by slightly darkened clay. Inclusions single-spaced, those with a long axis are weakly oriented parallel to vessel walls.

Groundmass
Not homogenous, pale brown to brown (92, 93) or slightly reddish brown (97) (ppl), yellow to yellow brown (92, 93) or red brown (97) (xpl) (40x), crystallitic b-fabric, optically slightly active.

Inclusions
c:f:$v_{0.2\ mm}$, 35:55:10 (92, 93), 50:40:10 (97). Well-sorted (92, 93) to moderately well-sorted (97), eq and el, sa-r, <1.5 mm, mode 0.3–0.7 mm, sometimes with calcite rims around inclusions; bimodal size distribution.

Coarse fraction
Dominant–frequent: Volcanic rock fragments, acid-intermediate, eq and el, sr-r, mode 0.3–0.7 mm. Fragments with trachytic, felsitic, and very rarely porphyritic textures, predominantly plagioclase phenocrysts, groundmass sometimes orange to red-brown. Volcanic glass, rarely with flow textures. Calcite, micrite lumps, eq and slightly el, r, mode 0.3–0.6 mm, occasionally with quartz/feldspar, glass(?), polycrystalline quartz, or birefringent orange inclusions; some of the smaller lumps may be microfossils, but the structure is not clear; a few possible shell fragments exist in 92.
Frequent–common: Metamorphic rock fragments, el, sa-sr, mode 0.3–0.7 mm. Mica schist with both biotite and white mica, occasionally with chlorite, brown material (clay?), and/or opaques; phyllite, usually brown, rarely with accessory tourmaline(?); polycrystalline quartz (sutured boundaries, undulose extinction), occasionally with calcite, titanite(?), opaques, and/or very weathered epidote(?); rarely schist with white mica or biotite and porphyroblastic feldspar. Schists in 92 and 93 are fine-grained, but coarser-grained examples are frequent in 97.
Common–few: Plagioclase, eq, sa-sr, mode 0.3–0.4 mm.
Very few: Pyroxene, eq, sr, mode 0.3 mm.
Rare: White mica aggregates, el, sr, mode 0.3 mm; epidote(?), eq and el, sa-sr, mode 0.3 mm.

Fine fraction
Frequent: Feldspar and monocrystalline quartz/feldspar, eq, sa-sr; calcite, micrite lumps, as above, rarely sparitic, eq, r.
Few–very few: White mica and biotite laths; opaques, eq and el, a-sr.
Few–rare: Birefringent orange-red grains, eq, sa.
Rare–absent: Metamorphic rock fragments, as above.
Very rare: Pyroxene, eq, sa; epidote/clinozoisite, eq, sa; amphibole (hornblende), el, sa.
Very rare–absent: Tourmaline(?), eq, sr (97); olivine(?), eq, r.

Tcfs

Frequent–few, pale yellow-brown (ppl), opaque or indistinguishable from groundmass (xpl), sharp to merging boundaries, optically neutral, eq and el, r, mode 0.1 mm.

Few–rare, red-brown (ppl), red (xpl), slightly diffuse boundaries, optically dense, sometimes with quartz/feldspar and/or birefringent orange inclusions, eq and el, r, mode 0.15–0.4 mm.

Variant: 124

Groundmass varies in color from yellow to brown (ppl) and yellow to dark greenish brown (xpl). Dominated by glassy rock fragments and metamorphics of a variety similar especially to those in sample 97, some possible serpentinite; extensive secondary calcite. While most calcite does not appear to be biogenic, one microfossil (foraminifera) is visible. White mica is relatively rare, but biotite is not uncommon in both the fine and coarse fractions. Appears closely comparable with Hilditch's (2004, 84) Group 10 Volcanic Metamorphic, tentatively suggested to be from Melos. Refired to red.

SUBGROUP E: RED-BROWN, VOLCANIC GLASS
Sample: 96

The red-brown groundmass color (ppl) is distinctive and unlike the previous subgroups. Volcanic rocks are mostly glass. Lava grains with porphyritic textures more regularly include pyroxene(?) phenocrysts, unlike previous groups. Micrite is rare and appears to be mainly lumps, although possible fine biogenics exist and the shape of at least one of the larger lumps is similar in outline to foraminifera. Metamorphic fragments are very rare. Mica appears to be almost entirely biotite, and a few very large biotite crystals appear. The sample is atypical for fabrics usually ascribed to Melos/Thera, but it also does not appear to be compatible with an Aeginetan provenance, owing to the abundance of glass as well as the presence of metamorphic inclusions. There are some similarities, especially in color variation and volcanic inclusions, with Hilditch et al.'s (2012, 81–84) Group V at Iasos (hypothesized to be Koan), although the parallel is not precise. Refired to variable pink.

Microstructure

Few voids, mostly macro-vughs, no preferred orientation, some calcite rims and infilling. Inclusions single- to double-spaced, no preferred orientation.

Groundmass

Not homogenous, red brown to brown (ppl), red-brown to dark yellow brown (xpl), slightly optically active.

Inclusions

c:f:$v_{0.2\,mm}$, 30:50:20. Moderately well-sorted, eq and el, a–r, <2.8 mm, modes 0.3–0.6 mm, 1.0–1.4 mm, bimodal size distribution.

Coarse fraction

Frequent: Feldspar, including common plagioclase, sometimes zoned, eq and el, a–sr, modes 0.3–0.6 mm, 1.0–1.3 mm, sometimes showing sericitization. Volcanic rock fragments, acid-intermediate, eq and el, a–r, mode 0.3–0.6 mm, 1.0–1.4 mm; mostly glass (some with perlitic cracks or flow textures) and lava with trachytic and porphyritic textures, including phenocrysts of plagioclase (sometimes zoned) and rarely hornblende or pyroxene(?); occasionally the groundmass has turned cloudy red. Calcite, micrite in round lumps and irregular patches, eq, r, mode 0.3–0.6 mm; an elongated fragment may be shell.

Very few: Metamorphic rock fragments, including biotite schist, el, sr, mode 0.3 mm.

Rare: Biotite laths, 0.3–0.6 mm.

Very rare: Serpentinite(?), red-orange with anomalous birefringence, el, r, 0.5 mm.

Fine fraction

Dominant: Quartz/feldspar, eq and el, sa, sometimes with calcite around the edges; glass, eq, r.

Few: Calcite, micrite, eq, r, some with dark rims, some may be microfossils but structure not clear and mostly opaque in xpl.

Very few: Metamorphic rock fragments, as above; biotite and more rarely white mica laths; polycrystalline quartz, el, r.

Very rare: Birefringent orange-red grains, eq, r; chert(?), eq, sa.

Tcfs

Few, red-brown (ppl), red (xpl), sharp to merging boundaries, eq and el, sa–r, <0.2–1.0 mm, sometimes with quartz/feldspar and/or tiny birefringent orange inclusions.

Rare, red brown or pale brown (ppl) to yellow brown or brown (xpl), in one case with swirls of red (ppl, xpl), sharp to merging or diffuse boundaries, optically neutral, el and irregular, r, 2.4–2.7 mm, with inclusions paralleled in the fine groundmass of the rest of the sample.

SUBGROUP F: INTERMEDIATE VOLCANIC, NON-CALCAREOUS
Sample: 95

This fabric, with predominantly intermediate volcanic rocks, is comparable with Kiriatzi, Geogakopoulou, and Pentedeka's (2011, 93–99) FG 1 at Kolonna. Aeginetan. Refired to red.

Microstructure
Rare voids, mostly macro-vughs, no alignment. Some cracks are probably the result of thin-sectioning. Inclusions single- to double-spaced, no preferred orientation.

Groundmass
Homogenous, brown (ppl), red-brown (xpl) (40x), optically active.

Inclusions
c:f:$v_{0.1\,mm}$, 33:65:2. Poorly sorted, eq and el, sr, <1.4 mm, mode 0.4–1.2 mm, roughly bimodal size distribution.

Coarse fraction
Predominant: Intermediate volcanic rock fragments, eq and el, sr, mode 0.4–1.2 mm. Primarily porphyritic lava grains composed of plagioclase (sometimes zoned) ± amphibole (hornblende, mostly green) ± opaques ± pyroxene ± sanidine ± biotite, some with brown or red-brown alteration; disaggregated fragments of similar rocks (plagioclase, amphibole, pyroxene, biotite grains).

Fine fraction
Frequent: Plagioclase, eq and el, a; quartz/feldspar (often indistinguishable from each other), eq, sa; volcanic rock fragments as above.
Few: Amphibole (hornblende, mostly green); opaques, eq, a–sr.
Very few: Mica laths (mostly biotite, very rarely white mica); pyroxene, eq, a.
Very rare: Birefringent orange grains, eq, sr.

Tcfs
Rare, brown (ppl), red-brown (xpl), sharp to merging boundaries, optically dense, eq, r, <0.1–0.5 mm, sometimes bearing small pyroxene, feldspar, tiny birefringent orange, and/or opaque inclusions.

SUBGROUP G: INTERMEDIATE VOLCANIC, CALCAREOUS
Samples: 121, 123, 125

This fabric contains mostly intermediate volcanic rocks and calcite. It is comparable with Kiriatzi, Geogakopoulou, and Pentedeka's (2011, 99–104) FG 2 at Kolonna. Aeginetan. Variable refiring colors. Sample 121 was pink with a well-defined yellow layer at the exterior; 123 refired to pale pink turning dark red at the surfaces; 125 refired to yellow.

Microstructure
Few voids, mostly macro-vughs and channels, roughly aligned parallel to vessel walls, some calcite rims and infilling. Large cracks in 121, perhaps from thin-sectioning; in 121, at least one large, slightly curving channel with well-defined edges appears to be result of burned-out organic. Inclusions double- to open-spaced; no preferred orientation in 121, very rough alignment parallel to vessel walls in 123, 125.

Groundmass
Not homogenous, pale orange-brown to brown (ppl), honey brown to brown (xpl) (40x), optically active to slightly active.

Inclusions
c:f:$v_{0.2\,mm}$, 20:65:15. Poorly sorted, eq and el, sa–r, <3 mm, mode 0.3–0.6 mm, bimodal size distribution.

Coarse fraction
Frequent–common: Calcite, mostly micrite lumps, rarely sparite or holocrystalline grains, eq and el, r, mode 0.3–0.6 mm; microfossils (foraminifera, rarely echinoderms, sponge spicules, and possible diatoms), eq and el, sr–r, mode 0.3–0.5 mm.
Frequent–few: Volcanic rock fragments, eq and el, sa–r, mode 0.3–0.6 mm. Plagioclase, often zoned; intermediate rock fragments with porphyritic texture and phenocrysts of plagioclase ± sanidine(? with simple twinning) ± amphibole (hornblende, mostly brown) ± clinopyroxene ± biotite (amphibole and biotite sometimes quite altered, with nearly opaque rims or turning almost entirely dark brown) ± opaques; rarely glassy fragments.

Very few–absent: Altered volcanic rock fragments(?), cloudy dark brown with feldspar, amphibole, and/or birefringent orange phenocrysts, slightly el, sr, mode 0.3–0.6 mm.

Rare–absent: Amphibole (green and brown hornblende), el, sa, mode 0.3 mm.

Very rare–absent: Quartz, eq, a, mode 0.3 mm; polycrystalline quartz with sutured boundaries and undulose extinction, with patch of birefringent red-orange material, slightly el, sr, 0.4 mm.

Fine fraction

Frequent: Quartz/feldspar (often indistinguishable from each other), altered untwinned feldspar and plagioclase, eq, sa–sr, in some cases with attached birefringent yellow-orange material (ppl, xpl) at edges; calcite, mostly micrite, lumps, eq, r; microfossils as above

Common: Birefringent yellow, orange, and red grains, eq, sr.

Few–very few: Biotite and white mica laths; opaques, eq, sa; amphibole (hornblende), el, a.

Rare–absent: Pyroxene(?), eq and el, sa–sr; volcanic rock fragments as above.

Very rare–absent: Tourmaline(?), eq, sa, pale blue-gray in ppl, nearly opaque in xpl.

Tcfs

Few; red, red-brown, or orange (ppl); red to nearly black or orange (xpl); sharp to merging boundaries; high–moderate optical density; eq and el, sr–r, <0.2–1.0 mm; sometimes with quartz/feldspar and/or birefringent yellow or orange inclusions.

Few to absent (only in 123), dark brown (ppl), honey brown to dark brown (xpl), sharp to merging boundaries, occasionally darker in color near edges, optically neutral, el, sr, 0.3–2.3 mm, with fine inclusions similar to those in the groundmass.

Variant: 109

Perhaps a higher-fired variant? Although inclusions are very similar to the main group, the groundmass is brown (ppl) to dark greenish brown (xpl) with no optical activity. Possible microfossils; large micrite grains (eq and el, r). Refired to pink, paler at core.

SUBGROUP H: CHALCEDONY
Sample: 111

This sample is unusual in the presence of chalcedony, partially filling pores but also as probable rock fragments. In addition, there are probable volcanics, non-micaceous quartz, feldspar, and coarse-grained quartz-feldspar aggregates showing strained grains and alteration of feldspars, in addition to rare mica schist and chert. The groundmass is very micaceous, although the inclusions are not. The prevalence of possible microfossils in combination with metamorphics and volcanics may suggest a Melian/Theran provenance. Chalcedony is reported from Melos (Stamatakis et al. 1996, 2010) and rarely appears in the main (presumed local) petrographic group of Phase A Akrotiri as well (Day, Müller, and Kilikoglou 2019, 329). Very rare chalcedony grains also exist in sample 90 (PFG 5B). Chemically, however, preliminary interpretation of the WD-XRF results suggests that this sample varies from the other proposed Melian/Theran fabrics (PFG 5A–D) across many elements. Refired to red.

Microstructure

Common voids, primarily meso- and macro-vughs, rarer macro-channels, several with chalcedony infilling; those with a long axis are roughly oriented parallel to vessel walls. Inclusions double- to open-spaced; those with a long axis are roughly oriented parallel to vessel walls.

Groundmass

Not homogenous, brown to red-brown at core (ppl), brown to red at core (xpl) (40x), optically slightly active.

Inclusions

c:f:$v_{0.15\,mm}$, 30:45:25. Moderately well-sorted, eq and el, sa–sr, <1.2 mm, mode 0.3–1.0 mm, bimodal size distribution.

Coarse fraction

Common: Quartz (mono- and polycrystalline), feldspar (occasionally showing albite or simple twinning), and aggregates thereof, with feldspars often altered, eq and slightly el, sa–sr, mode 0.3–1.0 mm.

Few: Calcite(?), extremely altered, often turning nearly completely brown in ppl and cloudy brown or opaque in xpl, sometimes with void at center, rarely angular and crystal-shaped, usually eq, r, mode 0.3–0.7 mm; biotite laths and tabular crystals, mode 0.2 mm (sometimes turning nearly opaque).

Very few: Chalcedony, eq and el, r, mode 0.2–1.0 mm, occasionally with red patches (ppl, xpl); altered volcanic(? dark gray to glassy yellow brown, sometimes with red streaks in ppl, opaque in xpl, with small quartz/feldspar and/or biotite phenocrysts).

Rare: Metamorphic rock fragments with chlorite, biotite, titanite, and needle-like, high-relief crystals (brown with slight pleochroism [ppl], first to low second-order birefringence [xpl]), slightly el, sr, 0.3–0.7 mm. Brown amphibole (hornblende), el, sa,

0.3 mm. Unknown mineral grains, yellow to orange or rarely red in ppl, sometimes with dark rim, pale gray, orange, or brown in xpl, no pleochroism, el, sa–r, mode 0.2 mm.

Very rare: Epidote(?), twinned, el, sr, 0.2 mm; chert(?), eq, r, 0.2 mm.

Fine fraction

Predominant: Calcite(?), very altered, might be better considered as a tcf, but the grain boundaries are quite distinct, generally round or slightly elongate, many have shapes that suggests they might be biogenic but no internal structure is preserved.

Common: Mica laths (biotite and less white mica); quartz/feldspar (often indistinguishable from each other) and aggregates as above, eq, sa.

Few: Unknown mineral grains as above.

Rare: Opaques, eq and el, sa–sr.

Very rare: Chalcedony as above; volcanic(?) rock fragments as above; epidote(?).

Tcfs

Few, very dark brown to opaque (ppl), brown to nearly opaque (xpl), sharp boundaries, optically very dense, eq and el, sa–r, <0.15 mm–0.3 mm.

Variant: 120

The color is similar, but this is less orange tinged in ppl; one chalcedony grain exists. This sample is much finer with a slightly siltier groundmass than 111 and more tcfs. Other inclusion types appear similar to those above. Refired to pink; paint refired to red.

GROUP 6: HIGH-FIRED, SAND-TEMPERED, MIXED INCLUSIONS

This group consists of sand-tempered fabrics with inclusions that seem to derive from geologically mixed deposits of the kind known on Crete; most (and perhaps all) of these probably derive from there. Preliminary interpretation of the WD-XRF results of samples 66 (PFG 6A) and 67 (PFG 6C) also suggests that they may be compatible with a Cretan provenance.

SUBGROUP A: OPHIOLITIC, METAMORPHIC, SEDIMENTARY

Sample: 66

This fabric is distinguished by a clean groundmass with rare fine inclusions and a mix of inclusion types including metamorphic, sedimentary, and igneous rocks. The fabric is comparable with descriptions of petrofabrics associated with central Crete (Day 2011, 52–56, 58–60. [Groups 8, 9, 11]; Nodarou 2015, 347–350 [Group 1]; Poursat and Knappett 2005, 21–24 [Group D]); the presence of fine-grained volcanic rock fragments may suggest a provenance in the Mesara more specifically (Day 2011, 60). Refired to yellow; paint refired to red-brown.

Microstructure

Common voids, meso- and macro-vughs, meso- and macro-channels, roughly oriented parallel to vessel walls. Inclusions single- to double-spaced, weakly oriented parallel to vessel walls.

Groundmass

Mostly homogenous; greenish gray (ppl); greenish brown (xpl) (40x); small patches and a couple of streaks of red, perhaps remnants of clay mixing; optically inactive; crystallitic b-fabric appears in amorphous patches (secondary calcite?).

Inclusions

c:f:$v_{0.03\ mm}$, 30:50:20. Poorly sorted, eq to el, sa–r, <2.1 mm, mode 0.3–1.2 mm, bimodal size distribution.

Coarse fraction

Common: Metamorphic rock fragments, eq and el, sa–r, mode 0.6–1.2 mm. Quartz-biotite schist; phyllite; polycrystalline quartz; amphibolite(?) and/or amphibole schist (fragments usually show some schistosity); elongated fragments with red-brown streaks. Untwinned feldspar and plagioclase, sometimes aggregates, eq, sa–sr, mode 0.3 mm, often weathered, occasionally with streaks of red material.

Few: Brown siltstones, eq, sr–r, mode 0.4 mm; igneous rock fragments composed of quartz, feldspar, and biotite, eq, mode 0.5–1.0 mm, some possibly metamorphosed; birefringent orange, sometimes fibrous (serpentinite?) grains (ppl, xpl), eq, sa–sr, 0.2–0.5 mm; altered calcite (one unaltered micrite grain, rimmed by cloudy red-brown material), r, mode 0.4 mm.

Very few: Sandstone (quartz arenite and subarkose), eq and el, sr–r, mode 1.0–1.1 mm; brown amphibole, eq, sa–sr, mode 0.1–0.2 mm.

Very rare: Chert, eq, sa, mode 1.3 mm. Altered volcanic(?) rock fragment with glassy groundmass turning muddy brown in xpl, with large birefringent orange-brown inclusions, perhaps altered phenocrysts(?), slightly el, r, 1.3 mm long; altered volcanic rock fragment, yellow-brown in ppl with variolitic texture in places, slightly el, r, 0.2 mm.

Fine Fraction
Dominant: Quartz/feldspar, eq, sa–sr; biotite laths.
Few: Calcite, el, sa.
Rare: Plagioclase, el, sr; polycrystalline quartz, el, sr.

Tcfs
Few, brown to red-brown (ppl), red-brown to red (xpl), sharp to merging boundaries, high optical density, eq to el, sr–r, 0.1–0.6 mm.

SUBGROUP B: ABUNDANT SEDIMENTARY
Sample: 77

This subgroup is distinguished by a clean groundmass and common sedimentary rocks, with rarer metamorphic and volcanic rocks. It is similar to PFG 6A, with more common sedimentary and less common metamorphic rocks. It is comparable with Day's (2011, 54–56, 58–60) Groups 9 and 11. Central Crete (Mesara?). Refired to pink, turning darker at core.

Microstructure
Common voids, meso- and macro-channels, meso- and macro-vughs, roughly oriented parallel to vessel walls, channels occasionally surrounding inclusions. Inclusions single- to double-spaced, weakly oriented parallel to vessel walls.

Groundmass
Mostly homogenous, honey brown to reddish brown at core (ppl), greenish brown to red at core (xpl) (40x), crystallitic b-fabric, optically slightly active.

Inclusions
$c:f:v_{0.03\ mm}$, 60:25:15. Poorly sorted, eq to el, sr–r, <3.5 mm, mode 0.2–1.8 mm, bimodal size distribution.

Coarse fraction
Frequent: Sedimentary rock fragments, mostly el, r, mode 0.6–1.8 mm. Brown and gray siltstones, some probably metamorphosed with weakly aligned mica, some encircled by thin red-brown rims. Sandstone (quartz arenite, litharenite, and arkose), sometimes quite poorly sorted, sometimes with angular inclusions in a red-brown matrix, occasionally with chloritic patches. Greywacke and chert also appear.

Few: Metamorphic rock fragments, mostly el, sr–r, mode 0.6–2.1 mm. Biotite schist, often with alteration, in one case opaque across much of grain; phyllite. Feldspar, individual grains and aggregates, eq, sa–sr, mode 0.2–0.6 mm, rarely twinned, sometimes with biotite attached, rarely attached to quartz. Quartz (mono- and polycrystalline), eq and el, sa–sr, mode 0.1–0.6 mm.

Very few: Altered calcite, mostly probably micritized but opaque or dark muddy brown in xpl, eq, rarely el, r, mode 0.1 mm, rarely larger, 0.3–0.4 mm; unclear if any might be biogenic.

Very few: Altered volcanic rock fragments, eq, sr–r, mode 0.3–0.6 mm, trachytic or variolitic textures, usually with cloudy red groundmass, in one case bright yellow-orange groundmass turning muddy yellow in xpl.

Fine Fraction
Dominant: Quartz/feldspar (often indistinguishable from each other), eq, sa–sr, some with mica and/or clay minerals adhering.
Few: Polycrystalline quartz, eq to el, sr; calcite, el, r, mostly altered and opaque in xpl; biotite laths; birefringent orange grains, eq, sa.

Tcfs
Very few, dark red brown to almost opaque (ppl), red to dark red-brown (xpl), sharp to merging boundaries, high to low optical density, eq to el, sr–r, 0.1–0.8 mm.

Variant: 73
Very similar to 77, but clear igneous inclusions do not exist and calcite inclusions are more common (although still altered). The shape of some grains suggests they may be altered microfossils. Slightly optically active. Refired to variable pink (perhaps clay mixing?); paint refired to dull red-brown.

SUBGROUP C: SILTY GROUNDMASS, PHYLLITE, SCHIST
Samples: 67, 81

The combination of metamorphic inclusions (schist to phyllite) and altered igneous inclusions would be consistent with origins in several parts of Crete, although no precise parallels have been located, and other sources are possible. Preliminary interpretation of the WD-XRF results of 67 suggests that it may be compatible with a Cretan provenance. Both samples refired to pink turning darker at core; paint on 67 turned red-brown.

Microstructure
Few–very few voids, meso- to macro-vughs, meso- and macro-channels, weakly oriented parallel to vessel walls (81) or no orientation (67). Inclusions single- to double-spaced; those with a long axis oriented generally parallel to vessel walls.

Groundmass
Not homogenous, varying across section from brown to red-brown to green-brown (ppl), red-brown to red to green-brown (xpl) (40x), optically slightly active.

Inclusions
$c:f:v_{0.08\,mm}$, 20:70:10. Poorly sorted, eq and el, sa–r, <2 mm, mode 0.2–0.7 mm, bimodal size distribution.

Coarse fraction
Dominant: Metamorphic rock fragments, el and more rarely eq, sa–r, mode 0.3–0.7 mm. Micaceous brown phyllite, sometimes showing crenulation textures. Quartz-mica schist, sometimes banded, biotite predominates ± chlorite ± feldspar ± brown amphibole ± angular opaques, sometimes with streaks of red-brown material, possible altered epidote(?) appears in one grain. Quartz-feldspar-amphibole aggregates ± biotite ± titanite(?), sometimes showing slight alignment of crystals, especially elongate amphibole and biotite; amphibolite (especially in 81); polycrystalline quartz. Quartz sometimes shows elongated boundaries and undulose extinction.

Few–very few: Calcite, nearly all micrite; in some cases altered with reaction rims or turning fully opaque or dark brown in xpl, eq and el, r, mode 0.2–0.5 mm. Feldspar, untwinned and usually altered, sometimes with mica or high relief acicular inclusions, eq, sa–sr, mode 0.2–0.6 mm.

Few–very rare: Chert, including radiolarian in 67, eq, sa–sr, mode 0.3 mm; monocrystalline quartz, eq or slightly el, sa–sr, mode 0.2 mm.

Few–absent: Igneous (intermediate, [grano]diorite) rock fragments, composed of plagioclase, alkali feldspar, quartz, hornblende and/or biotite, feldspars very altered, eq and el, sa–sr, mode 0.3–0.6 mm; biotite.

Very few–very rare: Brown to red mudstones/tcfs and siltstones with sa–sr quartz/feldspar, birefringent orange, and mica inclusions, generally sharp boundaries (and occasionally cracking around edges or in an irregular, polygonal fashion at interior), el, sr–r, mode 0.5 mm.

Rare–very rare: Yellow to orange to brown grains, birefringent in xpl, eq and el, r, mode 0.15–0.3 mm.

Rare–absent: Sandstone (quartz arenite), eq or slightly el, sa–sr, mode 0.3 mm.

Very rare: Altered volcanic(?), red with very altered possible elongate feldspar crystals, and mica, eq, r, 0.4 mm.

Fine Fraction
Dominant: Quartz/feldspar, eq and el, sa–sr.
Dominant–few: Quartz-feldspar-mica aggregates, eq and el, sa; mica laths, mostly biotite; birefringent red-orange grains, eq, r.
Common–very few: Calcite (micrite or altered), eq, r.
Very rare: Pyroxene(?), eq, sa.

Tcfs
Apart from those mentioned above, few–very few, red-brown to nearly opaque (ppl), red to dark red-brown (xpl), sharp to merging boundaries, optically dense to neutral, eq and el, sr–r, <0.1–0.5 mm, rarely with sa quartz/feldspar or mica inclusions, in one case streaking; probably clay pellets.

GROUP 7: HIGH-FIRED, TEMPERED, PREDOMINANTLY SEDIMENTARY

The fabrics in this group are sand-tempered and dominated by sedimentary-derived rocks, mostly mudstones and siltstones. Some bear very close similarities with known central Cretan fabrics. Others are difficult to assign a Cretan provenance on the basis of petrography alone, especially since Minoanizing Lustrous Decorated ware producers in Kythera and mainland Greece used similar sand-tempering techniques and appeared to have preferred similar sedimentary-derived inclusions (Kiriatzi 2010;

Kiriatzi, Georgakopoulou, and Pentedeka 2011, 141). Samples from PFG 7A (56), 7C (82), 7D (68), 7E (65), 7G (62, 70, 72), and 7H (75) were analyzed using WD-XRF. Preliminary interpretation of the WD-XRF results suggests that the samples from PFG 7A, 7C, 7D, and 7E may be compatible with a Cretan source. Samples from PFG 7G and 7H differ somewhat, chemically, which is perhaps indicative of a different and potentially non-Cretan provenance. One sample (72) of PFG 7G was a petrographic and chemical variant (below).

SUBGROUP A: FINE, MUDSTONES AND SILTSTONES
Sample: 56

This fabric, with a very fine groundmass and dominant mudstones and siltstones, is comparable with fabrics associated with central Crete in various publications, although a precise parallel has not been located. Compare with, e.g., Hilditch's (2019, 463–464) Group B subgroup A at Akrotiri, although PFG 7A is missing the volcanic rock fragments. Nodarou's (2015, 356–359) Group 1 is also similar, especially subgroup B; the whole group is hypothesized to be local to Kalochorafitis. Broad similarities exist with fabrics suggested to be from central Crete by Day (2011, especially 61–63, Fabric 13), although metamorphic rock fragments and amphibole are very rare, and phyllite is absent. Compare also with Kiriatzi, Georgakopoulou, and Pentedeka's (2011, 106–108) FG 4, especially 4B (hypothesized to be from Crete), although PFG 7A has more variety in inclusions. Preliminary interpretation of the WD-XRF results suggests that this may be compatible with a Cretan source. Refired to pink.

Microstructure
Few voids, meso- and macro-vughs and channels, some cracking around inclusions, some mud and possible calcite infilling, oriented more-or-less parallel to vessel walls. Inclusions single-spaced, oriented mostly parallel to vessel walls.

Groundmass
Homogenous; greenish brown (ppl, xpl) (40x); patches and streaks of red, probably mixed clay; very low optical activity.

Inclusions
c:f:$v_{0.01\ mm}$, 45:20:35. Poorly sorted, el and more rarely eq, sr–r, <3.0 mm, mode 0.3–0.8 mm, bimodal size distribution.

Coarse fraction
Dominant: Greenish brown to red-brown (ppl) mudstones/siltstones, often varying in color within the rock fragment, occasionally with dark rims, sometimes with faint layering, inclusions primarily of quartz and biotite in a fine-grained matrix, el, sr–r, mode 0.3–0.8 mm. Gray siltstones, primarily with fine quartz grains in gray matrix, occasionally with streaks of red-brown or golden-brown material that looks very similar to the matrix of the brown mudstones/siltstones, sr–r, mode 0.3–0.8 mm.
Rare: Micrite, lumps (eq, r, 0.2–0.4 mm) with alteration rims or fully altered (dark in xpl) and one large elongate (2.1 mm long) micritic area, probably secondary. Metamorphic rock fragments, el, sa–r, 0.2–1.0 mm. Quartz-biotite schist; polycrystalline quartz with undulose extinction and chlorite patches. Mica laths, mostly biotite, <0.05 mm.
Very rare: Altered yellow-green grain of unknown origin with dark patches and anomalous birefringence in xpl, slightly el, sr, 0.3 mm; sandstone (quartz arenite) set in red clay matrix, eq, r, 0.2 mm; brown amphibole, el, sr, 0.15 mm; altered untwinned feldspar, eq, sr, 0.08 mm.

Fine fraction
Predominant: Quartz, mostly monocrystalline, eq and el, sa–r.
Few: Mica laths.
Very few: Elongate amphibole(?) grains with inclined extinction; quartz-biotite and/or -amphibole aggregates, eq and el, sa–r.

Tcfs
Few, red-brown (ppl), red (xpl), generally diffuse boundaries, optically dense to neutral, eq to very irregular in shape, r, generally <0.3 mm; probably clay pellets.
Few, pale brown (ppl), opaque or speckled (xpl), sharp to diffuse boundaries, low optical density, eq and el, r, generally <0.2 mm.

SUBGROUP B: GRAY AND BROWN SILTSTONES
Sample: 55

This subgroup is similar to PFG 7A, but the groundmass is much siltier. Compare with Hilditch's (2019, 412–413) Group B (especially subgroup A), associated with central Crete. Refired to variable pink.

Microstructure
Few voids, mostly meso- and macro-vughs, oriented roughly parallel to vessel walls, occasionally cracking around edges of inclusions. At least one macro-channel in 60 has shape suggestive of organic origin. Inclusions generally double-spaced, oriented roughly parallel with vessel walls.

Groundmass
Not homogenous; brown to slightly paler at edges (ppl); red-brown (xpl) (40x); rounded red or red-brown patches or red to red-orange streaks; optically slightly active to inactive; crystallitic b-fabric, visible primarily at edges of slide (secondary?).

Inclusions
$c:f:v_{0.1\,mm}$, 30:55:15. Moderately well-sorted, eq and el, sa–r, <3 mm, modes 0.2–0.3 and 1.0–1.3 mm, bimodal size distribution.

Coarse fraction
Dominant: Siltstones, gray and brown, bearing quartz, chlorite, and occasionally calcite or bright birefringent orange-red inclusions; some siltstones have dark rim, some with biotite show general alignment of mica grains, perhaps slightly metamorphosed, el, r, mode 1.0–1.3 mm.
Common: Quartz, mono- and polycrystalline (sutured grain boundaries, undulose extinction), eq and slightly el, sa–r, mode 0.2–0.3 mm; feldspar, usually untwinned, eq and el, sa, mode 0.2–0.3 mm.
Few: Chert, eq and el, sa–r, mode 0.2–0.4 mm; birefringent orange grains, eq and el, sr, mode 0.2 mm.
Very few: Feldspar aggregates, sometimes with attached quartz, biotite, or amphibole, eq, sa, mode 0.2 mm; sandstone (arkose), el, sr, mode 0.3 mm.
Rare: Calcite, altered and opaque in xpl, eq and el, r, mode 0.2 mm.
Very rare: Biotite, mode 0.2 mm; igneous rock fragment with micrographic texture, eq, sr, 0.2 mm.

Fine Fraction
Dominant: Quartz (mono- and polycrystalline), feldspar (untwinned), and quartz/feldspar-biotite aggregates, eq and el, sa–sr; calcite (mostly altered, opaque in xpl), eq and el, r.
Few: Mica laths; birefringent orange grains, eq, sr.
Very rare: Radiolarian, eq, r.

Tcfs
Very few–very rare, brown (ppl), red to red-brown (xpl), sharp to merging boundaries, high optical density, eq and el, sr–r, <0.1–0.4 mm, rarely bearing quartz inclusions.

GROUP C: GREENISH GRAY WITH GRAY SILTSTONES
Samples: 82, 84

This fabric has a silty, dull greenish gray groundmass with small dark brown-red blobs, with dominant gray siltstones. It is comparable to FG 5 at Kolonna (Kiriatzi, Georgakopoulou, and Pentedeka 2011, 108–109) and appears very similar to, especially, KOL 247, fig. 102. The fabric is nonlocal there and has been associated with a fabric group found in EBA III–MBA contexts at Lerna and Asine, where it is not the predominant fabric but is nonetheless compatible with local geologies (Kiriatzi, Georgakopoulou, and Pentedeka 2011, 142; see also Spencer 2007, 144; Whitbread 2001, 372). An origin in the Corinthia or Argolid is, therefore, plausible. The sedimentary nature of the inclusions, however, is not distinctive enough to rule out a Cretan provenance, and the dominant inclusions, gray siltstones with dark rims, are also comparable with those from the previous subgroups PFG 7A and 7B. Although the macroscopic fabric was suspected to be from the mainland or Kythera, the sherds in this fabric are too poorly preserved to demonstrate whether the decoration or shapes associated with it can be securely described as Mainland/Kytheran Lustrous Decorated (i.e., cross-hatching, narrow-necked jars; see Zerner 1988, 2008) rather than Cretan Lustrous Painted ware. Sample 82 was analyzed using WD-XRF and appears to have more chemical similarities to PFG 7A and 7D (hypothesized to be from Crete) than 7G and 7H (perhaps from the mainland and/or Kythera), at least based on preliminary interpretation. Both samples refired to pale pink, turning slightly darker at the surfaces in places.

Microstructure
Few voids, mostly macro-vughs and channels, a few meso-vughs and channels, roughly oriented parallel to vessel walls, calcite infilling in some. Inclusions double- to open-spaced, oriented generally parallel to vessel walls.

Groundmass
Homogenous, greenish brown (ppl), greenish gray with common small red patches (xpl) (40x), optically inactive.

Inclusions
c:f:v$_{0.08\,mm}$, 20:55:25. Moderately well-sorted, mostly el, sa–sr, <3.2 mm, modes 0.15–0.7 mm, 1.7–2.1 mm, bimodal size distribution, only siltstones in largest mode.

Coarse fraction
Dominant: Siltstones (some grading to mudstone), gray, with quartz inclusions, regularly with dark rims, occasionally with some layering visible, occasionally with cracks filled with brown birefringent material, el, sa–sr, modes 0.3–0.7 mm, 1.7–2.1 mm. A few with somewhat larger inclusions may be better classed as sandstones (with abundant matrix), but otherwise they appear much the same as the finer-grained siltstone/mudstone fragments, and they usually have similar dark rims.
Common: Monocrystalline quartz and feldspar grains (untwinned and albite twinning), eq, sa, mode 0.1–0.2 mm.
Few: Polycrystalline quartz, undulose extinction, eq, sr, mode 0.15–0.2 mm.
Very few: Chert, eq, r, mode 0.15 mm.
Rare: Calcite(?), altered, pale yellow-brown to brown in ppl, yellow, dark brown, or opaque in xpl, eq and el, r, mode 0.3 mm; birefringent orange grains, el, sr, mode 0.1 mm.
Very rare: Sandstone composed of quartz and feldspar, sometimes with orange birefringent and possible altered calcite(?) grains, with red-brown slightly birefringent matrix; orange to red grains (ppl) that turn opaque in xpl, el, sa, mode 0.2 mm.

Fine fraction
Dominant: Polycrystalline quartz and monocrystalline quartz/feldspar, eq and el, sr.
Very few: Birefringent orange-red grains, eq, r.
Rare: Biotite laths.
Very rare: Titanite(?), high relief but very altered, slightly pleochroic brown, upper second-/low third-order interference colors, eq, r; quartz-biotite aggregate, eq, sa (84).

Tcfs
Common, brown to nearly opaque (ppl), red (xpl), generally diffuse boundaries, optically dense, eq, sr–r, mode 0.06–0.15 mm; probably clay pellets.

SUBGROUP D: ARGILLACEOUS GRAINS, SERPENTINITE
Samples: 68, 80

This fabric is distinguished by argillaceous grains (sedimentary rock fragments?) and probable serpentinite. It is somewhat similar to Kiriatzi, Georgakopoulou, and Pentedeka's (2011, 106–107) FG 4A at Kolonna (especially KOL 172 and 196), although that group is not reported as having microfossils, serpentinite is very rare, and the altered volcanic fragments are missing. Geologically, it could be compatible with central Crete, but it does not appear very similar to published descriptions and images of Cretan fabrics. Sample 68 was analyzed using WD-XRF; preliminary interpretation of the results suggests that it may be more similar to the potential Cretan (PFG 6A, 6C, 7A, 7C, 7E) than possible non-Cretan (PFG 7G, 7H) fabrics. Both samples refired to variable pink; paint on 80 refired to red-brown.

Microstructure
Few–very few voids, micro- and meso-vughs and channels, meso-vesicles, some infilled or rimmed with calcite. In 68, some appear to be burnt-out microfossils. Voids with a long axis roughly aligned parallel to vessel walls. Most inclusions are double- to open-spaced, but microfossils in many cases are close-spaced. Inclusions with a long axis oriented parallel to vessel walls.

Groundmass
Not completely homogenous, greenish brown to brown (ppl), brown to dark greenish brown (xpl) (40x), varying in color across section; optically slightly active.

Inclusions
c:f:v$_{0.1\,mm}$, 15:70:15. Well-sorted, eq and el, a–sr, <2.9 mm, mode 0.2–0.7 mm, bimodal size distribution.

Coarse fraction
Dominant: Micrite lumps, eq and el, sr–r, some quite amorphous, some are probably remnants of microfossils, a few are oblong and may be shell, mode 0.2–0.7 mm; at least one probable foraminifera in 68.
Dominant–few: Red-brown argillaceous grains, usually bearing silt- to sand-sized inclusions, with different combinations of quartz, feldspar, micrite, biotite, metamorphic rocks, and/or birefringent orange-red grains, often with cracking around edges and sometimes polygonal cracks at the interior, el and often irregular in shape, a–sr, mode 0.2–0.5 mm in 80, 0.2–2.1 mm in 68. Usually with sharp boundaries; optically dense; perhaps mostly rock fragments (mudstone–sandstone).

Few–very rare: Gray and brown siltstones, el, sr–r, 0.2–1.0 mm. Birefringent yellow to orange grains, at least some of which present a mesh-like texture and are probably serpentinite, eq and el, sr, mode 0.2 mm. Chert, rarely radiolarian, eq and el, sa, mode 0.2–0.3 mm. Sandstone, with poorly sorted sr to angular quartz, rare feldspar, brown and opaque minerals in a red-brown matrix, eq, r, mode 0.9–1.2 mm.

Very few–rare: Metamorphic rock fragments composed of quartz, feldspar, and occasionally biotite and/or possible amphibole, sometimes altered, rare titanite, rare calcite, el, sr, mode 0.2–0.3 mm. Feldspar grains, rarely with simple or albite twinning, eq and slightly el, sa–sr, mode 0.2–0.3 mm. Polycrystalline quartz with undulose extinction, mode 0.2–0.3 mm.

Rare–very rare: Altered volcanic rock fragments, cloudy dark brown with altered phenocrysts (mostly patchy birefringent orange) or glassy clear to pale yellow-brown with possible pyroxene, quartz(?), and/or mica phenocrysts and anomalous birefringence in xpl, eq and el, sr–r, 0.2–0.3 mm.

Very rare: Biotite mica laths, el, mode 0.15 mm; sponge spicules(?), silicified, el, mode 0.5 mm; epidote group minerals(?), el, sa, 0.4 mm.

Very rare–absent: Pyroxene(?), eq, sa, 0.2 mm; chalcedonic quartz, eq, sr, 0.2 mm.

Fine Fraction:
Dominant: Quartz/feldspar (often impossible to distinguish from each other) and quartz/feldspar-mica aggregates, eq and el, sa–sr; altered calcite (mostly black in xpl), eq and el, r, at least some of which may be degraded microfossils.
Common–rare: Chert, el, a; birefringent yellow to orange grains, eq, r.
Rare: Biotite laths.
Very rare–absent: Epidote group minerals(?), el, sa.

Tcfs
Few, brown to red-brown (ppl), brown to red (xpl), sharp to merging boundaries, high to moderate optical density, el, sr–r, mode 0.2–0.3 mm.
Few, orange-brown (ppl, xpl), merging boundaries, neutral optical density, eq, r, mode 0.2–0.3 mm, with quartz and yellow inclusions.
Common–few, pale brown (ppl), opaque or speckled (xpl), low optical density, irregular in shape, r, mode <0.2 mm.

SUBGROUP E: QUARTZ, RED TCFS/MUDSTONES
Sample: 65

This fabric appears to come from a somewhat mixed geological environment, probably dominated by sedimentary rocks. Broad similarities exist with Poursat and Knappett's (2005, 12–13) Group B1, hypothesized to be possibly local or from the Mesara (although the chert there is not described as radiolarian), as well as Graybehl's (2014) Group 6, which includes much later sherds and is hypothesized to come from the Corinthia and/or the Argolid. Preliminary interpretation of the WD-XRF results suggests that this sample is more similar to potential Cretan fabrics (PFG 6A, 6C, 7A, 7C, 7D) than possible non-Cretan fabrics (PFG 7G, 7H). Refired to very pale pink; paint refired to dull red.

Microstructure
Very few voids, meso- and macro-vughs, roughly oriented parallel to vessel walls. Inclusions double- to open-spaced, no clear orientation.

Groundmass
Relatively homogenous; greenish brown (ppl); brown (xpl) (40x); some red streaks, probably mixed clay; optically slightly active; patchy probably secondary calcite.

Inclusions
c:f:$v_{0.05\,mm}$, 55:30:15. Moderately well-sorted, eq and el, sa–r, <1.5 mm, mode 0.2–0.4 mm, bimodal size distribution, some inclusions are ringed by calcite (secondary?).

Coarse fraction
Dominant: Quartz, mono- and polycrystalline (undulose extinction), eq and el, sa–r, mode 0.3–0.4 mm. Feldspar, very rarely with albite twins, eq, sa, mode 0.2–0.3 mm.
Frequent: Quartz-feldspar aggregates, very weathered, rarely with biotite, red-brown clay, or epidote(?), el, sr, mode 0.2–0.3 mm.
Common: Brown siltstone, eq, r, mode 0.2–0.4 mm; red mudstones/tcfs, boundaries sharp to somewhat diffuse, eq, r, mode 0.4 mm.
Few: Calcite, eq, sa–r, mode 0.2 mm; chert, including radiolarian, eq and el, r, mode 0.2–0.3 mm.

Rare: Sandstone (quartz arenite), el, sa, 0.3 mm; grains of unknown origin, possible altered igneous(?), cloudy yellow brown in ppl, anomalous birefringence in xpl, slightly el, r, 0.2–0.3 mm.

Fine Fraction
Dominant: Quartz/feldspar, eq, sa–sr.
Common: Biotite laths; birefringent orange grains, eq, r.
Few: Calcite(?), eq, r.

Tcfs
Apart from those mentioned above, few, red (ppl), red-brown (xpl), merging boundaries, optically neutral, eq and el, r, mode 0.2–0.3 mm.

SUBGROUP F: GREENISH BROWN, CRACKING, MEDIUM COARSE
Sample: 64

The major inclusions apart from clay pellets are mudstones, siltstones, and chert (which may bear radiolaria), as well as micrite lumps and microfossils. The subgroup is distinctive in the presence of abundant fine cracks, some elongate and running parallel to the vessel walls and some closely spaced and latticed (Color Plate 3: j, k). It is very probably related to the next subgroup PFG 7G (Color Plate 3: l–o), which shows similar patterns of cracking but has many fewer coarse inclusions. Although the cracking that is evident in this and the next subgroup is quite distinctive, I know of no published parallels for that aspect of the fabric. With rather homogenous sedimentary-derived inclusions, it is difficult to determine provenance as these are widespread in the Aegean. The fabric seems comparable with two of Whitbread's (2011, 166–168) Mudstone groups from the Berbati Valley survey, as well as Day's (2011, 68–69) Fabric 17, hypothesized to be from the Argolid. Although neither microfossils nor shell are reported in those fabrics, neither is incompatible with an origin in the Argolid. Nevertheless, other origins, like Kythera, cannot be excluded. Although this sample was not analyzed using WD-XRF, it has close similarities to PFG 7G, which varies chemically from the other PFG 7 subgroups (apart from 7H) according to preliminary interpretation of the results; this may support the hypothesis that this fabric has a non-Cretan origin. Refired to slightly variable pink.

Microstructure
Common voids, meso- to mega-channels, meso- to macro- and rarely mega-vughs, oriented generally parallel with vessel walls. Inclusions single- and double-spaced, oriented generally parallel to vessel walls.

Groundmass
Relatively homogenous; greenish brown (ppl, xpl) (40x); a few red streaks and some red tcfs are elongated, probably evidence of clay mixing; optically inactive to slightly active in some places; patchy probably secondary calcite.

Inclusions
c:f:$v_{0.05\,mm}$, 50:20:30. Poorly sorted, eq and el, a–r, <2.25 mm, mode 0.1–1.4 mm, bimodal size distribution, cracking around some inclusions.

Coarse fraction
Dominant: Brown, red, and gray mudstones/siltstones, bearing quartz, biotite(?), birefringent orange-red inclusions, and rarely muscovite, sometimes with interior cracking, el, a–sr, mode 0.3–1.4 mm; some siltstones have a faint darker ring around the exterior; some mudstones bear radiolaria.
Common: Micrite lumps (in some cases altered), some appear to be degraded microfossils, eq and el, r, mode 0.1–0.3 mm. Red mudstones/tcfs, sharp to somewhat diffuse grain boundaries, eq and el, r, mode 0.3–0.5 mm.
Few: Chert, including radiolaria, eq, sr–r, mode 0.3–0.5 mm.
Very few: Polycrystalline quartz, el, sr, mode 0.3–0.5 mm; quartz-biotite schist, el, sr, mode 0.15–0.3 mm.
Rare: Shell(?), curving fragments, el, sa, mode 0.1–0.3 mm.

Fine fraction
Dominant: Quartz/feldspar (often indistinguishable from each other), eq and el, sa–sr; biotite and white mica laths (the white mica has very low birefringence colors).
Few: Micrite, eq and el, sr–r.
Very few: Polycrystalline quartz, el and eq, sr; birefringent yellow-orange, eq, r.

Tcfs
These tcfs are in addition to those mentioned above. Few, pale brown (ppl), opaque or speckled (xpl), somewhat diffuse boundaries, low optical density, eq and el, r, mode <0.4 mm.

Rare, greenish brown (ppl), reddish brown (xpl), sharp to merging boundaries, neutral to moderate optical density, eq, r, mode <0.3 mm; probably clay pellets.

SUBGROUP G: GREENISH BROWN, CRACKING, FINE
Samples: 61, 62

This fabric is probably related to PFG 7F, given the similar appearance of the clay, including the distinctive cracking. Cracks are sometimes accompanied by a kind of starburst feature in the groundmass, with undulating rays of dark red-brown clay radiating outward from a central point. It is possible that the "starbursts" represent natural variation in the clays. The fineness of this group combined with the rather nondistinctive inclusions makes it is impossible to pinpoint a production area. Macroscopically, they were hypothesized to be from the mainland or Kythera. Preliminary interpretation of the WD-XRF results suggests that samples from PFG 7G vary across several elements in comparison with PFG 7A and PFG 7C–E (which seem compatible with Cretan clays). It is possible, therefore, that PFG 7G may be from a non-Cretan source. Sample 61 fired pink, turning yellow at surfaces; 62 fired to yellow with pink margins. Paint of 61 refired to crackling red-brown; paint of 62 refired to dull red.

Microstructure
Common–few voids, meso- and macro-channels and vughs, generally parallel to vessel walls, sometimes with calcite rims or infilling. Sample 62 also contains mega-channels that might be shrinkage cracks. Inclusions open-spaced, no orientation.

Groundmass
Relatively homogenous, greenish brown (ppl), yellowish brown (xpl) (40x), optically slightly active to inactive.

Inclusions
c:f:v$_{0.05\,mm}$, 30:40:30, 15:50:35. Moderately well-sorted, eq and el, sr–r, <1.4 mm, mode 0.2–1.0 mm, bimodal size distribution.

Coarse fraction
Dominant: Mudstones/tcfs, brown in ppl, red in xpl, sharp to sometimes rather diffuse boundaries, eq and el, sr–r, mode 0.5–1.0 mm.
Frequent–very few: Altered calcite(?), clear to pale brown in ppl, speckled black in xpl, el, r, mode 0.2 mm (shape of some could suggest they are altered microfossils).
Few: Brown–gray mudstones/siltstones, bearing quartz/feldspar, biotite, birefringent orange inclusions, eq, r, mode 0.3–0.4 mm.
Very few: Feldspar (untwinned), el, sa, mode 0.1 mm; monocrystalline quartz, eq and el, a–sa, mode 0.08 mm.
Rare: Quartz-biotite schist, el, sa, mode 0.3 mm; polycrystalline quartz, eq, r, mode 0.15 mm.
Very rare: Chert, eq, r, mode 0.07 mm; micrite lumps, unaltered, el, r, and irregular, perhaps secondary(?), 0.5–0.7 mm.

Fine Fraction
Dominant: Quartz/feldspar (often indistinguishable from each other) and quartz/feldspar-mica aggregates, eq and el, sa–sr.
Frequent: Tiny biotite and more rarely white mica laths; the white mica has very low interference colors.
Few: Altered calcite(?), clear to pale brown in ppl, opaque or cloudy brown in xpl, eq, r.
Rare: Birefringent orange grains, eq, r.

Tcfs
These tcfs are in addition to those mentioned above. Few, patchy dark red-brown to nearly opaque (ppl), red to red-brown (xpl), merging boundaries, optically dense to optically neutral, eq and el, sa–r, mode 0.05–0.3 mm; clay pellets.
Few–very rare, gray-brown (ppl), yellow-brown (xpl), merging boundaries, sometimes with cracking around edges, optically neutral, el, r, mode 0.8–1.7 mm.

Variant: 63
Almost exactly as above in color, texture, and inclusions, but missing the cracking and with microfossils (mostly foraminifera). Optically moderately active, perhaps lower-fired version(?). Refired to very pale pink; paint refired to lustrous red.

Variant: 70
Fine with few recognizable inclusions, including chert and mudstones/tcfs. Shrinkage/cracking is rare, but is very similar to that in the main group, and there is a large area of "starbursts" as described above. Refired to pinkish yellow with pink margins; paint refired to crackling dark brown.

Variant: 72
Only one patch with "starburst" feature. Color is a warmer golden brown (ppl) to yellow-brown (xpl), and some large biotite grains exist. Refired to pink with red paint. According to preliminary interpretation of the WD-XRF results, sample 72 is also chemically different from the rest of PFG 7G.

SUBGROUP H: RED MUDSTONES, SILTSTONES
Sample: 75

This fabric bears common red mudstones/tcfs, red mudstones/siltstones, and brown and gray siltstones. The groundmass color is different and more optically active than PFG 7A–G. This subgroup appears somewhat similar to FG 5 at Kolonna, especially KOL 238 (Kiriatzi, Georgakopoulou, and Pentedeka 2011, 108–109, fig. 100). They hypothesized that FG 5 is associated with the Argolid or Corinthia, given comparisons at Lerna and Asine (Gauss and Kiriatzi 2011, 141–142; see also Spencer 2007, 144; Whitbread 2001, 372). Sample 75 contains chert, microfossils, and rare metamorphic rock fragments, which are not noted in FG 5 at Aegina. This fabric does not appear to be comparable to published descriptions of Cretan fabrics, and preliminary interpretation of the WD-XRF results suggests a potentially non-Cretan origin. Refired to variable pink; paint refired to red.

Microstructure
Few voids, meso- and macro-channels and vughs, some channels/cracking around edges of inclusions, some calcite infilling or rims around voids; voids with a long axis are generally parallel to vessel walls. Inclusions single to double-spaced, roughly oriented parallel to vessel walls.

Groundmass
Mostly homogenous; greenish brown (ppl); reddish brown (xpl) (40x); some red streaks are probably indicative of clay mixing; optically slightly active; patchy secondary calcite.

Inclusions
$c:f:v_{0.05\,mm}$, 35:40:25. Poorly sorted, eq and el, sa–r, <1.2 mm, mode 0.3–1.0 mm, bimodal size distribution.

Coarse fraction
Common: Red mudstones/siltstones, very rarely grading into sandstone, bearing quartz, biotite and white mica, sometimes chert, and birefringent orange inclusions, eq and el, sr–r, mode 0.4–1.0 mm; occasionally some alignment of clays and micas. Red mudstones/tcfs, with sharp to occasionally rather diffuse boundaries, eq, r, mode 0.3–0.7 mm. Chert, eq and el, sa–sr, mode 0.3–0.6 mm.
Few: Monocrystalline and polycrystalline quartz, eq, sa–sr, mode 0.2–0.3 mm. Micrite, partially altered, occasionally with small quartz inclusions, eq and el, r, mode 0.2–0.4 mm.
Very few: Metamorphic rock fragments composed of quartz and biotite or sometimes brown amphibole, generally appear to be quite low-grade, el and eq, sr, mode 0.1–0.3 mm.
Rare: Quartz-feldspar aggregates, with mica(?) inclusions in the feldspar; grains sometimes surrounded by red-brown material. Orange to yellow grains with anomalous birefringence, at least some may be serpentinite, eq and el, sa, mode 0.05–0.3 mm. Feldspar, untwinned and altered, eq, sr, mode 0.2 mm.
Very rare: Brown amphibole, el, sa, mode 0.1–0.3 mm; microfossils, foraminifera, micritic (altered), 0.6 mm.

Fine fraction
Common: Quartz/feldspar (often indistinguishable from each other) and quartz/feldspar-biotite aggregates, eq and el, sr; biotite and rarely white mica laths.
Very few: Birefringent orange grains, eq, sr.
Rare: Calcite (micrite), eq, sa–r, possibly secondary.

Tcfs
In addition to those described above, there are three kinds. Common, patchy dark red-brown to nearly opaque (ppl), red to red-brown (xpl), sharp to rarely merging boundaries, optically dense to optically neutral, eq and el though often irregular, sa–r, mode 0.05–0.6 mm; probably clay pellets.
Few, pale greenish brown (ppl), greenish gray (xpl), sharp to merging boundaries, low optical density, el, r, mode 1.0–2.4 mm.
Few, gray (ppl), gray-brown to very dark gray (xpl), clear boundaries, optically neutral, el, r, mode 0.3–2.4 mm, occasionally with red streaks and/or tiny inclusions of quartz and/or mica; perhaps clay pellets.

Variant: 74
Fine variant? The groundmass of this sample appears identical to that of 75, but it is much finer and is missing the chert. Refired to pink with a darker pink core; paint refired to red-brown.

GROUP 8: ABUNDANT CALCAREOUS ROCKS

The fabrics in this group are notable for bearing significant quantities of large decomposing or altered calcareous rock fragments. All are associated with earlier MBA Minoan/-izing wares, which suggests that they originate in Crete, Kythera, southern mainland Greece, or the southeastern Aegean. However, close parallels have not been located for any of the subgroups. Preliminary interpretation of the WD-XRF results suggests that samples from PFG 8 differ substantially from those in PFG 6 and 7 in their chemistry. Future chemical and petrographic study on a wider array of samples may help to resolve the origin(s) of this group.

SUBGROUP A: SPECKLED GROUNDMASS, LOW-GRADE METAMORPHICS
Sample: 83

This is a fine patchy greenish and reddish-brown fabric with common low-grade metamorphic rocks. Phyllites and low-grade metamorphic rocks are known from many regions, and no closely comparable fabrics have been located. Refired to pale pink, darker at core.

Microstructure
Very few voids, meso- to macro-vughs and channels, some with calcite infilling, no preferred orientation. Inclusions single- to open-spaced, no preferred orientation.

Groundmass
Not homogenous, brown to green-brown (ppl); brown to red-brown (xpl) (40x); color varies across section, with patches of red and green-brown (xpl) throughout, probably evidence of clay mixing; optically slightly active; patches of crystallitic b-fabric, perhaps from secondary calcite.

Inclusions
c:f:$v_{0.05\,mm}$, 60:20:20. Poorly sorted, eq to el, sr–r, <4.8 mm, mode 0.2–0.9 mm, bimodal size distribution.

Coarse fraction
Dominant: Low-grade metamorphic rock fragments, eq and mostly el, sr–r, mode 0.2–0.9 mm. Phyllite, mostly brown, rarely with crenulation textures. (Meta)sandstones to schist-like metamorphic rock fragments (with banding, alignment of minerals, and slightly elongated/deformed quartz grains), with similar compositions: variable quantities of quartz, feldspar (occasionally porphyroblastic), patches or bands of oxidized, opaque material, red-brown material, chlorite or sometimes biotite, rarely with possible calcitic inclusions altered to cloudy brown, and/or rare titanite. Polycrystalline quartz. Calcite, nearly all altered, most micrite, some with reaction rims, gold, brown, and nearly opaque in xpl, eq and el, r, mode 0.02–0.5 mm.
Common: Untwinned alkali feldspar and plagioclase grains, occasionally with alteration at edges, in some cases with acicular high-relief amphibole(?) inclusions, eq and el, sa, mode 0.2–0.6 mm.
Few: Red mudstones/tcfs with tiny quartz and birefringent orange inclusions, sharp boundaries and occasionally cracking around edges, el, sa–r, mode 0.3–0.6 mm.
Rare: Sandstone (quartz arenite), eq, r, mode 0.3 mm.
Very rare: Grain of unknown origin, mottled black in ppl, with rounded darker patches and streaky, cloudy red-brown material, el, sa, 0.6 mm.

Fine Fraction
Dominant: Quartz/feldspar (often indistinguishable from each other), eq and el, sa–sr.
Common: Calcite, altered, eq, r.
Few: Quartz-feldspar-mica or -opaque aggregates, eq and el, sr–r.
Rare: Birefringent orange grains, eq, sr.
Very rare: Mica laths, mostly biotite.

Tcfs
Apart from those mentioned above, few, brown to nearly opaque (ppl), red to dark red-brown (xpl), sharp to merging boundaries, high to moderate optical density, eq and el, sr–r, <0.1–0.7 mm.

SUBGROUP B: MOTTLED GROUNDMASS, BIOGENIC LIMESTONE
Sample: 58

This fabric is distinguished by its mottled red-brown groundmass with dense microfossils, metamorphic rock fragments, and red clay pellets. A very rare group from Lerna described by Myer, Betancourt, and Vaughan (1995, 686–688, Group 9) is broadly similar to this one, combining clay pellets, metamorphic rocks, and possibly biogenic limestone, although microfossils are not reported in the matrix. Geological formations in which metamorphic rocks are found in proximity to biogenic limestones, however, are widespread in the Aegean, and the provenance of this fabric cannot be determined with certainty. Refired pink, with streak of paler clay at core.

Microstructure
Common voids, micro- and meso-vesicles, many rimmed with calcite (burnt-out microfossils?), meso- and macro-vughs (very rarely, mega-vughs), rarely meso- and macro-channels. Voids with a long axis are roughly oriented parallel to vessel walls. Most inclusions single- to double-spaced, but microfossils in many cases are close-spaced. Inclusions with a long axis very roughly oriented parallel to vessel walls.

Groundmass:
Not homogenous, mottled brown (ppl) to red-brown (xpl) (40x), rounded red or red-brown patches or red to red-orange streaks, crystallitic b-fabric, optically slightly active.

Inclusions
c:f:$v_{0.1\,mm}$, 25:55:20. Moderately well-sorted, eq and el, sa–r, <1.2 mm, mode 0.3–0.6 mm; metamorphic fragments seem to have been added as a temper and have a more unimodal size distribution when considered independently of the microfossils and tcfs in the fabric.

Coarse fraction
Dominant: Limestone, micritic, in some cases with remnants of round bioclasts and/or small quartz inclusions, eq, r, mode 0.4 mm. Microfossils, including foraminifera, in some cases with voids or red material (clay) infilling chambers, r, mode 0.3–0.4 mm. Metamorphic rock fragments, mostly el, some eq, sa–sr, mode 0.4–0.6 mm. Mica schists, often but not always banded, biotite more common than muscovite, possible amphibole in one grain, possible calcite in a few grains (but no crystal structure, despite high birefringence colors, and pale brown in ppl). Phyllite, brown or with mica (muscovite or biotite, in some cases altered to chlorite); polycrystalline quartz with sutured boundaries and undulose extinction; quartz-feldspar-mica aggregates.
Few: Feldspar, untwinned, some with cracking or alteration, eq, sa, mode 0.3 mm.
Rare: Birefringent orange grains (including some serpentinite?), el, r, 0.2–0.3 mm.
Very rare: Tabular crystals of biotite or white mica, el, sa, mode 0.4 mm; epidote, eq, sr, 0.3 mm; red-brown siltstone, el, sr, 0.3 mm.

Fine Fraction
Dominant: Calcite, microfossils and micrite lumps, eq, r.
Common: Metamorphic fragments as above, mostly polycrystalline quartz, occasionally with mica adhering; quartz/feldspar.
Few: Mica laths.

Tcfs
Common, dark brown (ppl) to red brown (xpl), sometimes darker toward edges, often with micritic veins (infilling cracks?), mostly sharp boundaries, high optical density, el, sr–r, 0.3–1.5 mm, mode 0.6 mm, occasionally with sa–sr quartz inclusions or birefringent orange grains; probably clay pellets.
Common, dark brown to red (ppl), red or red brown (xpl), usually diffuse but sometimes sharp boundaries, high optical density, eq and el, sr–r, <0.1–0.5 mm, mode 0.3 mm, occasionally with small sparkling inclusions or quartz/feldspar.

SUBGROUP C: ABUNDANT SILTSTONES
Samples: 59, 60

This subgroup has relatively close similarities to the next subgroup (PFG 8D), but it contains more sedimentary inclusions and more probably ophiolite-derived inclusions. Sample 59 is a round-mouthed jug of a kind that has its closest parallels in the southeastern Aegean, and Rhodes, for example, where ophiolite outcrops occur in association with abundant limestones, would be a geologically compatible source. General parallels exist with Hilditch et al.'s (2012, 84–90) Group VI at Iasos, which they suggest might be from Rhodes, but this fabric and that one do not seem to be precisely the same, nor are there close parallels with later Rhodian amphora fabrics (Whitbread 1995, 60–67). The association in this case, therefore, must remain very tentative. Refired to pink, slightly variable in the case of 59; the paint of 60 refired to red-brown.

Microstructure
Few voids, mostly meso- and macro-vughs. Meso- and macro-channels also exist in 60. Long axis generally oriented parallel to vessel walls. Inclusions single- to double-spaced, weakly oriented parallel to vessel walls.

Groundmass
Not homogenous; pale reddish brown, grayish brown, yellow brown (ppl); red brown, brown, pale brown (xpl) (40x); some streaks of red in 59 (probably clay mixing); optically slightly active (60) to inactive (59); patchy crystallitic b-fabric, probably secondary.

Inclusions
c:f:v$_{0.1 mm}$, 30:40:30, 35:55:10. Poorly sorted, eq and mostly el, sa–r, <2.7 mm, mode 0.3–1.0 mm, weakly bimodal size distribution.

Coarse fraction
Frequent: Calcite-rich rock fragments, el, sr–r, mode 0.3–1.0 mm, often altered and opaque in xpl, and/or with a large void at the center. Limestone, micritic or very rarely sparitic or macrosparitic, occasionally with rare angular silt-sized quartz inclusions. Calcareous siltstones bearing poorly sorted angular quartz, mica (biotite or white mica), and rarely orange grains with anomalous birefingence. In 59, these rock fragments seem to grade into (proto)cataclastic rocks with varying proportions of calcitic matrix (which is sometimes altered and opaque in xpl), composed of a–sr often cracked fragments of quartz, feldspar (including plagioclase), and biotite together with red-brown and birefringent yellow or orange material. Greenish brown, gray, and brown siltstones sometimes grading into sandstones with less matrix, all rather poorly sorted, composed primarily of a–sr quartz, feldspar (including plagioclase), orange grains that are either opaque or birefringent in xpl, mica, and/or chlorite, occasionally with altered calcite(?), sometimes showing some alignment, el, sr, mode 0.3–1.0 mm. Red-brown mudstones/siltstones, bearing similar inclusions as the siltstones described above, sometimes showing some alignment, el, sr, 0.5–1.0 mm.
Few–very rare: Chert, very rarely radiolarian, eq and el, a–r, mode 0.3 mm.
Very few–rare: Birefringent orange grains, at least some of which may be serpentinite, eq and el, sa–r, mode 0.1–0.2 mm. Feldspar-quartz-biotite aggregates, el, a, mode 0.2–0.3 mm (all three elements are not always present, and the feldspar sometimes shows albite twinning).
Very few–very rare: Altered igneous rocks, mostly cloudy red-brown with phenocrysts of quartz, and/or altered feldspar, and golden to orange or red-brown grains with anomalous extinction, el, sr, mode 0.6 mm.
Very few–absent: Biotite and more rarely white mica, el, a, mode 0.1–0.2 mm.
Very rare–absent: Plagioclase, el, sa, 0.3 mm; black grain, red in xpl, slightly el, a, 0.6 mm.

Fine fraction
Predominant: Quartz/feldspar (often indistinguishable from each other), rarely with attached biotite, eq and el, a–sr.
Few–rare: Mica laths, biotite and white mica.
Very few–very rare: Birefringent orange grains, el, r.
Very rare–absent: Chert, el, sr.

Tcfs
Common; red-brown to very dark brown (ppl); red, dark brown, or dark red (xpl); sharp to sometimes diffuse boundaries; high to neutral optical density; eq and el, r; mode <0.1 mm; probably iron-rich clay pellets.
Few, pale brown (ppl), opaque or speckled (xpl), clear boundaries, low optical density, eq and el, often irregular, sr, mode <0.2 mm.
Common–few, gray (ppl), cloudy pale brown to gray (xpl), clear boundaries, moderate optical density, eq and slightly el, sr, mode <0.2 mm.

GROUP D: VARIOUS CALCAREOUS
Samples: 76, 78, 79

This fabric is typified by dominant calcareous inclusions in different forms, from micritic grains (probably limestone) to silt- and sandstones with calcareous matrix, to metamorphic rocks. It is similar to PFG 8C, especially in the presence of (proto)cataclastic rocks with a micritic matrix and possible serpentinite. Some similarities exist with FG 6A at Kolonna (Kiriatzi, Georgakopoulou, and Pentedeka 2011, 109–111, 142–143), which is tentatively associated with Thebes and/or Boeotia, although such an origin would be unexpected given the wares of these samples. The Kolonna samples refired brown but the PFG 8D samples refired red. This difference could support the hypothesis that the two groups have different sources. As with the previous subgroup, similarities also exist with Hilditch et al.'s (2012, 84–90) Group VI at Iasos, attributed to Rhodes, although, other sources are also possible. All refired red.

Microstructure
Few to very few, meso- and macro-vughs, micro- and meso-channels, no preferred orientation. Inclusions single- to double-spaced; no to weak orientation parallel to vessel walls.

Groundmass
Not homogenous between samples or across slides; pale brown, brown, or red brown (ppl); yellow, brown, brown gray, or red brown (xpl) (40x); optically active.

Inclusions
c:f:v$_{0.1\ mm}$, 40:40:20, 35:50:15. Poorly sorted, eq to el, sa–r, <4.4 mm, mode 0.3–1.3 mm, unimodal (76) to bimodal (78, 79) size distribution.

Coarse fraction
Predominant–common: Calcite-rich rocks, el and eq, sa–r, mode 0.3–1.3 mm. Micrite lumps, some with small sa quartz inclusions, rarely with sparitic areas, probably limestone. Calcareous siltstones/sandstones, with a–sr quartz, feldspar, mica, and/or birefringent orange inclusions, as well as red-brown material; some grading into (proto)cataclasites with similar if usually larger and more poorly sorted inclusions, which show in some cases significant cracking.
Common–few: Sedimentary rocks, eq and slightly el, sr, 0.3–1.3 mm. Red-brown to orange mudstones/siltstones with predominantly quartz, mica, and birefringent red inclusions (some alignment of mica, perhaps metamorphosed), varying proportions of matrix to clasts. Sandstones (quartz arenite); greywacke; rare chert (sa–r). Metamorphic rock fragments, el, sr, mode 0.3–0.8 mm. Some are composed of polycrystalline quartz (undulose extinction, sutured boundaries), mica (biotite and white mica), occasionally banded. Others are quartz-feldspar-mica aggregates with areas of undulose extinction, amphibole rarely appears (all minerals do not appear in all fragments).
Few–very rare: Monocrystalline quartz, eq, a–sr, mode 0.1–0.2 mm; feldspar grains, very rarely with simple or albite twinning, slightly el, a–sa, mode 0.1–0.2 mm.
Very few–rare: Mica, more biotite than white mica, el, 0.1–0.2 mm.
Rare–very rare: Birefringent yellow-orange to bright orange (ppl) grains, sometimes appear to have mesh-like texture in xpl, at least some may be serpentinite, el, sr–r, 0.2–0.3 mm.
Rare–absent: Micrite, el, possible shell fragments(?), 0.4 mm.

Fine Fraction
Dominant: Monocrystalline quartz/feldspar, eq and el, a–sr.
Frequent–few: Biotite and white mica laths.
Common–very few: Polycrystalline quartz and quartz/feldspar-mica aggregates as above.
Common–very rare: Birefringent yellow-orange grains as above; micritic lumps, eq and el, r, perhaps microfossils, although no internal structure is recognizable.

Tcfs
Common–few, red to red brown (ppl), red to nearly opaque (xpl), sharp to merging boundaries, high optical density, eq to el, sr–r, often bearing small quartz (mono- or polycrystalline) and/or mica and/or birefringent orange grains.

Variant: 57
Micrite is, for the most part, very altered and often amorphous; micrite lumps are substantially more common than other kinds of calcite-rich rocks. Color is more brown to orange-brown (ppl) than red. Refired to red.

SUBGROUP E: MIXED WITH VOLCANICS
Sample: 69

The presence of a few fresh-looking acid volcanic rock fragments in this fabric suggests an origin in the south Aegean volcanic arc. Substantial differences from Aeginetan and Melian/Theran fabrics suggest that the eastern Aegean may be a more likely source, which would also be plausible on the basis of the ware. Broad parallels exist with descriptions of Koan fabrics (Hilditch et al. 2012, 77–84; Whitbread 1995, 81–106), but they are not very precise, and other sources are possible. Refired to pink.

Microstructure
Common voids, meso- and macro-channels, meso-vesicles, meso- and macro-vughs, occasionally at edges of inclusions and regularly with calcite rims; channels weakly oriented parallel to vessel walls. Inclusions single- to double-spaced, no preferred orientation.

Groundmass
Mostly homogenous, greenish brown (ppl), reddish brown (xpl) (40x), optically slightly active, some patches of secondary calcite.

Inclusions
c:f:v$_{0.15\text{ mm}}$, 25:55:20. Poorly sorted, eq to el, sa–r, <3.2 mm, mode 0.3–0.9 mm, weakly bimodal size distribution.

Coarse fraction
Common: Feldspar (alkali and plagioclase), eq, sa, mode 0.3–0.5 mm, rarely with biotite attached, occasionally with sericite alteration, and rarely showing faint zoning. Chert, el, sa–r, mode 0.3–0.8 mm, some of which bear larger quartz grains and brown or red-brown material. Red to dark-brown mudstones/siltstones with sparkling tiny inclusions or larger inclusions of quartz, untwinned feldspar, and/or plagioclase and/or chert, mostly el, r, mode 0.6–0.9 mm. Metamorphic rock fragments, eq and el, sr–r, mode 0.3–0.6 mm and, for mica schist, also 1.4 mm. Quartz-feldspar aggregates, sometimes with clay or black/oxidized material, often very altered and cloudy, strained extinction, in some cases, porphyroblastic feldspars surrounded by quartz. Mica schist, usually with biotite (some altered), banded, occasionally grading into grains that are otherwise indistinguishable from the quartz-feldspar aggregates. Brown to golden phyllite, rarely with crenulation; micaceous brown phyllite is rarer.

Few: Calcite, mostly in the form of round lumps of micrite, much altered, eq, r, mode 0.3–1.2 mm, one very altered fragment, preserved primarily in the darkened ring around its edges, is in the shape of a microfossil (foraminifera). Acid volcanic rocks, some with trachytic texture, others porphyritic with feldspar phenocrysts, sometimes turning to cloudy red in places, el, r, mode 0.4 mm.

Rare: Sandstone (quartz arenite and arkose), grains sometimes showing strained extinction (partially metamorphosed?), eq, sr–r, mode 0.3 mm; greywacke, eq, r, mode 0.6 mm.

Very rare: Intermediate igneous rock (diorite?), very weathered, primarily composed of plagioclase, biotite, and quartz, eq, r, up to 1.2 mm; brown amphibole, el, 0.3 mm; pyroxene(?), eq, sa, 0.3 mm.

Fine Fraction
Dominant: Quartz (mono- and polycrystalline), feldspar, plagioclase, eq, sa–sr.
Common: Altered calcite, eq, r; biotite laths.
Rare: Volcanic rocks as above, eq, r; phyllite or mica aggregates, el, r; chert, el, r.
Very rare: Pyroxene(?), eq, sa; birefringent orange grains, eq and el, r, sometimes almost opaque in xpl.

Tcfs
Few, red brown to almost black (ppl), red to red brown (xpl), merging boundaries, high optical density, eq, sr–r, mode 0.15 mm.

GROUP 9: MICACEOUS, SILT-SIZED INCLUSIONS

Fabrics in this group have a silty, micaceous groundmass and relatively few coarse inclusions, especially compared to the groups above. The groundmass is colorful in xpl, owing to the presence of amphibole and birefringent orange grains, including serpentinite, at least in the case of PFG 9A.

SUBGROUP A: SERPENTINITE
Samples: 51, 87, 108

This group is not very homogenous and may well represent products from multiple places. All are associated with Cycladic wares. The mixed metamorphic and possible igneous inclusions could be compatible with several origins, although no precise petrographic parallels have been located. The abundant serpentinite, especially in 51, is very unusual. Serpentinite-rich fabrics have been found as part of other studies in the Aegean islands (Hilditch 2007, 241; Quinn et al. 2010, 1046) but neither of those fabrics seems very similar to the samples in this group. Although serpentinite and meta-serpentinite occur on several islands, the nearest major outcrops are on southern Euboea, Andros, and Tenos, which are in proximity also to metamorphic rocks (Hinsken et al. 2017; Katzir et al. 2007; Mehl et al. 2007). Talc, notably, appears with the serpentinites of Tenos, as well as in these samples, which may suggest that island as a more probable source. Such an origin, however, must remain hypothetical at this stage, especially since serpentinite is not mentioned as a significant component in a previous study of Hellenistic fabrics from Tenos (Etienne and Gautier 1983). Sample 51 refired to pink; 87 refired to red; 108 refired to variable pink.

Microstructure
Few–rare voids, mostly macro-vughs, some with calcite rims; a couple with darkening around void, perhaps burned-out organics (87); roughly oriented parallel to vessel walls. Inclusions single- to double-spaced; those with a long axis are roughly oriented parallel to vessel walls.

Groundmass
Not homogenous; yellow brown, pale reddish brown to brown or greenish brown (ppl); yellow or brown to very dark brown (xpl) (40x); optically slightly active to inactive.

Inclusions
c:f:v$_{0.15\,mm}$, 25:70:5 to 10:85:5. Moderately well-sorted, eq and el, a–r, <1.4 mm, mode 0.2–0.6 mm, unimodal size distribution.

Coarse fraction
Common: Biotite and white mica laths, rarely tabular crystals; rarely mica aggregates (which are sometimes surrounded by red-brown material), mode 0.2–0.3 mm, occasionally with titanite(?) inclusions, some of the white mica has first-order birefringence colors.
Common–few: Calcite, eq and el, a–r, mode 0.2–0.6 mm. Micrite lumps and angular fragments, perhaps recrystallized/micritized calcite crystals and some oblong and gently curving probable shell fragments, some with dark-brown rims. Feldspar-quartz-amphibole-mica aggregates, all minerals not always present, feldspars sometimes very altered, eq and el, sa–sr, mode 0.2–0.6 mm. Epidote/clinozoisite, eq, sa, 0.2 mm, rarely attached to quartz or mica.
Common–very rare: Serpentinite, bright orange, sometimes with mesh-like texture in xpl, eq, sa–sr, mode 0.2–0.3 mm. Grains of unknown origin, brown to orange-brown in ppl, appears micritic in some cases in xpl, although in some cases the birefringence is lower than typical, sometimes attached to bright orange material, probably serpentinite; perhaps altered carbonate of some sort (e.g., magnesite or ophicalcite)(?), el, sa–r, 0.2–0.5 mm.
Very few: Amphibole (mostly brown), altered, eq, a–sa, mode 0.2 mm.
Very few–absent: Talc(?), sometimes pale brown in ppl, slightly el, sr, 0.2–0.5 mm (51, 108); plutonic rock fragments, some may be metamorphosed, with alkali feldspar ± plagioclase ± biotite ± brown amphibole ± pyroxene, in one case with attached clinozoisite(? first-order interference colors), eq, sa, 0.2–1.0 mm (108).
Rare: Quartz, eq, a, mode 0.2 mm; quartz-mica schist, el, sa, 0.2–1.0 mm.
Very rare–absent: Volcanic rock fragments, eq and el, r, 0.15–0.6 mm. Lava fragment with porphyritic texture and quartz(?) and alkali feldspar phenocrysts (108); altered fragment with red-brown groundmass and variolitic texture (87).

Fine fraction
Dominant: Biotite and white mica laths; quartz/feldspar and more rarely quartz/feldspar-mica aggregates, eq, sa–sr.
Common–very few: Amphibole, eq, a; epidote/clinozoisite, eq, a–sr.
Common–very rare: Birefringent yellow-orange grains, eq, sa–sr; micrite lumps (eq, r) and probable shell fragments (el, sa).
Few–very rare: Talc(?) as above.
Very few: Opaques, eq, a.

Tcfs
Very few–absent, red to brown (ppl), red brown (xpl), sharp to merging boundaries, optically dense, el, sr, mode 0.3–0.6 mm, with quartz, calcite/micrite, epidote/clinozoisite and/or mica inclusions. (Absent from 51).
Dark brown to nearly opaque (ppl), birefringent shimmering red brown to opaque (xpl), sharp to rarely merging boundaries, optically dense, eq and el, a–sr, mode 0.2–0.3 mm.

Variant: 54
Much less amphibole and no serpentinite. Brown grains of unknown origin like those above exist, however, and the other inclusions appear similar to those above. Refired to pink, turning red at the surfaces.

SUBGROUP B: QUARTZ, PLAGIOCLASE, AMPHIBOLE
Sample: 147

Inclusions in this fabric are mostly fine, and many are not very distinctive (quartz and feldspar). In addition to mica, there are fairly common amphiboles and fresh-looking plagioclase in the fine fraction, which might suggest a volcanic origin, like Aegina. It is, however, impossible to be certain, especially with only one sample in this group. Refired to pink.

Microstructure
Few voids, meso- and macro-vughs and channels, with some voids in the shape of foraminifera; those with a long axis oriented parallel with vessel walls. Inclusions single-spaced, mostly fine; oriented parallel to vessel walls.

Groundmass
Homogenous, brown (ppl), dark red brown (xpl) (40x), optically inactive, patchy secondary calcite in places.

Inclusions
c:f:v$_{0.1\,mm}$, 5:70:25. Poorly sorted, eq and el, a–sr, <0.8 mm, mode <0.1 mm, unimodal size distribution.

Coarse fraction
Common: Feldspar, untwinned and albite twinning, eq and el, a–sr, 0.4–0.5 mm. Quartz (mono- and polycrystalline), eq and el, a–sr, 0.2–0.5 mm.
Few: Micritic and rarely sparitic lumps and rarely elongated sparitic grains (perhaps infilling voids?), some altered, eq, sr, 0.3–0.5 mm.
Rare: Chert, el, sa, 0.5 mm; quartzite, el, sa, 0.5 mm; dark-brown grain of unknown origin, el, sr, 0.6 mm; brown amphibole, el, a, 0.2 mm; mica laths, 0.2 mm.

Fine fraction:
Common: Quartz and feldspar, as above, including plagioclase and polycrystalline quartz; mica laths; amphibole, mostly brown, as above.
Few: Birefringent orange grains, sometimes opaque or with anomalous extinction in xpl, eq and el, r.
Rare: Chert, el, r; epidote(?), el, sr.

Tcfs
Few, red to red brown (ppl, xpl), sharp to diffuse boundaries, optically dense, eq and el, mostly fine (<0.1 mm) with a few larger elongated grains; probably clay pellets
Very few, very pale brown (ppl), opaque (xpl), sharp to diffuse boundaries, low optical density, eq and el, <0.1–0.3 mm.

GROUP 10: SPONGE SPICULES
Sample: 128

Macroscopically, this fabric resembles typical Melian/Theran fabrics in texture, if not in all inclusions, and the decoration of the object sampled strongly suggests a Cycladic provenance. No petrographic parallels for this fabric, however, are known. A Melian/Theran provenance is possible, given the metamorphic outcrops on those islands and the presence of spicules in sedimentary deposits there (Calvo et al. 2012; Fouqué 1879). Chemically, however, preliminary interpretation of the WD-XRF results suggests that this fabric differs significantly from proposed Melian/Theran fabrics in PFG 5. Refired to pink, varying in shade.

Microstructure
Few voids, mostly meso- and macro-vughs, roughly oriented parallel to vessel walls. Inclusions open-spaced, predominantly silty, no clear orientation.

Groundmass
Not homogenous, pale brown to brown at core (ppl), dark brown to pale yellow at core (xpl) (40x), slightly optically active.

Inclusions
c:f:v$_{0.2\,mm}$, 2:60:38. Moderately well-sorted, eq and el, sa–r, <1.1 mm, mode <0.2 mm, unimodal size distribution.

All inclusions considered together, all with mode <0.2 mm:
Frequent: Quartz/feldspar, most too small to tell the difference, although polycrystalline quartz, plagioclase, and probable quartz-feldspar aggregates exist; some with attached biotite, rarely, chlorite, titanite, and/or epidote(?), many of which are probably derived from metamorphic rock fragments, el and eq, sa–r.
Common: Birefringent yellow inclusions, eq, r; microfossils, including sponge spicules and possible diatoms.
Few: Biotite, and rarely white mica laths.
Very few: Calcite, altered, probably micritic, brown in ppl, speckled yellow/black in xpl in most grains, rarely with quartz and mica inclusions (probably limestone), eq and slightly el, r.
Rare: Amphibole (hornblende), el, r; birefringent orange grains, rarely with quartz inclusions, slightly el, r.
Very rare: Titanite(?), eq, r. Rock fragments of unknown origin, mostly brown, with included grains of epidote/clinozoisite(?) and mica, eq and slightly el, r; one fragment encased in red-brown material. Brown siltstone(?) with r quartz, feldspar, and birefringent yellow inclusions, eq, r.

Tcfs
Few, red, red brown or nearly opaque (ppl, xpl); sharp to somewhat diffuse boundaries; optically dense; eq to rarely el, r, up to 0.2 mm, but majority much smaller; occasionally with tiny quartz/feldspar inclusions; similar tcf in one case appears to be streaked.

GROUP 11: MODERATELY FINE, METAMORPHIC AND CALCAREOUS INCLUSIONS

This is a mixed group, for which few parallels exist. Fabrics derive from environments with metamorphic and calcite-rich rocks. Such a combination is typical for Attica and Euboea, although not exclusive to them. Additional research is needed to narrow down the origin(s) of this group.

SUBGROUP A: LOW-FIRED, REDUCED
Sample: 143

This fabric is low-fired, probably in a reducing environment. Its ware (Gray Minyan) suggests a source on mainland Greece or Euboea. Refired to pink.

Microstructure
Few voids, mostly macro-vughs and elongate macro-channels, sometimes with calcite infilling, one channel surrounded by darkened clay (perhaps burned-out organic), oriented parallel to channel walls. Inclusions open-spaced, oriented more or less parallel to vessel walls.

Groundmass
Not homogenous, yellow to dark brown, darker in patches and toward exterior surface (probably from reduction firing) (ppl, xpl) (40x), very optically active.

Inclusions
$c:f:v_{0.3\,mm}$, 20:65:15. Poorly sorted, eq and el, sr–r, <3.1 mm, mode 0.5–1.4 mm, bimodal size distribution.

Coarse fraction
Predominant: Calcite, el, a (shell) or r, mode 1.0–1.4 mm. Micrite, some sparite, some holycrystalline fragments. Limestone (probably), occasionally with small angular quartz or mica inclusions; shell fragments; some calcite has altered to dark brown (ppl, xpl) especially near exterior edge of sherd.
Very few: Metamorphic rock fragments, el, sr, mode 0.5–0.6 mm. Quartz-mica schist, with white mica and biotite, rarely with chlorite or epidote/clinozoiste; quartz (mono- and polycrystalline with sutured boundaries) with undulose extinction.
Very rare: Opaques, slightly el, irregular, a–sr, mode 0.5 mm.

Fine fraction
Dominant: White mica laths.
Frequent: Polycrystalline quartz and quartz/feldspar (often indistinguishable from each other), undulose extinction, eq and slightly el, sa.
Common: Calcite, as above. Includes microfossil (foraminifera) and shell fragments, with at least one probable bivalve.
Very few: Epidote/clinozoisite, eq and el, sa–sr; metamorphic rock fragments as above; opaques as above.

Tcfs
Few, brown, dark brown, or nearly opaque (ppl, xpl); sharp to rarely diffuse boundaries; optically dense; eq and el, r, up to 1.8 mm, occasionally with apparent crystallitic b-fabric and small quartz/feldspar, calcite, and mica inclusions that strongly resembles the browner edge of the sample groundmass, possibly grog(?).

SUBGROUP B: BIOGENIC LIMESTONE
Sample: 146

Biogenic limestone, which appears in this fabric, is noted as a primary component in one of the main fabrics at Lerna (Myer, Betancourt, and Vaughan 1995), but limestones are widespread in the Aegean, as are metamorphic rocks (Higgins and Higgins 1996). Macroscopically, an Attic origin was hypothesized, but a recent petrographic study of Attic fabrics does not contain a close parallel (Gilstrap 2015). Refired to pink; paint is red-brown.

Microstructure
Few voids, meso- and macro-vughs and channels, occasionally with calcite rims, roughly oriented parallel to vessel walls. One area of voids surrounding clay nodules that were probably not adequately hydrated during manufacture. Inclusions open-spaced, roughly oriented parallel to vessel walls.

Groundmass
Not homogenous, turning slightly darker toward one side, with a few red or red-brown streaks, otherwise orange-brown (ppl), orange (xpl) (40x), very optically active.

Inclusions
c:f:v$_{0.15\,mm}$, 20:65:15. Moderately well-sorted, eq and el, sr–r, <0.8 mm, mode 0.3–0.6 mm, bimodal size distribution.

Coarse fraction
Predominant: Calcite, mostly micritic, sometimes sparitic, eq and el, r, mode 0.3–0.6 mm. Limestone, altered, with small angular quartz inclusions, birefringent orange material, sometimes opaques, and rare foraminifera bioclasts; microfossils including foraminifera.
Rare: Quartz-mica schist, mostly biotite, el, sr–r, mode 0.3–0.6 mm; quartz, mono- and rarely polycrystalline, undulose extinction, el, sr, mode 0.4 mm.

Fine fraction
Dominant: Quartz/feldspar, eq, a.
Frequent: Calcite including limestone and microfossils as above, mostly micritic, although some sparitic and holocrystalline grains exist.
Few: Birefringent orange and red grains (clay?), eq and el, sr.
Very few: Metamorphic rock fragments including both biotite and white mica schists; mica laths (mostly white mica); epidote/clinozoisite, el, sa.
Rare: Chert, el, a–sa; opaques, eq, sa.
Very rare: Titanite(?), el, a.

Tcfs
Very few; red, red-brown or nearly opaque (ppl); orange, red, or nearly opaque (xpl); sharp to rarely somewhat diffuse boundaries; optically dense; eq and slightly el, up to 0.6 mm; occasionally with tiny quartz/feldspar or mica inclusions.

GROUP 12: SILTY

This group is mixed. The micaceous fabrics are dominated by fine sand- and silt-sized inclusions. It is difficult to assess their provenance on the basis of petrographic analysis alone.

SUBGROUP A: METAMORPHIC, RARE AMPHIBOLES
Sample: 154

This noncalcareous fabric is presumably derived from a geological area that includes metamorphic rocks of green- and blueschist (or transitional) facies, given the presence of both epidote/clinozoisite and rare blue amphiboles (glaucophane). The ware of this sample was hypothesized to be Euboean. A fabric with blueschist and greenschist facies inclusions at Eretria (FG 3) is hypothesized to be from part of the Cycladic/Aegean Blueschist Unit, whether the southern part of Euboea or the northwest Cyclades (Charalambidou et al. 2016); that fabric is much coarser than PFG 12A, so the two are not entirely comparable. Chemically, preliminary interpretation of the WD-XRF results demonstrates that this fabric is incompatible with an origin in the Lelantine Plain (FG 8), and there are also some chemical differences from FG 3 (compare with Charalambidou et al. 2016, table 2). Future analysis will be required to clarify the relationship (or not) between PFG 12A and the Eretrian fabrics. Refired to red.

Microstructure
Very few voids, mostly macro-vughs, rare meso- and macro-channels; those with a long axis oriented parallel with vessel walls. Inclusions single-spaced, nearly entirely fine, weakly oriented parallel to vessel walls.

Groundmass
Not homogenous, pale brown to red-brown (ppl), yellow to orange-red (xpl) (40x), optically active.

Inclusions
c:f:v$_{0.15\,mm}$, 10:80:10. Relatively densely packed, well-sorted, eq and el, a–sr, <0.2–0.3 mm, unimodal size distribution.

All inclusions considered together, all <0.3 mm:
Dominant: Quartz, feldspar (including plagioclase), and quartz/feldspar, eq and el, a–sa, occasionally with attached mica or pale green amphibole(?).
Common: Epidote/clinozoisite, some of which is green in ppl, eq and el, a–sr; mica laths, mostly white mica.
Very few: Metamorphic rock fragments, including schist with epidote and opaques and polycrystalline quartz with sutured boundaries and undulose extinction. Opaques, eq, sa–sr.
Rare: Amphibole (brown [hornblende?] and blue/lilac [glaucophane]), eq, sa.
Very rare: Tourmaline(?), eq, sr.

Tcfs
Few, red brown to nearly opaque (ppl, xpl), sharp to diffuse boundaries, optically dense, eq and el, r, <0.2 mm.

SUBGROUP B: FINE BROWN CALCAREOUS
Sample: 158

This fabric, which contains limestone(?) and microfossils, is not very petrographically distinctive. The origin of the ware is also unknown. Refired to pale pink.

Microstructure
Few voids, meso- and macro-vughs and channels, oriented generally parallel to vessel walls. Inclusions single-spaced, oriented generally parallel to vessel walls.

Groundmass
Not homogenous, brown to dark brown (ppl), yellow to dark brown (xpl) (40x), optically active.

Inclusions
$c:f:v_{0.15\,mm}$, 10:70:20. Moderately well-sorted, eq and el, sr–r, <0.3 mm, unimodal size distribution.

All inclusions considered together, all <0.3 mm:
Common: Quartz, feldspar, and aggregates thereof, rarely with attached mica, eq and el, sr–r. Calcite, small sparitic or holocrystalline fragments. Limestone(?); microfossils, generally micritic, including foraminifera, ostracods(?), and shell. Mica laths, primarily white mica, occasionally biotite or white mica aggregates, el, sr.
Very few: Opaques, eq and el, r–sr.
Rare: Birefringent yellow-orange to orange-brown grains, el, r; epidote/clinozoisite, eq, sr–r.
Very rare: Tourmaline(?), el, sa.

Tcfs
Few, dark brown to opaque (ppl), red brown to dark brown (xpl), sharp to rarely merging boundaries, optically dense, eq and el, r.

SUBGROUP C: SPECKLED RED AND BROWN, WITH SILTSTONE
Sample: 168

The groundmass of this fabric is speckled red and brown. It appears quite similar to Hilditch's (2004) Group 16 (Urfirnis and Yellow Mottled) from EBA Ayia Irini, especially sample 97/31, which is of unknown origin. Refired to pink.

Microstructure
Few voids, meso- and macro-vughs and channels, weakly oriented parallel to vessel walls. Inclusions nearly entirely fine, double- to open-spaced, oriented parallel to vessel walls.

Groundmass
Not homogenous, speckled red brown and greenish gray (ppl), red and dark greenish brown (xpl) (40x), optically slightly active.

Inclusions
$c:f:v_{0.15\,mm}$, 2:65:33. Well-sorted and entirely fine apart from one large oxidized siltstone grain (el, r, 2.7 mm long), eq and slightly el, sr–r, unimodal size distribution.

All other inclusions considered together (all apart from mica are eq or slightly el, sr–r), all <0.2 mm
Dominant: Quartz/feldspar (often impossible to distinguish from one another) and, more rarely, polycrystalline quartz and plagioclase; feldspars occasionally altered with attached biotite.
Frequent: Biotite and white mica laths.
Few: Birefringent orange-red grains.
Very few: Chert(?); yellow grains (ppl) that turn opaque or nearly opaque in xpl, altered calcite(?).
Very rare: Calcite, micrite lumps, altered and rimmed in black; altered brown amphibole(?).

Tcfs
Few, opaque (ppl), red brown (xpl), sharp to diffuse boundaries, eq and el, r, up to 0.4 mm, but most <0.15 mm; probably clay pellets.

GROUP 13: FINE, MICACEOUS, RED-BROWN ROUND TCFS

These fabrics are relatively fine with metamorphic inclusions. They have similarities to Euboean and Attic fabrics.

SUBGROUP A: FINE, DARK RED PELLETS
Samples: 140, 144, 155

This fabric and the next (PFG 13B) are very similar to each other. The major differences are that this fabric is more orange tinged in color (most visible looking at the slides without magnification), with red tcfs that are darker in color (ppl, xpl) than in PFG 13B and which sometimes bear inclusions (especially in 155). These tcfs are probably clay pellets. Coarse metamorphic rock fragments are very rare or absent. One of the variants (145) has similarities to Gilstrap's (2015, 80–86, 263–265; Gilstrap et al. 2016, 503–505) FG 1A and related Attic fabric groups. Preliminary interpretation of the WD-XRF results suggests that this group and the next group derive from different locations. Chemical and petrographic dissimilarities to the proposed fine local fabric (FG8) at Eretria (Charalambidou et al. 2016) suggest that the Lelantine Plain, at least, can be excluded as an origin for this group. Given the petrographic parallels between the variant 145 and Attic fabrics, Attica may be a more probable origin, but it is impossible to determine provenance on the basis of petrography alone. Refired to pink. Sample 155 refired to dark pink with a well-defined paler core.

Microstructure
Few voids, meso- and macro-vughs and channels, some calcite infilling especially in 140, voids with a long axis oriented parallel with vessel walls. Inclusions open-spaced, roughly oriented parallel to vessel walls.

Groundmass
Not homogenous; pale yellow or grayish yellow, pale orange brown, or red brown (ppl); orange, red, red brown, or gray (xpl) (40x); gray core in both 140 and 155; optically active to slightly active.

Inclusions
c:f:$v_{0.15\,mm}$, 20:60:20, 33:47:20. Well-sorted, eq and el, sa–r, <0.6 mm, mode <0.15–0.3 mm, unimodal size distribution.

All inclusions considered together:
Dominant: Monocrystalline quartz and/or feldspar (including rare plagioclase; some feldspars with tiny mica inclusions), eq and el, sa–r. Some polycrystalline quartz also appears, el, sa–r, mode <0.15–0.3 mm.
Frequent–very few: Mica laths, generally very fine (<0.1 mm), occasionally tabular crystals.
Very few–absent: Gray-brown siltstones with poorly sorted, angular inclusions of quartz/feldspar, mica, and birefringent orange grains, slightly el, r, 0.2–0.5 mm.
Rare–absent: Clinopyroxene(?), el, sa–sr, <0.15 mm; birefringent orange to red grains, el, sr, <0.15 mm.
Very rare: Brown amphibole, eq, sa, 0.15–0.2 mm.
Very rare–absent: Mica schist, el, sr, 0.3 mm; epidote/clinozoisite(?), eq, sa, <0.05 mm.

Tcfs
Common, red brown to nearly opaque (ppl), red to dark red or nearly opaque (xpl), sharp to diffuse boundaries, optically dense, most eq and slightly el, r, sizes as above, sometimes bearing small quartz/feldspar or birefringent orange grains; probably clay pellets.
Rare–absent, slightly paler yellow brown than primary groundmass (ppl), dark gray (xpl), clear to diffuse boundaries, optically neutral, bearing small quartz/feldspar grains, eq and el, r, 0.4 mm.

Variant: 145
Nearly entirely fine and somewhat darker brown (ppl) and darker orange-brown (xpl) than the main group. There are a few possible microfossils (foraminifera? rather degraded), more common white mica than biotite, some calcite/micrite lumps, and yellow-brown tcfs that appear to be similar to those discussed by Gilstrap (2015, 80–86, 263–265; Gilstrap, Day, and Kilikoglou 2016, 503–505) among Attic fabrics. Refired to pink; paint refired to red.

Variant: 151
Finer than the main group, with more common mica and less quartz/feldspar. Refired to pink.

SUBGROUP B: RED, COARSE METAMORPHIC ROCKS
Samples: 122, 150, 165, 166

This fabric and the previous one (PFG 13A) are very similar to one another. This fabric is darker red, with some micritic inclusions in the coarse and fine fraction. In addition, red tcfs are generally without inclusions, show a broader range of sizes, and are typically a paler, brighter red than those that appear in PFG 13A. Sample 122 has a cleaner groundmass and fewer voids. Preliminary interpretation of the WD-XRF results suggests that this fabric may derive from the Lelantine plain, given similarities to FG 8 at Eretria (Charalambidou et al. 2016). Most refired to pink; 166 refired to red. Sample 122 refired to variable shades of pink.

Microstructure
Few–very few voids, meso- and macro-vughs and more rarely channels; those with a long axis oriented parallel with vessel walls. Inclusions open-spaced, weakly oriented parallel to vessel walls.

Groundmass
Not homogenous; pale brown, red brown, brown or slightly greenish brown (ppl); orange, yellow, red, or red brown, often turning browner or grayish red at core (xpl) (40x); optically active.

Inclusions
c:f:$v_{0.15\,mm}$, 20:60:20, 10:65:25. Moderately well-sorted, eq and mostly el, sr–r, <1.4 mm, mode 0.3–0.5 mm, bimodal size distribution.

Coarse fraction
Predominant: Metamorphic rock fragments, mostly el, sr–r, mode 0.3–0.5 mm. Quartz-feldspar aggregates, sometimes with fine mica, red-brown material, amphibole, and/or opaques; some quite coarse-grained; one grain (122) with possible epidote/clinozoisite and radiating high-relief blades of an unidentified mineral; quartzite. Quartzes often show undulose extinction, sutured boundaries.
Few–rare: Red-brown tcfs, eq and slightly el, r, with sharp to diffuse boundaries, mode 0.3–0.5 mm. Calcite, altered, mostly micrite lumps, mostly opaque in xpl, eq, r, mode 0.4 mm, possible shell fragments in 122.

Fine fraction
Frequent–common: Quartz/feldspar and metamorphic rock fragments as above.
Frequent–few: Biotite and white mica laths; tcfs as above.
Few–rare: Birefringent orange and yellow grains, eq, sr.
Few–very few: Micrite lumps as above.
Few–absent: Microfossils (foraminifera?), altered, little internal structure, dark in xpl, eq, r.
Rare–absent: Chert, el, a–sa.

Tcfs
Described above; those with diffuse boundaries are especially likely to be clay pellets. A second kind exists: few–very few, gray-brown or pale yellow-orange (ppl), opaque or speckled (xpl), sharp to merging boundaries, low optical density, eq and el, r, up to 0.8 mm, most <0.3 mm, with small quartz/feldspar and mica inclusions.

Variant: 127
The groundmass appears very similar to the main group, but coarse metamorphic rocks are very rare. Tcfs are consistently diffuse at boundaries, and there are more elongate versions as well.

APPENDICES

GROUP 14: FINE

This is a mixed group of fine fabrics, for which provenance is impossible to determine on the basis of petrography alone. Owing to the small size of the original samples, it was not possible to submit all of these for WD-XRF analysis. Those that were analyzed using WD-XRF, apart from samples 157 (PFG 14Bv) and 148 (PFG 14Dv), seem to have relatively similar chemical profiles, according to preliminary interpretation of the results, especially samples 160 and 167 (PFG 14Bv), 159 (PFG 14C), and 169 (PFG 14D); such similarities could suggest a common origin for many of the subgroups. With one exception (sample 71), all associated wares were hypothesized to come from mainland Greece or Euboea.

SUBGROUP A: TCFS/MUDSTONES, HIGH-FIRED
Sample: 71

The majority of red tcfs have diffuse boundaries and are most likely to be clay pellets, though a few probable mudstones also exist. Other inclusions are extremely rare but appear to be entirely sedimentary. Refired to yellow with dark red-brown paint.

Microstructure
Very few voids, mostly macro-vughs, few meso-vughs, no orientation. Inclusions open-spaced, roughly oriented parallel to vessel walls.

Groundmass
Relatively homogenous; greenish brown (ppl, xpl) (40x); optically inactive; patchy crystallitic b-fabric, probably secondary calcite.

Inclusions
$c:f:v_{0.1\,mm}$, 15:75:10. Well-sorted, eq and el, sr–r <0.7 mm, mode 0.15–0.4 mm, unimodal size distribution.

Coarse fraction
Dominant: Tcfs, brown to dark red-brown (ppl), red (xpl), diffuse to sharp edges, rarely with inclusions of some combination of calcite, quartz/feldspar, mica, chert(?), birefringent orange grains, and/or yellow grains (black in xpl), optically dense to optically neutral, eq, rarely el, r, mode 0.15–0.4 mm. More rarely, possible mudstones (although in color they are much the same as the tcfs, with sharp boundaries and optically dense), eq and el, sr–r, mode 0.2–0.3 mm; these appear in both the clay body and slip layer.
Few: Micrite lumps, eq and irregular, r, mode 0.2–0.3 mm. Mudstones/siltstones, with a red-brown matrix identical to the mudstones and tcfs above, inclusions moderately well-sorted, a–r fragments of one or more of the following: quartz, chert, feldspar(?), occasionally biotite, and a yellow-orange grain that turns opaque in xpl; these mudstones/siltstones appear in both clay body and slip layer, eq, sa–r, mode 0.3–0.4 mm.
Very rare: White mica laths, 0.2 mm.

Fine fraction
Dominant: Quartz and/or feldspar, eq, sa; quartz/feldspar with red-brown clay or biotite attached, el, sr.
Common: Yellow-orange grains, either birefringent in xpl or turning opaque, eq, sa–r.
Few: Biotite and more rarely white mica laths.
Rare: Polycrystalline quartz, el, sr.
Very rare: Orange-red birefringent grains, eq, sr.

Tcfs
In addition to those described above, tcfs are common, pale brown (ppl), speckled gray or opaque (xpl), sharp boundaries, some of which have curving internal structure in ppl that resembles microfossils, low optical density, eq and slightly el, r, mode 0.05–0.08 mm; perhaps burned-out calcareous/microfossils(?).

SUBGROUP B: RED TCFS, MUDSTONES, FINE MICA
Samples: 152, 161, 162

Although they lack the distinctive cracking of PFG 7F and 7G, several samples of this subgroup (including the variants) appear quite similar to those subgroups in color, texture, and composition. Unfortunately, only variants 157, 160, and 167 could be analyzed using WD-XRF. Preliminary interpretation of the results suggests that these differ somewhat in their chemistry from the PFG 7G samples; future programs of study are required to clarify the relationship of PFG 14B and PFG 7G. All refired to pale pink, often with some variation, turning darker pink at the margin, paler at surface, or streaked dark and pale pink. When present, slip refired red.

Microstructure
Few–very few voids, meso- and macro-vughs, occasionally appear to be in shape of burned-out microfossils (esp. 152), occasionally cracking around inclusions (161) or around clay particles that may not have been fully hydrated during forming (152). Inclusions open-spaced, no orientation.

Groundmass
Not homogenous; yellow, pale brown, gray brown (ppl); yellow, gray, orange brown, yellow brown (xpl) (40x); some red clay streaking (152, 162); optically slightly active to nearly inactive.

Inclusions
c:f:v$_{0.1\,mm}$, 10:65:25, 15:50:35, 20:30:50. Well-sorted, eq and slightly el, sr–r, identifiable inclusions between 0.1–0.6 mm, unimodal size distribution.

All inclusions considered together, all are eq and slightly el, sr–r, mode 0.1–0.6 mm unless otherwise noted:
Dominant–common: Calcite, micrite lumps, mostly altered with black rim or almost entirely opaque in xpl; in finer fraction, some of the altered calcite may be microfossils since some are similar in shape to foraminifera.
Dominant–very few: Mudstones, red, el and more rarely eq, <0.15–0.6 mm; red tcfs with merging or diffuse boundaries, <0.15–0.6 mm; quartz (mono- and polycrystalline), sa, mode 0.1–0.2 mm, very rarely with attached biotite.
Very few–rare: Mica laths (most very fine, <0.1 mm, except in 157).
Rare–very rare: Birefringent orange-red grains, <0.15 mm.
Very rare–absent: Chert, eq, r, <0.1 mm; siltstone, sometimes with angular inclusions, 0.1–0.2 mm.

Tcfs
Discussed above.

Variant: 153
Red brown in xpl. Inclusions are primarily red tcfs and calcite, with much secondary calcite infiltration. A few siltstones and at least one possible altered igneous rock fragment exist, but otherwise the fabric appears very similar to the samples above. Refired to very pale pink, with slip refired to red.

Variant: 157
Pale yellow brown (ppl) and yellow (xpl), with high optical activity (low-fired). Tcfs are dominant and can be large (up to 1.3 mm) and quite amorphous; large (0.2 mm long) microfossils are rare. Chemically, this fabric also differs from the other PFG 14 fabrics, based on preliminary interpretation of the WD-XRF results. Refired to pink.

Variant: 160
Rare calcite (all opaque in xpl) and a few coarse siltstones/sandstones (poorly sorted with some angular grains), 0.6–1.0 mm. The shape of one elongate void suggests that it resulted from organic material burning out. Refired to very pale pink with a well-defined dark pink ring around the margin.

Variant: 167
Red to yellow or greenish brown in xpl, with prominent clay streaks. The most common identifiable inclusions are altered calcite and siltstones. Refiring showed streaks of dark and pale pink.

SUBGROUP C: GREENISH-YELLOW, SERPENTINITE(?)
Sample: 159

This fabric is somewhat similar to PFG 14B, but it is more green in color and with serpentinite(?); red tcfs are probably clay pellets. It may be from a geologically similar area. Future programs of study will be required to clarify the origin of the fabric. Refired to yellow; paint refired to red.

Microstructure
Few voids, meso- and macro-vughs and channels, most filled with secondary calcite, weakly oriented parallel to vessel walls. Inclusions, open-spaced, roughly oriented parallel to vessel walls.

Groundmass
Homogenous, greenish brown (ppl), greenish gray (xpl) (40x), some red streaking (clay mixing), optically slightly active, patches and streaks of secondary calcite throughout.

Inclusions
c:f:v$_{0.1\,mm}$, 40:30:30. Fine groundmass with a handful of identifiable rock fragments and red tcfs. Poorly sorted, eq and slightly el, sa–r, mode 0.1–0.6 mm, unimodal sizez distribution.

All inclusions considered together:
Dominant: Quartz/feldspar (often difficult to distinguish from one another), eq and el, sa–r, <0.1 mm; rarely, polycrystalline quartz.
Common: Calcite, mostly altered; some micrite/sparite lumps are better preserved but rimmed with brown or opaque material, eq, r, mode 0.1–0.6 mm.
Few: Mica laths, very fine (<0.05 mm). Birefringent yellow-orange to orange-red grains (serpentinite?), sometimes with dark-brown streaks and anomalous birefringence and extinction in xpl, eq and el, r, <0.05–0.3 mm.
Rare: Sedimentary rock fragments, eq and slightly el, r, 0.3–0.7 mm. Siltstones/sandstones, moderately poorly sorted with some angular grains, including quartz, feldspar, mica, and birefringent orange inclusions; brown mudstones/siltstones.

Tcfs
Very few, opaque (ppl), red brown (xpl), sharp to diffuse boundaries, optically dense, eq and el, r, rarely up to 0.5 mm, but most <0.15 mm; probably clay pellets.

GROUP D: FINE, CALCITE
Samples: 169, 170

This fabric, with predominant calcite inclusions, appears to be broadly similar to Hilditch's (2004, 36) Group 20 from EBA Ayia Irini, which she tentatively associated with the Lelantine Plain of Euboea. Given the wares represented, an origin in Euboea or Boeotia seems possible, and neither can be ruled out petrographically (see also Hilditch et al. 2008). Sample 169 was submitted for WD-XRF analysis, but preliminary interpretation of the results suggests that it is incompatible with the main local fine fabric (FG 8) at Eretria (Charalambidou et al. 2016, table 2). A variant, however (148), does appear to be chemically compatible with FG 8 at Eretria, according to preliminary interpretation of the WD-XRF results. Both samples refired to very pale pinkish yellow, turning dark pink to red in a thin band at the margins.

Microstructure
Few–rare voids, mostly meso-vughs and channels, rare macro-vughs, generally oriented parallel to vessel walls, some (169) appear to be filled with post-depositional clay/soil. Inclusions open-spaced, oriented generally parallel to vessel walls (169) or no orientation (170).

Groundmass
Not homogenous; dull greenish brown, pale yellow, or dark gray (ppl); yellow to greenish brown (xpl) (40x); slightly darker at core; optically very active (170) to slightly active (169).

Inclusions
c:f:v$_{0.1\,mm}$, 25:25:50, 45:45:10. Fine groundmass with a handful of identifiable inclusions and red tcfs. Moderately well-sorted to well-sorted, eq and el, a–r, mode 0.1–0.2 mm, unimodal size distribution.

All inclusions considered together:
Predominant–frequent: Calcite, mostly eq, r, <0.1–0.3 mm. Micrite lumps, occasionally with quartz inclusions, altered in 169 (including yellowish crystals that turn opaque in xpl); sa equant grains that are probably recrystallized/micritized calcite crystals; a few small grains might be microfossils (foraminifera?), based on their shape, but they do not have clear internal structure.
Frequent–very few: Quartz (mono- and polycrystalline), feldspar (untwinned or with albite twinning), and quartz/feldspar (too small to identify), occasionally with attached biotite, eq and el, a–r, mode 0.1–0.2 mm. Mica, mostly white mica (<0.05 mm) but occasionally strained aggregates (0.5 mm).
Rare: Birefringent yellow or orange-red grains (serpentinite?), anomalous extinction in xpl, el and eq, sr–r, <0.5–0.2 mm.
Rare–very rare: Chert(?), el, sr, 0.3–0.4 mm.
Rare–absent: Red-brown mudstones/tcfs with sharp boundaries, slightly el, r, mode 0.2 mm.
Very rare–absent: Siltstone with angular quartz inclusions, eq, r, mode 0.15 mm; brown birefringent grain, eq, sr, 0.3 mm; green amphibole, el, sa, 0.2 mm; opaque, eq, r, 0.2 mm.

Tcfs
Common–few, red to opaque (ppl), red to red brown (xpl), sharp to diffuse boundaries, optically dense, eq and el, r, rarely up to 0.2 mm, but most <0.1 mm.

Variant: 148
Entirely gray, with almost no coarse inclusions. Predominantly partially altered calcite/micrite lumps; very fine mica, quartz (mono- and polycrystalline), rare mica schist (mostly biotite), quartz-feldspar aggregates, chert, and birefringent yellow-orange grains. Red-brown to nearly opaque tcfs are nearly entirely fine (<0.15 mm). Refired to pink.

APPENDIX VI: FABRIC GROUP MUNSELL COLORS

Fabric group	Munsell range	Munsell color
RBMa	2.5YR 3/3–7/6, 5YR 4/4–5/6, 2.5Y 4/1–3/1–GLEY 1 3/	Red, reddish brown, dark reddish brown, yellowish red, reddish yellow, light red, black, dark gray, very dark gray
RBMb	2.5YR 4/4–5/6, 5YR 4/1–5/6	Red, reddish brown, reddish gray, yellowish red
RBMc	2.5YR 4/6–5/8	Red, reddish brown
RBMd	2.5YR 4/4–5/8	Red
RBMe	2.5YR 5/6	Red
FSTa	10YR 7/4–8/3	Very pale brown
FSTb	5YR 7/6–8/4	Reddish yellow, pink
FSTc	5YR 6/8–7/6–7.5YR 5/4–7/4	Reddish yellow, pink, brown
FSTd	5YR 6/4–7.5YR 8/3	Light reddish brown, pink
FSTf	2.5YR 5/6–5YR 6/6	Red, light red, reddish yellow
FSTg	2.5YR 7/4–8/3	Light reddish brown, pink
FSTh	10YR 8/3–7.5YR 8/3	Very pale brown–pink
FSTi	5YR 5/6–6/6	Yellowish red, reddish yellow
FSTj	7.5YR 7/4–10YR 7/4	Pink, very pale brown
FSTk	5YR 6/4–7.5YR 6/4	Light reddish brown, reddish yellow, light brown
DVa	2.5Y 7/4–10YR 8/4	Very pale yellow, pale yellow, very pale brown, pink
DVb	5YR 6/6–7.5YR 7/4	Reddish yellow, pink
DVc	10YR 7/3–8/3	Very pale brown
DVd	2.5Y 8/3–10YR 8/4	Pale yellow, very pale brown
DVe	5YR 6/6–7.5YR 7/6	Reddish yellow, pink
DVf	2.5YR 5/6–6/6	Red, light red
DVg	2.5Y 7/3–7/4	Pale yellow
MxMa	5YR 5/4–10YR 7/4	Very pale brown, reddish brown, yellowish brown, yellowish red, pink, reddish yellow
MxMb	2.5YR 5/8–6/6	Light red, red
MxMc	5YR 5/6–7.5YR 7/6	Reddish yellow
MxMd	2.5YR 5/6–6/6	Light red, red

Fabric group	Munsell range	Munsell color
MxMe	10YR 5/1–2.5YR 5/6	Gray, red
MxMf	2.5YR 5/4–5YR 6/4	Reddish brown, light reddish brown, reddish yellow, light red
MxMg	2.5YR 6/8–5YR 7/6	Light red, reddish yellow
CSWa	2.5YR 4/6	Red
CSWb	2.5YR 6/8–5YR 5/6	Light red, yellowish red
CSWc	GLEY 5/–5YR 6/6	Gray, reddish yellow
CSWd	GLEY 1 3/–5YR 5/6	Black, very dark gray, red, yellowish red
CSWe	2.5YR 5/6–5YR 7/8	Red, reddish yellow, yellowish red
PBS	2.5YR 5/6	Red
MFVa	7.5YR 6/4	Light brown
MFVb	7.5YR 5/1–10YR 6/1	Gray
MFVc	2.5YR 5/8–5YR 7/4–7/6	Red, reddish yellow, pink
MFVd	5YR 7/4–7/2	Reddish yellow
FVa	GLEY 1 6/–10YR 5/1	Gray, very dark gray
FVb	2.5Y 8/2–10YR 8/3	Pale yellow, very pale brown
FVc	5YR 7/6–7.5YR 7/6	Reddish yellow, pink
FVd	2.5YR 6/6–5YR 7/6	Light red, reddish yellow
FVe	7.5YR 7/4–10YR 8/3	Pink, very pale brown
FVf	2.5YR 6/4–5YR 6/4	Light reddish brown
FVg	5YR 6/6–10YR 6/6	Reddish yellow
FVh	5YR 6/6–7/2	Reddish yellow, pinkish gray

APPENDIX VII: RESULTS OF WAVE-DISPERSIVE X-RAY FLUORESCENCE

A "v" after the PFG code (e.g., 1Cv) designates a fabric variant.

Sample name	Macro group	PFG	Na2O (%)	MgO (%)	Al2O3 (%)	SiO2 (%)	P2O5 (%)	K2O (%)	CaO (%)	TiO2 (%)	V (PPM)	Cr (PPM)	Mn (PPM)	Fe2O3 (%)
SA_B001	RBMa	1C	2.19	2.99	20.55	55.45	0.270	2.16	2.13	0.883	188	251	1999	11.28
SA_B002	RBMa	1Cv	2.39	4.13	15.65	57.64	0.107	1.85	4.27	0.876	163	381	933	9.05
SA_B003	RBMa	1D	0.83	1.99	19.65	63.87	0.110	2.24	0.92	0.781	159	318	987	9.59
SA_B004	RBMa	1A	1.64	2.66	17.52	57.84	0.454	1.95	1.84	0.846	189	358	958	10.31
SA_B005	RBMa	1B	2.98	3.08	17.52	57.34	0.360	2.98	2.17	0.946	185	161	611	8.19
SA_B009	RBMb	1B	2.46	3.16	18.91	54.46	0.250	2.91	2.52	0.900	195	263	1170	10.18
SA_B010	RBMb/RBMc	2Av	0.89	2.57	15.99	66.08	0.372	2.32	0.90	0.717	143	296	974	8.74
SA_B015	RBMa	1Av	1.29	4.40	14.03	68.72	0.185	1.29	0.53	0.625	109	697	986	8.95
SA_B017	CSWe	4A	3.06	1.24	17.85	64.70	0.172	3.05	1.15	0.531	62	66	243	4.70
SA_B019	RBMav	2Bv	1.10	2.41	19.52	60.42	0.202	2.89	0.75	0.791	176	285	1327	11.19
SA_B020	RBMc	2Bv	0.84	6.90	17.58	62.45	0.055	2.20	0.39	0.469	97	329	1513	8.60
SA_B021	RBMc	2B	1.33	2.31	16.89	67.70	0.084	2.36	0.70	0.787	141	216	1061	8.20
SA_B022	RBMc	1Cv	1.72	2.13	17.34	55.84	0.143	2.55	3.91	0.558	137	221	1027	8.90
SA_B023	RBMd	1D	1.49	2.81	17.82	62.44	0.100	2.23	1.82	0.798	166	267	1322	10.04
SA_B024	RBMd	2Cv	2.31	4.62	16.54	61.53	0.068	1.78	3.13	0.941	182	367	890	9.15
SA_B026	RBMbv	1Bv	1.27	1.91	20.45	56.67	0.090	3.16	0.50	0.936	164	233	609	11.87
SA_B027	RBMav	1Cv	1.91	2.71	18.14	54.01	0.378	2.19	2.53	1.040	204	272	2019	13.51
SA_B028	RBMav	2B	0.87	4.69	17.59	62.61	0.162	1.80	1.18	0.615	143	718	943	9.89
SA_B030	RBMa	1A	2.55	2.20	16.75	61.50	0.417	2.16	1.80	0.987	147	195	717	8.89
SA_B032	RBMe	2Av	0.43	1.44	17.09	70.39	0.041	2.88	0.30	0.851	135	128	1391	6.45
SA_B033	RBMe	2A	2.02	3.20	17.66	62.24	0.075	2.31	1.57	0.903	150	291	1239	8.83
SA_B034	RBMe	2A	1.98	3.06	16.14	63.81	0.094	2.66	1.31	0.968	143	270	786	8.21
SA_B035	RBMa	1C	1.36	2.08	19.38	60.04	0.141	2.89	1.16	0.920	159	210	944	8.56
SA_B036	RBMa	1C	1.24	3.36	18.39	55.85	0.271	2.93	1.97	0.708	171	286	1189	9.93
SA_B038	RBMa	1Cv	1.39	1.83	17.73	61.19	0.511	2.51	1.09	0.485	137	215	942	8.93
SA_B039	RBMa	1Cv	1.34	1.81	18.46	62.64	0.266	2.68	0.79	0.506	122	201	1081	8.62
SA_B040	RBMa	1A	1.67	2.38	15.30	68.50	0.250	2.04	0.83	0.784	130	258	867	7.58
SA_B041	RBMa	1Bv	1.06	2.08	22.16	58.72	0.121	3.42	0.79	0.958	156	136	319	9.66
SA_B047	RBMd	2Cv	3.79	4.05	18.91	52.17	0.070	2.03	3.56	0.840	216	293	1067	11.56
SA_B048	RBMd	1A	2.55	2.67	17.41	60.60	0.114	2.73	0.90	0.910	150	368	840	9.80
SA_B049	RBMa	1D	1.11	2.73	16.93	65.40	0.210	2.38	1.22	0.742	151	256	1703	8.99
SA_B050	RBMa	2B	0.69	3.09	18.46	63.16	0.222	1.86	0.67	0.806	170	513	1057	10.60

APPENDIX VII: RESULTS OF WAVE-DISPERSIVE X-RAY FLUORESCENCE (CONT.)

Co (PPM)	Ni (PPM)	Cu (PPM)	Zn (PPM)	Rb (PPM)	Sr (PPM)	Y (PPM)	Zr (PPM)	Ba (PPM)	La (PPM)	Ce (PPM)	Nd (PPM)	Pb (PPM)	Th (PPM)	LOI (%)	Sum (%)
42	242	115	1560	81	145	38	116	388	28	42	22	839	10	2.37	100.88
44	251	89	81	58	122	30	113	173	24	50	21	17	7	5.18	101.40
41	294	101	99	93	58	47	129	352	41	58	41	40	10	0.80	101.06
38	238	99	86	65	225	40	93	246	34	55	40	229	11	6.01	101.37
36	104	73	87	63	186	30	148	259	26	53	30	52	10	5.37	101.15
39	189	68	96	90	162	52	128	269	42	65	54	54	10	5.16	101.20
40	274	119	101	84	110	39	123	287	36	58	40	72	13	2.55	101.42
61	573	103	101	55	55	31	97	188	24	50	38	43	9	1.04	101.39
15	27	48	45	103	188	13	185	548	25	40	17	30	19	4.97	101.58
39	213	165	144	114	78	40	122	485	42	54	43	134	12	1.78	101.40
25	257	71	103	77	37	50	118	364	37	55	43	49	12	1.63	101.44
34	174	61	76	88	53	47	144	324	34	57	38	24	13	0.80	101.42
31	187	91	145	91	103	54	99	299	49	63	50	80	13	7.69	101.06
44	259	79	105	79	112	73	114	236	62	59	60	89	8	1.44	101.31
50	209	57	77	50	177	29	130	212	23	38	29	27	7	0.91	101.24
37	153	128	109	117	152	31	191	296	34	67	32	72	16	3.95	101.05
41	193	143	120	72	212	60	126	333	51	63	57	51	13	4.51	101.33
47	449	59	101	63	68	34	98	256	31	44	29	39	8	1.75	101.48
34	103	103	109	64	184	26	146	1418	28	69	25	76	7	3.94	101.53
34	71	63	962	112	35	31	175	527	27	56	34	497	10	1.01	101.31
39	196	70	83	74	133	30	140	291	31	56	35	30	8	2.38	101.48
39	175	87	106	86	127	31	156	282	27	53	28	33	9	2.74	101.21
33	143	84	184	106	103	32	162	312	28	65	37	72	14	4.29	101.09
36	188	116	106	94	124	49	103	461	34	47	38	36	11	6.45	101.41
30	164	108	86	75	160	56	69	507	51	59	67	42	12	5.11	101.05
31	159	99	85	89	129	46	82	474	47	50	56	49	14	3.86	101.25
40	212	72	79	81	93	33	123	311	29	53	28	44	9	1.65	101.23
28	69	50	126	126	95	33	230	305	51	101	55	64	18	1.75	100.90
50	115	92	69	47	198	21	82	328	20	32	18	27	7	3.91	101.17
43	190	106	122	92	108	28	139	325	31	57	37	122	11	3.55	101.52
40	238	86	89	92	71	74	92	321	54	56	61	30	10	1.16	101.21
50	522	88	143	70	70	46	108	342	32	52	34	36	8	1.18	101.07

Sample name	Macro group	PFG	Na2O (%)	MgO (%)	Al2O3 (%)	SiO2 (%)	P2O5 (%)	K2O (%)	CaO (%)	TiO2 (%)	V (PPM)	Cr (PPM)	Mn (PPM)	Fe2O3 (%)
SA_B051	MxMa	9A	2.09	9.43	12.93	47.88	0.319	2.16	10.01	0.785	149	797	1160	8.41
SA_B053	MxMa	3C	2.23	4.00	15.34	48.51	0.087	2.09	9.48	0.746	163	173	986	8.45
SA_B054	MxMa	9Av	2.47	4.73	16.45	50.81	0.145	1.92	9.08	0.777	183	189	1027	9.27
SA_B056	FSTa	7A	1.29	6.88	16.19	53.77	0.224	2.42	7.87	0.833	144	416	1003	8.91
SA_B058	FSTiv	8B	1.03	1.94	15.08	52.78	0.624	2.34	12.57	0.787	128	230	1433	7.63
SA_B059	FSTiv	8C	1.69	3.08	18.64	56.06	0.305	3.56	6.95	0.793	143	94	1189	7.66
SA_B062	FSTh	7G	0.65	4.01	16.67	52.18	0.445	2.66	11.60	0.828	162	302	1129	7.75
SA_B065	FSTe	7E	1.03	7.07	14.52	55.59	0.153	2.46	9.15	0.749	113	458	774	7.87
SA_B066	FSTb	6A	1.41	7.08	14.09	54.23	0.166	2.06	12.09	0.728	126	480	1179	7.95
SA_B067	FSTe	6C	1.41	5.43	15.58	61.85	0.167	2.14	4.55	0.773	149	340	765	7.90
SA_B068	FSTc	7D	1.29	7.34	11.45	55.06	0.333	1.85	9.08	0.662	140	665	922	7.71
SA_B069	FSTiv	8E	1.98	1.95	17.56	61.71	0.259	2.93	5.05	0.826	108	145	1005	6.35
SA_B070	FSTj	7Gv	1.84	4.44	15.96	51.72	0.359	2.35	12.17	0.781	156	299	1535	8.27
SA_B071	FSTjv	14A	1.03	3.25	14.68	48.69	0.222	2.53	17.39	0.716	110	245	1057	6.83
SA_B072	FSTk	7Gv	0.93	9.53	16.23	50.22	0.138	2.82	8.20	0.805	147	441	1040	9.57
SA_B075	FSTd	7H	0.89	3.57	16.06	52.32	0.144	2.71	11.21	0.736	121	282	1106	8.47
SA_B076	FSTi	8D	1.07	2.53	15.97	64.63	0.256	3.21	3.66	0.726	92	85	638	5.74
SA_B078	FSTi	8D	1.07	2.69	16.75	55.57	0.245	3.43	8.19	0.758	130	119	439	6.78
SA_B082	FSTg	7C	1.90	6.56	14.19	55.33	0.239	2.00	9.94	0.797	143	464	735	7.53
SA_B089	MxMa	5C	2.20	2.47	16.94	58.96	0.542	3.60	3.69	0.746	103	242	609	6.23
SA_B090	DVa	5B	1.46	2.80	12.19	62.03	1.826	3.43	7.79	0.476	92	144	985	4.83
SA_B092	DVc	5D	1.80	2.01	11.53	42.57	0.186	1.71	19.46	0.445	62	118	638	3.55
SA_B093	DVc	5D	1.78	2.25	14.72	60.57	0.239	2.30	7.43	0.533	81	202	632	4.86
SA_B103	MxMc	4B	1.68	2.26	11.77	48.52	0.467	2.51	13.79	0.546	87	230	807	4.97
SA_B105	MxMc	3Cv	2.26	3.38	17.94	58.13	0.130	3.20	2.90	0.822	109	139	1079	7.54
SA_B107	MxMd	3D	2.46	3.50	12.28	53.90	0.280	1.73	8.97	0.778	128	367	1037	6.92
SA_B108	MxMe	9A	1.68	4.26	18.27	49.91	0.172	3.01	10.74	0.754	157	229	1685	8.61
SA_B110	DVdv	5Av	2.61	2.16	15.04	52.45	0.382	2.17	14.16	0.577	63	157	903	4.73
SA_B111	MxMf	5H	2.57	4.59	18.05	51.20	1.176	2.46	9.29	0.767	157	239	1038	8.78
SA_B113	MxMf	3C	2.76	4.62	16.41	46.87	0.439	2.74	8.21	0.773	161	248	771	8.41
SA_B114	CSWe	4C	2.52	2.69	17.83	61.69	0.090	3.50	2.98	0.760	83	80	904	6.61
SA_B119	MxMa	3Cv	2.60	3.47	12.59	55.42	0.987	2.03	7.73	0.794	139	387	727	7.05
SA_B122	MFVc/DVe	13B	2.04	2.64	21.01	55.89	0.209	3.95	4.87	0.851	145	166	1037	7.91
SA_B125	DVe	5G	1.49	3.45	9.31	49.65	0.357	1.89	16.32	0.551	83	406	573	5.33
SA_B126	DVa	5Bv	2.11	2.90	12.58	58.32	0.355	2.76	10.32	0.498	94	124	623	4.77
SA_B128	DVg	10	2.17	4.13	9.75	61.44	0.909	2.14	7.64	0.629	97	558	725	6.34

Co (PPM)	Ni (PPM)	Cu (PPM)	Zn (PPM)	Rb (PPM)	Sr (PPM)	Y (PPM)	Zr (PPM)	Ba (PPM)	La (PPM)	Ce (PPM)	Nd (PPM)	Pb (PPM)	Th (PPM)	LOI (%)	Sum (%)
60	521	78	105	61	199	24	120	282	16	40	24	6	6	6.56	100.93
36	86	93	106	53	177	24	105	311	24	38	17	16	5	9.61	100.78
41	84	74	103	54	196	26	107	314	20	37	17	20	6	4.96	100.87
49	399	64	102	96	240	21	129	349	28	57	23	28	9	2.16	100.86
43	149	115	143	86	429	35	204	391	43	74	43	56	10	5.9	101.03
36	55	65	107	139	198	30	175	510	42	75	43	39	14	2.01	101.05
47	316	69	90	108	276	28	122	480	34	70	26	72	9	3.77	100.90
48	407	64	99	99	173	21	124	303	25	53	27	26	8	2.23	101.11
45	423	60	88	82	265	23	110	239	26	48	26	33	8	1.24	101.37
41	278	46	92	81	182	23	157	289	26	50	28	22	8	1.20	101.26
36	530	70	101	70	211	23	116	305	26	45	19	20	6	4.20	99.31
20	88	55	94	115	262	29	249	519	43	86	40	37	17	1.87	100.78
50	324	77	110	101	348	26	119	347	30	64	28	43	10	2.71	100.96
47	247	75	89	105	561	23	117	374	23	62	33	12	9	5.56	101.22
60	525	91	115	111	161	24	119	290	24	50	20	72	10	2.26	101.04
48	297	91	101	137	266	25	117	346	32	61	29	21	9	4.35	100.77
27	45	48	93	119	141	30	217	303	37	67	35	29	14	3.26	101.25
30	94	68	104	141	155	28	175	442	32	59	34	36	12	5.61	101.32
42	347	64	77	78	281	23	146	570	31	48	24	18	10	1.85	100.63
32	173	90	85	142	323	33	264	704	53	108	37	56	29	5.34	101.03
26	97	52	104	111	225	24	137	386	30	53	26	62	11	3.65	100.75
11	78	51	81	47	323	20	124	538	20	42	24	16	9	17.13	100.61
31	101	49	104	79	282	19	139	516	27	52	23	36	10	6.15	101.08
29	202	75	78	80	355	25	166	932	34	61	26	23	11	13.78	100.62
32	85	71	134	137	214	27	229	390	38	76	35	237	17	4.70	101.28
29	251	58	84	47	262	24	127	228	23	41	26	10	4	9.99	101.06
42	144	96	105	92	175	30	134	426	30	52	30	33	8	2.96	100.70
28	87	54	75	67	498	21	158	668	28	68	27	12	10	6.42	100.99
45	120	91	113	65	197	29	123	407	31	56	25	24	7	1.89	101.04
43	125	94	89	70	292	25	110	790	31	51	23	9	6	9.32	100.85
28	43	49	87	159	251	30	215	405	54	101	40	43	30	2.37	101.30
34	226	94	70	49	290	24	129	374	21	40	19	10	5	8.08	101.01
34	104	56	103	144	118	31	143	665	36	75	35	38	15	1.21	100.88
29	277	61	109	52	326	21	124	319	23	38	17	21	5	12.4	100.98
25	84	49	73	94	298	24	144	388	31	51	29	20	11	6.31	101.14
31	333	92	75	64	287	24	140	218	19	44	20	10	7	5.79	101.22

Sample name	Macro group	PFG	Na2O (%)	MgO (%)	Al2O3 (%)	SiO2 (%)	P2O5 (%)	K2O (%)	CaO (%)	TiO2 (%)	V (PPM)	Cr (PPM)	Mn (PPM)	Fe2O3 (%)
SA_B129	CSWa	4A	3.26	0.99	18.92	62.73	0.314	2.75	1.67	0.654	75	90	179	5.83
SA_B130	CSWb	2C	3.05	4.93	19.21	55.73	0.053	1.29	3.12	1.306	200	518	1228	11.60
SA_B136	CSWd	2Cv	1.34	1.47	18.63	63.92	0.243	1.93	1.60	0.950	187	261	965	9.87
SA_B138	CSWe	4Av	3.25	1.41	15.87	71.18	0.025	1.85	0.36	0.648	41	112	879	5.37
SA_B139	CSWd	2C	1.65	2.22	18.55	61.31	0.127	2.67	1.50	0.891	185	220	1415	10.53
SA_B141	MFVa	3Cv	2.34	4.76	18.68	51.18	0.394	2.77	5.24	0.900	147	220	1073	9.03
SA_B142	MFVb	3H	1.54	2.73	15.24	61.24	0.323	2.33	4.86	0.637	142	301	724	7.83
SA_B144	MFVc	13A	1.21	5.19	18.46	56.78	0.141	3.13	4.39	0.909	138	453	715	8.84
SA_B145	MFVc	13Av	1.09	4.64	17.01	54.31	0.118	3.26	5.92	0.848	144	550	1088	8.16
SA_B147	No group	9B	2.07	4.33	17.26	57.95	0.444	3.78	5.81	0.728	117	283	478	6.54
SA_B148	FVa	14Dv	1.67	2.74	20.56	56.23	0.278	3.59	6.39	0.851	151	162	1067	7.55
SA_B151	FVf	13Av	1.68	3.36	20.21	55.51	0.292	3.91	5.02	0.878	157	322	1075	7.99
SA_B154	FVhv	12A	3.13	2.71	17.66	62.07	0.119	2.27	1.88	1.046	161	173	503	6.63
SA_B155	FVh	13A	1.06	3.14	19.73	58.14	0.248	3.00	4.19	0.847	153	328	1167	8.56
SA_B157	FVg	14Bv	0.49	5.90	18.51	58.68	0.092	3.22	1.98	0.442	105	500	1106	5.98
SA_B159	FVb	14C	1.35	3.77	16.17	48.98	0.156	2.43	16.10	0.789	132	237	930	7.41
SA_B160	FVc/FVe	14Bv	1.26	3.86	16.73	54.68	0.164	2.95	10.15	0.854	139	219	877	7.83
SA_B165	FVd/FVf	13B	1.70	2.51	20.49	57.26	0.165	3.83	4.69	0.852	123	157	1070	7.55
SA_B166	FVd/FVf	13B	1.49	2.74	20.67	56.26	0.198	3.84	5.51	0.858	145	169	1006	7.82
SA_B167	FVd	14Bv	1.32	4.26	17.97	49.78	0.309	3.59	11.46	0.815	157	223	1001	8.31
SA_B168	No group	12C	1.89	4.74	17.27	57.17	0.214	3.79	7.44	0.726	102	267	435	6.65
SA_B169	FVe	14D	1.14	3.78	17.15	50.76	0.297	3.09	12.96	0.814	174	222	1245	8.01

Co (PPM)	Ni (PPM)	Cu (PPM)	Zn (PPM)	Rb (PPM)	Sr (PPM)	Y (PPM)	Zr (PPM)	Ba (PPM)	La (PPM)	Ce (PPM)	Nd (PPM)	Pb (PPM)	Th (PPM)	LOI (%)	Sum (%)
9	16	63	45	81	238	16	166	559	23	39	26	59	22	4.03	101.31
50	274	123	84	55	104	26	103	82	11	21	16	18	4	1.09	101.69
27	128	67	88	74	117	39	166	274	36	63	35	35	12	0.90	101.11
8	132	21	61	74	41	28	249	475	27	81	25	36	9	1.30	101.51
26	187	72	104	90	120	57	145	298	42	56	52	53	11	1.22	100.98
28	156	82	160	128	228	34	169	631	35	72	39	40	13	5.66	101.28
18	179	71	82	78	208	33	125	423	30	49	32	47	9	4.49	101.47
36	352	88	148	146	164	31	149	481	35	66	33	35	13	1.62	100.98
39	382	77	121	135	215	26	137	533	34	63	26	39	11	5.06	100.77
20	229	45	85	157	432	31	250	702	57	107	46	53	26	2.00	101.22
24	122	30	111	137	126	32	157	681	43	77	35	32	15	0.78	100.95
27	152	52	101	155	132	29	143	604	33	72	24	51	13	1.28	100.43
17	72	60	99	65	137	30	236	342	28	61	34	61	9	3.42	101.15
29	236	51	118	127	108	35	187	500	40	80	44	36	13	1.60	100.85
29	324	67	291	148	84	19	116	331	25	49	22	111	13	5.66	101.30
28	182	65	96	114	453	24	123	382	29	58	27	14	10	3.61	101.05
26	167	72	98	132	287	24	139	317	28	61	29	27	11	2.27	101.01
22	114	42	87	146	130	31	164	658	43	82	37	46	14	1.55	100.90
23	134	51	99	150	123	32	155	682	40	80	37	50	14	1.38	101.06
30	174	79	104	162	435	26	116	409	31	64	32	29	12	3.01	101.13
24	235	37	106	161	406	32	248	637	57	103	48	61	26	0.96	101.15
28	177	61	106	147	473	25	120	466	30	57	31	34	10	2.62	100.95

APPENDIX VIII: EXCAVATION UNIT INFORMATION

Unit B03-	Location of unit	Kea Excavation Notebook	Page no.	↑ Elevation (m)	↓ Elevation (m)	CL
11	B.1–B.4, Alley AB	III	11–13	?	+3.10S/+2.50N	
18	B.1–B.4, Alley AB	III	27–28	+3.10S/+2.50N	+3.00S/+2.20N	
19	B.1–B.4	III	28	+3.40S, +2.20/2.05N	+2.90S, +2.20/+2.00N	604, 608, 609
20	B.1–B.4	III	31–33	+2.90S, +2.20/+2.00N	+2.40S, +2.00/+1.75N	604
21	Alley AB	III	31	?	?	
25	B.1	III	36	+2.45S, +2.00/+1.75N	+1.75	608
27	B.1	III	38	+1.75	+1.60	608
28	B.1	III	40	+1.60	+1.40	608
29	B.1	III	40	+1.40	+1.30	609
31	B.1	III	42	+1.30	+1.20	609
33	B.1	III	42	+1.20	+1.10	609
35	B.1	III	46	+1.10	+0.85	609
36	B.2/B.3 and B.4	III	49–52, 56	+2.70NE /+3.20SW	+2.40	604
37	B.2/B.3 and B.4	III	52	?	?	
39	B.1	III	55	+0.85	+0.75	609
40	B.2	III	57–58	+2.40	+2.00	605
41	B.1	III	59	+0.75	+0.59NE/+0.67NW/ +0.69SE/+0.75SW	609
42	B.2	III	61	+2.00	+1.80	605
43	B.2/B.3 and B.4	III	61	+2.40	+2.00	604
44	B.2/B.3 and B.4	III	62	+2.00	+1.60	604
46	B.2/B.3 and B.4	III	64–65	+1.60	+1.30	606
50	B.4	III	69	+1.40	+1.15	
51	B.2/B.3 and B.4	III	69	+1.30	+1.10	606
52	B.2	III	70–71	+1.80	+1.30	606
57	B.2/B.3 and B.4	III	73, 152	+1.30	+1.10	606
61	B.2/B.3 and B.4	III	75	+1.10	+1.00	606
64	B.2	III	78	+1.00	+0.68SE/+0.70SW/ +0.73NE/+0.73NW/ +0.78Mid	606
70	B.4	III	80, 82	+1.00	+0.65	

Unit B03-	Location of unit	Kea Excavation Notebook	Page no.	↑ Elevation (m)	↓ Elevation (m)	CL
71a	B.4	III	75, 78	+1.10	+1.00	
72	B.4	III	84	+0.65	+0.40	
73	B.4	III	84	+0.40	+0.20	602
74	B.4	III	84	+0.20	0.00	602
76	B.1	III	85	+0.70	+0.50	610
78	B.1	III	85	+0.50	+0.40	610
79	B.1	III	88	+0.40	+0.30	601
81	B.1	III	88	+0.30	+0.25	601
83	B.1	III	90	+0.25	0.00	602
87	Alley AB	III	94	+3.00S/+2.20N	+2.20	
88	Alley AB	III	94–95, 97	+2.20	+1.90	
93	B.1	III	102	+1.40	+0.59NE/+0.67NW/ +0.69SE/+0.75SW	609
94	Alley AB	III	97	+1.90	+1.60	
95	B.1	III	103–104	+0.70	+0.48	610
96	Alley AB	III	97	+1.60	+1.00	
97	Alley AB	III	105	+1.00	+0.70	
98	B.1	III	106	+0.70	+0.60	610
99	B.1	III	106–107	+0.60	+0.40	610
103	B.2, B.3	III	111	+0.70	+0.60	607
104	B.2	III	111	+0.60	+0.50	607
105	B.2	III	112	+0.50	+0.40	603
106	B.2	III	112	+0.40	+0.20	603
107	B.3	III	113	+0.60	+0.50	607
108	B.3	III	113	+0.50	+0.45	
109	B.2	III	113	+0.45	+0.20	603
114	B.2	III	115	+0.20	0.00	602
116	B.1	III	118	+0.48	+0.28	601
117	B.1	III	118	+0.28	+0.10	601
118	B.1	III	119	+0.10	-0.10	602
142	B.1	III	138	+0.48	+0.38	601
143	B.1	III	138	+0.38	+0.28	601
144	B.1	III	138–139	+0.28	+0.20	601
145	B.1	III	139	+0.28	+0.20	601

Unit B03-	Location of unit	Kea Excavation Notebook	Page no.	↑ Elevation (m)	↓ Elevation (m)	CL
146	B.1	III	140	+0.20	+0.10	602
147	B.1	III	140–141	+0.10	-0.20	602
148	B.8	III	146	+0.65	+0.15	
149	B.1	III	150	+0.28	+0.20	601
249	B.8	III	147	+0.15	+0.15	
250	B.4	III	148, 151	?	?	
506	B.8	XXXVIII	30–34	+0.39/+0.36	+0.20/+0.18	
764	Alley AB	III	164	?	+2.42SW/+2.35NE	
765	Alley AB	III	164–165	+2.42SW/+2.35NE	+2.27	
766	Alley AB	III	165	+2.27	+2.18	646
767	Alley AB	III	166	+2.18	+2.10	646
768	Alley AB	III	166	+2.10	+2.00	646
769	Alley AB	III	167	+2.00	+1.90	647
770	Alley AB	III	167	+2.00	+1.90	
771	Alley AB	III	167	+1.90	+1.60	647
772	Alley AB	III	168	+1.60	+1.40	647
773	Alley AB	III	168	+1.40	+1.25	647
774	Alley AB	III	168–169	+1.90	+1.90NE/+1.78SW	
775	Alley AB	III	169–170	+1.90NE/+1.78SW	1.78	
776	Alley AB	III	170	+1.78	+1.78NE/+1.73SW	648
777	Alley AB	III	170	+1.78NE/+1.73SW	+1.66	648
778	Alley AB	III	171	+1.75NE/+1.70SW	+1.70	648
779	Alley AB	III	171	+1.88	+1.70	
780	Alley AB	III	171	+1.73/+1.70	+1.64	
781	Alley AB	LVIII	8	+1.64	+1.58	
782	Alley AB	LVIII	8–9	+1.75E/+1.70W	+1.70E/+1.60W	648
783	Alley AB	LVIII	9	+1.70/+1.55	+1.70/+1.50	649
784	Alley AB	LVIII	10	+1.70	+1.50	649
785	Alley AB	LVIII	12	+1.57W/+1.50E	+1.50W/+1.43E	
786	Alley AB	LVIII	12	+1.50N/+1.43S	+1.43/+1.37	
787	Alley AB	LVIII	13	+2.30	+1.74	
788	Alley AB	LVIII	13	+1.43N/+1.37S	+1.38	
789	Alley AB	LVIII	14	+1.38	+1.30	
790	Alley AB	LVIII	15, 17	+1.30	+1.23	

Unit B03-	Location of unit	Kea Excavation Notebook	Page no.	↑ Elevation (m)	↓ Elevation (m)	CL
791	Alley AB	LVIII	15	+1.23	+1.15	791/793
792	Alley AB	LVIII	16	+1.70	+1.50	
793	Alley AB	LVIII	16	+1.15	+1.11	791/793
794	Alley AB	LVIII	16	+1.11	+1.06	
795	Alley AB	LVIII	18	+1.06	+0.90	795/a/796
795a	Alley AB	LVIII	18	+0.90	+0.90	795/a/796
796	Alley AB	LVIII	19	+0.90	+0.85	795/a/796
797	Alley AB	LVIII	19	+0.85	+0.75	797/798
798	Alley AB	LVIII	20	+0.75	+0.65	797/798
799	Alley AB	LVIII	20	+0.65	+0.56	
800	Alley AB	LVIII	21	+0.65	+0.54	800/801
801	Alley AB	LVIII	21	+0.54	+0.48	800/801
802	Alley AB	LVIII	21	+0.48	+0.39	
803	Alley AB	LVIII	22	+0.39	+0.34	
804	Alley AB	LVIII	23	+0.34	+0.25	
805	Alley AB	LVIII	23–25	+0.25	+0.15/+0.08	
806	Alley AB	LVIII	24–25	+0.15/+0.08	-0.30	
807	Alley AB	LVIII	27	+1.31	+1.25	
808	Alley AB	LVIII	27	+1.25	+1.13	
809	B.2	LVIII	31	+0.70	+0.50	
810	B.2	LVIII	31	+0.50	+0.30	
811	B.2	LVIII	31	+0.30	+0.25	
812	B.2	LVIII	32	+0.25	+0.20	
813	B.2	LVIII	34	+0.20	+0.14/+0.12	
814	B.2	LVIII	34	+0.14/+0.12	+0.09	
815	B.2	LVIII	35	+0.09	+0.05	
816	B.2	LVIII	35	+0.05	-0.05	
817	B.2	LVIII	35	-0.05	-0.15	
818	B.2	LVIII	36–37	-0.15	-0.05W/-0.34E	
819	B.2	LVIII	36	-0.30	-0.30	
820	B.2	LVIII	37	-0.34	-1.00	
821	B.2	LVIII	38, 41–43	-0.05	-0.40	
822	B.2	LVIII	39–41, 48	-0.27	-1.00	
823	B.2	LVIII	43–45	-0.50	-1.00	

Unit B03-	Location of unit	Kea Excavation Notebook	Page no.	↑ Elevation (m)	↓ Elevation (m)	CL
824	B.2	LVIII	45–46, 48–49	-1.00	-1.42	
825	B.1	LVIII	52	+0.50	+0.25	
825a	B.1	LVIII	52	+0.25	+0.25	
826	B.1	LVIII	53	+0.51	+0.30	
827	B.1	LVIII	53	+0.30	+0.22	
828	B.1	LVIII	53	+0.22	+0.15	
829	B.1	LVIII	54	+0.15	0.00	
830	B.2	LVIII	55	n/a	n/a	

REFERENCES

Abell, N. 2014a. "Migration, Mobility, and Craftspeople in the Aegean Bronze Age: A Case Study from Ayia Irini on the Island of Kea," *WorldArch* 46, pp. 551–568.

———. 2014b. "Reconsidering a Cultural Crossroads: A Diachronic Analysis of Ceramic Production, Consumption, and Exchange Patterns at Bronze Age Ayia Irini, Kea, Greece," PhD dissertation, University of Cincinnati.

———. 2016. "Minoanisation in the Middle Bronze Age: Evaluating the Role of Cycladic Producers and Consumers," *BSA* 111, pp. 71–93.

———. 2020. "Rethinking Household-Based Production at Ayia Irini, Kea: An Examination of Technology and Organization in a Bronze Age Community of Practice," *AJA* 124, pp. 381–416.

———. Forthcoming. "In Sync: Keian Insights on Pottery Chronologies at the Transition to the Late Bronze Age," *Hesperia*.

Abell, N., D. M. Crego, and J. C. Overbeck. Forthcoming. "The Cyclades and the Southeastern Aegean before the Late Bronze Age: A Keian Perspective," in *The Southeast Aegean/Southwest Coastal Anatolian Region: Material Evidence and Cultural Identity. I. The Early and Middle Bronze Age*, ed. T. Marketou and S. Vitale, Athens.

Abell, N., and M. Georgakopoulou. Forthcoming. "Metals and Metallurgy at Bronze Age Ayia Irini, Kea: A Preliminary Report," in *Third International Cycladological Conference, The Cyclades through Time: Space and People, Syros*, ed. E. Marmaras, D. Korres, G. Dardanos, L. Palaiokrassa, K. Chryssou, S. Psarras, and G. Gavalas.

Abell, N., and E. Gorogianni. 2019. "The Past in Practice: Craft Producers and Material Culture Change at Ayia Irini, Kea," in *MNHMH/MNEME: Past and Memory in the Aegean Bronze Age* (*Aegaeum* 43), ed. E. Borgna, I. Caloi, F. M. Carinci, and R. Laffineur, Liège and Leuven, pp. 655–658.

Abell, N., and J. Hilditch. 2016. "Adoption and Adaptation in Production Practices: Investigating Cycladic Community Interactions through the Ceramic Record of the Second Millennium B.C.," in *Beyond Thalassocracies: Understanding Processes of Minoanisation and Mycenaeanisation in the Aegean*, ed. E. Gorogianni, P. Pavúk, and L. Girella, Oxford, pp. 155–171.

Abramovitz, K. 1980. "Frescoes from Ayia Irini, Keos. Parts II–IV," *Hesperia* 49, pp. 57–85.

Åkerström, Å. 1987. *Berbati 2: The Pictorial Pottery* (*ActaAth* 4°, 36.2), Stockholm.

Alberti, M. E. 2008. "Textile Industry Indicators in Minoan Work Areas: Problems of Typology and Interpretation," in *Vestidos, textiles y tintes: Estudios sobre la producción de bienes de consume en la Antigüedad*, ed. C. Alfaro and L. Karali, València, pp. 25–35.

Andreadaki-Vlazaki, M. 1987. "Ομάδα νεοανακτορικών αγγείων απο τον Σταυρωμένο Ρεθύμνης," in *Ειλαπίνη: Τόμος τιμητικός για τον καθηγητή Νικόλαο Πλάτωνα*, ed. L. Kastrinaki, G. Orphanou, and N. Giannadakis, Herakleion, pp. 55–68.

———. 2011. "LM IB Pottery in Khania," in Brogan and Hallager 2011, pp. 55–74.

Andreou, S. 1978. "Pottery Groups of the Old Palace Period in Crete," PhD diss., University of Cincinnati.

Angelopoulou, A. 2008. "The 'Kastri Group': Evidence from Korfari ton Amygdalion (Panormos) Naxos, Dhaskalio Keros, and Akrotiri, Thera," in *Horizon: A Colloquium on the Prehistory of the Cyclades*, ed. N. Brodie, J. Doole, G. Gavalas, and C. Renfrew, Cambridge, pp. 149–165.

———. 2014. *Κορφάρι των Αμυγδαλιών (Πάνορμος) Νάξου: Μια οχυρωμένη Πρωτοκυκλαδική Ακρόπολη*, Athens.

Atkinson, T. D., R. C. Bosanquet, C. C. Edgar, A. J. Evans, D. G. Hogarth, D. Mackenzie, C. Smith, and F. B. Welch. 1904. *Excavations at Phylakopi in Melos*, London.

Augier, R., L. Jolivet, L. Gadenne, A. Lahfid, and O. Driussi. 2014. "Exhumation Kinematics of the Cycladic Blueschists Unit and Back-Arc Extension, Insight from the Southern Cyclades (Sikinos and Folegandros Islands, Greece)," *Tectonics* 34.1, pp. 152–185.

Bailey, A. S. 2007. "Appendix I: The Potters' Marks," in *Excavations at Phylakopi in Melos 1974–77* (*BSA* Suppl. 42), ed. C. Renfrew, N. Brodie, C. Morris, and C. Scarre, London, pp. 444–455.

Barber, R. L. N. 1974. "Phylakopi 1911 and the History of the Later Cycladic Bronze Age," *BSA* 69, pp. 1–53.

———. 1983. "The Definition of the Middle Cycladic Period," *AJA* 87, pp. 76–81.

———. 1984. "The Status of Phylakopi in Creto-Cycladic Relations," in Hägg and Marinatos 1984, pp. 179–182.

———. 1987. *The Cyclades in the Bronze Age*, Iowa City.

———. 2007. "The Middle Cycladic Pottery," in *Excavations at Phylakopi in Melos 1974–77* (*BSA* Suppl. 42), ed. C. Renfrew, N. Brodie, C. Morris, and C. Scarre, London, pp. 181–264.

———. 2008. "Unpublished Pottery from Phylakopi," *BSA* 103, pp. 43–222.

Barber, R. L. N., and O. Hadjianastasiou. 1989. "Mikre Vigla: A Bronze Age Settlement on Naxos," *BSA* 84, pp. 63–162.

Barley, N. 1994. *Smashing Pots: Works of Clay from Africa*, Washington, DC.

Barnard, K. A., and T. M. Brogan. 2011. "Pottery of the Late Neopalatial Periods at Mochlos," in Brogan and Hallager 2011, pp. 427–449.

Berg, I. 2007a. "Meaning in the Making: The Potter's Wheel at Phylakopi, Melos (Greece)," *JAnthArch* 26, pp. 234–252.

———. 2007b. *Negotiating Island Identities: The Active Use of Pottery in the Middle and Late Bronze Age Cyclades*, Piscataway, NJ.

Betancourt, P. P. 1985. *The History of Minoan Pottery*, Princeton.

———. 2011. "Pottery at Pseira in LM IB," in Brogan and Hallager 2011, pp. 401–412.

Bikaki, A. H. 1984. *Ayia Irini: The Potters' Marks* (*Keos* IV), Mainz.

Boulotis, C. 2000. "Travelling Fresco Painters in the Aegean Late Bronze Age: The Diffusion Patterns of a Prestigious Art," in *The Wall Paintings of Thera*, Athens, pp. 844–858.

———. 2009. "Koukonisi on Lemnos: Reflections on the Minoan and Minoanising Evidence," in Macdonald, Hallager, and Niemeier 2009, pp. 175–218.

Brogan, T. M. 2013. "'Minding the Gap': Reexamining the Early Cycladic III 'Gap' from the Perspective of Crete. A Regional Approach to Relative Chronology, Networks, and Complexity in the Late Prepalatial Period," *AJA* 117, pp. 555–567.

Brogan, T. M., and E. Hallager, ed. 2011. *LM IB Pottery: Relative Chronology and Regional Differences. Acts of a Workshop Held at the Danish Institute at Athens in Collaboration with the INSTAP Study Center for East Crete, 27–29 June 2007*, Århus.

Bronk Ramsey, C. 2009. "Bayesian Analysis of Radiocarbon Dates," *Radiocarbon* 51, pp. 337–360.

Bronk Ramsey, C., C. Renfrew, and M. J. Boyd. 2013. "The Radiocarbon Determinations," in *The Settlement at Dhaskalio* (The Sanctuary on Keros and the Origins of Aegean Ritual Practice: The Excavations of 2006–2008 1), ed. C. Renfrew, O. Philaniotou, N. Brodie, G. Gavalas, and M. J. Boyd, Cambridge, pp. 695–704.

Broodbank, C. 2000. *An Island Archaeology of the Early Cyclades*, Cambridge.

———. 2004. "Minoanisation," *PCPS* 50, pp. 46–91.

———. 2007. "Chapter 6: The Pottery," in *Keros, Dhaskalio Kavos: The Investigations of 1987–88* (Keros I), ed. C. Renfrew, C. Doumas, L. Marangou, and G. Gavalas, Cambridge, pp. 115–237.

———. 2008. "The Early Bronze Age in the Cyclades," in *The Cambridge Companion to the Aegean Bronze Age*, ed. C. W. Shelmerdine, Cambridge, pp. 47–76.

———. 2013. "'Minding the Gap': Thinking about Change in Early Cycladic Island Societies from a Comparative Perspective," *AJA* 117, pp. 535–543.

Burghardt, A. F. 1971. "A Hypothesis about Gateway Cities," *Annals of the Association of American Geographers* 61.2, pp. 269–285.

Burke, C., P. M. Day, and A. Kossyva. 2020. "Early Helladic I and Talioti Pottery: Is It Just a Phase We're Going Through?," *OJA* 39, pp. 19–40.

Caloi, I. 2019. "Breaking with Tradition? The Adoption of the Wheel-Throwing Technique at Protopalatial Phaistos: Combining Macroscopic Analysis, Experimental Archaeology and Contextual Information," *ASAtene* 97, pp. 9–25.

Calvo, J. P., M. V. Triantaphyllou, M. Regueiro, and M. G. Stamatakis. 2012. "Alternating Diatomaceous and Volcaniclastic Deposits in Milos Island, Greece: A Contribution to the Upper Pliocene-Lower Pleistocene Stratigraphy of the Aegean Sea," *Palaeogeography, Palaeoclimatology, Palaeoecology* 321–322, pp. 24–40.

Caskey, J. L. 1962. "Excavations in Keos, 1960–1961," *Hesperia* 31, pp. 263–283.

———. 1964. "Excavations in Keos, 1963," *Hesperia* 33, pp. 314–335.

———. 1971. "Investigations in Keos, Part I: Excavations and Explorations, 1966–1970," *Hesperia* 40, pp. 359–396.

———. 1972. "Investigations in Keos, Part II: A Conspectus of the Pottery," *Hesperia* 41, pp. 357–401.

———. 1979. "Ayia Irini, Keos: The Successive Periods of Occupation," *AJA* 83, p. 412.

———. 1982. "Koroni and Keos," in *Studies in Attic Epigraphy, History, and Topography Presented to Eugene Vanderpool* (Hesperia Supplement 19), pp. 14–16.

Caskey, J. L., M. E. Caskey, and J. G. Younger. 1975. "Kea, Ajia Irini," in *Corpus der Minoischen und Mykenischen Siegel V.2*, ed. I. Pini, Berlin, pp. 353–391.

Caskey, M. E. 1986. *The Temple at Ayia Irini: The Statues; Part 1* (*Keos* II), Mainz.

———. 1998. "Ayia Irini: Temple Studies," in Mendoni and Mazarakis Ainian 1998, pp. 123–129.

———. 2009. "Dionysos in the Temple at Ayia Irini, Kea," in ΔΩPON: Τιμητικός τόμος για τον καθηγητή Σπύρο Ιακωβίδη, ed. D. Danielidou, Athens, pp. 143–163.

Caskey, M., L. Meddoni, A. Papastamataki, N. Belogiannis. 1988. "Metals in Keos: A First Approach," in *Engineering Geology of Ancient Works, Monuments and Historical Sites*, ed. P. G. Marinos and G. C. Koukis, Rotterdam, pp. 1739–1745.

Caskey, M., and N. Tountas. 1998. "Ayia Irini: Some New Architectural Details," in Mendoni and Mazarakis Ainian 1998, pp. 695–697.

Catling, E., H. Catling, D. Smyth, G. Jones, and R. E. Jones. 1979. "Knossos 1975: Middle Minoan III and Late Minoan I Houses by the Acropolis," *BSA* 74, pp. 1–80.

Charalambidou, X., E. Kiriatzi, N. S. Müller, M. Georgakopoulou, S. Müller Celka, and T. Krapf. 2016. "Eretrian Ceramic Products through Time: Investigating the Early History of a Greek Metropolis," *JAS: Reports* 7, pp. 530–535.

Cherry, J. F., and J. L. Davis. 1982. "The Cyclades and the Greek Mainland in LC I: The Evidence of the Pottery," *AJA* 86, pp. 333–341.

———. 2007. "The Other Finds," in *Excavations at Phylakopi in Melos 1974–77* (*BSA* Suppl. 42), ed. C. Renfrew, N. Brodie, C. Morris, and C. Scarre, London, pp. 401–464.

Coldstream, J. N. 1978. "Kythera and the Southern Peloponnese in the LM I Period," in *Thera and the Aegean World I*, ed. C. G. Doumas, London, pp. 389–401.

Coldstream, J. N., and G. L. Huxley, ed. 1972. *Kythera: Excavations and Studies Conducted by the University of Pennsylvania Museum and the British School at Athens*, London.

———. 1984. "The Minoans of Kythera," in Hägg and Marinatos 1984, pp. 107–113.

Coleman, J. E. 1977. *Kephala: A Late Neolithic Settlement and Cemetery* (Keos I), Mainz.

Coleman, K. A. 1970. "A Study of Painted Wall Plaster Fragments from the Bronze Age Site of Ayia Irini in the Island of Keos," PhD diss., Columbia University.

Cosmopoulos, M. B. 1998. "Reconstructing Cycladic Prehistory: Naxos in the Early and Middle Late Bronze Age," *OJA* 17.2, pp. 127–148.

———. 2010. "The Middle Helladic Stratigraphy of Eleusis," in Philippa-Touchais et al. 2010, pp. 551–556.

Courty, M.-A., and V. Roux. 1995. "Identification of Wheel Throwing on the Basis of Ceramic Surface Features and Microfabrics," *JAS* 22.1, pp. 17–50.

Crego, D. M. 2007. "Exchange in Period IV at Ayia Irini on Kea," in *Middle Helladic Pottery and Synchronisms*, ed. F. Felten, W. Gauss, and R. Smetana, Vienna, pp. 333–338.

———. 2010. "Ayia Irini IV: A Distribution Center for the Middle Helladic World?" in Philippa-Touchais et al. 2010, pp. 841–845.

Crouwel, J. H. 1973. "Pot-Marks on Grey Minyan Ware," *Kadmos* 12.2, pp. 101–108.

Cummer, W. W., and E. Schofield. 1984. *Ayia Irini: House A* (Keos III), Mainz.

Cutler, J. 2012. "Ariadne's Thread: The Adoption of Cretan Weaving Technology in the Wider Southern Aegean in the Mid-Second Millennium BC," in *Kosmos: Jewellery, Adornment, and Textiles in the Aegean Bronze Age. Proceedings of the 13th International Aegean Conference/13ᵉ Rencontre Égéenne Internationale, University of Copenhagen, Danish National Research Foundation's Centre for Textile Research, 21–26 April 2010* (*Aegaeum* 33), ed. M.-L. Nosch and R. Laffineur, Liège, pp. 145–154.

———. 2016. "Fashioning Identity: Weaving Technology, Dress and Cultural Change in the Middle and Late Bronze Age Southern Aegean," in *Beyond Thalassocracies: Understanding Processes of Minoanisation and Mycenaeanisation in the Aegean*, ed. E. Gorogianni, P. Pavúk, and L. Girella, Oxford, pp. 172–185.

———. 2019. "Arachne's Web: Women, Weaving, and Networks of Knowledge in the Bronze Age Southern Aegean," *BSA* 114, pp. 79–92.

D'Agata, A. L., and S. De Angelis. 2014. "Minoan Beehives. Reconstructing the Practice of Beekeeping in Bronze Age Crete," in *Physis: L'environnement naturel et la relation homme-milieu dans le monde égéen protohistorique* (*Aegaeum* 37), ed. G. Touchais, R. Laffineur, and F. Rougement, Liège, pp. 349–357.

Davis, E. N. 1972. "Geological Structure of Kea Island," *Bulletin of the Geological Society of Greece* 9, pp. 252–265.

———. 1982. *Geological Map of Greece: Kea Island*, Institute of Geological and Mineral Exploration, Athens.

Davis, J. L. 1978. "The Mainland Panelled Cup and Panelled Style," *AJA* 82, pp. 216–222.

———. 1979a. "Late Helladic I Pottery from Korakou," *Hesperia* 48, pp. 234–263.

———. 1979b. "Minos and Dexithea: Crete and the Cyclades in the Later Bronze Age," in *Papers in Cycladic Prehistory*, ed. J. L. Davis and J. F. Cherry, Los Angeles, pp. 143–157.

———. 1984. "Cultural Innovation and the Minoan Thalassocracy at Ayia Irini, Keos," in Hägg and Marinatos 1984, pp. 159–166.

———. 1986. *Ayia Irini: Period V* (Keos V), Mainz.

———. 1992. "Review of Aegean Prehistory I: The Islands of the Aegean," *AJA* 96, pp. 699–756.

———. 2008. "Minoan Crete and the Aegean Islands," in *The Cambridge Companion to the Aegean Bronze Age*, ed. C. W. Shelmerdine, Cambridge, pp. 186–208.

Davis, J. L., and J. F. Cherry. 1984. "Phylakopi in Late Cycladic I: A Pottery Seriation Study," in *The Prehistoric Cyclades*, ed. J. A. MacGillivray and R. L. N. Barber, Edinburgh, pp. 148–161.

———. 1990. "Spatial and Temporal Uniformitarianism in Late Cycladic I: Perspectives from Kea and Milos on the Prehistory of Akrotiri," in *Thera and the Aegean World III: Proceedings of the Third International Congress, Santorini, Greece, 3–9 September 1989 3: Chronology*, ed. D. A. Hardy, C. G. Doumas, J. A. Sakellarakis, and P. M. Warren, London, pp. 185–200.

———. 2007. "The Cycladic Pottery from Late Bronze I Levels," in *Excavations at Phylakopi in Melos 1974–77* (*BSA* Suppl. 42), ed. C. Renfrew, N. Brodie, C. Morris, and C. Scarre, London, pp. 265–306.

Davis, J. L., and E. Gorogianni. 2008. "Potsherds from the Edge: The Construction of Identities and the Limits of Minoanized Areas of the Aegean," in *Horizon: A Colloquium on the Prehistory of the Cyclades*, ed. N. Brodie, J. Doole, G. Gavalas, and C. Renfrew, Cambridge, pp. 339–348.

Davis, J. L., and H. B. Lewis. 1985. "Mechanization of Pottery Production: A Case Study from the Cycladic Islands," in *Prehistoric Production and Exchange: The Aegean and Eastern Mediterranean* (Institute of Archaeology Monograph 25), ed. A. B. Knapp and T. Stech, Los Angeles, pp. 79–92.

Davis, J. L., E. Schofield, R. Torrence, and D. F. Williams. 1983. "Keos and the Eastern Aegean: The Cretan Connection," *Hesperia* 52, pp. 361–366.

Davis, J. L., and D. F. Williams. 1981. "Petrological Examination of Later Middle Bronze Age Pottery from Ayia Irini, Keos," *Hesperia* 50, pp. 291–300.

Dawkins, R. M., and J. P. Droop. 1910–1911. "Excavations at Phylakopi in Melos, 1911," *BSA* 17, pp. 1–22.

Day, P. M. 2011. "Petrographic Analyses," in *Transport Stirrup Jars of the Bronze Age Aegean and East Mediterranean* (*Prehistory Monographs* 33), by H. W. Haskell, R. E. Jones, P. M. Day, and J. T. Killen, Philadelphia, pp. 41–76.

Day, P. M., N. S. Müller, and V. Kilikoglou. 2019. "Phase A," in *Akrotiri, Thera, Middle Bronze Age Pottery and Stratigraphy* 1: *Stratigraphy, Ceramic Typology and Technology, Weaving Equipment*, by I. Nikolakopoulou, Athens, pp. 323–376.

Day, P. M., and D. E. Wilson. 1998. "Consuming Power: Kamares Ware in Protopalatial Knossos," *Antiquity* 71, pp. 350–358.

Demetriou, D. 2011. "What is an Emporion? A Reassessment," *Historia* 60, pp. 255–272.

Dickinson, O. T. P. K. 1972. "Late Helladic IIA and IIB: Some Evidence from Korakou," *BSA* 67, pp. 103–112.

———. 1977. *The Origins of Mycenaean Civilisation* (*SIMA* 49), Göteborg.

———. 2014. "Late Helladic I Revisited: The Kytheran Connection," in *KE-RA-ME-JA: Studies Presented to Cynthia W. Shelmerdine* (*Prehistory Monographs* 46), ed. D. Nakassis, J. Gulizio, and S. A. James, Philadelphia, pp. 3–15.

Dietler, M. 2001. "Theorizing the Feast: Rituals of Consumption, Commensal Politics, and Power in African Contexts," in *Feasts: Archaeological and Ethnographic Perspectives on Food, Politics, and Power*, ed. M. Dietler and B. Hayden, Washington, DC, pp. 65–114.

Dietz, S. 1991. *The Argolid at the Transition to the Mycenaean Age: Studies in the Chronology and Cultural Development in the Shaft Grave Period*, Copenhagen.

Dixon, J. 2013. "The Petrology of the Walls," in *The Settlement at Dhaskalio*, ed. C. Renfrew, O. Philaniotou, N. Brodie, G. Gavalas, and M. Boyd, Cambridge, pp. 309–323.

Domínguez Monedero, A. 2001. "La religión en el emporion," *Gerión* 19, pp. 221–257.

Donnan, C. B. 1971. "Ancient Peruvian Potters' Marks and their Interpretation through Ethnographic Analogy," *AmerAnt* 36, pp. 460–466.

Doumas, C. 1982. "The Minoan Thalassocracy and the Cyclades," *AA* 1982, pp. 5–14.

Driessen, J., and C. F. Macdonald. 1997. *The Troubled Island: Minoan Crete before and after the Santorini Eruption* (*Aegaeum* 17), Liège.

Earle, J. W. 2016. "Melos in the Middle: Minoanisation and Mycenaeanisation at Late Bronze Age Phylakopi," in *Beyond Thalassocracies: Understanding Processes of Minoanisation and Mycenaeanisation in the Aegean*, ed. E. Gorogianni, P. Pavúk, and L. Girella, Oxford, pp. 94–115.

———. 2018. "Coming to Terms with Late Cycladic II: Questions of Style and Stratigraphy at Phylakopi, Melos," in *Cycladic Archaeology and Research: New Approaches and Discoveries*, ed. E. Angliker and J. Tully, Oxford, pp. 43–55.

Etienne, R., and J. Gautier. 1983. "Recherches sur la céramique de Tenos: Étude pétrographique," in *Les Cyclades: Matériaux pour une étude de géographie historique*, ed. F. Rougement, Paris, pp. 191–200.

Evans, A. 1921. *The Palace of Minos* I, London.

———. 1928. *The Palace of Minos* II, London.

Evely, D. 1988. "The Potters' Wheel in Minoan Crete," *BSA* 83, pp. 83–126.

Felten, F., W. Gauss, and R. Smetana. 2012. "Project 15: F1415 Stratigraphic Project Aegina Kolonna," *The Synchronization of Civilizations in the Eastern Mediterranean in the 2nd Millennium B.C. 2000*, https://www.oeaw.ac.at/sciem2000/Pr15main.html (accessed Nov. 10, 2012).

Fishman, B., and B. Lawn. 1978. "University of Pennsylvania Radiocarbon Dates XX," *Radiocarbon* 20, pp. 210–233.

Fitzsimons, R., and E. Gorogianni. 2017. "Dining on the Fringe? A Possible Minoan-Style Banquet Hall at Ayia Irini, Kea and the Minoanization of the Aegean Islands," in *Minoan Architecture and Urbanism: New Perspectives on an Ancient Built Environment*, ed. Q. Letesson and C. Knappett, Oxford, pp. 334–360.

Forster, M. A., and G. S. Lister. 2005. "Several Distinct Tectono-Metamorphic Slices in the Cycladic Eclogite-Blueschist Belt, Greece," *Contributions to Mineralogy and Petrology* 150, pp. 523–545.

Fouqué, F. A. 1879. *Santorin et ses éruptions*, Paris.

Frizell, B. S. 1980. *An Early Mycenaean Settlement at Asine: The Late Helladic IIB–IIIA:1 Pottery*, Göteborg.

Furumark, A. 1941. *The Mycenaean Pottery: Analysis and Classification*, Stockholm.

Gale, N. H. 1998. "The Role of Kea in Metal Production and Trade in the Late Bronze Age," in Mendoni and Mazarakis Ainian 1998, pp. 737–758.

Gale, N. H., and Z. A. Stos-Gale. 1984. "Cycladic Metallurgy," in *The Prehistoric Cyclades: Contributions to a Workshop on Cycladic Chronology*, ed. J. A. MacGillivray and R. L. N. Barber, Edinburgh, pp. 255–276.

———. 2008. "Changing Patterns in Prehistoric Cycladic Metallurgy," in *Horizon: A Colloquium on the Prehistory of the Cyclades*, ed. N. Brodie, J. Doole, G. Gavalas, and C. Renfrew, Cambridge, pp. 387–408.

Gale, N. H., Z. A. Stos-Gale, and J. L. Davis. 1984. "The Provenance of Lead Used at Ayia Irini, Keos," *Hesperia* 53, pp. 389–406.

Gauss, W., and E. Kiriatzi. 2011. *Pottery Production and Supply at Bronze Age Kolonna, Aegina: An Integrated Archaeological and Scientific Study of a Ceramic Landscape* (Ägina-Kolonna, Forschungen und Ergebnisse V), Vienna.

Gauss, W., and R. Smetana. 2007. "Aegina Kolonna, the Ceramic Sequence of the SCIEM 2000 Project," in *Middle Helladic Pottery and Synchronisms*, ed. F. Felten, W. Gauss, and R. Smetana, Vienna, pp. 57–80.

———. 2008. "Aegina Kolonna and the Cyclades," in *Horizon: A Colloquium on the Prehistory of the Cyclades*, ed. N. Brodie, J. Doole, G. Gavalas, and C. Renfrew, Cambridge, pp. 325–338.

Georgakopoulou, M., A. Hein, N. S. Müller, and E. Kiriatzi. 2017. "Development and Calibration of a WDXRF Routine Applied to Provenance Studies on Archaeological Ceramics," *X-Ray Spectrometry* 46, pp. 186–199.

Georgiou, H. S. 1986. *Ayia Irini: Specialized Domestic and Industrial Pottery (Keos VI)*, Mainz.

Georma, F., I. Nikolakopoulou, and I. Bitis. 2017. "Το Κτήριο Βήτα στο Ακρωτήρι Θήρας: Τοιχογραφίες, κεραμική και αρχιτεκτονική," in *Το αρχαιολογικό έργο στα νησιά του Αιγαίου: Διεθνές επιστημονικό συνέδριο, Ρόδος, 27 Νοεμβρίου–1 Δεκεμβρίου 2013* T. B', ed. P. Triantafyllidis, Mitilene, 471–486.

Gercke, P., W. Gercke, and G. Hiesel. 1975. "Tiryns-Stadt 1971: Graben H," in *Tiryns: Forschungen und Berichte VIII*, Mainz, pp. 7–36.

Gill, M. C. N. 1981. "The Potter's Mark: Contemporary and Archaeological Pottery of the Kenyan Southeastern Highlands," PhD diss., Boston University.

Gillis, C. 1998. "Pottery and Statistics: A Pilot Study," in Mendoni and Mazarakis Ainian 1998, pp. 155–160.

Gilstrap, W. D. 2015. "Ceramic Production and Exchange in the Late Mycenaean Saronic Gulf," PhD diss., University of Sheffield.

Gilstrap, W. D., P. M. Day, and V. Kilikoglou. 2016. "Pottery Production at Two Neighbouring Centres in the Late Bronze Age Saronic Gulf: Historical Contingency and Craft Organisation," *JAS: Reports* 7, pp. 499–509.

Girella, L. 2007a. "Forms of Commensal Politics in Neopalatial Crete," *Creta Antica* 8, pp. 135–168.

———. 2007b. "Toward a Definition of the Middle Minoan III Ceramic Sequence in South-Central Crete: Returning to the Traditional MM IIIA and IIIB Division," in *Middle Helladic Pottery and Synchronisms*, ed. F. Felten, W. Gauss, and R. Smetana, Vienna, pp. 233–255.

———. 2010a. *Depositi Ceramici del Medio Minoico III da Festòs e Haghia Triada* (Studi di Archeologia Cretese VIII), Padova.

———. 2010b. "MH III and MM III: Ceramic Synchronisms in the Transition of the Late Bronze Age," in Philippa-Touchais et al. 2010, pp. 859–873.

Gorogianni, E. 2008. "Creation Stories: The Archaeological Site of Ayia Irini, Kea, and the Production of Archaeological Knowledge," PhD diss., University of Cincinnati.

———. 2009–2010. "Site in Transition: John L. Caskey, Ayia Irini, and Archaeological Practice in Greek Archaeology," *Aegean Archaeology* 10, pp. 105–120.

———. 2011. "Goddess, Lost Ancestors, and Dolls: A Cultural Biography of the Ayia Irini Terracotta Statues," *Hesperia* 80, pp. 635–655.

———. 2016. "Keian, Kei-noanised, Keicenaeanised? Interregional Contact and Identity in Ayia Irini, Kea," in *Beyond Thalassocracies: Understanding Processes of Minoanisation and Mycenaeanisation in the Aegean*, ed. E. Gorogianni, P. Pavúk, and L. Girella, Oxford, pp. 136–154.

———. 2020. "Finding Oikoi: Ayia Irini, Kea from the Household Perspective," in *Oikos: Archaeological Approaches to House Societies in the Bronze Age Aegean* (Aegis 19), ed. J. Driessen and M. Relaki, Louvain-la-Neuve, 257–274.

Gorogianni, E., and N. Abell. Forthcoming. "Insularity and Cosmopolitanism at Ayia Irini, Kea," in *Connectivity in the Ancient Mediterranean: Ceramic Perspectives on Island, Mainland, Coastland, and Hinterland*, ed. J. Hilditch, A. Kotsonas, C. Beestman-Kruijshaar, M. Revello Lami, S. Rückl, and S. Ximeri, Amsterdam.

Gorogianni, E., N. Abell, and J. Hilditch. 2016. "Reconsidering Technological Transmission: The Introduction of the Potter's Wheel at Ayia Irini, Kea, Greece," *AJA* 120, pp. 195–220.

———. 2017. "Aegean Fusion Cuisine: Ayia Irini, Kea as Cultural 'Middle Ground,'" in *From Cooking Vessels to Cultural Practices in the Late Bronze Age Aegean*, ed. J. A. Hruby and D. A. Trusty, Oxford, pp. 59–71.

———. 2020. "Kea and Attica: Connections in the Middle and Late Bronze Age," in *Athens and Attica in Prehistory*, ed. N. Papadimitriou, J. C. Wright, S. Fachard, N. Polychronakou-Sgouritsa, and E. Andrikou, Oxford, pp. 627–636.

Gorogianni, E., J. Cutler, and R. D. Fitzsimons. 2015. "Something Old, Something New: Non-Local Brides as Catalysts for Cultural Exchange at Ayia Irini, Kea?" in *Nostoi: Indigenous Culture, Migration, and Integration in the Aegean Islands and Western Anatolia during the Late Bronze Age and Early Iron Age*, ed. N. C. Stampolidis, Ç. Maner, and K. Kopanias, Istanbul, pp. 889–921.

Gorogianni, E., and R. D. Fitzsimons. 2017. "Social Complexity in the Late Middle Bronze Age and Early Late Bronze Age Cyclades: A View from Ayia Irini," in *Social Change in Aegean Prehistory*, ed. C. Wiersma and S. Voutsaki, Oxford, pp. 124–158.

———. Forthcoming. *Ayia Irini: Northern Sector: Stratigraphy and Architecture* (Keos).

Gorogianni, E., P. Pavúk, and L. Girella, eds. 2016. *Beyond Thalassocracies: Understanding Processes of Minoanisation and Mycenaeanisation in the Aegean*, Oxford.

Graziadio, G. 1988. "The Chronology of the Graves of Circle B at Mycenae: A New Hypothesis," *AJA* 92, pp. 343–372.

Graybehl, H. 2014. "The Production and Distribution of Hellenistic Ceramics from the Northeast Peloponnese at the Panhellenic Sanctuary at Nemea: A Petrographic Study," PhD diss., University of Sheffield.

Hadjianastasiou, O. 1989. "Some Hints of Naxian External Connections in the Earlier Late Bronze Age," *BSA* 84, pp. 205–215.

———. 1993. "Naxian Pottery and External Relations in Late Cycladic I–II," in *Wace and Blegen: Pottery as Evidence for Trade in the Aegean Bronze Age 1939–1989. Proceedings of the International Conference Held at the American School of Classical Studies, Athens, Dec. 2–3, 1989*, ed. C. W. Zerner, P. Zerner, and J. Winder, Amsterdam, pp. 257–262.

Hägg, R., and N. Marinatos, eds. 1984. *The Minoan Thalassocracy: Myth and Reality: Proceedings of the Third International Symposium at the Swedish Institute at Athens, 31 May–5 June, 1982* (*ActaAth* 4°, 32), Stockholm.

Hale, C. M. 2016. "The Middle Helladic Fine Gray Burnished (Gray Minyan) Sequence at Mitrou, East Lokris," *Hesperia* 85, pp. 243–295.

Hallager, B. 2011. "Response to Sinclair Hood," in Brogan and Hallager 2011, pp. 175–178.

Hamilakis, Y. 1999. "Food Technologies/Technologies of the Body: The Social Context of Wine and Oil Production and Consumption in Bronze Age Crete," *WorldArch* 31, pp. 38–54.

———, ed. 2002. *Labyrinth Revisited: Rethinking "Minoan" Archaeology*, Oxford.

Hatzaki, E. 2007a. "Ceramic Groups of Early Neopalatial Knossos in the Context of Crete and the South Aegean," in *Middle Helladic Pottery and Synchronisms*, ed. F. Felten, W. Gauss, and R. Smetana, Vienna, pp. 273–294.

———. 2007b. "Neopalatial (MM IIIB–LM IB): KS 178, Gypsades Well (Upper Deposit) and SEX North House Groups," in *Knossos Pottery Handbook: Neolithic and Bronze Age (Minoan)* (*BSA* Studies 14), ed. N. Momigliano, London, pp. 151–196.

Hayden, B. 2001. "Fabulous Feasts: A Prolegomenon to the Importance of Feasting," in *Feasts: Archaeological and Ethnographic Perspectives on Food, Politics, and Power*, ed. M. Dietler and B. Hayden, Washington, DC, pp. 23–64.

Heidenreich, R. 1935–1936. "Vorgeschichtliches in der Stadt Samos: Die Funde," *AM* 60–61, pp. 125–183.

Hekman, J. J. 2003. "The Early Bronze Age Cemetery at Chalandriani on Syros (Cyclades, Greece)," PhD diss., University of Groningen.

Hemingway, S., J. A. MacGillivray, and L. H. Sackett. 2011. "The LM IB Renaissance at Postdiluvian Pre-Mycenaean Palaikastro," in Brogan and Hallager 2011, pp. 513–530.

Hershenson, C. R. 1998. "Late Helladic IIB at Ayia Irini, Keos," in Mendoni and Mazarakis Ainian 1998, pp. 161–168.

Higgins, M. D., and R. Higgins. 1996. *A Geological Companion to Greece and the Aegean*, Ithaca.

Hilditch, J. 2004 "Petrographic Report on Early Bronze II Ceramics from Ayia Irini, Kea," Internal Report, BSA, Fitch Laboratory.

———. 2007. "Appendix D: Petrographic Analysis of the Ceramics from Kavos, Keros," in *Keros, Dhaskalio Kavos: The Investigations of 1987–88* (Keros I), ed. C. Renfrew, C. Doumas, L. Marangou, and G. Gavalas, Cambridge, pp. 238–263.

———. 2008. "Reconstruction of Technological Choice, Social Practice, and Networks of Exchange from a Ceramic Perspective in the Middle Bronze Age Cyclades," PhD diss., University of Exeter.

———. 2013. "The Fabrics of the Ceramics at Dhaskalio," in *The Settlement at Dhaskalio*, ed. C. Renfrew, O. Philaniotou, N. Brodie, G. Gavalas, and M. Boyd, Cambridge, pp. 465–482.

———. 2014. "Analyzing Technological Standardization: Revisiting the Minoan Conical Cup," in *Understanding Standardization and Variation in Mediterranean Ceramics Mid-Second to Late First Millennium BC*, ed. A. Kotsonas, Leuven, pp. 25–37.

———. 2015. "The Ceramic Fabrics of the Special Deposit South," in *Kavos and the Special Deposits*, ed. C. Renfrew, O. Philaniotou, N. Brodie, G. Gavalas, and M. Boyd, Cambridge, pp. 229–247.

———. 2019. "Phases B–C," in *Akrotiri, Thera: Middle Bronze Age Pottery and Stratigraphy 1: Stratigraphy, Ceramic Typology and Technology, Weaving Equipment*, by I. Nikolakopoulou, Athens, pp. 377–461.

———. Forthcoming. "Fabric Analysis," in *Ayia Irini: Northern Sector: Stratigraphy and Architecture* (Keos), by E. Gorogianni and R. D. Fitzsimons.

Hilditch, J., E. Kiriatzi, K. Psaraki, and V. Aravantinos. 2008. "Early Helladic II Pottery from Thebes: An Integrated Typological, Technological, and Provenance Study," in *Proceedings of the 4th Symposium of the Hellenic Society for Archaeometry* (*BAR-IS* 1746), ed. Y. Facorellis, N. Zacharias, and K. Polikreti, Oxford, pp. 263–268.

Hilditch, J., C. Knappett, M. Pirrie, and D. Pirrie. 2012. "Iasos Pottery Fabrics and Technologies," in *Bronze Age Carian Iasos: Structures and Finds from the Area of the Roman Agora (c. 3000–1500 BC)* (Missione Archeologica Italiana di Iasos 4, Archaeologica 166), ed. N. Momigliano, Rome, pp. 58–106.

Hiller, S. 1975. *Mykenische Keramik* (Alt-Ägina IV.1), Mainz.

Hinsken, T., M. Bröcker, H. Strauss, and F. Bulle. 2017. "Geochemical, Isotopic, and Geochronological Characterization of Listvenite from the Upper Unit on Tinos, Cyclades, Greece," *Lithos* 282–283, pp. 281–297.

Hirth, K. G. 1978. "Interregional Trade and the Formation of Prehistoric Gateway Communities," *AmerAnt* 43.1, pp. 35–45.

———. 2020. *The Organization of Ancient Economies: A Global Perspective*, Cambridge.

Hitchcock, L. A. 1998. "Blending the Local with the Foreign: Minoan Features at Ayia Irini, House A," in Mendoni and Mazarakis Ainian 1998, pp. 169–174.

Hood, S. 1996. "Back to Basics with Middle Minoan IIIB," in *Minotaur and Centaur: Studies in the Archaeology of Crete and Euboea Presented to Mervyn Popham*, ed. D. Evely, I. S. Lemos, and S. Sherratt, Oxford, pp. 10–16.

———. 2007. "Appendix F: The Middle Minoan Pottery," in *Excavations at Phylakopi in Melos 1974–77* (*BSA* Suppl. 42), ed. C. Renfrew, N. Brodie, C. Morris, and C. Scarre, London, pp. 248–264.

———. 2011. "Knossos Royal Road: North, LM IB Deposits," in Brogan and Hallager 2011, pp. 153–174.

Iglseder, C., B. Grasemann, A. H. N. Rice, K. Petrakakis, and D. A. Schneider. 2011. "Miocene South Directed Low-Angle Normal Fault Evolution on Kea Island (West Cycladic Detachment System, Greece)," *Tectonics* 30, TC4013.

Jeffra, C. D. 2011. "The Archaeological Study of Innovation: An Experimental Approach to the Pottery Wheel in Bronze Age Crete and Cyprus," PhD diss., University of Exeter.

———. 2013. "A Re-examination of Early Wheel Potting in Crete," *BSA* 108, pp. 31–49.

———. 2019. "Forming Technology," in *Akrotiri, Thera: Middle Bronze Age Pottery and Stratigraphy* 1: *Stratigraphy, Ceramic Typology and Technology, Weaving Equipment*, by I. Nikolakopoulou, Athens, pp. 471–477.

Johnson, A. W., and T. Earle. 1987. *The Evolution of Human Societies: From Foraging Groups to Agrarian State*, Stanford.

Joyce, R. A., and J. S. Henderson. 2007. "From Feasting to Cuisine: Implications of Archaeological Research in an Early Honduran Village," *American Anthropologist* 109, pp. 642–653.

Kaiser, I. 2009. "Miletus IV: The Locally Produced Coarse Wares," in Macdonald, Hallager, and Niemeier 2009, pp. 159–165.

Kalogeropoulos, K. 2010. "Middle Helladic Human Activity in Eastern Attica: The Case of Brauron," in Philippa-Touchais et al. 2010, pp. 211–221.

Karnava, A. 2008. "Written and Stamped Records in the Late Bronze Age Cyclades: the Sea Journeys of an Administration," in *Horizon: Ορίζων: A Colloquium on the Prehistory of the Cyclades*, ed. N. Brodie, J. Doole, G.Gavalas, and C. Renfrew, Cambridge, pp. 377–386.

———. 2018. *Seals, Sealings and Seal Impressions from Akrotiri in Thera* (CMS 10), Heidelberg.

Katzir, Y., Z. Garfunkel, D. Avigad, and A. Matthews. 2007. "The Geodynamic Evolution of the Alpine Orogen in the Cyclades (Aegean Sea, Greece): Insights from Diverse Origins and Modes of Emplacement of Ultramafic Rocks," in *Geological Society London Special Publications* 291.1, pp. 17–40.

Kemp, R. A. 1985. *Soil Micromorphology and the Quaternary* (Quaternary Research Association Technical Guide 2), Cambridge.

Kennedy, M. 2018. "Complex Engineering and Metal-Work Discovered beneath Ancient Greek 'Pyramid,'" *The Guardian*, January 13, 2018, https://www.theguardian.com/world/2018/jan/18/complex-engineering-and-metal-work-discovered-beneath-ancient-greek-pyramid (accessed May 7, 2019).

Kiriatzi, E. 2010. "'Minoanising' Pottery Traditions in the Southwest Aegean during the Middle Bronze Age: Understanding the Social Context of Technological and Consumption Practice," in Philippa-Touchais et al. 2010, pp. 683–699.

Kiriatzi, E., M. Georgakopoulou, and A. Pentedeka. 2011. "Pottery Production and Importation at Bronze Age Kolonna: The Ceramic Fabrics and the Island's Landscape," in *Pottery Production and Supply at Bronze Age Kolonna, Aegina*, by W. Gauss and E. Kiriatzi, Vienna, pp. 69–156.

Knapp, A. B., and J. F. Cherry. 1994. *Provenience Studies and Bronze Age Cyprus: Production, Exchange, and Politico-Economic Change* (Monographs in World Archaeology 21), Madison.

Knappett, C. 1999. "Tradition and Innovation in Pottery Forming Technology: Wheel-Throwing at Middle Minoan Knossos," *BSA* 94, pp. 101–129.

———. 2004. "Technological Innovation and Social Diversity at Middle Minoan Knossos," in *Knossos: Palace, City, State* (BSA Studies 12), ed. G. Cadogan, E. Hatzaki, and A. Vasilakis, London, pp. 257–265.

———. 2006. "Aegean Imports at MM III Knossos," in *Πεπραγμένα Θ' Διεθνούς κρητολογικού συνεδρίου, Ελούντα, 1–6 Οκτωβρίου 2001* T. 1.4: *Προϊστορική περίοδος, σύμμεικτα*, ed. E. Tabakaki and A. Kaloutsakis, Heraklion, pp. 109–117.

———. 2016. "Minoanisation and Mycenaeanisation: A Commentary," in *Beyond Thalassocracies: Understanding Processes of Minoanisation and Mycenaeanisation in the Aegean*, ed. E. Gorogianni, P. Pavúk, and L. Girella, Oxford, pp. 202–206.

———. 2018. "From Network Connectivity to Human Mobility: Models for Minoanization," *Journal of Archaeological Method and Theory* 25, pp. 974–995.

———. 2019. "The Cretan Imports," in *Akrotiri, Thera: Middle Bronze Age Pottery and Stratigraphy* 1: *Stratigraphy, Ceramic Typology and Technology, Weaving Equipment*, by I. Nikolakopoulou, Athens, pp. 295–316.

Knappett, C., and J. R. Hilditch. 2015a. "Colonial Cups? The Minoan Plain Handleless Cup as Iconic Inter-Regional Object," in *Pots, Palaces and Politics: The Evolution and Socio-Political Significance of Plain Ware Traditions in the 2nd Millennium BC Near East and East Mediterranean*, ed. C. Glatz, Walnut Creek, CA, pp. 91–113.

———. 2015b. "Milesian Imports and Exchange Networks in the Southern Aegean," in *Ein Minoer im Exil: Festschrift für Wolf-Dietrich Niemeier* (Universitätsforschungen zur Prähistorischen Archäologie 270), ed. D. Panagiotopoulos, I. Kaiser, and O. Kouka, Bonn, pp. 199–209.

Knappett, C., I. Mathioudaki, and C. F. Macdonald. 2013. "Stratigraphy and Ceramic Typology in the Middle Minoan III Palace at Knossos," in *Intermezzo: Intermediacy and Regeneration in Middle Minoan III Palatial Crete* (BSA Studies 21), ed. C. F. Macdonald and C. Knappett, London, pp. 9–19.

Knappett, C., and I. Nikolakopoulou. 2005. "Exchange and Affiliation Networks in the MBA Southern Aegean: Crete, Akrotiri and Miletus," in *Emporia: Aegeans in the Central and Eastern Mediterranean. Proceedings of the 10th International Aegean Conference/10e Rencontre Égéenne Internationale, Athens, Italian School of Archaeology, 14–18 April 2004* (Aegaeum 25), ed. R. Laffineur and E. Greco, Liège, pp. 175–184.

———. 2008. "Colonialism without Colonies? A Bronze Age Case Study from Akrotiri, Thera," *Hesperia* 77, pp. 1–42.

Knappett, C., D. Pirrie, M. R. Power, I. Nikolakopoulou, J. Hilditch, G. K. Rollinson. 2011. "Mineralogical Analysis and Provenancing of Ancient Ceramics Using Automated SEM-EDS Analysis (QEMSCAN®): A Pilot Study on LB I Pottery from Akrotiri, Thera," *JAS* 38, pp. 219–232.

Knappett, C., and I. Schoep. 2000. "Continuity and Change in Minoan Palatial Power," *Antiquity* 74, pp. 365–371.

Koehl, R. B. 2006. *Aegean Bronze Age Rhyta*. (Prehistory Monographs 19), Philadelphia.

Kosse, K. 1990. "Group Size and Societal Complexity: Thresholds in the Long-Term Memory," *JAnthArch* 9, pp. 275–303.

Kriga, D. 2018. "Η ΥΜ Ι εισηγμένη κεραμική στο Ακρωτήρι Θήρας και η ΥΚ Ι εισηγμένη κεραμική στην Κρήτη κατά τη Νεοανακτορική περίοδο: Νέα στοιχεία για τις περιοχές της Κρήτης, με τις οποίες είχαν εμπορικές σχέσεις οι Θηραίοι," in *Το αρχαιολογικό έργο στα νησιά του Αιγαίου: Διεθνές επιστημονικό συνέδριο, Ρόδος, 27 Νοεμβρίου–1 Δεκεμβρίου 2013* Τ. Α1.1, ed. P. Triantafyllidis, Mitilene, pp. 57–73.

Lamb, W. 1936. *Excavations at Thermi in Lesbos*, Cambridge.

Levi, D. 1976. *Festòs e la Civiltà Minoica* (Incunabula Graeca LX), Rome.

Levi, D., and F. Carinci. 1988. *Festòs e la civiltà minoica* II: *L'arte festia nell'età protopalaziale; Ceramica e altri materiali* (Incunabula Graeca LXXVII), Rome.

Lewis, H. B. 1983. "The Manufacture of Early Mycenaean Pottery," PhD diss., University of Minnesota.

———. 1986. "Appendix 1: Pottery Techniques and Surface Treatments," in *Ayia Irini: Period V* (Keos V), by J. L. Davis, Mainz, pp. 108–109.

Lindblom, M. 2001. *Marks and Makers: Appearance, Distribution, and Function of Middle and Late Helladic Manufacturers' Marks on Aeginetan Pottery*, Jonsered.

———. 2007. "Early Mycenaean Mortuary Meals at Lerna VI with Special Emphasis on Their Aeginetan Components," in *Middle Helladic Pottery and Synchronisms*, ed. F. Felten, W. Gauss, and R. Smetana, Vienna, pp. 115–135.

Lindblom, M., and S. W. Manning. 2011. "The Chronology of the Lerna Shaft Graves," in *Our Cups are Full: Pottery and Society in the Aegean Bronze Age. Papers Presented to Jeremy B. Rutter on the Occasion of His 65th Birthday*, ed. W. Gauss, M. Lindblom, R. A. K. Smith, J. C. Wright, Oxford, pp. 140–153.

Livingstone Smith, A. 2001. "Pottery Manufacturing Processes: Reconstruction and Interpretation," in *Uan Tabu in the Settlement History of the Libyan Sahara*, ed. E. A. A. Garcea, Florence, pp. 113–152.

Lolos, Y. G. 1990. "On the Late Helladic I of Akrotiri, Thera," in *Thera and the Aegean World III: Proceedings of the Third International Congress, Santorini, Greece, 3–9 September 1989* 3: *Chronology*, ed. D. A. Hardy, C. G. Doumas, J. A. Sakellarakis, and P. M. Warren, London, pp. 51–56.

Macdonald, C. F. 2004. "Ceramic and Contextual Confusion in the Old and New Palace Periods," in *Knossos: Palace, City, State* (BSA Studies 12), ed. G. Cadogan, E. Hatzaki, and A. Vasilakis, London, pp. 239–251.

———. 2013. "Between Protopalatial Houses and Neopalatial Mansions: An 'Intermezzo' Southwest of the Palace at Knossos," in *Intermezzo: Intermediacy and Regeneration in Middle Minoan III Palatial Crete* (BSA Studies 21), ed. C. F. Macdonald and C. Knappett, London, pp. 21–30.

Macdonald, C. F., E. Hallager, and W.-D. Niemeier, eds. 2009. *The Minoans in the Central, Eastern, and Northern Aegean—New Evidence. Acts of a Minoan Seminar 22–23 January 2005 in Collaboration with the Danish Institute at Athens and the German Archaeological Institute at Athens*, Athens.

Macdonald, C. F., and C. Knappett. 2007. *Knossos: Protopalatial Deposits in Early Magazine A and the South-West Houses*, London.

———, eds. 2013. *Intermezzo: Intermediacy and Regeneration in Middle Minoan III Palatial Crete* (BSA Studies 21), London.

MacGillivray, J. A. 1980. "Mount Kynthos in Delos: The Early Cycladic Settlement," *BCH* 104, pp. 3–45.

———. 1998. *Knossos: Pottery Groups of the Old Palace Period*, London.

———. 2007. "Protopalatial (MM IB–MM IIIA): Early Chamber beneath the West Court, Royal Pottery Stores, the Trial KV, and the West and South Polychrome Deposits Groups," in *Knossos Pottery Handbook: Neolithic and Bronze Age (Minoan)* (BSA Studies 14), ed. N. Momigliano, London, pp. 105–149.

Maniatis, Y. 1986. "Appendix I: Technological Examination of Samples of the Terracotta Statues," in *The Temple at Ayia Irini* 1: *The Statues* (Keos II), by M. E. Caskey, Mainz, pp. 109–113.

Maniatis, Y., A. Katsonas, and M. E. Caskey. 1982. "Technological Examination of Low-Fired Terracotta Statues from Ayia Irini," *Archaeometry* 24, 191–198.

Maniatis, Y., and M. S. Tite. 2007. "The Examination of Pottery from Phylakopi Using the Scanning Electron Microscope," in *Excavations at Phylakopi in Melos 1974–77* (BSA Suppl. 42), ed. C. Renfrew, N. Brodie, C. Morris, and C. Scarre, London, pp. 126–128.

Manning, S. W. 1995. *The Absolute Chronology of the Aegean Early Bronze Age: Archaeology, Radiocarbon, and History*, Sheffield.

———. 1997. "Cultural Change in the Aegean c. 2200 B.C.," in *Third Millennium B.C. Climate Change and Old World Collapse*, ed. H. Nüzhet Dalfes, G. Kukla, and H. Weiss, Berlin, pp. 149–171.

———. 2008. "Some Initial Wobbly Steps towards a Late Neolithic to Early Bronze III Radiocarbon Chronology for the Cyclades," in *Horizon: A Colloquium on the Prehistory of the Cyclades*, ed. N. Brodie, J. Doole, G. Gavalas, and C. Renfrew, Cambridge, pp. 55–59.

———. 2017. "Comments on Climate, Intra-Regional Variations, Chronology, the 2200 B.C. Horizon of Change in the East Mediterranean Region, and Sociopolitical Change on Crete," in *The Late Third Millennium in the Ancient Near East: Chronology, C14, and Climate Change*, ed. F. Höflmayer, Chicago, pp. 451–490.

Maran, J. 1992. *Kiapha Thiti: Ergebnisse der Ausgrabungen II.2, 2.Jt.v.Chr: Keramik und Kleinfunde* (Marburger Winckelmann-Programm 1990), Marburg.

———. 2011. "Lost in Translation: The Emergence of Mycenaean Culture as a Phenomenon of Glocalization," in *Interweaving Worlds: Systemic Interactions in Eurasia, 7th to 1st Millennia BC*, ed. T. C. Wilkinson, S. Sherratt, and J. Bennet, Oxford, pp. 282–293.

Marangou, L., C. Renfrew, C. Doumas, and G. Gavalas. 2008. "Markiani on Amorgos: An Early Bronze Age Fortified Settlement—Overview of the 1985–91 Investigations," in *Horizon: A Colloquium on the Prehistory of the Cyclades*, ed. N. Brodie, J. Doole, G. Gavalas, and C. Renfrew, Cambridge, pp. 97–106.

Marinatos, S. 1971. *Excavations at Thera IV (1970 Season)*, Athens.

———. 1972. *Excavations at Thera V (1971 Season)*, Athens.

Marketou, T. 2009. "Ialysos and Its Neighboring Areas in the MBA and LB I Periods: A Chance for Peace," in Macdonald, Hallager, and Niemeier 2009, pp. 73–96.

Marketou, T., E. Karantzali, H. Mommsen, N. Zacharias, V. Kilikoglou, and A. Schwedt. 2006. "Pottery Wares from the Prehistoric Settlement at Ialysos (Trianda) Rhodes," *BSA* 101, pp. 1–55.

Marthari, M. 1980. "Ακρωτήρι, κεραμεική μεσοελλαδικής παρόδοσης στο στρώμα της ηφαιστειακής καταστροφής," *ArchEph*, pp. 182–211.

———. 1984. "The Destruction of the Town at Akrotiri, Thera, at the Beginning of LC I: Definition and Chronology," in *The Prehistoric Cyclades*, ed., J. A. MacGillivray and R. L. N. Barber, Edinburgh, pp. 119–133.

———. 1987. "The Local Pottery Wares with Painted Decoration from the Volcanic Destruction Level of Akrotiri, Thera: A Preliminary Report," *AA* 1987.3, pp. 359–379.

———. 1990. "The Chronology of the Last Phases of Occupation at Akrotiri in the Light of the Evidence from the West House Pottery Groups," in *Thera and the Aegean World III: Proceedings of the Third International Congress, Santorini, Greece, 3–9 September 1989* 3: *Chronology*, ed. D. A. Hardy, C. G. Doumas, J. A. Sakellarakis, and P. M. Warren, London, pp. 57–70.

———. 1993. "The Ceramic Evidence for Contacts between Thera and the Greek Mainland," in *Wace and Blegen: Pottery as Evidence for Trade in the Aegean Bronze Age 1939–1989. Proceedings of the International Conference Held at the American School of Classical Studies, Athens, Dec. 2–3, 1989*, ed. C. W. Zerner, P. Zerner, and J. Winder, Amsterdam, pp. 249–256.

———. 1998. "The Griffin Jar from Ayia Irini, Keos, and Its Relationship to the Pottery and Frescoes from Thera," in Mendoni and Mazarakis Ainian 1998, pp. 140–153.

———. 2008. "Aspects of Pottery Circulation in the Cyclades during the Early EB II Period: Fine and Semi-Fine Imported Ceramic Wares at Skarkos, Ios," in *Horizon: A Colloquium on the Prehistory of the Cyclades*, ed. N. Brodie, J. Doole, G. Gavalas, and C. Renfrew, Cambridge, pp. 71–84.

———. 2009. "Middle Cycladic and Early Late Cycladic Cemeteries and Their Minoan Elements: The Case of the Cemetery at Skarkos on Ios," in Macdonald, Hallager, and Niemeier 2009, pp. 41–58.

Mathioudaki, I. 2010. "'Mainland Polychrome' Pottery: Definition, Chronology, Typological Correlations," in Philippa-Touchais et al. 2010, pp. 621–633.

———. 2014. "Shifting Boundaries: The Transition from the Middle to the Late Bronze Age in the Aegean under a New Light," *Aegean Studies* 1, pp. 1–20.

———. 2019. "Other Imports," in *Akrotiri, Thera: Middle Bronze Age Pottery and Stratigraphy* 1: *Stratigraphy, Ceramic Typology and Technology, Weaving Equipment*, by I. Nikolakopoulou, Athens, pp. 317–322.

Mathioudaki, I., and I. Nikolakopoulou. 2018. "Η ΥΜ ΙΑ κεραμική από το Συγκρότημα Δ στο Ακρωτήρι Θήρας," in *Πεπραγμένα του ΙΑ' Διεθνούς Κρητολογικού Συνεδρίου* Τ. Α1.4, ed. E. Gavrilaki, Rethymno, pp. 65–75.

McGovern, P. E. 2009. *Uncorking the Past: The Quest for Wine, Beer, and Other Alcoholic Beverages*, Berkeley.

Mehl, C., L. Jolivet, O. Lacombe, L. Labrousse, and G. Rimmele. 2007. "Structural Evolution of Andros (Cyclades, Greece): A Key to the Behaviour of a (Flat) Detachment within an Extending Continental Crust," in *The Geodynamics of the Aegean and Anatolia* (Geological Society, London, Special Publications 291), ed. T. Taymaz, Y. Yilmaz, and Y. Dilek, London, pp. 41–73.

Mendoni, L., and A. Mazarakis Ainian, eds. 1998. *Kea-Kythnos: History and Archaeology. Proceedings of an International Symposium Kea-Kythnos, 22–25 June 1994*, Athens.

Mendoni, L., and N. Belogiannis. 1991. "Μεταλλευτικές και μεταλλουργικές δραστηριότητες στην αρχαία Κέα," *Archaiognosia* 7, pp. 91–104.

Michailidou, A. 1995. "Investigating Metal Technology in a Settlement: The Case of Akrotiri at Thera," *Archaiognosia* 8, pp. 165–180, pls. 22–26.

———. 2008. *Weight and Value in Pre-Coinage Societies* 2: *Sidelights on Measurement from the Aegean and Orient* (Meletemata 61), Athens.

Mizera, M., and J. H. Behrmann. 2016. "Strain and Flow in the Metamorphic Core Complex of Ios Island (Cyclades, Greece)," *International Journal of Earth Sciences* 105, pp. 2097–2110.

Momigliano, N. 2007. "Late Prepalatial (EM III–MM IA): South Front House Foundation Trench, Upper East Well and House C/Royal Road South Fill Groups," in *Knossos Pottery Handbook: Neolithic and Bronze Age (Minoan)* (BSA Studies 14), ed. N. Momigliano, London, pp. 79–103.

———. 2012. *Bronze Age Carian Iasos: Structure and Finds from the Area of the Roman Agora (c. 3000–1500 BC)*, Rome.

Morgan, L. 2020. *Ayia Irini: The Wall Paintings of the Northeast Bastion; Social Context and the Miniature Frieze* (Keos XI), Philadelphia.

———. n.d. "Area B Fresco Notes," unpublished.

Morris, C., and R. Jones. 1998. "The Late Bronze Age III Town of Ayia Irini and Its Aegean Relations," in Mendoni and Mazarakis Ainian 1998, pp. 189–199.

Mountjoy, P. A. 1981. *Four Early Mycenaean Wells from the South Slope of the Acropolis at Athens* (Miscellanea Graeca 4), Gent.

———. 1983. "The Ephyraean Goblet Reviewed," *BSA* 78, pp. 265–271.

———. 1984. "The Marine Style Pottery of LM IB/LH IIA: Towards a Corpus," *BSA* 79, pp. 161–219.

———. 1985. "The Pottery," in *The Archaeology of Cult: The Sanctuary at Phylakopi*, by C. Renfrew, P. A. Mountjoy, E. French, J. G. Younger, J. F. Cherry, A. Daykin, J. Moody, L. Morgan, N. Bradford, C. Macfarlane, R. Torrence, C. Gamble, and T. Whitelaw (*BSA* Suppl. 18), London, pp. 151–208.

———. 1986. *Mycenaean Decorated Pottery: A Guide to Identification*, Göteborg.

———. 1988. "The LH IIIA Pottery from Ayios Stephanos, Laconia," in *Problems in Greek Prehistory*, ed. E. B. French and K. A. Wardle, Bristol, pp. 185–191.

———. 1995. *Mycenaean Athens*, Jonsered.

———. 1999. *Regional Mycenaean Decorated Pottery*, Rahden, Westfalia.

———. 2004. "Knossos and the Cyclades in LM IB," in *Knossos: Palace, City, State*, ed. G. Cadogan, E. Hatzaki, and A. Vasilakis, London, pp. 399–404.

———. 2007. "The Mycenaean and Late Minoan I–II Pottery," in *Excavations at Phylakopi in Melos 1974–77* (*BSA* Suppl. 42), ed. C. Renfrew, N. Brodie, C. Morris, and C. Scarre, London, pp. 307–370.

———. 2008a. "The Cyclades during the Mycenaean Period," in *Horizon: A Colloquium on the Prehistory of the Cyclades*, ed. N. Brodie, J. Doole, G. Gavalas, and C. Renfrew, Cambridge, pp. 467–477.

———. 2008b. "The Late Helladic Pottery," in *Ayios Stephanos: Excavations at a Bronze Age and Medieval Settlement in Southern Laconia*, ed. W. D. Taylour and R. Janko, London, pp. 299–387.

———. 2011. "Response to Philip P. Betancourt," in Brogan and Hallager 2011, pp. 413–423.

Mountjoy, P. A., and M. J. Ponting. 2000. "The Minoan Thalassocracy Reconsidered: Provenance Studies of LH II A/LM I B Pottery from Phylakopi, Ay. Irini, and Athens," *BSA* 95, pp. 141–184.

Müller, K. 1909. "Alt-Pylos II: Die Funde aus den Kuppelgräbern von Kakovatos," *AM* 34, pp. 269–328.

Müller, N. S., A. Hein, M. Georgakopoulou, V. Kilikoglou, and E. Kiriatzi. 2018. "The Effect of Inter- and Intra-Source Variation: A Comparison between WD-XRF and NAA Data from Cretan Clay Deposits," *JAS: Reports* 21, pp. 929–937.

Müller, N. S., A. Hein, V. Kilikoglou, and P. M. Day. 2013. "Bronze Age Cooking Pots: Thermal Properties and Cooking Methods," *Préhistoires Méditerranéennes* [Online] 4, http://journals.openedition.org/pm/737 (accessed October 2, 2020)

Müller, N. S., V. Kilikoglou, and P. M. Day. 2015. "Home-Made Recipes: Tradition and Innovation in Bronze Age Cooking Pots from Akrotiri, Thera," in *Ceramics, Cuisine and Culture: The Archaeology and Science of Kitchen Pottery in the Ancient Mediterranean World*, ed. M. Spataro and A. Villing, Oxford, pp. 37–48.

Myer, G. H., P. P. Betancourt, and S. J. Vaughan. 1995. "Appendix II, Petrography, A: Ceramic Petrography of Selected Pottery Samples from Lerna V," in *The Pottery of Lerna IV* (Lerna: A Preclassical Site in the Argolid III), by J. B. Rutter, Princeton, pp. 666–693.

Mylonas, G. E. 1934. "Excavations at Hagios Kosmas: Preliminary Report," *AJA* 38, pp. 258–279.

———. 1959. *Aghios Kosmas: An Early Bronze Age Settlement and Cemetery in Attica*, Princeton.

———. 1972–1973. *Ο Ταφικός Κύκλος Β των Μυκηνών*, Athens.

Nakou, G. 1997. "The Role of Poliochni and the North Aegean in the Development of Aegean Metallurgy," in *Η Πολιόχνη και η Πρώιμη Εποχή του Χαλκού στο Βόρειο Αιγαίο/Poliochni e l'antica età del Bronzo nell'Egeo settentrionale*, ed. C. G. Doumas and V. La Rosa, Athens, pp. 634–648.

———. 2000. "Metalwork, Basketry, and Pottery in the Aegean Early Bronze Age: A Meaningful Relationship," in *Dorima: A Tribute to the A. G. Leventis Foundation on the Occasion of Its 20th Anniversary*, ed. A. Serghidou, Nicosia, pp. 27–57.

———. 2007. "Absent Presences: Metal Vessels in the Aegean at the End of the Third Millennium," in *Metallurgy in the Early Bronze Age Aegean* (Sheffield Studies in Aegean Archaeology 7), ed. P. M. Day and R. C. P. Doonan, Oxford, pp. 224–244.

Niemeier, W.-D. 1995. "Aegina—First Aegean 'State' outside of Crete?" in *Politeia: Society and State in the Aegean Bronze Age. Proceedings of the 5th International Aegean Conference* (*Aegaeum* 12), Austin, pp. 73–80.

———. 2011. "Closing Comments," in Brogan and Hallager 2011, pp. 627–628.

Nikolakopoulou, I. 2007. "Aspects of Interaction between the Cyclades and the Mainland in the Middle Bronze Age," in *Middle Helladic Pottery and Synchronisms*, ed. F. Felten, W. Gauss, and R. Smetana, Vienna, pp. 347–359.

———. 2009. "'Beware Cretans Bearing Gifts': Tracing the Origins of Minoan Influence at Akrotiri, Thera," in Macdonald, Hallager, and Niemeier 2009, pp. 31–39.

———. 2019. *Akrotiri, Thera: Middle Bronze Age Pottery and Stratigraphy*, Athens.

Nikolakopoulou, I., F. Georma, A. Moschou, and P. Sofianou. 2008. "Trapped in the Middle: New Stratigraphic and Ceramic Evidence from Middle Cycladic Akrotiri, Thera," in *Horizon: A Colloquium on the Prehistory of the Cyclades*, ed. N. Brodie, J. Doole, G. Gavalas, and C. Renfrew, Cambridge, pp. 311–324.

Nikolakopoulou, I., and C. Knappett. 2016. "Mobilities in the Neopalatial Southern Aegean: The Case of Minoanization," in *Human Mobility and Technology Transfer in the Prehistoric Mediterranean*, ed. E. Kiriatzi and C. Knappett, Cambridge, pp. 102–115.

Nodarou, E. 2015. "Petrographic Analysis," in *Kalochorafitis: Two Chamber Tombs from the LM IIIA2–B Cemetery* (Studi di Archeologia Cretese XII), by A. Karetsou and L. Girella, Padua, 343–362.

Nye, J. S. 2021. "Soft Power: The Evolution of a Concept," *Journal of Political Power* 14, pp. 196–208.

Oka, R., and C. M. Kusimba. 2008. "The Archaeology of Trading Systems, Part 1: Towards a New Trade Synthesis," *Journal of Archaeological Research* 16, pp. 339–395.

Orton, C., and M. Hughes. 2013. *Pottery in Archaeology*, Cambridge.

Overbeck, G. F. 1974. "Graves and Burial Customs at Ayia Irini," PhD diss., State University of New York at Albany.

———. 1989. "The Cemeteries and the Graves," in *Ayia Irini: Period IV. Part 1: The Stratigraphy and Find Deposits* (Keos VII), by J. C. Overbeck, Mainz, pp. 184–205.

Overbeck, J. C. 1982. "The Hub of Commerce: Keos and Middle Helladic Greece," *TUAS* 7, pp. 38–49.

———. 1984. "Stratigraphy and Ceramic Sequence in Middle Cycladic Ayia Irini, Kea," in *The Prehistoric Cyclades*, ed. J. A. MacGillivray and R. L. N. Barber, Edinburgh, pp. 108–113.

———. 1989a. *Ayia Irini: Period IV. Part 1: The Stratigraphy and Find Deposits* (Keos VII), Mainz.

———. 1989b. *The Bronze Age Pottery from the Kastro of Paros*, Jonsered.

———. 2007. "The Middle Bronze Age Sequences of Kea and Aigina," in *Middle Helladic Pottery and Synchronisms*, ed. F. Felten, W. Gauss, and R. Smetana, Vienna, pp. 339–346.

———. 2010. "The Middle Helladic Origin of 'Shaft Grave Polychrome' Ware," in Philippa-Touchais et al. 2010, pp. 615–619.

Overbeck, J. C., and D. M. Crego. 2008. "The Commercial Foundation and Development of Ayia Irini IV (Kea)," in *Horizon: A Colloquium on the Prehistory of the Cyclades*, ed. N. Brodie, J. Doole, G. Gavalas, and C. Renfrew, Cambridge, pp. 305–309.

Overbeck, J. C., and G. F. Overbeck. 1979. "Consistency and Diversity in the Middle Cycladic Era," in *Papers in Cycladic Prehistory*, ed. J. L. Davis and J. F. Cherry, Los Angeles, pp. 106–120.

Papadimitriou, N. 2001. *Built Chamber Tombs of Middle and Late Bronze Age Date in Mainland Greece and the Islands*, Oxford.

Papagiannopoulou, A. G. 1991. *The Influence of Middle Minoan Pottery on the Cyclades*, Göteborg.

Papagiannopoulou, A., A. Grimanis, and V. Kilikoglou. 1985. "Analysis of Melian and Theran Pottery: A Preliminary Report," *Hydra* 1, pp. 59–65.

Pavúk, P. 2002. "Troia VI and VIIa: The Blegen Pottery Shapes; Towards a Typology," *Studia Troica* 12, pp. 35–71.

———. 2007. "What Can Troia Tell Us about the Middle Helladic Period in the Southern Aegean?" in *Middle Helladic Pottery and Synchronisms*, ed. F. Felten, W. Gauss, and R. Smetana, Vienna, pp. 295–308.

Petruso, K. M. 1992. *Ayia Irini: The Balance Weights* (Keos VIII), Mainz.

Philippa-Touchais, A. 2007. "Aeginetan Matt Painted Pottery at Middle Helladic Aspis, Argos," in *Middle Helladic Pottery and Synchronisms*, ed. F. Felten, W. Gauss, and R. Smetana, Vienna, pp. 97–113.

Philippa-Touchais, A., and A. Balitsari. 2020. "Attica in the Middle: Middle Helladic Pottery Traditions and the Formation of Cultural Identity," in *Athens and Attica in Prehistory*, ed. N. Papadimitriou, J. C. Wright, S. Fachard, N. Polychronakou-Sgouritsa, and E. Andrikou, Oxford, pp. 387–398.

Philippa-Touchais, A., G. Touchais, S. Voutsaki, and J. Wright, eds. 2010. *Mesohelladika: La Grèce continentale au Bronze Moyen. Actes du colloque international organisé par l'École française d'Athènes, en collaboration avec l'American School of Classical Studies at Athens et le Netherlands Institute in Athens, Athènes, 8–12 Mars 2006* (*BCH* Suppl. 52), Athens.

Popham, M. 1967. "Late Minoan Pottery, a Summary," *BSA* 62, pp. 337–351.

———. 1969. "The Late Minoan Goblet and Kylix," *BSA* 64, pp. 299–304.

———. 1974. "Trial KV (1969), A Middle Minoan Building at Knossos," *BSA* 69, pp. 181–194.

Poursat, J.-C. 2013. "Ustensiles divers de terre cuite," in *Vie quotidienne et techniques au Minoen Moyen II* (*ÉtCret* 34), by J.-C. Poursat, Athens, pp. 129–135.

Poursat, J.-C., and C. Knappett. 2005. *La poterie du minoen moyen II: Production et utilisation* (*ÉtCret* 33), Athens.

Poursat, J.-C., and M. Loubet. 2005. "Métallurgie et contacts extérieurs à Malia (Crète) au Minoen Moyen II: Remarques sur une série d'analyses isotopiques du plomb," in *Emporia: Aegeans in the Central and Eastern Mediterranean. Proceedings of the 10th International Aegean Conference/10ᵉ Rencontre égéenne internationale, Athens, Italian School of Archaeology, 14–18 April 2004* (*Aegaeum* 25), ed. R. Laffineur and E. Greco, Liège, pp. 117–121.

Puglisi, D. 2011. "From the End of LM IA to the End of LM IB: The Pottery Evidence from Hagia Triada," in Brogan and Hallager 2011, pp. 267–290.

Quinn, P. S. 2013. *Ceramic Petrography: The Interpretation of Archaeological Pottery and Related Artefacts in Thin Section*, Oxford.

Quinn, P., P. Day, V. Kilikoglou, E. Faber, S. Katsarou-Tzeveleki, and A. Sampson. 2010. "Keeping an Eye on Your Pots: The Provenance of Neolithic Ceramics from the Cave of the Cyclops, Youra, Greece," *JAS* 37, pp. 1042–1052.

Rabillard, A., L. Arbaret, L. Jolivet, N. Le Breton, C. Gumiaux, R. Augier, B. Graseman. 2015. "Interactions between Plutonism and Detachments during Metamorphic Core Complex Formation, Serifos Island (Cyclades, Greece)," *Tectonics* 34, pp. 1080–1106.

Raymond, A. 2001. "Kamares Ware (and Minoans?) at Miletus," *Aegean Archaeology* 5, pp. 19–26.

Raymond A., I. Kaiser, L.-C. Rizzotto, and J. Zurbach. 2016. "Discerning Acculturation at Miletus: Minoanisation and Mycenaeanisation," in *Beyond Thalassocracies: Understanding Processes of Minoanisation and Mycenaeanisation in the Aegean*, ed. E. Gorogianni, P. Pavúk, and L. Girella, Oxford, pp. 58–74.

Renfrew, C. 2006. "Markiani in Perspective," in *Markiani, Amorgos: An Early Bronze Age Fortified Settlement. Overview of the 1985–1991 Investigations* (*BSA* Suppl. 40), by L. Marangou, C. Renfrew, C. Doumas, and G. Gavalas, London, pp. 247–256.

———. 2007. "The Development of the Excavation and the Stratigraphy of Phylakopi," in *Excavations at Phylakopi in Melos 1974–77* (*BSA* Suppl. 42), ed. C. Renfrew, N. Brodie, C. Morris, and C. Scarre, London, pp. 5–13.

―――. 2015. "The Sanctuary at Kavos," in *Kavos and the Special Deposits* (The Sanctuary on Keros and the Origins of Aegean Ritual Practice: The Excavations of 2006–2008 2), ed. C. Renfrew, O. Philaniotou, N. Brodie, G. Gavalas, and M. J. Boyd, Cambridge, pp. 555–560.

Renfrew, C., and R. K. Evans. 2007. "The Early Bronze Age Pottery," in *Excavations at Phylakopi in Melos 1974–77* (*BSA* Suppl. 42), ed. C. Renfrew, N. Brodie, C. Morris, and C. Scarre, London, pp. 129–180.

Renfrew, C., O. Philaniotou, N. Brodie, G. Gavalas, and M. J. Boyd, eds. 2015. *Kavos and the Special Deposits* (The Sanctuary on Keros and the Origins of Aegean Ritual Practice: The Excavations of 2006–2008 2), Cambridge.

Renfrew, J., G. Gavalas, M. Ugarković, J. Haas-Lebegyev, and C. Renfrew. 2013. "The Other Finds from Dhaskalio," in *The Settlement at Dhaskalio* (The Sanctuary on Keros and the Origins of Aegean Ritual Practice: The Excavations of 2006–2008 1), ed. C. Renfrew, O. Philaniotou, N. Brodie, G. Gavalas, and M. J. Boyd, Cambridge, pp. 645–665.

Rethemiotakis, G., and P. M. Warren. 2014. *Knossos: A Middle Minoan III Building in Bougadha Metochi* (*BSA* Studies 23), Athens.

Rice, A. H. N., C. Iglseder, B. Grasemann, A. Zámolyi, K. G. Nikolakopoulos, D. Mitropoulos, K. Voit, M. Müller, E. Draganitis, M. Rockenschaub, and P. I. Tsombos. 2012. "A New Geological Map of the Crustal-Scale Detachment on Kea (Western Cyclades, Greece)," *Austrian Journal of Earth Sciences* 105.3, pp. 108–124.

Rice, P. M. 1976. "Rethinking the Ware Concept," *AmerAnt* 41, pp. 538–543.

―――. 2015. *Pottery Analysis: A Sourcebook*, 2nd ed., Chicago.

Roux, V. 2003. "Ceramic Standardization and Intensity of Production: Quantifying Degrees of Specialization," *AmerAnt* 68, pp. 768–782.

―――. 2011. "Anthropological Interpretation of Ceramic Assemblages: Foundations and Implementations of Technological Analysis," in *Archaeological Ceramics: A Review of Current Research* (*BAR-IS* 2193), ed. S. Scarcella, Oxford, pp. 80–88.

Roux, V., and D. Corbetta. 1989. *The Potter's Wheel: Craft Specialization and Technical Competance*, New Delhi.

Roux, V., and M.-A. Courty. 1998. "Identification of Wheel-Fashioning Methods: Technological Analysis of 4th–3rd Millenium BC Oriental Ceramics," *JAS* 25, pp. 747–763.

Rupp, D. W., and M. Tsipopoulou. 1999. "Conical Cup Concentrations at Neopalatial Petras: A Case for a Ritualized Reception Ceremony with Token Hospitality," in *Meletemata: Studies in Aegean Archaeology Presented to Malcolm H. Wiener as He Enters His 65th Year*, ed. P. P. Betancourt, V. Karageorghis, R. Laffineur, W.-D. Niemeier, Liège, pp. 729–739.

Rutter, J. B. 1983. "Some Observations on the Cyclades in the Later Third and Early Second Millennia," *AJA* 87, pp. 69–76.

―――. 1990. "Pottery Groups from Tsoungiza of the End of the Middle Bronze Age," *Hesperia* 59, pp. 375–458.

―――. 1993a. "A Group of Late Helladic IIA Pottery from Tsoungiza," *Hesperia* 62, pp. 53–93.

―――. 1993b. "Review of Aegean Prehistory II: The Prepalatial Bronze Age of the Southern and Central Greek Mainland," *AJA* 97, pp. 745–797.

―――. 1995. *The Pottery of Lerna IV* (Lerna: A Preclassical Site in the Argolid III), Princeton.

―――. 2011. "Late Minoan IB at Kommos: A Sequence of at Least Three Distinct Stages," in Brogan and Hallager 2011, pp. 307–344.

―――. 2013. "'Minding the Gap': From Filling Archaeological Gaps to Accounting for Cultural Breaks; A 2013 Perspective on a Continuing Story," *AJA* 117, pp. 593–597.

―――. 2015. "Ceramic Technology in Rapid Transition: The Evidence from Settlement Deposits of the Shaft Grave Era at Tsoungiza (Corinthia)," in *The Transmission of Technical Knowledge in the Prodution of Ancient Mediterranean Pottery* (Österreichisches Archäologisches Institut Sonderschriften 54), ed. W. Gauss, G. Klebinder-Gauss, and C. von Rüden, Vienna, pp. 207–223.

―――. 2020. "Middle Helladic III–Late Helladic II Pottery Groups," in *The Mycenaean Settlement on Tsoungiza Hill* (Nemea Valley Archaeological Project III), by J. C. Wright and M. K. Dabney, Princeton, pp. 473–818.

Rutter, J. B., and M. Lindblom. Forthcoming. "A Shape for Few Seasons: The Rapid Appearance and Disappearance of the Mainland Greek Panel Cup," *Hesperia*.

Rutter, J. B., and S. H. Rutter. 1976. *The Transition to Mycenaean: A Stratified Middle Helladic II to Late Helladic IIA Pottery Sequence from Ayios Stephanos in Lakonia* (Monumenta Archaeologica 4), Los Angeles.

Sakellarakis, Y., and E. Sapouna-Sakellaraki. 1997. Αρχάνες. Μία νέα ματιά στη Μινωϊκή Κρήτη, Athens.

Sarri, K. 2010a. "Minyan and Minyanizing Pottery: Myth and Reality about a Middle Helladic Type Fossil," in Philippa-Touchais et al. 2010, pp. 603–613.

―――. 2010b. *Orchomenos IV: Orchomenos in der Mittleren Bronzezeit* (Bayerische Akademie der Wissenschaften, Philosophisch-Historische Klasse, Abhandlungen, Neue Folge 135), Munich.

Schachermeyr, F. 1976. *Die ägäische Frühzeit: Forschungsbericht über die Ausgrabungen im letzten Jahrzehnt und über ihre Ergebnisse für unser Geschichtsbild* 1: *Die vormykenischen Perioden des griechischen Festlandes und der Kykladen*, Vienna.

Schallin, A.-L. 1997. "The Late Bronze Age Potter's Workshop at Mastos in the Berbati Valley," in *Trade and Production in Premonetary Greece* (*SIMA-PB* 143), ed. C. Gillis, C. Risberg, B. Sjöberg, Jonsered, pp. 73–88.

Scheffer, C., O. Vanderhaeghe, P. Lanari, A. Tarantola, L. Ponthus, A. Photiades, and L. France. 2016. "Syn- to Post-orogenic Exhumation of Metamorphic Nappes: Structure and Thermobarometry of the Western Attic-Cycladic Metamorphic Complex (Lavrion, Greece)," *Journal of Geodynamics* 96, pp. 174–193.

Schiffer, M. B. 1996. *Formation Processes of the Archaeological Record*, Salt Lake City.

Schofield, E. 1982. "The Western Cyclades and Crete: A 'Special Relationship,'" *OJA* 1, pp. 9–25.

―――. 1984a. "Coming to Terms with Minoan Colonists," in Hägg and Marinatos 1984, pp. 45–48.

———. 1984b. "Destruction Deposits of the Earlier Late Bronze Age from Ayia Irini, Kea," in *The Prehistoric Cyclades*, ed. J. A. MacGillivray and R. L. N. Barber, Edinburgh, pp. 179–183.

———. 1990. "Evidence for Household Industries on Thera and Kea," in *Thera and the Aegean World III: Proceedings of the Third International Congress, Santorini, Greece, 3–9 September 1989* 1: *Archaeology*, ed. D. A. Hardy, C. G. Doumas, J. A. Sakellarakis, and P. M. Warren, London, pp. 201–211.

———. 1998. "Town Planning at Ayia Irini, Kea," in Mendoni and Mazarakis Ainian 1998, pp. 117–122.

———. 1999. "Conical Cups in Context," in *Meletemata: Studies in Aegean Archaeology Presented to Malcolm H. Wiener as He Enters His 65th Year* (*Aegaeum* 20), ed. P. P. Betancourt, V. Karageorghis, R. Laffineur, and W.-D. Niemeier, Liège, pp. 757–760.

———. 2011. *Ayia Irini: The Western Sector* (Keos X), Mainz.

Scholes, K. 1956. "The Cyclades in the Later Bronze Age: A Synopsis," *BSA* 51, pp. 9–40.

Schumacher, J. C., J. B. Brady, J. T. Cheney, and R. R. Tonnsen. 2008. "Glaucophane-Bearing Marbles on Syros, Greece," *Journal of Petrology* 49, pp. 1667–1686.

Sherratt, S. 2000. *Catalogue of Cycladic Antiquities in the Ashmolean Museum: The Captive Spirit*, Oxford.

Siedentopf, H. B. 1991. *Mattbemalte Keramik der Mittleren Bronzezeit* (Alt-Ägina IV.2), Mainz.

Sotirakopoulou, P. 1993. "The Chronology of the 'Kastri Group' Reconsidered," *BSA* 88, pp. 5–20.

———. 1996. "The Dating of the Late Phylakopi I as Evidenced at Akrotiri on Thera," *BSA* 91, pp. 113–136.

———. 2008. "Akrotiri, Thera: The Late Neolithic and Early Bronze Age Phases in the Light of Recent Excavations at the Site," in *Horizon: A Colloquium on the Prehistory of the Cyclades*, ed. N. Brodie, J. Doole, G. Gavalas, and C. Renfrew, Cambridge, pp. 121–134.

———. 2010. "The Cycladic Middle Bronze Age: A 'Dark Age' in Aegean Prehistory or a Dark Spot in Archaeological Research," in Philippa-Touchais et al. 2010, pp. 825–837.

———. 2016. *The Pottery from Dhaskalio*. (The Sanctuary on Keros and the Origins of Aegean Ritual Practice: The Excavations of 2006–2008 4), Cambridge.

Spencer, L. C. 2007. "Pottery Technology and Socio-Economic Diversity on the Early Helladic III to Middle Helladic II Greek Mainland," PhD diss., University College London.

Stamatakis, M. G., D. Fragoulis, S. Antonopoulou, and G. Stamatakis. 2010. "The Opaline Silica-Rich Sedimentary Rocks of Milos Island, Greece and Their Behaviour as Pozzolanas in the Manufacture of Cement," *Advances in Cement Research* 22, pp. 171–183.

Stamatakis, M. G., U. Lutat, M. Regueiro, and J. P. Calvo. 1996. "Milos: The Mineral Island," *Industrial Minerals* 341, pp. 57–61.

Stos, Z. A., and N. H. Gale. 2006. "Lead Isotope and Chemical Analyses of Slags from Chrysokamino," in *The Chrysokamino Metallurgy Workshop and Its Territory* (*Hesperia* Supplement 36), by P. P. Betancourt, Princeton, pp. 299–319.

Stos-Gale, Z. A., and C. F. Macdonald. 1991. "Sources of Metals and Trade in the Bronze Age Aegean," in *Bronze Age Trade in the Mediterranean* (*SIMA* 90), ed. N. H. Gale, Göteborg, pp. 249–288.

Stouraiti, C., P. Mitropoulos, J. Tarney, B. Barreiro, A. M. McGrath, E. Baltatzis. 2010. "Geochemistry and Petrogenesis of Late Miocene Granitoids, Cyclades, Southern Aegean: Nature of Source Components," *Lithos* 114, pp. 337–352.

Tankosić, Ž., and I. Mathioudaki. 2011. "The Finds from the Prehistoric Site of Ayios Nikolaos Mylon, Southern Euboea, Greece," *BSA* 106, pp. 99–140.

Tartaron, T. F. 2013. *Maritime Networks in the Mycenaean World*, Cambridge.

Televantou, C. A. 2008. "The Early Cycladic Cemetery at Rivari on Melos," in *Horizon: A Colloquium on the Prehistory of the Cyclades*, ed. N. Brodie, J. Doole, G. Gavalas, and C. Renfrew, Cambridge, pp. 209–216.

Tsipopoulou, M., and M. E. Alberti. 2011. "LM IB Petras: The Pottery from Room E in House II.1," in Brogan and Hallager 2011, pp. 463–498.

Vakirtzi, S. 2019. "Spindle Whorls and Loomweights," in *Akrotiri, Thera: Middle Bronze Age Pottery and Stratigraphy* 1: *Stratigraphy, Ceramic Typology and Technology, Weaving Equipment*, by I. Nikolakopoulou, Athens, pp. 479–500.

van de Moortel, A. 2006. "Middle Minoan IA and Protopalatial Pottery," in *The Monumental Minoan Buildings at Kommos* (Kommos V), ed. J. W. Shaw and M. C. Shaw, Princeton, pp. 264–377.

———. 2007. "Middle Minoan Pottery Chronology and Regional Diversity in Central Crete," in *Middle Helladic Pottery and Synchronisms*, ed. F. Felten, W. Gauss, and R. Smetana, Vienna, pp. 201–214.

———. 2011. "LM IB Ceramic Phases at Palaikastro and Malia: A Response to Seán Hemingway, J. Alexander MacGillivray, and L. Hugh Sackett," in Brogan and Hallager 2011, pp. 531–548.

van de Moortel, A., and P. Darcque. 2006. "Late Minoan I Architectural Phases and Ceramic Chronology at Malia," in *Πεπραγμένα Θ' Διεθνούς Κρητολόγικου Συνεδρίου, Ελούντα, 1–6 Οκτωβρίου 2001* T. A1.4, Herakleion, pp. 177–188.

van Doosselaere, B., C. Delhon, and E. Hayes. 2014. "Looking through Voids: A Microanalysis of Organic-Derived Porosity and Bioclasts in Archaeological Ceramics from Koumbi Saleh (Mauritania, Fifth/Sixth-Seventeenth Century AD)," *Archaeological and Anthropological Sciences* 6.4, pp. 373–396.

Vaughan, S. J. 1989. "Appendix 2: Petrographic Analysis of Mikre Vigla Wares," in "Mikre Vigla: A Bronze Age Settlement on Naxos," by R. L. N. Barber and O. Hadjianastasiou, *BSA* 84, pp. 150–159.

———. 2006. "B. Macroscopic and Petrographic Studies of Pottery from Markiani on Amorgos," in *Markiani, Amorgos: An Early Bronze Age Fortified Settlement. Overview of the 1985-1991 Investigations* (*BSA* Suppl. 40), ed. L. Marangou, C. Renfrew, C. Doumas, and G. Gavalas, London, pp. 99–101.

Vaughan, S. J., and D. Williams. 2007. "The Pottery Fabrics," in *Excavations at Phylakopi in Melos 1974–77* (*BSA* Suppl. 42), ed. C. Renfrew, N. Brodie, C. Morris, and C. Scarre, London, pp. 91–128.

Vaughan, S., and D. Wilson. 1993. "Interregional Contacts in the Aegean in Early Bronze II: The Talc Ware Connection," in *Wace and Blegen: Pottery as Evidence for Trade in the Aegean Bronze Age 1939–1989. Proceedings of the International Conference Held at the American School of Classical Studies, Athens, Dec. 2-3, 1989*, ed. C. W. Zerner, P. Zerner, and J. Winder, Amsterdam, pp. 169–186.

Vlachopoulos, A. G. 2016. "Neither Far from Knossos nor Close to Mycenae: Naxos in the Middle and Late Bronze Age Aegean," in *Beyond Thalassocracies: Understanding Processes of Minoanisation and Mycenaeanisation in the Aegean*, ed. E. Gorogianni, P. Pavúk, and L. Girella, Oxford, pp. 116–135.

Voigtländer, W. 2004. *Teichiussa: Näherung und Wirklichkeit*, Westfalen.

Wace, A. J. B. 1932. *Chamber Tombs at Mycenae* (*Archaeologia* LXXXII), Oxford.

Wagner, U., F. E. Wagner, W. Häusler, and I. Shimada. 2000. "The Use of Mössbauer Spectroscopy in Studies of Archaeological Ceramics," in *Radiation in Art and Archeometry*, ed. D. C. Creagh and D. A. Bradley, Amsterdam and New York, pp. 417–443.

Walberg, G. 1976. *Kamares: A Study of the Character of Palatial Middle Minoan Pottery*, Uppsala.

Wall, S. M., J. H. Musgrave, and P. M. Warren. 1986. "Human Bones from a Late Minoan IB House at Knossos," *BSA* 81, pp. 334–388.

Walter, H., and F. Felten. 1981. *Die vorgeschichtliche Stadt: Befestigungen, Häuser, Funde* (*Alt-Ägina* III), Mainz.

Warren, P. M. 1980–1981. "Knossos: Stratigraphical Museum Excavations, 1978–1980; Part I," *AR* 27, pp. 73–92.

———. 1987. Review of *Ayia Irini: Specialized Domestic and Industrial Pottery* (*Keos* VI), by H. S. Georgiou, *AntJ* 67.1, pp. 142–143.

———. 1991. "A New Minoan Deposit from Knossos, c. 1600 B.C., and Its Wider Relations," *BSA* 86, pp. 319–340.

———. 1999. "LM IA: Knossos, Thera, Gournia," in *Meletemata: Studies in Aegean Archaeology Presented to Malcolm H. Wiener as He Enters His 65th Year* (*Aegaeum* 20), ed. P. P. Betancourt, V. Karageorghis, R. Laffineur, W.-D. Niemeier, Liège, pp. 893–903.

———. 2002. "Political Structure in Neopalatial Crete," in *Monuments of Minos: Rethinking the Minoan Palaces* (*Aegaeum* 23), ed. J. Driessen, I. Schoep, and R. Laffineur, Liège, pp. 201–205.

———. 2007. "A New Pumice Analysis from Knossos and the End of Late Minoan IA," in *The Synchronisation of Civilisations in the Eastern Mediterranean in the Second Millennium B.C. 3*, ed. M. Bietak and E. Czerny, Vienna, pp. 495–499.

———. 2011. "Late Minoan IB Pottery from Knossos: Stratigraphical Museum Excavations, the North Building," in Brogan and Hallager 2011, pp. 183–196.

———. 2014. "Aromatic Questions," *CretChron* 34, pp. 13–41.

Warren, P. M., and V. Hankey. 1989. *Aegean Bronze Age Chronology*, Bristol.

Whitbread, I. K. 1995. *Greek Transport Amphorae: A Petrological and Archaeological Study* (Fitch Laboratory Occasional Paper 4), Athens.

———. 2001. "Petrographic Analysis of Middle Bronze Age Pottery from Lerna, Argolid," in *Archaeometry Issues in Greek Prehistory and Antiquity*, ed. Y. Bassiakos, E. Aloupi, and Y. Facorellis, Athens, pp. 367–377.

———. 2011. "Petrographic Analysis of Ceramics from the Berbati Valley," in *Mastos in the Berbati Valley: An Intensive Archaeological Survey* (ActaAth 4°, 54), ed. M. Lindblom and B. Wells, Stockholm, pp. 143–176.

Whitelaw, T. 2004. "The Development of an Island Centre: Urbanization at Phylakopi on Melos," in *Explaining Social Change: Studies in Honour of Colin Renfrew*, ed. J. Cherry, C. Scarre, and S. Shennan, Cambridge, pp. 149–166.

———. 2005. "A Tale of Three Cities: Chronology and Minoanisation at Phylakopi on Melos," in *Autochthon: Papers Presented to O. T. P. K. Dickinson on the Occasion of His Retirement, Institute of Classical Studies, University of London, 9 November 2005*, ed. A. Dakouri-Hild and S. Sherratt, Oxford, pp. 37–69.

Wiener, M. H. 1990. "The Isles of Crete? The Minoan Thalassocracy Revisited," in *Thera and the Aegean World III: Proceedings of the Third International Congress, Santorini, Greece, 3–9 September 1989* 1: *Archaeology*, ed. D. A. Hardy, C. G. Doumas, J. A. Sakellarakis, and P. M. Warren, London, pp. 128–161.

———. 1991. "The Nature and Control of Minoan Foreign Trade," in *Bronze Age Trade in the Mediterranean*, ed. N. H. Gale, Göteborg, pp. 325–350.

———. 2007. "Neopalatial Knossos: Rule and Role," in *Krinoi kai Limenes: Studies in Honor of Joseph and Maria Shaw* (Prehistory Monographs 22), ed. P. P. Betancourt, M. C. Nelson, and H. Williams, Philadelphia, pp. 231–242.

———. 2011. "Conical Cups: From Mystery to History," in *Our Cups are Full: Pottery and Society in the Aegean Bronze Age: Studies Presented to Guenter Kopcke in Celebration of His 75th Birthday* (Prehistory Monographs 43), ed. W. Gauss, M. Lindblom, R. A. K. Smith, and J. C. Wright, Oxford, pp. 355–368.

———. 2013. "Realities of Power: The Minoan Thalassocracy in Historical Perspective," in *Amilla: The Quest for Excellence*, ed. R. B. Koehl, Philadelphia, pp. 149–173.

———. 2016. "Aegean Warfare at the Opening of the Late Bronze Age in Image and Reality," in *Metaphysis: Ritual, Myth and Symbolism in the Aegean Bronze Age* (*Aegaeum* 38), ed. E. Alram-Stern, F. Blakolmer, S. Deger-Jalkotzy, R. Laffineur, and J. Weilhartner, Leuven-Liège, pp. 139–146.

Wiersma, C. 2013. "Building the Bronze Age: Architectural and Social Change on the Greek Mainland during Early Helladic III, Middle Helladic, and Late Helladic I," PhD diss., University of Groningen.

Wild, E. M., W. Gauß, G. Forstenpointner, M. Lindblom, R. Smetana, P. Steier, U. Thanheiser, and F. Weninger. 2010. "14C Dating of the Early to Late Bronze Age Stratigraphic Sequence of Aegina Kolonna, Greece," *Nuclear Instruments and Methods in Physics Research Bulletin* 268, pp. 1013–1021.

Williams, D. F. 1978. "A Petrological Examination of Pottery from Thera," in *Thera and the Aegean World III: Proceedings of the Third International Congress, Santorini, Greece, 3–9 September 1989* 3: *Chronology*, ed. D. A. Hardy, C. G. Doumas, J. A. Sakellarakis, and P. M. Warren, London, pp. 507–514.

———. 1981. "Heavy Mineral Analysis of Bronze Age Pottery from Melos and Thera: A Preliminary Report," *Revue d'Archéométrie* 3, pp. 321–323.

Wilson, D. E. 1987. "Kea and East Attike in Early Bronze II: Beyond Pottery Typology," in *ΣΥΝΕΙΣΦΟΡΑ McGill: Papers in Greek Archaeology and History in Memory of Colin D. Gordon*, ed. J. M. Fossey, Amsterdam, pp. 35–49.

———. 1999. *Ayia Irini: Periods I–III. The Neolithic and Early Bronze Age Settlements* (Keos IX), Mainz.

———. 2013. "Ayia Irini II–III. Kea: The Phasing and Relative Chronology of the EB II Settlement," *Hesperia* 82, pp. 385–434.

Wilson, D. E., and M. Eliot. 1984. "Ayia Irini, Period III: The Last Phase of Occupation at the E.B.A. Settlement," in *The Prehistoric Cyclades*, ed. J. A. MacGillivray and R. L. N. Barber, Edinburgh, pp. 78–87.

Wohlmayr, W. 2007. "Aegina Kolonna MH III–LH I: Ceramic Phases of an Aegean Trade-Domain," in *Middle Helladic Pottery and Synchronisms*, ed. F. Felten, W. Gauss, and R. Smetana, Vienna, pp. 45–56.

Xypolias, P., I. Iliopoulos, V. Chatzaras, and S. Kokkalas. 2012. "Subduction- and Exhumation-Related Structures in the Cycladic Blueschists: Insights from South Evia Island (Aegean Region, Greece)," *Tectonics* 31.2, TC2001.

Zerner, C. W. 1988. "Middle Helladic and Late Helladic I Pottery from Lerna: Part II, Shapes," *Hydra* 4, pp. 1–51.

———. 2008. "The Middle Helladic Pottery, with the Middle Helladic Wares from Late Helladic Deposits and the Potters' Marks," in *Ayios Stephanos: Excavations at a Bronze Age and Medieval Settlement in Southern Laconia*, ed. W. D. Taylour and R. Janko, London, pp. 177–298.

INDEX

Page numbers in *italics* represent figures, while page numbers in **bold** represent tables.

Achaea, 91
Acropolis Burnished ware, *see* pottery
Acropolis wells, 84, 89, 214, 217
Aegean, maps, 2
Aegina, 1, 91, 152, **179–180**, 181, 189, **198**, 215, 227–231, 238
    see also pottery, Aegina
Akroterion Ourion, 230
Akrotiri, 4, 41, 67, 89, 151, 154, 157, 167, 175, 178–181, 195, 198–199, 214, 227, 229–233, 235–237, 260, 283–284, 287, 290, 294
    see also pottery, Melos/Thera, Thera
Alley AB, 16, 22, 25, 27, 113–144, 173, 175, 207, 324–327
    Period III, 113–114, **115**, 141
    Period IV, 6, 20, 31, 113–120, 141–142
    Period V, 6, **117**, 120, 142
    Period VI, 23, **117**, 120–121, 142–143
    Period VII, 24, **118**, 121, 143–144
    test pits, 4, 6, 7, 15–16, 27, 113–114, 141
Amorgos, *see* pottery
Anatolia, 1, 227, 229–230
    see also Miletus, Troy
Anatolianizing wares, *see* pottery
Andros, *see* pottery
Archanes, 180–181
Argive Minyan ware, *see* pottery
Argolid, 222
    see also pottery
Asine, 58, 216, **217**, 295, 300
Attica, 1, 148, 151, 154–156, 199, 227, 231, 233, 237, 250, 270
    see also pottery
Ayia Irini
    abandoned, 1, 3, 148, 153, 156, 167, 171, 173, 189, 228, 237–238
    earthquake impacts, 3, 120–121, 142–145, 144, 207
    overview, 1–6
Ayia Triada, 180, 211
Ayios Kosmas, 141
Ayios Nikolaos Mylon, 231
Ayios Stephanos, 84, 91, 216, **217**, 254

Barber, R. L. N., 118
Berbati, 222, 298
Berg, I., 199

Bikaki, A., 3–4, 7–9, 27, 31–32, 58–59, 63, 109, 114, **116**, 119–121, 140, 143–144, 166, 181, 227
Black and Red style, *see* pottery
Black Burnished ware, *see* pottery, EBA Black Burnished ware
Boeotia, *see* pottery, Boeotia, central Greece
bone, 42, 47, 69, 77, 104, 119–120
    awls, 32, 47, 66–67, 106, 111, 123, 135, 141
    bovid, 37, 55, 66–67, 93, 111
    burnt, 15, 106, 111–112
    ovicaprid, 34, 38, 77, 123, 135
    peg, 55
Broodbank, C., 227–228

Carinci, F., 180
Caskey, J. L., 1, 10, 144, 191, 197, 199, 207, 215–216
Central Greece, *see* pottery, Attica, Boeotia, central Greece, Euboea
ceramic lots, 4, 324–328
    B03-19, 55, 58, 63, 94
    B03-20, 33, 53, 55, 57–58, 63, 94–95, 98
    B03-25, 33, 58
    B03-27, 33
    B03-28, 33, 57
    B03-29, 33, 48, 85
    B03-31, 33
    B03-33, 33
    B03-35, 33
    B03-36, 63, 95, 97–99, 101
    B03-39, 33, 48–49, 51
    B03-40, 63, 101, 103
    B03-41, 33, 48–49, 55
    B03-42, 63
    B03-43, 63, 98–99
    B03-44, 63, 98–99
    B03-46, 63, 85, 85–89, 91
    B03-50, **106**
    B03-51, 63, 85–87, 91
    B03-52, 63
    B03-55, **62**
    B03-57, 63, 87, 91, 93
    B03-61, 63, 88, 91, 93–94, 216
    B03-64, 63–64, 88, 91, 216
    B03-70, 105, 106, *108*, 109, 111, 207, **219–222**, **224**

B03-71a, 106, 110, 111–112, 207, **219–222**, 224
B03-72, *102*, 104, **105**, 107, 109, 173
B03-73, 104
B03-74, 104
B03-76, 32–33
B03-78, 31–32
B03-81, 31, 41
B03-83, 31
B03-87, 118, 138, 140
B03-88, 118, 138, 140
B03-93, 33, 48
B03-94, 117, 134, 137, 139
B03-95, 42–43, 45, 47
B03-96, 117, 134, 136–137
B03-97, 116–117, 118, 121, 134, 135–136
B03-98, 32–33
B03-99, 32, 43, 47
B03-103, 63, 65, 83–84, 93
B03-104, 65, 83
B03-105, 60, 79
B03-106, 60
B03-107, 65, 83
B03-108, 61, 65, 84, 207, **224**
B03-109, 60, 79
B03-114, 37, 59–60
B03-116, 31–32, 39
B03-117, 31, 39
B03-142, 32, 39
B03-143, 31, 42
B03-144, 32, 42
B03-145, 31, 39
B03-148, 33, *110*, 112–113, 207, **219–222**
B03-249, 113
B03-250, 104
B03-506, 113
B03-765, 121
B03-766, 121, 139
B03-767, 121, 139
B03-768, 121, 139
B03-769, 121
B03-771, 121, 139
B03-772, 121, 139
B03-773, 121
B03-774, 120
B03-775, 120
B03-776, 120, 135
B03-777, 120, 135
B03-778, 120, 135
B03-780, 120
B03-781, 120
B03-782, 120, 135
B03-783, 120
B03-784, 120
B03-785, **117**, 119, 130, 133, 175, **182**, 184
B03-786, **117**, 119, 130, 132–133, **182**, 184
B03-788, 116, 119, *130*, 132, **182**, 184
B03-789, 116, 119, 130, 132, **182**, 184
B03-790, 116, 119, 130, 131–132, 176, **182**, 184
B03-791, 119, 131

B03-793, 119
B03-794, 116, 118, 129, **184**
B03-795, 118
B03-795a, 118
B03-796, 118
B03-797, 118, 126
B03-798, 118
B03-799, 114, 115, 124, 125–126, **182**, **184**
B03-800, 114
B03-801, 114
B03-802, 113, 115, 124, 125
B03-803, 113, 115, 123–125, 165, **168–169**
B03-804, 113, 115, 123, 124, 165, **168–169**
B03-805, 110, 113, 115, 122–123, 124, 165, **168–169**
B03-806, 110, 115, 122, 165, **168–169**
B03-807, 119
B03-808, 119
B03-809, 59–60, 61, 63, 84–85, 207
B03-810, 61, 65, 71, 74, 77–78
B03-811, 60, 61, 77
B03-812, 59, 61, 65–66, 69, 71, 74, 75–77
B03-812 etc., 77, 165, **168–169**
B03-813, 59, 61, 74, 76–77
B03-814, 61, 65–66, 69, 71, 74, 76, 165, **168–169**
B03-814 etc., 76, 165, **168–169**
B03-815, 61, 69, 75, 165, **168–169**
B03-815 etc., *74*, 75–76, 165, **168–169**
B03-816, 59, 61, 65–66, 69, 71, 75, 77, 165, **168–169**
B03-817, 59, 61, 65, 67, 69, 71, *74*, 75, 77, 165, **168–169**
B03-818, 59, 61, 65–67, 69, 71, 73–74, 75–78, 165, **168–169**
B03-819, 59, 61, 69, 71, 73
B03-820, 59, 61, 65–67, 69, 71, *72*, 75, 77, 165, **168–169**
B03-821, 59, 61, 65–66, 69–71, 76, 165, **168–169**
B03-821 etc., 69, *70*, 165, **168–169**
B03-822, 59, 61, 65–69, 71, 75, 165, **168–169**
B03-823, 59, 61, 65–69, 71, 75–77, 165, **168–169**
B03-824, 59, 61, 65–66, 68, 69, 165, **168–169**
B03-825, **29**, 31, 34–35, 36
B03-825a, **29**, 31, 34
B03-826, **30**, 32, 36, 38
B03-827, **29**, 31
B03-828, **29**, 31, 34, 36
B03-829, 28, **29**, 34, 36, 165, **168–169**
B03-830, 59, 61, 65–66, 69, 71, 75–78, 165, **168–169**
B601CL, *12*, *16*, *17*, 28–30, 31–32, 36, 38–42, *44*, 191, **200–202**
B602CL, *12*, *14*, *16–18*, **28–29**, 31, 35–37, 59, 60–61, 104, 105
B603CL, *14*, *18*, 60–61, 74, 78–83, 104, 173
B604CL, *17–19*, 33, 53, 60, 62, 63, 65, *92*, 94–101, *102*, 106, 207, **219–222**, 224
B605CL, *18*, 60, 62, 63, 94, 101–103, **219–222**, 224
B606CL, *18*, 60–62, 63–64, 85–94, 103, 105–106, 207, **219–222**, 224
B607CL, *14*, *18*, 59–63, 65, 82, 83–84, *86*, 207, **219–222**, 224
B608CL, 7, *12*, *17*, **28**, **30**, 33, 54, 55–58, 94, 101, **219–222**, 224

INDEX

B609CL, *12*, *17*, **28**, 30, 33, 43, *46*, 48–55, 85, 94, 112, 207, **219–222**, 224
B610CL, *12*, *16*, *17*, **28**, 30, 31–33, 42–49, 191, **200–202**
B646CL, *19*, 114, 118, 121, 138, 139–140, 207, **219–222**, 224
B647CL, *19*, 114, 117–118, 121, 138, 139, 191, **200–202**
B648CL, *19*, 114, 117, 120, *130*, 134, 135, 191, **200–202**
B649CL, *19*, 114, 117, 120, 133, 173, 181, 184
B791/793CL, *19*, 114, 116, 119, 128, 129, 131, 175–176, **182**, 184
B795/a/796CL, *19*, 114, 116, 118, 126–129, 175–176, **182**, 184
B797/798CL, *19*, 114–115, 124, 126, 175–176, **182–184**
B800/801CL, *19*, 114–115, 124, 125
combined lots, 7–8, 28, 60, 114
notations, 10, 27
see also excavation units
ceramics:
  Final Neolithic, 1
  synchronisms of, 8, 165–167, 173, 178–181, 191, 197–199, 216, **217**
  see also ceramic lots; pottery
Chalandriani, 227
Cherry, J. F., 199, 230–231, 235
chronological periods, 3, 4
  Archaic, 7, 28, 62, 63–64, 94, **105–106**
  EBA, 1, 3, 4, 20, 27–28, **29**, 31, 34–38, 59–60, **61**, 64–83, 95, 104, 107, 109, 112–114, 122–125, 133, 136–137, 141, 143, 148, 150–157, 165–171, 173, 175, 184, 189, **201**, 218, **219**, 227–231, 238
    see also chronological periods, Period II, Period III
  LBA, 1, 3, 4, 5, 7–8, 10, 20, 27–28, **29**, 31, 33–35, 45, 59–64, 67, 71, 78–83, 94, 101, 103–104, 107, 112–114, 120–121, 135, 141–144, 148, 150–157, 176, 185, 191, 195, 197–199, 207, 216, **217**, 227, 229–230, 232–238
    see also chronological periods, Period VI, Period VII, Period VIII
  MBA, 1, 3, 4, 7, 28, **29–30**, 31, 34–35, 59, **61**, 64, 71, 76–78, 104, **105**, 107–109, 118–120, 136–137, 139, 141–142, 150–157, 171, 173–189, 205, 227–238
    see also chronological periods, Period IV, Period V
  Period I, 1, **3**, 141, 148, 167, 238
  Period II, 1, **3**, 4, 27, 141, 148, 165–167, 169, 170–171, 227–228, 238
  Period III, 1, **3**, 4, 6, 8, 20, 27–28, **29**, 31, 33–37, 59–60, **61**, 65–83, 104, 105, 112–114, **115**, 122–125, 135–136, 141, 148, 150–151, 153–156, 165–171, 173, 183–184, 189, 203, 227–228, 230–231, 238, 250–252, 258, 260–261, 264
  Period IV, 1, **3**, 4, 6–8, 20, 27, **29**, 31–32, 34–35, 38–39, 41–42, 59–60, **61**, 75–76, 78–83, 85, 104, 113–114, **115**, 118, 123, 125, 133, 135–136, 141–143, 148, 150–157, 165, 167, 173–179, 181–186, 189, 199, **200**, 201, 203–205, 211, **219**, **221**, 227–233, 236–238, **247**, **249**, 250–259, 261–263, 271
  Period IVa, 4, 31–32, 60, 114, **115**, 118–119, 125–126, 129, 141–142, 175–179, **185**, 186, 229
  Period IVb, 4, 115–117, 118–119, 125–133, 142, 175–179, 185–186
  Period IVc, 4, 107, **116**–117, 119, 132–133, 142, 175–179, 181, **185**, 186
  Period V, 1, **3**, 4, 6–8, 27, 31–32, 35, 38, 43, 59–60, 61, 76, 78–83, 85, 104, 107, 113, 117, 118–120, 133, 135, 141–143, 148, 150–157, 165, 173, 176–181, 186–189, 199, 203–205, 211, 214, 227, 229, 230, 232–238, **249**, 250–252
  Period VI, 1, **3**, 4, 6–8, *22–23*, 28, **29–30**, 31–32, 35, 38–48, 59–62, 77, 81, 85, 101–103, 113, **117–118**, 120, 135–139, 141–143, 148, 150–157, 165, 173, 178, 180–181, 184, 186, 189, 191–205, 207, 211, 213–214, 218, 222–223, 225–227, 229, 230, 232–238, **249**, 250–259, 261–263, 268
  Period VI early, **29–30**, 31–32, 38–42, **117–118**, 120, 135–139, 178, 180–181, 191–193, 195, 197–199, 201
  Period VI late, **30**, 42–48, 191, 193–195, 197–199, 201
  Period VII, 1, **3**, 4, 6–8, 16, *24–25*, 27–28, **30**, 31–33, 35, 42–43, 55, 58–60, 62–64, 84–85, 101–104, **105**, 111, 113, 117–118, 120–121, 139–144, 148, 150–157, 165, 173, 186, 189, 191, 195, 197, 201, 203, 205, 207–227, 229, 230, 233–23, **249**, 250–252, 254–260, 262–264
  Period VIIa, 4, 30, 61, 63, 65, 83–85, 133, 143, 207, *208*, 211, 213–216, **217**
  Period VIIb, 4, 30, 33, 48–58, 61–62, 63, 65, 85–101, 104, 105–106, 109–113, 121, 140, 144, 207, *209*, 211, 214–216, **217**
  Period VIIc, 4, 30, 55–58, 62, 94–101, 105–106, 207, 211, 213, 215–216, **217**
  Period VIII, 3, 4, 30, 58, 62, 101–103, 105–106, 144–145, 216, 234–235, 238
Coldstream, J. N., 84, 139, 155
Coleman, K. A., 64
communal events, 9, 186, 228, 231–232, 234, 236–237
Corinthia, *see* pottery
Courty, M. -A., 156
Crego, D. M., 175–176, 183, 229
Crete, 1, 2, 84, 142, 155–157, 180, 229–230, 232, 235
  technologies of, 3, 157, 229, 233–235
  see also pottery, Crete, Cretan wares, Mesara, Minoan/-izing, Minoan published wares
Cummer, W. W., 113, 119–120, 143, 191, 192
Cyclades, 1, 3, 156–157, 173, 175–176, 189, 205, 215, 222, 226–238
  chronology of, 3
  geology, 147–148, 151, 153–155
  maps, 2
  and Minoanization, 232–235
  see also pottery, Amorgos, Andros, Cyclades, Ikaria, Ios, Melos, Melos/Thera, Naxos, Paros, Seriphos, Sikinos, Siphnos, Syros, Tenos, Thera
Cycladic White ware, *see* pottery

Dark-Brown Slipped and Burnished ware, *see* pottery, EBA Dark-Brown Slipped and Burnished
Dark Burnished ware, *see* pottery

Davis, J. L., 147, 173, 187, 189, 198–199, 230, 234–235
Day, P. M., 154, 170
deposits, 4
    disturbances to, 6–7, 28, 31, 33, 55, 59–60, 63, 65, 94, 101, 104, 107, 113, 121, 135, 140, 141, 144
    summaries of, **29–30, 61–62, 105–106, 115–118**
Dhaskalio, 79, 142, 167, 169–170, 227–229, 258
Dickinson, O. T. P. K., 231
Dietz, S., 181
Drain 1, 7, 19, 25, 118, 121, 138, 140, 143–144
Drain 2, 19, 21, 27, 114, 116, 119, 128, 129–132, 142
Drain from A.34, 25
drains, 142–144

Early Bronze Age, 3
    plan, 20
    deposits, 28, 29, 31, 34, 59–60, **61**, 65–81, 104, **105**, 113–114, **115**, 122–125, 141
    and RBMb/PFG 1, 153
    see also chronological periods; pottery, EBA wares
earthquakes, 3, 120–121, 142–145, 207, 216
east Aegean, 1, 66–67, 151, 155, 177, 183–184, 195, 228, 230–231, 234–235, 255, 301–302
    see also Miletus; pottery, east Aegean, Kos, Rhodes; Troy
eating/drinking practices, 1, 9, 141, 166, 171, 185–186, 189, 205, 211, 226, 228, 231–232, 234–235, 237–238
Eleusis, 51, 199
Euboea, 1, 152, 156–157, 169, 171, 227, 231, 237
    geology of, 148, 151, 153–155
    see also pottery, central Greece, Euboea
excavation notebooks, 27, 32, 62, 121
excavation units, 4, 11–14, 16, 324–328
    B03-11, *17–19*, 33, 63, 113, 121, **324**
    B03-18, *11, 14, 17–19*, 33, 63, 113, 121, **324**
    B03-19, *11, 14, 17–19*, 28, 33, **60**, 63, 101, **324**
    B03-20, *11, 14, 17–19*, 33, **60**, 63, 101, **324**
    B03-21, *19*, 113, 121, **324**
    B03-25, *11, 12, 17*, 28, 33, 58, **324**
    B03-27, *11, 12, 17*, 28, 33, **324**
    B03-28, *11, 12, 17*, 28, 33, **324**
    B03-29, *11, 12, 17*, 28, 33, **324**
    B03-31, *11, 12, 17*, 28, 33, 55, **324**
    B03-33, *11, 12, 17*, 28, 33, 55, **324**
    B03-35, *11, 12, 17*, 28, 33, 55, **324**
    B03-36, *11, 13, 14, 18, 19*, **60**, 63–64, 101, 106, **324**
    B03-37, *18, 19*, 63, 106, **324**
    B03-39, *11, 12, 17*, 28, 33, 55, **324**
    B03-40, *11, 13, 14, 18*, **60**, 63–64, 94, 103, **324**
    B03-41, *11, 12, 17*, 28, 33, **324**
    B03-42, *11, 13, 14, 18*, **60**, 63–64, 94, **324**
    B03-43, *11, 13, 14, 18, 19*, **60**, 63–64, 101, 106, **324**
    B03-44, *11, 13, 14, 18, 19*, **60**, 63, 101, 106, **324**
    B03-46, *11, 13–15, 18, 19*, **60**, 63–64, 94, 106, **324**
    B03-50, *15, 19*, 106, 112, **324**
    B03-51, *11, 13–15, 18, 19*, **60**, 63, 93, 106, **324**
    B03-52, *11, 13, 14, 18*, **60**, 63–64, 98–94, **324**
    B03-55, *18*, 64
    B03-57, *11, 13, 14, 18*, **60**, 63–64, 94, **324**
    B03-61, *11, 13–15, 18, 19*, **60**, 63–64, 94, 106, 216, **324**
    B03-64, *11, 13, 14, 18*, **60**, 62–64, 93, 216, **324**
    B03-70, *11, 14, 15, 19*, 106, 111, **324**
    B03-71a, *11, 14, 15, 19*, 106, 112, **325**
    B03-72, *11, 14, 15, 19*, 104, **325**
    B03-73, *11, 15, 19*, 28, **60**, 37, 104, **325**
    B03-74, *11, 15, 19*, 28, **60**, 104, **325**
    B03-76, *11, 17*, 28, 32, 47–48, **325**
    B03-78, *11, 17*, 28, 31–32, 47, **325**
    B03-79, *17*, 28, 31, 42, **325**
    B03-81, *11, 17*, 28, 31, 42, **325**
    B03-83, *11, 17*, 28, 37, **60**, **325**
    B03-87, *19*, 121, **325**
    B03-88, *15, 19*, 113, 121, 140, **325**
    B03-93, *17*, **28**, 33, **325**
    B03-94, *15, 19*, 113, 121, **325**
    B03-95, *11, 17*, 28, 32, 47–48, **325**
    B03-96, *15, 19*, 113, 121, **325**
    B03-97, *15, 19*, 113, 118, 121, **325**
    B03-98, *11, 17*, 28, 47–48, **325**
    B03-99, *11, 17*, 28, 32, 47–48, **325**
    B03-103, *11, 13, 14, 18*, **60**, 62–63, 65, **325**
    B03-104, *11, 14, 18*, **60**, 62, 65, 84, **325**
    B03-105, *11, 14, 18*, 60, 62, **325**
    B03-106, *11, 14, 18*, 60, 81, 83, **325**
    B03-107, *11, 18*, **60**, 62, 64–65, **325**
    B03-108, *14, 18*, 64–65, **325**
    B03-109, *11, 14, 18*, 60, 81, 83, **325**
    B03-113, *18*, 62
    B03-114, *11, 18*, 28, 59–60, **325**
    B03-116, *11, 17*, 28, 31–32, 42, **325**
    B03-117, *11, 12, 17*, 28, 32, 42, **325**
    B03-118, *11, 17*, 28, 37, **60**, **325**
    B03-142, *11, 17*, 28, 31–32, 42, **325**
    B03-143, *11, 17*, 28, 31, **325**
    B03-144, *11, 17*, 28, 32, **325**
    B03-145, *11, 17*, 28, **325**
    B03-146, *11, 17*, 28, **60**, **326**
    B03-147, *11, 17*, 28, 37, **60**, 141, **326**
    B03-148, *12*, 112, **326**
    B03-149, *17*, **28**, **326**
    B03-249, 112–113, **326**
    B03-250, *15, 18, 19*, 104, **326**
    B03-506, 112, **326**
    B03-764, *19*, 113, **326**
    B03-765, *16, 19*, 121, **326**
    B03-766, *16, 19*, 114, 121, **326**
    B03-767, *16, 19*, 114, 121, 140, **326**
    B03-768, *16, 19*, 114, 121, **326**
    B03-769, *16, 19*, 114, 121, **326**
    B03-770, *16, 19*, 120, 142, **326**
    B03-771, *16, 19*, 114, 121, **326**
    B03-772, *19*, **114**, 121, **326**
    B03-773, *16, 19*, 114, 121, **326**
    B03-774, *16, 19*, 120, **326**
    B03-775, *19*, 120, **326**
    B03-776, *19*, **114**, 120, **326**
    B03-777, *19*, **114**, 120, **326**
    B03-778, *19*, **114**, 120, **326**

B03-779, *19*, **326**
B03-780, *19*, 120, 135, **326**
B03-781, *19*, 120, **326**
B03-782, *16*, *19*, **114**, 120, 135, **326**
B03-783, *16*, *19*, **114**, 120, **326**
B03-784, *16*, *19*, **114**, 120, 133, **326**
B03-785, *16*, *19*, 119, **326**
B03-786, *16*, *19*, 119, 133, **326**
B03-787, *19*, **326**
B03-788, *16*, *19*, 119, **326**
B03-789, *16*, *19*, 119, **326**
B03-790, *16*, *19*, 119, 132, **326**
B03-791, *16*, *19*, 119, 131, **327**
B03-792, *19*, **327**
B03-793, *16*, *19*, 119, 131, **327**
B03-794, *16*, *19*, 118, **327**
B03-795, *16*, *19*, 118, 129, **327**
B03-795a, *19*, 118, **327**
B03-796, *16*, *19*, 118, **327**
B03-797, *16*, *19*, 114, 118, **327**
B03-798, *16*, *19*, 114, 118, **327**
B03-799, *16*, *19*, 114, 184, **327**
B03-800, *16*, *19*, 114, **327**
B03-801, *16*, *19*, 114, **327**
B03-802, *16*, *19*, 113, **327**
B03-803, *16*, *19*, 113, **327**
B03-804, *16*, *19*, 113, **327**
B03-805, *16*, *19*, 113, 123, **327**
B03-806, *16*, *19*, 113–114, **327**
B03-807, *19*, 119, **327**
B03-808, *19*, 119, **327**
B03-809, *18*, 63, **327**
B03-810, *18*, 59–60, **327**
B03-811, *18*, 60, 77, **327**
B03-812, *18*, 59, **327**
B03-813, *18*, 59, 77, **327**
B03-814, *18*, 59, **327**
B03-815, *18*, 59, **327**
B03-816, *18*, 59, **327**
B03-817, *18*, 59, **327**
B03-818, *18*, 59, **327**
B03-819, *18*, 59, **327**
B03-820, *18*, 59, **327**
B03-821, *18*, 59, 69, **327**
B03-822, *18*, 59, 67, **327**
B03-823, *18*, 59, 66–67, **327**
B03-824, *18*, 59, 66, **328**
B03-825, *17*, 31–32, 35, **328**
B03-825a, *17*, 31, **328**
B03-826, *17*, 32, 38, **328**
B03-827, *17*, 28, 31, **328**
B03-828, *17*, 28, 31, **328**
B03-829, *17*, 28, 34, **328**
B03-830, *18*, 65–66, **328**
exogamy, 227–230

field numbers, 9
Fitch Laboratory, 9, 147, 154, 250, 265, 272, 274, 276, 282, 287

floors, 7, 32, 59, 60, 62, 64, 114, 141–144
   see also specific surfaces
fortification walls, 1, 3, 27, 118–119, 141–142, 144, 173, 229

Georgakopoulou, M. A., 154, 257, 294, 296
Georgiou, H. S., 144, 233
Gilstrap, W. D., 155, 311–312
globalization, 236
Gorogianni, E., 189, 199
graves, 1, 32, 133, 157, 177
Gray/Black Burnished ware, *see* pottery
Gray Minyan ware, *see* pottery

Harris matrices, 6, 17–19, 27
Hearth 1, 11–12, 17, 22–23, **30**, 32, 43, 142–143
hearths, 106, 129, 165, 169, 171, 228–229
Hilditch, J., 49, 148, 152, 154, 236–237, 250, 258, 275, 283–
       284, 287–288, 294, 302–303, 310, 315
Hood, S., 231
House A, 3–4, *6–7*, *14–16*, 22–25, 27–28, 33, 58, 64, 85, 100,
       113, 119–121, 141–144, 191, 193, 207, 211,
       214–215, 236
   and the location of the Alley AB test pit, 113
   entrance in Period VI, 142
   painted floor plaster in, 64
   Period IV, 3
   Period VII, 64
   wall painting in, 64
House B, 3–4, *6–7*, 11, 27–28
   and B03T, 3–4
   construction, 7, 142
   destruction, 8, 144–145
   facade, 143, 236
   phase one, 22, **30**, 31–32, 38–42, 142
   phase two, 23, **30**, 32, 42–48, 143
   phases three and four, *24–25*, **30**, 33, 48–58, 60–65,
       83–85, 104–106, 109–111, 143–144
   see also specific rooms or walls
House C, 3, 144, 236
House D, 141
House ED, 141
House F, 3
Huxley, G. L., 84, 148

Iglseder, C. B., 147
Ikaria, *see* pottery
Ios, 227, 273, 276
   see also pottery

Jeffra, C. D., 156

Kastri phase, 1, **3**, 167
Kea, 151, 227–228, 231, 236
   geology, 147
   maps, 2–3
Keros, 154, 227–228, 258, 275, 281, 283
Kiapha Thiti, 4, 178–181, **198**, 199, 216, **217**
Kilikoglou, V., 154
Kiriatzi, E., 154, 257, 294, 296

"kitchen," *see* Room B.4
Knapp, A. B., 231
Knappett, C., 156, 178, 236–237, 297
Knossos, 4, 178–181, 197–199, **217**, 232
Koehl, R. B., 139, 215
Kolonna, 4, 125, 151–152, 155, 167, 173, 175, 177–181, 198, 199, 228–230, 238, 289, 295–296, 300, 303
Korakou, 4, **198**, 216, **217**
Korfari ton Amygdalion, 227
Kos, *see* pottery
Kounadis, N., 67
Kusimba, C. M., 230
Kythera, 4, 142, 155, 177, 180, 184–185, 198, 216, 217
 see also pottery
Kythnos, 227

Laconia, 91, 224
Late Bronze Age, 3
 plans, 22–25
 deposits, **29–30**, 31–33, 35–58, 60–65, 83–106, 109–113, **117–118**, 120–121, 135–140, 142–145
 see also chronological periods
Lavrion, 1, 154, 227–231, 237–238, 273
Lefkandi, 228
Lefkandi I phase, 167
Lerna, 4, 167, 178–181, 198–199, 254, 295, 300, 302, 308
Levi, D., 180
limonite, 48
Linear A, 232
local wares, *see* pottery, local and local region production
looms, 229–230, 233
lots, *see* ceramic lots
Lustrous Decorated ware, *see* pottery
Lustrous Painted ware, *see* pottery

macroscopic fabric groups, 9, 148, 195, 250–315, 316–323
 Coarse, with Shiny White Inclusions (CSW), 148, 150, 151–152, 250, 260–261
  CSWa, 38, 55, 112, 137, 150, 152, 154, 160, 218, 221, 260, **322–323**
  CSWb, 37, 42, 107, 135–136, 140, 150, 152, 154, 159, 201, 260, **322–323**
  CSWc, 34, 55, 85, 150, 152, 154, 160, 218, 222, 260–261
  CSWd, 35, 71, 77, 81, 123, 150, 152, 154, 159–160, 167, 169, 201, 261, **322–323**
  CSWe, 34–35, 37–38, 41, 69, 77–79, 99, 122–123, 125, 131, 133, 150, 152, 154, 160–161, 167, 168, 182, **201**, 218, 222, 261, **318**, **320**, **322–323**
 Dusty, Volcanic (DV), 148, 149, 151, 250, 256–258
  DVa, 34–35, 37, 39, 41–42, 48, 55, 57, 65, 71, 75–78, 81, 83, 85, 89, 94, 99, 101, 107, 109, 122–123, 126, 129, 131, 135–137, 139–140, 149, 151–155, 161, 167, 168, 182, 184, 199–201, 203, 218, 220, 222, 256–257, **320–321**
  DVb, 15, 35, 43, 45, 48–49, 51, 78, 89, 99, 103, 111, 140, 149, 151, 154, **161**, 199, 200, 218, 221, 256
  DVc, 34, 38, 41, 65, 75–76, 81, 85, 89, 107, 109, 133, 135, 137, 149, 151, 154, **161**, 167, 169, 182, 184, 199, 200, 218, 221, 256, **320–321**
  DVd, 41, 45, 55, 65, 71, 83–85, 125, 132, 136, 149, 151–152, 154, 161, 167, 169, 182, 184, 200, 201, 218, 221–222, 224, 256–257, **320–321**
  DVe, 34–35, 37, 39, 41–42, 45, 48, 51, 55, 57, 77–78, 83–85, 89, 94, 101, 107, 109, 113, 127, 131, 135–137, 139–140, 149, 151, 154, 161, 163, 182, 184, 200, 201, 218, 220, 222, 224, 257, **320–321**
  DVf, 51, 107, 126, 131, 137, 149, 151, 161, 182, 184, 222, 257
  DVg, 39–41, 107, 149, 151, 163, 200, 201, 203, 218, 222, 257–258, **320–321**
 Fine, Non-Micaceous, Sand-Tempered (FST), 148–151, 183, 250, 252–255
  FSTa, 42, 47–48, 55, 58, 101, 126, 133, 136–137, 139–140, 149, 151, 155, 162, 182, 183–184, 200, 201, 203, 218, 221, 224, 252–254, **320–321**
  FSTb, 93–94, 101, 133, 136–137, 139–140, 149, 151, 155, 161, 182, 183–184, 201, 218, 221, 224, 252–254, **320–321**
  FSTc, 34, 39, 42, 55, 75, 126, 129, 135–137, 140, 149, 151, 162, 169, 182, 183–184, 200, 201, 203, 222, 253, 255, **320–321**
  FSTd, 39, 53, 94, 101, 112, 126, 137, 149, 151, 155, 162, 201, 203, 218, 222, 253, **320**
  FSTe, 131–133, 135, 149, 151, 155, 162, 182, 183, 201, 203, 253, **320–321**
  FSTf, 35, 42, 78, 85, 94, 101, 125–126, 129, 131–132, 135–137, 140, 149, 151, 155, 162, 182, 183–184, 201, 203, 222, 224, 253–254
  FSTg, 42, 81, 111, 127, 136–137, 139, 149, 151, 155, 162, 182, 183–184, 201, 218, 222, 254, **320–321**
  FSTh, 47–48, 53, 55, 93–94, 100–101, 111, 140, 149, 151, 155, 162, 201, 218, 221–222, 224, 254–255, **320–321**
  FSTi, 55, 75, 78, 126, 129, 131–132, 135–137, 139–140, 149, 151, 162–163, 169, 182, 183–184, 203, 255, **320–321**
  FSTj, 39, 42, 47–48, 53, 55, 58, 83–85, 93–94, 100–101, 107, 109, 111–112, 139–140, 149, 151, 155, 162, 164, 200–201, 203, 218, 219, **222**, 224, 255, **320–321**
  FSTk, 42, 47–48, 53, 55, 84–85, 94, 100–101, 109, 112, 127, 129, 131–133, 139–140, 149, 151, 155, 162, 182, 183, 201, 218, 221–222, 255, **320–321**
 Fine, Varied (FV), 148, 150, 151–152, 156, 167, 169, 250, 262–264
  FVa, 38–39, 41–42, 78, 81, 91, 107, 109, 125–126, 132, 136–137, 140, 150, 152, 164, 182, 184, 200, 201, 203, 222, 263, **322–323**
  FVb, 48, 51, 53, 55, 57–58, 85, 91, 94, 100–101, 112, 140, 150, 152, 164, 218, 220, 263, **322–323**
  FVb/FVc, 57–58, 91, 140, 218, **220**, 222, 263

FVc, 45, 48, 53, 55, 57–58, 85, 91, 94, 100–101, 109, 111–112, 135, 140, 150, 152, 164, 201, 203, 218, 220, 222, 263–264, **322–323**

FVd, 35, 42, 45, 48, 51–53, 55, 57–58, 77, 83–85, 91, 94, 100, 112, 136, 139–140, 150, 152, 160, 164, 200, 201, 203, 218, 219, 222, 263, **322–323**

FVd/FVf, 57, 127, 135–137, 150, 152, 155, 164, 182, 184, 218, 221, 222, 263–264, **322**

FVe, 42, 53, 55, 77–78, 94, 100, 136, 150, 152, 164, 167, 169, 201, 218, 221–222, 264, **322–323**

FVf, 45–47, 55, 57, 91, 93–94, 100–101, 107, 111, 137, 140, 150, 152, 155, 163, 201, 218, 220, **222**, 264, **322–323**

FVg, 34, 65, 71, 75, 81, 122, 140, 150, 152, 164, 167, 169, 264, **322–323**

FVh, 65, 75, 78, 122–123, 150, 152, 163, 167–169, 264, **322–323**

Micaceous, Fine, Varied (MFV), 148, 150, 151–152, 250, 261–262

MFVa, 77, 93–94, 127, 135, 150, 152, 160, 182, 203, 218, 222, 262, **322–323**

MFVb, 35, 58, 81, 91, 93, 126, 136, 150, 152, 155, 160, 163, 182, 222, 262, **322–323**

MFVc, 51, 84, 91, 94, 99, 107, 137, 150, 152, 155, 163, 218, 221–**222**, 224–225, 257, 262, **320**, **322–323**

MFVd, 139–140, 150, 152, 164, 222, 262

Mixed Micaceous (MxM), 148, 149, 151–152, 250, 258–260

MxMa, 35, 38, 42–43, 45, 49, 55, 57, 71, 75–76, 85, 88–89, 99, 101, 107, 113, 122, 135–136, 139–140, 149, 151–152, 154–155, 160–161, 163, 167, 169, 200, 201, 203, 218, 220, 222, 258, **320–321**

MxMb, 77–78, 135, 149, 152, 154, 160, 167, 169, 258

MxMc, 35, 38, 48–49, 65–66, 75–77, 79–81, 83, 85, 89, 94, 99, 122–123, 127, 135, 137, 140, 149, 151–152, 154, 160–161, 163, 167, 168, 182, 203, 218, 221–222, 258–259, **320–321**

MxMd, 35, 38, 41, 78–79, 85, 131, 136–137, 149, 151–152, 160, 182, 201, 218, 222, 259, **320–321**

MxMe, 53, 65, 149, 152, 163, 218, 222, 259, **320–321**

MxMf, 41, 49, 57, 77–78, 85, 89, 112, 125, 129, 137, 140, 149, 151–152, 160–161, 182, 201, 218, 221, 259, **320–321**

MxMg, 34, 71, 77, 79, 149, 152, 154, 161, 167, 169, 260

Pink-Brown Soapy (PBS), 35, 65, 67, 71, 77, 148, 150, 151–152, 167, 168, 250, 261

Red-Brown Metamorphic (RBM), 148, 149, 150–151, 181, 183, 211, 218, 250–252

RBMa, 34–35, 37–39, 42–43, 45, 48–49, 53, 55, 57–58, 65–67, 69, 71, 75–79, 81, 83–85, 87–88, 93–95, 97–99, 101, 103, 107, 109, 111–113, 122–123, 125–127, 129, 131–133, 135–137, 140, 148–151, 153–154, 158–159, 167, 168, 182, 183–185, 199, 200, 218, 219, 250–251, **318–319**

RBMb, 34–35, 38, 65–67, 69, 71, 75–79, 81, 83, 95, 109, 122–123, 125, 131–133, 135–136, 140, 149, 150–151, 153, 158–159, 167, 168, 183–184, 199, 218, 219, 250–251, **318–319**

RBMc, 34–35, 51, 65–67, 69, 71, 75–79, 83, 89, 103, 107, 123, 126, 135, 149, 150–151, 153–154, 158–159, 165, 167, 168, 171, 182, 183, 199, 218, 219, 250–251, **318**

RBMd, 34–35, 37, 39, 65–67, 69, 71, 76–78, 83, 87–88, 97–99, 103, 107, 109, 122–123, 125–127, 135, 149, 150–151, 153–154, 158–160, 167, **168**, 171, 182, 183, 199, 200, 218, 219, 250–252, **318–319**

RBMe, 37, 78, 122–123, 149, 150–151, 153–154, 159, 167, 168, 171, 250, 252, **318–319**

Mainland Greece, 1–3, 66–67, 142, 157, 199, 227–228, 230, 232–233, 235–238

see also pottery, Aegina, Argolid, Attica, Boeotia, central Greece, Corinthia, Euboea, mainland

Mainland Polychrome ware, *see* pottery

maps:
    Aegean, 2
    Ayia Irini, 5, 6
    Kea, 2–3

Margaritis, E., 67

Markiani, 227

Matt Painted ware, *see* pottery

Melos, 166, 189, 227, 229
    see also pottery, Melos, Melos/Thera

Mesara, *see* pottery

metal, 1, 141–142, 227–231, 237–238
    copper-based, 55, 66, 93
    lead, 66
    ore, 48
    slag, 67, 229
    vessels, 170–171, 228

metalworking, 1, 3, 141, 229, 236–237

micro-regional networks, 228–229

Middle Bronze Age, 1, 3, 28, 31
    plans, 21
    deposits, 4, 7, 28–31, 34–37, 59–60, **61**, 77–83, 104, **105**, 107–109, 119–120, 125–136, 141–142
    see also chronological periods

Mikre Vigla, 151, 154, 258, 282–284

Mikro Vouni, 230

Miletus, 180, 230, 234

Minoan wares, *see* pottery, Crete, Mesara, Minoan/-izing, Minoan published wares

Minoanization, 1, 3, 148, 150, 156–157, 232–236

Minoanizing, definition, 1

Mitrou, 81, 178, 181

mobility, 157, 227–230, 233

Mountjoy, P. A., 216

Müller, N., 147, 154, 250, 265

Mycenae, 93, 191, 222, 232, 263

Mycenaean palaces, 1, 235, 237–238

Myrtos Fournou Korifi, 141

Nakou, G., 170
Naturalistic style, *see* pottery
Naxos, 151, 216, 227, 229, 236
    see also pottery
Northeast Bastion, 3, 144, 236
Northern Sector, 3, 9, 148, 152, 184, 189, 195, 199, 213, 250
notation systems, 9, 10

Oka, R., 230
Orange-Buff wares, *see* pottery, EBA Orange-Buff wares
Overbeck, J. C., 27, 104, 114, 118–119, 121, 173, 175–176, 186, 189, 229–231

Panormos, 227
papsing, 7, 10
Paroikia, 151–152, 175, **179**, 231, 259
Paros, *see* pottery
pavement packing, 118–119, 126, 132
pavements, 118
Pentedeka, A., 154, 257, 294, 296
perforated disks, 48
petrographic fabric groups (PFG), 152–156, 265–316
    PFG 1, 35, 39, 43, 45, 48, 57, 69, 71, 76, 78–79, 83, 122–123, 126–127, 129, 135, 140, 148, 150–154, 158–159, 183, 185, 199, 218, 250–251, 265–272, **318–319**
    PFG 2, 34, 37, 39, 43, 51, 55, 77–78, 81, 89, 107, 122–123, 126, 135–136, 151, 153–154, 159–160, 199, 218, 250–252, 260–261, 265–266, 269–274, **318–319**, **322–323**
    PFG 3, 38, 41, 45, 49, 76–77, 89, 93, 99, 127, 131, 154, 160, 258–259, 262–263, 274–281, **320–323**
    PFG 4, 41, 79, 112, 125, 127, 129, 131, 154, 160–161, 258, 260–261, 282–284, **318–323**
    PFG 5, 37, 41, 45, 49, 51, 107, 125–127, 131, 133, 135, 139, 151, 154, 161, 201, 256–257, 284–291, 307, **320–321**
    PFG 6, 127, 129, 132–133, 155, 161–162, 252–255, 291–293, 296, 301, **320–321**
    PFG 7, 47, 53, 101, 111, 125–127, 129, 131, 133, 136, 155, 162, 252–255, 293–301, 313, **320–321**
    PFG 8, 81, 126, 129, 131–132, 151, 155, 162–163, 254–255, 301–305, **320–321**
    PFG 9, 45, 53, 57, 122, 131, 155, 163, 258–259, 305–307, **320–323**
    PFG 10, 41, 155, 163, 257, 307, **320–321**
    PFG 11, 81, 84, 155, 163, 262, 308–309
    PFG 12, 75, 93, 139, 155, 163, 264, 309–311, **322–323**
    PFG 13, 45, 47, 51, 75, 84, 111, 123, 127, 135, 140, 155–156, 163–164, 257–258, 262–264, 311–313, **320–323**
    PFG 14, 53, 57, 65, 81, 84–85, 100, 111, 132, 156, 164, 255, 263–264, 313–316, **320–323**
petrographic studies, previous, 152–153
Phaistos, 178, 180–181
phase plans, 6, *20–26*
Phylakopi, 4, 37, 85, 91, 95, 118, 135, 151, 157, 167, 175, 178–181, 195, **198**, 199, 211, 214, 216, **217**, 227, 229–232, 235–237, 256

Phylakopi I phase, 167, 175, 178
Pink-Orange ware, *see* pottery
Pinkish Buff ware, *see* pottery, EBA Pinkish Buff
Pit 1, 11–12, *17*, 23, 30, 32, 143
plaster fragments, 12–15, 32–33, 55, 63–65, 94, 101, 103, 106, 111, 118, 129, 135, 139, 142, 233
Platform 1, 11–13, 17, 22–23, 28, 30, 32, 34, 38, 142
potter's marks, 38, 51, 53, 83, 113, 125–127, 129, 176–177, 185–186, 203
potter's wheel, 3, 150, 153, 156–157, 176, 185–186, 189, 203–204, 223, 229–230, 233–235
    see also pottery forming methods
pottery
    Acropolis Burnished, 152, 213, 215, 262
    Aegina, ceramic connections to, 34–35, 39, 42, 48, 55, 83, 85, 94, 101, 107, 109, 126, 136–137, 141, 151–152, 154, **161**, 167, 170, 177, 183, 184–186, 189, 193, 195, 197, 200–202, 204–205, 213–214, 218, 220, 223, 224–225, 230–231, 233–235, 247, 249, 256–257, 289, 306
        catalogued, 37, 40, 41, 45, 46, 51, 52, 56, 57, 83–84, 89, 90, 102, 107, 113, 125, 127, 128, 131–132, 135, 138, 139
        see also pottery, Aeginetan wares, Matt Painted, Standard Matt Painted
    Aeginetan Bichrome, 85, 101, 195, 197, 218, **220**, 247
    Aeginetan Burnished, 51, 214, 218, **220**, 247
    Aeginetan Painted, 35, 39, 41, 42, 83, 85, 94, 101, 107, 109, 136–137, 193, 197, **200**, 218, 220, 247
    Aeginetan plain, 35, 51, 55, 84–85, 107, 113, 126–127, 131, 136, 151, 177, **182**, 184, 197, 213–214, 218, **220–222**
    Aeginetan(?) Yellow Slipped, 51, 55, 84–85, 218, **220**, 247
    alabastra, 48, 55, 85, 101, 201, 208–210, 215–216, **219–220**, 225
        catalogued, 45, 46, 90, 91
    Alternating style, 100–101, 215–216
    Amorgos, ceramic connections to, 77, 151, 154, 167, 169–171, 227, 258, 275, 281
    amphoras, 194, 197, 209, 214–215, 302
    Anatolianizing wares, 1, 166–167, 170–171, 228
    Andros, possible ceramic connections to, 305–306
    applied decoration, 85, **247–248**
        bands, 37, 55, 112
        disks, 35, 37, 49, 55, 71, 76, 79, 99, 107, 123, 135, 165
        double axe, 113
        pellets, 67, 69, 78, 141, 166
        rope-bands, 37, 55, 67, 69, 77, 112, 165
    Archaic, 63–64, 94
    Argive Minyan, *174*
    Argolid, ceramic connections to, 91, 152, 155, 181, 214, 218, 222, 224–225, 236, 253–254, 295, 297–298, 300
        catalogued, 53, *54*, 81, 85, 101, *108*, 111
        see also pottery, Argive Minyan, Lustrous Painted, mainland wares
    askoi, 65–66, 76, 109, 164, 166, **168**, 171, 193–195, 197, 204–205, 208–210, 213, 215, **219**, 221–222, 225
        catalogued, 96, 99–100

Attica, ceramic connections to, 55, 140, 152, 154, **159–160**, **163**, 166–167, **170**, 171, 199, 201, **202**, 205, 214, 218, **223**, 224–225, 227–228, **249**, 258–264, 273–274, 278–280, 308, 311–312
 catalogued, 34, *36*, 37, 45–47, 51, 52, 75, 79, 80, 89, 90, 91–93, 96, 99, 102, 107, 122–123, *124*, *134*, 135
 see also pottery, Acropolis Burnished, EBA Yellow Mottled, Lustrous Painted, mainland wares
baking pans/trays, 66, 74, 75–76, 78, 96, 99, 127, *128*, 153, **168**, *174*, 176, **182**, *187*, *192*, 193, *209–210*, 214, **220**, 234
barrel jars, 79, 126–127, *130*, 132, 174, 176–177, **182**, 187, **219**
basins, 34, 38, 41, 48, 65–66, 71, 75–78, 101, 122–123, 125, 136, 141, 148, 153, 165, 167–171, *174–175*, 176–177, 181–184, 186, 187–188, 192, 194–196, **200**, *209–212*, 213–214, **219–221**, 222, 229
 catalogued, 34–37, 56, 57, 92, 95, 123, 124, 126, 130, 131, 134, 135–136
 see also pottery, bathtubs, kalathoi
basket-handled vessels, 49, 50, 110, 111, 214, **219–220**, 234
bathtubs, *92*, 95, 195, 214, **219**
beaked jugs, 83, *174*, 176–178, 186, *187*, 195, *208–210*, 231
bell cups (LBA), 48, 55, 63, 83, 101, 197, 200, 208–210, 213–215, 218, **219–221**, 225
 catalogued, 42, *44*, 53, 54, *82–86*, 89, 100–101, 102
bell-shaped cups (EBA), 71, 78–79, 80, 165–167, **168**, 170–171, 228
Black and Red style, 177–178, 181, 195
blossom bowls, 211
body sherds and quantification, 8–9, 166
Boeotia, ceramic connections to, 91, 231, 262, 303, 315
 see also pottery, central Greece, Gray Minyan, Mainland Polychrome, mainland wares, Pink-Orange
bowls (general), 35, 48, 65, 83, 85, 94, 101, 107, 112, 135–136, 157, 163–164, 165, 168–**169**, 171, 174–*175*, 176–177, 181, **182**, 185–186, 187, 192–194, 195, 197–198, 200, 208–210, 211, 213–216, **219–220**, **222**, 228, 260
 catalogued, *36*, 37–38, *40*, 41, 45, 56, 57, 71, 73–74, 76–77, 79–81, *82*, 89–91, *92*, 101, 102, 107–109, *128*, 131–133, 134, 136–137, 138, 140
 see also pottery, blossom bowls, carinated bowls, deep bowls/open jars, flaring saucers, footed bowls, ledge-rim bowls, Melian bowls, ogival bowls, pedestaled bowls, saucers, shallow bowls, spouted bowls/kraters, spreading bowls
bridge-spouted jars, 48, 85, 136, 181, **182**, 187, **188**, 191–197, 200, 204, 205, 208–210, 212, 213–215, **219**, **221**, **225**, 226
 catalogued, 37, 85–87, 112, 130, 135
bridge-spouted jugs, 109, **188**, **200**, 204, *209–210*, 212, 213–216, **219–221**, 225
 catalogued, 46, 47–49, 56, 58, 89, 90

carinated bowls, 78, 129, 158, 161, 174, 176–177, **182**, 184, 186, **188**, 189, **225**, 228, 231
 catalogued, 79, 80, 126, 128, 130, 133–135
carinated cups, *174*, 176, 178, 180, *187*, 189, 214
central Greece, ceramic connections to, 91, 152, 155–156, 164, 177, 183, 184, 186, 189, 201, 202, 205, 218, 223, 224, 229–231, **248–249**, 262–264, 303, 315
 catalogued, 53, *54*, *92*, 93, *96*, 100, *130*, 132
 see also pottery, Acropolis Burnished, Attica, Boeotia, EBA Pinkish Buff, Euboea, Gray Minyan, Lustrous Painted, Mainland Polychrome, mainland wares, Pink-Orange
collar-neck jars, 101, **168**, **220**
collared jugs, 79, 85
conical cups, 10, 193, 234
 see also pottery, handleless cups
conical rhyta, 112, *194*, 197, *209*, *210*, 215, **220**, **225**
 depicted in wall painting, *14*, 64, 94
cookware, 38, 48, 55, 83–84, 89, 106, 109, 113, 148, 150–151, 153–154, 156–157, 165, 167, 171, 176, 187–188, 189, 193, 203, 212, 213–214, 218, **219**, **222**, **225**, 229, 233–234, 257
 catalogued, 51, *52*, 58, *108*, 109, 110, 112, 123, 124, 127, 128
 see also pottery, baking pans/trays, deep bowls/open jars, plates, tripod jars, tripods, tripod tables, tripod trays, wide-mouthed jars
Corinthia, ceramic connections to, 155, 218, 253–254, 295, 297, 300
 catalogued, 53, *54*, 101
 see also pottery, mainland wares
Cretan Lustrous Painted, 35, 39, 42, 47, 53, 55, 58, 83–85, 93–94, 100–101, 107, 109, 111, 125–127, 131–133, 136–137, 139, 151, 176–177, 181–184, 193, 195, 197, 199–201, 203, 213, 215, 218, **219**, **221–222**, 224
Cretan Non-Lustrous Painted, 42, 55, 107, 129, 137, 151, 177, **182**, 183–184, 195, 197, **200**, 201, **219**, **221–222**
Cretan plain, 34, 42, 101, 107, 137, 139–140, 151, 177, **182**, 184, 197, **200**, 201, 215, **219**, **221**
Cretan Slipped, 55, 93, 215, **221–222**
Crete, ceramic connections to, 1, 8–10, 34–35, 39, 41–42, 55, 71, 83, 85, 89, 94, 107, 109, 127, 137, 139–140, 150–152, 155–157, **161–162**, 173–189, *192*, 193–205, 207–218, 221–223, 224–225, 227, 229–237, 248–**249**, 252–255, 275, 291–297, 299, 301
 catalogued, 42, 44, *46*, 47–48, 53, 54, *56*, 58, 82, 83–84, *86*, 92, 93, 100–101, 102, 108, 109, 111, *124*, 125–133, 134, 136–139
 see also pottery, Cretan wares, Lustrous Painted, Mesara, Minoan published wares
cup-rhyta, 164, *194*, 195, 197, 200, *209–210*, 211, 214–215, **219**, **221–222**, 225
 catalogued, 53, 54, 85, 86, 96, 99–100, 138, 139
cups, 65, 83, 101, 133, 153, 157, 166, 168, 169, 174, 176, 178, 181, **182**, 185–186, 187, 189, 192–194, 197,

200, 204–205, 208–210, 214–216, **219–222**, 224, 231
  catalogued, 44, 45, 56, 57, 75, 84–85, 100, *102*, 127–129
  see also pottery, bell cups, bell-shaped cups, carinated cups, conical cups, Cycladic cups, depas cups, Ephyraean goblets, goblets, handleless cups, kantharoi, Keftiu cups, kylikes, ogival cups, one-handled cups, paneled cups, pedestaled cups, piriform cups, Pteleon goblets, ring-handled cups, rounded cups, saucers, shallow cups, stemmed cups, stippled cups, straight-sided cups, tankards, tumblers, Vapheio cups
cutaway neck jugs, 197
Cyclades, ceramic connections to, 2–3, 8–10, 34–35, 38–39, 42, 48, 55, 76–78, 83, 85, 94, 101, 126, 133, 135–137, 151–152, 166–167, 170, 171, 175, 177, **179–180**, 181, 183, 184–189, 191, 193–197, **198**, 200–202, 203–205, 207, 211–215, **217**, 218, 222, **223**, 225–231, 233–238, 258–262, 264, 270, 274–284, 305, 307, 309–310
  catalogued, 34–45, 46, 49, *50*, 51, 53–57, 74, 75–76, 79, 80, 86, 88–89, 90, 96, 99, 102, 107, 110, 112–113, 122–123, 124, 127–131, 134, 135–140
  see also pottery, Amorgos, Andros, Cycladic wares, Dark Burnished, EBA Black Burnished, EBA Dark-Brown Slipped and Burnished, EBA Orange-Buff wares, EBA Red-Brown wares, EBA Talc, EBA Urfirnis, Ikaria, Ios, Melian wares, Melian/Theran wares, Naxos, Paros, Seriphos, Sikinos, Siphnos, Syros, Tenos, Thera
Cycladic Burnished, 35, 48, 119, 137, 177, 193, *194–196*, **222**, 248
Cycladic cups, 42, 78, 85, 107, 137, 176, **182**, 184, *187*, **188**, 189, *192*, 193–195, **200**, 203–205, **220**, 224, **225**, 233
  catalogued, *36*, 38–39, 43–45, 79, *80*, *130*, 133–137
Cycladic Painted, 8–9, 35, 41–42, 45, 48–49, 53, 55, 83, 85, 89, 94, 99, 101, 136–137, 191–193, *194–196*, **200–201**, 207–214, 218, 220–222, 248, 258–259
  and quantification, 191, 207
Cycladic plain, 34, 37–39, 41, 43, 45, 49, 51, 55, 78–79, 89, 99, 107, 112, 129, 131, 133, 135–138, 151, 177, **182**, 184, *192–196*, **200–201**, *208–210*, *212*, 213–214, 218, **220–222**, 258–259
Cycladic Slipped, 34–35, 38, 79, 85, 135, 193, 195, **200**, 214, **248**
Cycladic Slipped and Burnished, 127, 131, 152, *174–175*, 177, **182**, 184, 186, **221**, **248**
Cycladic Yellow Slipped, 38, 49, 55, 57, 78, 88–89, 99, 112–113, 135, 140, 195, **200**, **220–222**, 248
Cycladic White, 34–35, 76, 94, 126, 129, 131, 136, 152, *174–175*, 176–178, **182**, 184–186, 231, 248
Dark Burnished, 231, 283
deep bowls/open jars, 34–37, 65–67, 69–71, *74*, 75–78, 80, 107–109, 122–123, 125, 141, 153, 165–167, **168**, 171, **219**

depas cups, 165–166, 170–171
double-rimmed jugs, 211
East Aegean, ceramic connections to, 155, 177, 195, *209–210*, *212*, 231, 234
EBA Black Burnished, 35, 65, 71, *74*, 76–81, 108–110, 122, *124*, **158**, **160**, **163**, 165–171, **219**, 247, 261
EBA Dark-Brown Slipped and Burnished, 122, *124*, 166–167, 168, 170–171, 248
EBA Orange-Buff Semifine to Coarse, 35, 65, 69, 71, *74*, 75–77, 79–81, 122–123, 125, 137, 166–167, 168–169, 171, 248
EBA Orange-Buff Painted, *36*, 37, 71, *74*, 75–76, 123, *124*, 166, **168–169**, 171, **248**
EBA Pinkish Buff, 65, 71, 75, 77–78, *80*, 81, 122, 152, 155, 166–171, **201**, 248, 264
EBA Red-Brown Burnished, 35–37, 65–66, *68*, 69, 71, *72–74*, 76–79, 122–125, 165, 168, 170, 247
EBA Red-Brown Coarse, 34–37, 65, 67, 69–71, *72–73*, 76–79, *80*, 165, 219, 247
EBA Red-Brown Semifine to Semicoarse, 34–35, 37–38, 65–67, 69, 71, 75–79, 95, 107, 122–123, 125, 153, 165, 167–170, 219, 247, 252, 258
EBA Talc ware, 35, 65, 67, *68*, 71, 77, 141, 152, 166–167, 168, 170–171, 229, **248**, 261
EBA Urfirnis, 34, 65, 71, 81, 122, 152, 166–171, **248**, 264, 310
EBA Yellow Mottled, 78, 123, 152, 166, 168, 169, 171, **248**, 264, 310
EBA Yellow Slipped, 165
Ephyraean goblets, 51–53, *54*, 111, 214–216
Ephyraean jugs, 94, 215
Euboea, ceramic connections to, 152–157, 166–167, 169, 171, 177, 183, 184, 186, 201, 202, 205, 218, 223, 224, 231, 248, 250, 255, 257, 261–264, 270, 274, 276–281, 305, 308–311, 313, 315–316
  catalogued, *36*, 37, 65, 74, 75, *82*, 84, *92*, 93, *96*, 99, *108*, 111, 122, 127, *128*, *134*, 135, 140
  see also pottery, central Greece, EBA Pinkish Buff, Gray Minyan, Mainland Polychrome, mainland wares, Pink-Orange
ewers, 63–64, 85, 144, 187–188, 194, 196, 205, *209–210*, *212*, **221**
  catalogued, *56*, 58, 91, 108, 111
feature sherds, 8
fireboxes, 3, 144, 193, 194, 208–212, 213–214, **219**, **221**, 233
  catalogued, 49, 54, 55, 88, 92, 95
flaring saucers, 39, 40, 44, 45, 55, 89, 90, 193, **200**, 213, **219**
  see also pottery, saucers
footed bowls, 71, 73, 168
fruit stands, 84–85, 109
globular jars, 168, *174*, 176–177, 180, **182**
  catalogued, 34, 69, 70, 76, 124, 125
goblets, 33, 35, 48, 55, 63, 83, 85, 94, 101, 107, 112, 114, 126, 129, 132, 135–137, 152, 174, 176–178, 181, **182**, 184–189, 192–194, 197, 199, 200, 204, 205, 208–210, 211, 213–216, 218, **219–222**, 225, 231, 233–235, 237, 262

catalogued, 36, 38–42, 50, 51–58, 63, 79–81, 82, 84–
      85, 86, 89–91, 92, 96, 99–100, 102, 107–109,
      111, 114, 124, 125–132, 138, 139
   see also pottery, Ephyraean goblets, Pteleon goblets
Gray/Black Burnished, 56, 58, *92*, 93, 136, 152, 155, 197,
      208–212, 213, 215, 221–222, 248
Gray Minyan, 7, 35, 38–39, 41–42, 48, 55, 78, 81–85, 91,
      92, 101, *102*, 107, 109, 114, 118, *124*, 125–126,
      129, *130*, 132, 136–137, 152, *174–175*, 176–177,
      181, 184–186, *187–188*, 191–193, *194*, *196*, 197,
      199–201, 205, *209–210*, 211–214, 222, 230–231,
      248, 262–263, 308
   pseudo-Gray Minyan, 35, 211
   see also pottery, Boeotia, central Greece, Euboea
Griffin Jar, 195
handleless cups, 7–8, 10, 13, 27, 32, 38, 42, 48, 55, 62–63,
      65, 78, 83–85, 94, 106–107, 109, 111, 148, 157,
      174, 176–178, 185–189, 191–195, 199, 200–201,
      203–205, 207–211, 213–215, 218, **219–221**,
      223–226, 234–237
   catalogued, 36, 38–43, 44, 46, 47–51, 57, 62–63, 65,
      79, 80, 82, 83–89, *90*, 93, 95–99, 101–103,
      107–112, 134, 137, 140
hole-mouthed jars, 48, 135, *174–175*, 176–177, 181, **182**,
      186, 187–188, 191–197, 204, 205, 208–210, 212,
      213, 215, **219**, 225, 226, 234
   catalogued, 102, 107, 123, 124, 128, 129–132, 137
hydrias, 55, 112, 187, 192, 194, 197, 200–201, 204, 208–
      210, 214, **221–222**
   catalogued, 40, 41, 45, 46, 134, 135
Ikaria, possible ceramic connections to, 273
incense burners, 208–210, 213, **219**, 233, 265
   catalogued, 82, 83
incised surfaces, 166, 175, **247–248**
   bands, 45, 81, 83, 87, 213
   curved grooves/fingernail marks, 125
   lines, 38, 51, 71, 78, 107, 127
   triangles, 81
   zigzag, 122
Ios, possible ceramic connections to, 273, 276
jar-shaped rhyta, 89–91, *194*, *209–210*, 211, 214–215,
      218, **220–221**, 224
jars, 34–35, 47, 65–67, 69, 75, 77–78, 83, 112, 125, 129,
      136–137, 141, 148, 150–151, 153, 155–156,
      165–171, *174–175*, 176–177, 180, **182**, 183–184,
      186–189, *192–196*, 197, 200, 201, 204–205, 208–
      210, 212, 213–215, **219–222**, 224–225, 229
   catalogued, 48–51, 52, 56, 57, 71–79, *80*, 85, 86, *92*,
      93, 101, 108, 109–111, 113, 123, 125–131,
      138, 140
   see also pottery, barrel jars, bridge-spouted jars,
      collar-neck jars, deep bowls/open jars,
      globular jars, hole-mouthed jars, hydrias,
      jars with two-stage necks, narrow-necked
      jars, open jars, Palace Style jars, pedestaled
      jars, piriform jars, pithoi, rim-handled jars,
      Roman grooved jars, spouted jars, stemmed
      jars, stirrup jars, tripod jars, wide-mouthed
      jars

jars with two-stage neck, 78, 123, *124*, 165
juglets, 154, 187, 192–194, 200, *208–210*, 213, **219**
   catalogued, 95, 96, 134, 135
jugs, 35, 42, 65–66, 76, 83, 85, 86, 94, 107, 140, 151, 154,
      165–170, *174–175*, 176–178, 180, **182**, 184, 186,
      187–188, *192*, 194–196, 197, **200**–201, 204–205,
      208–212, 213–215, **219–222**, 224–225
   catalogued, 34, *36*, 37, 49–51, 56, 58, 79, 85–87, 96,
      100, 108, 111, 126–129, 130, 133, 134, 136
   see also pottery, askoi, beaked jugs, bridge-spouted
      jugs, collared jugs, cutaway neck jugs, double-
      rimmed jugs, Ephyraean jugs, ewers, juglets,
      lentoid jugs, paneled jugs, round-mouthed
      jugs, spouted jugs
kalathoi, 194
kantharoi, 136, *174*, 177, 186, *187*, 194, 197, 231
Keftiu cups, 10
Kos, possible ceramic connections to, 155, 257, 288,
      304–305
kraters, 34, 55, 83, 136, 193, 194, 196, 197, 205, 208–210,
      212, 214, **220**, 225, 235
   catalogued, 56, 57
   see also pottery, spouted bowls/kraters
kylikes, 56, 58, 100–101, *102*, 214–216, **219–220**
Kythera, ceramic connections to, 41, 48, 55, 84, 94, 100–
      101, 137, 139, 151, 155, 177, 180, 183, 184–185,
      198, 201, 202, 211, 215–218, 223, 224, 248–**249**,
      252, 254–255, 293–295, 298–299, 301
   catalogued, 42, *44*, *46*, 47, 53, *54*, 81, 93, 100, 102,
      108, 111, 127, *134*, 136, 139
   see also pottery, Lustrous Decorated
lamps, 175, 187–188, 192–194, 196, 197–199, 200
   catalogued, 36, 38, 42, 44, 123, 124
   handleless cups as, 193, 234
   see also pottery, stick-handled lamps
leaf impressions, *36*, 37, 79, *80*, 95, 169–170
ledge-rim bowls, 41, 112, 181, 195
lentoid jugs, 180, *187*
lids, 75, 136, **168**, *174–175*, 187, 192, 193–195, 197, **200**,
      208–210, 211, 215, **220**, 222
   catalogued, 35, *36*, 39, 42, *56*, 58, 74, 77, 138, 139
local and local region production, 1–3, 7–8, 148–154,
      156–157, 165, 167, 169–171, 184–186, **188**,
      191–193, 203–204, 207–211, 213, 223, **225**, 227,
      247, 250–252, 265–274
   Burnished, 34, 38–39, 77–78, 81, 83, 87, 101, 107,
      125–126, 129, 131–132, 135–137, *174*, 176,
      182, 183, 186, *187*, 189, 191–193, *194*, 197,
      200, 207–211, 213, 219, 233, 247
   Painted, 55, 85, 94, 101, 135–137, *187*, 191–195, 205,
      207, *208–210*, 213, 219
   plain, 34–35, 37–39, 42–43, 45, 48–49, 51, 55, 57,
      77–79, 83, 87–88, 94–98, 101–103, 107, 109,
      111–113, 123, 125–127, 129, 131, 133, 135–
      137, 140, 173, *174*, 176, **182**, 183, *187*, 189,
      191–193, *194*, 200, 207–211, 213, **219**
   Red Coated, 193, 197
   Slipped, 35, 38–39, 77, 79, 135, 137, 191, 193
   Slipped and Burnished, 43, 177, 193, **200**

White-on-Gray, *174*, 176
White-on-Red, *174*, 176
Yellow Painted, 38–39, *40*, 85, 87, 89, *90*, *92*, 95, *130*, 135, 181, 191, 193, **200**, 211, **219**, 247
Yellow Slipped, 34–35, 38–39, 43, 48, 55, 77–79, 83, 85–87, 89, 94–95, 101, 107, 109, 111, 126–127, 132–133, 135–137, 165, *174*, 176, **182**, 183, *187*, 189, 191, 193, **200**, 207, 211, 214, **219**, 233
    see also pottery, EBA Black Burnished, EBA Red-Brown wares
Lustrous Decorated, 42, *44*, 81, 127, 136, 139, 151, 155, 175, 177, **182**, 184, 193, 197–198, **248**, 254, 293, 295
    see also pottery, Kythera, mainland Greece
Lustrous Painted, 10, 35, 39, 42, 44–46, 47–48, 51–58, 78, 83–85, 89–94, 100–101, 102, 107, 109, 111–112, 125–127, 129, 131–133, 135–137, 139–140, 144, 151–152, 155, 176–177, 181–184, 191, 193–201, 203, 205, 207–215, 218, 219–222, 224, 249, 255, 263–264, 295
    see also pottery, Crete, mainland Greece
mainland Greece, ceramic connections to, 35, 39, 42, 48, 55, 83, 85, 94, 107, 109, 112, 136–137, 151–152, 155–157, 165, 167, 170, 171, 173, 176–177, **179–180**, 181, 183, 184–186, 189, 191, 193, 195, 197–199, 201–205, 207, 213–218, 222–231, 233–237, 248–249
    catalogued, 45–47, 51–53, *54*, *56*, 57–58, 80–82, 83–85, 90, 91–93, 96, 100–101, 102, 107–112, 124, 125–127, 130, 132, 134, 135–140
    see also pottery, Acropolis Burnished, Aegina, Aeginetan wares, Argive Minyan, Argolid, Attica, Boeotia, central Greece, Corinthia, EBA Pinkish Buff, EBA Urfirnis, EBA Yellow Mottled, Euboea, Gray Minyan, Kythera, Lustrous Decorated, Lustrous Painted, mainland wares, Matt Painted, Pink-Orange, Red Coated, Standard Matt Painted, Yellow Minyan
Mainland Burnished, 42, 48, 58, 85, 94, 100, 111–112, 136–137, 193–197, 200, 201, 205, *209–210*, *212*, 213–214, 218, 219–222, 247, 263–264
Mainland Lustrous Painted, 10, 39, 45–47, 51, 53, 55, 57, 83–85, 91, 93–94, 100–101, 109, 111–112, 140, 152, 191, 193–199, 200–201, 203, 205, *208–210*, *212*, 213–215, 218, 219–222, 224, 249, 263–264
Mainland Non-Lustrous Painted, 48
Mainland Painted, 156, *187–188*, **222**, 247
Mainland plain, 35, 39, 45–47, 55, 58, 85, 93–94, 107, 136–137, 139, 152, 156, *192*, 193–197, 201, 205, *208–210*, *212*, 213–215, 218, 219–221, 263–264
Mainland Polychrome, 136–137, 152, 155–156, *192*, 193–197, 199, 205, *208–210*, *212*, 213–214, 249, 263–264
Mainland Red Coated, 42, 55, 57, 84–85, 91, 94, 109, 136, 193, 197, 199, 213–214, 218, 219–221, 263–264

Mainland Slipped, 48, 58, 83, 91, 100, 135, 193, 197, **200**, 201, 213–214, 218, 219–222, 249, 263
Marine style, 58, 214–216
mat impressions, 34–35, 75, *110*, 122, 165, 169–170
Matt Painted, 38, 48, 55, 83–85, 100–101, 112, 125, *128*, 131, 136, 151–152, *174–175*, 176–177, 181, 182, 184–186, *187–188*, 191–193, *194*, *196*, 197, 205, 207, *208–210*, *212*, 213–214, 218, 221, 222, 231, 249, 254
    see also pottery, Aegina, mainland Greece, Standard Matt Painted
Melian bowls, *44*, 45, 177, 193, 195, **200**
Melian Painted, 45, 75, *208–210*, *212*, 213–214, 218
Melian plain, 213–214, 218
Melian Slipped and Burnished, 133
Melian/Theran Painted, 34, 37, 41–42, 45, 48–49, 55–57, 81, 83, 85, 89, 94, 101, 107, 109, 123, 135–137, 139, *187–188*, 189, *192–196*, 199, **200**, 220–221, 248
Melian/Theran plain, 38, 39, 41–43, 45, 51, 55, 77–78, 81, 89, 99, 103, 107, 109, 111, 135–137, 177, *187–188*, *192–196*, 199, 200, 205, 220–221
Melian/Theran Red Coated, 45, 107
Melian/Theran Slipped, 34, 85, 107, 205, **248**
Melian/Theran Slipped and Burnished, 41, 133, 177, 184, 186, *187–188*, *192*, 193, 195, *196*, 199, **248**
Melian/Theran Yellow Slipped, 34, 49–51, 220–221, 248
Melos, ceramic connections to, 37, 41, 45, 74, 75–76, 85, 91, 95, 133, 135, 151–152, 154, 157, 166, 170–171, 175, 178–181, 191, 195, 198, 199, *208–212*, 213–214, 216–218, 223, 224–225, 227, 230–231, 235–237, 248, 256, 261, 287–288, 290–291
    see also pottery, Cycladic White, EBA Orange-Buff wares, Melian wares, Melian/Theran wares, Melos/Thera
Melos/Thera, ceramic connections to, 34, 39, 41–42, 48, 55, 77–78, 83, 85, 94, 101, 107, 109, 123, 135–137, 151–152, 154–155, 157, 167, **168–170**, *174–175*, 177, 183, 184–185, *187–188*, 189, 191, 193, 195, 199–205, 220–221, 234–237, 248, 256–257, 259, 284–287, 290–291, 307
    catalogued, 35–38, 40, 41, 43–45, 49, 50, 56, 57, 79–81, 89, 90, *96*, 99, 102, 103, 107, 109, 111, 126, 130, 131, 133–137, 139
    see also pottery, Cycladic White, EBA Orange-Buff wares, Melian wares, Melian/Theran wares, Melos, Thera
Mesara, possible ceramic connections to, 127, 130, 132–133, 155, 180, 184, 291–292, 297
Minoan published wares, 8, *187–188*, *192*, *194*, *196*, 204–205, *208–210*, *212*, 249
    see also pottery, Crete, Cretan wares, Lustrous Painted, Mesara, Minoan/-izing
Minoan/-izing, 126, 129, 131–132, 135–136, 155, 173–178, 183–186, 189, 203, 231, 249
motifs, painted, 10, 178, 181, 193, 195, 197–199, 205, 207, 211, 214–215, 233–234
    arcade, 111

INDEX

bands, 34–35, 37, 39, 41–43, 45, 47–49, 51, 53, 57–58, 75, 81, 83–85, 87, 89, 91, 93, 95, 99–101, 109, 111–113, 125–140, 176, 193, 195, 197, 214
bars, 43, 58, 85, 89, 99, 125–126, 131
blooms, 47, 197–198
bracket, 195
chevrons, 49, 111, 137, 139
circles, 34, 41, 43, 45, 49
crocuses, 100
curved stripes, 195, 197, 215
disks, 41, 49, 91, 129, 177
dots, 51, 53, 84, 87, 89, 91, 93, 99, 101, 111, 139, 176, 181, 195, 215
double axes, 93, 180, 215
festoons, 78, 89, 95, 100–101
figure-eight shields, 58
floral, 53, 137, 193, 195, 197, 199
foliate band, 42, 49, 58, 85, 95, 195, 197, 214
hatched loops, 55, 101, 215
irises, 84, 101
ivy, 140
lilies, 111, 215
loops, 41, 43, 49, 51, 84, 113
net, 55, 75, 215
ogival canopy, 51, 93, 215
ovals, 113
palm, 51, 53, 111, 216
rays, 41
reeds, 47, 53, 100–101, 112, 197–198, 214–215
ripple pattern, 39, 43, 45, 51, 53, 57, 88–89, 100–101, 137, 140, 181, 193, 195, 197, 199, 214, 216
rock pattern, 53, 91, 100–101, 140, 215
rosettes, 41, 111, 176, 195, 215
scale pattern, 84, 111, 215
semicircles, 78–79, 93, 214
spirals, 34, 43, 45, 47, 49, 51, 84, 87, 89, 91, 99–100, 109, 111–112, 135–137, 140, 193, 195, 197–199, 211, 214–215
stipple, 55, 57
stone pattern, 84, 91, 215
swastikas, 84
trefoil, 101
trickle, 47, 126, 129, 131–133, 137, 177
vertical bars, 137, 195
wheel, 45, 91
zigzags, 214
narrow-necked jars, 45, *46*, *134*, 135, *138*, 139, 197, **200**, 214, **220**, 295
Naturalistic style, 178, 181
Naxos, ceramic connections to, *40*, 41, 79, 96, 99, 112, 123, 125, 131, 151–152, 154, 166–167, 169–171, 183, 201, 202, 216, 218, 223, 231, 235–236, 258, 260–261, 273, 282–283
   see also pottery, Cycladic wares, EBA Orange-Buff wares
notebook descriptions, 7
ogival bowls, 42, *44*, 197, 200
ogival cups, 10, *96*, 99
one-handled cups, 34, *36*, 66, 165, 168

open jars, 35, *36*, 38, 71, *72*, 78, *82*, 83–84, 89, *90*, 123–125, *130*, 135–137, 139, **168**, 182, 193, **200–201**, 214, 218, **219–220**
Palace Style jars, 33, 53–55, 101, 112, 215, 253
paneled cups, 10, 53, 100, 214, **221**, 237
   see also piriform cups
paneled jugs, 53, *54*, 213, **222**
pans, *see* pottery, baking pans/trays
Paros, possible ceramic connections to, 151–152, 175, 259, 273
pedestal bases and feet, 34–35, 66–67, 69, 75–78, 109, 126, 136, 176
pedestaled cups, 74, 75, 166, **168**, 171, 197
pedestaled bowls, 43, 44, *108*, 109, 187, 188, 191–193, 194, 200, *208–210*, 211, **219**
pedestaled jars, 211
perforated shapes, 83, 109, 141, 168, 187, 194, 209–212, 213–215, **221**, 225–226, 234
   catalogued, 49, *50*, *56*, 58, 71, *72*, 109
   see also pottery, conical rhyta, cup-rhyta, fireboxes, incense burners, jar-shaped rhyta, rhyta, spreading bowls, strainers, strainer-pyxides
Pink-Orange, 127, *128*, 152, 156, *174–175*, 177, **182**, 184–186, 205, 249
   see also pottery, Boeotia, central mainland, Euboea
piriform cups, 10, 78, *174*, 177, 181, 186–189, 191–195, 197, 200, 201, 204, 205, 208–210, 211, 213–214, 224–226, 231, 237
   catalogued, 35, *36*, 40, 41, 44, 45, 89, *90*, 137, 139
piriform jars, 89–91, *92*, 208–210, 211, 214–215, **219**
pithoi, 7–8, 34, 35, 38, 48, 55, 59, 65, 67, 69, 71, 75, 77, 83, 85, 107, 112, 125, 135, 141, 144, 148, 154, 165–167, 168, 171, 174, **182**, 187, 192–194, 208–210, 213, **219**, 229
   catalogued, *36*, 37, 67–71, 73, 76, 78–79, 80, 113
plates, 66, 169
   pedestaled, 75–76, **168**
   wheelmade, 157, 166, 171
Pteleon goblets, 125, 177–178
pyxides, 65, 122, 141, 154, 165–166, 168, 169–171, *194*, *209–210*, 213, **219**, **221**
   catalogued, 49, *50*, 54, 57, 74, 75–76, 80, 81, 110, 122, 124
   see also strainer-pyxides
Red and Black style, 48–51, 53, 57, 85–87, 89, 94, 101, 113, 137, 140, 195, 211, 214
Red Coated, 42, 45, 48, 51, 55, 57, 83–85, 91, 94, 99, 107, 109, 136–137, 139–140, 151, 193–197, 199, **200**, 201, 205, *208–210*, *212*, 213–214, 218, 219–222, 249, 262–264
   see also pottery, mainland wares, Melian/Theran wares, local and local region production
reworked sherds, 65, 78
   as rubbers/polishers, 35, 75, 140
Rhodes, possible ceramic connections to, 155, 302–304
rhyta (various), 101, *194–196*, 204–205, *209–212*, 214–215, **225**, 226, 234, 236–237
   see also conical rhyta, cup-rhyta, jar-shaped rhyta

rim-handled jars, 35
ring-handled cups, 48, **220**
Roman grooved jars, 140
rounded cups, 35, 48, 78, 101, 135, *174*, 176–177, 180–181, 186–189, 191–195, 197, 199, 200–201, 204, 205, 208–210, 211, 214–215, 218, **219–221**, 225, 237
    catalogued, 36, 39, 45–47, 57, 81, *82*, 84–87, 89, 90, 92, 93, 96, 99, 101, 102, 107, 108, 111
round-mouthed jugs, *128*, 129, 155, *174*, 176–177, **182**, 302–303
sauceboats, 35, 65–66, 78, 125, 141, 165–167, **168–169**, 171, 228
    catalogued, 78, 80, 81, 110, 122–123, 124
saucers, 34–35, 65–67, 71, 75, 77–78, 122–123, 125, 141, 165–167, **168–169**, 171, 176, 178, **182**, 187, 194, 208–210, 213, **219**, 228
    catalogued, 35–37, 79, 80, 95, 110, 122–123, *124*, 127, 128
    see also pottery, flaring saucers
Seriphos, possible ceramic connections to, 154, 273
shallow bowls, 35, 36, 65–69, 71, *72*, 75–78, 122–125, 141, 165–167, **168–169**, 171, 228
shallow cups, 55, 109, *209–210*, 214, **220**
Sikinos, possible ceramic connections to, 154, 273
Siphnos, ceramic connections to, 67, 68, 152, 166, **170**, **248**, 261, 276
Slipped and Burnished, *see* pottery, Cycladic, Melian/Theran, local and local region production
spouted bowls/kraters, *212*, 214, **220**, **225**, 235
    see also pottery, kraters
spouted jars, 42, 94, *194*, **200**, **219**
spouted jugs, *54,* 55, 85, **219**
spreading bowls, 84, 111–112, *192–194*, *208–210*, 213
Standard Matt Painted, 40, 41, 45, 46, 55, 193–197, **200**, 201, 205, *208–210*, *212*, 213–215, 218, 221, 224, 249
    see also pottery, Aegina, Matt Painted
stemmed cups, *208–210*, **219**
stemmed jars, 89, *90*, 214, 224
stick-handled lamps, 35, 130, 135
    see also pottery, lamps
stippled cups, 55
stirrup jars, 87, 208–210, 213, 215, **219**
straight-sided cups, 10, 55, 151, 174, 176, 180, **182**, 187, 188, 189, 191–195, 197–198, 200–201, 203–205, 208–210, 214–215, **219–222**, 225, 226, 237
    catalogued, 36, 38–39, 40, 42–43, 44, 81, 86, 88–89, 91–93, 95, 96, 109, 110, 112, 130, 133, 134, 137, 139
strainer-pyxides, *208–210*, 211, 213
strainers, *196*, 208–212, 213–214, 225
Syros, possible ceramic connections to, *36*, 38, *40*, 41, *44*, 45, 49, *50*, 76, *86*, 89, 127, *128*, 154, 167, 170, 227, **248**, 258–259, 262, 276–277
    see also pottery, EBA Dark-Brown Slipped and Burnished
tankards, *36*, 37, 71, 76–77, 79, 80, 122–123, 124, 141, 165–171, 228

Tenos, possible ceramic connections to, 45, 53, *54*, *56*, 57, 122, *124*, 154–155, 167, 230, 258–259, 273, 276, 305–306
Thera, ceramic connections to, 41, 89, 151, 154, 157, 167, 175, 178–181, 195, 198–199, 214, 230–231, 235–237, 260, 283–284, 290, 294
    see also pottery, Cycladic White, Melian/Theran wares
tripod jars, *22*, 32, 83–84, 111, 142, 157, *174*, 176, *187–188*, 189, 193, 194, 200, *208–210*, 213, **219**, 229, 233–234
    catalogued, 39, 40, 44, 45, *82*, 83, 110, 111–112, 134, 137
    see also pottery, tripods
tripods, 8, 34–35, 39, 48, 78, 83–85, 94, 173, 174, 176, 187, 189, *194*, 208–210, 213, 229, 233–234
    see also pottery, tripod jars, tripod tables, tripod trays
tripod tables, *187*, 192–194
tripod trays, 102, 107–109, 187, 193, 213, **219**, 234, 257
tumblers, 40, 41, 44, 45, 178, **182**, 195, 198, 201
unfired/low-fired, 108, 109, 150–151, 219
Vapheio cups, 10, 55, 101, 151, 191–195, 197–199, 200–201, 203–205, 208–210, 214–215, **219–221**, 225, 226
    catalogued, 42–47, 51–53, 56, 57, 86, 88–89, 91, 100, 102
    Kythera types, 197
wide-mouthed jars, 124, 126–127, 128, 134, 136–137, *174*, 176, **182**, 183, 189, 193
Yellow Minyan, 192–194, 196, 197, 205, **249**
    see also ceramics
pottery forming methods, 156–157, 158–164, 169–170, 184–186, 203–204, 223–224, 229
  coil-built, 156–157, 169, 184–185, 199, 224
    catalogued, 35, 39, 41, 43, 45, 55, 57, 76, 79, 81, 83, 87, 89, 95, 99, 107, 109, 112, 129, 131–133, 137
  handmade, 148, 156, 169, 184–185, 203–204, 223–224, 234
    catalogued, 34–35, 37–39, 41–43, 45, 49, 51, 53, 57, 65, 75–76, 78–79, 81, 83, 85, 88–89, 91, 93, 95, 100, 107, 111–113, 122, 125–127, 129, 131–133, 135–137, 139–140
  push-through handles, 170, 184–185, 203, 229
    catalogued, 69, 71, 75–76, 125–126, 131
  terminology, 156
  wheel-coiled, 148, 153, 156–157, 176, 178, 185, 203, 223–224
    catalogued, 37, 39, 41–43, 45, 48–49, 51, 53, 57, 77–79, 83–85, 87–89, 91, 93, 95, 97–101, 103, 107, 109, 111–112, 126–127, 129, 135–137, 139, 140
  wheelmade, 156–157, 166, 169, 171, 176, 178, 185, 199, 203–204, 223–224
    catalogued, 38–39, 41–43, 45, 47, 49, 51, 53, 57–58, 78, 81, 83–85, 87–89, 91, 93, 95, 97–101, 103, 107, 109, 111–113, 125, 127, 131–132, 135–137, 139–140
  see also potter's wheels

INDEX

Red and Black style, *see* pottery
Red-Brown wares, *see* pottery, EBA Red-Brown wares
Red Coated ware, *see* pottery
refiring tests, 153, **158–164**
Rhodes, *see* pottery
Rice, A. H. N., 147
rituals, 141, 211, **225**, 226, 228, 231–232, 237
Room A.18, *5*, 191, 198
Room A.26, *5*, 118, 195
Room A.34, *5*, 121
Room A.36, 4, *5*, 7, 113, 120, 141–142
Room A.37, *5*, 118, 121
Room A.39, 4, *5*, 7, 113, 121
Room B.1, 4, *5*, 7, 11–13, *16–17*, 21–25, 28–58, 60, 64, 94, 104, 109, 114, 118, 120–121, 141–144, 216, 239, 324–**326**, **328**
    combined lots, 28, **60**
    MBA, 28, **29**, 31
    Period III, 28, **29**, 31, 34–37, 141
    Period VI, *22–23*, **30**, 31–32, 38–48, 142–143
    Period VII, 16, *24–25*, **30**, 33, 48–58, 143–144
Room B.2, 4, *5*, 7, 11, *13–14*, 18, 24, 28, 31, 33, 35–38, 59–104, 141–144, 239, 324–**325**, **327–328**
    combined lots, 28, **60**
    MBA, 60, **61**, 78–83
    Period III, 59–60, **61**, 65–83, 141
    Period VI, 62
    Period VII, 60–63, 83–85, 143
    test pit, 7, *15*, 59–60
Room B.2/B.3, *5*, 7, *11*, *13–14*, 18, 25, 33, 59–64, 85–106, 144, **324**
    combined lots, **60**
Room B.3, *5*, 7, 11, *13–14*, 18, 24, 28, 33, 59–65, 78–84, 104, 141, 143, 239, 325
    combined lots, **60**
Room B.4, *5*, 11, *14–15*, 19, 24, 25, 28, 31, 33, 35–38, 59–64, 85–112, 114, 141–144, 239, 324–**326**
    combined lots, 28, **60**
Room B.5, *5*, 24–25, 28, 143, 239
Room B.8, *5*, 24–25, 28, 33, 112–113, 142–143, 207, 239, 326
Room F.3, *5*, 32
Roux, V., 156

Schiffer, M. B., 4
Schofield, E., 113, 119–120, 143, 191, 207
sea level rises, 7, 59
Seriphos, 227
    see also pottery
shells, 42, 47, 77, 93, 119
Sikinos, *see* pottery
Siphnos, 227
    see also pottery
Skarkos, 227
Slipped and Burnished ware, *see* pottery
South Alley, *5*, 28, 113
stairways, 143
Standard Matt Painted ware, *see* pottery
Stone Feature 1, 17, 22–23, 30, 32, 142–143

stone objects, 1, 32, 65–66, 69, 71, 101, 133, 141–142
    basins, 101
    denticulates, 32, 47
    disks, 67
    drill-cores, 55, 93, 101, 103
    figurines, 47
    flint fragments, 32, 47, 131
    hammer stones, 67, 141
    lids, 67
    millstones, 32, 47, 67, 141
    mortars, 32, 47, 69
    obsidian, 28, 32, 37–38, 42, 47, 55, 67, 81, 93, 101, 103, 112–113, 131, 136–137, 141, 227
    palettes, 66–67, 69, 141
    perforated, 66
    pestles, 55, 66–67, 93, 101, 141
    pounders/grinders, 67, 101, 141
    pumice, 37
    rubbers/polishers, 35, 66–67, 71, 141
    saddle quern, 67, 141
    sealstones, 92, 93
    tools, 47
    weights, 38, 65, 69, 141
    whetstones, 66–67, 141
Street 1, *19*, **118**, 121, 139–140
Street 2, *19*, **116–117**, 119–120, 132–133, 142
Surface a, 11–12, *16–17*, 30, 31–33, 42, 47–55, 106, 143–144
Surface b, 11–13, *16–17*, 30, 31–33, 38, 42–48, 142
Surface c, 7, 11–13, *16–17*, 28, 29, 31–37, 60, 114, 141
Surface d, 11, 13, 18, 61, 62–63, 65, 83–85, 106, 144
Surface e, 11, 18, 61, 62–63, 65, 83–85, 143
Surface f, 11, 18, 60–64, 83–85, 143
Surface g, 11, 18, 61, 62–63, 65, 83–84, 143
Surface h, 11, 18, 61, 62–65, 84, 143
Surface i, 7, 11, 15, 19, 35–37, 60, 104, 105, 107–109, 114, 141
surfaces, 7, 27
Syros, 227
    see also pottery

Talc ware, *see* pottery, EBA Talc
Temple, 1, 3–4, *5*, 27–28, 33, 63–64, 85, 91, 143–145, 211, 231–232, 236–237
    Period IV, 3, 229, 231–232
    statues, 153, 234
Temple Lane, 4, *5*, 24–25, 28, 33, 48, 113, 121, 142–144
Tenos, *see* pottery
terracotta
    disks, 32, 48, 93
    buttons, 93
    drains, 121
    figurines, 140
    loom weights, 32, 38, 47–48, 55, 62, 83–84, 93–94, 111, 113, 133, 229–230, 233
    rubbers/polishers, 140
    spindle whorls, 27, 32, 37–38, 42, 48, 58, 81, 83, 94, 109, 132, 141, 233
    spools, 58, 137, 233
    spoons, 77
    weights, 140

test pits, 4, 8, 31, 166
    Alley AB, 4, 6, 7, 15–16, 27, 113–114, 118–142
    Platform 1, 34
    Room B.1, 4, 13, 28, 31–32, 34
    Room B.2, 7, *15*, 59, 65–78
textile production, 3, 141–142, 144, 233
Thera, volcanic eruption, 3, 199, 235
    see also pottery, Melian/Theran wares, Melos/Thera, Thera
Tiryns, 51, **217**
tombs, 142, 230, 233
tools
    of marble, 32, 47
    of pottery, 35, 75, 78, 140
    of slag, 67
    of stone, 66, 141
    see also bone, stone
trade patterns, 170–171, 186–189, 204–205, 224–237
    tramping, 230
trenches, 3–4, 6, **10**
    Troy, 191, 199
    Tsoungiza, 57, **180**, 181, **198**, 211, 216, **217**, 236, 254

Urfinis ware, *see* pottery, EBA Urfirnis

Vaughan, S. J., 154
violent destruction, lack of evidence for, 143

Wall 57, *see* Wall E1
Wall AA, 11, 14, 18, 24–25, 59–65, 143–144
Wall AB, 11, 14, 18, 20, 35, 59–60, 61, 141
Wall AC, 11–12, 16, *17*, 20, 28, 29, 31–32, 34–35, 114, 141
Wall AD, 13, 15, 18–20, 35, 59, 61, 104, 105, 141
Wall AE, *11*, *14*, 19–20, 35, 104, 105, 141
Wall AF, 11, 15, 18, 20, 35, 59, 61, 141

Wall E, 7, 15–16, 19, 27, 113, 118, 119–121, 142
Wall E1, 16, *19*, 27, 116–117, 119–121, 142–143
Wall H, 7, 12–19, 24–26, 28, 30, 32–34, 59–65, 104, 106, 113–114, 117–118, 118–121, 143–144
    foundation trench, *16*, **117**, 118–121, 135–139, 143
Wall H foundation, 13, 16, 17–*19*, 21–23, 27, 29–30, 31–34, 60, 104, 114, 118, 141–143
Wall I, 11–13, 17, 24–25, 28, 30, 31–33, 48, 64, 113, 143–144
Wall J, 12, 14, 16–18, 24–*25*, 28, 30, 31–33, 59–60, 61–62, 64–65, 104, 113, 143–144
Wall K, 11–12, 14, 17–*18*, 24–26, 28, 30, 31, 33, 59–63, 84, 143
Wall O, 11, 14, 19, 24–26, 62, 63, 104, 105, 106, 143
    foundation trench, 104, 105, 107
Wall P, 11, 13–15, 18–19, 25–26, 59, 61–62, 63, 65, 104–106, 144
Wall Q, 7, 11, 13–14, *18*, 26, 28, 59, 62, 63–64, 94, 101, 145
Wall R, 11, *14*, 18, *25*, 61–62, 63, 65, 144
Wall T, 11, 13–14, *18*–19, 24, 59, 61, 63–65, 104–106, 143–144
Wall X, 7, 12, 15–16, 19, 21, 27, 31–32, 60, 113–114, 115, 116, 118–120, 125–129, 135–136, 141–143
    foundation trench, 114, 115, 125–126
Wall Y, 11–12, 17, 22–23, 30, 31–32, 142–143
ware-based classifications, 8–9, 247–249
Warren, P. M., 198
weaving, 229–230, 233
Western Sector, 3, 32, 91, 133, 141–144, 166, 191, 198, 207, 211
Williams, D. F., 154
Wilson, D. E., 165–167, 169–170, 173
wine, 141, 186
women, 229
wood, burnt, 65

Yellow Mottled ware, *see* pottery, EBA Yellow Mottled
Yellow Minyan, *see* pottery

a. Areas A and B at the beginning of excavation from the east-northeast.
b. Room B.2/B.3 during excavation in 1961 from the northeast. Note the steep decline in preserved wall height from west to east, toward the sea.
c. Rooms B.1 and B.2/B.3 from the east, showing the Period VII destruction deposit.

PLATE 2

a. Room B.2/B.3 from the east, showing the Period VII destruction debris.
b. Rooms B.1 and B.2/B.3 from the northeast, showing the Period VII destruction deposit.
c. Room B.1 from the west, showing the Period VII destruction debris.

PLATE 3

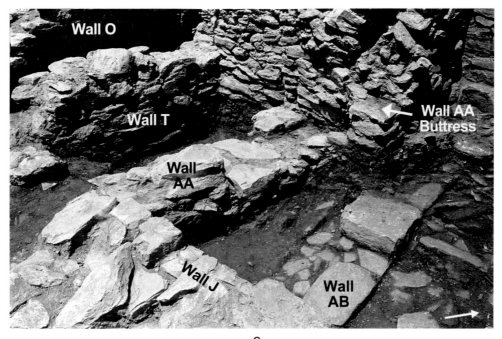

a. Room B.1 from the southwest, showing the lower part of the Period VII destruction debris.
b. Room B.1 from the northeast, showing architecture from House B: Phases 1 and 2. The lower elevation of the excavated area is at the approximate level of Surface b. The upper elevation area shows Wall Y from the first phase of the house, stones probably fallen from Wall Y, as well as Pit 1 and Stone Feature 1, which seem to have been used in the second phase of the house, before Rooms B.2–B.4 were added to the building.
c. Room B.2/B.3 from the east, showing EBA Wall AB and Walls O, T, AA, and J from Phases 3 and 4 of the LBA house.

PLATE 4

a. Rooms B.2 and B.1 from the southwest, showing EBA Wall AB and Walls I, J, K, and AA from Phases 3 and 4 of the LBA house.
b. Eastern edge of Rooms B.3 and B.4 from the southwest, showing EBA Wall AD extending under Period VII Walls T and J.
c. Room B.2 from the north, showing EBA Wall AB and Walls AA and J from Phase 3 of the LBA house.

a. House B from the east, with LBA cross walls labeled.
b. House B from the southeast, with LBA walls (except long walls H and J) labeled.
c. House B from the south, showing Rooms B.1, B.2, and B.8.

PLATE 6

a. Room B.1 from the southeast, showing LBA Wall H built on top of the Wall H foundation, a possible Period IV wall.
b. Rooms B.2/B.3 and B.4 from the east.
c. Room B.2/B.3 from the southeast, showing Walls P, T, R, AA, and the Wall AA buttress.

PLATE 7

a. Room B.2/B.3 from the southeast, showing Walls P, T, R, AA, and the Wall AA buttress.
b. Room B.2 from the southeast, showing the large stones of the Wall H foundation under Wall H.
c. Room B.1 from the southwest, showing the corner of Walls I and J.

PLATE 8

a. Room B.1 from the south, showing the large stones of the Wall H foundation under Wall H.
b. Room B.1 from the northeast, after excavation.
c. Room B.8 from the south-southeast, showing the intersection of Walls I and J.

a. Northeast part of Alley AB in 1975 from the northeast, before the test pit was opened.
b. Area of the 1975 test pit in Alley AB, below the four stones in the center of the photograph from the northwest.
c. Northeast part of Alley AB in 1975 from the southwest, before the test pit was opened.

PLATE 10

a. Northeast part of Alley AB in 1975 from the northeast, before the test pit was opened. Note the vertically-placed slabs that line the alley and form the sides of Drain 1.
b. Flat stones embedded in red mud under the slabs of Drain 1 in Alley AB (B03-766), from the northwest.
c. At a level slightly lower than in the previous photo from the northwest, showing more tightly packed stones, probably a walkway (Street1) (B03-766).

a. After excavation unit B03-767 from the southeast, showing the relationship of Street 1 to House A Wall E.
b. End of excavation unit B03-767 from the southeast, showing the relationship of Street 1 to House A Wall E.
c. Upper part of the loose soil and stones in the Wall H foundation trench (B03-769), from the northeast. Note that the stones do not continue all the way to Wall E in the foreground of the photo; this soil was firmer and was dug separately, starting with B03-770.

PLATE 12

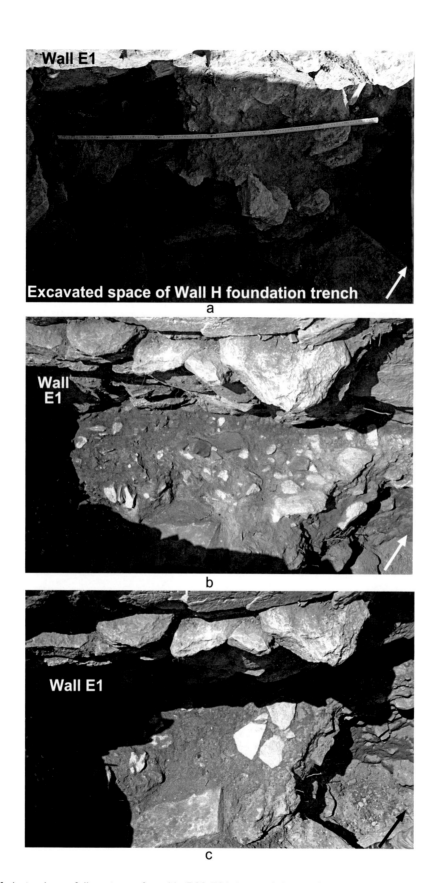

a. Upper part of photo shows fallen stones found in B03-781, beneath layer of red soil, from the southeast.
b. Pebble layer (Street 2) found in B03-785 from the southeast.
c. Second paving level of Street 2 (B03-786), from the southeast.

PLATE 13

a. A shallow layer of packed stones that abutted Wall E1 (B03-789) beneath Street 2, from the southeast. These stones may have served as a packing layer for Street 2. Their position suggests Wall E1 and Street 2 were in use at the same time.
b. Wall X beneath Wall H from the northwest.
c. Test pit in Alley AB from the northeast. Drain 2 probably postdates Wall X and runs underneath Wall E1. A pavement that abutted Wall X (B03-796) was laid above a packing level (B03-797 and B03-798).

a. Test pit in Alley AB from the southwest, showing Wall H above Wall X and the northeast scarp.
b. Test pit in Alley AB from the south. The stones that make up the northeast face of Drain 2 seem to be part of a wall. Both the wall and drain run under Wall E1.
c. Period IV Wall E1 beneath Period VI Wall E of House A, from the east.

a. Test pit in Alley AB from the northeast, showing Wall H above Wall X, a possible Period III wall in the southwest scarp, and Wall E1 beneath Wall E of House A.
b. Test pit in Alley AB from the southwest. Bikaki thought that the stone marked with * might be part of a Period III wall, but since soil runs under it (visible in this photo and in sections [Pl. 20:a]), it is not considered a wall in this text.
c. Test pit in Alley AB from the east, showing Period IV walls and Drain 2, as well as a possible Period III wall in the southwest corner of the test pit.
d. End of the test pit in Alley AB, from the northeast.

PLATE 16

a. Test pit in Room B.2 from the southwest, showing Wall AF below Wall K and Period III destruction debris to the south of Wall AF.
b. Test pit in Room B.2 from the southeast, showing Period III destruction debris between Walls AB and AF.
c. Test pit in Room B.2 from the northwest, showing Period III destruction debris between Walls AB and AF.

PLATE 17

a. Test pit in Room B.2 from the southwest, showing pithos (**232**) underwater.
b. Test pit in Room B.2 from the southwest, showing pithos (**232**) half submerged in seawater.
c. Test pit in Room B.2 from the northeast, showing Wall AB.

a. Bikaki and a workman pumping water from the flooded test pit in Room B.2.
b. Test pit in Room B.2 during excavation from the northwest. Note the widening of Walls AF and AB at the lower elevation, possibly evidence for an earlier building phase.
c. Test pit in Room B.2 from the southwest, showing large, flat slab found at elevation −0.42 m below sea level.

PLATE 19

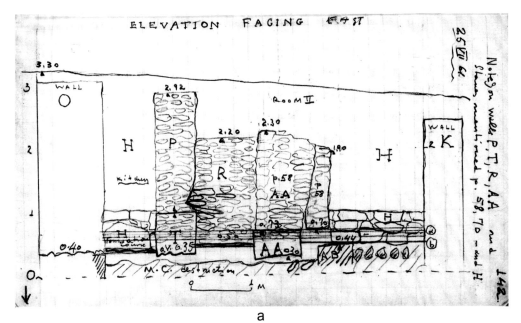

a

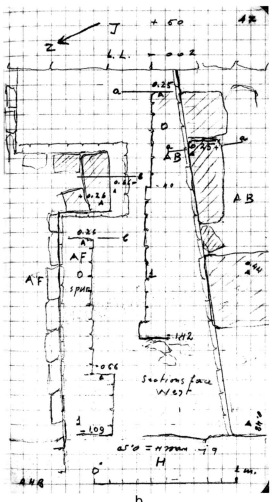

b

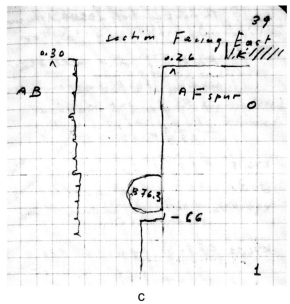

c

a. Sketch of Room B.2/B.3 and B.4 showing the relationships between walls and "Floors" a and b (Kea Excavation Notebook III, 142).

b. Section and plan of Wall AB and the spur of Wall AF, from the west (Kea Excavation Notebook LVIII, 47).

c. Sketch of Walls AB and AF below Room B.2, with sections showing jogs in the profiles of both walls and the position of a marble mortar (**239**; B-76.3 [K76.27]; Kea Excavation Notebook LVIII, 39).

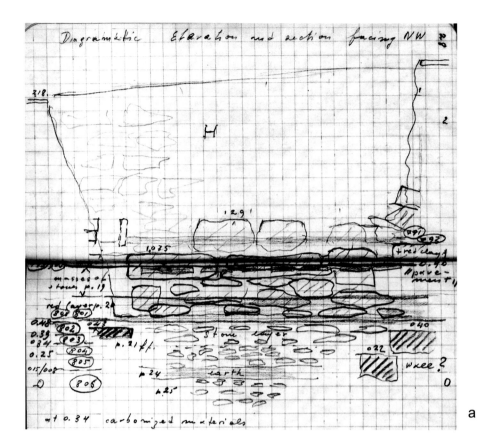

a

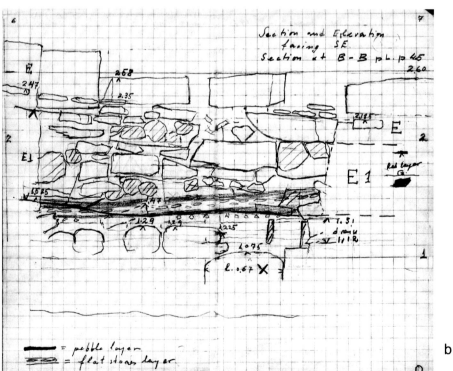

b

a. Section of test pit in Alley AB, showing the relationship of strata and architectural features to Walls H and X (Kea Excavation Notebook LVIII, 28–29).
b. Section of test pit in Alley AB, showing the relationship of strata and architectural features to Walls E and E1 (Kea Excavation Notebook LVIII, 6–7).

PLATE 21

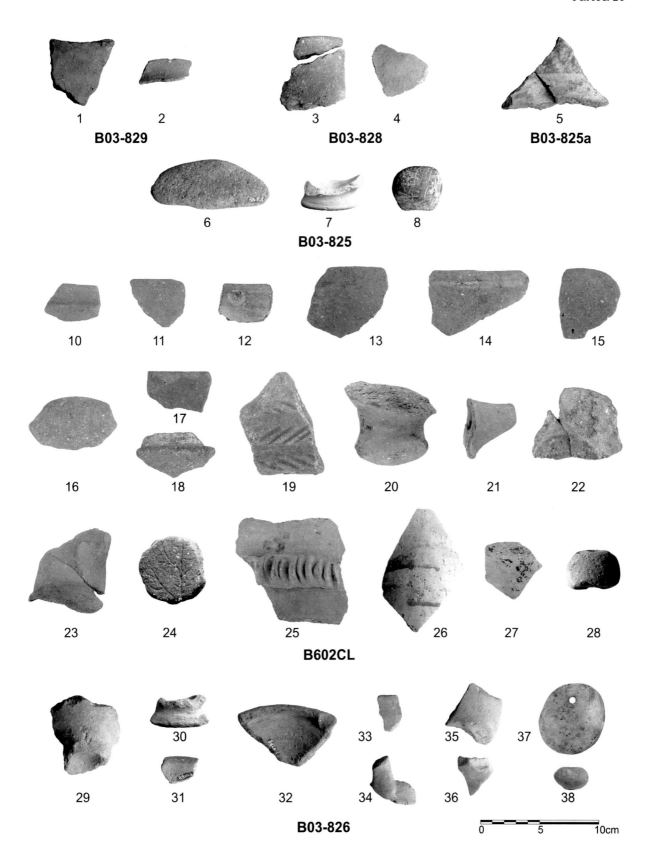

Objects from B03-829 (**1**, **2**), B03-828 (**3**, **4**), B03-825a (**5**), B03-825 (**6–8**), B602CL (**10–28**), and B03-826 (**29–38**). Photos of **1–23**, **25–27**, **29–36** by the author.

PLATE 22

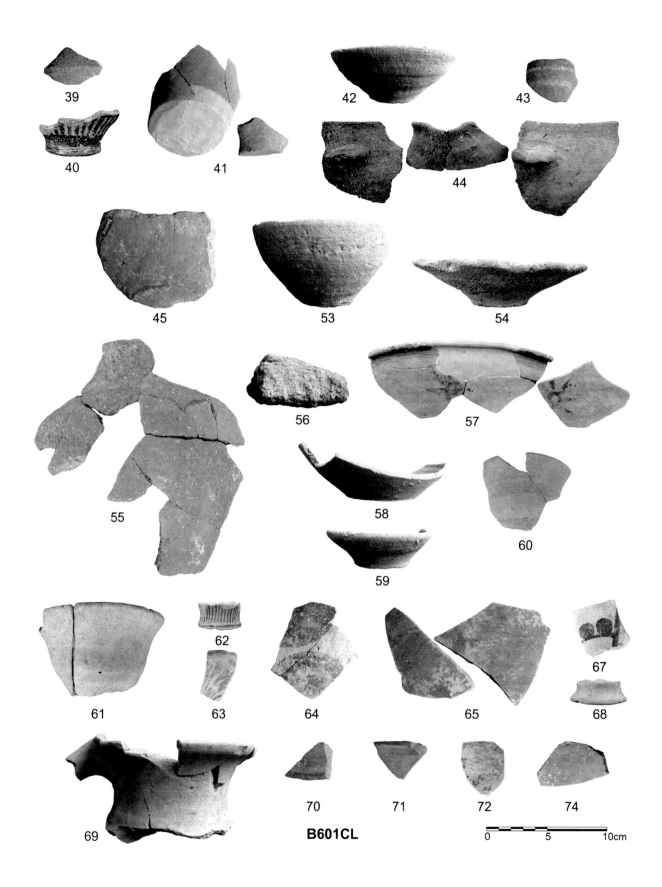

Objects from B601CL (**39–45**, **53–65**, **67–72**, **74**). Photos of **39–43**, **45**, **53–56**, **58–65**, **67–72**, **74** by the author.

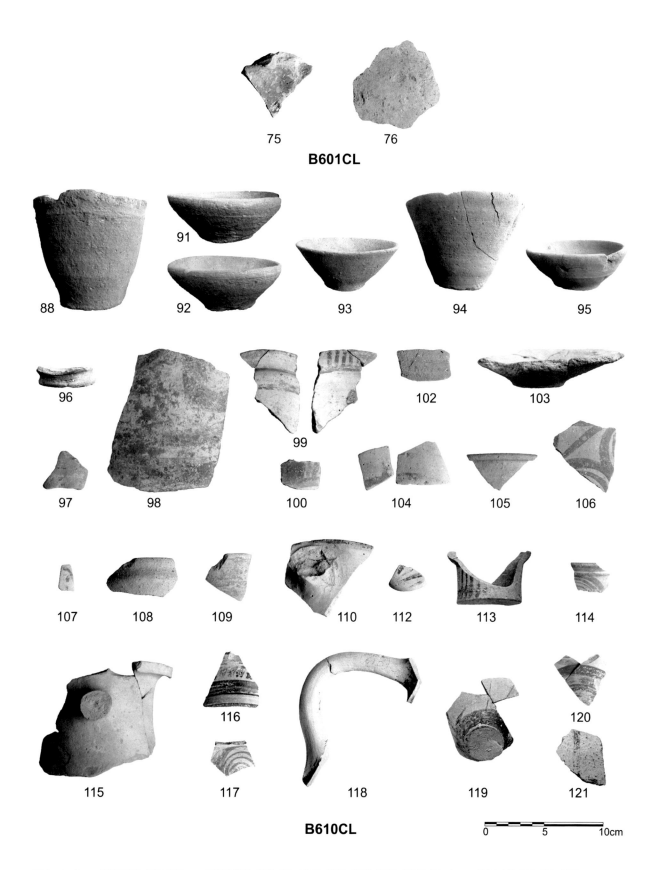

Objects from B601CL (**75**, **76**) and B610CL (**88**, **91–100**, **102–110**, **112–121**). Photos of **75**, **76**, **88**, **91–100**, **102–110**, **112**, **114–118**, **120**, **121** by the author.

PLATE 24

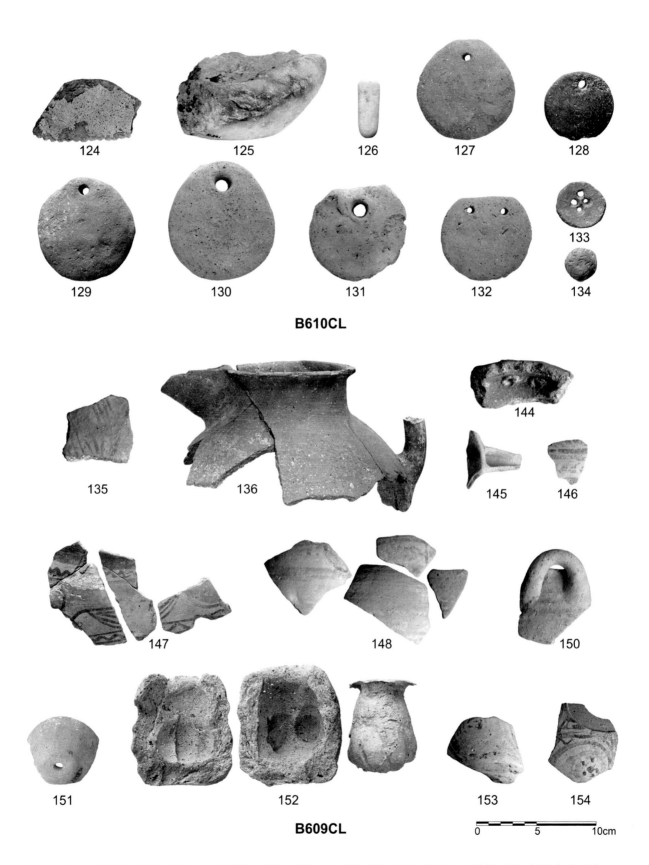

Objects from B610CL (**124–134**) and B609CL (**135**, **136**, **144–148**, **150–154**). Photos of **135**, **144–146**, **148**, **150**, **151**, **153**, **154** by the author.

PLATE 25

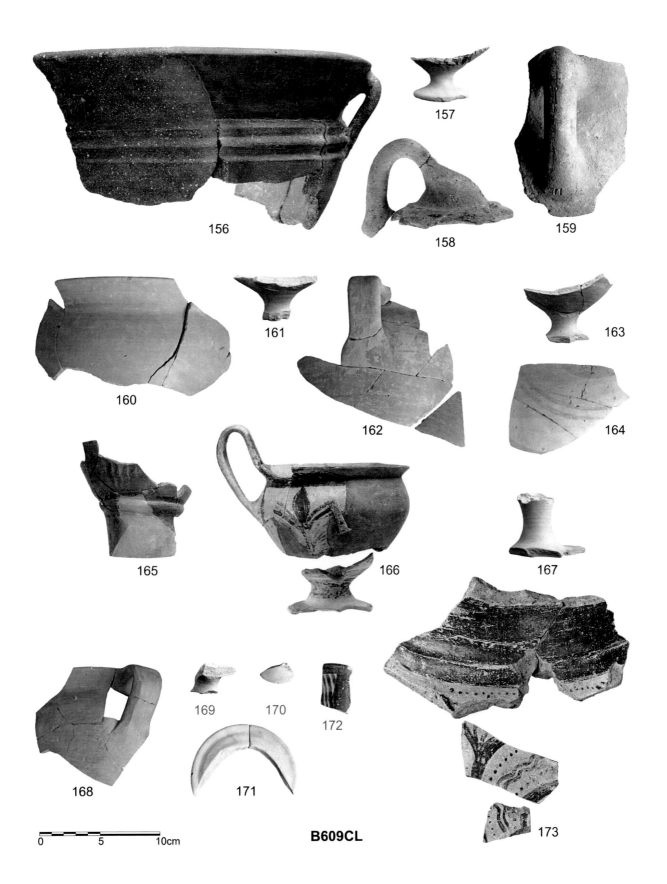

Objects from B609CL (**156–173**). Photos of **157**, **160–164**, **167–172** by the author.

PLATE 26

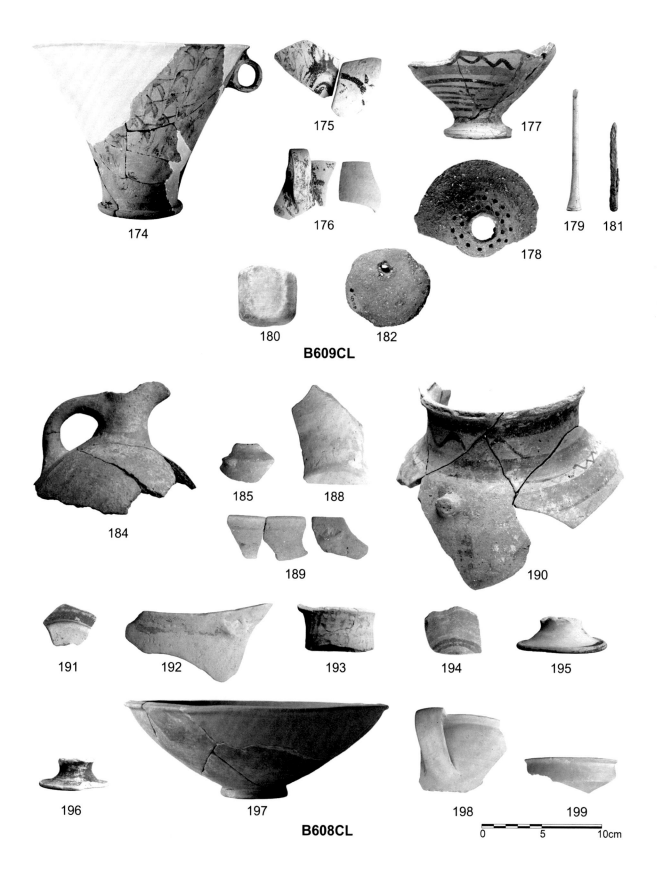

Objects from B609CL (**174–182**) and B608CL (**184**, **185**, **188–199**). Photos of **175**, **176**, **184**, **185**, **188**, **189**, **191–196**, **198**, **199** by the author.

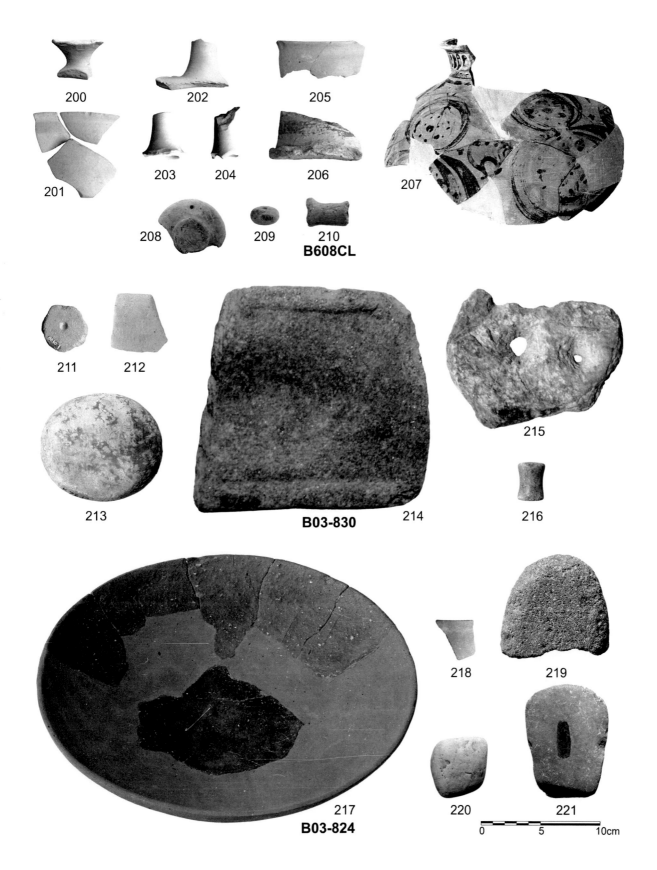

Objects from B608CL (**200–210**), B03-830 (**211–216**), and B03-824 (**217–221**). Photos of **200–206**, **211**, **212**, **218** by the author.

PLATE 28

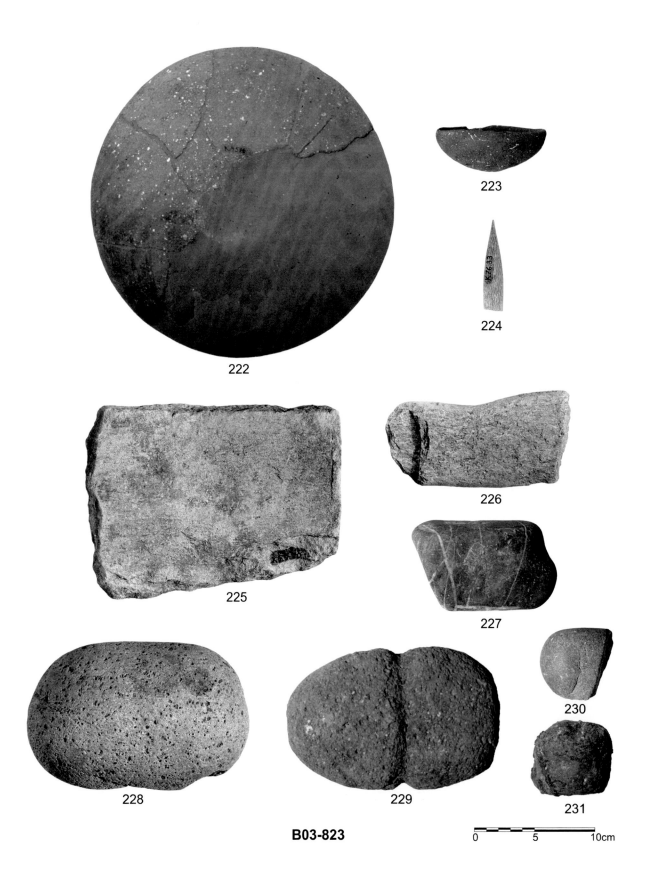

Objects from B03-823 (**222–231**).

PLATE 29

232

B03-822

Object from B03-822 (**232**).

PLATE 30

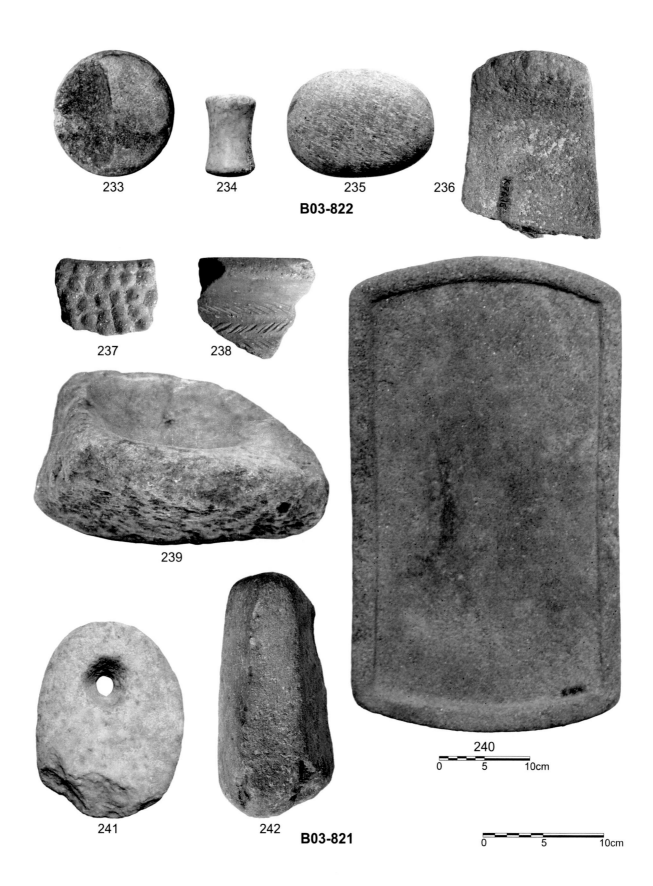

Objects from B03-822 (**233–236**) and B03-821 (**237–242**). Photos of **237**, **238** by the author.

PLATE 31

Objects from B03-821 etc. (**243–245**).

PLATE 32

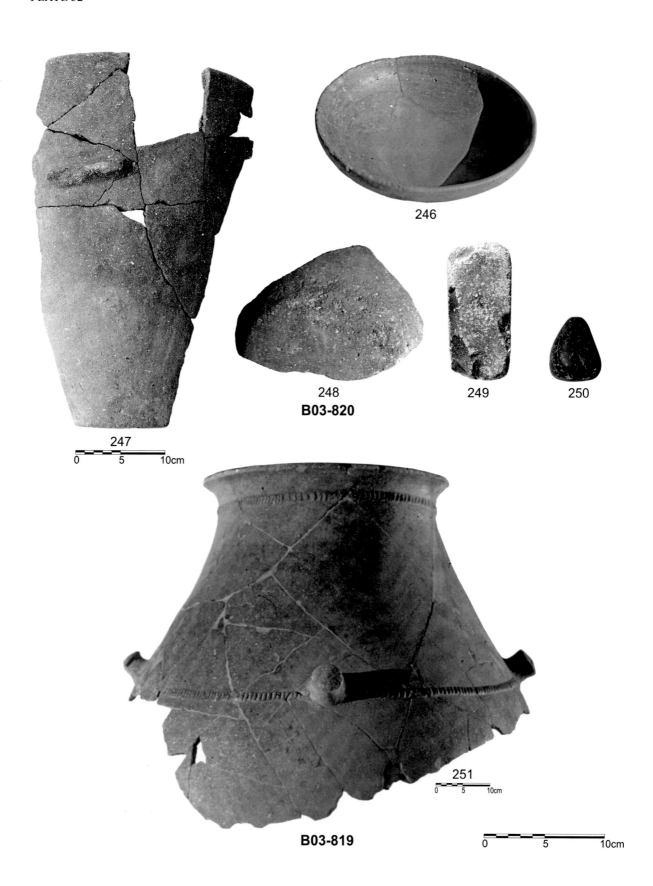

Objects from B03-820 (**246–250**) and B03-819 (**251**). Photo of **248** by the author.

PLATE 33

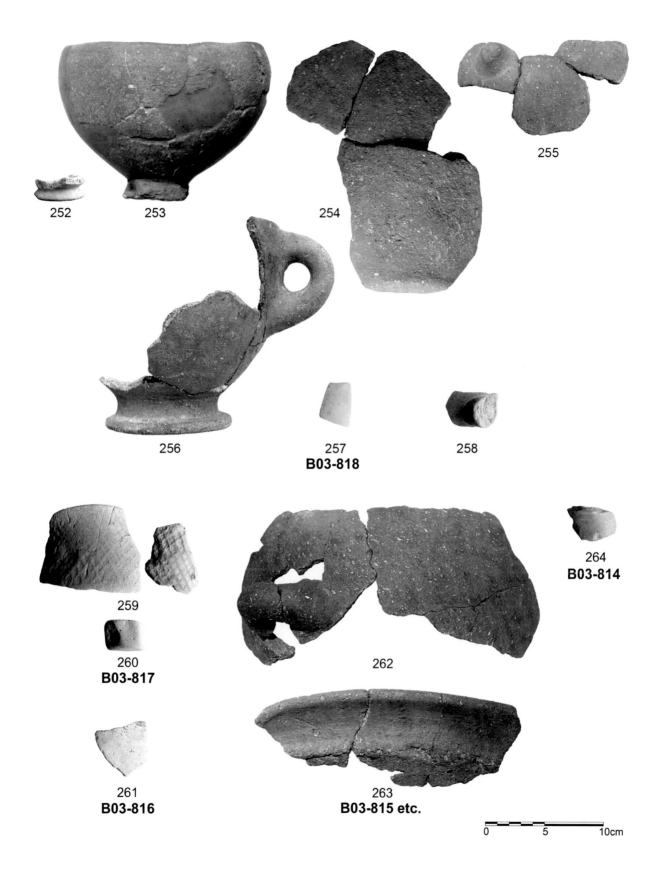

Objects from B03-818 (**252–258**), B03-817 (**259**, **260**), B03-816 (**261**), B03-815 etc. (**262**, **263**), and B03-814 (**264**). Photos of **252**, **254**, **255**, **257–261**, **264** by the author.

PLATE 34

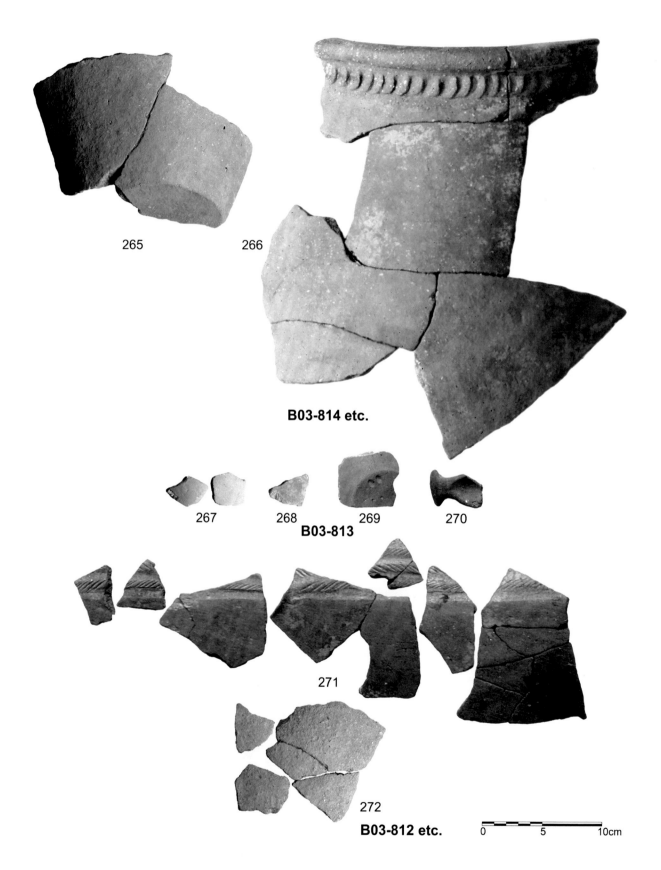

Objects from B03-814 etc. (**265**, **266**), B03-813 (**267–270**), and B03-812 etc. (**271**, **272**). Photos of **265**, **267**, **268**, **272** by the author.

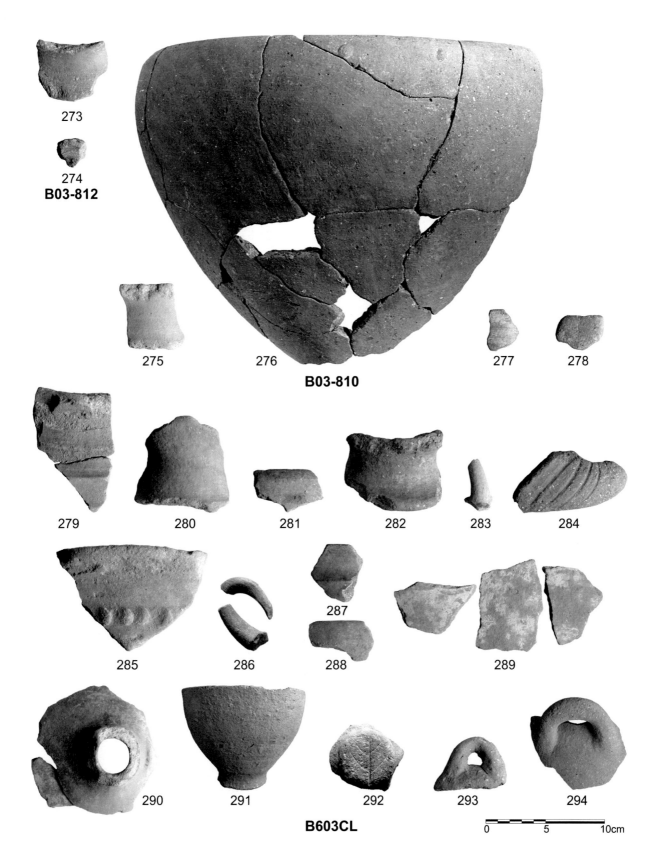

Objects from B03-812 (**273**, **274**), B03-810 (**275–278**), and B603CL (**279–294**). Photos of **273–275**, **277–285**, **287–291**, **293**, **294** by the author.

PLATE 36

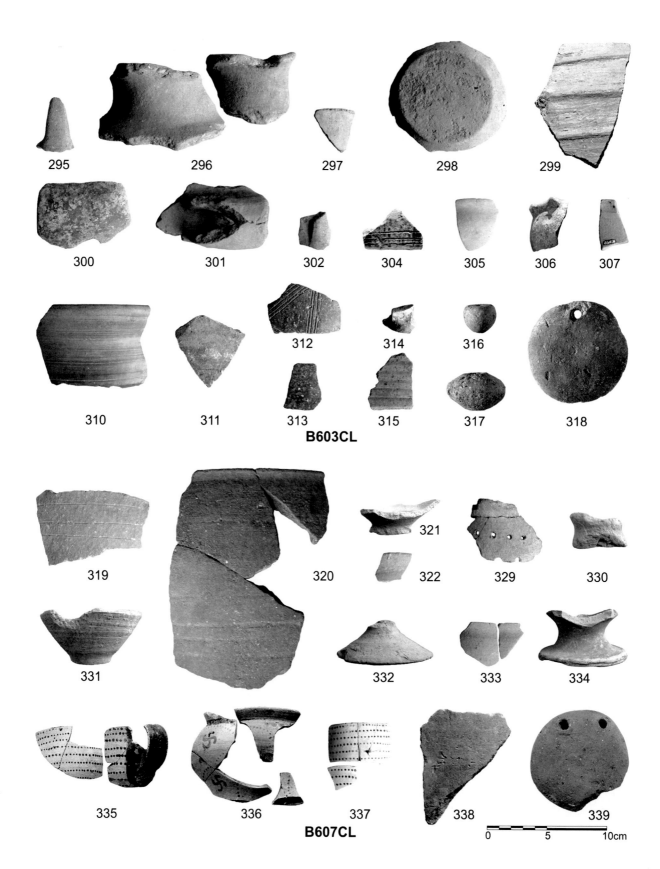

Objects from B603CL (**295–302, 304–307, 310–318**) and B607CL (**319–322, 329–339**). Photos of **295–298, 300–302, 305, 307, 310–315, 319–322, 329–337** by the author.

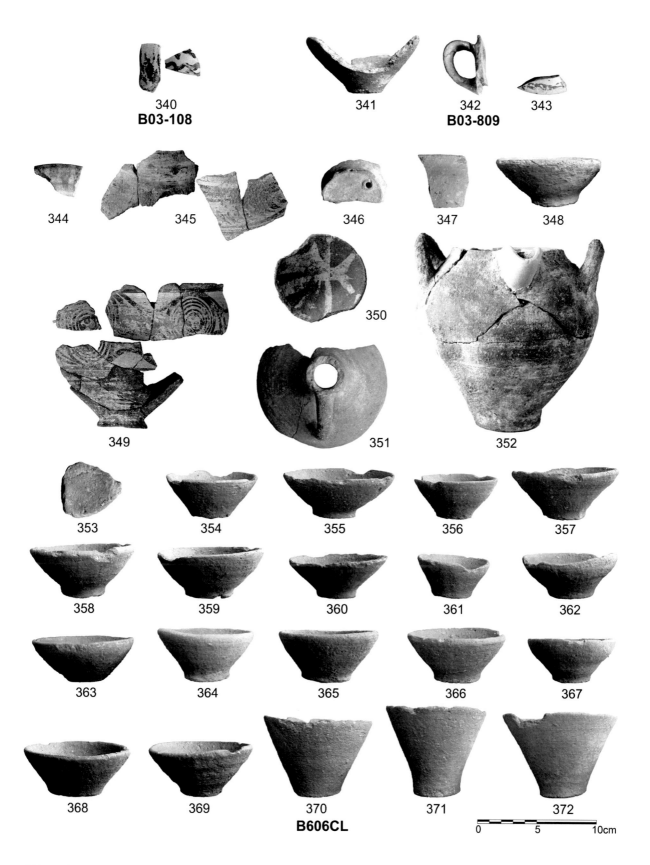

Objects from B03-108 (**340**), B03-809 (**341–343**), and B606CL (**344–372**). Photos of **340**, **341–344**, **346–348**, **351**, **353–372** by the author.

PLATE 38

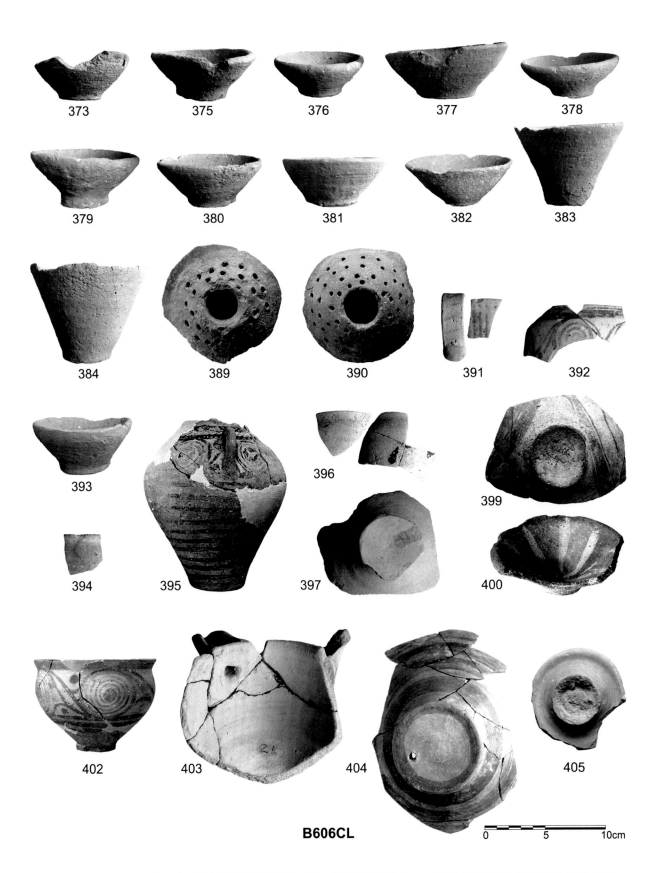

B606CL

Objects from B606CL (**373**, **375–384**, **389–397**, **399**, **400**, **402–405**). Photos of **373**, **375–384**, **391–394**, **396**, **397**, **403**, **405** by the author.

PLATE 39

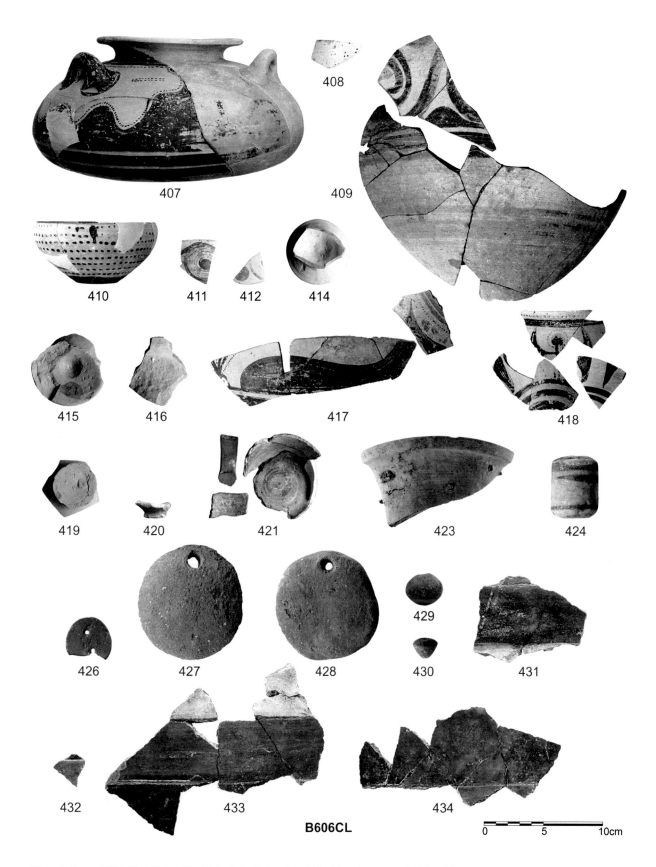

Objects from B606CL (**407–412, 414–421, 423, 424, 426–434**). Photos of **408, 411, 412, 414–416, 419–421** by the author.

Objects from B606CL (**435–439**) and B604CL (**440–462, 464**). Photos of **436, 439–443, 446, 449–462, 464** by the author.

Objects from B604CL (**465, 466, 468, 470, 471, 473, 475, 478, 479, 485, 487, 492, 494, 495, 501, 502, 512–515, 517–538**). Photos of **465, 466, 468, 470, 471, 473, 475, 478, 479, 485, 487, 492, 494, 495, 501, 502, 512, 514, 515, 517, 523, 524, 526** by the author.

PLATE 42

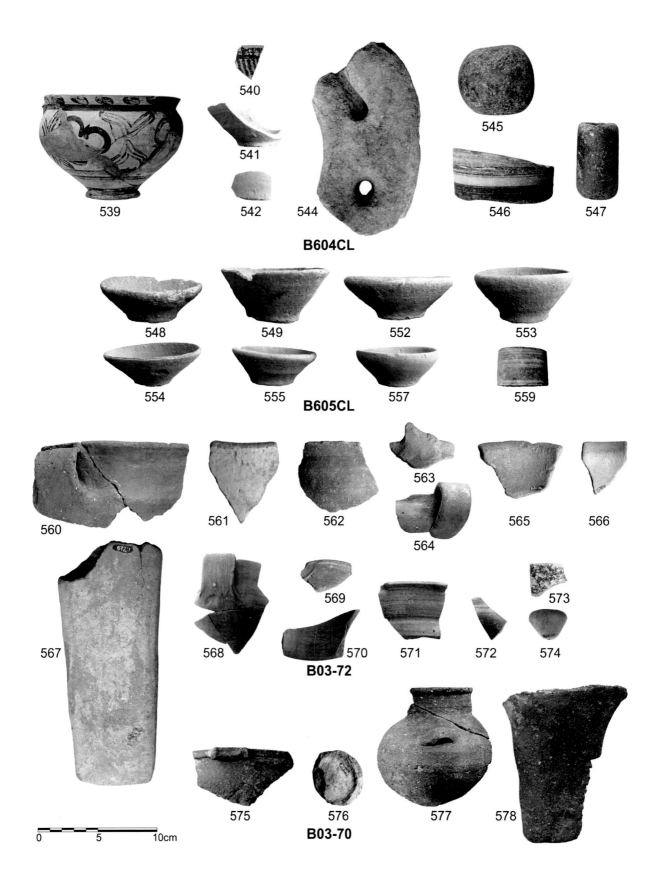

Objects from B604CL (**539–542, 544–547**), B605CL (**548, 549, 552–555, 557, 559**), B03-72 (**560–574**), and B03-70 (**575–578**). Photos of **541, 542, 548, 549, 552–555, 557, 561–569, 571–576** by the author.

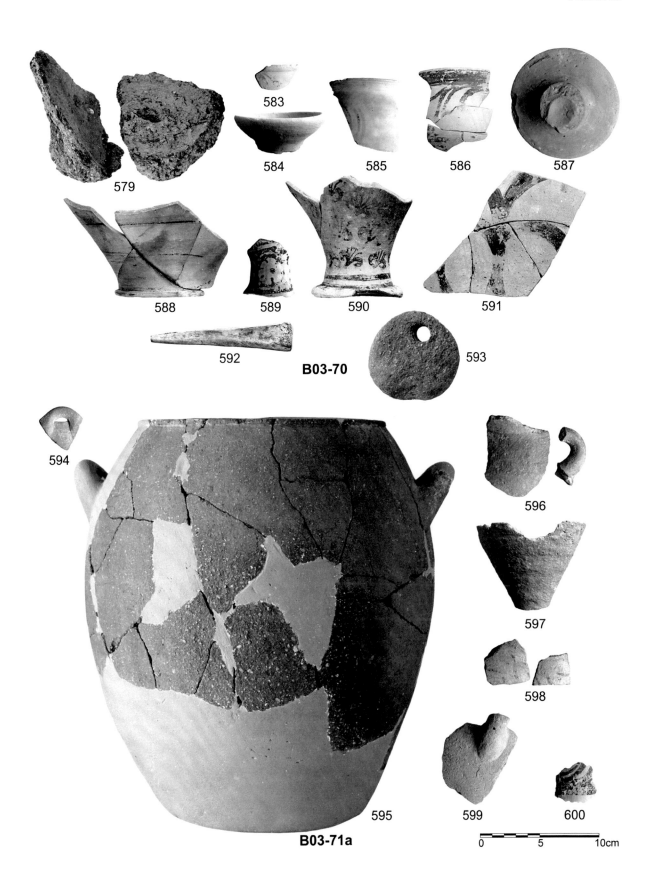

Objects from B03-70 (**579**, **583–593**) and B03-71a (**594–600**). Photos of **583–587**, **589**, **594**, **596–600** by the author.

PLATE 44

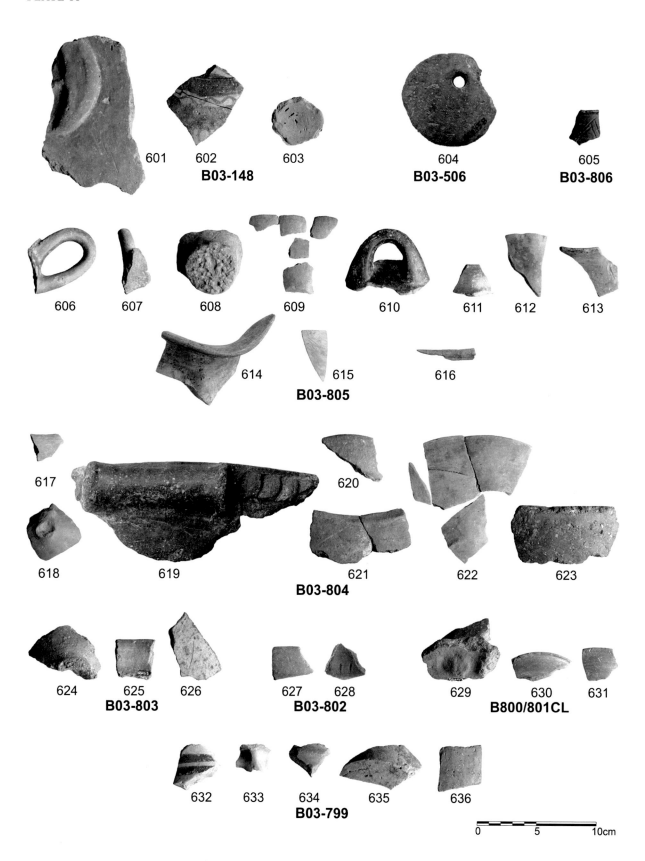

Objects from B03-148 (**601–603**), B03-506 (**604**), B03-806 (**605**), B03-805 (**606–616**), B03-804 (**617–623**), B03-803 (**624–626**), B03-802 (**627, 628**), B800/801CL (**629–631**), and B03-799 (**632–636**). Photos of **601, 602, 605–613, 615, 617, 618, 620–627, 629–636** by the author.

PLATE 45

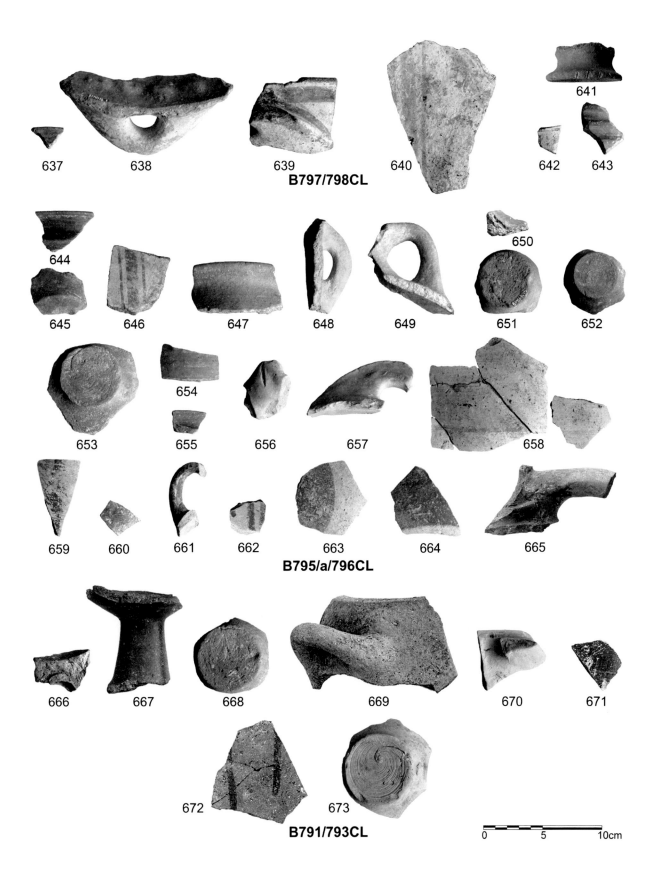

Objects from B797/798CL (**637–643**), B795/a/796CL (**644–665**), and B791/793CL (**666–673**). Photos of **637–640**, **642–664**, **666**, **668**, **670**, **671**, **673** by the author.

PLATE 46

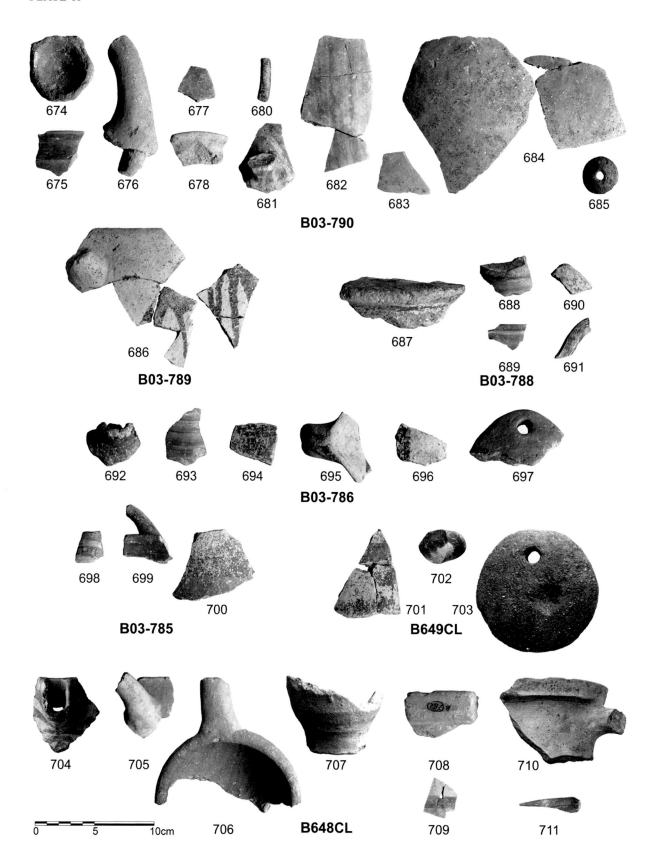

Objects from B03-790 (**674–678**, **680–685**), B03-789 (**686**), B03-788 (**687–691**), B03-786 (**692–697**), B03-785 (**698–700**), B649CL (**701–703**), and B648CL (**704–711**). Photos of **674–678**, **680–684**, **686–701**, **705–709** by the author.

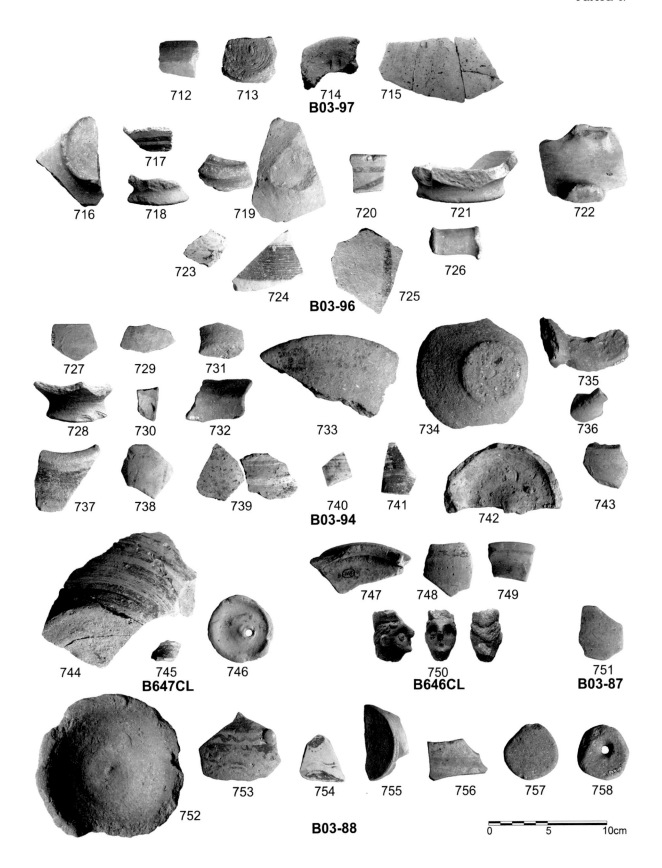

Objects from B03-97 (**712–715**), B03-96 (**716–726**), B03-94 (**727–743**), B647CL (**744–746**), B646CL (**747–750**), B03-87 (**751**), and B03-88 (**752–758**). Photos of **712**, **713**, **716–749**, **751–758** by the author.

COLOR PLATE 1

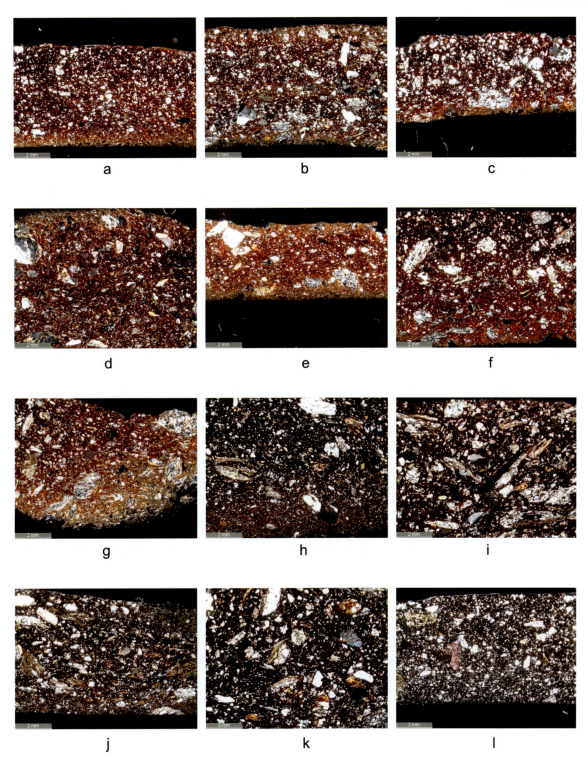

Photomicrographs of probable and possible local fabrics, with sample number in parentheses. Period and forming method are included to illustrate the similarities through time and across other variation in the *chaîne opératoire*. All images taken with crossed polars; gray bars are 2 mm. a. PFG 1A (4) (Period III, handmade), with mica schist and epidote group minerals; b. PFG 1A (40) (Period IV, wheel-coiled); c. PFG 1A (48) (Period VII, wheelmade); d. PFG 1B (9) (Period III, handmade), very micaceous, with common clinozoisite; e. PFG 1C (35) (Period III, handmade), with micrite/sparite; f. PFG 1C (37) (Period IV, handmade); g. PFG 1C (18) (Period VI, wheel-coiled); h. PFG 1D (23) (Period III, handmade), with common voids; i. PFG 2A (34) (Period III, handmade), with white mica schists bearing opaque material and rare talc; j. PFG 2B (28) (Period VII, handmade), with chaotic, fine-grained schist and phyllite; k. PFG 2C (139) (Period III, handmade), with coarse, amphibole-bearing metamorphic rocks; l. PFG 2Cv (136) (Period III, handmade), darker in color with less amphibole than the main group.

COLOR PLATE 2

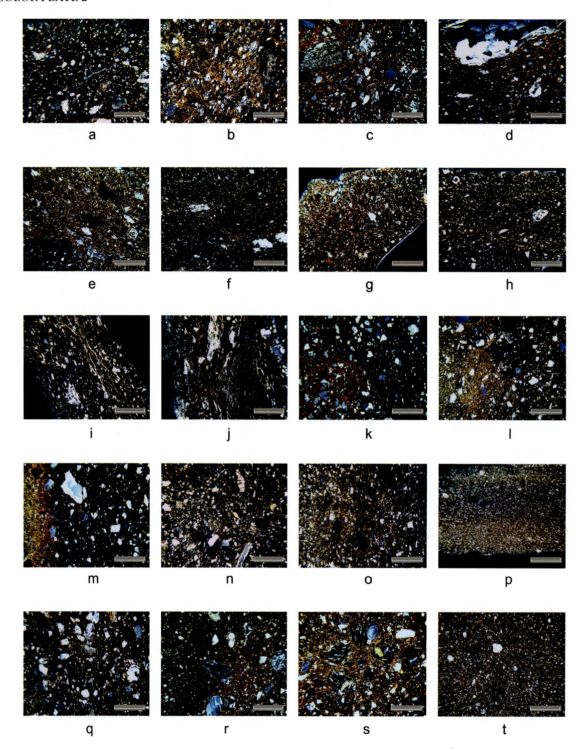

Photomicrographs of imported fabrics. The sample number is indicated in parentheses. All images taken with crossed polars; scale bars are 500 μm. a. PFG 2D (16), with biotite-rich metamorphic and rare igneous rocks; b. PFG 3A (102), with quartz-rich metamorphic rocks; c. PFG 3B (106), with mica schists, phyllite, and feldspars; d. PFG 3C (53), with white mica, glaucophane schist, and microfossils; e. PFG 3D (107), similar to PFG 3C, with possible grog; f. PFG 3E (101), with biotite schist; g. PFG 3F (164), with biotite schist and dense micrite lumps; h. PFG 3G (52), greenish brown with phyllite; i. PFG 3H (142), greenish brown, very micaceous; j. PFG 3I (14), with abundant phyllite; k. PFG 4A (129), with angular quartz and feldspar; l. PFG 4B (103), with quartzofeldspathic rocks, calcite, and microfossils; m. PFG 4C (114), with granite; n. PFG 5A (85), with acid–intermediate volcanic rocks and microfossils; o. PFG 5B (90), with abundant volcanic glass; p. PFG 5C (89), fine volcanic; q. PFG 5D (97), with acid–intermediate volcanic rocks and non-biogenic calcite; r. PFG 5E (96), red-brown with volcanic glass; s. PFG 5F (95), non-calcareous with intermediate volcanic rocks; t. PFG 5G (125), calcareous with intermediate volcanic rocks.

COLOR PLATE 3

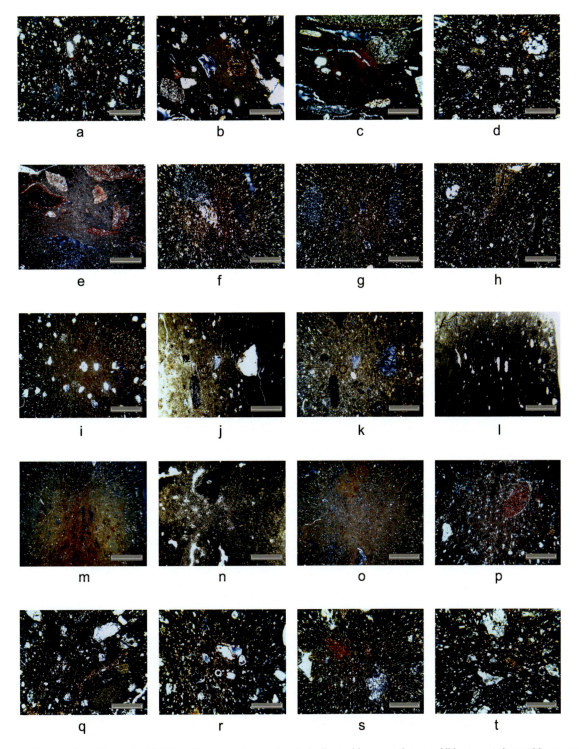

Photomicrographs of imported fabrics. The sample number is indicated in parentheses. All images taken with crossed polars unless otherwise noted; scale bars are 500 μm. a. PFG 5H (111), with chalcedony; b. PFG 6A (66), with mixed sand; c. PFG 6B (77), with abundant sedimentary rocks; d. PFG 6C (81), with a silty groundmass, phyllite, and schist; e. PFG 7A (56), with mudstones and siltstones; f. PFG 7B (55), with gray and brown siltstones; g. PFG 7C (82), greenish gray with gray siltstones; h. PFG 7D (68), with argillaceous grains and serpentinite; i. PFG 7E (65), with quartz and red tcfs/mudstones; j. PFG 7F (64) (ppl), greenish brown, with clay pellets, mudstones, chert, and cracking; k. PFG 7F (64) (xpl); l. PFG 7G (61) (ppl), greenish brown, with cracking, showing "starburst" feature; m. PFG 7G (61) (xpl); n. PFG 7G (62) (ppl); o. PFG 7G (62) (xpl); p. PFG 7H (75), with red mudstones and siltstones; q. PFG 8A (83), speckled groundmass with low-grade metamorphic rocks and calcite; r. PFG 8B (58), mottled groundmass with biogenic limestone; s. PFG 8C (59), with calcite-rich rock fragments and siltstones; t. PFG 8D (76), with various calcareous rocks.

COLOR PLATE 4

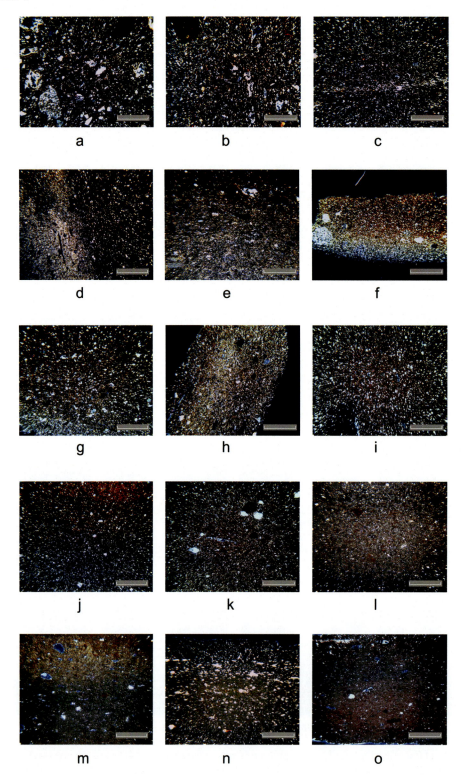

Photomicrographs of imported fabrics. The sample number is indicated in parentheses. All images taken with crossed polars; scale bars are 500 μm. a. PFG 8E (69), silty groundmass with sedimentary, metamorphic, and volcanic rocks; b. PFG 9A (51), with serpentinite; c. PFG 9B (147), with quartz, plagioclase, and amphibole; d. PFG 10 (128), with sponge spicules; e. PFG 11A (143), low-fired, reduced, with calcite and quartz-mica schists; f. PFG 11B (146), with biogenic limestone; g. PFG 12A (154), with metamorphic rocks and rare amphiboles; h. PFG 12B (158), brown, calcareous, micaceous; i. PFG 12C (168), speckled red and brown, micaceous, with siltstone; j. PFG 13A (140), orange-red, with dark red clay pellets; k. PFG 13B (122), red, with coarse metamorphic rocks; l. PFG 14A (71), fine, with tcfs/mudstones; m. PFG 14B (152), with red tcfs, mudstones, and fine mica; n. PFG 14C (159), greenish yellow with serpentinite(?); o. PFG 14D (169), with calcite.

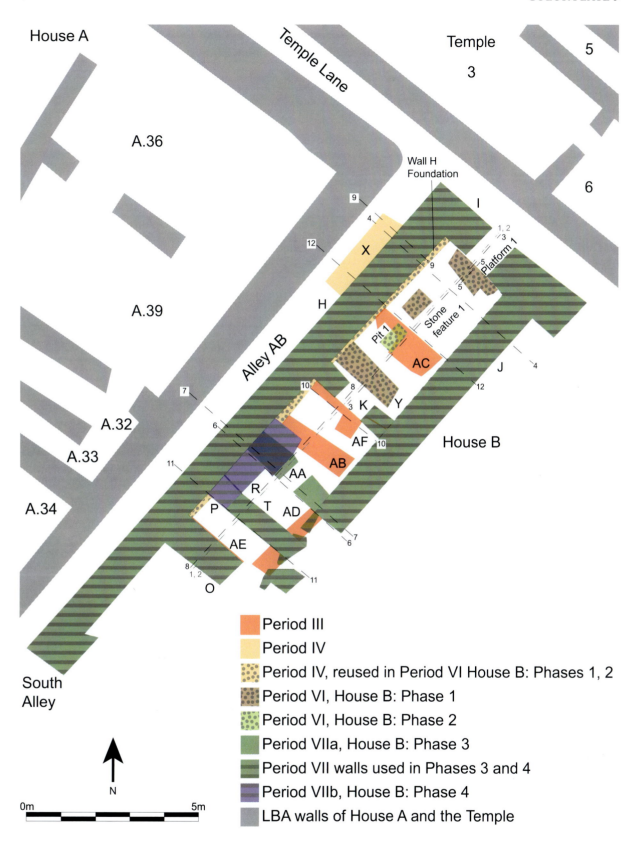

Plan of the southeastern part of Ayia Irini, showing walls and major features of all Bronze Age phases in Area B. After architect's field sheets.